W9-APF-807

UP
AGAINST
THE
CORPORATE
WALL

Other Books by S. Prakash Sethi:

Business Corporations and the Black Man (1970)

Advanced Cases in Multinational Business Operations (1972)

The Corporate Dilemma (with Dow Votaw, 1973)

Management of the Multinationals (with Richard H. Holton, 1974)

*The Unstable Ground: Corporate Social Policy
in a Dynamic Society* (1974)

Japanese Business and Social Conflict (1975)

Advocacy Advertising and Large Corporations (1976)

Third Edition

UP AGAINST THE CORPORATE WALL

Modern Corporations and Social Issues of the Seventies

S. PRAKASH SETHI

School of Business Administration
University of California, Berkeley

PRENTICE-HALL, INC., ENGLEWOOD CLIFFS, NEW JERSEY

Library of Congress Cataloging in Publication Data

SETHI, S PRAKASH.
    Up against the corporate wall.

    Includes bibliographies.
    1. Industry—Social aspects—United States—Case
studies.   I. Title.
HD60.5.U5S47 1976   301.5'1   76-15277
ISBN   0-13-938217-8

© 1977, 1974, 1971 by PRENTICE-HALL, INC.,
Englewood Cliffs, New Jersey

Printed in the United States of America

10   9   8   7   6   5   4   3   2   1

PRENTICE-HALL INTERNATIONAL, INC., *London*
PRENTICE-HALL OF AUSTRALIA PTY. LIMITED, *Sydney*
PRENTICE-HALL OF CANADA, LTD., *Toronto*
PRENTICE-HALL OF INDIA PRIVATE LIMITED, *New Delhi*
PRENTICE-HALL OF JAPAN, INC., *Tokyo*
PRENTICE-HALL OF SOUTHEAST ASIA PTE. LTD., *Singapore*

To
those "haves" and "have-nots" among us
who still have hopes
that when men of reason get together
they will plan the survival
and not the extinction
of the human race and of humanity
this book is affectionately dedicated.

Contents

I

THE QUALITY OF LIFE   1

A

POLLUTION CONTROL

B

CONSERVATION OF THE NATURAL ENVIRONMENT

II

THE CHANGING NATURE OF GOVERNMENT AND BUSINESS RELATIONSHIPS   81

A

CORPORATIONS AND UNITED STATES DOMESTIC POLITICS

B

CORPORATIONS, UNITED STATES FOREIGN POLICY, AND THE ETHICS OF OVERSEAS OPERATIONS

C

BUSINESS LOBBYING AND SOCIAL GOALS

D

INDIRECT/DIRECT USE OF THE PRESIDENT'S EXECUTIVE AUTHORITY

E

GOVERNMENT AND BUSINESS AS PARTNERS

III

CORPORATIONS, THEIR DEPENDENCIES, AND OTHER SOCIAL INSTITUTIONS   279

A

CORPORATIONS AND THE STOCKHOLDERS

B

CORPORATIONS AND THEIR EMPLOYEES

C

CORPORATIONS AND THE CITIZEN-AT-LARGE

D

CORPORATIONS AND THE CONSUMER

E

CORPORATIONS AND THEIR AUTHORIZED DEALERS AND FRANCHISES

F

CORPORATIONS, ETHNIC MINORITIES, AND DISCRIMINATION

G

CORPORATIONS AND THE NEWS MEDIA

H

CORPORATIONS AND THE CHURCH

Preface
to
the Third Edition

The constant questioning into the activities of large corporations by various segments of society has continued unabated since the publication of the first edition in 1971. Also, the basic nature of the conflict between large corporations and other social institutions has remained unchanged. This conflict has to do with the society's changed expectations of business in general and large corporations in particular, on the one hand, and business's willingness and ability to modify its behavior to meet these expectations, on the other hand.

There seems to be a sincere desire on the part of many businesses to attempt to attack various social problems for which they have rightly or wrongly been blamed. Even where there is a meeting of minds between business and social elements on objectives, there are considerable differences of opinion as to who should do the job and how the costs should be shared.

The efforts of business notwithstanding, the pace of the conflict seems to have accelerated and is manifested in many more directions—directions that were only vaguely discernible when the first edition was being prepared. There is a growing suspicion of the power of large corporations and its real or alleged abuse by them, the nature of corporate profits, and more important, the means by which they are earned.

The present edition takes cognizance of these dimensions by including new case studies dealing with such issues as pollution control, business lobbying, consumer and product safety, and age discrimination on the domestic front. Overseas activities of U.S. multinational corporations are covered, especially those dealing with political interference and large-scale bribery abroad in order to secure business on favorable terms, and subsequent attempts to conceal this information from stockholders, boards of directors, and appropriate government regulatory authorities.

In addition, the case studies from the earlier editions have been brought up to date by incorporating latest developments. Admittedly, some of the material from the earlier editions had to be dropped to keep the book to a manageable size. However, the core of those editions has been retained, and it is therefore hoped that this edition will be more representative of the spectrum of business and society controversies.

Subsequent to the publication of the first edition, many readers and reviewers questioned the omission not only of success stories in business-society controversies but also of my analysis of the issues and recommended courses of action for business to follow. These exclusions were based on the following considerations:

1. The nature of success in dealing with business and social problems has been sporadic and inconsistent. Therefore, in two apparently similar situations, there is no guarantee that similar policies will be successful. No theoretical framework has yet been developed to understand the total phenomena in a manner that would yield consistent interpretation. Moreover, the nature of the problem is so complex and multifaceted that it is not clear we have identified all the important variables—a necessary precondition to the development of a theoretical framework.

2. The instances of business failure to handle social controversies have been far greater in number and magnitude than the instances of success. Consequently, although we may not be able to say "what works," we are in a better position to say "what is not likely to work," based on our study of the failures.

3. Since learning is as much a function of the availability of data as it is of their interpretation, I have refrained from prejudicing the reader's mind by imposing my own interpretations. Instead, I have tried to provide the reader with an accurate picture of the particular incident; the sociopolitical environment in which it took place, which must be taken into account to understand the *what, how,* and *why* of the incident; and the viewpoints of the parties involved in as objective a manner as possible. The book provides the reader interested in doing further research or seeking the opinions of various experts with ample suggestions for additional reading that will help him to arrive at his own conclusions.

4. Although I have refrained from giving my own analysis and recommendations in the book, I have given considerable thought to the nature of these conflicts and to the precautions that business and other social groups could take to avoid them in the future. Analyses of specific case studies are presented in a teacher's manual, which is available on request from the publisher. My analysis of the general nature of social conflicts and possible approaches to their solution has been presented in various articles that have appeared in the *California Management Review* and *Business and Society Review* during the last five years. Some of these articles have since been collected and published in Dow Votaw and S. Prakash Sethi, *The Corporate Dilemma: Traditional Values and Contemporary Problems* (Englewood Cliffs, N.J.: Prentice-Hall, Inc., 1973). Readers may also wish to review the material contained in my book *Japanese*

Business and Social Conflict: A Comparative Analysis of Response Patterns with American Business (Cambridge, Mass.: Ballinger Publishing Company, 1975).

I am grateful to various educators and business executives who were kind enough to write me about their reactions to the first two editions. In addition, many corporations and their executives, lawyers, and government administrators contributed their time and also provided me with data for the development of the new cases included in this edition. Their contributions are acknowledged at the appropriate places in the book.

I also wish to thank Dr. Peter P. Gabriel, Dean, School of Management, Boston University, and Professor Joseph W. Garbarino, Director, Institute of Business and Economic Research, University of California, Berkeley, for providing partial financial support for research and secretarial services. Much of the work on this edition was done during a year as visiting professor at the School of Management, Boston University. The assistance of Mr. Hamid Etemad, Mrs. Linda Myers, Mrs. Wendy Quinones, and Ms. Christine Rehfuss in researching parts of this book is appreciated.

Typing of the numerous drafts of this book was variously done by Mrs. Betty Kendall, Ms. Dena Brown, and Ms. Patricia Murphy at the University of California, Berkeley, and Ms. Patty Sherman at Boston University. I am grateful for their assistance and forbearance.

S. PRAKASH SETHI

Preface
to
the First Edition

As the United States enters the seventies and the decades beyond, it carries a plethora of new problems and social conflicts that have added to the nation's rhetoric. These include the protection of our environment by restricting both the amount of pollution and the amount of destruction, the concern for social justice, the search for relevance in our work and play, the protection of individual rights from abrogation by large institutions—public and private—and the reordering of national priorities.

Most of these problems have been with us for quite some time, but during the past ten years a variety of factors has brought them new importance:

1. The population mix has changed and a large segment is now composed of people born in the postdepression era, who are not haunted by the fear of scarcity, are not motivated by the specter of ever-increasing consumption, and are not willing to accept without question a system whose primary concerns are based on economic rationality.

2. A communications explosion, especially of television, has made millions of people aware of the inequities in social justice, the differences between the "haves" and the "have-nots," and the frustration and anger caused by social and economic deprivation.

3. A benign neglect of the problems of pollution and the exploitation of natural resources without regard to their effect on our environment have brought about a dangerous situation which cannot be ignored. Issues become salient to the public by personal experience, and the deterioration of the environment can no longer be hidden or wished away.

4. Economic, social, and political institutions have increasingly become less responsive to the changing needs of their constituents, leading the dissatisfied members of society to conclude that their grievances cannot be redressed without a restructuring of social institutions and a reordering of national priorities.

Another remarkable change has been the emergence of large business corporations as the main culprits, in the eyes of the public, for major social ills. In this context, the large business corporation has assumed a place equal to, if not higher than, that of big government as the villain. The corporations have been accused of creating "values" that are highly materialistic and thus undermine the normative values of the "good life." They have been accused of polluting the environment for their own financial gain, undermining the individual intellectual activity and creativity of the human mind by trivializing its work and achievement; bureaucratizing a large part of human activities and standardizing products, culture, and performance to the lowest common denominator of economic efficiency; exercising considerable authority—along with the Congress and the Pentagon—over the prosperity or decline of various communities and their inhabitants; sapping the political vitality of the middle class; and contributing to the alienation of faceless masses from the democratic processes.

The ills of the society cannot be attributed solely to large business corporations. Those who loudly accuse the corporations of prostituting the physical, social, and political environment cannot escape part of the blame, for they also share in the ill-gotten gains of the corporations. However, the corporations are responsible because of their close identity with the economic goals of society. Their loud disclaimers notwithstanding, corporations have not given consumers "what they want," because the selection processes of consumers are determined by the number of alternatives available to them and by their ability to evaluate the alternatives: both these factors are considerably influenced by the corporations. The large size of individual corporations and their control, individually and collectively, of the nation's productive facilities make it difficult to believe that they are passive instrumentalities subject to the control of market mechanisms.

It is therefore understandable that segments of the population have increasingly resorted to confrontation tactics in their efforts to involve corporations in activities that are nonprofit-oriented and might very well force these corporations to offer new rationales for their activities, change their manner of operation, and even increase the cost of doing business.

The corporations have to some extent recognized their partial immunity from competition, their increased economic and social power, and their responsibility for contributing to a better community life within which they must exist. However, this recognition has come hesitantly, in insufficiently small doses, invariably as partial cure rather than as preventive measure, and above all, only if it did not hurt the firm's profitability. Thus corporations have insisted on complete independence in determining products and profits, have fought measures of public control in pollution and other areas as economically prohibitive, and have demanded tax and other incentives for going into "nonprofit" activities. The emphasis has been on measuring the effect of these "nonprofit" activities on the profit potential of the corporation rather than on evaluating the effect of their "for profit" activities on the larger social goals. It is like allowing one department of a large company to exploit all the other departments to increase its own profitability.

The results have been predictable and disappointing. During the past few years business corporations have started, jointly and individually, a host of programs in community help—urban renewal, minority hiring, beautification, pollution control, communication with students—but their success, taken in the aggregate and in relation to their capacity, and barring a few isolated instances, has been either negligible or negative.

Conflicts between large corporations and other segments of society are likely to be intensified because neither the corporations nor other ruling members of the establishment seem willing to perceive these changes or to take bolder steps to revitalize the system. Their efforts are still directed at putting down brush fires and repairing occasional leaks to make the system work in its present form. As Neil Chamberlain pointed out in "The Life of the Mind in the Firm" (*Daedalus,* Winter 1969):

> It is still considered a high economic virtue that our major corporations behave like somewhat softened, but scrimping Scrooges or modest, but misanthropic misers—whose actions are governed only by the test of whether they are efficient in adding to a revenue stream and whose only purposes are limited dispersal to a limited stockholder clientele and reinvestment to maintain or augment the profit flow.
>
> . . . The argument is concerned with the standards that apply to the conduct of those organizations which give our society its special character. If our corporations were wholly government-owned, but still applied only the profit efficiency test to their operations, the result would be the same. . . . There is much to be said for leaving control over our giant corporations in private hands—diffusion of discretion and power is a value not to be given up lightly—if we can broaden the standard by which we judge their activity, if we can free them from a test of efficiency more relevant to the past than to the present.

The objective of this book is to expose the student, through a series of case studies involving business corporations, to a variety of problems that are increasingly becoming the prime concern of both business and society. It is aimed at developing in the reader a sensitivity to the issues involved, an awareness of the complexity of the motives of various parties, and a familiarity with the success and failure of their strategies and tactics. The areas covered can be broadly divided into business and the quality of life, business and other social institutions, business and the community, business and the individual, business and government, the military industrial complex, and business and foreign policy.

Case studies were selected on the basis of their timeliness and their ability to bring out as many facets of the problem as possible. I have tried to provide equal depth in every topic covered, but because of the difficulty in gathering data I might not have been uniformly successful. I have also tried to make the material as factual and objective as possible so as not to bias the reader with my own opinions and prejudices.

This book is primarily designed for executive development programs and for readers interested in business and society, business and public policy, business and government, and management policy. The issues involved are complex and of broad social import, and the case studies are somewhat long because they cover many facets of the conflicts and parties involved.

This book would not have been possible without the cooperation of many corporations and their executives, who generously contributed their time and information. However, the responsibility for material included in the cases and for errors of omission and commission is strictly my own. Thanks are especially due to Allen-Bradley Company, Bank of America, Crown Zellerbach Corporation, Dow Chemical Company, Eastman Kodak Company, Fairchild Camera and Instrument Corporation, and Motorola, Incorporated. Chandler Publishing Company graciously permitted the use of copyrighted material from my book, *Business Corporations and the Black Man*. A debt of gratitude is due also to Professor Ivar Berg (Columbia University), Professor Michael Conant (University of California), Professor Rick Pollay (University of British Columbia), Professor Lee E. Preston (State University of New York), and Professor Dow Votaw (University of California) for their valuable comments in the preparation of this book.

In addition to my research assistant, Michael Hawkins, other graduate students contributed in varying degrees, especially Peter Stoppello, Norbert Schaefer, and Rodney Gully. Their assistance is gratefully acknowledged. I also want to thank my editor, Mrs. Jan Seibert, who contributed greatly to the readability of the manuscript, and Patricia Murphy, who typed it in many drafts. Acknowledgments are also due to the School of Business Administration and to the Institute of Business and Economic Research, University of California, Berkeley, for typing and clerical assistance in the preparation of the manuscript.

And finally, I am grateful to my wife, Donna, who in the months immediately preceding and following our marriage encouraged me with affection and helped me with constructive criticism by reading the various drafts of the manuscript.

S. Prakash Sethi
Berkeley, California

UP
AGAINST
THE
CORPORATE
WALL

THE QUALITY
OF LIFE

Pollution
Control

THE SANTA BARBARA OIL SPILL

WHAT PRICE ENERGY?

It is one of your [Congress's] responsibilities as custodians of our federal government to provide for the general welfare. Do you honestly feel that the general welfare is being served when an area is being forcibly destroyed and its entire character changed? Is it right for the federal government and the oil industry to enjoy enormous revenues while we here continue to pay high taxes, high gas prices, and suffer the loss of our basic sources of revenue? We don't think so, and I don't think you can either.[1]

—ALLAN R. COATES, JR.
Mayor of Carpinteria, California

[1] U.S. Congress, House, *Hearings before the Subcommittee on Flood Control and the Subcommittee on Rivers and Harbors, Committee on Public Works, Oil Spillage—Santa Barbara, California,* 91st Cong., 1st sess., February 14, 1969, p. 13. (Hereafter cited as *Oil Spillage,* followed by page number.)
My description of the events is reconstructed primarily from this and the following sources (specifically identified in the text only where directly cited): U.S. Senate, *Hearings on S.1219 before the Subcommittee on Minerals, Materials, and Fuels, Committee on Interior and Insular Affairs, Santa Barbara Oil Spill,* 91st Cong., 1st sess., May 19–20, 1969. (Hereafter cited as *Santa Barbara,* followed by page number.) U.S. Senate, *Hearings on S.7 and S.544 before the Subcommittee on Public Works, Water Pollution—1969,* 91st Cong., 1st sess., part 2, February 5–6, 1969; part 3, February 24–25, 1969. (Hereafter cited as *Water Pollution,* followed by part and page number.) A. E. Keir Nash, Dean E. Mann, and Phil G. Olsen, *Oil Pollution and the Public Interest: A Study of the Santa Barbara Oil Spill* (Berkeley, Calif.: Institute of Governmental Studies, University of California, 1972). (Hereafter cited as *Oil Pollution,* followed by page number.)

THE INCIDENT

On the morning of January 28, 1969, drilling was completed on the fifth well from offshore platform A, owned jointly by Union Oil Company, Mobil, Texaco, and Gulf, and located 5 miles seaward of the city of Santa Barbara, in the Santa Barbara Channel. After drilling to the maximum depth of 3,479 feet, the crew was removing the drill pipe from the well. Suddenly, mud began trickling up through the pipe; soon it became a geyser of natural gas and mud. With tremendous effort, the crew successfully sealed the well in less than fifteen minutes, apparently preventing the danger of an explosion. No sooner had this been accomplished, however, than the sea began to churn and bubble violently. Apparently the attempt to contain the tremendous pressure in the well had somehow caused a rupture in the ocean bottom, and a black mass began to surge vigorously and to cover the surface.

The following two weeks, which brought disaster of unprecedented proportions to the beautiful coastline of Santa Barbara, for the first time brought home to the nation the nature of the damage that can be caused by oil spillage during offshore drilling activities.

THE ISSUES

The case points out certain still unresolved problems. It poses dilemmas that must be faced somehow if we are to evolve possible solutions and make livable accommodations among various economic, social, and political interests. Furthermore, on narrower grounds, an analysis of the case should help to develop a programmatic framework that will minimize the adverse effects of similar occurrences in the future.

The questions pertaining to managerial actions and strategy include these:

1. In the case of Santa Barbara, were there adequate planning, foresight, strict preventive measures, and rigorous law enforcement that could have prevented a blowout or minimized the impact on the environment and the surrounding communities?
2. What were the main elements of Union Oil's strategy in dealing with various public and private groups both before and after the oil spillage? Were these strategies effective?
3. How should one evaluate the preventive measures designed by Union Oil and other companies to avoid oil spillage? Were they effective? Were there any changes made in Union Oil's strategies as a result of the Santa Barbara case?
4. Given the fact that offshore drilling for oil is likely to continue and

increase in the future, what types of policies and strategies should a firm develop in order to deal with issues similar to those raised by the Santa Barbara oil spill?

5. How does the company evaluate the objectives and strategies of other groups involved in the conflict—namely, citizen groups, local government, state and federal government?

The questions pertaining to broad public policy and the interaction between various groups include these:

1. How should we satisfy national energy needs and measure the assumable costs and risks? How might one go about developing a national energy policy?
2. In satisfying the nation's energy needs, is it possible that we have been overemphasizing the supply side of the equation and have paid inadequate attention to the demand side?
3. What other types of major national issues raise similar concerns of setting up national priorities?
4. How are the often conflicting interests of industry, local community, and supposedly overall national interest to be balanced?
5. Is there a fragmentation of decision making among city, state, and federal agencies that leads to jurisdictional squabbling and impotence and the inability to take decisive measures, thereby unnecessarily increasing the dangers and costs that result from catastrophes such as the Santa Barbara oil spill? If so, how could these jurisdictional disputes be minimized in order to develop a smoothly run operation and enforcement program?

WHAT HAPPENED?

Parcel 402 of submerged lands was acquired by Union Oil Company and its partners on February 6, 1968. Union paid the federal government a bonus of $61.4 million, the highest single bid for one of the lots in the offering. The offer for competitive bids was announced by the Department of the Interior on December 21, 1967, despite opposition from the Santa Barbara community. On the tracts receiving acceptable bids, the government realized a record-breaking total of $602.7 million plus royalty payments of nearly 17 percent on future oil production.

Activity on parcel 402 began soon after the completion of the lease sale, with Union Oil as the operating partner. After drilling three exploratory wells and after discussions with the U.S. Geological Survey, Union determined that there would be three platforms on the parcel and that the first, platform A, would contain fifty-six wells. By January 14, 1969, three wells were finished and waiting for completion of onshore receiving facilities; a fourth well was being completed; and work on the ill-fated fifth well, A–21, had begun.

By 9 A.M. of January 28, 1969, drilling had been proceeding smoothly on A–21 for two weeks, and the well had reached its maximum designated depth of 3,479 feet. The crew began removing the lengths of pipe to which the drill bit was attached. At 10:45 A.M., after 720 feet of pipe had been removed, mud and gas began to escape through the pipe remaining in the well. On the platform was a blowout preventer designed to be attached to the end of the pipe for just such emergencies; however, the high volume of the escaping mud and gas made it impossible to connect the device. During the twelve to thirteen minutes that elapsed during this effort, the air was filled with a hydrocarbon mixture that reduced visibility and carried with it the threat of fire and explosion. The drill pipe was dropped back into the well and the shutdown valves attached to the well itself were closed. About fifteen minutes later, gas boils appeared in the water a few hundred feet from the platform. Gas was being forced upward by pressure from below and was escaping from the uncased well hole through a fissure or highly porous area in the ocean floor.

When the initial efforts to control the well failed, Union Oil called the famed blowout specialists, Red Adair, Inc., of Houston, Texas. On January 30, Red Adair personnel took over the task of regaining control of the well. The problem was compounded by the drill pipe being plugged and stuck at the bit. It could be neither pumped through nor removed. On February 2, the drill pipe was perforated near the bottom of the well, bypassing the plugged bit, and 3,000 barrels of drilling mud were forced into the well, noticeably slowing but not killing the well. Finally, ninety-seven holes 0.34 inches in diameter were perforated in the pipe from 2,860 feet down to 2,883 feet. More than 10,000 additional barrels of mud were required to kill the well, which was finally brought under control on February 7, at 7 P.M. Subsequently, over 4,000 sacks of cement were used to close the well permanently.

But Union's troubles were not over. On February 9, gas bubbles and oil began seeping from the ocean floor near platform A. A Union Oil spokesman later testified: "This was not unexpected since there were obviously openings in the ocean bottom connected to shallow sands which would have been pressurized during the time the well was out of control" (*Water Pollution,* part 3, p. 554). To relieve the pressure, Union proposed drilling wells from platform A into the pressurized shallow sands. Interior approved the plan, and Union was by the end of February producing approximately 450 barrels per day from these wells. Seeps continued, however, and there was an effort to bring the seepage up to the platform through a hose to dispose of it. Efforts were also made to close holes in the ocean floor with cement. By March 3, there appeared to be no more leakage from the original site, 800 feet from the platform, although oil continued to appear closer to the platform itself. Further efforts to relieve pressure were made by perforating the well that had been almost completed when A–21 was being drilled. By this time only a minor seep, estimated at 20 barrels per day, remained.

THE SIZE OF THE SPILL AND ITS AFTERMATH

Estimates of how much oil was lost into the water vary widely. Union people estimated on January 29 that the flow was 5,000 barrels per day. On January 30, they claimed they had been misquoted and reduced the estimate to 500 barrels per day.[2] The U.S. Geological Survey also estimated some 500 barrels per day, based on Union's estimate; it later admitted that this estimate was off by a factor of 2.[3] Santa Barbarans noticed the consistent discrepancy between government and Union estimates and those of Allen A. Allen, an executive of the General Research Corporation, a local research and development firm. His estimates, based on "a comprehensive sampling and scaling of the thickness of oil on the water," were five to ten times higher than the others (*Oil Pollution,* pp. 21–22). He estimated that between 13,000 and 63,500 barrels spilled into the channel in the first two days. By February 3, six days after the blowout, oil covered 251 square miles of the channel: 86 square miles were covered with heavy, dark oil, and the rest with a thinner film.

It should be noted here that both Union Oil and the U.S. Geological Survey consider Allen's estimates to be unrealistically high. In a communication to the author, a spokesman for Union Oil stated: "The most productive well on Platform A produced slightly in excess of 3,000 b/pd under conditions conducive to production, i.e., flow through pipe rather than fissures in the rock. This is less than 50 percent of Allen's low estimate." [4] A technical paper proposed by the U.S. Geological Survey indicated that Allen's estimates of spill were based on aerial reconnaissance mapping of the oil slick. The experience of U.S. Geological Survey with similar technique indicates that "an overestimate of the volume of oil is obtained from the extent of the slick . . . [which] ranges between a factor of 4 and 10, depending on wind and current conditions and the rate of leaking. Reducing Allen's estimates of about 5,000 b/pd by a factor of four would give an estimate of 1,250 b/pd and a reduction by a factor of 10 would suggest 500 b/pd. The latter figure is in agreement with visual estimates made by Union Oil Company and independently by engineers and inspectors of the Geological Survey's Conservation Division but they may be too conservative." [5]

Through February 3, the oil slick remained confined in an area gen-

[2] "Oil Firm Figure on Leakage Is Challenged by Researcher," *Santa Barbara News-Press,* February 2, 1969, p. A–3.
[3] "Channel Is Still Buzzing as Oil Still Flows," *Santa Barbara News-Press,* June 21, 1970, p. B–3.
[4] Letter to the author from Mr. Neal A. Schmale, an attorney with the Union Oil Company of California, dated June 17, 1975. Unless otherwise specified, all references to Union Oil spokesman refer to written or oral communications with the author.
[5] U.S. Geological Survey, "Geology, Petroleum Development, and Seismicity of the Santa Barbara Channel Region, California," Geological Survey Professional Paper 679 (1970), p. 44.

erally to the east of Santa Barbara proper, with small projections hitting the beaches lightly in the Ventura area. This was apparently due to advantageous offshore winds. On February 4, the U.S. Coast Guard reported that the slick had hit the beach in the western part of the city of Santa Barbara. Eventually the oil spread over 40 miles of some of the finest beach area in the country, and by February 5 it was several inches thick in places. There was a noticeable odor several miles inland; 660 square miles of the channel were now covered by the slick, 160 square miles with the heavy, dark oil. By the end of April, the best estimate indicated that at least 3 million gallons of oil had spilled into the channel (*Oil Pollution,* p. 22). The flow tapered off in March to an estimated 650 barrels per day by the end of the month; in April, it was 130 to 260 barrels per day. At the end of March, Union estimated the flow of oil at one barrel per hour.

Even the Coast Guard was skeptical about this estimate and warned that it might make the public and those responsible for action think that the situation was improving, thus slowing down their efforts. For example, in one of their official situation reports (SITREPS), dated March 26, 1969, the Coast Guard stated:

> There is evidence and testimony of credible witnesses that show Union Oil Co.'s original estimate of 500 bbl/day [being spilled] is ultra conservative. Present flow estimates should be treated likewise. . . . The minimizing image being presented by Union Oil Co. is lulling the local population into thinking the situation is improving and will be back to normal soon. (*Water Pollution,* part 3, p. 846)

During the late summer and early fall, the flow continued to decline to a relatively stable 13 barrels per day, with occasional greater spurts due to seismic activity.

Ecological Effects

The oil damage was not limited to esthetics. Many lives were lost—not human lives, to be sure, but those of an undetermined number of fish and other wildlife. According to marine biologist Carl Hubbs of La Jolla's Scripps Institution of Oceanography, "What we're seeing happen here is the creation of a dead sea. Some of the creatures affected by the disaster won't die for months, and it will be years, even decades, before this area of the ocean returns to normal." [6] According to a Union Oil spokesman, "Mr. Hubbs' statement was reported on February 21, 1969. This is a scant three weeks after the blowout. Time has shown that a 'dead sea' was not created. This area of the ocean has returned to normal. Although initial estimates of ecological damage were high, subsequent studies indicated that there were no lasting ill effects."

The long-range effects on wildlife of the spill and of the chemicals used

---

[6] *Life,* February 21, 1969, p. 60.

for controlling the oil remain to be evaluated. David Snell, a *Life* correspondent, went to San Miguel Island on an inspection tour and counted more than a hundred dead elephant seals and sea lions, mostly newborn pups.[7] Death was apparently caused either by ingestion of toxic oil or pneumonia resulting from oil inhalation. A spokesman for Union Oil responded:

> There is absolutely no basis for any conclusions that any dead elephant seals and sea lions were killed by ingestion of oil or pneumonia resulting from oil inhalation. To the contrary, all studies made of this matter failed to incriminate oil contamination as the cause of any deaths.

Ms. Jodi Bennett of the University of California, Santa Barbara, Museum of Zoology, made an independent study of the dead sea lions on San Miguel Island. In her opinion, oil caused a number of these deaths and had a serious impact on the breeding cycle of these animals (*Oil Pollution,* p. 124).

Immediate action was taken for the thousands of birds coated with the oil. On January 30, three bird-cleaning stations were set up by the U.S. Department of Fish and Game, with the cooperation of the U.S. Fish and Wildlife Service, the Audubon Society, the Humane Society, and Union Oil (which supplied equipment, chemicals and supplies, and a staff of ten men). During the first month after the spill, 1,575 affected but alive birds were brought into the centers, though estimates of the total number of birds killed ran as high as 8,000.

First estimates were that 20 percent of the birds brought to the centers were saved; a year later, however, the survival rate had declined to less than 11 percent. Estimates of the total number of birds affected had also declined to some 3,600. These were considered by wildlife experts to be relatively moderate losses. However, this may have been fortuitous due to seasonal and weather conditions. As Jack E. Hemphill of the California Bureau of Sport Fisheries and Wildlife emphasized: "Where oil facilities lie within or adjacent to [avian] wintering, feeding, or nesting areas, the potential peril of oil contamination is severely magnified" (*Water Pollution,* part 3, p. 848).

Paul de Falco, Jr., regional director for the Southwest Region, Federal Water Pollution Control Administration (FWPCA), stated early in February:

> . . . minimal acute effects have been experienced thus far by sea life. Planktonic and intertidal plants and invertebrate animals have maintained their abundance and variety; no fish kills have been observed as yet and the kelp beds are still in a reasonably healthy condition.

One of the marine animals observed by us to have demonstrated

[7] "Environment of Death," *Life,* June 13, 1969, pp. 23–26.

some sensitivity to the changes in their environment is a species of mollusk. (*Water Pollution,* part 3, p. 808)

Dr. Dale Straughan of the Allen Hancock Foundation of the University of Southern California said that her research failed to indicate effects on zoo- and phytoplankton, or on sea plants, fish, and larvae. One variety of barnacle, however, had been smothered by the oil. Her findings were hotly disputed even by members of her own staff. A study financed by the FWPCA and directed by Professor Michael Neushull of the Department of Biological Sciences, University of California, Santa Barbara, showed heavy damage in intertidal areas both to barnacles and to surf grass.

Woods Hole Oceanographic Institute, which has conducted careful research on the general chemical and biological effects of oil spills, feels that many statistical studies, such as those conducted in the Santa Barbara Channel, are not sensitive enough to reveal the real extent of damage done by oil. Their studies indicate grave effects on the marine environment from oil contamination.[8]

THE ACTIONS OF THE PARTIES INVOLVED

The Union Oil Company

The Union Oil Company of California was incorporated in California on October 17, 1890. In 1969 it ranked 58 among the *Fortune* 500 top industrial manufacturing companies and 13 among U.S. oil companies.[9] By 1972, these rankings had changed to 52 and 12, respectively.[10] In 1972 it had capital assets of $2.7 billion, with sales of $2.4 billion and net earnings of $122 million.[11]

But Union Oil's record in Southern California is not spotless. During the latter part of January 1969, a mud slide broke a Union Oil pipeline near the Santa Ana River. An estimated 1,500 barrels of crude oil was discharged into the river. Twice in 1967 the company bumped heads with the California fish and game statutes, the infraction being the pollution of Los Angeles harbor. These incidents, coupled with the *Torrey Canyon* disaster (at the time of its sinking Union was the tanker's operator), have given Union something of a reputation as a polluter. According to *Time,* Union is "known in Southern California as 'the go-go company' . . . [and] its competitors complain that Union is giving the industry a bad name." [12]

Union's frankness in informing the affected communities about the magnitude of the disaster and its possible effects was less than exemplary

8 Max Blumer, Howard L. Sanders, J. Fred Grassle, and George R. Hampson, "A Small Oil Spill," *Environment,* 13, 2 (1971), 3. Cited in *Oil Pollution,* p. 27.
9 *Fortune,* May 1970, p. 182.
10 *Fortune,* May 1973, pp. 222–24.
11 Union Oil Company of California, 1972 Annual Report.
12 "Environment: Tragedy in Oil," *Time,* 93:23–5 (February 14, 1969), p. 24.

at best. While the spill and the pollution of Santa Barbara beaches continued through the spring of 1969, both Union and the Santa Barbara Chamber of Commerce fostered a nationwide impression to the contrary.

> *Advertising Age* took the Santa Barbara Chamber of Commerce to task for engaging in misleading advertising, which Union had helped pay for. . . . Such advertising had already been roundly denounced as shortsighted by local citizens, conservationists, the local newspaper, and particularly by the "Get Oil Out" Committee [GOO], led by a former Democratic state senator, Alvin Weingand. (*Oil Pollution,* p. 114)

Union Oil's Cleanup Effort.   Lt. George H. Brown of the Coast Guard was notified of the problem at platform A on January 28 by Don Craggs of Union Oil, although at that time only natural gas was leaking. At 6:10 P.M. the same day, Craggs notified Lt. Brown that the leaking gas now contained oil and that there would be a pollution problem. Lt. Brown made an aerial survey of the area the following morning. At the ensuing briefing between Union and the Coast Guard, Union explained its problems with recirculating the drilling mud and added that Red Adair had been contacted to advise them on controlling the well.

It is ironic that during this critical period neither the company nor the Coast Guard informed the people whose lives might be severely affected by the spill. It was as if the problem were a purely technical one that should be attended to by experts without creating any panic in the public, whose interests were, from this viewpoint, best served by being kept ignorant of the impending disaster. As Allan Coates, the mayor of the city of Carpinteria, California, poignantly stated at the congressional hearings on February 14, 1969:

> In regard to the current oil spill, I want to raise a few questions: Why did the industry and the Coast Guard keep the spill a secret for 22 hours? They still haven't announced that it happened—a newsman told us. Why didn't they announce the second leak for 30 hours and why didn't they tell us that when the well was sealed we could expect some additional seepage as they now claim? Why was no effort made, other than futile spraying, to contain the oil slick, and prevent its spread with the use of booms, sweeping or burning? . . . It appears that the primary concern might have been to protect the platforms rather than the local communities. Why must the experts within the interior department be so partial to the oil industry? If they aren't, at least it certainly looks that way. (*Oil Spillage,* pp. 12–13)

Union Oil from the start assumed the responsibility for all control and cleanup operations. However, Union was quite aware of the potential for damage claims. Its president pointed out that, by accepting responsibility for the cleanup costs, the company was in no way acknowledging legal responsibility for damage costs that could run into hundreds of millions of dollars.[13] Hundreds of Union Oil employees were brought into the massive cleanup operation, which was eventually to cost the oil industry $5 million.[14] However, if well control and oil collection costs are included, the cleanup cost exceeded $10 million.[15] In this the company was assisted by the Coast Guard and other federal agencies.

Regardless of Union's intentions, its ability to cope with the problem of dispersion and containment was brought into question throughout the literature I surveyed. The present condition of the area may be a testimony to their diligence, but one is left with the overriding impression that the Santa Barbara spill was, in many respects, a laboratory in which to experiment with various cleanup methods. The operations, hampered by inadequate preparation and less than effective government leadership, were not reassuring. With the full use of beaches denied until June 1 and a seawall cleanup continuing until August 15, the public had a constant reminder of government and industry ineffectiveness. Nevertheless, T. H. Gaines of Union Oil detailed the company's efforts and findings during the postspill period. He prefaces his report: "In spite of all difficulties encountered, the beaches, harbors . . . have been restored to, and in some cases exceed their original beauty and cleanliness."[16]

Union's first effort at dispersing the oil was the use of Standard Oil of New Jersey's Corexit. This chemical is intended to put oil into solution in the water so that it will not be deposited on beaches or seabirds. Manufacturer's specifications state that the chemical is nontoxic at concentrations up to 10,000 parts per million; Union used a weak solution of only 25 parts per billion. The Coast Guard warned that dispersant chemicals are ineffective when used in small amounts and damaging to wildlife when used in quantities sufficient to break up a slick.[17] Chemicals were nevertheless used for approximately a week and a half, with no noticeable success. It was finally decided that enough chemicals had been used, according to the manufacturer's recommendations, to disperse four times the amount of oil that Union estimated to be present. On February 1, the FWPCA had ordered Union to halt spraying, except in the immediate area of platform A, but this decision was reversed later in the day, partly because of pressure from chemical companies who wanted opportunities to use their products. Spraying was continued with Corexit and Hal Kasden & Co.'s Polycomplex A–11. Controversy over the use of these chemicals was severe. The Sierra Club and the Audubon Society demanded that their use be halted; the oil and chemical companies demanded that it be continued. The Sierra Club complained that, since the chemical companies had proprietary rights not to place the formulas on their labels,

13 "Maybe a Few Nuts," *New Republic*, February 22, 1969, pp. 8–9.
14 Santa Barbara Chamber of Commerce, *The Santa Barbara Oil Story: Fact Sheet* (1969).
15 Mr. Schmale's letter, *op. cit.*
16 T. H. Gaines, *Pollution Control at a Major Oil Spill*, Union Oil Company (n.d.), p. 7.
17 "Oil Leak Report Delay Explained," *Santa Barbara News-Press*, January 30, 1969, p. A–4.

claims that the chemicals were nontoxic were meaningless.[18] The Interior Department had no regulatory power over these chemicals, since it lacked authority to certify them as safe for use. In addition, pilings were obtained from Los Angeles, and construction was begun on two 2,000-foot booms to be used to contain oil at the platform. The storm of February 5 and 6 broke the 1-inch steel cables holding these booms together. On February 14 and 16, after the well itself had been plugged, Union tried using 20-inch steel pipe booms to control the residual seepage, but again bad weather intervened. Unable to be contained, the oil coated 28 miles of beaches.

Cleanup operations on the beach, although more effective, were primitive and slow. During the first few days of the spill, offshore winds predominated, and most oil stayed out to sea. At 3:30 P.M. on February 4, the wind shifted and increased, and within two hours the beaches and harbor of Santa Barbara were coated with oil. The Coast Guard ordered a plastic inflated boom to protect the harbor. This boom, however, was punctured by a boat and sank, and the harbor filled with oil.

Natural clays and talc were of no help, and mulchers were utilized to spread straw on the beaches. The retrieval of the straw was the problem with this method—the attempt to burn the material failed. Rocks and seawalls were cleaned by hydroblasting and sandblasting.

The Oil Industry. The oil industry in general took steps to abate public displeasure in the form of a $150,000 grant from the Western Oil and Gas Association to the Hancock Foundation of the University of Southern California to study for one year the effects of oil pollution on the channel's ecology. The association emphasized that there were absolutely no strings attached to this grant, that it sincerely wanted to evaluate the effects of the leak.

The *Oil and Gas Journal* chastised the critics for not praising the cleanup efforts of Union Oil and other companies, and indicated that such risks are inevitable in major operations of this kind and must be borne in view of the economic returns and the country's growing petroleum needs. In an article entitled "Calm Appraisal Is Needed to End Santa Barbara Hysteria," the *Journal* stated:

> The hysteria whipped up over the Santa Barbara Channel blowout is beyond belief.
>
> Descriptions of the unusual accident by the general news media as a disaster and a tragedy are just out of touch with reality. The demand by some politicians for punitive moves against the entire oil indusrty is self-serving at its worst.
>
> A disaster—it wasn't. No lives were lost, no extensive destruction of property occurred. A regrettable mess—of course. Expensive— very. But the resulting pollution is something that can and is being cleaned up. Any damage to shipping or installations can be repaired.

[18] *Santa Barbara News-Press,* February 3, 1969, p. A–5.

Everyone deplores the loss of seagulls and other birds. But the first dead fish is yet to be discovered, and the strict use of approved cleanup materials should prevent damage to the marine ecology of the area.

The government doesn't ban commercial flying in this country after tragic air crashes. It doesn't halt highway travel even though thousands consistently die in accidents every year. Yet the first serious accident among some 1,100 wells drilled off Santa Barbara County and hundreds more in other waters inspires a cry for halting offshore drilling.

Union Oil Co. and its industry associates deserve praise—not malignment—for their efforts under difficult circumstances. They strained every muscle to plug the leak, prevent spread of the slick, and clean up the mess. They showed genuine concern and a high sense of responsibility.[19]

The Santa Barbara Community

Santa Barbara was a particularly unhappy location for an oil spill of any magnitude. The city is a wealthy town of about 147,000; it is situated amid spectacular scenery and perfect beaches. Since early in the century it has made the most of its natural assets and now lives primarily by tourism, which in 1968 was a $53 million industry.

Oil has always been with Santa Barbara, with the first systematic exploitation beginning in 1895: "By 1901 approximately 350 small wells had been drilled. Santa Barbara then did not object to being the world's first site for offshore oil development" (*Oil Pollution,* p. 14). However, in the early 1920s Santa Barbara's economy began to change to that of a wealthy resort and retirement community. This trend was accentuated in the middle 1950s by the establishment of a General Electric research and development center attracting light industry and the conversion of Santa Barbara College into a full-fledged campus of the University of California in 1958. This opened up another major sector for the service and light-industry-oriented economy—higher education (*Oil Pollution,* p. 15).

It would be no exaggeration to state that the people of Santa Barbara and neighboring communities were extremely angry at Union Oil and various agencies of the federal government, whom they jointly blamed for the spill. Their feelings were amply aired before the congressional hearings in Santa Barbara on February 14, 1969; in Washington, D.C., on February 5 and 6; and again in Santa Barbara on February 24 and 25, 1969.

Perhaps the most dramatic activity after the spill was the formation of the group called Get Oil Out! (GOO). James Bottoms, a local artist, and Marvin Stuart, a public relations expert, had the original idea for the group and asked Alvin Weingand, a former state senator, to assume active

---

[19] *Oil and Gas Journal,* February 17, 1969, p. 35.

leadership. Within a month after the spill, an estimated 70 percent of the south coast adult population had signed GOO petitions, and the group boasted 50,000 members in Santa Barbara alone. The objectives of GOO were these (*Water Pollution*, part 3, pp. 622–23):

First: Stop all present oil operations in the Santa Barbara Channel.
Second: Cancel all leases.
Third: Issue no new leases.
Fourth: Remove all offshore platforms.
Fifth: Declare the Santa Barbara Channel a national sanctuary.

Weingand presented to Senator Muskie's subcommittee a petition to ban all offshore drilling in the channel. The petition contained 100,000 signatures, 50,000 collected on the first day of circulation. GOO did not stop with this petition. On Easter Sunday, a mass meeting was held near Stearn's wharf. After the speeches, about 500 people spontaneously marched onto the wharf and took peaceful possession of the oil facilities. When a large truck loaded with new casings drove onto the wharf to make delivery, a group of protestors sat down in front of the truck to stop it. Police ordered the truck off the wharf. Following this incident, regarded as a symbolic victory by its participants, a group of 74 people picketed the wharf for fifteen days. On a smaller and more immediate scale, GOO held a meeting on February 1, only two days after the spill, to destroy oil company credit cards.[20]

GOO also sought a court injunction against further drilling and the installation of a new platform by the Sun Oil Company. This request was reviewed and denied by the U.S. Supreme Court on November 25, 1969. According to GOO, Sun's attorneys had told the court that the platform was already on its site, and "its removal at this point would be an immensely costly and laborious operation." [21] When, in December, Sun attempted actually to install the platform, GOO tried again to intervene. It held a "fish-in" with several boats from the Santa Barbara harbor anchoring on the drilling site. This maneuver was ultimately unsuccessful; when the boat that had been left to occupy the site drifted off, the platform was quickly anchored in place. GOO also initiated a suit in the U.S. Circuit Court of Appeals to force the U.S. Corps of Engineers to hold public hearings before any drilling permits were issued to oil companies. And on Earth Day, April 22, 1970, GOO sent the White House a petition, with 200,000 signatures, demanding complete cessation of oil development in the Santa Barbara Channel.

The Federal Government

The federal government responded to the Santa Barbara situation by dispatching teams of experts from various federal agencies to the scene.

---

20 "GOO Group to Meet to Destroy Cards," *Santa Barbara News-Press,* January 31, 1969, p. A–4.
21 "Oil: GOO Fishes In," *Newsweek,* December 8, 1969, p. 100.

Cleanup and surveillance activities were coordinated by the Coast Guard under the National Multiagency Oil and Hazardous Materials Contingency Plan approved by President Johnson in 1968.

In retrospect, however, one is struck by the length of time it took for any national significance to be attached to Union's accident. The only immediate public response from Washington was Secretary Hickel's reply to a wire from Santa Barbara County Supervisor George Clyde demanding that drilling be halted. Hickel shared Clyde's concern and pointed out that he had sent a team of experts to help control the well and was asking for recommendations for stricter drilling regulations. However, as the magnitude of the oil spill became apparent, Hickel himself flew out on Sunday, February 2, 1969. He was shocked by the scene and immediately asked for a voluntary moratorium on all drilling operations. The purpose of this moratorium was to draft a new and stricter set of drilling regulations. But when the oil companies objected that standby status cost between $10,000 and $20,000 per platform per day, the draft was announced as complete and the moratorium lifted the following day.

The next two days, however, apparently brought new evidence to Hickel's attention, and on February 7, reversing his stand again, he stated:

> I have directed all of the oil companies involved to reduce their platform operations to a standby condition until it can be shown . . . that we are not risking another blowout. . . .
>
> . . . It has become increasingly clear that there is a lack of sufficient knowledge of this particular geological area.
>
> This lack leaves us no other reasonable course of action than to halt drilling until Union's ruptured well can be sealed and until the required geological knowledge is secured.[22]

The president's first public acknowledgment of the spill came in a February 6 news conference, at which time he mentioned only changes in drilling regulations as the likely result of the spill. Perhaps as a result of this lack of attention from national figures, the national press was also somewhat delayed in carrying the story; the first major article in *The New York Times,* for example, did not appear until February 2, a full week after the blowout. On February 11, the president issued another statement, expressing his concern for the Santa Barbara tragedy and "directed the president's science advisor, Dr. DuBridge, to bring together at the earliest possible time a panel of scientists and engineers" to recommend ways in which the federal government can best assist "in restoring the beaches and waters around Santa Barbara." The DuBridge panel was also to "submit their views as to how best to prevent this kind of sudden and massive oil pollution." [23]

22 "Channel Oil Operations Are Ordered Shut Down," *Santa Barbara News-Press,* February 7, 1969, p. A–1.
23 U.S. General Services Administration, National Archives and Records Service, *Weekly Compilation of Presidential Documents,* 5, no. 7 (February 17, 1969), 254.

The DuBridge Panel. The panel convened in Santa Barbara on February 19 amid hopes that the community and "outside, nonbiased, nondefensive and outstandingly qualified people" [24] would be heard. After a closed-door morning session, however, Dr. John C. Calhoun, the panel's chairman, informed the press that Secretary Hickel had appointed a committee of his own in the Department of Interior to review existing drilling regulations. In order to avoid prejudicing this review, Hickel further instructed the panel "to avoid consideration of detailed drilling techniques or safety regulations in the Santa Barbara Channel. . . . *In no sense should you regard your mission as an investigation of this incident.*" [25] The panel was also to meet behind doors closed even to the press, and with testimony only from oil industry and Interior Department spokesmen. Santa Barbarans were outraged—the oil industry had access to the decision-making process; they were excluded entirely.

Interior formulated several significant changes in both drilling and administrative procedures: Drillers faced unlimited liability for damages, whether negligent or not; drilling and inspection requirements were tightened; variance authority was centralized in Washington; the companies had to submit full geological data to Interior to determine if the channel was safe for further drilling. Again with little opportunity for public participation in the decision, Secretary Hickel announced on April 2 that drilling would be resumed on the five active leases, but the ban would continue on the others.

The *News-Press,* in a front-page editorial, expressed the community's sense of betrayal:

> Interior Secretary Hickel has bluntly and unconscionably rejected the appeal of thousands of Santa Barbarans and their friends across the United States to stop oil drilling in the Santa Barbara Channel.
>
> Today he lifted his drilling ban on five of the Federal leases. . . . He says he had been assured that the drilling can now take place with a "minimum of hazard."
>
> What does he mean by a "minimum of hazard?" Any hazard is too great, in light of what has occurred. What happened to his announcement in February that all channel drilling had to be halted until Union Oil's ruptured well was sealed and until the required geological knowledge could be obtained?
>
> *   *   *
>
> What geological knowledge has been obtained in the past few weeks that in any way justifies resumption of drilling in this earthquake zone? [26]

---

24 Testimony of George Clyde, in *Oil Spillage,* p. 77.
25 Lee Dye, *Blowout at Platform A* (Garden City, N.Y.: Doubleday, 1971), p. 83. Emphasis added.
26 "An Editorial," *Santa Barbara News-Press,* April 2, 1969, p. A–1.

The questions went unanswered. Interior cited exemptions from the Freedom of Information Act as its justification for withholding information. The industry repeatedly offered proprietary rights and competitive position in similar justification.

The DuBridge panel report, released on June 2, further aggravated this conflict over information and access to decisions. The short report, in the form of a memorandum to the president, recognized that:

> There are a variety of different procedures that might be considered, ranging from:
>
> (a) immediate suspension of all oil drilling and pumping operations in the vicinity of the Union Oil platform, sealing up, if possible, existing leaks and abandoning the operation to:
>
> (b) proceeding to pump the oil as rapidly as possible to remove the oil and reduce its pressure and thus forever prevent future spillage.
>
> There are, of course, a variety of intermediate procedures that might be examined.

The panel concluded that:

> The maximum safety would be attained by proceeding approximately in accordance with alternative b. Specifically, they recommend that suitable structures be placed over existing leakage areas so the oil now leaking can be contained, and that removal of the oil from the various layers under the Santa Barbara Channel be expedited in order that pressures be reduced which force the oil upward into the ocean, with the eventual idea of removing the oil from the reservoir.[27]

The report specifically recommended underwater receptacles to collect the seeping oil (already used with minimal success), sealing the leaks through shallow drilling, pumping, and grouting (also tried without complete success), reviewing earthquake hazards, determining ease of oil migration between reservoirs, reducing pressures to hydrostatic or less, and, through use of additional wells, depleting all reservoirs under the channel as rapidly as was safe. Hickel commented: "It is clear to me that this distinguished panel had concluded that it would be more hazardous to withdraw from this lease than to proceed with the removal of all the oil in the reservoir to prevent oil leakage forever." [28]

In Santa Barbara, however, the response to the report was shock and anger. Rather than ceasing operations, more wells would be drilled! Further, the only voices to have been heard—surely not completely objective—came from the ranks of the lessor (including the Geological Survey), and the leaseholder. The affected communities and outside experts had been ignored. A protest meeting called by GOO for the

27 Dye, *Blowout at Platform A*, p. 84.
28 "Teague Urges Hickel to Reject Panel's Oil Report," *Santa Barbara News-Press*, June 3, 1969, p. A–1.

following Sunday brought together about 1,500 Santa Barbarans to denounce the panel and demand remedial action. Alvin Weingand of GOO dismissed both the panel and the theory, stating that he found it "utterly incomprehensible that a group of scientists would come to this tragic conclusion. We've had oil in this fissure for eons and until Union Oil started drilling there were no significant spills due to the so-called pressures." [29]

The question of what rights and whose should be protected is, of course, at the heart of the dilemma. In a precedent-setting decision, the U.S. Supreme Court held in the case of *U.S.* v. *California* (322 U.S. 19 [1946], since reaffirmed in more recent decisions),[30] that the federal government and not the state or localities has the right to the resources under the outer continental shelf. Even under the Submerged Lands Act (1953, as amended in 1970) the states have only limited rights within the 3-mile territorial limit.[31]

Thus, should interests located immediately adjacent to this country's offshore resources have either the right to block or exclusive call on the revenues from offshore development? How and by whom are the rights of landlocked states to be protected? Further, are the "development of oil" and the "interests of the people" mutually exclusive? The tougher question is: Should some areas be excluded from development and if so, who makes this decision and upon what criteria is the decision based? The question is not limited to either oil or Santa Barbara but is of broader import; should certain areas bear all the burden of development? Is strip mining in Arizona preferable to oil development in the Santa Barbara Channel?

Congress.   Congressional response to the blowout at A–21 began with a flurry of activity. The Subcommittee on Air and Water Pollution of the Senate Public Works Committee, which had been holding hearings on unrelated water pollution bills, heard testimony on the Santa Barbara situation on February 5 and 6 in Washington, and on February 24 and 25 in Santa Barbara. In the House of Representatives, the Subcommittee on Flood Control and the Subcommittee on Rivers and Harbors met in Santa Barbara on February 14 to hear testimony on both the spill and the flood that had ravaged the area just before Union's accident. These hearings produced information on what had happened, a great deal of public exposure for the various individuals involved, and very little else.

Santa Barbara's Congressman Teague, who was not generally given to espousing liberal causes with potentially antibusiness implications, nonetheless introduced three bills: to prohibit all future channel leases and rescind those in effect; to amend the FWPCA Act to impose strict liability for oil spills; and to bar the secretary of the interior from permitting any

29 "Panel Calls for More Wells to End Oil Seepage," *Santa Barbara News-Press,* June 2, 1969, p. A–1.
30 See, for example, *U.S.* v. *Maine,* 95 S. Ct. 1155 (1975), and *U.S.* v. *State of Alaska,* No. 73–1888 (1975).
31 43 U.S.C. 1301 et. seq.

mineral exploration or development within the two-mile federal buffer zone around the Santa Barbara sanctuary. Alan Cranston, the state's freshman senator, introduced bills that would end all drilling in the Santa Barbara Channel, suspend all other offshore drilling on the outer continental shelf leases off California, and initiate a study of methods of drilling, producing, and transporting oil to end the threat of pollution (*Oil Pollution*, pp. 7, 116–17).

These bills, however, were opposed by the administration and were not even reported out of their respective committees. Activity continued in 1970. The administration, through Senator Murphy, introduced its own bill, which would rescind, with compensation, twenty channel leases in favor of an ecological preserve. This bill was opposed both by the oil industry and the environmentalists, the former considering it to go too far; the latter, not far enough.

But 1970 produced no more success than had 1969. Even Humble Oil's discoveries in waters 1,100 feet deep could not bring any bills out of committee.[32] Indeed, despite administration support for some limited measures, congressional interest in Santa Barbara seemed to be waning. All bills introduced in the 91st Congress died upon its adjournment without any having been reported out of committee; bills introduced into the 92nd Congress were unable even to obtain hearings.

The State of California

Governor Reagan reacted immediately to the news of the spill. In a press release on January 30, he pledged "the full resources of the State of California" to aid federal personnel in cleaning up the oil.[33] The governor announced his support for a resolution by State Senator Robert Lagomarsino asking the federal government for state control of offshore development in federal waters. He also ordered all state agencies involved in oil regulation to institute a review of their own drilling standards and emergency procedures. Until the review could be completed, the State Lands Commission unequivocally suspended all leasing, drilling, and exploratory activities, allowing only the continuation of production on already completed wells. Apparently the commission was ultimately unconvinced that regulations that would prevent another spill could be drafted, *for this suspension has continued in state-owned tidelands, and no new operations have been permitted to this date.*

Very little happened after the initial activity by the governor and the State Land Commission. By late spring 1969, pressures were building for some stronger form of state response. During hearings on Senator Cranston's bill to ban channel drilling, other senators pointedly asked why Santa Barbarans were making demands in Washington while there was no action in the state itself.

[32] U.S. Congress, Senate, Subcommittee on Minerals, Materials, and Fuels, Committee on Interior and Insular Affairs, *Hearings on S.1219, S.2516, S.4017, S.3516, and S.3093,* 91st Cong., 2nd sess., July 21–22, 1970, section A, p. 2.
[33] Office of the Governor, State of California, News Release 56, January 30, 1969.

Senator Cranston reiterated this problem in a letter asking the governor to support state legislation as the best way to encourage federal action. Along with Cranston's plea to the governor came the first state action: Democratic Assemblyman Jesse Unruh announced that he would introduce a bill banning drilling off Santa Barbara in June 1969. Bills were introduced to, among other things, create new sanctuaries, allow the state to ban all offshore drilling, and increase criminal liability in the event of accidents. None passed. Again in 1970 the same bills were defeated, despite Governor Reagan's plea for a federal ban on drilling.[34] The year's only legislative accomplishment was the California Senate's Joint Resolution 2, which was virtually a repeat of the resolution passed in 1969. It asked the federal government and Congress to apply California's stricter standards to oil and gas drilling in federal waters, and also to halt drilling permanently in the Santa Barbara Channel. It was not until 1971 that binding legislation was passed relating to Santa Barbara, creating a new sanctuary of approximately 400,000 acres around the islands in the channel. This bill is to date the state's only legislative accomplishment.

Lawsuits

Virtually all the parties involved, even peripherally, in the Santa Barbara oil spill took legal action. The result was a jumble of lawsuits in every direction and jurisdiction. Class actions were filed by property owners, fishermen, boat owners, and other groups; individual damage suits proliferated. But the larger issues were dealt with primarily in suits by and against various government bodies.

Suits seeking monetary compensation were the first to be filed. In civil actions, the City and County of Santa Barbara, the City of Carpinteria, and the State of California jointly sued Union Oil and the other operators of platform A for a little over $560 million in damages. The State of California, alleging negligence, sued the Department of the Interior for another $500 million.

In July 1974, Union Oil, Mobil Oil, Gulf Oil, Texaco, and Peter Bawden Drilling Co. agreed in an out-of-court settlement to pay $9.7 million in damages—$4.5 million to the state, $4 million to Santa Barbara, $775,000 to Santa Barbara County, and $200,000 to Carpinteria. In announcing the settlement, a spokesman for Union Oil pointed out that it covered only actual damages. "We were always willing to pay actual damages," he said.[35] The suit against the Department of the Interior was dropped at this same time. By July 1974 the four oil companies had paid about $6.3 million in damages to private individuals and companies.[36]

The district attorney of Santa Barbara filed criminal actions against the companies charging that the spill was a public nuisance and seeking $500

---

[34] Reagan, State of the State Message, January 6, 1970, p. 3.
[35] "Oil Concerns Agree to Settle Lawsuit on California Spill," *The Wall Street Journal*, July 24, 1974, p. 5.
[36] "Channel Blowout Oil Suit Settled," *San Francisco Chronicle*, July 24, 1974, p. 2.

per day in fines for the duration of the spill which eventually continued for almost a year. This suit was tried in municipal court in 1971. The judge was brought in from outside Santa Barbara County. The companies pleaded guilty to the charges for *one* day only. By this time a number of individual and class suits had been settled at considerable cost to the companies and the judge, saying that they had already been punished enough, dismissed the remaining charges and fined the companies $500.

These suits, however, did not touch upon the larger issue that had been brought to national attention by the spill: the issue of the rights and needs of a community versus the rights and needs of the federal government. In one of the first actions of its kind, the city and county sought a permanent injunction against all drilling in the channel, asserting that drilling endangered the community's environmental rights. The suit further questioned the constitutionality of the Interior Department's issuing leases and permits while denying public hearings and access to information.

The American Civil Liberties Union brought a similar suit, *Weingand* v. *Hickel,* on behalf of GOO and seventeen individual Santa Barbarans. This was ACLU's maiden effort in the field of environmental litigation. Both suits made the same—now timeworn—arguments: that the community should have the same right of access as the oil industry to the decision-making process and the information that led to decisions. These claims were vindicated to a degree by passage of the 1970 National Environmental Policy Act (NEPA), which made mandatory the public participation and release of information that these suits asked for and, in the words of Martin Levine, deputy counsel for Santa Barbara, "provide the due process protection that we have always insisted we were entitled to." [37] The suits were amended after the passage of NEPA to ask for an injunction against further drilling and platform installation permits until the Interior Department complied with the act's provisions. Interior and the oil industry, maintaining a united front, contended that since the channel leases had been negotiated before the act was passed, the leases remained in effect. Finally, however, bowing to legal pressure on other fronts as well (especially the Alaska pipeline case), Interior capitulated. It agreed that NEPA would be complied with before any further activity was allowed in Santa Barbara. Having been granted by legislation what they had sought through the courts, Santa Barbara and the ACLU dropped their suit.

Environmentalists were not alone in complaining of Interior's actions. Several small oil companies, headed by Pauley Petroleum, also argued that their rights were violated. Had the new and stiffer regulations— especially the high-risk unconditional liability for damages—been in force originally, these companies maintained they would never have submitted bids. Accordingly, they sued Interior for recision of their leases, for return of the bonuses and rent already paid, as well as for payment of

[37] "The Santa Barbara Saga—Pre- and Post-N.E.P.A.," *Lincoln Law Review,* December 1971, p. 79.

profits expected at time of bidding. This suit, which has been heard and is presently awaiting decision by the Court of Claims, should be of considerable interest to both the oil industry and the federal government, for it will set a precedent for financial compensation to the oil companies in the event of lease termination.

In one final ironic twist, Union, after steadfastly maintaining that the accident at platform A had been unforeseeable and unpreventable, sued its drilling contractor, the Peter Bawden Company, for negligence, which Union charged had caused the spill.

COULD THE BLOWOUT HAVE BEEN AVOIDED?

The Broad Question: Jurisdictional Disputes— How Not To Administer a Program

A study of the administration of federal oil leases leads to the conclusion that federal concern is primarily with the recovery of oil in the most expeditious and economic manner. Little provision exists either for protecting the interests of other affected parties or for resolving the conflicts that inevitably arise from the development of the leases by the oil companies.

The entire administration of the leasing program can best be described as a "jurisdictional quagmire and competition between multiple agencies with restricted responsibilities" (*Oil Pollution*, p. 50). Since the Outer Continental Shelf Lands (OCSL) Act of 1953, leasing authority is divided: from the 3-mile limit, states control shoreward leases; Interior, seaward leases. In the Interior Department, the actual administration of the leasing program is divided among several agencies. The leases themselves are issued by the Bureau of Land Management; exploration and technical operations of drilling and production are authorized and supervised by the U.S. Geological Survey; regulations to reduce hazards to navigation are considered by the Coast Guard; and the placement of platforms is reviewed and authorized by the Army Corps of Engineers, which also issues permits for exploration and drilling activities.

The secretary of the interior is authorized by the OCSL Act to require the prevention of pollution in offshore drilling activities. However, the pollution control facilities of the Interior Department in 1969 were highly limited. FWPCA (now the Federal Water Quality Administration) was charged with cooperating with, and coordinating the activities of, the states in designing programs to improve the quality of interstate waters. It was not designed, and did not function, as a watchdog over the activities of other agencies within the department. At the same time, the administrative structure of the leasing program facilitated the agencies' avoidance of the issue. The result was characterized by one California official as "Federal schizophrenia" (*Water Pollution*, part 3, p. 455).

The Corps of Engineers, although it has a specific mandate to administer the Refuse Act of 1899, which applies to virtually all discharges into navigable waters, similarly managed to escape responsibility for the pollution aspects of the leasing program in Santa Barbara. The corps did not consider its responsibility under the Refuse Act relevant to its granting of permits for a program primarily administered by the Department of the Interior (*Water Pollution*, part 3, p. 541). But the mineral resources section of the department viewed pollution control as peripheral to its primary concern of resource development (*Water Pollution*, part 2, p. 281).

The State of California's agency, the State Lands Commission, is required by statute, in contrast to the Department of the Interior, to balance competing interests in determining whether a lease is in the best interests of the state. Responding to this requirement, the state had respected the Santa Barbara community's own decision to base its economy on tourism and light industry rather than oil. A Union Oil spokesman, however, suggests this is only partly true:

> A map of the Santa Barbara Channel would show that the sanctuary is of limited size. Furthermore, there are four platforms located in state waters off the Summerland/Carpenter area, there is a drilling island located off the Rincon and there are oil drilling piers located off the Rincon. All of the above are in state waters. In addition, platforms are located in state waters off the Goleta area and westward along the coast. I think you should also be aware that the Federal Government has created a sanctuary slightly outside the Santa Barbara/State sanctuary.

Furthermore, in 1966, largely as a result of citizen pressure, the state legislature established a 3-mile-wide sanctuary for sixteen miles along the Santa Barbara coast, and the city and county promptly enacted zoning controls that similarly prohibited onshore drilling.

When the Supreme Court in 1965 settled a long-standing dispute over the ownership of the submerged lands in the channel and established as federal territory the lands seaward of the 3-mile limit, the stage was set for the coming conflict.[38] The local concern over federal leases was twofold: (1) Pollution and esthetic degradation would be caused by the wells in federal waters; (2) establishment of platforms in waters adjacent to the sanctuary would inevitably lead to the authorization of drilling by the state within the sanctuary.

The community began to press its case as early as February 1967, expressing its opposition to leases in the channel on grounds that the economy of the community depended on the unspoiled beauty of the area and that uncontrolled erection of platforms would severely damage tourist, convention, and vacation industries. It asked for public hearings; for a year's moratorium so a study could be made of the impact leasing would have on the area; for reduction of the size of the area opened for

[38] See, for example, *U.S.* v. *California*, 381 US 139 (1965), and *Gulf Oil* v. *Morton*, 493 F.2d 141 (1973).

leasing, pending future developments in technology; and for regulations to limit the number of platforms that would be built. Interior responded that it was unwilling to accept a delay in calling for bids; that the oil industry would certainly protest any delay; and that there could well be pressures on Congress from the industry if the request for a moratorium was pursued. Santa Barbara was eventually granted sixty days for its report, a 2-mile buffer zone around the state sanctuary, and the requirement that no platform be constructed to hold fewer than twenty wells. But the buffer zone did not include all the area that had been requested (which would have included the spot on which A–21 was drilled), and it appeared that the twenty-well minimum would be a meaningless requirement, since the $5 to $6 million cost of each platform dictated more intensive use of the platforms (platform A, for instance, was designed for fifty-six wells).

Santa Barbara did succeed, however, in obtaining one public hearing, although this was under the aegis of the Army Corps of Engineers, not the Interior Department. The hearing was held in November 1967 on the emplacement of a platform by Phillips Petroleum, which had obtained the first lease after the 1965 Supreme Court decision. Nonetheless, it was a mere formality—the platform was already on a barge on the way to its site in the channel.[39] It was after this hearing that the departments of Army and Interior determined that questions of pollution would be handled by Interior. No further public hearings were held by either department, despite repeated requests.

The Narrow Question: Unenforced Regulations and Insufficient Inspection Equal No Protection

The State of California had consistently attempted to gain some jurisdiction over the federal leasing program in the area. The state felt that its own drilling regulations were more adequate for the protection of its coastline than federal regulations. However, California's requests for regulatory authority over drilling operations were consistently dismissed as impossible, despite precedents for such cooperation between federal and state authorities in Texas and Louisiana (*Water Pollution*, part 3, pp. 606–8).

A factor undoubtedly contributing to Interior's disallowance of state participation was the absolute confidence of the industry and its regulators in the state of offshore technology. Even after the spill, this confidence was unshaken. A Union spokesman stated at one point that "no prudent engineer could guarantee against this recurring," but followed this statement by saying that with additional safeguards, drilling could continue safely (*Water Pollution*, part 3, p. 582). Another stressed that storm chokes were available to shut off the flow of oil in a well even if the platform were completely destroyed in a hurricane; he also pointed out later

39 "Complex Oil Suits History Is Traced," *Santa Barbara News-Press*, September 13, 1970, p. A–12.

that neither the government nor industry had the proper apparatus to take oil off the ocean in a massive spill (*Water Pollution,* part 2, p. 336). Donald W. Solanas, regional oil and gas supervisor of the Geological Survey testified that he had enforced "what I would consider stricter requirements" regarding pollution control, especially "because of the 'hostility' of the residents of the Santa Barbara coastline to any oil operation being conducted in the Channel." When pressed for the specific requirements, he stated that he had required "more alertness and more caution in every person's mind that was involved in this operation in the Santa Barbara Channel" (*Water Pollution,* part 3, pp. 678–79). He was also confident of the industry's ability to conduct safe operations, even after the spill (*Water Pollution,* part 3, p. 685).

Those responsible for controlling wells after the failure of these devices (Red Adair's crew) were perhaps understandably more skeptical of their efficacy (*Water Pollution,* part 3, p. 635; *Oil Spillage,* p. 273). According to Interior estimates, a blowout rate of 2.5 per thousand wells has been the norm in offshore drilling. At that rate, with a potential of 4,000 or more wells in the Santa Barbara Channel as a result of the leases, Santa Barbarans could anticipate as many as ten more blowouts.[40]

According to a Union Oil spokesman, significant improvements have been made in the technology of prevention and control of oil spillage that considerably reduce the danger of future blowouts and oil spills in the outer continental shelf.[41]

The issue hinged on the question of casing requirements. Oil wells are "cased" by lengths of steel pipe cemented together to enclose the hold from surface to oil pool, the first length or "string" going from platform to ocean floor. Within the casing, drilling mud is circulated to carry away the drill cuttings. Casing is ordinarily heavy enough to offset any upward pressure from the oil- and gas-bearing strata below. When the "string" is set, drilling recommences and continues to a depth usually specified by state and federal regulations (variable according to the final anticipated well depth), when the "surface casing" is set. Very deep wells may require intermediate casing strings to be set before oil is reached.

In wells the depth of A–21, federal regulations specify that surface casing be set at approximately 800 feet below the ocean floor. But Union's investigation showed that, at this location, the oil sands were extremely shallow. Complying with federal regulations would have meant that they would have had to drill 800 feet directly into the producing area; with no surface casing cemented in place above 800 feet, there would have been no way to control the flow of oil. Union felt that the surface casing needed to be set in place before that point was reached. They requested and were granted a variance by Donald Solanas. As a result of the variance, the surface casings of well A–21 and the other wells from platform A were cemented at 239 feet, and the well was then drilled to its final depth of

---

[40] Ross MacDonald and Robert Eaton, "Thou Shalt Not Abuse the Earth," *The New York Times Sunday Magazine,* October 12, 1969, passim.
[41] "Critique of Bureau of Land Management Draft EIS for Lease Sale 35, May 1975," prepared by Dames and Moore for the Western Oil and Gas Association.

3,479 feet. The blowout occurred as the drilling equipment was being removed preparatory to cementing a complete string of casing in the well (*Water Pollution,* part 3, pp. 552–65). The uncased hole allowed the escape of oil to the surface of the water.

The importance of this casing program was underscored in an exchange between Senator Baker and Fred Hartley of Union Oil (*Water Pollution,* part 2, p. 344):

> *Senator Baker:* "Are you saying then, that had the well been cased to a level of 2,000 feet, the escape of oil through a fissure in the sea floor would not have occurred?"
>
> *Mr. Hartley:* "That is correct. That is what we think for sure and, of course, you have now joined the great group of people who are using hindsight."

The state insisted that its own requirements would not have allowed this variance. In reviewing their own drilling program, state officials checked the twenty-five offshore wells drilled under state leases between 1967 and 1969, and stated: *"In all cases, both a conductor casing string and a surface casing string were set prior to deeper drilling"* [emphasis added] (*Water Pollution,* part 3, p. 617).

A further question over the adequacy of federal regulation was raised by comparing federal and state inspection schedules. The California State Lands Division Field Office for Santa Barbara and Ventura counties alone had ten people on its staff. The U.S. Geological Survey had only ten petroleum engineers and two technicians for the approximately 2,000 miles of the Pacific Region (California, Oregon, Washington), with only one engineer and one technician assigned to the Santa Barbara Channel exclusively. The state required frequent, sometimes daily, inspections (as it would have for A–21). Solanas testified that the Geological Survey tried to inspect a well at least once during drilling operations. He stressed that his office received and reviewed daily the drilling log from all wells. There were, however, no inspections of platform A during the drilling of A–21. However, he maintained:

> We could have had an engineer on that platform 24 hours a day, 7 days a week, and he could have been right on that drilling floor at the time this accident happened and he could not have done any more about this than the people on the platform did do to try to correct this accident that happened and was blowing out on that rig floor. (*Water Pollution,* part 3, p. 673)

Later evidence, however, cast doubt on Solanas's assertions. A year after the spill, the Geological Survey released its Professional Paper 679, entitled "Geology, Petroleum Development, and Seismicity of the Santa Barbara Channel Region, California." This was a comprehensive review of the Santa Barbara Channel and the drilling operations there. The report presented an interesting fact not previously brought out. On each of the four wells drilled from platform A before A–21, there had been a loss of circulation of drilling mud. At a depth of about 2,000 feet, the mud would flow away from the drilling shaft through the porous surrounding rock. The paper stated:

> This repeated loss of circulation indicated qualitatively that some part or parts of the capping strata above the shallowest major reservoir of the Dos Cuadras field were permeable to drilling fluid and cement, or perhaps were fragile enough to be fractured by the pressure of the drilling mud.[42]

It therefore seems highly probable that a more rigorous inspection program would have discovered this problem, recognized its implications, and perhaps initiated action that would have prevented the blowout.

EPILOGUE: A CHANGE IN POLICY OR MORE OF THE SAME?

On January 1, 1970, the National Environmental Policy Act became law. It stated that it was national policy "to create and maintain conditions under which man and nature can exist in productive harmony, and fulfill the social, economic and other requirements of present and future generations of Americans." [43] This act required that every federal agency

> include in every recommendation or report on proposals for legislation and other major Federal actions significantly affecting the quality of the human environment, a detailed statement by the responsible official on:
>   (i) the environmental impact of the proposed action,
> (ii) any adverse environmental effects which cannot be avoided should the proposal be implemented,
> (iii) alternatives to the proposed action,
> (iv) the relationship between local short-term uses of man's environment and the maintenance and enhancement of long-term productivity, and
>   (v) any irreversible and irretrievable commitments of resources which could be involved in the proposed action should it be implemented.[44]

The act also provided that these impact statements be made available to the public.

Thus it seemed that the primary issue underlying Santa Barbara's demands was resolved in this legislation. Indeed, it was through the applica-

---

[42] Dye, *Blowout at Platform A*, p. 43.
[43] National Environmental Policy Act, reproduced in the Bureau of National Affairs, *Environment Reporter: Federal Law* (1970), p. 71:0101.
[44] *Ibid.*

tion of this act to the leasing program, as described above in the section on legal actions, that Santa Barbara achieved its first significant success in preventing further oil development in the channel. A draft environmental impact statement was released in May 1971 on applications to install two new platforms in the channel. One of these was Union's platform C, which had been built and waiting in Vancouver for two years. The impact statement appeared to favor building the platforms, but on September 20, Secretary of the Interior Rogers Morton announced that the permits would be denied. Union has challenged this denial in court, and the suit is presently on appeal; in an ironic shift of alliances, the city and county of Santa Barbara are intervenors in the case on behalf of the government.

But much of the fate of the channel is still to be decided. The original two mile federal buffer zone around the state sanctuary was made into an ecological preserve after the spill, and an executive moratorium on exploratory operations in the adjoining area was imposed by Secretary Hickel in February 1969. The oil companies challenged this moratorium, and on June 21, 1972, a federal judge in Los Angeles declared that Secretary Morton did not have legal authority to suspend drilling. On April 21, 1971, Secretary Morton announced that the moratorium would end on January 1, 1973, unless Congress took some action. Interior, however, appealed the court decision and also declared that no drilling would be allowed until after its appeal was heard by the courts. Santa Barbara also appeared on behalf of the federal government in this case. Subsequently, a Court of Appeals held that the reason for any suspension terminated when the 92nd Congress adjourned in 1972 without taking action on the legislation.[45]

The moratorium, however, was to be a temporary solution pending legislative action by Congress on an administration bill, introduced each year since the spill, to terminate thirty leases directly opposite Santa Barbara and around the channel islands. The bill has not found support in Congress. The administration's bill died in the 92nd Congress and was not introduced in the 93rd. During this period, development has been allowed in other areas of the channel.

On April 13, 1973, the U.S. Department of Interior announced that it was allowing oil companies with leases in the buffer zone to combine their lease tracts for joint operations. This was seen as the beginning of the steps necessary to allow new drilling in the future in an area that the Nixon administration once proposed as an oil-free sanctuary.

The reaction of state and city officials was swift, though predictable. A spokesman for the State Lands Commission stated that a resumption of federal drilling in the area would "increase the pressure [from the companies] on us to do something" about the state's own drilling moratorium, still in effect since 1969.[46]

Perhaps it was the changed environment of the "energy crisis" or a more realistic assessment of the situation, but GOO had softened its

---

[45] *Gulf Oil* v. *Morton*, 493 F.2d 141 (9th Cir., 1973).
[46] "New Santa Barbara Drilling Move," *San Francisco Chronicle*, April 14, 1973, p. 14.

position somewhat on the question of drilling: it stated that it was "willing to tolerate test drilling to find out what oil reserves are available for tapping only in the event of a national crisis. But we remain utterly opposed to any new oil production in the channel." [47]

In September 1974 the Senate passed and sent to the House a bill that would have given coastal states a share of federal offshore oil revenues. It would also have set up a $200 million fund to be used to compensate states for any adverse environmental, social, and economic effects of drilling in federal waters.[48] The bill did not pass.

The mood of the city remains anti-oil (a public opinion poll held in November 1973 showed that two-thirds of the population wanted oil drilling stopped),[49] but its intensity may be lessening. For example, in a recent referendum in Santa Barbara County as to whether or not Exxon should be allowed to construct an onshore processing plant for their proposed Santa Ynez Unit, the voters by a slight margin of approximately 835 votes out of some 70,215 voted to allow the building of this facility.[50] Only time will tell whether or not there has been a permanent change in local sentiment or just a temporary one because of current circumstances.

New suits, however, continue to be filed. In August and September 1974, GOO tried to block Atlantic Richfield and Standard Oil of California from drilling more wells in the channel. GOO sued the California Coastal Zone Conservation Commission for exempting ARCO and Standard from having to have permits to drill. Both companies had constructed platforms at the new sites prior to the 1972 Coastal Act. This became the basis for their claim to begin drilling.[51] A California Superior Court later issued a temporary restraining order halting the Standard program.[52] The matter is now in the hands of the all-new California State Lands Commission.[53]

The deciding factor in the "to drill or not to drill" controversy will inevitably turn out to be the energy crisis. Regardless of the issues involved, increased production of oil, and thus at least partial independence from the Arab countries, will be the dominant theme. Shared revenues and greater safeguards may temper the blow, but the fact that will probably remain is that offshore drilling will shortly be on the increase.

SELECTED REFERENCES

BEAM, FLOYD A., and PAUL E. FERTIG, "Pollution Control Through Social Cost Conversion," in *The Accounting Sampler,* ed. Thomas J. Burns and Harvey S. Hendrickson (New York: McGraw Hill, 1972).

47 *Ibid.*
48 "Senate OKs Offshore Oil Bill," *San Francisco Chronicle,* September 19, 1974.
49 "Old Animosities Rise Again in Santa Barbara as Oilmen Eye Channel," *The Wall Street Journal,* November 26, 1973, p. 1.
50 *Oil and Gas Journal,* June 2, 1975, p. 43.
51 "New Channel Drilling Suit," *Oil and Gas Journal,* September 11, 1974, p. 2.
52 *Oil and Gas Journal,* December 9, 1974, p. 44.
53 *Oil and Gas Journal,* January 13, 1975, p. 15.

BLUMER, MAX, HOWARD L. SANDERS, FRED J. GRASSLE, and GEORGE R. HAMPSON, "A Small Oil Spill," *Environment,* 13, 2 (1971).

DAVIES, J. CLARENCE, III, *The Politics of Pollution* (New York: Pegasus, 1971).

DILLEY, STEVEN C., "Case of the Nebulous Numbers," *Harvard Business Review,* November–December 1974, pp. 42–52.

DOWNS, ANTHONY, "Up and Down With Ecology—The Issue Attention Cycle," *The Public Interest,* 28 (summer 1972), pp. 38–50.

———, et al., *The Political Economy of Environmental Control* (Berkeley, Calif.: Institute of Business and Economic Research, University of California, 1972).

DYE, LEE, *Blowout at Platform A* (Garden City, N.Y.: Doubleday, 1971).

GAINES, H. T., *Pollution Control at a Major Oil Spill* (Union Oil Company, Los Angeles, California, n.d.).

HICKEL, WALTER, *Who Owns America?* (Englewood Cliffs, N.J.: Prentice-Hall, 1971).

KNEESE, ALLEN V., "Why Water Pollution Is Economically Unavoidable," *Transaction,* April 1968, pp. 31–36.

MACDONALD, ROSS, and ROBERT EATON, "Thou Shalt Not Abuse the Earth," *The New York Times Sunday Magazine,* October 12, 1969.

McELRATH, DENNIS C., "Urban Differentiation: Problems and Prospects," *Law and Contemporary Problems,* 30 (winter 1965), 103–10.

McKEE, JACK EDWARD, "Water Pollution Control: A Task for Technology," *California Management Review,* 14, 3 (spring 1972), 88–91.

MEAD, WALTER J., "The System of Government Subsidies to the Oil Industry," article presented before the Subcommittee on Antitrust and Monopoly, Senate Committee on the Judiciary, Washington, D.C., March 11, 1969, pp. 121–30.

———, and PHILIP E. SORENSEN, "The Economic Cost of the Santa Barbara Oil," paper prepared for the Santa Barbara Oil Symposium, University of California, Santa Barbara, December 1970.

MOLOTCH, HARVEY, "Oil in Santa Barbara and Power in America," *Sociological Enquiry,* 40 (1970), 131–44.

MURDOCH, WILLIAM, and JOSEPH CONNELL, "All About Ecology," *Center Magazine,* 3 (January–February 1970), 56–63.

NASH, A. E., KEIR MANN, E. DEAN, and PHIL G. OLSEN, *Oil Pollution and the Public Interest: A Study of the Santa Barbara Oil Spill* (Berkeley, Calif.: Institute of Governmental Studies, University of California, 1972).

"National Environmental Policy Act," reproduced in the Bureau of National Affairs, *Environment Reporter: Federal Laws, 1970.*

NETSCHERT, BRUCE C., "Energy vs. Environment," *Harvard Business Review,* January–February, 1973, pp. 24–36.

POTTER, FRANK M., JR., "Everyone Wants to Save the Environment but No One Knows Quite What to Do," *Center Magazine,* 3 (March–April 1970), 34–40.

———, "Pollution and the Public," *Center Magazine,* 3 (May–June 1970), 18–24.

U.S. v. State of California, 332 U.S., 19–46.

U.S. Congress, House, *Hearings Before the Subcommittee on Flood Control and the Committee on Rivers and Harbors, Committee on Public Works, Oil Spillage—Santa Barbara, California,* 91st Cong., 1st sess., February 14, 1969.

U.S. Congress, Senate, Subcommittee on Minerals, Materials, and Fuels, Committee on Interior and Insular Affairs, *Hearings on S.1219, S.2516, S.4017, S.3516, and S.3093,* 91st Cong., 2nd sess., July 21–22, 1970, Sec. A.

U.S. Congress, Senate, *Hearings on S.7 and S.544 Before the Subcommittee on Public Works, Water Pollution–1969*, 91st Cong., 1st sess., February 5–6, 1969, part 1; February 5–6, 1969, part 2; and February 24–25, 1969, part 3.

U.S. Congress, Senate, *Hearings on S.1219 Before the Subcommittee on Minerals, Materials, and Fuels, Committee on Interior and Insular Affairs, Santa Barbara Oil Spill*, 91st Cong., 1st sess., May 19–20, 1969.

U.S. Geological Survey, "Geology, Petroleum Development and Seismicity of the Santa Barbara Channel Region," Geological Survey Professional Paper, No. 679 (1970), pp. 1–44.

Conservation
of the Natural
Environment

GEORGIA-PACIFIC CORPORATION, PORTLAND, OREGON

REDWOOD NATIONAL PARK CONTROVERSY

When you've seen one redwood tree, you've seen them all.

Ronald Reagan,
Governor of California

In September 1964 the National Park Service of the U.S. Department of the Interior completed a survey of the redwood region of Northern California.[1] The survey was made in an attempt to assess the remaining stock of coast redwood (*Sequoia sempervirens*), the need for its further preservation, and the possible establishment of a redwood national park. The Park Service found that 85 percent of the original coast redwood forests had been logged, mostly since 1900. Only 2.5 percent of the original stock was preserved in state parks. The survey estimated that if the remaining old-growth redwoods were not preserved they would, at present logging rates, be completely gone in thirty years. George B. Hertzog, Jr., director of the National Park Service, stated in the foreword that "on June 25, 1964, a meeting was held with President Johnson to brief him on the progress of the study. The President . . . requested the Secretary of the Interior to formulate recommendations for his consideration."[2] This

---

[1] U.S. Congress, Senate, Report 641, 90th Cong., 1st sess., October 12, 1967.
[2] "The Redwoods: A National Opportunity for Conservation and Alternatives for Action," report prepared by the National Park Service, U.S. Department of the Interior, under a grant provided by the National Geographic Society, September 1964, p. 3.

study proved to be a major catalyst in the reaction that was to result eventually in the formation of a redwood national parkland and in the controversy that surrounded its creation.[3]

A flood of legislation dealing with the establishment of a redwood park was begun. Proposals ranged from the 90,000-acre plan favored by the Sierra Club, and introduced by several senators and congressmen, to the 39,264-acre proposal transmitted to Congress by the secretary of the interior as the administration's recommendation and introduced as S. 2962 by Senator Thomas Kuchel of California. All interested parties were agreed that a park should be established, but controversy raged over questions of where and how large it should be. The park proposed in S. 2962 was primarily located in the north unit on Mill Creek in Del Norte County, with a small 1,600-acre strip along Redwood Creek in the south unit in Humboldt County. The 90,000-acre proposal consisted of large acquisitions in both the north unit and the south unit. The private lands of the north unit were primarily owned by Miller-Rellim Lumber Company and Simpson Timber Company. The south unit lands were held by Arcata Redwood Company, Simpson Timber Company, and Georgia-Pacific Corporation (G-P).

THE ISSUES FOR ANALYSIS

The larger concern of society raised in the case was best typified by a statement made by Dr. David Gates before the Subcommittee on Science, Research and Development of the House Committee on Science and Astronautics: "We will go down in history as an elegant technological society struck down by biological disintegration for lack of ecological understanding." [4] With the growing need and concern for conserving natural environmental resources, we must ask who is responsible for achieving these goals and meeting this challenge.

Should conservation continue on an *ad hoc* basis?

What role should government play?

If government has the ability to regulate access to raw materials as it did in this case, how should the needs of conflicting interests be made

---

[3] In a personal communication, a spokesman for G-P stated: "If the Park Service report failed to indicate the true park quality redwoods were almost entirely protected and that the remainder of the redwoods still not harvested were quite ordinary forests, the report was grossly misleading . . ." This was one of the basic issues through the battle. To put it another way, the great redwoods the public really cared about were flatlands along creek beds where the largest and most unique are located. The vast acreage of ordinary commercial redwoods contains specimens that are generally younger and smaller and are situated on slopes.

[4] U.S. Congress, Senate, Subcommittee on Parks and Recreation of the Committee on Interior and Insular Affairs, *Hearings on S. 1370, S. 514, and S. 1526*, 90th Cong., 1st sess., 1967.

manifest and weighed? through lobbying? through mobilization of public opinion?

Since conservation issues always raise the problem of our responsibility to future generations, how can the interests of these generations be brought to bear and balanced against present needs?

Is Congress an impartial or impressionable decision-making body in resolving these conflicts?

How do power considerations affect the outcome of this and similar conflicts?

Is it feasible to replace the kind of *ad hoc,* noninstitutionalized conflict that this controversy represents with an institutionalized framework for conflict resolution such as that developed for labor-management disputes?

In terms of specifics, an analysis of the strategies and tactics employed by Georgia-Pacific, the Sierra Club, and other groups should provide us with an understanding about their possible use in similar situations.

WHY GEORGIA-PACIFIC OPPOSED THE ESTABLISHMENT OF NATIONAL REDWOOD PARK

The lumber companies wanted as small a park as possible, preferably containing little more land than was already preserved in existing state parks, so that their commercial operations would be unchanged. Georgia-Pacific put forth the following reasons for this position: (1) The "park-like" redwoods had already been saved. More than 100,000 acres were preserved in state parks and the nation did not need to save more. The expenditure of public funds for the acquisition of more redwood land would be a misuse. (2) The redwoods that existed on commercial lands were not of parklike quality. Existing groves of that quality were already in the state parks. (3) In any event, the existence of the redwoods was not threatened because lumber companies were reseeding and converting to sustained-yield practices.

G-P's position is further understood in the light of some of the company's background. Georgia-Pacific as an organization has exhibited fantastic growth. An article in *Dun's Review* cites the company's "seven-fold growth in a scant ten years." [5] Much of the credit, the article says, was due to Owen Cheatham, then G-P's chairman, who had taken it from a company largely dependent upon lumber to a diversified corporation with over 250 products. This transition was made by Cheatham's adroit use of debt leverage and the company's unique circumstances. He first used long-term debt to acquire timberland in an industry that was rapidly consolidating. This debt was also used to diversify the company into manufacturing, thus giving it an outlet for its raw materials.

5 "Second Growth at Georgia-Pacific," *Dun's Review,* May 1965, p. 48.

G-P pioneered several industry trends. It was the first to use technological breakthroughs that made pulp production a major factor in the wood products industry. With this technology in mind, it was the first to buy land in southern United States for timber production. But neither of these moves could have been made without long-term debt financing, and this debt could not have been possible without the unique advantages of the lumber industry. Some of these advantages are mentioned in the *Dun's Review* article—"tax advantages that accrue to the timber grower, depletion allowances that enable him to deduct the cost of his timber from his sales prices before paying taxes, and the capital gains tax that applies to all profits from timber." The result of these advantages is that while most corporations pay an average 48 percent tax, G-P in 1964, with 20 percent of its operations in lumber, paid a 34.4 percent tax on its profits. Giving further credit for the company's performance, the article states that "it is because of its first rate management team, not because of one man alone, that G-P ranks as one of the most skillfully run companies in the country." The article concludes: "But however expert its management, there is no questioning the fact that timberlands are still the true source of G-P's prosperity. For it is on timber that the company's three great weapons—its high borrowing ability, its low tax rate, and its spectacular cash flow are based."

G-P's unique organizational situation was not the only reason for its position on the redwood park. Resistance to the removal of private lands from commercial timber production for park purposes was strengthened by the conditions that prevailed in the timber industry, especially in the redwood industry, which was consolidating and converting to pulp production. The following testimony by C. Davis Weyerhaeuser, retired from the Weyerhaeuser Corporation but still chairman of the board of Arcata Redwood Company, indicates the situation in the redwood region:

> We are opposed to the removal or withdrawal of any further redwood-producing lands from redwood production. . . . We have a selfish reason. Because from a marketing standpoint there is a limited amount of redwood being placed on the market. Our promotional expenses are consequently very high. And when a market is thin, people tend to lose interest in the product. And I am afraid that if a substantial producer of redwood is removed from the market, we might have real difficulty selling our product.[6]

Weyerhaeuser Corporation and U.S. Plywood closed their plants in Humboldt County in 1966. In the ten-year period from 1952 to 1962, 110 mills in Del Norte and Humboldt counties ceased operations. However, G-P recently invested over $50 million in a new redwood pulp plant, and Simpson Timber invested almost $20 million in a similar enterprise.

In addition to conversion to pulp production, the redwood industry was

---

[6] U.S. Congress, Senate, Subcommittee on Parks and Recreation of the Committee on Interior and Insular Affairs, *Hearings on S. 1370, S. 514* and *S. 1526,* 90th Cong., 1st sess., 1967, p. 250.

making the transition to sustained-yield operations. According to the National Park Service study, new growth would equal cut growth by 1985.[7] Second-growth redwood grows fast but matures slowly. It is inferior to old growth for lumber, but it is ideally suited to pulp production. To make the transition as easy as possible, the lumber companies needed their old-growth lands. Although G-P had total holdings of several million acres, the loss of several thousand acres in the redwood region jeopardized the profitability of operations in that area. The following testimony by William J. Moshofsky, assistant to the chairman of G-P, indicates what the effect of the park might be on G-P's operations:

> *Mr. Johnson:* Mr. Moshofsky, if the large park in the Sierra Club plan were to be adopted by the Congress of the United States, you stated in your statement you would liquidate . . .
>
> *Mr. Moshofsky:* That is correct. We would not be able . . .
>
> *Mr. Johnson:* (continuing) Humboldt County.
>
> *Mr. Moshofsky:* That is correct. We would not be able to continue.
>
> *Mr. Johnson:* How many employees do you have in Humboldt County at the present time?
>
> *Mr. Moshofsky:* 1,400.
>
> *Mr. Johnson:* 1,400 people. You operate how many facilities?
>
> *Mr. Moshofsky:* We operate a relatively new kraft pulpmill, the redwood sawmill in Samoa, that is across the bay from Eureka, another sawmill at Big Lagoon, a plywood plant, a stud mill plus, of course, our woods operations.
>
> *Mr. Johnson:* If Senate bill 2515 were to be adopted, what effect would that have on your company's operations in Humboldt County?
>
> *Mr. Moshofsky:* It would have an impact but not nearly as serious as the Sierra Club 90,000 acre proposal. The big problem is that every acre of old-growth mature timber that is taken from our operations will make it more difficult for us to make a transition from old-growth type of operation to a second growth. In other words, we are waiting for these stands of second growth to come up to enough maturity to process effectively in our present operations, and every acre that you remove from this old-growth base makes it more difficult and it is hard to project exactly what would happen.[8]

SUPPORTERS OF A LARGE REDWOOD PARK: CONSERVATION ORGANIZATIONS

The proposals for a large redwood park faced strong opposition from the lumber industry, yet they received strong support from conservation

---

7 "The Redwoods," p. 23.

8 U.S. Congress, House, Subcommittee on Parks and Recreation of the Committee on Interior and Insular Affairs, *Hearings on H.R. 1311 and Related Bills,* 90th Cong., 2d sess., April 16 and 18, 1968, p. 487.

groups and organizations. The establishment of a redwood national park had long been a goal of conservation organizations. In reviewing the history of preservation of the coast redwoods, the National Park Service cited the efforts of the Save-the-Redwoods League, a private conservation organization founded in 1918 and supported primarily by funds from the Rockefeller Foundation. The league's activities are noteworthy not only for their effectiveness but also for the manner in which they achieved their objectives. The league performed the delicate task of reaching conservation goals without alienating, and in fact often by cooperating with, private business interests. The National Park Service study quotes the following statement about the league:

> The Save-the-Redwoods League has done excellent work, not alone in the purchase of redwood areas and in the development of the park project in northern California, but in furnishing evidence that an organization of this character can secure the widest cooperation of the agencies of the state and nation, including both the nature lovers and the men of business concerned with lumber operations. I am sure that the Save-the-Redwoods League has the respect and confidence of the people.[9]

As of January 1964, 102,689 acres were preserved in twenty-eight redwood state parks. Of this total, 48,383 acres were estimated to be virgin-growth redwood. These lands represented approximately $19 million, of which nearly $10 million was donated through the Save-the-Redwoods League.[10] The only thing that had consistently escaped the league was the establishment of a redwood national park of worthwhile size and stature.

The Sierra Club, however, emerged as the leading park proponent in the redwood national park controversy. In 1963, prior to the National Park Service study, the Sierra Club published *The Last Redwoods,* a book in its Exhibit Format series, which eloquently presented the case for preservation of the coast redwoods. In 1965 the club designated five major conservation issues as prime objectives. Among these was the establishment of a redwood national park. The club's aim was to establish as large a park as possible, preserving and protecting in ecological units as much old-growth acreage as possible. It favored a park consisting of redwood groves in both a north unit along Mill Creek in Del Norte County and a south unit along Redwood Creek in Humboldt County. The Sierra Club considered the park a now-or-never proposition. Repeated efforts over the past century had failed to establish a redwood national park, and National Park Service estimates indicated that the remaining virgin redwoods not already preserved would be completely gone in thirty years. The club repeatedly took the position that what could be rescued today, this hour, this very minute was the most that could ever be saved.

The philosophy and objectives of the Sierra Club are fundamentally

9 "The Redwoods," p. 28.
10 *Ibid.*

preservationist. In the words of David Brower, then the club's executive director:

> The Sierra Club owes its beginnings to one of America's most famous naturalist—John Muir. In 1892 he founded the club in order to make certain that wilderness and wildlands would continue to exist in our civilization. . . .
>
> However, even John Muir could not fully realize the tremendous demands that the 20th century would be making on the remaining wilderness areas. Already many of the most magnificient natural areas have been lost forever—all in the name of "progress." . . . That is why the Sierra Club has adopted . . . "not blind opposition to progress, but opposition to blind progress" . . . as its motto.[11]

To achieve its objectives the organization researched the complex issues involved in the establishment of the park, and promulgated information to club members, political figures, and the general public. The club's 90,000-acre proposal was presented to several congressmen and was first introduced in October 1965. In its early attempts to mobilize public opinion in support of the park, the Sierra Club had not singled out any of the lumber companies for criticism. But there was clearly a fight on between the lumber companies and the Sierra Club. The club decried industry practices and the companies' opposition to park proposals, and it saw the lumber industry as the major reason for the failure of previous efforts to establish a redwood national park. In the October 1965 issue of the *Sierra Club Bulletin,* in an article entitled "The Redwood National Park—A Forest of Stumps?" the club president, Edgar Wayburn, made the following plea for passage of a park bill before Congress adjourned:

> Consider what has happened in the past two and one-half years, since the National Park Service and the National Geographic Society started their study of the redwoods. Reliable statistics suggest an increase of 34 percent in logging of virgin redwoods. In recent testimony before the California State Park Commission, it was stated that in Humboldt County, over 50 percent of privately owned virgin timber that was present in 1963 had now been logged off. In boosting its output, the redwood industry has razed some of the last and finest river flats. It has invaded almost the last pristine watersheds. And it has laid bare many partially timbered slopes.
>
> This logging has respected neither the proposed national park boundaries nor the irreplaceable values—both scenic and scientific— that it has destroyed. The consequent loss to park potential is obvious and staggering.
>
> Because of the vast extent of past logging in the redwood region, it has been necessary already to include cutover lands within the

[11] David Brower, Sierra Club promotional literature.

boundaries of the proposed national park. But Congress hardly can be expected to appropriate millions of dollars for a forest newly bereft of its trees. If cutting on the present scale and in the present random pattern continues, it is obvious that chances for an adequate Redwood National Park will become progressively more bleak. As members of the redwood industry have said, in five years there won't be much worth worrying about.

It can still be hoped that the redwood industry will cooperate; failing this, the use of condemnation or of a moratorium on cutting may be essential. Otherwise we may leave to future generations only a memory of another national park—and a forest of stumps! [12]

The club then moved outside its own immediate membership to mobilize public opinion in favor of the park on a larger scale. On December 17, 1965, the Sierra Club took out a full-page ad in five newspapers with the headline "An open letter to President Johnson on the last chance to really save the redwoods."

THE LEGISLATIVE STRUGGLE

On February 23, 1966, Secretary of the Interior Stewart L. Udall transmitted the administration's 39,264-acre, $60 million proposal to Congress. In doing so, he said that he "wanted to pick a park and not a fight." [13] It appeared that Secretary Udall's strong 1963 support of the creation of a redwood national park, expressed when he wrote the foreword to *The Last Redwoods,* had diminished. The Sierra Club, disappointed with the overall size and location of the administration's proposal, speculated that lumber interests were lobbying strongly in Washington and getting results. The club stepped up its efforts.

The first hearings on the park legislation (S. 2962) were held in Cresent City, California, in June 1966 and in Washington, D.C., in August 1966. During these hearings the Sierra Club raised the question of cutting in the prospective park areas. On September 7 a moratorium on cutting in proposed park areas was agreed to by the Senate and five lumber companies. According to Congressman Don H. Clausen, of the First District in California, which includes the redwood region, "the action removes the need for the rather drastic and somewhat punitive bill recently proposed by the President and Secretary Udall." [14] Following is the text of a

12 Edgar Wayburn, *Sierra Club Bulletin,* October 1965. In a personal communication William J. Moshofsky, assistant to the chairman of G-P, stated: "We strongly disagree with and question the accuracy of the statements attributed to Dr. Wayburn particularly without presenting the material correcting the misstatements. We consider these statements libelous. While they may be privileged in a plea to Congress, we do not think the privilege extends to reprinting. At the least there should be an indication that what they said was considered by others to be most inaccurate."
13 *Sierra Club Bulletin,* August 1967, p. 8.
14 *Humboldt Times-Standard* (California), September 8, 1966.

telegram sent to Senator Kuchel of California by Gray Evans, vice-president of Georgia-Pacific, agreeing to the moratorium:

It has been the long standing policy of Georgia-Pacific Corporation that the special interests of the Corporation, its employees and their families must be sacrificed if the national interest requires it. We earnestly believe however, that this national interest must be clearly established before such a sacrifice is required. Under pending national park proposals Georgia-Pacific Corporation could lose as much as 75 percent of its timber reserves in the redwood region. This loss would jeopardize our entire industrial complex in Humboldt County representing 1500 jobs and an annual payroll of $8 million.

Our opposition to the further acquisition of privately held lands for redwood park purposes is a matter of record with you and the Congress. All of the park-like groves are already preserved in existing parks or are voluntarily set aside by industry awaiting public acquisition. Existing redwood parks are largely unused and undeveloped. Most of our Redwood Creek holdings are commercial timber lands which are unsuitable for national park purposes.

Nevertheless, we recognize that some people believe it is in the public interest to establish a national redwood park on our land and that they are concerned that our harvesting operations might impair the alleged park-like quality of the land pending Congressional action. We wish to let you know Georgia-Pacific Corporation is and always has been willing to work out any reasonable adjustment in our harvesting program on our redwood lands in order to minimize cutting in proposed redwood park areas. We believe a one-year period would give everyone sufficient time to study·carefully the needs for more redwood parks and the suitability or unsuitability of our land for such parks.[15]

The first hearings on redwood park legislation brought out a number of difficult and complex obstacles to the creation of a park. The question of whether any of the lumber companies would be forced to liquidate their operations was of major concern to the members of Congress responsible for formulating the park boundaries. As a result, the problems and conditions of the lumber industry in the redwood region were thoroughly aired. In addition, the impact on the local area was given consideration. The issue was whether the unemployment and loss of tax revenues caused by establishment of the park would be offset by increased tourist trade and in-lieu payments made to the counties. The Sierra Club maintained that the timber economy was unstable and that the area needed the diversification that a park and tourist economy would provide. G-P claimed that the short tourist season made park projections overly opti-

---

[15] Gray Evans, vice-president, G-P, telegram to Senator Thomas Kuchel, September 7, 1966.

mistic.[16] It pointed to recent investment as a sign of stability and emphasized the impact of the loss of timber-producing lands on its ability to continue operations.

Anticipating these obstacles, the National Park Service asked Arthur D. Little, Inc., to prepare reports on the projected impact of the creation of a park on Del Norte and Humboldt counties.[17] Both reports indicated that both counties were largely dependent on the timber industry, but employment was already declining. This decline was due primarily to three factors: (1) depletion of old-growth timber, (2) reduction of timber cut to sustainable levels, and (3) automation. The reports also indicated, however, that the removal of lands for park use would result in further short-term decline in employment until the early 1970s. In addition to the problem of overall employment was the problem of labor mobility. Some of the people employed in the lumber industry would have to find work in the tourist industry. As one industry employee put it, "When you have to tell a lumberjack that he's out of a job because of the park, it doesn't help much to tell him that in five years he'll be able to get a job selling redwood burls to tourists."

Further complications were brought out in the hearings. The land acquisition procedures posed difficult problems. Congress had recently encountered tremendous problems in the acquisition of land at Point Reyes and wanted to avoid the same situation in the redwood region. Once plans for land acquisition are announced, land prices increase tremendously. The assurance of funding through the use of land-and-water-fund revenues was in doubt. Not only was it not clear how much land could be acquired for a given sum, it was not even clear how much could be allocated for acquisition.

In addition, it was not clear whether the state of California was willing to contribute the three state parks in the region for inclusion in a national park. Governor Edmund G. Brown had strongly supported the establishment of a park but was seeking an exchange of U.S. Forest Service lands in return for the state parks, an arrangement that the Forest Service opposed. Ronald Reagan, in the 1966 California gubernatorial campaign, was reported to have said, "When you've seen one redwood tree, you've seen them all." When he was elected in November, the chances of including the California parks looked even more doubtful.

All the problems in establishing a redwood park seemed to favor those interested in a small park, and after the moratorium on cutting was agreed to, the Sierra Club once again increased its efforts. When the club mem-

16 According to a G-P spokesman, the company's statement of a short tourist season "had its foundation in Chamber of Commerce figures and an economic study done for the Redwood Park and Recreation Committee by Dr. H. DeWayne Kreager, an independent industrial economist based in Seattle." It was following his study that the National Park Service decided to hire Arthur D. Little, Inc., to do one for them. Kreager and Little were in wide disagreement on a number of points.
17 A. D. Little, Inc., "The Impact of the Proposed Redwood National Park on the Economy of Del Norte County," report to the National Park Service, March 1966; and "The Economic Impact of Possible Additions to a Redwood National Park in Humboldt County," April 1967.

bers realized that Congress was unlikely to appropriate sufficient funds for a 90,000-acre park, they substituted a 72,000-acre, $100 million proposal, although still advocating the desirability of their original plan. They continued to supply information to members of Congress, answers to industry arguments, and solutions to the problems raised.

On January 25, 1967, the Sierra Club resumed its full-page ad campaign in four major newspapers. The ad read in part: "History will think it strange that America could afford the Moon and $4 billion airplanes while a patch of primeval redwoods—not too big for a man to walk through in a day—was considered beyond its means." The ad contained bar charts of the redwoods that once existed, those yet uncut, and the portion that the park would save. The ad also contained coupons to be sent to G-P, Arcata Redwood Company, and Governor Ronald Reagan of California expressing support for the park, and readers were urged to write to their congressmen and the president.

On February 24, and again on July 1, 1967, the club placed an ad with the headline: "Mr. President: There is one great forest of redwoods left on earth; but the one you are trying to save isn't it. . . . Meanwhile they are cutting down both of them." [18]

On April 17 and 18, 1967, the Senate held further hearings on the park bills before it, and in June and July the House held its first hearings on park legislation. William J. Moshofsky of G-P made the following statement to the House Parks and Recreation Subcommittee, reasserting the company's position on the park:

> In summation of our position, Mr. Chairman, Georgia-Pacific (1) Does not oppose creation of a Redwood National Park if that should be the decision of the U.S. Congress. (2) Georgia-Pacific does most strongly oppose the taking of privately owned commercial forest land for inclusion in a Redwood National Park. This has been our position throughout this controversy. We believe it is a justifiable position and one truly in the national interest.[19]

The company also began to put forth this position in letters responding to letters and coupons it received and in a full-page ad responding to the Sierra Club ad.

On August 10, 1967, the Committee on Interior and Insular Affairs met in executive session and ordered a clean bill, S. 2515, to be reported. S. 2515 authorized a two-unit, 66,384-acre park at an estimated cost of $76 million. The committee stated the following advantages of the new bill:

> The committee, after considering all of the many proposals, accepted S. 2515 introduced by Senators Jackson, Kuchel and Bible. In the judgment of the committee, S. 2515 is superior to S. 1370 [the administration proposal] as introduced. It saves more of the remaining un-

18 *The New York Times,* January 25, 1967.
19 U.S. Congress, House, *Hearings,* p. 485.

protected superlative stands of virgin redwoods. It spreads the impact of land acquisition over four companies, rather than concentrating on only one company's holdings. If enacted, as introduced, S. 1370 probably would have forced the largest employer in Del Norte County out of business. The committee believes that no company which has a genuine interest in staying in the redwood timber business will be obliged to cease operations as a result of the enactment of S. 2515.

The committee believes that any initial adverse impact of the creation of the park on the local economy will be temporary. S. 2515 will shift the bulk of the land acquisition to Humboldt County, which has a much sounder tax base than Del Norte County. Seventy-one percent of the land in Del Norte County is already owned by the State or Federal Government. The bulk of the land acquisition program authorized by S. 2515 is in Humboldt County where only 21 percent of the land is owned by the State and Federal Governments.[20]

On September 5, 1967, the *Humboldt Times-Standard* reported that the moratorium on cutting had been extended. The paper also reported the following comment on the possibility of swift congressional action:

In asking for extension of the moratorium, [Senators] Jackson and Kuchel told the companies they expected the Senate to act on legislation to authorize a Redwood National Park before adjourning for the year.

However, Chairman Wayne H. Aspinall, D. Colo., of the House Interior Committee has said he has "no desire" to take up redwood national park legislation this year and his committee has not yet acted on the bill.[21]

On November 1, 1967, S. 2515 passed the Senate by a vote of seventy-seven to six. On November 16 the Sierra Club charged in a press release that "the Georgia-Pacific Corporation has begun logging operations in a key part of the Redwood National Park approved recently by the Senate. He [Edgar Wayburn] said the operation was started before the expiration of a moratorium agreement." [22] The *Humboldt Times-Standard* reported on November 24 that Georgia-Pacific claimed that "the boundary line on the map is 600 feet wide when enlarged to ground size. With the knowledge we have now, we've been falsely accused." [23] To try to clarify things further, the paper reported the following events:

20 *Ibid.*, p. 1.
21 *Humboldt Times-Standard*, September 6, 1967.
22 *San Francisco Chronicle* (California), November 16, 1967.
23 *Humboldt Times-Standard*, November 24, 1967. Mr. Moshofsky further comments: "It was proven to the satisfaction of the National Park Supervisor from Crater Lake and others we were not in the park area approved by the Senate, indeed had a minimum safety factor of about 1,500 feet, but they declined to make this public. In any event, a clear detail map never was supplied to us in spite of repeated requests to the National Park Service."

June 1967—G-P advised Senator Jackson that "in order to avoid irrevocable damage to our long-range plans it would be necessary to resume operations in some of these areas."

July 1967—Rock was placed on road L–2–2.

August 1967—Cutting started in the L–2–2 area, above MacArthur and Elam Creeks.

September 1, 1967—G-P president R. B. Pamplin wired Senator Jackson, extending the cutting "moratorium" 60 days. "This does not mean that at the end of the period the timber involved would be harvested," Pamplin said. "It simply means that intelligent management calculated to maintain redwood forests forever on all the land would be put back into effect."

October 26, 1967—Hauling logs in the area started, including right-of-way trees cut prior to February 1965.

November 1, 1967—S. 2515 passed the Senate, 77–6.

November 9, 1967—G-P forester A. H. Merrill received a copy of the map specified in the park bill (NP-RED-6112). Cutting was halted east of station 38 on the L–2–2 road, some 1,900 feet from where G-P thinks the park boundary is and about 6,200 feet from the center of Redwood Creek.

November 14, 1967—Kuchel and Jackson wired Pamplin, implying that G-P cutting flies in the face of overwhelming public opinion and in a manner calculated to frustrate consideration of the bill by the House. The statements were made on the basis of ground and air surveys by the National Park Service.

November 16, 1967—The Sierra Club and Citizens for a Redwood National Park charged that G-P had cut inside the park boundary.

November 17, 1967—G-P vice-president Harry A. Merlo stated, "from the sketchy park outline we have received some part of this [cutting] may be within it [the park]. We have stopped all cutting in that area and are hopeful a more precise location for park boundaries will be made available to us."

On November 29 Georgia-Pacific rejected a request from thirty-four congressmen to stop cutting timber in a large area adjacent to that in the proposed Senate bill pending House action.

The Sierra Club took another full-page ad in *The New York Times* on January 18, and in *The Wall Street Journal* on January 23, 1968, entitled "Legislation by Chain-saw?" The ad read, in part, as follows:

Georgia-Pacific, in committing these acts, may not be violating any laws. Nor is it violating the wording of promises it has made. To explain: A year ago, after tremendous public pressure, G-P and three other logging concerns agreed to halt logging within redwood areas proposed as parks, until the Senate had acted to define the boundaries. Now the Senate has done so. But the House has not. G-P, therefore (unlike the other three redwood companies) feels it may now quickly cut down everything beyond the Senate lines. Then, you see, there will be no point in having the House, or Secretary Udall add the Emerald Mile or the MacArthur-Elam Creek area, or others. The trees will already have become patio furniture.

On December 4, Rep. Jeffery Cohelan reported, with outrage, his exchange with G-P on this question. (From the *Congressional Record):*

Cohelan: Adjacent to the Senate park boundaries are virgin redwoods lovely enough to grace the best redwood national park. . . . These trees are now being fed to the sawmills of the Georgia-Pacific Corp., forever blocking the opportunity for us to choose them to dignify a park worthy of its name . . . We thus wrote the following letter to Georgia-Pacific (signed by Cohelan and 34 other congressmen):

"Since the entire question of the precise lines and acreage of the proposed park should be finally determined some time next spring, we hope that this request to suspend further logging (in some 3,000 acres adjacent to the Senate boundary) will be favorably considered."

Georgia-Pacific answered:

". . . it is necessary for us to do some harvesting in this area in order to run our plants on an economically sound basis. For the above reason and in the interest of our employees, our stock holders and good forest management and indeed as a corporate citizen, we respectively must decline your request."

Mr. Cohelan then said, "The second largest lumbering concern in the world says it cannot accord the House the same concern it voluntarily gave the Senate. . . . I deplore this indifference to the public interest."

The ad also contained five coupons, as some of the earlier ads had, which the reader could clip and send to the president of Georgia-Pacific, the president of the United States, Representative Wayne Aspinall (chairman of the House Interior Committee), his congressman, and the president of the Sierra Club requesting information or membership.

On January 23, 1968, it was reported that the president of G-P had threatened to sue the Sierra Club and had stated that "the Congress of the United States should immediately conduct a full investigation of the Sierra Club and the vendetta tactics being employed by the Club." [24]

Both the Sierra Club and Georgia-Pacific became increasingly im-

[24] *San Francisco Chronicle,* January 23, 1968.

patient as the controversy dragged on. The delay was clearly attributable to political malingering. Nearly five years passed between the completion of the NPS study and the final passage of legislation.

On January 8, 1968, the following statements, which indicate the growing impatience with congressional intransigence, were reported:

> A Georgia-Pacific Corporation vice-president has denied a statement released by United Press International, in which he allegedly went on record supporting the Senate Redwood National Park bill.
>
> UPI, in a story distributed on its wire service for release today, quoted Georgia-Pacific executive Robert O. Lee, Portland, as saying, "We are not going to fight this any more. We hope the House will accept the Senate bill."
>
> ". . . it has created uncertainty in the local economy," said Fred Laudenberger, the North Coast Timber Association's secretary-manager. "It has held up private investment. People are waiting to see what is going to happen."
>
> Echoing the feelings of most North Coast businessmen and timber operators, a Georgia-Pacific spokesman said: "It's got everybody upset and has got to be resolved. We hope Congressional action will be completed in 1968." [25]

The House held additional hearings on April 16, 1968; and in June, when the park bill was about to be brought to the House for a vote, the most dramatic political maneuvering in the long controversy was performed by the chairman of the House Interior Committee, Representative Wayne Aspinall. Several major conservation bills were before Congress. Included among these was a North Cascades Park in the state of Washington. Washington's Senator Henry Jackson was chairman of the Senate Interior Committee. Other major bills concerned Colorado River water projects, in which Representative Aspinall was extremely interested. These bills were to be worked out in Joint House-Senate conferences, and Aspinall wanted to increase his bargaining power. The redwood national park gave him the opportunity.

Representative Aspinall forced an amended version of S. 2515 out of committee on June 25, 1968. This version limited the park to 28,000 acres. When this happened, the Sierra Club's fears grew. Its members redoubled their efforts. A floor fight was threatened by several congressmen, but it never materialized because if a fight developed, Aspinall had the power to kill the park legislation completely. Aspinall brought the bill before the House on July 15, under suspension of the rules. This meant that it could not be amended. He said that a compromise bill would be worked out in a House-Senate conference committee. A vote against the bill under suspension of the rules again ran the risk of losing a park of any size. After a bitter debate, the bill passed 388 to 15. The joint conferences were held

[25] *Humboldt Times-Standard,* January 8, 1968.

in August, and in September the House and Senate passed a 58,000-acre compromise. The compromise included 30,000 acres of old-growth redwoods of state redwood parklands, and 28,000 acres of private timberlands of which 3,450 acres belonged to Georgia-Pacific In retrospect it seems unlikely that Aspinall ever had any intention of creating a 28,000-acre park.

On September 11, 1968, the following comment appeared in *The New York Times* in an article entitled "Redwood Victory." "However, because of insistent pressures from Georgia-Pacific and other timber companies, the park will be considerably less than ideal in its layout." [26]

On October 2, 1968, the bill was signed into law (PL 90–545) along with three other major pieces of conservation legislation, thus ending the redwood national park controversy. President Johnson at the signing made the following statement about the park and its establishment:

> I believe this act of establishing a Redwood National Park in California will stand for all time as a monument to the wisdom of our generation—The Redwoods will stand because men of vision and courage made their stand, refusing to suffer any further exploitation of our natural wealth, or any greater damage to our environment.[27]

POSTSCRIPT

This case was written for inclusion in the first edition of this book. I sent a copy of the case to G-P as a matter of courtesy, and also to check the accuracy of certain statements and facts. A spokesman from G-P responded with clarification as to certain facts and asked that the case be changed in a manner that I felt would have impinged on my prerogative of a fair presentation of material. The G-P communication also carried an implied threat of legal action if all the changes desired by the company were not made. Although I was willing to make changes to clarify various points, I was not willing to make the other type of changes.

Since the case was entirely based on published material, G-P had no ground for legal action. However, rather than risk a long delay in the publication of the book, the G-P case was deleted from the first edition. This case is being included in the current edition with clarifying statements presenting the G-P viewpoints in footnotes wherever pertinent. Following are two communications that have a bearing on the controversy.

[26] *The New York Times*, September 11, 1968. In a communication to the author Mr. Moshofsky retorts: "It should be noted that the Editorial Page editor of The New York Times was a Sierra Club official. In fact, this editor wrote a number of strongly biased editorials during the Redwood Park controversy."
[27] Statement by President Johnson, October 2, 1968.

GEORGIA-PACIFIC CORPORATION
900 S.W. Fifth Avenue
Portland, Oregon 97204

WILLIAM J. MOSHOFSKY
Assistant to the Chairman

January 6, 1971

Mr. S. Prakash Sethi
Assistant Professor of
    Business Administration
School of Business Administration
University of California, Berkeley
Berkeley, California 94720

Dear Mr. Sethi:

I was distressed to receive your December 28 letter and wish to reiterate that we strongly object to your publishing your inaccurate and damaging paper in book or any other form without the corrections included in my letter of December 16. You were certainly aware of this in some detail many weeks ago as a result of our early conversation on the subject.

I would appreciate knowing whether your book is being written and published on university time and at university expense. I also suggest that the document be removed from the presses until appropriate corrections can be made.

While I can understand your desire to proceed and regret the delay in getting our written comments to you, I find it hard to believe any kind of urgency from your standpoint could justify publishing educational material so inaccurate. This strongly suggests academic irresponsibility which cannot be sanctioned in our school system.

It seems to me that institutions of higher education—particularly those schools teaching business administration—should bend over backwards to present objective, accurate material particularly in light of the many, unjustified attacks on business from so many quarters.

Sincerely,

(Signed) William J. Moshofsky

UNIVERSITY OF CALIFORNIA, BERKELEY
School of Business Administration   Berkeley, California 94720

January 25, 1971

Mr. William J. Moshofsky
Georgia-Pacific Corporation
900 Southwest Fifth Avenue
Portland, Oregon 97204

Dear Mr. Moshofsky:

I was quite unhappy to read your letter of January 6, 1971. However, I delayed answering it until today as I wanted to think over its contents. Moreover, I did not wish to respond to you in anger.

Your absurdly amateurish attempt at threatening me would have been comical but for the issue involved and for the air of injured innocence you exuded. Let me say here, unequivocally, that I believe your allegations to be without any merit whatsoever. However, rather than argue with you and risk costly delay in the publication of my book, my publisher (who, it may surprise you to learn, is a commercial publisher) and I have decided to delete the Georgia-Pacific case from the book. You can now believe that the purity and virtue of Georgia-Pacific have been saved from the invading barbarians.

In your letter you accuse me of "academic irresponsibility which cannot be sanctioned in our school system." However, if your letter is an indication of the kind of "business responsibility" that you would like the country to applaud, God save us all. You want business schools "to bend over backwards to present objective, accurate material particularly in light of the many, unjustified attacks on business from so many quarters." I suggest that *you* do some serious soul searching. Obviously, in your view "objective" and "accurate" mean "favorable to" Georgia-Pacific. You do not want independent or objective inquiry. You apparently do want institutions of higher learning to be the public relations arm of the business corporations.

While preparing my book, I had the opportunity of working with top executives from some of the largest and best known American corporations. I found them to be mature and objective enough to accept honest criticism and concede the fallibility of human beings and even of their own organizations. You may be interested to learn that you are the only one of the many corporate officers to whom I talked or corresponded, who threatened, demanded, refused clearance or opposed my comments because they did not show their companies in a completely favorable light. But for my experience with the others, your conduct would really have been a depressing forecast for the future of American business and its important place in our society.

Yours truly,

(Signed) S. Prakash Sethi
Assistant Professor of
Business Administration

SELECTED REFERENCES

HENDERSON, HAZEL, "Ecologists versus Economists," *Harvard Business Review,* July–August 1973.

HERFINDAHL, ORRIS C., and ALLEN V. KNEESE, *Quality of the Environment: An Economic Approach to Some Problems in Using Land, Water, and Air* (Washington, D.C.: Resources for the Future, Inc., 1965).

KNEESE, ALLEN V., "Protecting Our Environment and Natural Resources in the 1970's." Testimony before the Subcommittee on Conservation and Natural Resources, Committee on Government Operations, U.S. House of Representatives, February 6, 1970.

A. D. Little, Inc., "The Impact of the Proposed Redwood National Park on the Economy of Del Norte County," report to the National Park Service, March 1966; and "The Economic Impact of Possible Additions to a Redwood National Park in Humboldt County," April 1967.

"The Redwoods: A National Opportunity for Conservation and Alternatives for Action," report prepared by the National Park Service, U.S. Department of the Interior, under a grant provided by the National Geographic Society, September 1964, p. 3.

"Second Growth at Georgia-Pacific," *Dun's Review,* May 1965, p. 48.

U.S. Congress, House, Subcommittee on Parks and Recreation of the Committee on Interior and Insular Affairs, *Hearings on H.R.1311 and Related Bills,* 90th Cong., 2nd sess., April 16 and 18, 1968, p. 487.

U.S. Congress, Senate, Subcommittee on Parks and Recreation of the Committee on Interior and Insular Affairs, *Hearings on S.1370, S.514 and S.1526,* 90th Cong., 1st sess., 1967, p. 250.

U.S. Congress, Senate, Report 641, 90th Cong., 1st sess., October 12, 1967.

PACIFIC GAS & ELECTRIC COMPANY, SAN FRANCISCO

ATTEMPT TO CONSTRUCT A NUCLEAR POWER PLANT AT BODEGA BAY

> To hell with posterity! After all, what have the unborn ever done for us? Nothing. . . .
> To hell with posterity! That, too, can be arranged.
>
> —A statement made facetiously by LORD RICHIE-CALDER, noted newspaperman and author long concerned with problems of ecology

In 1973, the Pacific Gas & Electric Company (PG&E), finally abandoned its efforts to construct a nuclear power plant at Bodega Bay in northern California. The project included plans for constructing two nuclear generating units of more than 1 million kilowatts each. The project was budgeted at $830 million and scheduled for completion in 1979–1980. The effort by PG&E stretched over a decade and cost millions of dollars in plans, studies, presentations before various regulatory bodies, and exploratory construction. In addition, it embroiled the company in fierce and acrimonious conflict with various community and political groups, and left scars in terms of loss of credibility and public goodwill that will take time to erase.

On a broader level, one of the most important issues has to do with the use of nuclear power for developing electricity. The case provides an excellent framework within which one can study

1. The mechanism by which new technology is introduced into the society; the criteria used in evaluating its benefits to different groups, and assessment of future costs and potential hazards associated with the use of such technology.
2. The interplay between different social groups and institutions—the corporation, the regulatory agencies, the communities involved, and the university—that have a bearing on the possible outcomes and that have often conflicting goals.

On a narrower level, an analysis of the strategies and tactics employed by PG&E and its opponents should throw light on the relative strengths and weaknesses of these strategies and their possible use by other companies and groups faced with similar situations.

An important point to note here is that PG&E was actively involved in the communities in which it had operations. The company encourages its executives and employees to take part in local government and community-related activities. This made the company quite conscious of the needs of various communities and also allowed it to take positive steps in improving community welfare. But the question remains of whether the functional advantages of a business corporation having close relations with the community and its leaders outweigh the problems that can arise —for example, community leaders serving company rather than constituents interests because of such relationships. To put it differently, what should be the role of a business corporation in the community in which it operates? Can a power position be avoided if a corporation plays an active role in civic affairs?

BACKGROUND

Bodega Head is a thumblike peninsula jutting out of the California coastline approximately fifty air miles north of San Francisco. Until 1959, the headland was privately owned by three families, and as a result its natural beauty and ecology remained intact. Two of these private holdings, 648 acres owned by Mrs. Rose Gaffney and the tip of the headland owned by Mrs. Garry Stroh, could be traced to the original Spanish land grant.

Because the headlands had been preserved, the State of California Division of Beaches and Parks became interested in acquiring the land for a recreation area and, independently, the University of California became interested in the area as a site for a northern California marine facility. The site was also chosen by the Pacific Gas & Electric Company, a private California utility, as being suitable for the location of a generating plant to provide electrical power to the rapidly growing metropolitan San Francisco Bay Area.

In 1953 an informal faculty committee was formed at the University of California (U.C.), Berkeley, to obtain a marine facility in northern

California. Dr. Cadet Hand, a marine biologist at U.C., was a member of
the committee and was influential in its organization. Dr. Hand discovered the beauty and richness of the peninsula when he first visited it
shortly after World War II. "I was overwhelmed with it," Hand said later.
"There were the ocean, the cliffs, the tidepools, and over here those rich
mudflats in the harbor. It was a biologist's paradise."[1] The committee was
given formal recognition by the university administration in 1955, and in
the summers of 1956 and 1957 classes were held in a rented shack at
Bodega Bay. Spurred by Dr. Hand and awed by what they saw, the
committee began actively pursuing plans for a permanent marine laboratory on the headland.

In this attempt the committee first learned of the state of California's
interest in Bodega Head for a recreational park. The State Division of
Beaches and Parks had included the headland in its 1955 master plan for
park development, and $350,000 was appropriated in the 1956–57 budget
for acquisition of the land. However, under California's "home rule" law,
which requires local concurrence with state proposals, the Sonoma County
Board of Supervisors held absolute veto power over the state's park plan.
The board requested that Bodega Head be included in the master plan
for the county, but County Planning Director Jack Prather refused. The
board upheld this decision and approved the plan without Bodega Head.

In April 1957 the state, still seeking the inclusion of Bodega Head in its
park system, agreed to meet with the university to coordinate their plans,
and in May a joint committee reached a mutually acceptable plan of
action. Three months later, however, in July 1957, the Division of Beaches
and Parks reported cryptically that its plans for Bodega Head had "been
forestalled by planned purchase of a major portion of the headland by a
private utility company."

PG&E STEPS IN

Pacific Gas & Electric moved quickly in the acquisition of the permits
and rights necessary for a generating plant on Bodega Head. Experience
over the years had taught it that this was the best way to handle the delicate task of establishing a generating plant. The first public announcement
of PG&E's plans was not made until May 1958. PG&E president M. R.
Sutherland issued a brief statement to the effect that "preliminary purchasing negotiations" were underway for a site on which to build a
"steam-electric" generating plant.[2]

Although no mention was made of a nuclear facility, there were rumors
that the plant would be atomic. These rumors were fueled when in
September 1958 Kenneth Diercks, the company's land agent in Sonoma
County, told the supervisors: "No decision can be made as to when actual

[1] David Pesonen, "A Visit to Atomic Park," unpublished manuscript. San Francisco,
California. Used with permission of the author.
[2] *Santa Rosa Press Dispatch,* May 23, 1958.

construction of this facility will commence or as to the type of plant to be constructed, whether conventional or nuclear, until the time of installation is much nearer at hand." [3] However, the previous month a PG&E spokesman had told a meeting of the American Institute of Electrical Engineers that PG&E was committed to a course that would lead the utility to large-scale use of economic nuclear power.[4] And only six months later President Sutherland told reporters at a press conference in San Francisco that "an atomic power plant will be built in one of the nine Bay Areas counties . . . as soon as it can be done at reasonable cost" and that it was to be in operation "by 1964 or 1965." [5] Although he would not say that he was referring to Bodega Head, no other acquisitions were being made that would have been remotely feasible for an atomic power plant.[6]

PG&E continued to acquire the necessary rights and permits for a conventional generating plant. In September 1958 the county supervisors granted a delay in the improvement of a small airstrip that was in the proposed path of high-power lines from Bodega Head as requested by PG&E, even though the company owned no property in the county at that time.[7] In October 1958 the company filed condemnation proceedings against all of Mrs. Gaffney's property and indicated that the Stroh ranch would also be acquired. It stated that it needed all this land for site access for borings and so on. No mention was made of the AEC requirement for a three-quarter-mile radius around a nuclear installation (a reactor at Horseshoe Cove would necessitate owning approximately 600 acres of headland).[8]

On October 15, 1959, the company announced that the site had been changed to the tip of the headland to get away from the San Andreas Fault zone, although the type of plant was still unannounced.[9] The suit against Mrs. Gaffney was modified to include only 65 acres, and plans were made to purchase the Stroh ranch. This modification of land area coincided with an AEC revision stating that only a one-half-mile radius was required around a nuclear installation—the revised property line followed such a radius.[10] Although the ranch had been in Mrs. Stroh's family for over a century and the family repeatedly stated that it did not want to sell, a grant deed to PG&E was filed in the Sonoma County Courthouse less than one month following the announced site change.[11] Allegations that Stroh was intimidated into selling via a party-crashing incident causing "great violence, destruction and bloodshed" [12] were stoutly denied by PG&E,

[3] Pesonen, "A Visit to Atomic Park."
[4] *San Francisco Chronicle,* August 20, 1958.
[5] *Santa Rosa Press Dispatch,* April 5, 1959.
[6] Pesonen, "A Visit to Atomic Park."
[7] Joel W. Hedgpeth, "Bodega Head—A Partisan View," *Bulletin of the Atomic Scientists,* 3 (March 1965), 3.
[8] Pesonen, "A Visit to Atomic Park."
[9] Hedgpeth, "Bodega Head—A Partisan View," p. 4.
[10] *Ibid.*
[11] Pesonen, "A Visit to Atomic Park."
[12] *Ibid.*

which stated in 1961, in answer to the charge, that "the transaction was concluded in terms satisfactory to Mrs. Stroh." [13]

Then, in November 1959, the Sonoma County Board of Supervisors granted a use permit to PG&E for power lines over Doran Park, a sandspit running northeast from Bodega Head. The supervisors deemed a public hearing unnecessary despite a petition carrying 1,300 signatures in opposition.[14]

Gene Marine, writing in *The Nation,* cited this as only one of many instances of flagrant disregard for the public interest:

> Then there's Doran Park, a sandspit which, with Bodega Head, makes Bodega Bay one of the only five safe harbors along 300 miles of tortuous, treacherous Pacific Coast. Doran Park was turned over to Sonoma County by the State of California on condition that it be preserved as a park. At its widest point, it's less than 350 feet wide. PG&E will run power lines down the center of the park; its easement is 180 feet wide. Why don't they put the wires underground? "Uneconomical." [15]

In February 1960 the Sonoma County Board of Supervisors granted the company a use permit to build a steam-electric plant on Bodega Head, again without public hearings and without the submission of plans, as this would "impose a hardship on the company." [16]

REACTION BY THE UNIVERSITY OF CALIFORNIA, BERKELEY

Meanwhile, neither the state nor the university faculty committee had given up on Bodega Head. The state announced in July 1958, one year after abandoning the Head, that it had been negotiating with PG&E to buy whatever portion was left for the park system.[17] The university's reaction, at the faculty level at least, was less submissive. The faculty committee wanted to fight the company and asked permission to seek the governor's intervention. The administration declined this request and told the committee to find another site for the marine facility.[18]

Since July 1958 the University of California faculty committee had investigated the possibility of acquiring alternate sites for a marine laboratory and had further investigated the impact the PG&E facility would have on the Bodega Bay marine environment. Members of the committee

[13] *Ibid.*
[14] *Ibid.*
[15] Gene Marine, "Outrage on Bodega Head," *The Nation,* June 22, 1963, p. 525.
[16] J. B. Neilands, "Industrial Radiation Hazard," unpublished manuscript. University of California, Berkeley, February 1963.
[17] Pesonen, "A Visit to Atomic Park."
[18] Hedgpeth, "Bodega Head—A Partisan View," p. 3.

asked two professors from the Scripps Institute of Oceanography to meet with PG&E to assess the impact of the plant on the surrounding environment. They indicated that the discharge from the plant might not disperse as rapidly as originally thought but might displace normal tidal flows for a considerable period of time.[19] Chancellor Seaborg reported in a letter to Philip Flint of the Sierra Club:

> Horseshoe Cove might be expected to be bathed for periods of some hours in the essentially unmixed effluent at near discharge temperatures. . . . The fact that the ecological future of Bodega Head was unpredictable made it undesirable to locate a marine laboratory at Horseshoe Cove, in view of the plans for the power station.[20]

However, on November 29, 1960, the committee told Chancellor Seaborg that despite the obvious drawbacks, Bodega Head was still the best site available for the marine laboratory.[21] The committee still felt that the university ought to oppose PG&E's proposed plant officially. The committee summed up this negative feeling by concluding:

> Weighing all relevant aspects, we agreed unanimously that there was not a single one of these sites that was equal to Bodega Head as it now stands. Bluntly stated, a unique Class A site for a marine facility is being exploited for power production.[22]

As a result of this decision, a portion of the headlands was purchased and plans were made to share the peninsula with PG&E. No official position of opposition was taken by the university. The following comment on the report appeared in *The Nation:*

> In fact nothing was done about that report at all. It was written twenty-three days after the election of John Kennedy; a short time later the Chancellor [Seaborg] became the chairman of the AEC.[23]

The article also noted that the AEC contributed a sizable sum to the university.

PG&E ANNOUNCES A NUCLEAR FACILITY

In July 1961, after obtaining county permits for a conventional steam generating plant, PG&E announced its intention to build a nuclear power

19 J. D. Frautschy and D. L. Inman, Preliminary Report of Investigation of Bodega Head, made to Professor Roger Y. Stenier, Department of Bacteriology, University of California, Berkeley, June 14, 1960.
20 Marine, "Outrage on Bodega Head," p. 526.
21 *Daily Californian* (UCB), December 14, 1962, p. 3.
22 *Ibid.*
23 Marine, "Outrage on Bodega Head," p. 22.

plant on Bodega Head.[24] Prior to this announcement the controversy centered primarily on the best use of the land—for research and recreation or for power generation—and secondarily on the manner in which the land-use issue was being decided. However, with the formal announcement of a nuclear facility, public safety became a major issue. Three problem areas were associated with establishing this nuclear facility:

1. The geological instability of the Bodega Head and the proximity of the reactor to the San Andreas Fault zone
2. The location of a nuclear reactor near a major population center
3. The problem of radioactive waste discharge

Geological Instability of Bodega Head

PG&E apparently chose the site without much advance consideration of its geologic features.[25] To study it in detail, however, it hired a competent staff of experts, which included Dr. Dan Tocher, a consulting seismologist from U.C.; Dr. William Quaide, a consulting geologist from Claremont; the firm of Dames and Moore, soil mechanics engineers; and Dr. George Housner of Cal Tech, PG&E's principal consultant on structural design.

Drs. Tocher and Quaide filed a report to the company on September 18, 1960. This study showed the reactor site to be approximately 1,000 feet from the western edge of the San Andreas Fault [26] and indicated that the headland is "strongly jointed and is faulted on old minor faults. However, there have been no movements in these faults in the past few thousand years . . . [which] strongly implies, but does not guarantee, that there will be no movements throughout the life-expectancy of a power plant." [27] It also revealed that "the intensity of the faulting and jointing in the rock is so great that the formerly massive rock is now broken into a mosaic of blocks with average dimensions of approximately one foot." [28] In June 1960 Dr. Housner wrote to Mr. Worthington, PG&E's civil engineer: "As regards gross ground movement produced by faulting, I would say that if there appeared even a small likelihood of this happening, then the site should not be used. The investigation of Dr. Tocher and Dr. Quaide should be aimed at assessing the likelihood that active movement will occur in the San Andreas Fault zone near the site on Bodega Head. . . .[29] "No evidence was found in the geologic examination to indicate the existence of a *large fault* beneath the plant or tunnel sites. Chances of

24 William E. Bennett, "Dissenting Opinion in the Order Denying Reopening of Hearings on the Application for a Certificate of Public Convenience and Necessity for the Bodega Bay Atomic Park," Decision No. 65706.
25 Hedgpeth, "Bodega Head—A Partisan View," p. 3.
26 California Public Utilities Commission, Application 43808, Appendix IV.
27 *Ibid.*, Sec. 8, p. 12.
28 *Ibid.*, Sec. 7, p. 5.
29 *Ibid.*

disruption of the sites by breakage along a large fault are therefore small." [30]

Dames and Moore filed three reports, with the last the most definitive. From borings at the test site, they found the bedrock to be of poor quality and much deeper than originally thought.[31] As a result, they concluded that the reactor pit, designed to be 90 feet deep, could be excavated without blasting, except for the last 20 to 35 feet.[32] Furthermore, the generating plant and other surface installations would be based on approximately 65 feet of sands and clays at the point of juncture with the reactor.[33] This despite Tocher and Quaide's earlier admonition:

> It is important from the standpoint of ability to withstand strong ground shaking that the buildings and any other large appurtenances be constructed on foundations resting on the hard quart-diorite bedrock. Should the borings reveal that bedrock will not be reached at practicable depths where it is proposed to erect structures, serious consideration should be given to alternate sites.[34]

Proximity of Plant to Urban Centers: Dangers of Radiation

The location of the plant in an earthquake fault area compounded the ordinary problems of public safety generally associated with the location of a nuclear facility near large population concentrations. The first such problem can arise when an accident caused by seismic activity or other origins results in a major failure of the nuclear safety systems. The company based its safety system on "pressure suppression containment," a novel design used to replace the traditional dome. One of the factors leading to the adoption of this system seems to have been its significantly lower cost.[35] The AEC originally rejected this type of system when it was proposed for the Humboldt County nuclear facility; it reversed itself four months later, however,[36] and called it an improvement over traditional containment systems, even though there was no operational experience upon which to base this opinion.[37] Dr. James E. McDonald questioned the integrity of the safety system on the basis of testimony given by PG&E witnesses to the effect that if an earthquake caused movement of 2 feet the first two barriers could be punctured, but the critical system would be undamaged; he argued that "the *triple* barrier to escape of volatiles is admitted to be, potentially, reduced to a single barrier [the reactor vessel itself] in event of major seismic displacements. . . . [This] clearly de-

30 *Ibid.*, Sec. 8, p. 9. (Emphasis added.)
31 *Ibid.*, Sec. 17, log of boring shaft 16.
32 *Ibid.*, Sec. 17, conclusions.
33 *Ibid.*, Sec. 12.
34 *Ibid.*, Sec. 8, p. 11.
35 Neilands, "Industrial Radiation Hazard," p. 8.
36 Marine, "Outrage on Bodega Head," p. 524.
37 AEC Docket No. 50–205, p. 12.

mands that very serious consideration be given to the . . . consequences of fission-product release at Bodega. . . ." [38]

No one knows what would happen if the core melted down. In 1963 the AEC was given $19 million to build a reactor in Idaho and allow it to suffer the maximum credible accident to see what would happen. Until this is done, all assumptions will be mere speculation. However, one recognized study conducted by the AEC in 1957, known as the Brookhaven Report, gives some startling statistics. Based on a 100 to 200 megawatt capacity reactor (much less than the 325 megawatt capacity of PG&E's reactor) located 30 miles from a major city, it theorizes the following results of a major accident: 3,400 deaths, 43,000 injuries not including several hundred thousand cases of long-term radiation damage, and property damage of from $2 billion to $4 billion. [39] Dr. McDonald's study of meteorological conditions on the Bodega coast stated that due to the prevailing wind patterns and temperature inversion traps, radioactive gases from the site could easily be funneled into the San Francisco Bay Area without appreciable diffusion. [40] Thus, the conditions surrounding the Bodega reactor were, if anything, more extreme than the hypothetical Brookhaven case. Dr. Samuel Glasstone, in commenting on a boiling water reactor slightly smaller than the one proposed for Bodega, wrote: "Some doubt has been expressed concerning the stability of a boiling water reactor operating at such a high power, but the problem can be resolved only by experience." [41] There have been several major reactor accidents in the past, and seldom has there been a full explanation of the causes: Great Britain's Windscale in 1957; Arco, Idaho's, incident in 1955, in which three people were killed; the Chalf River reactor in Canada, in which nine hundred safety devices did not prevent a meltdown that released 10,000 curies of fission products. [42] Of course, design changes have been made that make these particular types of accidents unlikely, but it is presumptuous to assume that no new imperfections will arise. [43]

Problems of Waste Disposal

Another significant hazard of the Bodega reactor was the nuclear wastes that were to be discharged into the water and air. Dr. McDonald outlined some of the problems of radioactive wastes in the air. Included among the

[38] Dr. James E. McDonald, "Meteorological Aspects of Nuclear Reactor Hazards at Bodega Bay," published by the Northern California Association to Preserve Bodega Head and Harbor, June 1964, p. 43.
[39] Adolph J. Ackerman, "Atomic Power, a Failure in Engineering Responsibility," *Journal of Professional Practice, Proceedings of the American Society of Civil Engineers,* October 1961, p. 48.
[40] McDonald, "Meteorological Aspects," p. 51.
[41] Samuel Glasstone, "Sourcebook on Atomic Energy," *AEC,* p. 471.
[42] Lindsay Mattison and Richard Daly, "A Quake at Bodega," *Nuclear Information,* VI, 5 (April 1964), 3.
[43] David E. Lilienthal, "When the Atom Moves Next Door," *McCall's,* XCI, 1 (October 1963), 228.

hazards were a plume-down wash for the stack directly into the channel traveled by the fishing boats [44] and fog- and drizzle-borne contamination due to shifts in prevailing winds.[45] With regard to this second point, an excerpt from an article by C. Auerbach in *Nature* disclosed that milk samples taken in the Windscale area *"before* the accident contained 44 μμc. of Iodine—131/1, as compared with 5.6 in the United Kingdom as a whole." [46] Dr. Neilands, professor of biochemistry at U.C., calculated that based on the discharge control system at Humboldt Bay, the exhaust valve (which closed automatically if the release rate of radioactive noble and activation gases exceeded 2 million microcuries per second over a ten-minute period) would not have been activated until after over 7.8 billion microcuries had been discharged.[47]

The other type of waste release, that is, through the cooling system into the ocean, also presented a hazard. Although the annual discharge rate was very small, comprising only one-third of the natural radiation in the sea water, the elements produced by the plant were far different from those occurring naturally. More important is the remarkable ability of shellfish, in which the area abounds, to concentrate radioactive ions that can then be ingested by people.[48]

The concern regarding nuclear hazards was also related to the issue of solid waste disposal. David Lilienthal, former chairman of the AEC, stated the problem very clearly in a *McCall's* article in 1963:

> The AEC tells us that in another fifteen years or less a substantial percentage of the electricity of the country will be produced in atomic power plants. Dr. Donald R. Chadwick, Chief of the Division of Radiological Health of the U.S. Public Health Service, estimated in April 1963, that "the accumulated volume of radioactive wastes from nuclear installations. . . . will increase from about one and a half million gallons, the estimated 1965 volume, to two billion gallons in 1995." These huge quantities of radioactive wastes *must somehow be removed* from the reactors, must—without mishap—be put into containers that will never rupture; then these vast quantities of poisonous stuff must be moved either to a burial ground or to reprocessing and concentration plants, handled again and disposed of by burial or otherwise, *with a risk of human error at every step.*[49]

He further stated that to continue to project as our goal ten or twelve full-scale power plants in a dozen years, before a safe method of meeting this problem had been demonstrated, was irresponsible financially and revealed a questionable attitude toward public health and safety.[50] Not

---

44 McDonald, "Meteorological Aspects," pp. 28–29.
45 *Ibid.,* pp. 30–31.
46 C. Auerbach, "Effects of Atomic Radiation," *Nature,* April 27, 1963, p. 343.
47 Neilands, "Industrial Radiation Hazard," p. 6.
48 *Ibid.,* p. 6.
49 Lilienthal, "When the Atom Moves Next Door," p. 52.
50 *Ibid,* p. 228.

only did the wastes have to be disposed of, but they had to be kept out of circulation for centuries.[51] This created another problem:

> At the present time, these wastes are mainly stored in stainless steel tanks, the life of which is expected to be much less than the duration problem. It is thus possible that we are passing on to future generations a formidable commitment to guard and juggle our atomic garbage.[52]

THE ROLE OF THE ATOMIC ENERGY COMMISSION

The responsibility for ensuring the public safety with regard to nuclear power has been vested in a federal agency, the Atomic Energy Commission (AEC). In 1954 the Atomic Energy Act charged the AEC to promote civilian uses of nuclear power as well as to license and regulate privately operated reactors. In 1955 the AEC announced a demonstration program in which it offered to underwrite part of the cost of certain atomic power projects. This program was expanded in 1957 to include all types of projects, as long as (1) they could make significant contributions toward the achievement of commercial atomic power and (2) construction could be completed by June 1962.[53] The requirement for early completion was motivated by the agency's desire to show concrete results in its development program as insurance for its continued funding. Government aid and subsidies to civilian commercial reactors were considered necessary to ensure continued development of nuclear power that was not competitive with conventional power.

On January 31, 1961, the AEC optimistically predicted that more than 1 million kilowatts of nuclear power would be available by the end of 1963, compared with 350,000 kilowatts then available. Most of the new generating capacity would be added in 1961–62 when fifteen nuclear power plants were expected to start up.[54]

The AEC's dual role of regulating and promoting civilian reactors carried an inherent conflict, which the *Wall Street Journal*, on March 20, 1961, reported that the agency recognized and was trying to alleviate:

> The AEC announced it is reorganizing in order to separate its regulatory and promotional functions.

> The aim is to ensure that the AEC's regulatory responsibilities concerned with such matters as the location and licensing of atomic reactors and licensing of industrial use of radioisotopes, are not jeopardized by the commission's eagerness to promote industrial use of the atom. . . .

[51] Ackerman, "Atomic Power," p. 47.
[52] Neilands, "Industrial Radiation Hazard," p. 5.
[53] Ackerman, "Atomic Power," p. 46.
[54] *The Wall Street Journal,* January 31, 1961, p. 15.

The [House-Senate Atomic Energy] committee will also publish the record of a University of Michigan Law School study on AEC organization conducted by two former AEC attorneys, William H. Berman and Lee M. Hydeman. Their report will urge that the preferred step is total separation of the AEC's regulatory and promotional functions.[55]

The AEC did not totally separate the two functions and even under its reorganization could not eliminate the conflict in responsibilities. At the 1962 hearings pursuant to Section 202 of the Atomic Energy Act, Congressman Chet Holifield, chairman of the Joint Committee on Atomic Energy, read a letter he had written to AEC Chairman Seaborg earlier that month, in which he expressed concern and disappointment at the pace and extent of the atomic power program. In commenting on budget requests, he said that the AEC had shown a lack of enthusiasm for "our civilian atomic power program" and recommended accelerated development of a number of projects including Bodega Bay.[56] The committee then spent the entire day chiding Seaborg for distorting press releases, emphasizing weapons and space, and delaying programs by "studying them to death." In defending himself, Seaborg mentioned several times that the Bodega Bay plant was one situation in which the commission was moving ahead.[57]

Dr. Seaborg cited another source of pressure in a report to the president in 1962:

It should be recognized that, largely as a result of early optimism, we have, in a short space of time, developed a competitive nuclear equipment industry which is over-capitalized and under-used at the present time. . . . Fortunately, it now appears that only relatively moderate additional government help will be necessary to insure the building of a substantial number of large, *water-type* power reactors that will be economically competitive in the high-fuel-cost areas of this country and the world. This would increase public acceptance, keep the nuclear industry healthy and help to furnish the plutonium necessary for a breeder reactor economy as soon as it can be adequately developed.[58]

In response to pressure from Congress and the industry, the AEC granted concessions to PG&E, some of which could adversely affect the public safety:

1. In the interim between PG&E becoming interested in Bodega Head

55 "A.E.C. Reorganizing in Effort to Separate Its Regulatory, Promotional Functions," *The Wall Street Journal*, March 20, 1961, p. 7.
56 Marine, "Outrage on Bodega Head," p. 525.
57 Pesonen, "A Visit to Atomic Park."
58 United States Atomic Energy Commission, *Civilian Nuclear Power*, a report to the president (Washington, D.C.: Government Printing Office, 1962).

and its filing with the AEC, regulations regarding locating a site near an active earth fault were liberalized three times.[59] Even so, the Bodega site was less than the currently required one-quarter mile distance, and nothing had been said.

2. The pressure suspension containment system used at both PG&E plants, which cost considerably less than the traditional dome, was approved after having been rejected as unsafe.

3. Shortly after PG&E announced interest in the site, the AEC reduced fuel charges by 34 percent.[60]

It also apepared likely that the AEC had tacitly agreed to license the Bodega Bay reactor before the case ever began. As noted, the commission was using the plant as evidence that it was "moving ahead" long before the application was even submitted; even more persuasive was the fact that PG&E had spent over $4 million before the hearings were even scheduled.

THE CONTROVERSY

In November 1961 PG&E overcame the final hurdle at the county level when the Sonoma County Board of Supervisors approved, again without public hearing, the company's suggested route for the access road, which followed the tidelands around the bay. When the tidelands road was proposed, the university objected.

One of the university's basic considerations in acquiring this particular facility was the variety of organisms to be found in the mudflats of the bay. Chancellor Strong wrote a letter of protest outlining the university's position to the Army Corps of Engineers, who had to approve the route since it might affect navigation in the bay.[61] The County Board of Supervisors was apoplectic at this opposition [62] and ordered the Harbor Commission to meet with the chancellor and "explain the facts of life to him." [63] There is no account of this meeting, but it seems to have had an effect on the chancellor's position, for in January 1962 he wrote to Ray Ruebel, secretary-manager of the Bodega Bay Chamber of Commerce, stating that the university was interested only in that portion of the road crossing the university's property and that the remainder was of less importance.[64] The faculty committee did not share this view, however (which was, in fact, contrary to Strong's position less than two months earlier): At the public hearings on the road in February, Dr. Cadet Hand

[59] Pesonen, "A Visit to Atomic Park."
[60] *Ibid.*
[61] Letter to Col. John A. Morrison, Army Corps of Engineers, from Chancellor Edward Strong, University of California, Berkeley, December 1961.
[62] *Santa Rosa Press Democrat,* December 15, 1961.
[63] *Ibid.*
[64] Letter to Mr. Ray Ruebel, Bodega Bay Chamber of Commerce, from Chancellor Edward Strong, University of California, Berkeley, January 31, 1962.

opposed the tidelands route in its entirety, stating that any disturbance of the mudflats would affect the ecology of an area vital for effective research.[65] Dr. J. B. Neilands made the following statement concerning the tidelands road to the northern section of the University Academic Senate:

> Not long after a firm decision to locate at Horseshoe Cove had been reached, it was announced that a tidelands access road would be built around the inner rim of the harbor in order to connect the southern tip of Bodega Head to the mainland. This roadway proved to be a convenient arrangement between PG&E and certain Sonoma County officials, the latter now completely dazzled by the prospect of acquiring a giant tax bonanza for the county. The tidelands in question had been leased to the county from the State with the provision that, for final transfer of title, a major improvement must be placed thereon within a certain time period. The lease was running out on the county. PG&E required an access road as well as a convenient place to dump their fill and rip-rock from the excavation. The townspeople were, and still are, much opposed to the roadway and with some difficulty they succeeded in forcing the county to apply to the Army Engineers for the necessary permit.
>
> The hearing was held on February 15; the entire proceedings have been transcribed and the transcription exists as a public document. It describes a bitterly fought contest between Sonoma County officials on one side and the fishermen of Bodega Bay plus certain expert marine biologists on the other side. On this occasion the Acting Director stated that he had the authority of the Chancellor to oppose the roadway "in its entirety" and that a *previous realignment arrangement* with the county did not prevent the destruction of "some of the very values which led us to choose this headland as our site in the first place." In this stand he is strongly supported by the Western Society of Naturalists and by a number of other marine biologists.[66]

Professor Neilands suggested the possibility that a "family relationship" between the university and PG&E may have prevented the university from "fighting to preserve its biological integrity." He pointed out that:

1. PG&E Board Chairman James Black raised $2.4 million for the campus student union in 1958.
2. Walter Haas, who contributed the money to build the Walter Haas Clubhouse at Strawberry Canyon, was on the Board of Directors of PG&E.
3. The senior attorney for the company was John Sproul, son of R. Gordon Sproul, president emeritus of the university.
4. The university could cut its $2 million annual electric bill in half if

[65] Letter to Chancellor Edward Strong, University of California, Berkeley, from Dr. Cadet Hand, acting director, Bodega Marine Laboratory, February 21, 1962.
[66] *Daily Californian*, October 29, 1964, p. 3.

it bought power directly from the Central Valley Project, but inexplicably had not.[67]

Dr. Neilands said:

> Unfortunately I can find not a shred of evidence that the University
> has taken advantage of this cordial relationship in order to persuade
> the company to place the proposed power plant where it would be
> less destructive to scenic, recreational and possible scientific values.[68]

In October 1961, PG&E filed an application with the California Public
Utilities Commission for a "certificate of public convenience and necessity
to construct, install, operate and maintain Unit #1, a nuclear power unit,
at its Bodega Bay Atomic Park." [69] Hearings were held on March 7, 8, and
9, 1962, with little opposition, and it appeared as if the company had
surmounted another major hurdle without encountering any significant
opposition.

At the Public Utilities Commission hearings, Richard Ramsey, Sonoma
County counsel, submitted a booklet containing all twenty-six of the
county's resolutions involving the plant, none of which even remotely
suggested that it would be atomic.

The company was obviously not eager to delve too deeply into the
geology and seismology of the Bodega Bay area at these PUC hearings.
When asked if the consultants' reports were to be placed in evidence,
PG&E counsel John Morrissey replied:

> Well, we didn't intend to put any of them in. They are quite lengthy,
> they are quite voluminous. Certainly, they are available for the Com-
> mission staff to look at and to study. Indeed, if we can get extra
> copies, we will give you an extra copy. . . .[70]

PUC counsel Bricca then argued that, without documentation and
direct testimony of the consultants, the assurances given by Mr.
Worthington constituted hearsay.[71] But this line of inquiry was interrupted by a recess and not raised again until the close of the proceedings, three months later. At that time, Worthington rather reluctantly
agreed to submit the reports [72] and subsequently filed the compilation
known as Exhibit 48 on July 9, 1962.

At this point, however, public sentiment began to grow in opposition
to PG&E's use of Bodega Head. PG&E's repeated refusals to hold public
hearings made people more and more critical. Dr. Wayne Olson of
Sonoma State College was quoted as saying, "The decision to build was

---

[67] *Ibid.*
[68] *Ibid.*
[69] California Public Utilities Commission, Application 43808, Preface, p. 1.
[70] California PUC Hearings, Application 43808, transcript, pp. 37–38.
[71] *Ibid.*, p. 38.
[72] *Ibid.*, pp. 1402–13.

made not by the people, but by a power elite—the AEC, the PG&E and the county supervisors." [73]

In response to an article entitled "Nature vs. the Atom," [74] printed February 11, 1962, Karl Kortum, director of the San Francisco Maritime Museum and a native of Sonoma County, wrote a letter to the editor of the *San Francisco Chronicle*, protesting the process through which engineers were making the decisions on the establishment of social priorities. The letter, which appeared on March 14, 1962, presented the following imaginary dialogue between PG&E officials:

> Conservationists from the State Park Commission and the National Park Service came in the last decade to walk among the lupine and decide that this should be a public preserve.
>
> But about the same time came men of a different type. They too walked out on the point and gave it the triumphant glance of demigods.
>
> I am reconstructing. These men are engineers from a public utility and as a member of the public it is my privilege and duty to speculate. The scene shifts to the home office.
>
> "Our engineering boys think we ought to grab Bodega Head."
>
> "They do? (low whistle) That might be a little rough."
>
> "Why? Why more than Moss Landing or Humboldt Bay?"
>
> "Well it's more scenic. There will be more protest. The State Park people and the National Park people are already on record for public acquisition."
>
> "Our engineers say we need it. We'll just buy fast. Get in ahead of them. It's legal."
>
> "Well . . ."
>
> "What we can't buy we'll condemn."
>
> "What about the public protest? This one could get a little noisy."
>
> "Keep it at the county level. Or try to. Every service club in every town has got our people in it rubbing shoulders. In the county, opinion is made at the weekly luncheon . . ."
>
> "How about the newspapers?"
>
> "It's the local businessmen who buy the space. Oh, I don't say we haven't got some work to do. But those guys have got other things on their minds—they're scratching out a living."
>
> "Have you got an angle? I mean apart from the fact that we want it."
>
> "Oh sure. We'll get out some releases and speeches on how the county tax base will be improved. We might even try calling it a tourist attraction."
>
> "And the county officials?"

[73] K. S. Roe, "Bodega, Symbol of a National Crisis," *American Forests*, 69, December 1963, 25.
[74] "This World," *San Francisco Chronicle*, February 11, 1962.

"They're O.K. We'll set the tone up and they'll respond to it. Just as elected representatives should. Oh you might get some idealist . . ."

What is the matter? Why do these things come to pass?

The answer is simple. Our engineer demigods are obsolete.

The idea of shaking their pedestals to see if they will topple over has only lately come upon us. (A covey bit the dust lately when the Tiburon Bridge was cancelled.)

The engineers of this public utility may find their callousness has crested at Bodega Head. Just as the Toll Bridge Authority engineers crested with the bridge that sags frugally from Richmond to San Rafael. Or the highway engineers with the two deck freeway that spoils the Embarcadero.

An atomic plant doesn't have to be built at Bodega Head. Without any expertise whatsoever, I can make that statement categorically. It is just a matter of whose engineers you listen to.

Engineers have amazing resources. They have been able to prove that it is mechanically impossible for a bee to fly.

"You can't lick the biggest 'city hall' of them all . . ." wrote Ed Mannion in his column in the *Petaluma Argus Courier* on February 17, pointing out that two friends, one a member of the county grand jury and the other a prominent newspaper reporter, had urged him to give up the fight.

Well, Ed, you can lick them. If everyone reading this would take five minutes to write a letter they would be licked. But a licking is not what to ask for; regulation is sufficient—regulation in the full breadth of the public interest. We have a Public Utilities Commission charged with doing just that.[75]

As a result of Mr. Kortum's letter, the Public Utilities Commission received over 2,500 letters protesting the atomic plant at Bodega Head.[76] In response to this public outcry, the hearings were reopened in May and ran into June 1962.

The second set of hearings was very vocal and the "record gives the clear impression that the vast majority of the public does not want this unit at this place at this time." [77] Nevertheless, the company ultimately received a certificate of convenience from the PUC subject to AEC approval of the construction.

AFTERMATH OF HEARINGS

After PUC approval came on November 8, 1962, an *ad hoc* organization quickly entered the fray—the Northern California Association to Preserve Bodega Head and Harbor, headed by David Pesonen. On December

[75] *San Francisco Chronicle,* March 14, 1962.
[76] Hedgpeth, "Bodega Head—A Partisan View," p. 4.
[77] Bennett, "Dissenting Opinion," p. 3.

28 PG&E applied to the AEC for a construction permit and with it filed a Preliminary Hazard Report. This report had the same basic documentation as Exhibit 48, filed with the PUC. Noting some fundamental differences between the two and some major discrepancies in Mr. Worthington's testimony, the Northern California Association to Preserve Bodega Head and Harbor filed a request to reopen the hearings before the PUC. The association pointed out that Mr. Worthington had testified that (1) the San Andreas Fault was "approximately a mile" from the reactor vessel; (2) the foundation would be located "in solid granodiorite"; [78] and later, responding to a question concerning his reasons for believing that the Bodega site would be better than the company's site in Humboldt Bay, "Why it's on solid rock." [79] Both statements contradicted the Dames and Moore report, which was omitted from the Preliminary Hazard Report analysis. Some of Tocher and Quaide's conclusions had been significantly changed.[80] The report was finally forwarded to the AEC more than a year after the original analysis had been filed.

In July 1963 the *ad hoc* group's application for a rehearing was denied by a four-to-one vote. William M. Bennett, president of the commission, stated in his dissenting opinion:

> We are here dealing so far as seismic activity is concerned with a voluntary exposure to risk. It is obvious that few ventures are entirely risk free, but this is not to say that risk should be courted unnecessarily . . . only blind compulsion would insist upon placing this plant in the heart of one of nature's choice areas and in frightening proximity to an active fault line.[81]

Following the rehearing denial, the association brought suit in the Supreme Court of the State of California to force a rehearing. It also sued in Superior Court to have the county permits rescinded on the grounds that no public hearings were held.

As indicated at the second PUC hearings, public opposition to the Bodega Head atomic power plant was widespread. The fact that no local, state, or federal agency or organization had opposed the plant—either in its own interest or in the public interest—created an atmosphere of doubt and suspicion about the degree to which the public safety and interest were being served. The Association to Preserve Bodega Head served as a focal point for the widespread but unorganized opposition to the atomic plant. The association began to document the case for preserving Bodega Head and the dangers involved in establishing a nuclear facility there. It also began to prepare and distribute literature presenting this documentation to the press and the public.

To counter the complex technical reports provided by PG&E on the stability of the Bodega Head area, the association requested further

[78] California PUC Hearings, Application 43808, transcript, p. 42.
[79] *Ibid.*, p. 1004.
[80] California Public Utilities Commission, Memorandum of Action Concerning Late Filed Exhibit 48 and Related Evidence, May 6, 1963, pp. 39–41.
[81] Bennett, "Dissenting Opinion," p. 7.

studies. Dr. Pierre Saint-Amand, a consultant seismologist from the Naval Ordnance Test Station, China Lake, and expert analyst of Chile's 1960 quake, was asked to investigate the site. His conclusion was that "Bodega Head is a very poor location for a reactor. . ." [82] "Each time the San Andreas Fault has moved, it has jumped a distance of four to eight meters. Strain is estimated to be accumulating at a rate of about six to seven meters per century across the Fault. Hence one could expect at least one great earthquake per century." [83] He stated that as the reactor site was on the "zone of fling" it would undergo a horizontal movement of some three to four meters [84] and "a worse foundation situation would be difficult to imagine." [85] He concluded:

> It is surprising, in view of the expert advice given by Tocher and Quaide, and by Housner, that another site was not chosen and that construction has gone ahead.[86]

At this time another study was undertaken, this one sponsored by the United States Geological Survey. The investigators, Julius Schlocker and Manuel Borilla, first inspected the site in the summer of 1963. Their work was completed in September, and they found no evidence of active faulting through the reactor site.[87] However, the company continued its excavation, and the AEC reported in October that a fault through the site itself had been discovered. Schlocker and Borilla returned and conducted a three-month investigation. They reported in January that the fault was comparable to that on Point Reyes, which had had considerable movement in 1906.[88]

PG&E responded to these findings with reports of its "own consultants" who advised them that the plant could still be built safely.[89] It is significant to note that two of the four reports predated the discovery of the new fault and that Dr. Quaide had developed severe doubts as to the advisability of the project:

> There is a chance that the fault could break beneath the plant's site in case of an earthquake. I still think the probability is low . . . but it is necessary to face the moral issue: "If there is even a slight chance of danger should we go ahead and build the plant?" [90]

On the other hand, Dr. Tocher stated:

[82] Pierre Saint-Amand, "Geologic and Seismologic Study of Bodega Head," published by the Northern California Association to Preserve Bodega Head and Harbor, 1963, p. 20.
[83] *Ibid.*, p. 14.
[84] *Ibid.*, p. 17.
[85] *Ibid.*, p. 19.
[86] *Ibid.*, p. 20.
[87] USGS TE-884, December 1963. As cited in David Pesonen, "A Visit to Atomic Park."
[88] *Ibid.*, p. 14.
[89] *San Francisco Chronicle,* January 28, 1964.
[90] *Ibid.*

We are firmly of the opinion that movements of this nature ["minor vibrations" associated with an earthquake along such "auxiliary faults"] will in no way constitute a hazard to the plant.[91]

As a direct result of the discovery of the shaft fault in January 1964, and possibly because of the full array of geologic and seismologic reports, the company revised its proposed structure in March 1964. To compensate for horizontal movements of from one to two feet, the pit would be packed with a compressible material of a then undetermined type.[92] This decision was a complete reversal of Mr. Worthington's earlier statement: ". . . the one thing that will not change is the fact that we are founding the reactor structure on solid rock and surrounding it with very heavy concrete structures." [93] The approach was novel and could well have been very effective according to the staffs of the AEC Division of Reactor Licensing [94] and the AEC Advisory Committee on Reactor Safeguards.[95] However, the former felt that as "experimental verification and experience background" were lacking, "we do not believe that a large nuclear power reactor should be the subject of a pioneering construction effort based on unverified engineering principles, however sound they may appear to be." [96]

At the same time, the Association to Preserve Bodega Head had published a number of booklets and pamphlets recounting the events and actions that had occurred in PG&E's attempt to establish the plant. This literature was bad publicity for the company, and the public increasingly began to view PG&E and the various public agencies and organizations as irresponsible. The mounting pressure of negative public opinion as mobilized by the association began to influence the AEC.

On October 27, 1964, the AEC issued two reports regarding the Bodega Bay reactor. One, from the commission's Advisory Committee on Reactor Safeguards, stated that, in its opinion, the company's plant could be operated with reasonable assurance that it would not constitute an undue hazard to the health and safety of the public. The other, from the commission's Division of Reactor Licensing, stated that, in its opinion, "Bodega Head is not a suitable location for the proposed nuclear power plant at the present state of our knowledge." Its reason for this conclusion was the feeling that there was not enough experimental and actual operating data on the proposed design [97] to ensure that it would withstand an earthquake of potential intensity. Immediately following the AEC reports, PG&E announced that it was abandoning the project, in which the company had invested several million dollars and which had caused

91 *Ibid.*
92 U.S. Atomic Energy Commission Application Docket, No. 50–205 by Pacific Gas and Electric Company, Amendment.
93 California PUC Hearings, Application 43808, transcript, p. 383.
94 AEC Docket, No. 50–205.
95 Advisory Committee on Reactor Safeguards, "Report on Bodega Bay Atomic Park, Unit No. 1," October 20, 1964, p. 2.
96 AEC Docket, No. 50–205, p. 13.
97 *Ibid.*

controversy for nearly seven years. PG&E's decision was surprising since under AEC licensing procedures a final decision on the company's $61 million project would not be made until a public hearing had been held by an Atomic Safety and Licensing Board, appointed by the AEC. The initial decision of the three-member board could be protested by the company, the public, or other interested parties before final action was taken.[98]

On November 2, 1964, the following explanation for the company's decision was reported in *The Wall Street Journal:*

> Robert Gerdes, PG&E president, said the doubt raised by the AEC staff "although a minority view, is sufficient to cause us to withdraw our application: We would be the last to desire to build a plant with any substantial doubt existing as to the public safety."
>
> Mr. Gerdes stated that PG&E has made provisions "for adequate electrical generating capacity elsewhere to take care of our customers' needs for the several years immediately ahead."
> The company said it has spent $4 million at the site for grading, excavating and road building.[99]

PG&E MAKES A SECOND RETREAT

It seems the problems of PG&E were not over with the cancellation of the Bodega Bay nuclear plant. On January 19, 1973, PG&E announced withdrawal of its applications, without prejudice, to the AEC and the California Public Utilities Commission for authority to construct the $830 million plant at Point Arena on the Mendocino coast. The project included plans for constructing two nuclear generating units of more than 1 million kilowatts each which were scheduled for completion in 1979 and 1980, respectively.[100]

Among the reasons cited were the "unresolved geological and seismological questions recently raised by the U.S. Geological Survey (USGS) and further uncertainties caused by the passage of Proposition 20, the Coastal Initiative." [101] PG&E's John F. Bonner announced that "all work has stopped at the Mendocino site, except for completing geologic and seismic investigations already in progress." [102]

The USGS, which had been serving as a consultant to the AEC, told PG&E in September 1972 that it had "uncovered evidence indicating strong possibility of previously unsuspected active earthquake faulting at or near the 586-acre Point Arena plant site." [103] As a result, the AEC ex-

98 *The Wall Street Journal*, October 28, 1964, p. 30.
99 *Ibid.*, November 2, 1964, p. 7.
100 Dale Champion, "PG&E Drops Point Arena A-Plant Plan," *San Francisco Chronicle*, January 20, 1973, p. 1.
101 PG&E press release, January 19, 1973.
102 *Ibid.*
103 Champion, "PG&E Drops Point Arena A-Plant Plan."

pressed serious reservations as to the acceptability of the site and directed PG&E to conduct further studies. The company has since supplied the AEC with progress reports for evaluation by the USGS. On January 8, 1973, USGS sent another report to AEC which concluded that "given the present state of the art of off-shore geophysical techniques and considering the physical characteristics of the Point site it was not now possible to resolve all questions as to suitability of the site." [104]

Another reason for withdrawing the application cited by the company was the passage of the Coastal Initiative in 1972, which was designed to control the development of the California coastline for three years while regional commissions drew up land-use regulations. Popularly known as Proposition 20, the Coastal Initiative was passed in the teeth of strong opposition from many large industrial corporations, land developers, agribusiness and utilities, including PG&E (which contributed in excess of $25,000 to the campaign against its passage).

In a letter to the author a company spokesman stated:

> In regards to coastal siting, PG&E is cooperating fully with the Coastal Zone Conservation Act and the newly established Coastal Zone Conservation Commissions. The effect of the Act on utility operations, however, is delaying construction of needed new power plants at coastal sites which already have been acquired and which have been zoned by local authorities for power plants. Because of this, and for the short-term, we will probably have to build alternative plants at yet unselected sites not subject to the Coastal Zone Conservation Act. Unfortunately, the alternatives to coastal nuclear power plants are less desirable environmentally and economically.

> Included in the Coastal Zone Conservation Act is the development of a Coastal Plan, including a power plant siting element. We will endeavor to assist the Coastal Zone Conservation Commissions in identifying coastal sites within our service area which should be considered for inclusion in the Plan.[105]

David E. Pesonen of the Sierra Club, who was one of the leaders in the fight against PG&E on its Bodega Bay nuclear plant construction, commended the company "for acknowledging the inevitable before a bitter fight which would have ended with the same result." However, he severely criticized company officials "for attempting to set Proposition 20 up as any basis for their decision. Proposition 20 is really a smokescreen addressed to the company's stockholders." Pesonen went on to say: "In the light of this new case and Bodega it is clear that no more coastal sitings should be permitted in California. PG&E has a duty to explore the technology of alternate sources of energy and alternate inland siting of thermal plants, fossil and nuclear." [106]

104 *Ibid.*
105 Letter from Christopher C. Newton, Nuclear Information, PG&E, San Francisco, March 28, 1973.
106 Champion, "PG&E Drops Point Arena A-Plant Plan."

EPILOGUE

The outcome of the controversy was that PG&E leased its Bodega Head land to Sonoma County, which now operates the area as a county park. The tidelands road, which represented a major part of the company's $4 million investment in the project, and which the university originally strenuously opposed, is used for access to the park. The university operates a marine facility on the Head, on land acquired during the controversy. No systematic attempt has been made to assess the effect of the road on marine life. The reactor pit is still there, but no nuclear radiation threat to public safety exists.

APPENDIX

HOW HAZARDOUS
ARE THE NUCLEAR PLANTS?

More than fifteen years of nuclear power plant construction and the experience of more than twenty operating nuclear power plants have not silenced or even diminished the intensity of the controversy associated with their potential hazards. Although some fears about nuclear plant operation have been partially alleviated, new concerns have surfaced in the light of experience: lack of data on the potential hazards associated with increasing the size of individual plants and using untested technologies; and public doubt and apprehension about the Atomic Energy Commission, nuclear equipment manufacturers, and nuclear plant operators and their motives and concern for safety.

A perusal of the available nonclassified material leaves one with the impression that although the proponents of nuclear power have generally underestimated the potential hazards, its critics have frequently used scare tactics by resorting to exaggerated estimates of loss of life and property. The result has been a lack of the serious discussion that must precede any balanced evaluation of risks, benefits, and ways to minimize the hazards of building and operating nuclear power plants.

HAZARDS ASSOCIATED WITH MANUFACTURING
AND OPERATING PROCEDURES

The most frequently occurring hazards in the construction and operation of nuclear power plants are those associated with deficiencies in technology and operating procedures, and these may be the most dangerous hazards.

In a recent article, *The Wall Street Journal* cited numerous examples of plant shutdowns, slowdowns, and delays caused by deficient and shoddily made equipment. "Basically the hardware industry in this country isn't in very good health," according to Milton Shaw, the director of reactor development for the AEC.[1] The big utility companies, lured by the cost advantages of nuclear power plants over fossil fuel and hydroelectric plants and by the availability of nuclear fuel, have been increasing the size of their nuclear plants. Equipment manufacturers have further encouraged this expansion by offering "turn-key" projects. However, the larger plants have been achieved by "scaling up former technology instead of developing new technology," causing costly plant slowdowns or shutdowns and increasing the cost of building and operating plants. The problems caused by these "design deficiencies" are augmented and aggra-

---

[1] Thomas Ehrich, "Atomic Lemons: Breakdowns and Errors in Operation Plague Nuclear Power Plants," May 3, 1973, p. 1.

vated by operating procedures that reflect a "lack of training and an attitude in conflict with good safety practices." [2]

ENVIRONMENTAL HAZARDS

Apart from the problems associated with the operation of nuclear power plants, some environmental problems, such as waste disposal, radiation leaks, and contamination, are caused simply by their very existence.

Waste Disposal

The wastes from nuclear reactors are radioactive and highly toxic substances. They are routinely removed from the reactors and replaced by new nuclear fuel. Removal of the wastes from the reactor sites for ultimate disposal in underground storage tanks is also a routine operation. Although they are no longer usable in the plants, these wastes remain radioactive for a long time. According to AEC Commissioner William O. Doub, "some have half-lives in the decades and are present in amounts that make them potentially dangerous for hundreds of years." [3]

The problems of transportation, storage, and safekeeping of nuclear waste are of grave importance, even to the AEC. Its recent unsuccessful bid to use abandoned Kansas salt mines as a burial ground is one example, as is the realization that a Nagasaki-type bomb can be made in an ordinary laboratory using the available public information and only 11 to 22 pounds of one of these wastes—plutonium. Another aspect is highlighted by the fact that a plane carrying a package of plutonium was hijacked to Cuba. Although the AEC has issued very tough standards for the future handling of radioactive materials, the problems associated with waste disposal cannot be considered solved.

Unpredictable Factors

The San Fernando Valley earthquake of 1971 destroyed an "earthquake-proof" concrete hospital, with the loss of a number of lives. Should the "quake-proof" structure of the nuclear power plants fracture in the event of an earthquake, causing a rupture in vital parts of the backup cooling system of the reactor, the consequences could be so staggering that they must be considered—regardless of what we are told about the infinitesimal chances of such an occurrence. Unpredictable natural phenomena in the past caused damage that was, at least to some degree, repairable, but the existence of nuclear power plants radically changes the type, extent, and repairability of the damage that may be caused. The question

2 *Ibid.,* p. 18.
3 "Why It's a Good Idea to Break Up the AEC," *Business Week,* June 30, 1973, p. 41.

then becomes, How safe are our nuclear power plants? Would they withstand an earthquake? How reliable and trouble-free are our most reliable emergency systems? Finally, is the risk to the environment and to mankind itself worth the benefits gained from nuclear power?

The China Syndrome and Related Safety Issues

Basically, a nuclear reactor is like a firebox for the fossil fuel combustion chamber of conventional electric plants. Instead of the coal or fuel oil used in conventional plants, nuclear plants use a compact maze of fuel rods filled with thimble-sized pellets of nuclear fuel. Each of the 7 to 9 million tiny pellets contained in the reactor's heart—the reactor vessel— generates power equal to a ton of coal. Once coal is burned, the remains are only ashes; but the remains of nuclear fuel stay hot even after the plant is shut down, resulting in an "after-heat" problem whether the plant is working or not. Should the coolant substance, normally water, be lost to the reactor vessel, a loss-of-coolant-accident known as LOCA, the heat generated by the continuing nuclear reaction would increase the temperature and cause a meltdown. Without proper coolant circulation, some of the fuel cladding would deform, blocking coolant circulation to other claddings and causing an increase in the rate of temperature rise and possibly a total meltdown of the claddings.

In a meltdown situation, the fuel will be exposed to the water. With a temperature increase of a thousand degrees every few seconds, it would not take long to reach 4982°F., the melting point of uranium oxide. The melting of the fuel would cause hot, active nuclear fuel and cladding material to fall to the bottom of the reactor vessel, melt through the foot-thick steel at the bottom, and drop onto the concrete below, shattering the concrete and burning into the ground. Due to the direction of its travel, this phenomenon is known as the *China syndrome*. Under the least favorable conditions, radiation thus released would be dangerous to an exposed population over an area of nearly 100 miles downwind, resulting in hundreds of human fatalities, thousands of injuries, and billions of dollars in property losses. To be exact, according to the Brookhaven report, 3,400 fatalities, up to 43,000 injuries, $7 billion in property damage, and the long-term contamination of an area as large as the state of California could be expected.

The China syndrome is the most serious potential problem with nuclear power plants. To prevent its occurrence, an emergency backup cooling system, technically known as the Emergency Core Cooling System (ECCS), must start operating immediately to avert a temperature rise in the reactor vessel. Any delay or malfunctioning of the ECCS could result in the China syndrome, with its dangerous consequences. Thus, the reliability of ECCS becomes the central point in nuclear power plant safety.

At this time there are only twenty-nine commercial nuclear power plants in operation; they account for 4 percent of the nation's total power. However, nuclear power plants are projected to provide 60 percent of the nation's required power by the year 2000, and one thousand power plants might be in operation by the year 2025.[4] Obviously, as the reactors proliterate, the dangers multiply and the chances of accidents rapidly increase.

The ECCS's reliability depends primarily on two things: (a) the design of the system, which is restricted by available technology, and (b) the reliability of quality control in the construction of the system. The frequent shutdowns of the existing twenty-nine power plants due to equipment failures make one doubt the engineering safety of the ECCSs that is claimed by their designers and the AEC.[5] Existing nuclear power plants operate at less than 50 percent of capacity because of immature design technology and inadequate quality control in their construction. Examples of these problems are valve blowouts, seawater seepage corroding the reactor, and fuel impurities.

Under such circumstances, can or should the nation rely on the AEC's and industry's safety claims? On the one hand, the leading nuclear reactor manufacturers claim that their designs and equipment are foolproof; on the other hand, the buyers of the plants, the utility companies, do not agree. "We think there's a real question about [the quality of equipment] we're buying," says Donald Allen, president of Yankee Atomic Electric.[6] However, most utility men believe that most atomic plants will deliver on their promise of cheap, abundant electric power once the "learning-curve" stage is over.[7] With no "hard" experimental data, the designs of emergency safety systems are based on computer-simulated data or tests. However, in practice, the reliability of these systems is not supported.

The central question is, will the ECCS work in a loss-of-coolant accident? The nuclear industry asserts that it will. However, Ralph Nader thinks it will not and has joined Friends of the Earth in a suit seeking to shut down twenty of the twenty-nine nuclear power plants on the grounds that they are unsafe.

BREAKUP OF THE ATOMIC ENERGY COMMISSION

The dual role of the AEC as both promoter and regulator of the use of nuclear energy and the resultant conflict of interests has been one of the major causes of criticism of the AEC from the time it was first established. Over the years this criticism has grown as the commission has been accused by respected, well-informed scientists, by members of Congress, and by the general public of sacrificing concern for public safety to the promotion of nuclear power plants for commercial use.

The government has finally heeded this criticism. In June 1973 President Nixon recommended to Congress that it break up the AEC into two

---

4 "The Uninsurable Risk," *San Francisco Chronicle,* June 18, 1973, p. 17.
5 Ehrich, "Atomic Lemons," pp. 1, 18.
6 *Ibid.,* p. 1.
7 *Ibid.*

separate groups. Under his proposal, AEC's research and development staff would become part of a new agency to be fashioned after the National Aeronautics and Space Administration and to be called the Energy Research and Development Administration. Safety and regulatory functions of the AEC would be handled by a new nuclear energy commission.[8] At the time of this writing, Congress has not acted on the proposal.

REFERENCES

ALEXANDER, TOM, "The Big Blowup over Nuclear Blowdowns," *Fortune,* May 1973, p. 216.

LAPP, RALPH E., "Nuclear Power Safety—1973," *New Republic,* April 28, 1973, pp. 17–19.

"Nuclear Reactor Safety: A Skeleton at the Feast," *Science,* May 28, 1971, p. 918.

People's Lobby, "A Condensation of Nuclear Reactor Safety: An Evaluation of New Evidence," by IAN A. FORBES, DANIEL F. FORD, HENRY W. KENDALL, and JAMES J. MacKENZIE. Washington, D.C., July 1971.

——, "A Critique of the New AEC Design Criteria for Reactor Safety Systems," by DANIEL F. FORD, HENRY W. KENDALL, and JAMES J. MacKENZIE. Washington, D.C., October 1971.

U.S. Congress, Senate, Committee on Interior and Insular Affairs, *Hearings Pursuant to S.R.45, A National Fuels and Energy Policy on Environmental Constraints and the Generation of Nuclear Electric Power: The Aftermath of the Court Decision on Calvert Cliffs,* parts 1 and 2, serial no. 92–14, 92nd Cong., 1st sess., November 3, 1971.

SELECTED REFERENCES

ACKERMAN, ADOLPH J., "Atomic Power, a Failure in Engineering Responsibility," *Journal of Professional Practice, Proceedings of the American Society of Civil Engineers,* October 1961, p. 48.

ALEXANDER, TOM, "The Big Blowup over Nuclear Blowdowns," *Fortune,* May 1973, p. 216.

BARKLEY, PAUL W., and DAVID W. SECKLER, *Economic Growth and Environmental Decay: The Solution Becomes the Problem* (New York: Harcourt Brace Jovanovich, 1972).

BEAM, FLOYD A., and PAUL E. FERTIG, "Pollution Control Through Social Cost Conversion," in *The Accounting Sampler,* ed. Thomas J. Burns and Harvey S. Hendrickson (New York: McGraw-Hill, 1972).

California Public Utilities Commission, Application 43808, Appendix IV.

DAVIES, J. CLARENCE, III, *The Politics of Pollution* (New York: Pegasus, 1971).

DOWNS, ANTHONY, et al., *The Political Economy of Environmental Control* (Berkeley, Calif.: Institute of Business and Economic Research, University of California, 1972).

[8] *Business Week,* June 30, 1973, p. 40.

HEDGPETH, JOEL W., "Bodega Head—A Partisan View," *Bulletin of the Atomic Scientists,* 3 (March 1965), 3.

HERFINDAHL, ORRIS C., and ALLEN V. KNEESE, *Quality of the Environment: An Economic Approach to Some Problems in Using Land, Water, and Air* (Washington, D.C.: Resources for the Future, Inc. 1965).

KNEESE, ALLEN V., "Protecting Our Environment and Natural Resources in the 1970's." Testimony before the Subcommittee on Conservation and Natural Resources, Committee on Government Operations, U.S. House of Representatives, February 6, 1970.

LILIENTHAL, DAVID E., "When the Atom Moves Next Door," *McCall's,* XCI, 1 (October 1963), 228.

McDONALD, JAMES E., "Meteorological Aspects of Nuclear Reactor Hazards at Bodega Bay," published by the Northern California Association to Preserve Bodega Head and Harbor, June 1964, p. 43.

McKEE, JACK EDWARD, "Water Pollution Control: A Task for Technology," *California Management Review,* 14, 3 (spring 1972), 88–91.

MURDOCH, WILLIAM, and JOSEPH CONNELL, "All about Ecology," *Center Magazine,* 3 (January–February 1970), 56–63.

NETSCHERT, BRUCE C., "Energy vs. Environment," *Harvard Business Review,* January–February 1973, pp. 24–36.

POTTER, FRANK M., JR., "Everyone Wants to Save the Environment But No One Knows Quite What to Do," *Center Magazine,* 3 (March–April 1970), 34–40.

————, "Pollution and the Public," *Center Magazine,* 3 (May–June 1970), 18–24.

U.S. Atomic Energy Commission, *Civilian Nuclear Power,* a report to the president (Washintgon, D.C.: Government Printing Office, 1962).

THE CHANGING NATURE
OF GOVERNMENT
AND BUSINESS RELATIONSHIPS

Corporations and United States Domestic Politics

THE ITT AFFAIR (A)

INFLUENCE OF BIG BUSINESS IN POLITICS AND GOVERNMENT: ANTITRUST CASE SETTLEMENT AND CAMPAIGN CONTRIBUTION

We are not talking here [in the ITT affair] about isolated encounters between the government and a huge corporation from which deals would be likely to emerge. Rather these are on-going relationships in which the Very Rich buy goodwill day in day out, the year around and it cuts both ways.

—Editorial, *Washington Post,* March 14, 1972

As a businessman, fundamental in my mind is the question of "What does a diversified company such as IT&T do that is good for the economy and/or bad for the economy?"
On this basis, knowing the degree of effort that our company has consistently in the last 12 years expended as well as the personal effort of our management and myself to strengthen the company within the domestic economy . . . I am surprised to find a company such as ours, and there are others, without much chance of stating its case, but in the category of nonconstructive and fearsome force within our society.

—HAROLD S. GENEEN, Chairman and Chief
Executive of ITT, in a statement
before the U.S. Senate Judiciary
Committee on March 16, 1972

The ITT affair, as it has since come to be known, involved contributions by a large corporation to a presidential political campaign for the alleged purpose of securing favorable settlement of antitrust cases involving the company. At the time of the disclosure and the attendant

[handwritten annotation: ITT - only tip of iceberg. dep. of fed. policy. what gout. happen will]

subsequent publicity, it was widely held that ITT was a unique case, or at best one of the very few large corporations alleged to have been engaged in activities that were not only of doubtful legal validity, but were clearly unprofessional and socially undesirable.

However, later disclosures in the Watergate investigation and also in hearings before the Subcommittee on Multinational Corporations of the Committee on Foreign Relations revealed a broad pattern of illegal activities by such a large number of U.S. blue chip corporations that in retrospect, ITT's revelations seemed pale by comparison, and only the tip of the iceberg. The activities included political contributions both in the United States and abroad, and bribes and payoffs to foreign governments. Furthermore, elaborate and ingenious schemes were developed by the managements of these companies to conceal the nature, amount, and beneficiaries of these payments from the corporate board of directors, stockholders, and appropriate government regulatory agencies such as the Securities and Exchange Commission.

A partial list of corporations convicted or accused of political contributions, political payoffs, and bribery in the United States or one or more countries abroad include: American Airlines, Ashland Oil, American Shipbuilding, Bethlehem Steel, California Standard, Carnation, Diamond International, EXXON, General Motors, Goodyear Tire & Rubber, Gulf Oil, Indiana Standard, Lockheed Aircraft, Northrop Corporation, Phillips Petroleum Co., 3M, United Brands, Wilson & Co.

It is unlikely that attempts by large corporations to buy political influence and channel it to their own economic advantage can ever be completely eliminated. The very nature and diversity of activities pursued by large corporations in general and conglomerates in particular are such that their interests are inevitably linked with and dependent upon the general public policies pursued by the federal government, as well as the specific courses of action determined by various government bodies. However, the timing of the ITT incident was so sensitive, the level of public officials and corporate executives so high, and the nature of the incidents, both before and after the disclosure, so bizarre that it brought into the limelight all the various facets of business-government interaction that had hitherto been known only by a select few.

THE ISSUES

The case raises broad questions of public policy and deals with the issue of business-government interaction and its consequences both for business and society, which deserves serious discussion and analysis.

1. Although it is the recognized right of all citizens, including business corporations, to argue their side before elected political bodies, government agencies, and high officials, it is not clear whether the

channels of appeal are equally open to all concerned. Given the unequal strength and sophistication of various petitioners, how should the public interest be protected in government decision making?

2. Is there something in the processes of government decision making and public policy formulation that makes it possible—laws to the contrary and without an attempt to corrupt—for large corporations and vested interests to secure easy access to government attention to make their views known, and also to secure more favorable decisions?

3. Is it possible that constant and continuous interaction between government officials and business leaders becomes so pervasive that a different and more lenient set of criteria are applied in the enforcement of laws concerning large corporations?

4. To the extent that modern large corporations are private governments, which to be effective must interact with public governments, do conditions exist in their internal governance that make them behave in a particular manner in their outside dealings? If so, can their internal governance be modified to make their external behavior more acceptable to social standards and expectations?

On a more specific level, there are questions that deal with the internal structure of a corporation and its response to external environments that might suggest alternative approaches to restructuring the external environment or internal management processes to make the corporate system more responsive to social needs. For example:

1. Is there anything in the nature of a company's objectives, character and management style of its top leadership, past history, and internal decision-making structure and processes that make it behave in a manner that is legally dubious, unprofessional, and socially undesirable, while another company similarly situated is less likely to respond in the same way?

2. What was the nature of the strategies and tactics employed by ITT in securing a favorable settlement of its antitrust cases with the Department of Justice and also in its subsequent efforts to squelch the unfavorable publicity and a possible termination of the original settlement by the government? Are there any guidelines in ITT's behavior that can be used by other corporations in their own conduct?

3. Are there any environmental conditions—for example, competition in general or in a specific industry, the type of industry (regulated versus unregulated), industrial concentration, or the absolute size of a corporation relative to other companies—that make a corporation respond to external conditions in a manner which might be contrary to its long-term interests or those of the society?

ENTER JACK ANDERSON: THE DITA BEARD MEMO

On February 29, 1972, only five days after the Senate Judiciary Committee voted to confirm the nomination of Acting Attorney General Richard G. Kleindienst to succeed John Mitchell as Attorney General,[1] the following appeared in the "Washington Merry-Go-Round," the nationally syndicated column by Jack Anderson:

> We now have evidence that the settlement of the Nixon administration's biggest anti-trust case was privately arranged between Attorney General John Mitchell and the top lobbyist for the company involved.
>
> We have this on the word of the lobbyist herself, crusty, capable Dita Beard of the International Telephone and Telegraph Co. She acknowledged the secret deal after we obtained a highly incriminating memo, written by her, from ITT's files.
>
> The memo, which was intended to be destroyed after it was read, not only indicates that the anti-trust case had been fixed but that the fix was a payoff for ITT's pledge of up to $400,000 for the upcoming Republican convention in San Diego.
>
> Confronted with the memo, Mrs. Beard acknowledged its authenticity. . . .

The memo detailed a meeting between Mrs. Beard, Attorney General John Mitchell, and Republican Governor Louis Nunn at the governor's Kentucky mansion. It [the memo] is addressed to W. R. (Bill) Merriam, head of ITT's Washington office. It is marked "Personal and Confidential" and its last line asks, "Please destroy this, huh?"

The memo warns Merriam to keep quiet about the ITT cash pledge for the Republican convention. "John Mitchell has certainly kept it on the higher level only," the memo says, "we should be able to do the same. . . .

"I am convinced, because of several conversations with Louis (Gov. Nunn) re Mitchell that our noble commitment has gone a long way toward our negotiations on the mergers coming out as Hal (ITT President Harold Geneen) wants them.

"Certainly the President has told Mitchell to see that things are worked out fairly. It is still only McLaren's mickey-mouse that we are suffering. . . .

"If (the convention commitment) gets too much publicity, you can believe our negotiations with Justice will wind up shot down. Mitchell is definitely helping us, but cannot let it be known."

---

[1] U.S. Congress, Senate, Committee on the Judiciary, *Hearings on Nomination of Richard G. Kleindienst, of Arizona, to be Attorney General,* Part 2, 92nd Cong., 2nd sess., March 1972, pp. 392–93. References to this source will hereinafter be referred to in the text as *Hearings,* followed by part and page number.

The implications of this memo were explosive, and the timing of its publication left little doubt that its allegations would be fully investigated. The year 1972 was a presidential election year, with the incumbent Republican administration strongly identified as a friend of big business.

ITT immediately issued a statement categorically denying the existence of any deal in the settlement of its antitrust cases. It maintained that "the San Diego contribution of the Sheraton Hotels was made as a non-partisan joint effort of the San Diego community and was purely in support of a local situation" (Hearings, part 2, p. 393). Kleindienst also denied any wrongdoing during the 1971 settlement and requested that his confirmation hearings be reopened immediately so that he would not take office "with a cloud over my head, so to speak" (*Hearings,* part 2, p. 96). The Judiciary Committee, with a majority of Democrats, including some very vocal administration critics, was quite willing to oblige.

To keep the facts of the case straight and the sequence of events comprehensible, the narrative that follows has been divided into two sections. The first section deals with the ITT contribution to the Republican convention and the attempts at its coverup. The second section deals with settlement of the antitrust case involving ITT and the Hartford Insurance Company.

I. GOP CONVENTION PLEDGE

The hearings were reopened on March 2, 1972, with Richard Kleindienst as the lead-off witness. In his testimony Kleindienst admitted to some general discussions about the ITT case with Felix Rohatyn, an ITT director. He emphatically denied putting any pressure on McLaren or having any part in the settlement of the ITT case. He went on to state:

> I would like to conclude my remarks by saying categorically and specifically that at no time, until some time in December 1971, did I have any knowledge of any kind of a contribution to the city of San Diego or to the Republican Party with respect to the prospective national convention of the Republican Party in San Diego. I never talked to a person on the face of this earth about any aspect of the San Diego Republican National Convention or the I.T.&T. Corp. I never talked to Mr. Mitchell about any aspect of this case. He never mentioned any aspect of this case, . . . I had nothing whatsoever to do with anything that the Department of Justice, the Government of the United States, myself, or Judge McLaren, in connection with these matters. (*Hearings,* part 2, p. 100)

Little did Kleindienst realize that in asking for a reopening of his hearings, he was opening a Pandora's box. Once started, the hearings assumed a life of their own and led into things that if Kleindienst had known earlier would be brought up, he would never have wished anyone to investigate. What finally emerged from the hearings was not a clarification or a denial of any specific deal, but revised and "refreshed" testimony, lapses of memory, and conflicting testimony by witnesses, which so obscured the truth about what might or might not have been arranged between ITT and the Nixon administration that little could be determined with any certainty. But what did emerge with great clarity was the picture of a corporation sparing no effort or expense to influence events in its own favor and an administration apparently receptive to such efforts.

The Memo and Its Allegations

The two events around which the memo centered were hardly secret, and each was controversial in its own right. In July 1971 the Antitrust Division of the Justice Department abruptly accepted an out-of-court settlement of three cases against ITT. These were suits in which the government sought the divestiture of three of ITT's recently acquired subsidiaries: Canteen Corporation, the leading company in vending machine production; Grinnell Corporation, a leader in production and sales of fire protection devices; and Hartford Fire and Casualty Insurance Company, the nation's sixth largest insurance concern. Richard McLaren, then assistant attorney general in charge of antitrust, repeatedly stressed his intention of taking these cases to the Supreme Court, for they were based on a departure from traditional legal interpretation of the antitrust laws as they applied to conglomerate mergers, and McLaren wanted his theories clarified and vindicated in the Court. ITT's acquisition of Hartford Fire was the largest corporate merger in history, and McLaren had been adamant that any settlement with ITT would have to include complete divestiture of Hartford. Nevertheless, the 1971 consent decree by which all three cases were settled allowed ITT to keep Hartford while divesting itself of approximately $1 billion of other assets. This sudden change in McLaren's position left many wondering if the close ties between ITT and the administration (both President Nixon and Attorney General Mitchell had been attorneys in a firm that had represented an ITT subsidiary) did not have something to do with McLaren's change of mind.

The abandonment of these cases even caused expressions of disappointment in some business circles. *Business Week,* for example, commented, in an editorial entitled "The Antitrusters Cop Out":

> The sudden settlement last weekend of the government's package of antitrust cases against International Telephone & Telegraph Corp. is a singularly unsatisfying end to an important episode in government-business relations.

> The ITT cases were promoted by the Nixon Administration as an attempt to establish a clear judicial definition of the limits on corporate growth in a modern society. By suddenly agreeing to accept the settlement, the government antitrusters have thrown away

the chance to do that. . . . <u>Clarification not only of the law but of the economics of mergers is badly needed.</u> . . . It will take a major series of legal tests, ending in the Supreme Court, to prompt the rigorous analysis necessary to determine how big and how fast a company can grow without endangering the public interest.[2]

At approximately the same time, in "shining green coincidence," [3] it was announced that ITT, through its subsidiary Sheraton Hotels, had made a generous contribution to the financing of the Republican National Convention by underwriting a $400,000 cash guarantee to bring the convention to San Diego.[4] The contribution's size, although Sheraton later said the $400,000 figure was "highly exaggerated," [5] made it extremely conspicuous and legally questionable.

On December 13, 1971, Lawrence F. O'Brien, the Democratic national chairman, raised questions concerning the link between ITT's antitrust settlement and convention pledge in a letter to Attorney General Mitchell, which was passed on to Kleindienst: O'Brien specifically asked whether there was any connection between ITT's sudden largesse to the Republican party and the out-of-court settlement of its merger case. He also asked whether San Diego Congressman Bob Wilson, who was also the chairman of the House Republican Campaign Committee, had either talked with ITT officials in New York or discussed the merger case with Deputy Attorney General Kleindienst prior to the selection of San Diego as the host city for the Republican convention.

In his reply, which was later to haunt him, Kleindienst wrote O'Brien that he had no prior knowledge, direct or indirect, of ITT's subsidiary Sheraton Corporation of America's pledge of $400,000 to San Diego for hosting the GOP convention. He also stated:

> *The settlement between the Department of Justice and ITT was handled and negotiated exclusively by Assistant Attorney General Richard McLaren.* . . . Mr. McLaren kept me generally advised as to the course of negotiations . . . prior to the final conclusion of these settlement negotiations and the effectuation of a settlement between the Department of Justice and ITT, Mr. McLaren made his final recommendation in the matter to me with which I concurred. [Emphasis added] (*Hearings,* part 2, pp. 120–21)

However, in later hearings before the Judiciary Committee (Watergate Hearings), <u>Kleindienst admitted not only to knowing about ITT's anti</u>trust case settlement but also to playing an active part in bringing it about. <u>His admission came out only after Jack Anderson had made allegations in his column accusing him of actually lying.</u> → *newspaper brought out the truth*

2 *Business Week,* August 7, 1971; also cited in *Hearings,* part 2, p. 575.
3 "The ITT Affair: Politics and Justice," *Newsweek,* March 20, 1972, p. 24.
4 "Sheraton's GOP Parley Aid Affirmed," *San Diego Union,* August 6, 1971.
5 "San Diego Is Split on Convention Aid," *The New York Times,* September 13, 1971, p. 38.

The Repercussions of the Memo:
The Justice Department

Denials that there had been any impropriety in the settlement came immediately, first from John Mitchell and then from Kleindienst himself. Attorney General Mitchell issued the following statement:

> I was not involved in any way with the Republican National Committee convention negotiations . . . when the Department of Justice first brought action against ITT, I removed myself from all consideration of such matters. I have not discussed the subject with anyone from ITT or in the Department, with one exception, . . . with respect to the allegations that the President discussed the matter with me, there would be no occasion for him to do so and he did not. (*Hearings,* part 3, p. 1269)

The exception referred to by Mitchell was that of a conversation (see Jack Anderson's memo) with Dita Beard at a party where he refused to discuss with her any business relative to ITT and suggested that she approach the appropriate people in the Department of Justice.

In the reopened hearings, Kleindienst was accompanied by McLaren, at that time a federal judge in Illinois, and Felix Rohatyn, the director of ITT with whom Kleindienst had had the meetings that Anderson reported. The three men described a chronology in which Rohatyn had contacted Kleindienst in April 1971 to persuade him that the Antitrust Division should hear an ITT presentation that a forced divestiture of Hartford would be "almost a fatal blow" [6] to the company and would also damage the national economy. As a result of this meeting, a larger meeting was held, with staff members from the Antitrust Division and the Treasury Department, various ITT representatives, Kleindienst, and Rohatyn. McLaren thereafter arranged for an analysis of ITT's presentation by an outside consultant and, chiefly, he said, on the basis of that consultant's report, McLaren decided that divestiture of Hartford should not be required. He then recommended a settlement proposal to Kleindienst, and they made a joint call to Rohatyn to say that if the broad outlines of the proposal were acceptable, negotiations over its smaller details could begin. Negotiations started during the latter part of June 1971 and culminated in the consent decree of July 31, by which ITT retained Hartford.

All three men insisted that there had been no undue pressure on McLaren to change his mind. McLaren himself testified that

> the decision to enter into settlement negotiations with ITT was my own personal decision; I was not pressured to reach this decision. Furthermore, the plan of settlement was devised, and the final terms

---

[6] "ITT's Arrogance," *New Republic,* April 8, 1972, p. 4.

negotiated, by me with the advice of other members of the Antitrust Division, and by no one else. (*Hearings,* part 2, p. 113)

But flaws began to appear almost immediately in this categorical testimony, and it rapidly became "one of those maddening exercises in which every loose end seems to unravel itself into half a dozen more." Testimony was revised and refreshed, omissions were corrected, conflicting evidence was presented, and relevant information was refused to the committee without any change in the Justice Department's posture of studied indifference. It became easier and easier to believe that witnesses were admitting only what was impossible to hide and resorting to forgetfulness and such drastic measures as "executive privilege" when no other means of preventing the discovery of embarrassing facts could be found. ITT's own actions (discussed in the next section) exhibited an arrogance whose chief characteristic was an apparently "unlimited faith in the gullibility of the public." [7]

The events that Kleindienst did not at first remember significantly enlarged his own role in the events, showed in greater detail the efforts ITT was making to pressure McLaren into a settlement favorable to the company, and, even more important, outlined White House involvement in the settlement, through a presidential aid known as "Mr. Fixit" for big business, Peter M. Flanigan.[8]

Among the more glaring examples of the events that Kleindienst did not remember were the following:

1. He had been approached at a neighborhood social event by one of his neighbors, John Ryan, deputy director of ITT's Washington office, who described himself as the company's antitrust "listening post," or "focal point" (*Hearings,* part 3, p. 1068). Ryan asked Kleindienst if he would listen to an ITT economic presentation; Kleindienst agreed, and Rohatyn was assigned to make the presentation. Kleindienst did not remember this contact independently, but he had his "recollection refreshed" by Rohatyn (*Hearings,* part 2, p. 133).

2. Just before his meeting with Rohatyn, Kleindienst received a plea from an ITT lawyer to delay the case against ITT's acquisition of Grinnell, which was scheduled to be filed before the Supreme Court. Kleindienst requested the solicitor general to apply for the thirty-day delay, which was granted, and during that period, McLaren heard the financial and economic arguments that allegedly changed his mind. Even more important than these bare facts is the identity of the lawyer who requested the delay: Lawrence Walsh was deputy attorney general (the position Kleindienst held) during the Eisenhower administration; he was appointed by President Nixon to be deputy chief negotiator at the Paris peace talks in 1969, and he was chairman of the American Bar

---

[7] See, for example, "The ITT Case; End of the Affair?" *Newsweek,* April 10, 1972, p. 17; "Know-Nothing Mitchell," *New Republic,* March 25, 1972, p. 5. Editorial, *St. Louis Post-Dispatch,* March 22, 1972.

[8] "Is He the White House 'Mr. Fixit'?" *The Wall Street Journal,* March 21, 1972, p. 18.

Association Committee on the Federal Judiciary, which was responsible for clearing administration nominees for all federal judgeships. Kleindienst, as deputy attorney general, was in charge of judicial appointments, and through their contact on that matter, he and Walsh were close friends.

Further complicating Walsh's relationship with Kleindienst and with these cases, and highlighting the question of the propriety of his contacts with Kleindienst, is the fact that when Richard McLaren was nominated to be a federal judge several months after the settlement of these cases (raising questions of the judgeship's being the carrot that induced McLaren to allow the settlement), it was Walsh's committee that reviewed his candidacy and cleared him in a matter of hours.

3. Kleindienst was repeatedly questioned about any contacts he might have had with the White House over these cases, and he repeatedly answered that there had been none. It later appeared, however, that the role of presidential aide Peter Flanigan was quite important. Flanigan was White House liaison with business and was supposed to help businessmen in their problems with the federal government and Congress.

However, later in a letter to Judiciary Committee Chairman Senator Sam Erwin, Flanigan admitted calling Kleindienst about the Ramsden report. He also acknowledged that Kleindienst was present when he personally delivered the report to McLaren (*Hearings,* part 3, p. 1639).

Departing Attorney General John Mitchell's testimony showed the same pattern of initial omissions and subsequent corrections as Kleindienst's, although Mitchell's was also characterized by flat statements that were widely disbelieved and by statements that contradicted other witnesses, with no resolution ever advanced.[9]

New fuel was soon added to this flickering suspicion. California's Lieutenant Governor Ed Reinecke and his aide, Edgar Gillenwaters, stated to Jack Anderson's aide, Brit Hume, to several other reporters, and to Senator John V. Tunney that they had briefed Mitchell fully on San Diego's prospects as host for the convention in May 1971, with the briefing including a discussion of the ITT financial commitment.[10] Senator Tunney, a political colleague and friend, called Reinecke to point out to him that his testimony conflicted with what Mitchell had said. An obviously disturbed Tunney recounted the telephone call in the hearings:

> You [Reinecke] said that unless you were subject to a failing memory, there was no question that you had brought up the $400,000 to be given to the city of San Diego to bring the convention to San Diego. When I pointed out to you that Mr. Mitchell was probably going to testify to the contrary you said, "Well, all a person has is his integrity," and you indicated that you recalled the conversation. (*Hearings,* part 3, p. 1524)

That call was on Thursday, March 2. On Friday, March 3, Reinecke called a press conference and stated:

[9] "Mitchell Gearing Up to Steer Campaign," *Washington Post,* October 10, 1971.
[10] "Lieutenant Governor Reinecke's Shift on ITT Story," *Sacramento Bee,* March 3, 1972.

On the May 16, 1971, trip to Washington, D.C. we did not meet with Attorney General John Mitchell as I had previously reported. . . . My discussions with Attorney General Mitchell concerning the convention was at 9:30 A.M. on September 17, 1971. . . . This would have been the first time either of us (Reinecke or Gillenwaters) discussed any such offer with the Attorney General.[11]

But this correction, like those of other witnesses, only served to cloud the issue further. Even Reinecke's corrected version of events did not coincide with the version given by Mitchell who, in a great show of indifference to the entire topic, *failed to remember any discussion whatever with Reinecke about the convention (Hearings,* part 2, pp. 547–69).[12]

In June 1973 Reinecke gave yet another version of events to the FBI which, at the request of special Watergate prosecutor Archibald Cox, was investigating the possibility of perjury by either Reinecke or Mitchell. Reinecke now said he had told Mitchell of Sheraton's pledge during a telephone call in May or June 1971 before the settlement of ITT's cases had been reached. (Recall that Reinecke's first version indicated that he had had a *meeting* with Mitchell in May.) Asked whether his statement did not contradict Mitchell's repeated denials of knowledge of this pledge, Reinecke said, "It would appear to be in contradiction, yes." [13]

Another part of Mitchell's earlier denial stated that he had "not discussed the subject [of ITT's antitrust cases] with anyone from ITT" except Mrs. Beard. He admitted in testimony, however, that he had, after all, had a thirty-five-minute meeting with Harold Geneen, ITT's president, on August 4, 1970. Mitchell testified that he "assented to the meeting on the express condition that the pending ITT litigation would not be discussed. Mr. Geneen agreed to this condition. The pending ITT litigation was not discussed at the meeting" (*Hearings,* part 2, p. 540). Instead, they had discussed the department's antitrust policy with respect to conglomerates. Furthermore, ITT Vice-President Edward J. Gerrity told the committee that the purpose of the meeting was to take another try at seeing "if we could move the Justice Department toward some sort of reasonable attitude toward our position" on a settlement involving ITT's antitrust suits (*Hearings,* part 2, p. 1198). A summary of ITT documents prepared by the SEC was released to the public by another congressional committee almost a year after Kleindienst's hearings supported

---

11 *Ibid.*
12 For the reaction of the press on the hazy memories and evasiveness of Mitchell, Kleindienst, and other witnesses, see, for example, the following sources, most of which are contained either in the *Hearings,* in the "Separate Report of Senators Bayh, Kennedy, and Tunney on the Supplementary Hearings Regarding the Nomination of Richard Kleindienst as Attorney General (as Revised and Supplemented)," or in *Editorials on File,* 1972; editorial, *Arkansas Gazette,* April 23, 1972; editorial, *Louisville Times,* April 24, 1972; "Kleindienst: Without a Doubt," *New Republic,* May 13, 1972; editorial, *Arkansas Democrat,* March 24, 1972; editorial, *St. Louis Post-Dispatch,* April 28, 1972; and "Lofty Discussions: How Mitchell Kept His Door Open," *San Francisco Chronicle,* March 16, 1972.
13 "ITT's Offer: I Told Mitchell, Reinecke Insists," *San Francisco Chronicle,* June 28, 1973, p. 11.

Gerrity's statement. It contained a summary of a memo from Gerrity to Vice-President Spiro Agnew, dated August 7, 1970. The memo consisted of a thank-you letter concerning an attached memo and a suggestion that Mitchell get the facts relating to ITT's position to McLaren. It indicated that there was a friendly session between Geneen and Mitchell, in which Mitchell told Geneen that Nixon was not opposed to the merger and that Nixon believed that mergers were good. Mitchell apparently said that ITT had not been sued because bigness is bad.

This memo contradicted another part of Mitchell's statement and supported a vigorously disputed remark of Mrs. Beard's. Mitchell had at first stated: "With respect to the allegations that the President discussed the matter with me, there would be no occasion for him to do so and he did not."

See the Rabbits Run: Actions of ITT

ITT officials moved rapidly to cover their tracks following the publication of Dita Beard's memo. The combination of denials, retractions, and other shenanigans was often so outrageous and bizarre that ITT became identified in the public as the author of events external to the hearings that "reached the full stance of a comic opera . . . a full grown Amos 'N Andy minstrel with Mrs. Beard in the role of Madame Queen." [14]

For starters, Mrs. Beard immediately disappeared from Washington after publication of her memo and was unavailable when hearings reopened on March 2, 1972. A subpoena was then issued by the committee, and the FBI was assigned the task of locating her. ITT officials denied knowledge of Mrs. Beard's whereabouts. Jack Anderson, however, reported that when his office talked to Mrs. Beard a few days previously, she told them, "ITT has told me to get out of town." [15]

On March 4 Mrs. Beard was located in Denver, in the Rocky Mountain Osteopathic Hospital, where she had been admitted on March 3 for treatment of angina pectoris. Through an agreement with her doctors, arrangements were made for a select committee of senators to question her in Denver later in the month.

It was later alleged during the Watergate hearings that G. Gordon Liddy, then counsel for CREEP and one of the chief convicted conspirators in the Watergate bugging case, had whisked Mrs. Beard out of Washington.[16] Furthermore, E. Howard Hunt, also convicted in the Watergate case, visited Denver in disguise to talk to Mrs. Beard prior to her testimony before the select panel of senators from the Judiciary Committee.

ITT itself did not long remain in the shadow of Mrs. Beard's dramatic sickbed reappearance. Anderson charged that ITT officials, after being shown the memo, sent security officers from New York to put Mrs. Beard's

14 Editorial, *Chicago Daily Defender*, April 25, 1972.
15 "Kleindienst Says He Set Up Talks on ITT Accord But Denies It Was Tied to GOP Convention Fund," *The New York Times*, March 3, 1972, p. 20.
16 "Other Break-Ins Reported," *San Francisco Chronicle*, June 4, 1973, p. 8.

files through a document shredder "to prevent their being subpoenaed after disclosure of the memo" (*Hearings,* part 2, p. 392). On March 15 Geneen testified that although he knew no details about the incident, it was "probably more a reaction to the feeling that our files were suddenly open to the public . . . and certainly not any kind of action to, you might say, prevent a review of our files by any legitimate agency" (*Hearings,* part 2, p. 666). He promised a full report by the following day.

On March 16 Geneen and several ITT lawyers faced the committee to continue their detailed testimony on the memo's allegations and the shredding incident. Howard J. Aibel, vice-president and general counsel for ITT, testified that William Merriam, ITT's Washington office chief, had instructed his staff the day after he saw the memo "to remove any documents which, if put into Mr. Anderson's possession, could be misused and misconstrued by him. . . ." (*Hearings,* part 2, p. 704). This was, he stated, in accordance with a long-standing company policy of destruction of noncurrent confidential and other material, which had not been previously complied with in the Washington office.

Aibel described the documents as primarily tourist brochures about San Diego, newspaper clippings, copies of speeches, and material relating to past Congresses. These were, he said, the only documents in the files that related to the San Diego convention. He admitted, however, that he could say only in a general way which documents were actually destroyed and that John Ryan from ITT's Washington office had helped Mrs. Beard in deciding which documents from her files were to be destroyed. Geneen and the other ITT witnesses insisted that there had been no intention to impede the committee's investigations and that there had been no documents in the files relevant to the investigation (*Hearings,* part 2, pp. 713–28).

Geneen and Aibel had been questioned in detail about Mrs. Beard's memo and its allegations. In two days of testimony, March 15 and 16, there was never a suggestion of doubt about the memo's authenticity. Suddenly, on March 17, Mrs. Beard issued the following statement:

> Mr. Anderson's memo is a forgery, and not mine. I did not prepare it and could not have since to my knowledge the assertions in it regarding the antitrust cases and former Atty. Gen. (John N.) Mitchell are untrue. I do not know who did prepare it, who forged my initial on it, how it got into Jack Anderson's hands or why. But, I repeat, I do know it is not my memo and is a hoax.
>
> I did prepare a memo at about the time indicated, at the request of (W. R.) Bill Merriam, to him concerning plans for the Republican convention in San Diego. However, it was not the memo Jack Anderson has put in evidence before the Senate.[17]

Mrs. Beard's lawyer, who later stated that ITT was paying his fees

[17] "ITT Lobbyist Calls Memo a 'Forgery'; Evidence Promised," *Los Angeles Times,* March 18, 1972.

($15,000 was his initial retainer), hinted that evidence to prove the forgery charge would be forthcoming.

ITT immediately came to Mrs. Beard's support. On March 20 ITT turned up what it called the "genuine" memo, carrying the same date as the Anderson memo; but this one, an innocuous job description, was so different from what Mrs. Beard said she had written that the company was forced to admit the next day that they had made an error and that their genuine memo was not the original after all. At that time the FBI produced a report that offered its expert opinion that the Anderson memo had been prepared in the ITT office at the time indicated. ITT countered with its own experts' report that it could *not* have been prepared in June 1971 but was more likely written in January 1972.

On March 26 Mrs. Beard herself finally testified before that "bunch of little bums," [18] as she referred to the senators who had come to interview her. She continued to deny that she had written the memo or that there was any connection between ITT's campaign pledge and the antitrust settlement. But she admitted to authorship of sections of the memo that linked Mitchell to the convention planning he had denied being part of and that stated that he knew of ITT's pledge. She also claimed to have written the last paragraph of the memo, which *specifically* linked the two events.

But after several hours of testimony, Mrs. Beard collapsed with a sudden recurrence of her heart symptoms. It would be at least six months before she could testify again, said her doctors, and the senators, understandably disturbed at what they had heard, went back to Washington to continue the hearings without her.

Mrs. Beard's illness also became a subject of controversy. Her condition was attested to by several doctors, including two cardiologists—Dr. Victor Liszka, her long-time personal physician in Washington, and Dr. Leo Radetsky in Denver. Dr. Liszka appeared before the committee on March 6 amid rumors that ITT would be making an all-out effort to discredit Mrs. Beard. His testimony did little to contradict this rumor as he described Mrs. Beard's excessive drinking and heavy use of tranquilizers. (*Hearings,* part 2, p. 232).

This testimony, which would have provided ITT with a convenient explanation for Mrs. Beard's memo, was seriously questioned. The following day the medical director of the American Heart Association termed Dr. Liszka's testimony about the side effects of cardiac problems "nonsense." [19] But even more damaging, the Justice Department informed the committee the day *after* Dr. Liszka's testimony that earlier in the year he had been under investigation for alleged fraud in receiving excess Medicare payments. Although Dr. Liszka had been cleared of these allegations, at the time of the hearings a grand jury was considering similar evidence against his wife, also a doctor, with whom he operated a joint practice.

It was subsequently discovered that Dr. Radetsky, Mrs. Beard's Denver

[18] "Dita Beard on Dita Beard," *Time,* April 3, 1972, p. 16.
[19] "Ex-Governor of Kentucky Asserts Mitchell Rebuffed ITT Lobbyist," *The New York Times,* March 8, 1972, p. 21.

cardiologist, was the subject of a similar investigation, still in progress at the time he cared for Mrs. Beard. Inasmuch as Dr. Radetsky was responsible for terminating Mrs. Beard's testimony and for making the decision that she would not be available to testify again for six months the discovery that he was under investigation for fraud made his reliability questionable. A week after her "collapse," Mrs. Beard checked out of the hospital for an evening, during which she was interviewed by CBS newsman Mike Wallace. Although she had left the hospital in a sweater and skirt, she wore a hospital gown for the interview. It was too much to accept without a snicker, and newspaper editorials and columns took advantage of the rare opportunity to view what the *St. Louis Post-Dispatch* called the "squirming of this 6.7 billion dollar conglomerate under the light of public scrutiny." [20]

II. THE HARTFORD FIRE COMPANY ACQUISITION

The ITT pledge of financial contributions to the GOP convention was allegedly linked to a favorable settlement of the Justice Department's antitrust suit against ITT involving the Hartford Fire Insurance Company. In this section I shall examine the merits of the case, the circumstances that led up to it, and the real or suspected efforts made by ITT to persuade various public officials and agencies to act in ways favorable to ITT.

The Consent Order

On July 31, 1971, Assistant Attorney General Richard W. McLaren announced the details of a consent order settling the government's antitrust suit against ITT involving the latter's acquisition of Canteen Corporation, Grinnell Corporation, and Hartford Fire Insurance Company. Under the terms of the consent order, ITT was required:

1. To divest Canteen Corporation and the Fire Protection Division of Grinnell Corporation within two years.
2. To divest (a) Hartford or (b) Avis Rent-A-Car, ITT-Levitt and Sons, Inc., and its subsidiaries, ITT Hamilton Life Insurance Company and ITT Life Insurance Company of New York.
3. To refrain from acquiring any domestic corporation with assets of more than $100 million and to refrain from acquiring leading companies in concentrated U.S. markets without the approval of the department or the court. Under the agreement, a leading company was defined as one with annual sales of more than $25 million and holding 15 percent of any market in which the top four companies accounted for more than 50 percent of total sales.

[20] Editorial, *St. Louis Post-Dispatch,* March 22, 1972.

4. To refrain from acquiring any substantial interest in any domestic automatic sprinkler company or any domestic insurance company with insurance assets exceeding $10 million

5. To discontinue the practice of reciprocity—using purchasing power to promote sales—by ITT and all its subsidiary companies.

McLaren declared it to be a significant victory for the government in that it "obtained very substantial divestiture, the largest ever in an antitrust case, and strong injunctions against ITT's making any more of the giant and leading firm mergers" (*Hearings,* part 2, p. 254).

A significant number of people, however, were disappointed by the government's willingness to settle and considered it a reversal of the policy that was so forcefully enunciated by the Nixon administration when it first came to power. McLaren had consistently maintained, and so stated at his confirmation hearings before the Senate Judiciary Committee on January 29, 1969, that he believed that "the antitrust laws, more particularly Section 7 of the Clayton Act, are able to reach conglomerate mergers." [21] Perhaps the best and most articulate summary of McLaren's views is in his testimony before the House Ways and Means Committee:

Let me state briefly how I conceive the responsibility of the Antitrust Division in the light of current developments.

Our basic antitrust statutes are few in number; their provisions are relatively concise; and they have been the subject of major amendments on but few occasions since the Sherman Act was passed in 1890. . . .

Perhaps the cardinal reason for the achievements of antitrust has been the capacity of the basic law to adapt to changing circumstances. . . . In short, antitrust law seeks always to remain equal to the vital task entrusted to it—the protection of a free competitive society.

The evolving nature of antitrust law is, I think, particularly relevant to a discussion of conglomerate mergers, for two principal reasons. First, there is every indication that conglomerate mergers are increasing in both frequency and magnitude at an unparalleled rate and are bound to have a significant impact on business activity. Second, if we define conglomerate mergers to mean those which are neither horizontal nor vertical, it is apparent that different conglomerate

[21] Quoted in "Separate Report of Senators Bayh, Kennedy, and Tunney on the Supplementary Hearings Regarding the Nomination of Richard Kleindienst as Attorney General (as Revised and Supplemented)," p. 31. Hereinafter referred to as "Separate Report." See also "Antitrust—Republican Style," *Dun's Review,* October 1969; "Conglomerates Under Attack," *Newsweek,* March 10, 1969; "Antitrust Chief McLaren Promises Suits to Block Large Conglomerate Mergers," *The Wall Street Journal,* March 7, 1969, p. 2; and "McLaren Clarifies Administration Policy in Antitrust War on Conglomerate Mergers," *The Wall Street Journal,* March 28, 1969, p. 5.

mergers may present different kinds of threats to competition and thus may require different kinds of analyses.[22]

McLaren also stated: "We are willing to risk losing some cases to find how far Section 7 will take us in halting the current accelerated trend toward concentration by merger." [23]

In his oft-quoted speech to the Georgia Bar Association in Savannah, Mitchell, who was then attorney general, strongly backed McLaren's get-tough antitrust policy and claimed that "the future vitality of our free economy may be in danger because of the increasing threat of economic concentration by conglomerate corporate mergers." [24]

Therefore, McLaren's announcement of the settlement of the antitrust cases against ITT left many observers puzzled and dissatisfied. *Business Week* called its editorial on the settlement "The Antitrusters Cop Out." [25] In the following months two further events were to take place that cast a grave shadow of doubt on the settlement and the propriety of the actions of the parties involved.

The first event was the announcement by Congressman Bob Wilson, on August 5, that the $400,000 pledge to the San Diego Convention and Tourist Bureau came from the Sheraton Corporation of America, an ITT subsidiary.[26] The second event was the nomination by the White House, and the subsequent confirmation "in record time" by the Senate, of McLaren as a federal judge. Although all parties vehemently denied at that time—and still deny—any connection between these two events and McLaren's antitrust policy or the ITT settlement, doubts arose about the strange coincidence of events.

The Background of the Antitrust Cases

In early 1969 ITT decided to acquire the Canteen Corporation; with $240 million in assets, Canteen was the leading vending machine producer in the country. The Justice Department considered this merger a violation of antitrust laws. The merger of ITT, the largest pure conglomerate in the United States, with the leader of the vending machine business was obviously more than a "foothold" or "toehold" acquisition and could have anticompetitive implications.

McLaren's policy on such mergers was reflected in the guidelines issued by the department and was repeatedly stressed by Justice Department officials: "The Department of Justice will probably oppose any merger by one of the top 200 manufacturing firms or any leading producer in any

22 U.S. Congress, House, *Hearings Before the Committee on Ways and Means on the Subject of Tax Reform,* 91st Cong., 1st sess., p. 2389.
23 *Ibid.*
24 "News Analysis and Interpretation: ITT Log Book: Names, Dates . . . and Questions," *St. Louis Post-Dispatch,* March 26, 1969, p. 3E. See also *The Wall Street Journal,* March 28, 1969, p. 5.
25 August 7, 1971.
26 *San Diego Union,* August 6, 1971.

concentrated industry" (*Hearings,* part 2, p. 141). As early as April 7, 1969, ITT was formally informed by McLaren of his intention to bring suit against the merger. The thrust of this suit was apparently the merger's ability to facilitate reciprocity or a reciprocity effect.

ITT, therefore, was very well aware of its antitrust violation. Nevertheless, it went ahead and consummated the merger on April 25, 1969. The Justice Department filed suit, asking for the divestiture of Canteen, on April 28, 1969. Shortly after the announcement of this suit, plans for two more mergers that apparently violated the administration's policy guidelines were made public by ITT. The company announced its intention to acquire (1) the Grinnell Corporation, a leading company in the sales and production of fire protection devices, industrial piping, and sprinkler systems, and (2) the Hartford Fire and Casualty Insurance Company, the nation's sixth largest insurance company and second largest fire insurance company.

The Justice Department opposed both mergers. Its intention to bring suits against ITT was announced on June 23 and 30, 1969, and the suits, seeking preliminary injunctions, were filed on August 1, 1969. The Justice Department's opposition was again based on the reduction of competition and the threat of reciprocity that might be caused by the mergers. Specifically, in *Grinnell,* the main thrust of the suit was that once acquired by ITT, Grinnell would be entrenched as the dominant company in the manufacture and installation of automatic sprinklers, with ITT's immense resources at its disposal. All other suppliers were small regional companies or contractors. ITT could provide or finance huge contracts to Grinnell through its various subsidiaries, such as ITT-Levitt—the leading real estate developer and home builder; ITT-Hamilton Insurance; and ITT-Hartford. This could make it virtually impossible for the small competitors to survive, much less compete.

In the Hartford case, reciprocity was argued as the basis for suit. It was contended that the immense purchasing power of ITT, spread across every branch of the economy, could not but help Hartford, with a resultant powerful effect on the insurance industry. Furthermore, because of the special nature and structure of the insurance business, most of ITT's suppliers would favor doing business with Hartford even if no pressures to do so were applied. Vertical integration aspects of the merger could trigger other similar mergers.

The government also argued that ITT's three acquisitions of large and leading companies were part of its growth and concentration of economic power, as stated by McLaren:

> . . . we expect to argue that the three acquisitions are not only part of ITT's program of acquiring large leading companies, but are part of a general merger trend which, if continued, will have substantial anticompetitive effects upon the economy as a whole. . . .

It is interesting to note that ITT ended 1969 as Number 9 on

FORTUNE's list of 500 Largest Industrial Corporations (up from Number 11 in 1968). It has continued to make acquisitions—albeit smaller ones than those at issue—and it is my opinion that if we lose these cases against ITT, or do not obtain meaningful relief, we will have to seek new legislation which will be effective to stop the resurgence of big-firm mergers which will almost inevitably result. (*Hearings,* part 2, p. 1245)

Due to the novelty and complexity of these cases, the Justice Department in both the Hartford case and the Grinnell case was denied its request for preliminary injunctions against the mergers, thereby opening the way for a direct government appeal to the Supreme Court. These cases, as well as *Canteen,* which had similarly been initially decided against the government, were brought to trial and appealed very quickly.

In November 1970, while the cases were in progress, ITT proposed an out-of-court settlement involving its retention of Hartford, but divestiture of Canteen, Grinnell, ITT-Levitt, and some other insurance operations of ITT. This would have, to some extent, eliminated the reciprocity and vertical integration effects of the acquisitions. To be specific, ITT was the major consumer of Canteen's "in-plant feeding program" (15 percent of its sales). Therefore, divestiture of Canteen would eliminate the reciprocity and anticompetitive aspects of this merger. Divestiture of Levitt, ITT's real estate and home builder, along with the fire protection division of Grinnell, would also eliminate some apparent vertical integration and reciprocity. Finally, divestiture of small insurance operations would remove the obvious possibility of horizontal integration in the insurance business. Retention of Hartford, however, would leave untouched ITT's movement toward more economic concentration and a tendency toward vertical integration in the insurance of other ITT subsidiaries.

This settlement was rejected by the Antitrust Division, and the appeals continued. To no one's surprise, the court rejected the government's contentions in *Grinnell* on December 31, 1970, on the grounds that there was no legal precedent. This was the final lower court decision, and the case could now be appealed to the Supreme Court. This procedure was recommended by McLaren to Solicitor General Erwin N. Griswold on February 24, 1971, and although Griswold did not agree with McLaren's theories, he approved the appeal, and preparations for the submission of the jurisdictional statement to the Court were begun.

Canteen, being tried in Chicago, suffered a similar fate. In July 1971 the government's case was rejected by the District Court.

Hartford Fire Insurance Company

Hartford Fire Insurance Company was a leading writer of property and liability insurance. Pertinent financial data for Hartford as of 1969 were as follows:

Consolidated assets	$ 1.98 billion
Premium receipts	968.80 million
Net income	53.30 million
Excess cash over required reserves	400.00 million

The ITT-Hartford merger was the largest corporate merger in history. The acquisition had to be approved by the Connecticut insurance commissioner. Even before the start of these proceedings, in June 1969, the Justice Department announced its opposition to the merger. In August 1969 the department sought a preliminary injunction against the merger in the Connecticut District Court, but this was denied in November 1969 after lengthy hearings.

The Connecticut insurance commissioner was charged with the responsibility for protecting policyholders from possible risks from such a merger. In December 1969 Commissioner William R. Cotter ruled against the merger, a move that surprised many observers and enraged many Hartford shareholders, as well as financial concerns that had bought Hartford stock on the expectation that the merger would be approved. Although Commissioner Cotter did not give his reasons for rejecting the merger, the *Hartford Times* noted that Cotter "suggested that a tender offer, directly to the stockholders, would have been more appropriate," thus bringing the merger under the provisions of Public Act 444.[27]

Public Act 444 was basically designed to make it as difficult as possible for an outsider, especially a noninsurer, to take over Connecticut's rich insurance companies. When raids by acquiring companies into the giant surplus funds of some insurance companies were reported, Connecticut felt the need for action. However, ITT had consistently denied that Hartford's huge cash flow and reserves were its reasons for acquiring the company.

On January 28, 1970, Cotter's decision was appealed to the Connecticut Superior Court, ITT, Hartford, and three of Hartford's stockholders sued the commissioner, seeking an injunction and claiming that the commissioner's decision was unfounded.[28] Cotter's decision had not discouraged ITT's acquisition plans, and it renewed its effort to take over Hartford, this time through a new tender offer that was more generous to Hartford shareholders, thereby forcing the commissioner to reconsider his decision.

Throughout the lengthy hearings, ITT claimed that it was immensely strong financially and economically. ITT stated that it intended to pump money into Hartford for further growth. The soundness of ITT's management team and its intention to improve upon Hartford's management were persistent arguments. There was no indication that ITT wanted to take advantage of any of Hartford's assets, excess available cash, or borrowing power. However, as it turned out later, during its negotiations with the Justice Department over an antitrust settlement, ITT argued that a

27 "Cotter vs. ITT: Strong Image Unfolds," *Hartford Times*, December 18, 1969.
28 "Cotter Sued on Merger," *Hartford Times*, January 29, 1970.

divestiture of Hartford would inflict a severe and crippling financial blow on ITT stockholders in particular and the U.S. economy in general.

During the hearings, ITT promised help with the financing of the proposed Civic Center in Hartford and committed the company to building a Sheraton Hotel there.[29] On May 23, 1970, the commissioner reversed his earlier decision and approved the merger.

Settlement Negotiations

With two lower court decisions in hand on February 24, 1971, McLaren urged the solicitor general to push the *Grinnell* case to the Supreme Court. Griswold later testified that he considered it a "difficult case to win." However, "there was no way that we could find out whether the existing statute . . . was adequate to deal with conglomerate mergers except by taking the case to the Supreme Court and seeking their decision" (*Hearings,* part 2, p. 372).

By April 19, 1971, the case was ready for submission to the Supreme Court. However, on that date, in response to a phone call and letter from ITT attorney and personal friend Lawrence Walsh, Acting Attorney General Richard Kleindienst asked the solicitor general to request an extension of time from the Supreme Court. Although McLaren and the solicitor general did not relish the idea of requesting a delay, for different reasons, the extension was nonetheless requested and granted.

One day later, although Kleindienst "did not associate the two" (*Hearings,* part 2, p. 348), Kleindienst met for the first time with Felix Rohatyn to discuss the impact that a Hartford divestiture would have upon ITT. Kleindienst was sufficiently impressed, he said, by Rohatyn's presentation to make arrangements for a second, larger meeting. On April 29, 1971, Kleindienst, McLaren, a representative of the Treasury Department, and attorneys and staff of the antitrust division met with Rohatyn, two ITT attorneys—Howard J. Aibel and Henry Sailer—and others representing ITT. ITT's argument was not based on the merits of antitrust statutes or their applicability. Its new approach was a financial one with three basic arguments, all dealing with the results of a divestiture of Hartford:

1. The divestiture of Hartford was impractical; a forced spinoff, the only feasible way of divestiture, would have a devastating effect—a reduction by as much as 45 percent—on the liquidity and cash position of ITT.

2. The divestiture of Hartford would also affect ITT's credit rating and therefore its borrowing position abroad. This could have an adverse effect on the U.S. balance of payments, to which ITT was a substantial positive contributor.

[29] "ITT Replies to Attack from Nader," *Hartford Courant,* April 29, 1970; "Cotter Denied Hotel Plans Swayed ITT Decision," *Hartford Courant,* March 11, 1972. See also "Hartford Fire, ITT Sue Cotter," *Hartford Times,* January 29, 1970.

3. The divestiture of Hartford would cause an immediate diminution of approximately $1.2 billion in the price of ITT stock. This not only would wreak hardship on the owners of ITT stock but could have a substantial unsettling impact—a "ripple effect"—on the stock market and possibly the economy as a whole.

For the Justice Department's further study, the ITT group left behind a set of documents meant to substantiate their arguments. In addition, Rohatyn forwarded a letter to McLaren acknowledging the meeting and stressing the points he had raised.

Independent Analysis

After the April 29 meeting, McLaren decided to check the merit of ITT's arguments. Bypassing the economists on his own staff, McLaren chose an independent outside consultant, Richard Ramsden. Ramsden had previously been a White House Fellow and, during that time, had prepared for McLaren an analysis that was used for the settlement of the controversial Ling-Temco-Vought–Jones & Laughlin merger case. In both instances, White House aide Peter Flanigan was involved in securing Ramsden's services. According to McLaren, at the time of the ITT presentation he did not know how to reach Ramsden and therefore asked Flanigan to contact him. For reasons never clarified, Ramsden's sole contact in Washington regarding the preparation of his analysis of ITT's presentation was with Flanigan, labeled by *The Wall Street Journal* as business's "Mr. Fixit."

According to Ramsden's testimony, he met Flanigan in the latter's office at the White House for about twenty minutes. Flanigan informed him that his assignment was to be ITT and that McLaren wanted Ramsden to examine *solely* "the financial consequences of divestiture of Hartford Insurance Company by ITT" (*Hearings,* part 3, p. 1352). Flanigan also gave Ramsden a document for study entitled "Memorandum on Economic Consequences of a Hartford Divestiture by ITT" (*Hearings,* part 3, p. 1356). As to the nature of this document, Ramsden stated:

> I can make two comments about the memorandum: First of all, it was obviously written by someone who thought there were some financial consequences that were bad for ITT in the divestiture of Hartford. That was obvious.
>
> The second thing that was very obvious about the memorandum was that it was in no way based on any facts; it was in no way based on any analysis. It was basically unsubstantiated opinion. . . . (*Hearings,* part 3, p. 1356)

Ramsden testified that he spent a total of five days preparing the report but charged the government for only two days—the time he was actually away from his normal work. Ramsden did not talk to McLaren directly;

he analyzed what Flanigan told him McLaren wanted. Ramsden also testified that he was not told what the purpose of the analysis was; nor did Flanigan tell him that the "memo" was prepared by Felix Rohatyn, an ITT director.[30]

Ramsden's report weighed heavily in McLaren's decision, and in his later testimony he repeatedly referred to it as a solid and substantive piece of analysis. In his memorandum to the deputy attorney general dated June 17, 1971, recommending the settlement, McLaren noted:

> We have had a study made by financial experts and they substantially confirm ITT's claims as to the effects of a divestiture order. Such being the case, I gather that we must also anticipate that the impact upon ITT would have a ripple effect—in the stock market and in the economy.
>
> Under the circumstances, I think we are compelled to weigh the need for divestiture in this case. . . . Or, to refine the issue a little more: Is a decree against ITT containing injunctive relief and a divestiture order worth enough more than a decree containing only injunctive relief to justify the projected adverse effects on ITT and its stockholders, and the risk of adverse effects on the stock market and the economy?
>
> I come to the reluctant conclusion that the answer is "no." I say reluctant because ITT's management consummated the Hartford acquisition knowing it violated our antitrust policy; knowing we intended to sue; and in effect representing to the court that we need not issue a preliminary injunction because ITT would hold Hartford separate and thus minimize any divestiture problem if violation were found. (*Hearings,* part 2, p. 111)

In later testimony, McLaren defended the settlement as being good for the economy. However, Ramsden testified that his report could not be used to draw any such conclusion. A similar conclusion, that a divestiture of Hartford would not be detrimental to the economy, was arrived at independently by some economists and financial experts both within the Justice Department and in academic circles (*Hearings,* part 3, pp. 1374–95). As to the protection of ITT's stockholders, the Supreme Court, in *United States* v. *E. I. Du Pont de Nemours & Co. et al.* (1961), held that this hardship argument was not admissible:

> Those who violate the Act may not reap the benefits of their violations and avoid an undoing of their unlawful project on the plea of hardship or inconvenience.
>
> If the Court concludes that other measures will not be effective to redress a violation, and that complete divestiture is a necessary ele-

---

[30] "ITT Report's Author Undercuts Rationale of Justice Agency on Anti-trust Accord," *The Wall Street Journal,* April 18, 1972, p. 4.

ment of effective relief, the Government cannot be denied the latter remedy because economic hardship, however severe, may result. (*Hearings,* part 3, p. 1404)

The Aftermath

A final agreement was announced on July 31, 1971, thereby ending three years' hard work by the Antitrust Division in the interests of getting a landmark Supreme Court Decision. However, many questions remained unanswered:

Why did the government settle at all?
Why should ITT be allowed to keep Hartford's $1.98 billion by divesting only $796 million in other assets?
What was the effect of the settlement on competition?
Why did McLaren, with his twenty-five years of deep commitment to antitrust, approve the shift so rapidly?

The agreement was in the form of a consent decree and was thus subject to Court approval. On August 23, 1971, the Justice Department announced that the agreement had been filed for the approval of the Court and would become final in thirty days. Attempts were made by Ralph Nader's group both before the Justice Department and later in the courts to block the merger. However, they were unsuccessful. The decree was approved and finalized on September 24.[31]

THE SEC'S ROLE IN THE ITT AFFAIR

It appears that no government agency that had dealings with ITT could avoid the long shadow of doubt about decisions favorable to ITT, decisions that were seemingly contrary to the agency's established policies. This section briefly covers the SEC's involvement in another dimension of the government's antitrust case against ITT.

The SEC Suit

On Friday, June 16, 1972, the Securities and Exchange Commission charged that ITT and two of its top executives had violated federal securities laws in June and July 1971. This occurred, the SEC charged, while the Justice Department and ITT were privately negotiating a settlement of three antitrust cases. The SEC suit, in the federal court for the Southern District of New York, accused ITT of failing to disclose the settlement

---

[31] "Approval Is Seen for ITT Merger," *The New York Times,* September 24, 1971, p. 57. See also *Hearings,* part 3, p. 1283.

talks with the Justice Department in a supplement to a prospectus filed with the SEC. The prospectus covered 26,668 shares of ITT stock sold in July 1971 by a unit of Hartford. Two ITT executives, Senior Vice-President Howard J. Aibel and Secretary and Counsel for Corporate Affairs John J. Navin, were also charged with selling stocks on the basis of inside information.

In the same suit, the SEC brought charges against ITT and two investment banking institutions, Lazard Frères & Company of New York and Mediobanca of Milan, Italy. The SEC charged that they had violated securities laws in the unregistered distribution of $1.7 million worth of ITT Series N preferred stock between November 1970 and May 1971 under a fee-splitting arrangement through which Lazard Frères and Mediobanca divided $2.17 million.

The suit against ITT and its executives was a relatively mild one. The SEC did not seek any sanctions other than restraining those charged from future securities law violations. However, according to the agency's Rule 10B–5, the SEC could have brought fraud charges against the company and its officers and required repayment of the profits made by the executives' sales.[32]

Commenting on charges against ITT and its officials, the SEC stated that *they had been filed after two years of investigating ITT's acquisition of Hartford*. It was therefore a matter of some surprise when "two days later, the SEC suit was settled by consent agreement under which the defendants, without conceding past violations, agreed they wouldn't violate securities laws in the future." [33] As *Business Week* cynically pointed out, "People who violate securities laws seldom go to jail; instead they often consent to an injunction—that is, they agree not to do in the future what they neither admit nor deny doing in the past." [34] Commenting on the settlement, *Business Week* editorialized:

> The penalty assessed by the Securities and Exchange Commission . . . is woefully inadequate. . . . The SEC could have asked the court to order the two executives to pay the corporation back the $7-a-share additional profit that they made by selling their stock before a public announcement that the company had entered into a consent decree with the Justice Dept.—an action that proved bearish for the stock. But the SEC's general policy is not to ask defendants such as these to pay back profits. Instead, the commission feels that its action may trigger civil suits where the real damage will be inflicted.
>
> The commission needs to reevaluate this policy. The SEC should not expect somebody else to do its painful dirty work.[35]

---

32 For a detailed explanation of Rule 10B–5, see "Securities and Exchange Commission versus Texas Gulf Sulphur Company," pp. 296–97 of this book.
33 "Handling of 'Politically Sensitive' ITT Files to Be Reviewed by House Commerce Unit," *The Wall Street Journal,* December 18, 1972, p. 3.
34 "The 34 Boxes of Dynamite," *Business Week,* October 21, 1972, p. 61.
35 "Make the Penalty Fit," *Business Week,* July 1, 1972, p. 60.

The Background

Between June 18 and July 31, 1971, heavy sale of ITT stock by ITT officers and other associates came to Wall Street's attention. From the beginning of 1971 through June 18, 1971, ITT executives had been heavy buyers of ITT stock. This trend did not continue, however. Reports filed with the SEC by ITT insiders show that in six weeks, between June 18 and July 31, 1971, ITT executives dumped a total of $3.1 million in ITT stock. SEC regulations require that all major stockholders and officers of a company report their stockholdings every month.

This change in the trend of insider transactions was called a coincidence by company spokesmen. The Senate hearings, however, revealed that a telephone call on June 17, 1971, from the Justice Department to Felix Rohatyn could well have been the turning point for these transactions. Rohatyn, under intense questioning by Senator Edward M. Kennedy, testified that he had informed Geneen and Aibel within twenty-four to forty-eight hours after the call from Justice. Testimony during the hearings showed that at least a few ITT officials learned by June 18, 1971, or thereabouts that the government had proposed a settlement which was then unacceptable and undesirable to ITT, although it would not require divestiture of Hartford. This settlement eventually caused a $7-per-share drop in the price of ITT stock, from $62 to $55 per share, on the first day of trading after it had been announced. The officers, however, enjoyed prices ranging from $62 to $68 per share by selling before the announcement.

Trading on the basis of inside material information, undisclosed to the public, is prohibited by SEC Rule 10B–5. The ITT officials involved and other corporate spokesmen denied any charges of trading based on inside information. On the contrary, they all claimed that their sales were for reasons having nothing to do with information about the negotiations with Justice.

It is interesting to note that ITT failed to disclose its settlement negotiations with Justice to the SEC. ITT issued a prospectus on July 22, 1971, with not even a hint about the negotiations that concluded nine days later. In fact, concerning the antitrust cases it states: "ITT is asserting a vigorous defense. Trial on the merits in this case is expected to begin in September, 1971." [36] The prospectus was originally issued on April 19, for registration of certain letter stock, and was updated on July 22 when additional shares were added. In its defense, ITT stated that the reason there was no mention of negotiations was that "the agreement in principle was rejected on July 6," [37] although such a rejection was not mentioned during the Senate hearings.

---

[36] "ITT: Emerging Contradictions," *The Wall Street Journal*, March 22, 1972, p. 16.
[37] *Ibid.*

The Thirty-four Boxes of SEC Files

During its investigation of ITT's possible violation of SEC regulations, the SEC subpoenaed documents and papers from ITT files. However, when the SEC quietly settled its case within a week after filing formal charges, the state of Ohio and Ralph Nader's group demanded that the hearings be made public or SEC might wind up in court. Both groups wanted access to SEC files. Almost simultaneously, Representative Harley Staggers, chairman of the House Interstate and Foreign Commerce Committee, and Representative John Moss decided they wanted to look at the files also in connection with their own investigations.

SEC Chairman William Casey refused to hand over the files to the congressional investigators, claiming that the case was still under investigation. Soon after (October 6, 1972), the SEC packed every scrap of the ITT files into thirty-four boxes and sent them to the Justice Department. Two days later Casey wrote to Staggers that "he couldn't deliver the files because Justice had asked for them—'for possible criminal prosecution.' " Justice, however, told two newspaper reporters "it hadn't asked for the files, Casey had offered them." [38]

In later testimony before Congressman Stagger's committee, Casey stated that he feared that if the ITT material in SEC files were prematurely made public, it might interfere with the possible prosecution of a criminal case against ITT by the Justice Department. In later questioning, however, it was revealed that Casey had discussed with White House Counsel John Dean the possibility of the extension of executive privilege to SEC for its refusal to furnish congressional committees with the ITT files, including the plans for the transfer of the files to the Justice Department. Charles Whitman, Casey's administrative assistant, testified that he kept a few documents out of the thirty-four boxes after informing Casey, because they were "politically sensitive." [39]

Staggers's request for the files was made on September 23 and was repeated on September 28, and the discussion between Dean and Casey took place on October 3, 1972; SEC voted for the transfer of the files to Justice on October 4, and the actual transfer took place on October 6.

When he testified, Casey provided the House committee with a summary of ITT papers contained in the thirty-four boxes, as well as with a secret SEC working paper on the case. This paper, later made public by Staggers, indicated that "several key Nixon administration officials were instrumental in helping International Telephone and Telegraph Corp. reach the controversial 1971 antitrust settlement with the Justice Department." The officials named were Vice-President Spiro Agnew, Treasurer Secretary John Connally, former Commerce Secretary Maurice Stans, and

[38] *Business Week,* July 1, 1972, p. 60.
[39] "Casey Says Politics Affected SEC Decision to Keep Files on ITT Case from Congress," *The Wall Street Journal,* December 15, 1972, p. 3.

former Commerce Secretary Peter Peterson.[40] This disclosure thus raised the possibility that Connally and others may have perjured themselves in their earlier testimony concerning their roles in the ITT affair. The paper also mentioned a Mitchell statement to the effect that President Nixon knew of the merger and considered it "good."

The entire matter seemed to be headed for final unraveling, however, when special Watergate prosecutor Archibald Cox was assigned the task of reopening the case. Attorney General Elliot Richardson instructed Cox to investigate ITT and its executives for possible obstruction of investigation or commission of perjury.[41]

Internal Revenue Service—Favorable Tax Ruling

For the ITT-Hartford merger to go through, it was important that ITT receive a favorable tax ruling from IRS so that the merger could be tax-free. That is, so that the Hartford stockholders would not be required to pay a capital gains tax on the exchange of their Hartford stock for ITT stock. An unfavorable ruling could have killed the merger.

To gain such a ruling, ITT made an application in "routine fashion" claiming that it had fulfilled all the IRS requirements, and the ruling was granted forthwith. However, it later appeared that ITT may not have fulfilled all the IRS requirements and may have been in technical violation of the regulations, and that in these and "in other aspects of the sale, too, the IRS tended to make things as easy as possible for ITT." [42]

The regulations for a tax-free type B merger, by which ITT intended to acquire Hartford, required that ITT pay for Hartford stock *only in stock*. However, at that time ITT already owned 1.7 million shares, or about 8 percent, of Hartford's outstanding stock, which it had acquired for cash in the open market. IRS had earlier informed ITT that only if this stock was first disposed of, under conditions acceptable to IRS, could the merger become tax-free.[43] Earlier IRS rulings in such cases had held that such a sale must be an *unconditional divestiture of the stock to unrelated third parties prior to the tender offer by the acquiring corporation or the vote of the shareholders of the acquired corporation* (whichever is appropriate) for a stock-for-stock acquisition (*Hearings,* part 3, p. 1303, emphasis added). ITT was thus required to divest itself of its holdings of 8 percent of Hartford stock.

ITT reached an agreement with Mediobanca through Lazard Frères and presented it to the IRS to satisfy the requirements of Section 368(1) (B). Under the agreement with the bank:

[40] "ITT Saga (Cont'd): Agnew, Connally, Stans Linked to ITT Effort in the Hartford Case," *The Wall Street Journal,* March 19, 1973, p. 1.
[41] "ITT Antitrust Accord Still a Political Issue as Possible Link to GOP Pledge Is Studied," *The Wall Street Journal,* June 11, 1973, p. 8.
[42] "How ITT Maneuvered to Get a Tax Ruling in the Hartford Deal," *San Francisco Chronicle,* October 12, 1972, p. 1.
[43] "ITT Tax Ruling Linked to Complex Maneuvering," *The New York Times,* March 26, 1972, pp. 1, 52.

1. Mediobanca was guaranteed against any losses in the transaction if it resold the stock through Lazard Frères at any time during the eighteen months prior to May 31, 1971. (This was the basis of the fee-splitting charge by the SEC.)
2. Mediobanca was guaranteed a profit of 25.5 cents per share if it sold the stock during the second half of 1970, but 51 cents per share if it sold it during the first five months of 1971.
3. As an inducement for Mediobanca to enter into the contract, ITT *paid* a premium of 76.5 cents per share.
4. The price of the stock was not fixed at the time of the agreement but was to be determined by one of three options, from which the bank was to choose one, provided in the contract:

The first option called for the bank to pay $51 a share or the market price for the huge block on the day of closing as determined by Lazard Frères, if that price was higher. . . .

The second option would have set the price at the "fair market value" of the stock during a two-week period in May 1971, more than 18 months after the stock was supposedly to change hands, in November 1969. . . .

The third option . . . provided that the price would be whatever the bank could sell the Hartford shares for, or ITT shares it might receive in a merger, whenever the bank chose to sell up to May 31, 1971.[44]

It was reported that the bank had ruled out the first option on the day it signed the contract. By doing this, the only normal business option was deleted immediately. With this option eliminated, the actual content of the transaction as specified in the contract was as follows:

1. Mediobanca did not have to pay anything to ITT but a credit on its own books, if this was deemed appropriate.
2. ITT would not receive any money because prices were not set and, in fact, the transaction could not have been completed without the stock prices, which had not been determined at that time.
3. The buyer, Mediobanca, did not have to take *any risk*, even a normal one, associated with the stock transactions. On the contrary, ITT, the seller, accepted all risk in addition to an unreasonably high inducement and an unusual profit guarantee.

It could be argued, therefore, that there was no arm's-length transaction between Mediobanca and ITT and that the bank never bought the stock at all. As *The Wall Street Journal* stated:

[44] "Easing a Merger," *The Wall Street Journal*, October 12, 1972, pp. 1, 19.

Even before signing a contract to buy them, Mediobanca got $1.3 million in fees. Later, when Mediobanca got ITT stock in exchange for those Hartford shares, it sold the ITT stock and passed the proceeds (about $100 million plus accumulated dividends) along to ITT as payment for the original Hartford stock. So it could be argued in substance that the bank merely held the Hartford stock for ITT until the tax problem was resolved and there was no longer any possibility that it might fall into unfriendly hands opposed to a merger, pocketing a $1.3 million fee for its trouble. In fact, this is essentially what the SEC has concluded, a reading of its complaint in the now-settled suit makes clear.[45]

Apparently Mediobanca had converted the Hartford stock into ITT's Series N preferred stock after the merger had taken place. In late 1970 Mediobanca sold the stock to the Dreyfus Marine Midland Corporation, a New York mutual fund now known as the Dreyfus Fund. This stock, according to the provisions of the contract, was sold through Lazard Frères. In mid-1970 ITT named Dreyfus to manage an estimated $10 million in ITT pension fund assets. This transaction generated $2.2 million in fees, of which Mediobanca received $1.3 million, thus providing the grounds for the SEC investigation that revealed the details of this transaction.

When pressed by a reporter from *The Wall Street Journal*, IRS refused to discuss the case on the grounds that "its rulings in such cases are private matters between it and the taxpayer." However, it conceded that "private rulings are made strictly on the basis of facts as presented by the taxpayer involved [and] any verification is done when and if the taxpayer's returns are audited." [46]

In another aspect of the case, IRS was proved to be lenient with ITT. It has been IRS policy, in stock-for-stock mergers, to require the company to sell previously acquired stock "before an offer is made" to other shareholders. This could mean "the deadline is when the acquiring company first publicizes the terms of its offer." [47] However, in the case of ITT, the offer was first publicized on December 23, 1968; proxy solicitations were mailed to Hartford stockholders on July 24, 1969; and yet it was not until October 14, 1969, that ITT submitted the Mediobanca contract to IRS for approval. Only a week later it was cleared by IRS. When asked for an explanation, an IRS official responded: "That's a technical point; it isn't the kind of thing I've ever heard discussed." [48]

The IRS ruling was a private one and subject to reversal at the time of audit, should the company then prove to be in violation of IRS regulations. In July 1972 a class action suit was filed by a former Hartford stockholder, Hilda Herbst, asking that the merger be set aside because ITT's circular to Hartford stockholders did not mention the risk to them in the

45 *Ibid.*, p. 1.
46 *Ibid.*, p. 18.
47 *Ibid.*
48 *Ibid.*

event of an unfavorable tax ruling. The suit asked for a rescinding of the merger and payment of damages to Hartford stockholders.

The contradictions in IRS's handling of ITT were further compounded when, in another case of stock ownership, IRS challenged a woman's claim to ownership as starting when the stock was delivered to her rather than four months earlier when she signed an agreement entitling her to stock. IRS argued, and the court agreed, that she owned the stock from the earlier date because she carried the risk of ownership and also received dividends. Yet in the case of ITT, the transfer of Hartford stock to Mediobanca had been considered a sale even though ITT carried all the risks of ownership.[49]

The Watergate scandal and the subsequent hearings changed the political fortunes of individuals and institutions that were in any way involved with the Nixon Administration. ITT was no exception. On April 19, 1973, ITT announced that IRS Washington headquarters was "reconsidering" the favorable tax ruling it made in late 1969, permitting the ITT-Hartford merger. The reconsideration was requested by the New York office of the IRS. There was no comment by the IRS.[50]

EPILOGUE

ITT's reputation has continued to suffer since the campaign contribution fiasco. Although no direct causal links can be demonstrated, ITT has been facing a loss of credibility in the marketplace. According to *The New York Times*, ITT "has become a three-letter symbol for corporate subterfuge and raw political power. . . ."[51]

ITT has a long history of continuous earnings growth of around 15 percent, which puts it in the category of growth and glamour stocks. Despite tremendous public relations efforts, however, ITT's stock has never commanded the high price/earning multiples accorded other glamour stocks. This has been one of Geneen's major gripes against security analysts, and he has often complained about their reluctance to accord ITT the kind of glamour status that gets lofty p/e multiples, thereby making acquisitions possible and highly profitable.[52] Even before the campaign contribution scandal, some Wall Street analysts were questioning the quality and stability of ITT's earnings. They suspected that ITT was using certain accounting practices to smooth out its earning curve and maintain its upward direction.[53]

49 "Attention ITT Fans: Here's Another Curious Wrinkle on That Curious Tax Ruling," *The Wall Street Journal*, April 18, 1973, p. 1.
50 "IRS Favorable Tax Ruling in ITT Purchase of Hartford Fire Is Being 'Reconsidered,' " *The Wall Street Journal*, April 19, 1973, p. 4.
51 "ITT's Woes Increase as Stock Slips," *The New York Times*, August 6, 1973, pp. 43–44.
52 "Harold Geneen's Money Making Machine Is Still Humming," *Fortune,* September 1972, pp. 88–92, 212–21.
53 *Ibid.*

The Colson Memorandum

On August 2, 1973, the Senate Watergate Committee disclosed a memorandum, written by Charles W. Colson, then a White House special counsel, to H. R. Haldeman, then White House chief of staff, that directly linked high government officials with the settlement of the antitrust case and helped to elucidate how the settlement was reached. The memorandum, dated March 30, 1972, discusses Colson's concern that, if certain memorandums came to light, the president as well as Agnew and several other officials would become involved in the antitrust settlement. As one White House aide said, after the memorandum was disclosed, "Writing these memos may be the most stupid act of all the stupid acts performed in this whole mess." [54]

Colson suggested that it might be best to withdraw Kleindienst's nomination rather than risk any further exposure of the ITT affair during the hearings. He said that neither Kleindienst nor Mitchell realized how many incriminating documents existed. One memo, from Herbert G. Klein, then director of communications, to H. R. Haldeman, dated June 30, 1971, sets forth the $400,000 arrangement with ITT. Of this Colson wrote: "This memo puts the A.G. on constructive notice at least of the ITT commitment at that time and before the settlement, facts which he has denied under oath." A memo from Ehrlichman to Mitchell on May 5, 1971, alludes to discussions between Nixon and Mitchell as to the "agreed upon ends" in the resolution of the ITT case. Colson wrote that this would once again contradict Mitchell's testimony and directly involve the president.[55]

The Colson memorandum is important for four major reasons: It confirmed the arrangement between ITT and the White House for a campaign contribution in return for favorable settlement; it suggested that Mitchell had committed perjury; it implicated Agnew and Kleindienst in interceding on behalf of ITT; and it "blot [ted] Richard Nixon's copybook one more time." [56]

President Nixon's Response

Intense public pressure and growing rumors finally forced the president to respond to these as well as other allegations as part of a new White House strategy dubbed Operation Candor. On January 8, 1974, the White House released a White Paper in explanation of the president's role in the ITT affair. It stated that on April 19, 1971, Nixon ordered then Deputy

---

54 "ITT: Back on the Doorstep," *Newsweek*, August 13, 1973, p. 21.
55 "Colson '72 Memo Warns Records Could 'Directly Involve' Nixon in I.T.T. Trust Case Settlements," *The New York Times*, August 2, 1973, pp. 1, 18.
56 "ITT: Back on the Doorstep," *Newsweek*, August 13, 1973, p. 21; see also ". . . Illuminating Nothing." *The New York Times*, January 10, 1974, p. 36.

Attorney General Kleindienst to instruct McLaren to drop a pending appeal on the Grinnell case. (This information had been made public two months previously, much to the irritation of the White House.) He rescinded this order two days later when either Solicitor General Griswold or Kleindienst, depending on one's source, threatened to resign. The president's intervention was based on his belief that bigness per se was the basis of the suits and that bigness per se is not bad. The white paper did not deal directly with the campaign contribution issue.[57] Thus, it revealed nothing new. Nixon tried to establish that his involvement in the case had nothing to do with ITT's financial pledge, about which he knew nothing until after the settlement was made.

Actions by the Special Prosecutor's Office

First Archibald Cox and then Leon Jaworski investigated the ITT case. In addition, the House Judiciary Committee's impeachment inquiry delved into the ITT affair. Archibald Cox's investigation led him to declare that, in his opinion, the terms of the ITT settlement "were a perfectly good bargain from the point of view of the government. And that's the opinion I get from most antitrust lawyers."[58]

On May 16, 1974, at the instigation of Special Watergate Prosecutor Leon Jaworski, Kleindienst pleaded to a federal misdemeanor charge for making false or misleading sworn statements in connection with testimony made during his confirmation hearings. The relatively minor charge carried a maximum penalty of a month in jail. Judge George L. Hart, the federal judge presiding over the case, not only let Kleindienst off virtually scot free by giving him a thirty-day jail term and a $100 fine, both suspended, but he also praised him in court for being, among other things, "loyal and considerate." The favorable treatment accorded Kleindienst led to friction and discontent among Jaworski's lawyers working on the case. In many quarters it also led to criticism of the judge and American courts that "go easy on the rich and powerful while coming down hard on the poor and the weak."[59]

On May 30, 1974, Jaworski stated that his office had found no evidence of any criminal violation of law by ITT executives in connection with the 1971 settlement of the government's suits against the conglomerate. However, he did not rule out the possibility of prosecution of ITT executives and government officials on charges of perjury, obstruction of justice, and improper influence should continuing investigations warrant filing of

57 "Nixon Says He Considered Politics In Milk Rise But Denies Any Deal: He Also Rejects Charges On I.T.T." *The New York Times,* January 9, 1974, pp. 1, 21; see also "Nixon's Own Views on Antitrust Policy, Big Business Didn't Require ITT Lobbying Blitz, Documents Show," *The Wall Street Journal,* July 22, 1974, p. 3; "Legal Brief Submitted to House Panel on Behalf of the President," *The New York Times,* July 24, 1974, pp. 27–28.
58 "Cox Says He May Be Source of ITT Leak," *Oakland Tribune,* October 30, 1973, p. 1.
59 "Furor Over Handling of Kleindienst Case Dismays Judge Hart," *The Wall Street Journal,* July 11, 1974, p. 1.

such charges.[60] Jaworski's statement came on the heels of the news that three of the four attorneys responsible for the ITT investigation in Jaworski's office had resigned, supposedly in protest against Jaworski's decision to allow Kleindienst to plead guilty to a relatively minor charge in the ITT case.[61] Another figure, H. Edwin Reinecke, lieutenant governor of California, a relatively minor character in the ITT affair, was also charged with a felony for perjuring himself during the Kleindienst hearings. After a trial, Reinecke was found guilty. He is appealing the decision.

The Internal Revenue Service

Developments on other fronts were also continuing. On March 6, 1974, the IRS announced that it had decided to rescind ITT's tax-free status on its 1969 purchase of Hartford, charging that ITT made a conscious and initially successful effort to mislead the IRS concerning the complex stock transaction between it and Mediobanca. The ruling had permitted the 17,000 former Hartford shareholders to exchange their stock—worth more than $1 billion at that time—for ITT stock without immediately paying capital gains taxes.[62]

The company immediately announced that it would reimburse Hartford shareholders for any net tax liability they might incur as a result of the IRS action.[63] Authorities said that this could be as much as $30 to $50 million. The amount could go higher if shareholders were awarded additional damages. The IRS followed its announcement with a letter to all former Hartford shareholders asking for a collection of the capital gains tax. Since the statute of limitations was to run out on April 15, 1974, a matter of a few weeks from then, the IRS gave the shareholders the option to pay immediately or sign an enclosed form extending the assessment deadline to December 31, 1976.[64]

Securities and Exchange Commission

In an earlier section, we discussed the disposition of the SEC case against ITT on the matter of insiders' trading, and also the manner in which thirty-four boxes of SEC files relating to ITT were transferred to the Department of Justice on October 6, 1972, to forestall their delivery to a House subcommittee investigating the affair. The committee hear-

[60] "Jaworski Clears I.T.T. of Crimes in Trust Case," *The New York Times,* May 31, 1974, p. 1.
[61] "3 of 4 Investigating I.T.T. Resign Jobs With Jaworski," *The New York Times,* May 30, 1974, p. 24.
[62] "IRS Rescinds ITT Tax-Free Status on 1969 Purchase of Hartford Fire," *The Wall Street Journal,* March 7, 1974, p. 3.
[63] "ITT to Reimburse Ex-Hartford Holders If Taxes Are Owed," *The Wall Street Journal,* March 8, 1974, p. 2.
[64] "IRS Acts in ITT-Hartford Case to Collect Taxes From Ex-Holders of Insurance Unit," *The Wall Street Journal,* March 27, 1974, p. 3.

ings that eventually took place in May and June 1973 provided revealing insights into the influence of the White House on the activities and decisions of regulatory agencies, in this case the SEC. The hearings revealed that a part of the SEC draft complaint containing fraud charges against ITT had been deleted before the complaint was filed in court. The fraud charges, which were made in connection with ITT's failure to inform the SEC and the public of the details of the stock transaction between Lazard Frères and Mediobanca, were deleted from the draft complaint by a unanimous decision of the commission, led by then Chairman William J. Casey. The charges had been supported by the commission's two top staff officials and then General Counsel G. Bradford Cook, but the commissioners apparently felt there was insufficient evidence to support these charges. Cook later succeeded Casey as SEC chairman, but resigned after a brief tenure when the SEC, and Casey in particular, was alleged to have acted improperly regarding a secret and illegal campaign contribution during the 1972 presidential campaign.[65]

The Merger Game:
The Consent Decree and Its Aftermath

Since 1959, when Geneen took over, ITT has acquired more than 275 companies. Because of this, ITT has changed from little more than an overseas telecommunications company with sales of $765 million into a conglomerate with sales reaching $10 billion.[66] However, because of the terms of the consent decree, acquisitions will now have to be on a much smaller scale. ITT is still buying companies, but is restricted for the next ten years to buying relatively minor ones. There was no control put on foreign acquisitions, and ITT has continued to make investments abroad. According to Carol Loomis in *Fortune,* the company has been forced into change. Instead of its strategy of acquiring company after company, it now has to grow from within.[67] But ITT seems to be having difficulty sustaining the type of growth it has enjoyed for so long. In 1974, ITT suffered a 13 percent drop in profits and earnings per share. First half figures for 1975 indicate a continuance of this trend, with ITT earnings down 17 percent.[68]

It is interesting to see how ITT went about complying with the terms of the consent decree. As mentioned earlier, the price of ITT stock fell from $60 in August 1972 to $20 in July 1974. This has had a bad effect on ITT, since it was during this time that it had to divest itself of many subsidiaries in accordance with the conditions of the consent decree.

[65] U.S. Congress, House, Special Subcommittee on Investigations, Committee on Interstate and Foreign Commerce, *Hearings on Legislative Oversight of SEC: Agency Independence and the ITT Case,* Serial No. 93068, 93rd Cong., 1st sess., May–June 1973.
[66] "Harold Geneen's Tribulations," *Business Week,* August 11, 1973, p. 102.
[67] "Harold Geneen's Moneymaking Machine Is Still Humming," *Fortune,* September 1972, p. 88.
[68] "ITT Profit Fell 13% in Second Quarter," *The New York Times,* August 14, 1975, pp. 43–45.

Levitt was particularly hard to sell. ITT acquired Levitt, a highly successful house-building and land development company, for over $100 million in stock in 1968. It then instigated several new projects: the construction of a new factory for manufacturing modules for housing; the acquisition of United Homes, a Seattle-based building company; the acquisition of $100 million of undeveloped land; and the construction of rental apartments to be sold as tax shelters. Unfortunately, each of these projects proved unsuccessful and very costly. It was in the midst of these ventures that the order to sell Levitt was handed down. Since Levitt was in no shape to sell, ITT brought in a former ITT officer, Austrian-born Gerhard R. Andlinger, to shape it up as quickly as possible. But because of the building slump, caused by the rise in mortgage interest rates and by the inflation-caused rise in construction costs, Levitt's operating losses have risen.[69]

In November 1972, Pennsylvania Life bought ITT Hamilton Life Insurance and ITT Life Insurance of New York for $21.2 million. This price was below book value, creating a loss, on ITT's financial statements, of $6.3 million. Notwithstanding, ITT had to pay $3.3 million in taxes. ITT's tax accounting had kept the value of its investment in the companies so low that the sale created a gain, according to IRS. Thus ITT reported a net loss of $9.6 million on the sale.[70]

The fate of Canteen Corporation was not very different. ITT first planned to make a public offering of Canteen stock at $33 a share. However, this offering had to be postponed for want of takers. The public offering was made in January 1973 for one-third of the shares of Canteen at $22 per share. ITT earned a gain of $4.5 million on proceeds of $44 million from the public sale of one-third of Canteen's shares. However, the investors who bought the stock took a severe beating, as the price of Canteen stock soon fell to about $12 a share. ITT, however, stepped in to salvage the situation. In August 1973, ITT completed an agreement with TWA by which the latter agreed to buy all Canteen's shares for $22 a share, the original public offering price. The payment to ITT was made in notes, whereas the public shareholders were to get theirs in cash. ITT received $88 million in five-year notes, which it sold at a discount to raise $78.3 million in cash. The company's net gain on the TWA deal was only $2.5 million, less that an originally expected $4 million because of a higher-than-anticipated tax rate.[71]

After an aborted attempt to sell the company back to its original owner, William Levitt, ITT failed to meet the divestiture deadline and Levitt was placed in the charge of a trustee, Victor Palmieri and Company, in January 1975. Continued operating losses, $51.3 million in 1974, and the depressed state of the construction industry have not made Levitt an attractive purchase. ITT, required to support Levitt's operating "via-

[69] "ITT Finds It Difficult to Earn Top Dollar in Divestiture Program," *The Wall Street Journal*, January 8, 1974, pp. 1, 19.
[70] *Ibid.*
[71] *Ibid.*

bility" until sold, has covered these losses with loans totaling $42 million.[72]

Even the prize of the consent decree, Hartford Fire, after showing strong profits in the first years after the merger, has turned sour on ITT. The year 1974, a bad one for the insurance industry as a whole, was a disaster for Hartford. In its underwriting operations alone, Hartford experienced a loss of $123 million. An aggressive push to increase premiums resulted in an annual growth rate in written premiums of 17 percent for the three years 1970 to 1972. The industry rate during that time was 10 percent a year. It was not until 1973 that Hartford began to feel the effects of its growth. New claims against these premiums began to come in at a higher frequency than had been expected and were being settled at higher costs. In effect, the reserves that had been set aside for these claims were inadequate. Therefore, Hartford was forced to draw on its current income in order to pay the claims. In 1974 the reserves again proved inadequate, and Hartford has yet to recover.[73]

Although not directly affecting its net income or its balance sheet, a loss of assets has hit Hartford Fire. Owing to the problems of the stock market, Hartford's stock portfolio, into which it has been pouring money all along, had a cost of about $880 million and a market value of $240 million less than that by the end of 1974. Its bond portfolio, which cost about twice its stocks, was worth, on the market, about $340 million less.[74] According to Carol Loomis of *Fortune,* judging from the performance of Hartford Fire, it appears that

> ITT has not "managed" Hartford with anything like the energy it has expended on its other operations. Geneen himself plainly does not understand Hartford well. In fact, his behavior in connection with the insurance company seems . . . as if he had one set of standards for all the other businesses he oversees and another, flabbier set for Hartford. . . .
>
> It seems reasonable to ask whether ITT is now sorry it ever acquired Hartford. . . . Because of Hartford, ITT has had its political reputation wrecked, and fought a never ending stream of legal battles. . . .
>
> So, is Geneen sorry? He says not.[75]

SELECTED REFERENCES

ANDREWS, KENNETH R., "Application of the Sherman Act by Attempts to Influence Government Action," *Harvard Law Review,* 81 (February 1968), 847.

[72] "Levitt's '74 Loss From Operations Was $51.3 Million," *The Wall Street Journal,* August 7, 1975, p. 5.
[73] Carol J. Loomis, "ITT's Disaster in Hartford," *Fortune,* May 1975, pp. 201+.
[74] *Ibid.,* p. 203.
[75] *Ibid.,* pp. 202–11.

————, "Can the Best Corporations Be Made Moral?" *Harvard Business Review*, May–June, 1973, pp. 57–64.

BURNS, THOMAS, *Tales of ITT: An Insider's Report* (Boston: Houghton Mifflin, 1974).

Business Week, "The View from Inside," Special Report, November 3, 1973, p. 43.

CHERINGTON, PAUL W., and RALPH L. GILLEN, "The Company Representative in Washington," *Harvard Business Review*, May–June, 1961, pp. 109–15.

CRISPO, JOHN, *The Public Right to Know: Accountability in the Secretive Society* (New York: McGraw-Hill, 1975).

DAHL, R., "Governing the Giant Corporation," in *Corporate Power in America*, ed. Ralph Nader and Mark J. Green (New York: Grossman, 1973).

DEMARIS, OVID, *Dirty Business: The Corporate-Political Money Power Game* (New York: Harper Magazine, 1974).

EPSTEIN, EDWIN M., *Corporations, Contributions, and Political Campaigns: Federal Regulation in Perspective* (Berkeley, Calif.: Institute of Governmental Studies, May 1968).

————, *The Corporation in American Politics* (Englewood Cliffs, N.J.: Prentice-Hall, 1969).

————, "Dimensions of Corporate Power, Part 1," *California Management Review*, XVI, 2 (winter 1973), 9–23.

————, "Dimensions of Corporate Power, Part 2," *California Management Review*, XVI, 3 (spring 1974), 32–47.

Fortune, "The Fallout from the ITT Affair," Editorial, January 1968.

GOULDEN, JOSEPH C., *The Super Lawyers: The Small and Powerful World of the Great Washington Law Firms* (New York: Weybright and Talley, 1972).

GREEN, M., "The Politics of Antitrust: Pardons for the Powerful," *Business and Society Review*, 11 (autumn 1974), 27–33.

————, "Washington Lawyers: A Study in Power," *Business and Society Review*, 14 (summer 1975), 55–62.

————, BEVERLY C. MOORE, and BRUCE WASSERSTEIN, eds., *The Closed Enterprise System* (New York: Grossman, 1972), Part II.

JACOBY, NEIL H., *Corporate Power and Social Responsibility* (New York: MacMillan, 1973), Chaps. 4, 6, 7, 8.

LOOMIS, CAROL J., "Harold Geneen's Moneymaking Machine Is Still Humming," *Fortune*, September 1972, p. 220.

————, "ITT's Disaster In Hartford," *Fortune*, May 1975, p. 201.

MUELLER, WILLARD F., "The Rising Economic Concentration in America: Reciprocity's Conglomeration, and the New American 'Zaibatsu' System," *Antitrust and Economics Review*, spring 1971, pp. 15–50.

NADER, RALPH, and MARK J. GREEN, eds., *Corporate Power in America* (New York: Grossman, 1973), Chaps. 3, 6, 13.

NICHOLAS, DAVID, *Financing Elections: The Politics of an American Ruling Class* (New York: New Viewpoints, a division of Franklin Watts, 1974).

PLATTNER, MARC F., "Campaign Financing—The Dilemmas of Reform," *The Public Interest*, 34 (fall 1974), 112–30.

RICHARDSON, M. E., "Lobbying and Public Relations—Sensitive, Suspect or Worse?" *Antitrust Bulletin*, 10 (July–August, 1965), 507–18.

Rodgers, William, "ITT's Geneen: How to Succeed in Business by Really Trying," *Ramparts,* March 1973.

Sampson, Anthony, *The Sovereign State of ITT* (New York: Stein and Day, 1973), Chaps. 4, 5, 6.

Sethi, S. Prakash, *The Unstable Ground: Corporate Social Policy in a Dynamic Society* (New York: Wiley, 1975).

Silk, Leonard S., "Business Power Today and Tomorrow," *Daedalus,* winter 1969, pp. 174–90.

Votaw, Dow, and S. Prakash Sethi, *The Corporate Dilemma: Traditional Values Versus Contemporary Problems* (Englewood Cliffs, N.J.: Prentice-Hall, 1973).

Watzman, Sanford, *Conflict of Interest: Politics and the Money Game* (Chicago: Cowles, 1971).

Winter-Berger, Robert N., *The Washington Pay-Off* (New York: Dell, 1972).

U.S. Congress, House, *Hearings Before the Committee on Ways and Means on the Subject of Tax Reform,* 91st Cong., 1st sess., 1970.

U.S. Congress, Senate, Committee on Judiciary, *Hearings on Nomination of Richard G. Kleindienst, of Arizona, to be Attorney General,* part 2, 92nd Cong., 2nd sess., March 1972.

Corporations, United States Foreign Policy, and the Ethics of Overseas Operations

THE ITT AFFAIR (B)

INTERFERENCE IN THE CHILEAN PRESIDENTIAL ELECTIONS

Let's stop apologizing for America's wealth and power. Instead let's use it aggressively to attack those problems that threaten to explode the world.

We *can* win the race with change. We *can* preserve our leadership. But to do so we have to recapture the faith and trust of a world in ferment. We have to revitalize the American dream, and cast it in terms that the new people of a new world can understand and appreciate and aspire to.

—RICHARD M. NIXON

All that ITT did was to present its views, concerns, and ideas to various departments of the U.S. government. This is not only its right but also its obligation. The right is a very important constitutional right, and . . . it is not wrong for a citizen to try to approach government officials to discuss with them his problems and concerns.

—HAROLD S. GENEEN, chairman
and chief executive of ITT, in a
statement before the U.S. Senate
Subcommittee on Multinational
Corporations

ITT's involvement in Chile is now history. The issues raised by the case, however, belong to a class with which the multinational corporations (MNCs), notwithstanding their intentions, seem constantly to be getting involved. In most countries, MNC operations tend to be large and deal with products that make their influence on the local economies quite dominant. Consequently, they become vulnerable to the pressures of host country governments and to various and often rapidly changing political alignments. Conversely, the size of MNC assets in a given country and their worldwide operations makes it very tempting for the multinational corporations to use their economic leverage to extract unusual and often excessive advantages from host country governments.

Thus, in the case of ITT, there was a large and allegedly ruthless corporation scheming to bring down the freely elected government of a foreign nation and undermine its entire economic base, all in the name of protecting the company's vital interests and preserving freedom in Latin America. On the other hand, we see the specter of scores of large multinational corporations of all national shades and colors succumbing to the pressures of Arab countries without so much as a whimper and devising various schemes to avoid doing business with Israel or with companies that, for one reason or another, find themselves on the Arab blacklist. The weak-kneed response would be hilarious if it were not so pathetic and at the same time so full of serious implications.[1]

In a somewhat different vein, but still confronting the same dilemma, there was the case of United Brands, which paid a bribe of $1.25 million to the president of Honduras in order to persuade the Honduran government to reduce its proposed export taxes on bananas, a potential saving to the company of $7.5 million a year. The discovery of the bribery ultimately led to a coup in Honduras and the deposition of President General Oswaldo Lopez.[2] It might also be noted here that bribery is not confined to less developed countries but has also been practiced by multinationals in industrially advanced countries of Western Europe.[3]

---

[1] For references to the earlier and unsuccessful Arab boycott attempts, see the case "Coca-Cola and the Middle East Crisis." For the more successful boycott attempts during the post-1973–74 oil blockade and resulting energy crisis, see the *Hearings of the Subcommittee on Multinational Corporations of the Senate Foreign Relations Committee,* March 1975. Subcommittee chairman Senator Frank Church disclosed that there were about 1,500 American companies on the Arab blacklist. It was also disclosed by the Army Corps of Engineers that Jewish personnel were excluded from projects in Saudi Arabia. Some U.S. employers were also found to be voluntarily discriminating against Jewish workers, or withdrawing or withholding from developing business arrangements with Israel, in order to curry favor with the Arabs. Furthermore, the situation was not confined to U.S. companies alone, but was found to be prevalent with French and British multinational companies as well. For further references on the Arab boycott and its influence on the multinational corporations, see "The Furor over the Black List," *Newsweek,* March 10, 1975, p. 59; Richard J. Levine, "Israeli Businessmen Grow More Fearful over Rising Pressures from Arab Boycott," *The Wall Street Journal,* March 28, 1975, p. 20; "Boycott by Arabs Affecting Israel," *The New York Times,* April 20, 1975, p. 6.

[2] For references, see *The Wall Street Journal:* "United Brands Paid Bribe of $1.25 Million to Honduran Official," April 9, 1975, p. 1; "United Brands Accused by SEC of Second Payoff," April 10, 1975, p. 2; "United Brands Named in Suit Filed by Holder," April 11, 1975; "Senate Panel Will Study United Brands Bribe Case," April 11, 1975; "Calm on the Surface, Hondurans Are Ready for Political Turmoil," April 14, 1975, pp. 1, 12; "U.S. Looks for Possible Criminal Charges in United Brands' Payment in Honduras," April 16, 1975, p. 16; "Honduran President Ousted by Military in Bloodless Coup; Successor Is Named," April 23, 1975, p. 34; "United Brands' Net Loss Widened in First Period," April 23, 1975, p. 34.

[3] In April 1975 the managing director of ITT's Belgium subsidiary was accused of bribing the head of the Belgian government's Telephone and Telegraph Administration. See "World Roundup," *Business Week,* April 21, 1975, p. 43.

Many U.S. and British multinationals are being pressured by various church groups and other socially conscious investor groups to withdraw from South Africa because of its apartheid policies and from Namibia (South West Africa) because of the latter's illegal control by South Africa in defiance of the United Nations mandate and world opinion.[4]

The point of all these instances is that whether multinational companies like it or not, they cannot avoid getting involved in host country economic and political affairs, as well as in conflicts of international dimension. It is a specious argument to suggest that multinational corporations are apolitical or politically neutral, and that all that is needed for the world to utilize the tremendous resources of multinational companies for human welfare is for the national governments to avoid narrow politics and xenophobic nationalism. To accept this view is to disregard the institutional reality of both the multinational corporation and the nation-state.

THE ISSUES

The issue for analysis, therefore, is not the *avoidance* but the *control* of involvement in a country's economic and political affairs. What are the acceptable limits of such involvement? As an editorial in *Business Week* points out, "It is one thing to pay a few hundred dollars to get a cargo off the pier; it is something entirely different to buy a government and dictate its economic policies. . . . [MNCs] should reject the cynical conclusion that all men are corruptible and a smart man should make the most of his opportunities. For the smart men today are in danger of outsmarting themselves."[5]

The implications for management decision making for an analysis of ITT's case are quite important. For example:

1. What lessons can be drawn from our analysis of strategies and tactics pursued by ITT both in Chile and the United States from the viewpoint of a large multinational that has to deal in the vastly changed world of the late 1970s and 1980s?

2. What were the objectives of ITT in Chile? Is it possible that ITT confused its goals as a private company and acted as a sovereign power? Is it in the nature of large multinational companies to do so or was it unique in the case of ITT?

3. Can the multinationals count on the economic, political, and intelligence resources of their home countries, along the lines utilized by ITT, in their overseas conflicts with host countries?

4. How should a company plan for the protection of its assets and

4 See, for example, "Namibia—Foreign Companies Are Running Scared," *Business Week,* May 5, 1975, p. 47.
5 "A Question of Ethics," editorial *Business Week,* May 5, 1975, p. 108.

overseas operations given the new expectations of performance and ethical standards of behavior both at home and abroad?

On a broader level of public policy, the case ,raises, among others, the following issues:

1. Is there a need for international control of multinational corporations? If so, how might it be brought about, and what form should it take?
2. What role should government play in protecting the interests of its citizens—individuals and corporations—from expropriation by foreign governments?
3. To what extent should government-sponsored insurance organizations such as the Overseas Private Investment Corporation (OPIC) facilitate private direct foreign investments? What are the liabilities involved in such arrangements in the sense of aggravating conflicts between MNCs and host countries, or between the governments of various countries? Is it possible that such arrangements would influence foreign policy and thereby be likely to adversely affect the vital foreign policy interests of the insuring country's government?
4. What are the avenues open to multinational corporations to seek redress for expropriation by foreign governments?
5. How much direct and indirect influence do large U.S. multinational corporations exercise in the molding of American foreign policy to serve their private needs? To what extent should the foreign policy of a country be guided by the interests of the overseas operations of its business institutions?

THE INCIDENT

On September 11, 1973, Chilean President Salvador Allende was killed. His government was overthrown by the Chilean army and was replaced by a military junta. Charges and countercharges were made about the CIA and ITT's involvement in the coup. They were vigorously denied by both the U.S. government and the company. However, in later testimony before the Senate Judiciary Committee, it was discovered that the CIA was indeed involved in the attempts aimed at the overthrow of Allende. The company's part in the coup remains unproved. The role that ITT and the United States government played in the events leading up to Allende's death provide an interesting insight into the clandestine actions of both big business and big government.

Up until 1970, ITT and the United States government had enjoyed friendly relations with Chile and Eduardo Frei, Chile's exceedingly popular president. Due to a provision in the constitution, however, Frei could not succeed himself; thus a new president had to be elected. Because of the strong Marxist socialist convictions of Allende, the leading presidential contender, ITT was very worried. If Allende got in, ITT/Chile would be nationalized. The lengths to which ITT went to try to prevent this were first revealed in 1972 by Jack Anderson.

Jack Anderson Again

It seems that ITT had not heard the last of Jack Anderson with his publication of the Dita Beard memorandum. Three weeks after the first memo appeared, Jack Anderson exploded another bomb in his column when he accused ITT of attempting to plot against the 1970 election of leftist Chilean President Salvador Allende, to trigger a military coup, and to create economic chaos in Chile. The column read, in part:

> Secret documents which escaped shredding by International Telephone and Telegraph show that the company, at the highest levels, maneuvered to stop the 1970 election of leftist Chilean President Salvador Allende.
>
> The papers reveal that ITT dealt regularly with the Central Intelligence Agency and, at one point, considered triggering a military coup to head off Allende's election.
>
> These documents portray ITT as a virtual corporate nation in itself with vast international holdings, access to Washington's highest officials, its own intelligence apparatus and even its own classification system. . . .
>
> They show that ITT officials were in close touch with William V. Broe, who was then director of the Latin American division of the CIA's Clandestine Services. They were plotting together to create economic chaos in Chile, hoping this would cause the Chilean army to pull a coup that would block Allende from coming to power.
>
> ITT Director John McCone, himself a former CIA head, played a role in the bizarre plot. . . .
>
> The plot to bring about a military coup by applying economic pressure is spelled out in a confidential telex, dated September 29, 1970, to ITT's President Harold S. Geneen from one of its vice presidents, E. J. Gerrity. Here is Gerrity's description of the plot:
>
> 1. Banks should not renew credits or should delay in doing so.
> 2. Companies should drag their feet in sending money, in making deliveries, in shipping spare parts, etc.
> 3. Savings and loan companies there are in trouble. If pressure were applied they would have to shut their doors, thereby creating stronger pressure.
> 4. We should withdraw all technical help and should not promise

any technical help in the future. Companies in a position to do so should close their doors.

5. A list of companies was provided and it was suggested that we approach them as indicated. I was told that of all the companies involved ours alone had been responsive and understood the problem. The visitor (evidently the CIA's William Broe) added that money was not a problem. . . . [6]

ITT's immediate response was that Anderson's allegations had "no foundation in fact." [7] As subsequent columns appeared, quoting more ITT documents, the company had no comment to make.

A State Department spokesman also denied that the U.S. government had tried to prevent Allende's election. The spokesman stated that the Nixon administration had "firmly rejected" any ideas of "thwarting the Chilean constitutional processes," [8] and that the government's actions were firmly in line with the president's stated policy that the United States was willing to live with "a community of diversity in Latin America: we deal with governments as they are. Our relations depend not on their internal structures or social systems, but on acts which affect us in the Inter-American system." [9]

But these denials had little effect on the tide of events that followed Anderson's new revelations. The Senate Foreign Relations Committee voted immediately to investigate the charges and created a subcommittee on multinational corporations, headed by Senator Frank Church (D, Idaho), to study the impact of these corporations on the formulation of American foreign policy. Although hearings were not scheduled to begin until after the 1972 presidential election, the committee immediately asked ITT for all documents relating to Chile during the turbulent period surrounding Allende's accession to power.

And in Chile itself, the accusations were a "political windfall" for Allende,[10] allowing him to divert public attention from the country's severe economic troubles to the ever-present fears in Latin America of American domination and subversion by the CIA (see Appendix A). He was also able to link the alleged plotting by ITT and the CIA to the earlier assassination of the army commander. "The revelations in the United States of the documents should convince every Chilean that the nation's independence is at stake today," said one Allende supporter.[11] Furthermore, the negotiations between ITT and the Chileans over compensation for the company's expropriated property were abruptly terminated, and the Chilean government began to consider the possibility of confiscating all the company's assets in Chile.

[6] "The Washington Merry-Go-Round: Memos Bare ITT Try for Chile Coup," *Washington Post*, March 21, 1972, p. B–13.
[7] "ITT Said to Seek Chile Coup in '70," *The New York Times*, March 22, 1972, p. 25.
[8] "Intervention in Chile Is Denied," *San Francisco Chronicle*, March 24, 1972, p. 14.
[9] Richard M. Nixon, *U.S. Foreign Policy for the 1970's, A Report to the Congress*, February 25, 1971, p. 53.
[10] "Allende Finds ITT Story Useful," *San Francisco Chronicle*, March 24, 1972, p. 14.
[11] *Ibid.*

Even though ITT's efforts were unsuccessful in preventing Allende's election, the very nature of the involvement, the audacity with which the plans were conceived, the contempt in which ITT held all other parties, and, more important, the extent to which ITT sought and received entree into the CIA and other government agencies to pursue its objectives raise serious issues of far greater import than the particular incident in question.

Background History: ITT in Chile

ITT's involvement in Chile began in 1927 when it acquired the Chile Telephone Company, Ltd., an English company founded in 1899. In 1930, ITT was granted a fifty-year concession to operate the company, and under that contract the present Compañía de Teléfonos de Chile was organized. Its 37,607 telephones in operation in 1930 increased to 360,000 by 1971, when the company had a book value of $153 million, almost 5,900 employees, and a monthly payroll of approximately $3.8 million. Two years of negotiations between ITT and the Chilean government culminated in 1967 in an agreement by which the Corporación de Fomento de la Producción (CORFO, the government development agency) and other Chilean nationals could purchase up to 49 percent of ITT's stock in the company. By 1971 the Chilean government owned approximately 24 percent, the Chilean public 6 percent, and ITT 70 percent of the company's stock.

In support of its telephone system, ITT owned in 1971 a number of related enterprises. Standard Electric-Chile was established in 1942 for the production of telecommunications equipment. The company, a $2.2 million investment on ITT's part, had approximately 800 Chilean employees and an annual payroll of over $2 million in 1971. ITT World Directories operated a subsidiary in Chile for four years prior to 1971, Guías y Publicidad, which published telephone directories. It also owned All America Cable and Radio-Chile, an international telegram company with assets of $600,000.

After its 1927 purchase of the Chile Telephone Company, ITT World Communications laid a cable across the Andes in 1928, providing Chile's first international service to Argentina and Uruguay, and linked the country to the rest of the world by radio through its terminus in Buenos Aires. As of 1971, ITT World Communications assets in Chile had a book value of $3 million. In 1968 the Chilean government negotiated a purchasing agreement, this time a total buy-out through ENTEL, the government international communications unit. As of 1971, ENTEL owned about 10 percent of the company. Finally, in 1968, ITT purchased the Carrera and San Cristóbal hotels, agreeing to integrate them into the Sheraton Hotel system. These hotels represented in 1971 an investment of $8.4 million.

ITT explains, in a public relations brochure that emphasizes its value to the country, that the Chile Telephone Company is a regulated public utility, with three members of its board of directors appointed by the Chilean government, by which the government participates in the formulation of the company's operating and financial policies. The company's books have been audited annually by an independent accounting firm, and these audits have each year been approved not only by the government's representatives on the board, but also for more than forty years by the Chilean Ministry of Finance. Thus, ITT states, the Chilean government has "not only certified the value of the Chile Telephone Company but has also thereby in effect confirmed the amount of ITT's investment of approximately $153 million in the company." [12] Between 1961 and 1970, ITT asserts that its reinvestment in the company and payment of withholding taxes amounted to more than $84 million, plus an additional $40 million of supplier financing through the ITT system and foreign bank loans, while it withdrew during the same period only $19 million in net remittances. Thus, for every dollar taken out of Chile, ITT reinvested or paid in taxes more than 6 dollars.[13]

In addition, the company contributed to "no less than 50 cultural, civic and educational organizations throughout the country." [14] These included blood bank efforts; the Red Cross; help for the blind; support for the national symphony, philharmonic orchestra, and other performing arts; on-the-job training programs provided without charge to students of high schools, professional training schools, and colleges; a university-level scholarship program; and support for major sporting events.

This record of public service, however, was not sufficient to counteract the Chileans' resentment over the extent of foreign ownership of capital and industry in their country. During the 1970 presidential campaign only one of the three candidates, Jorge Alessandri Rodríguez, former president and candidate of the right-wing National party, supported the private free enterprise system that made such foreign ownership possible. Radomiro Tomic Romero, supported by the ruling Christian Democratic party, advocated a continuation of then president Eduardo Frei Montalvo's policies of gradual "Chileanization" of important sectors of the economy.[15] Dr. Salvador Allende Gossens, a long-time Socialist and candidate of the Popular Unity party (a coalition of Communists, Socialists, Social Democrats, Radicals, and dissident Christian Democrats), campaigned on a platform that called for extensive land reform and rapid nationalization of monopolies and vital industries, many of which were controlled by foreign capital (see Appendix B, Exhibit 1).

In spring 1970, with the presidential campaign in progress, ITT's political information indicated that Allende would win the popular election in the fall. ITT's total assets in Chile were valued at approxi-

---

[12] *ITT History in Chile,* International Telephone and Telegraph Company, p. 3.
[13] *Ibid.*
[14] *Ibid.,* p. 4.
[15] U.S. Congress, Senate, Report to the Committee on Foreign Relations by the Subcommittee on Multinational Corporations, *The International Telephone and Telegraph Company and Chile, 1970–71,* June 21, 1973, p. 2. All citations from this source will hereinafter be referred to in the text as *Report,* followed by page number.

mately $160 million, about $100 million of which was insured against expropriation by the Overseas Private Investment Corporation (OPIC). Allende had made clear the probable fate of these assets in any administration he would head, and ITT became understandably concerned over this eventuality (see Appendix A).

ITT Swings into Action

ITT was apparently unwilling to let the situation drift and give up its Chilean assets without a fight. The actions ITT took, the way it went about them, and the ultimate outcome are vividly detailed in ITT inter-office memorandums, cables, and letters, and the company's communications with various government officials and representatives of other businesses. These documents were first made public by Jack Anderson. Some of these were later inserted into the *Congressional Record* by Senator Fred Harris. ITT also furnished copies of these documents to Senator Church's subcommittee, at the latter's request, and these were made public record by the subcommittee. (See footnote 21 for the complete citation of the subcommittee hearings.) A few of these documents are reproduced in Appendix B.

The Senate hearings opened on March 20, 1973, almost a year after the initial disclosure of these documents, and they raised as many questions as they answered. The record shows that ITT executives were particularly prone to loss of memory and vagueness over detail. In cases of apparent contradictions and conflicts in their testimony, ITT executives blandly attributed these to failure of communication within the organization, an incredible admission in view of ITT's reputation of being an extremely tightly run ship and Geneen a genius at administration. ITT actions, as culled from the documents and testimony of witnesses at the hearings, can be divided into three significant time periods: the pre-election period, the period between the popular election and the congressional election, and the period after Allende came to power.[16]

The Period Preceding the Popular Election of September 4, 1970

During May and June 1970, ITT Director John McCone (see Table 1 for cast of characters) held a series of meetings with his successor at the CIA, Richard Helms. McCone pointed out to Helms the magnitude of both business investments and OPIC guarantees that were at stake if Allende were elected and asked whether the United States would interfere to encourage support for "one of the candidates who stood for the principles that are basic to this country" (*Report,* p. 3). Helms indicated that, although this matter had been considered by the "40 Committee," the interdepartmental committee that oversees CIA covert activities, the de-

16 The format in this section is the same as that followed in the *Report.*

cision had been to do nothing. [17] Although the CIA could still undertake certain minimal actions, Helms was pessimistic about the chances of defeating Allende in the popular election. (It is interesting to note that the U.S. embassy at this point was predicting that the conservative Alessandri would win a plurality of 40 percent in the popular vote. ITT's information predicted a plurality for Allende, and it was ITT's intelligence that was accurate.)

At one of these meetings, McCone suggested to Helms that someone on his staff should be in contact with Geneen. According to the subcommittee, "it was McCone, through his suggestion to Helms, who set in motion a series of contacts between the ITT and CIA in connection with Chile" (*Report,* p. 3). The *Washington Post* quoted one government official involved with the case as saying, "ITT's relationship with the CIA is no mystery. If you have John McCone on your board it gives you a certain kind of entree." [18]

On July 16, 1970, Geneen met with William V. Broe, director of the Latin American division of the CIA's Clandestine Services, for the first time. At this meeting, Broe testified, Geneen offered to assemble a "substantial" election fund for Alessandri, to be controlled and channeled through the CIA. Broe said he refused the offer and informed Geneen that the CIA was not supporting any candidate in the election. Geneen, who is consistently described as having almost total recall of facts and figures, testified

> that he did not recall having offered a "substantial" sum of money to the CIA. . . .
>
> But Mr. Geneen told a Senate subcommittee that, since he had "no recollection to the contrary," he would accept the testimony of . . . Broe. . . .
>
> Mr. Geneen said that, assuming he did make the offer of cash to Mr. Broe, it was probably an "emotional reaction" to learning from their conversation that the United States was planning no action to attempt to defeat Dr. Allende. . . .[19]

[17] The 40 Committee, formed in 1948 to oversee the year-old CIA's activities and to make sure that they were worth the political risks, at the time of this writing comprised Secretary of State Henry Kissinger, CIA chief William E. Colby, Deputy Defense Secretary William Clements, Under Secretary of State Joseph Sisco, and Air Force General George Brown, chairman of the Joint Chiefs of Staff. The committee reviews CIA proposals. Some of the projects it has approved over the years include the spy flights of the U-2, the Bay of Pigs invasion, and the secret war in Laos. It has not been credited with approving CIA actions to sabotage Allende's Marxist regime. Kissinger's growing power has reduced the committee's impact, since it is said that he dominates the meetings. When he exhibits a personal interest in a project, such as U.S. involvement in Chile, that project is almost certain to gain approval despite doubts about it held by others. (For more information on the 40 Committee, see "Supervising the Spooks," *Newsweek,* September 23, 1974, p. 52.)

[18] "Congress, OPIC Probe, ITT's Efforts Against Chile's Allende," *Washington Post,* February 19, 1973, p. A–4.

[19] "Geneen Concedes ITT Fund Offer to Block Allende," *The New York Times,* April 3, 1972, pp. 1, 17.

TABLE 1   CAST OF CHARACTERS

AIBEL, H. J.	ITT's senior vice-president and general counsel
ALESSANDRI, JORGE	Candidate for the presidency of the republic
ALLENDE, SALVADOR	Senator, candidate for the presidency of the republic
BARTLETT, CHARLES	Columnist of conservative tendencies of the *Evening Star* and other North American newspapers
BENNETT, R. E.	ITT's executive vice-president
BERRELLEZ, ROBERT	ITT's chief of Latin American public relations, situated in Buenos Aires
BERTINI, JORGE	Member of the Economic Committee of Unidad Popular
BRITTENHAM, RAYMOND LEE	ITT's senior vice-president
BROE, WILLIAM	Director of CIA Latin American Clandestine Services
DUNLEAVY, F. J.	ITT's vice-president, situated in Brussels
EDWARDS, AGUSTIN	President of board of *El Mercurio,* an anti-Communist newspaper in Chile
FISHER, JOHN	U.S. State Department director for the area of Bolivia-Chile
FREI, EDUARDO	President of the republic until November 3, 1970
GENEEN, HAROLD S.	ITT's chairman and chief executive
GERRITY, EDWARD J.	ITT's senior vice-president, corporate relations and advertising
GUILFOYLE, JACK	ITT's vice-president in New York, and ITT's president for Latin America
HENDRIX, HAL	ITT's director of public relations for Latin America
HERRERA, FELIPE	President of Inter-American Development Bank
KORRY, EDWARD	U.S. ambassador to Chile
MATTE LARRAIN, ARTURO	Brother-in-law of Jorge Alessandri and director of his presidential campaign
McCONE, JOHN	Ex-CIA director and member of ITT's board of directors
MERRIAM, WILLIAM R.	ITT's vice-president in charge of the Washington office
NAVIN, J. J.	ITT's secretary
NEAL, JACK D.	ITT's director of international relations
PERKINS, KEITH	ITT's director of public relations
PORTA ANGULO, FERNANDO	Commander in chief of the Chilean navy
PRATS, CARLOS	Chief of staff of the Chilean army; commander in chief of the army following the assassination of General Schneider
SCHNEIDER, RENE	Commander in chief of the Chilean army (assassinated)
THEOFEL, N.	ITT's vice-president
TOMIC, RADOMIRO	Christian Democratic party candidate for the presidency of the republic
VAKY, VIRON PETER	Adviser to Henry Kissinger for Latin American affairs
VALDES, GABRIEL	Minister of foreign affairs in the government of Frei
VIAUX, ROBERTO	Ex-general of the army
WALLACE, EDWARD R.	ITT's vice-president and assistant director, corporate relations and advertising.

Geneen also testified that he had made a similar offer in 1964, and the CIA had also rejected that offer (*Report*, p. 4). And when Broe refused his offer to support Alessandri, Geneen stated, the matter "died right there." [20]

The Period between September 4, 1970 and the Congressional Election of October 24, 1970

As ITT had predicted, Allende won a narrow plurality in the September 4 popular election. These results stimulated immediate activity. Allende's narrow victory did not ensure his ultimate election. Since he had not won a majority of votes, the Chilean congress would have to choose between him and Alessandri, who had received the next highest number of votes. This congressional election was set for October 24. On September 9 Alessandri announced that if he were elected by the congress, he would immediately resign. This would enable outgoing President Eduardo Frei, who was constitutionally prohibited from succeeding himself, to run against Allende in a new election. In such a two-way contest, many believed that Frei would win a clear majority of the popular vote. This plan became known as the "Alessandri formula" (see Appendix B, Exhibit 2, and *Hearings*).[21]

ITT, however, was unwilling to accept Allende's election as a *fait accompli* (*Hearings*, part 2). A memo from ITT's Chile office to Gerrity (Appendix B, Exhibit 2) inluded a list of recommendations to promote "stop Allende" activities. According to McCone's testimony, Geneen again called upon him and told him that

> he [Geneen] was prepared to put up as much as a million dollars *in support of any plan that was adopted by the government for the purpose of bringing about a coalition of the opposition to Allende* so that when confirmation was up, which was some months later, this coalition would be united and deprive Allende of his position. (*Report*, p. 4; emphasis added)

On Geneen's urging, McCone communicated this offer to both Henry Kissinger and Helms.

At roughly the same time, another ITT official, International Relations Director Jack Neal, communicated the same offer to both Viron Peter Vaky, Kissinger's assistant for Latin American Affairs, and Assistant Secretary of State Charles Meyer (*Hearings*, part 2).

[20] "ITT Head Talks about Chile Case," *San Francisco Chronicle*, April 2, 1972, p. 1.
[21] U.S. Congress, Senate, *Hearings Before the Subcommittee on Multinational Corporations of the Committee of Foreign Relations, The International Telephone and Telegraph Company and Chile, 1970–71*, March 20, 21, 22, 27, 28, 29, and April 2, 1973. The Hearings are in two parts. Part 1 contains the testimony of various witnesses. Part 2 is an appendix and contains copies of various exhibits. In the text of this case, all citations of this source from part 1 will hereinafter be referred to as *Hearings*, part 1, followed by page number. The citations from part 2 will be referred to simply as *Hearings*, part 2, except where a direct quote is used, when the appropriate page number will be given.

Geneen's purpose in offering these funds was the subject of heated controversy in the hearings. Geneen himself testified that "it was intended to be a very open offer," to be used either to finance an anti-Allende coalition in the Chilean congress or for development aid.[22] According to McCone,

> at no time had Mr. Geneen contemplated that the proffered fund . . . would be used to create "economic chaos," despite recommendations to that effect from various people within ITT and others within the CIA.

> "What he had in mind was not chaos," Mr. McCone said, "but what could be done constructively. The money was to be channeled to people who support the principles and programs the United States stands for against the programs of the Allende-Marxists."

> These programs, he said, included the building of needed housing and technical assistance to Chilean agriculture.[23]

E. J. Gerrity, senior vice-president for corporate affairs and advertising, similarly stressed that the funds were for constructive uses.

Other ITT witnesses, however, as well as the documents of the period, make these assertions highly dubious. Despite ITT's highly effective internal communication system, there is no evidence that such constructive intentions were ever communicated to several key individuals. Gerrity admitted that he had not included any constructive purposes in his instructions to Merriam, who had subsequently instructed Jack Neal on his contacts with Kissinger's office and the State Department. Neal testified that he had no knowledge of what the money was to be used for, and stated that when he spoke to Meyer at the State Department, "I didn't elaborate" on the potential uses of the funds. "We didn't go into it," he said:[24] Vaky of Kissinger's office said he had understood the offer to be toward helping block Allende's election. Gerrity also admitted that he could not remember having discussed this issue with Geneen (*Report,* p. 5).

Furthermore, Chile had been the recipient of more than $1.5 billion in aid between 1961 and 1971 (Appendix C), and the senators found it impossible to believe that ITT would think $1 million more would have a serious impact on Chile's economic situation. According to Senator Case:

> The whole body of evidence, memoranda, internal communications in the company, communications among all of you shows great disillusionment on the part of ITT with a program of aid to Chile [Appendix B, Exhibit 4] . . . this adds to the difficulty of believing that a relatively small amount of additional aid would be of any value. (*Report,* p. 5)

22 "ITT Head on Chile," *San Francisco Chronicle,* April 3, 1973, p. 24.
23 "McCone Defends ITT Chile Fund Idea," *The New York Times,* March 22, 1973, p. 1.
24 "ITT Officials Offer Conflicting Views," *The New York Times,* March 23, 1973, p. 8.

The subcommittee concluded in its report that Gerrity's assertions had

all the earmarks of an afterthought. As Senator Percy put it, "The implausibility of this story is what bothers us. It just does not hang together. It does not make sense for reasonable, rational men . . . to really feel that this assistance could have an impact. (*Report*, pp. 5–6)

The communications from ITT's observers in Chile during the period following the popular election contain no mention of any constructive aid or the results of such aid. They do, however, contain detailed analyses of the political situation and the possible consequences of ITT's intervention (Appendix B, Exhibits 2, 3; *Hearings*, part 2). For example, a week before Allende won the congressional runoff, Gerrity received word from Chile that former Brigadier General Roberto Viaux, who had led an unsuccessful insurrection by members of a regiment the year before in a demand for more pay and better working conditions and had been promptly dismissed from the army, was going to try to stage a coup in the very near future. The memo stated in part:

It is a fact that word was passed to Viaux from Washington to hold back last week. It was felt that he was not adequately prepared, his timing was off and he should "cool it" for a later, unspecified date. Emissaries pointed out to him that if he moved prematurely and lost, his defeat would be tantamount to a "Bay of Pigs in Chile."

As part of the persuasion to delay, Viaux was given oral assurances he would receive material assistance and support from the U.S. and others for a later maneuver. It must be noted that friends of Viaux subsequently reported Viaux was inclined to be a bit skeptical about only oral assurances. (*Hearings*, part 2, p. 659)

ITT officials continued their efforts to block Allende's election. Robert Berrellez and Hal Hendrix, two ex-newspaper reporters responsible for reporting on Chile's political situation, cabled their recommendations to New York on September 17 (Appendix B, Exhibit 2). Merriam showed a copy of this cable to Broe and solicited his assessment of their recommended actions. According to Merriam, Broe "agreed with the recommendations." [25]

A week later, on September 29, Broe met with Gerrity in New York. This was the first in the series of CIA-ITT meetings that were initiated by the CIA; Broe had, in fact, arranged the meeting at the instruction of CIA Director Helms. The content of this meeting raises substantial questions about the *actual* policy the U.S. government might have been following as opposed to its *stated* policy and about its possible use of ITT as an instrument of covert actions, contrary to stated policy. Stated policy, both before and after Allende's election, was that the United States

[25] "CIA-ITT Plans on Chile Reported," *The New York Times*, March 21, 1973, p. 1.

would take no position on the election. Yet at this meeting Broe, *on the instructions of Helms,* presented a plan of action "to accelerate economic chaos in Chile as a means of putting pressure on Christian Democratic Congressmen to vote against Dr. Allende or in any event to weaken Dr. Allende's position in case he was elected" (*Report*, p. 9). The suggested actions included those listed in Jack Anderson's column. Gerrity told Geneen after the meeting that he did not think this plan was workable and later wrote to Merriam that Geneen "agrees with me that Broe's suggestions are not workable. However, he suggests that we be very discrete in handling Broe" (*Hearings*, part 2, p. 636).

Charles Meyer of the State Department later attempted to explain that Broe's suggestions were "merely the exploration of a possible policy option" (*Report*, p. 10), although he later conceded that had these suggestions been carried out, they would have constituted a change in policy that would have needed government approval at a higher level than CIA Director Helms. But he would not disclose whether the 40 Committee had specifically approved the plan, and thus whether it did represent policy or, as Senator Church suggested, whether "ITT did successfully lobby the CIA on behalf of a covert operation, without policy approval." [26]

The question of policy was further confused by the September 17 telegram from Berrellez and Hendrix, which stated: "Late Tuesday night (September 15), Ambassador Edward Korry finally received a message from the State Department giving him the green light to move in the name of President Nixon" and gave him authority to do "all possible—short of a Dominican Republic-type action—to keep Allende from taking power" (Appendix B, Exhibit 2). Hendrix later explained that the source of this information was a Chilean who was not connected with the American Embassy and that the source had mentioned neither President Nixon nor the Dominican Republic. Then-Ambassador Korry testified that he had cabled the State Department that an Allende victory would not be in the best interests of the United States (*Hearings*, part 2). The subcommittee stated in its report:

> When Ambassador Korry was questioned about the "green light message" he refused to tell the Subcommittee what his instructions from Washington were. Assistant Secretary of State Meyer also refused to say what the Ambassador's instructions were and the Department refused to furnish copies of the cables it sent to Santiago. In the face of the refusal of the State Department to cooperate, it is impossible for the Subcommittee to determine definitely whether the Ambassador in fact received a cable substantially along the lines described by Hendrix. (*Report*, p. 7)

This, in turn, made it impossible to determine whether ITT and the CIA

[26] "CIA's Action on Chile Unauthorized, Ex-Aide Says," *The New York Times*, March 20, 1973, p. 3.

were acting with or without official approval—in other words, who was using whom for what.

Meetings between Broe and ITT officials continued during October 1970, resulting in a regular exchange of information about the Chilean situation. Cables that ITT received from Santiago were passed along to Broe, and Broe kept Merriam informed of the CIA's assessment of the situation. Other contacts continued as well. Meetings between ITT's Jack Neal and Ambassador Edward Korry led to a letter from Merriam to Kissinger on October 23 (*Hearings,* part 2), the day before the congressional vote, outlining the measures that ITT felt the government should take. The government did not respond to the suggestions. On October 18, Alessandri had withdrawn from the congressional runoff, and Allende's victory was a foregone conclusion. In a confidential memo to Geneen on October 20, 1970, Gerrity stated:

> State has been absolutely wrong on the outcome in Chile, as other Government agencies have, but State has the fundamental responsibility for the U.S. position and it has been wrong consistently. It is our assumption that it will also, based on its record, probably be wrong about the effects of the Allende presidency. (*Hearings,* part 2, p. 665)

Allende in Power

On October 24 the Chilean congress confirmed Allende as president, and he was sworn in on November 4. ITT now had to face the unpleasant reality it had hoped to avoid. Its strategy changed to attempting to weaken his power (perhaps causing the collapse of his government) and to securing favorable terms in the inevitable Chilean takeover of Chiltelco. The suggestions made earlier by Broe and rejected by both Gerrity and Geneen seemed to take root after Allende was actually in power. ITT's point of view after the election became this: Allende would be forced farther to the left by American economic and political reprisals. His move to the left, however, would eventually be forced on him regardless of what Washington's tack was. In any case, a popular and military reaction against the new government would be unlikely. The military had not shown any indications of moving against the Allende coalition even in defense of the constitution. Nor did it show a capacity for carrying off general strikes or urban guerilla warfare such as the extreme left faction was capable of.

Fear was growing at this time among ITT officials that the United States was growing soft. In a memo to Hendrix from Berrellez, October 25, it is stated thus:

> Having just recently given Tito a personal presidential blessing, Washington will certainly arouse liberals everywhere if it turns its back on Allende. Such inconsistencies are fodder for the editorial

pages. . . . However, if Washington just sits there and does nothing to thwart Allende, it will be inviting a sharper turn toward leftist nationalism—which translates into more danger for foreign investments—among other Latin American countries. (*Hearings,* part 2, pp. 679–80)

In a fit of ITT-type passion, Gerrity exclaimed to Merriam:

> Three years ago, Allende said: "The United States is in trouble, everywhere. The wave of the future is Marxist-Leninism." If that is so, freedom is in danger, everywhere. (*Hearings,* part 2, p. 684)

In a memo to Geneen, he said: "Freedom is dying in Chile and what it means to Latin America, and to us—to free men everywhere—is not pleasant to contemplate." (*Hearings,* part 2, p. 665)

At the suggestion of a representative of the Anaconda Company, ITT's Merriam invited Washington representatives of major companies with interests in Chile to form the Ad Hoc Committee on Chile. This committee began meeting in January 1971 and included representatives of Anaconda, Kennecott, Ralston Purina, Bank of America, Pfizer Chemical, and Grace and Company. The Bank of America representative wrote that

> the thrust of the meeting was toward the application of pressure on the (U.S.) Government, wherever possible, to make it clear that a Chilean take-over would not be tolerated without serious repercussions following. . . . ITT believes the place to apply pressure is through the office of Henry Kissinger. (*Report,* p. 12)

This representative, as well as Ralston Purina's, withdrew from these meetings, feeling that any program such as ITT was advocating would compromise its ability to negotiate successfully on its own properties in Chile (*Report,* p. 13). Banks interviewed by the subcommittee also indicated their opposition to the kind of policy being pursued by ITT. According to the subcommittee's report:

> Several of the bank witnesses said that, from their perspective, creating economic chaos would have been counterproductive. The banks had large amounts outstanding in loans to the Chilean Government, as well as to Chilean businessmen. Economic chaos might have meant that the loans could not have been repaid.
>
> A number of bank witnesses said that in order to operate in a large number of countries around the world they have adopted strict policies of non-involvement in the political affairs of the countries where they do business. . . . Involvement in host country politics would inevitably mean impairment of their ability to function. (*Report,* p. 12)

ITT's own internal memoranda show that other companies were not cooperating with its efforts (*Hearings,* part 2).

It might be noted here that some members of ITT's legal department who were responsible for ITT's Chilean activities did not agree with the company's strategy and tactics, which were then largely directed by the company's public relations department, because they felt these would lessen chances of a settlement with Allende and might also jeopardize their claims with the Overseas Private Investment Corporation (OPIC) (Appendix B, Exhibit 6). But, characteristically, ITT persevered in its own program, disregarding protests from its own legal department, its observers in Chile, other companies with which it was in contact, and the inaction and disinterest of government agencies other than the CIA (*Hearings,* part 2).

One of the ways in which it intended to influence U.S. government figures was by sending letters to key administration personnel asking what U.S. policy in Latin America was; what was being done to halt the continuous expropriation in Latin America; and why protective statutes such as the Hickenlooper Amendment were not being used. In a memo from Hendrix to Gerrity shortly after Allende was confirmed as president, Charles Meyer, then assistant secretary for inter-american affairs, was discussed at length. Hendrix complained about Meyer's ineffectiveness and lack of imagination and said:

> The general theme has been don't make any waves; don't rock the boat. . . . In retrospect Meyer may, of course, be the victim of the new Latin area strait jacket called the "low profile of the U.S. in Latin America," which when applied to Chile today could be a salient reason why the United States failed even to head off in 1970 that which it so successfully and energetically aided Chileans to avoid in 1964—the emergence of a Marxist president. Meyer and Crimmons jointly led the effort to make certain that the U.S. this time did nothing with respect to the Chilean election. Meyer's public statements in Latin America all seem to be flavored with apology, which certainly doesn't reflect U.S. strength. As stated in the beginning, I consider Meyer one of the weakest yet in the long string of Assistant Secretaries. I also believe it would be better for us if he returned to Sears Roebuck. (*Hearings,* part 2, p. 745)

Negotiation over Chiltelco's fate began in March 1971, and it is possible to question the good faith of ITT's negotiating stance on two points. First, there is evidence that ITT was negotiating with the attitude that if a satisfactory settlement could be arranged over its own property, these arrangements might be used against other American interests in Chile. Geneen testified during the subcommittee hearings that he hoped "some sort of plan might be developed by our Government that might induce Dr. Allende to proceed with nationalization in a way that would permit orderly recovery of the vast U.S. investments, including ITT's, that were at stake." [27] But the company's internal memoranda indicate that ITT expected to receive a purchase offer similar to one it had earlier negotiated successfully with the Peruvian government. In that settlement, as described by the subcommittee, ITT had persuaded the Peruvian government that

> a satisfactory agreement with ITT would demonstrate that it was not inherently hostile to foreign investments. ITT persuaded the Peruvian government that it could then argue that its decision to expropriate, without compensation, the property of the International Petroleum Company (IPC) a wholly owned subsidiary of the Exxon Corporation, was a special case and not an indication of general financial irresponsibility. (*Report,* p. 14)

An ITT officer described the company's hopes in Chile:

> When Allende signs the copper legislation and formally expropriates Anaconda and Kennecott, there must be increased international resentment against the Government of Chile, and, as in the case of Peru, on their expropriation of IPC, we were able to capitalize on this and eventually arrive at a deal which allowed them to announce internationally that copper and IPC were special cases and here is an arrangement we made in reasonable negotiation with ITT. (*Report,* p. 14)

Efforts To Get Other U.S. Companies Involved

An important component of ITT's strategy was to seek the cooperation of other U.S. businesses operating in Chile in its efforts to slow down and otherwise damage the Chilean economy. However, as in the earlier periods, the company was unsuccessful in these efforts (Appendix B, Exhibits 5, 7; *Hearings,* part 2). Nevertheless, the company continued its plans even after its meetings with Allende, when it became clear that such a strategy could backfire.

Geneen later testified that during this period ITT "and other companies" made

> suggestions and representations to the U.S. Government, including Congress, concerning the expected and actual expropriations, and the fact that Dr. Allende seemed to be moving in a direction to avoid fair payment. These suggestions sought to enlist U.S. Government support to make it clear that the U.S. would not lightly accept arbitrary and unlawful action by Dr. Allende, and that the U.S. would take *all lawful steps* to protect the property of U.S. nationals in Chile. (*Hearings,* part 1, p. 461; emphasis added)

[27] "No Interference with Chile Elections, Top ITT Official Tells Senate Committee," ITT press release, April 2, 1972, p. 3.

Meetings with President Allende and
Negotiation with the Chilean Government

On March 10 Jack Guilfoyle and Francis Dunleavy of ITT met with President Allende, at which time Allende said he had not yet decided what to do about Chiltelco. He further stated that he did not then plan to seize control of Chiltelco and that he might even be interested in a mixed company. In a memo dated March 24, 1971, to Hendrix, Berrellez updated the Chiltelco takeover situation (*Hearings*, part 2). He stated that the Chilean Public Service Commission was starting to compile information on Chiltelco in order to reach a figure that it would offer ITT for Chiltelco. The price would be based on the book value less the total remitted abroad for loan interest repayments and profits since 1931. The total would run to about $80 million. The memo said how Allende would use this transaction to support and strengthen his regime. Also mentioned was the state-controlled news media pressure toward nationalizing the San Cristobal Sheraton and strong attacks against ITT relating to the poor service supplied by Chiltelco.

After this meeting, the Chilean press and the government began to attack the company, alleging that it was deliberately allowing service to deteriorate, that equipment was obsolete, that engineers and technicians were not receiving adequate training, that the rate increase requested by the company was exorbitant, and that the company was generally not fulfilling its obligations under the concession originally granted to it. ITT naturally denied these charges, pointing out the sharp cash squeeze caused by shortfalls in the previously agreed-upon purchasing plan by CORFO and by the mandatory 35 percent wage increase decreed by the government in early 1971, while at the same time there had been no action on the rate-increase petition that would offset these pressures.

On May 26 another meeting was held between Allende and ITT officials. Allende now said that he had decided to proceed immediately with nationalization. ITT was offered $24 million for its interest in the company, and Allende stated that once agreement in principle was reached over the terms of the sale, the government would expect to take over operation of the company at once. ITT refused the $24 million offer, insisting that the government pay the full book value of $153 million. This was despite the fact that ITT had been fully prepared for an offer based on book value less the total remitted abroad since 1931 (*Hearings*, part 2). ITT also opposed the idea of government control of the company during arbitration, fearing its value would deteriorate during this period.

Negotiations thus ended in an impasse, and the government, stressing its eagerness to take control of the company, charged that ITT was deliberately delaying settlement. Even the anti-Communist newspaper *Mercurio*, while denouncing the government's actions, complained of Chiltelco's inferior service and the distribution of service—telephones were still so expensive in Chile that only middle-class and wealthy families could afford them. These attacks continued and increased during the summer while ITT officials continued to meet with the government commission authorized to carry out negotiations. Both sides never wavered: ITT insisted on payment of full book value, and the Chileans insisted that book value was not an appropriate criterion on which to base compensation. Finally, in August, the government wrote that it would accept ITT's suggestion of international arbitration over the value of Chiltelco.

No further action was taken until September 1, however, when Chiltelco's bank accounts were frozen by the government for nonpayment of taxes. The company blamed its admitted inability to pay these taxes on the government's inaction on its rate-increase request, and on the falloff in remittances to the company because of Allende's policies and attitudes toward it. The government, however, had earlier charged that ITT had been siphoning off Chiltelco profits through its telephone directory company, Guías y Publicidad. On September 25 Benjamin Holmes, the Chilean manager of Chiltelco, and officials from Guías y Publicidad were arrested on fraud charges. Finally, on September 29, the government of Chile officially expropriated the Chile Telephone Company.

Although the Chilean government had given every indication that it intended to pursue negotiation and arbitration over compensation for ITT's interest in the company (in fact, negotiations were resumed in December, only to be terminated again after publication of Jack Anderson's column), ITT had no faith that a settlement could be arrived at which could be considered satisfactory from its viewpoint. Accordingly, the company once more swung into action, and Merriam, through presidential aide John Ehrlichman, obtained a meeting between Geneen and General Haig, Henry Kissinger's deputy, and Secretary of Commerce Peter Peterson. Peterson later testified that at this short luncheon meeting Geneen had given a straightforward presentation of what had happened in Chile. Immediately after this meeting, Geneen instructed Merriam to forward to Peterson ITT's suggested actions. The result was Merriam's October 1 letter to Peterson (Appendix B, Exhibit 8), to which was attached an eighteen-point action plan designed "to see that Allende does not get through the crucial next six months." Among Merriam's specific suggestions:

> Continue loan restrictions in the international banks such as those the Export/Import Bank has already exhibited.
>
> Quietly have large U.S. private banks do the same.
>
> Confer with foreign banking sources with the same thing in mind.
>
> Delay buying from Chile over the next six months. Use U.S. copper stockpile instead of buying from Chile.
>
> Bring about a scarcity of U.S. dollars in Chile.
>
> Discuss with CIA how it can assist the six-month squeeze.
>
> Get to reliable sources within the Chilean Military. Delay fuel delivery to Navy and gasoline to Air Force (This would have to be

carefully handled, otherwise would be dangerous. However, a false delay could build up their planned discontent against Allende, thus, bring about necessity of his removal.)

Help disrupt Allende's UNCTAD plans.

It is noted that Chile's annual exports to the U.S. are valued at $154 million (U.S. dollars). As many U.S. markets as possible should be closed to Chile. Likewise, any U.S. exports of special importance to Allende should be delayed or stopped. (*Report,* p. 15)

What's Wrong with Taking Care of Number One?

According to the subcommittee, the company's attitude, motivation, and strategies with regard to its Chilean investment could best be summed up by Gerrity's question: "What's wrong with taking care of No. 1?" (*Report,* p. 17). The subcommittee went on to state:

> This is not to say that there was no reason for concern on the company's part over the fate of its investments in Chile. . . . Whether compensation would be paid, or, if paid, whether such compensation would be adequate was not clear. . . . So the company's concern was perfectly understandable.

> So, too, was its desire to communicate that concern to the appropriate officials of the U.S. Government and to seek their judgment as to how the United States would view the possible eventuality of a seizure of company property without adequate compensation. It is also understandable that the company would wish to have the U.S. Government's assessment of the likelihood of an Allende victory, so that it could plan for such an eventuality in terms of negotiations, investment strategy, and corporate profitability targets.

> But what is not to be condoned is that the highest officials of the ITT sought to engage the CIA in a plan covertly to manipulate the outcome of the Chilean presidential election. In so doing the company overstepped the line of acceptable corporate behavior. If ITT's actions in seeking to enlist the CIA for its purposes with respect to Chile were to be sanctioned as normal and acceptable, no country would welcome the presence of multinational corporations. Over every dispute or potential dispute between a company and a host government in connection with a corporation's investment interests, there would hang the spectre of foreign intervention. No sovereign nation would be willing to accept that possibility as the price of permitting foreign corporations to invest in its territory. The pressures which the company sought to bring to bear on the U.S. Government for CIA intervention are thus incompatible with the long-term existence of multinational corporations; they are also incompatible with the formulation of U.S. foreign policy in accordance with U.S. national, rather than private interests. (*Report,* pp. 17–18)

The End of Allende

The September 1973 coup was the culmination of the political unrest that had continuously rocked the nation since Allende came to power. It had consistently grown in intensity as a result of Allende's policies, which had led to inflation, economic stagnation, and a strong split between various political factions. The political disorder began in March 1972 and continued until the coup. A right-wing plot against Allende was discovered in March. In October, the opposition organized a big "March for Democracy," and the truck owners and trade and craft unions began a strike that lasted until November. Allende tried to secure the help of the army by including three generals in his cabinet. Augusto Pinochet became commander in chief of the army. The congressional elections of March 1973 failed to provide Allende's opposition with enough votes to impeach him. In April 1973, riots erupted in the copper mines, causing another strike. A second truckers' strike was carried out. In June a coup by an army division was crushed, and workers took over factories to protest against the coup. In August, Allende, in a concession to the right, named military officers, including Pinochet, to government positions. On September 11, the same Pinochet led the military coup that overthrew Allende.

The post-Allende period was initially marked by extreme political repression, torture, and large-scale execution of Allende supporters. Chief of State Pinochet and the three other members of the junta have established a repressive, authoritarian political style, with economic policies that are conservative and austere. Tales of torture and death continue to this day.[28]

In September 1974 it came to light that the CIA had spent $8 million in fostering political unrest and social chaos in Chile during Allende's presidency. This was in direct contradiction to the testimony of high government officials during the 1973 hearings of the Subcommittee on Multinational Corporations.[29]

[28] For an analysis of the causes that led to Allende's downfall and an analysis of post-Allende Chile, see "Overthrow of Allende Seen as No Guarantee of a Return to Stability," *The Wall Street Journal,* September 12, 1973, p. 1; "Chile's Reconstruction Formula," *The Wall Street Journal,* June 3, 1974, p. 10; Paul E. Sigmund, "The 'Invisible Blockade' and the Overthrow of Allende," *Foreign Affairs,* January 1974, pp. 322–40; Paul N. Rosenstein-Rodan, "Why Allende Failed," *Challenge,* May–June 1974, pp. 7–13; Jonathan Kandell, "Chile's Junta after a Year," *The New York Times,* September 13, 1974, p. 1; Victor Perera, "Law and Order in Chile," *The New York Times Magazine,* April 13, 1975, p. 15.

[29] Refer to the following articles for more detailed information on U.S. involvement in Allende's overthrow: "The CIA: Time to Come In from the Cold," *Time,* September 30, 1974, p. 16; "The War over Secret Warfare," *Newsweek,* September 30, 1974, p. 37; "The CIA's New Bay of Bucks," *Newsweek,* September 23, 1974, p. 51; Seymour M. Hersh, "Washington Said to Have Authorized a 'Get-Rougher' Policy in Chile in '71" *The New York Times,* September 24, 1974, p. 2; Seymour M. Hersh, "C.I.A. Is Linked to Strikes in Chile That Beset Allende," *The New York Times,* September 20, 1974, p. 1;

Economic Developments in Post-Allende Chile

The military junta has given top priority to rebuilding the Chilean economy, which was badly damaged during Allende's regime. To revitalize the economy, the junta is encouraging private enterprise, promoting exports, and adopting an open-door policy to foreign investment. To stimulate competition and efficiency, about 2,400 items have been removed from tariff protection.[30] About 500 companies that were "intervened," that is, taken over by Allende's government but never legally purchased, are to be returned to their former owners. Fifty of these were American-owned or controlled. By October 1973, 88 firms had been returned to their former owners. However, the takeovers legally completed by the Allende government were not to be reversed. These included the assets of Bank of America, Citibank, and three big copper mines seized from Kennecott Copper, Anaconda, and Cerro Corporation, which will clearly stay in government hands.[31] In 1974 the Chilean government settled with the three copper companies. Anaconda received a compensation of $253 million, Kennecott received $68 million, and Cerro received $42 million.[32] One reason why the junta settled so equitably is so that they could more readily establish world credits. In January 1974, Chile returned two plants to Dow Chemical valued at $31 million.[33] Other U.S. companies that are likely to resume their former operations include Ford, PPG Industries, Phelps Dodge, and General Tire & Rubber.

The efforts of the junta to restore the nation's economy and attract private foreign investment, however, have been only partially successful. Most of the plants and operations were so badly mismanaged by the Allende-appointed Chilean managers that they will need sizable new investment to repair the damage. Also, the junta has set some stiff conditions that must be met before control can revert to the former owners. These include renouncing all legal action against the state; recognizing

Seymour M. Hersh, "Kissinger Called Chile Strategist," *The New York Times*, September 15, 1974, p. 1; Laurence R. Birns, "Allende's Fall, Washington's Push," *The New York Times*, September 15, 1974, Sec. 4, p. 23; Seymour M. Hersh, "C.I.A. Chief Tells House of $8-Million Campaign Against Allende in '70–73," *The New York Times*, September 8, 1974, p. 1.

30 "Chile's Reconstruction Formula," *The Wall Street Journal*, June 3, 1974, p. 10.

31 "A Future for Business in Chile," *Business Week*, September 29, 1974, p. 30. For an analysis of the legal arguments of nationalization of copper mines, see Samuel A. Stern, "The Judicial and Administrative Procedures Involved in the Chilean Copper Expropriations," *American Journal of International Law*, 66 (September 1972), 205–13; F. A. Vicuña, "Some International Law Problems Posed by the Nationalization of the Copper Industry by Chile," *American Journal of International Law*, 67 (October 1973), 711–27.

32 "In Business This Week—Anaconda's Reparations," *Business Week*, August 3, 1974, p. 25; "Kennecott Says Chile Will Pay It $68 Million Total," *The Wall Street Journal*, October 25, 1974, p. 6; "Cerro Corporation Says Chile Agrees to Repay at Least $41.9 Million for Seized Mine," *The Wall Street Journal*, March 13, 1974, p. 2.

33 "Chile Returns 2 Plants of Dow Chemical Co. Seized in October 1972," *The Wall Street Journal*, January 7, 1974, p. 3.

all debts contracted during intervention; and accepting whatever social statutes the government promulgates to regulate the worker-management relationship. The workers probably will get a share in company profits.[34]

On July 9, 1974, OPIC announced the settlement of two claims totaling $3 million by the Bank of America against two Chilean companies.[35] In December 1974 the Chilean government formally expropriated ITT's 70 percent interest in Chiltelco. This was described as a "procedural" step to be taken before the government would compensate ITT.[36] Shortly thereafter, ITT announced that it expects to receive $125.2 million, only $37 million less than the total book value. ITT also announced that it would be investing $25 million over a ten-year span in a research facility near Santiago. The topics to be researched are nutrition and communications.[37]

THE OPIC GUARANTEE

Another element of ITT's investment in Chile involved the company's claim against the Overseas Private Investment Corporation (OPIC), which had insured ITT's investment in Chile against expropriation.

OPIC was established by Congress in January 1971 to take over the expropriation-guarantee program from the Agency for International Development, which had operated similar programs since 1958. OPIC has the responsibility of "promoting American business investment in less developed countries by insuring investments against expropriation, blocked currencies, and war risks." [38] OPIC has insured business ventures in ninety countries for a total of $2.1 billion, with $400 million of reinsurance with Lloyd's of London. Its staff numbers 133 and its budget is $4 million. OPIC charges a premium rate of 1.5 percent to insure against the three types of risks it covers. It does not insure investments in Indochina, Cuba, China, the Soviet Union, some of the East European countries, Western Europe, Canada, or any other developed country.

OPIC has had rough going since its inception, and in 1972 the House "came within 26 votes of cutting off the OPIC's authority to make new insurance commitments, loans, or loan guarantees. . . . Some members of Congress doubt that the U.S. government should shoulder any of the risk of investment abroad, especially for big corporations," [39] because it

34 "Chile: An Uphill Struggle to Revive Business," *Business Week,* November 17, 1973, p. 41.
35 "OPIC Settles Two Claims by Bank of America Against Chilean Firms," *The Wall Street Journal,* July 10, 1974, p. 2.
36 "Chile Formally Takes ITT Stake in Phone Firm," *The Wall Street Journal,* December 12, 1974, p. 4.
37 "ITT to Receive $125.2 Million from Chile to Settle Expropriation of Its Phone Unit," *The Wall Street Journal,* December 23, 1974, p. 6.
38 "Washington Report: Insurance for ITT?" *The New York Times,* April 8, 1973, Sec. 3, p. 6.
39 *Ibid.*

will drag the United States into conflicts between private industry and foreign governments where it is frequently not clear who is to blame, and where foreign policy considerations may make it undesirable to meddle at a particular time.

OPIC's former chief, Bradford Mills (Marshall T. Mays took over as OPIC president in the fall of 1973), strongly defended the concept of government insurance to cover such private risks on three grounds:

1. If the United States is to help the poor countries develop, and also maintain its present leadership position in the world markets, it must protect U.S. corporations against unusual nonbusiness risks so that they will invest in these countries.

2. Other European countries are providing similar coverage to their businesses and at rates that are about one-third those charged by OPIC. For example, for the three standard risks, Denmark, Germany, and Norway charge only 0.5 percent; Japan, 0.55 percent; France and Holland, 0.8 percent; and the United Kingdom, 1.0 percent.[40] Mills maintained that such low premiums amount to indirect subsidy, and if the U.S. government were to withdraw its guarantees, it would put U.S. business in an unfair competitive position against companies from other countries for a share of trade and investment in less developed countries.

3. The less developed countries are less likely to take illegal and confiscatory actions against U.S. companies and will settle claims on a more businesslike basis when such investments are insured by an agency of the U.S. government. Not to do so would lead to a confrontation with the U.S. government where the stake, in terms of cutoff of foreign aid and development loans, is much higher than capital funds from a single company.

Such arguments, however, draw equally strong counterarguments. American labor protests that such assistance is contributing to the export of American jobs and contends that multinationals go to less developed countries for cheap labor. Some congressmen believe that, given the situation at home, helping poor lands is a luxury that they "can no longer afford." [41]

European authorities also reject the arguments of low premium rates by suggesting that investment risks in less developed countries may be different for multinationals from different countries. Furthermore, low premiums must be evaluated as part of total assistance provided by governments to multinationals. States one international expert: "All the programs are subsidies in the sense that governments are the final guarantors of private risks." [42]

---

[40] Richard F. Janssen, "The Problem of Expropriation Risks," *The Wall Street Journal*, May 9, 1973, p. 18.
[41] *The New York Times*, April 8, 1973, Sec. 3, p. 6.
[42] Janssen, "The Problem of Expropriation Risks."

At the time of Allende's election, OPIC had a total commitment in Chile of approximately $500 million in guarantees against expropriation: $105 million of that commitment was to ITT, with other large policies held by Anaconda, Kennecott, and Cerro de Pasco. ITT's insurance contract, its amount and conditions, became a part of the negotiations with the Chilean government when the government demanded, in August 1971, that it receive copies of the contract for study before further negotiations could take place. ITT refused to allow the contract to be released and forwarded the demand to OPIC.

Following Chile's nationalization of ITT properties, the company filed a claim with OPIC for $92.5 million. The company had every reason to expect sympathetic treatment from OPIC's Mills. When the Senate subcommittee was hearing testimony on ITT's attempt to enlist the CIA's help to block Allende's election, Mills pointedly refused to advise Congress of OPIC's opinion of ITT's claim, saying that a decision would soon be forthcoming.

On April 9, 1973, OPIC rejected ITT's insurance claim on the grounds that ITT "failed to comply with its obligations under the OPIC contracts to disclose material information to OPIC. In addition, ITT increased OPIC's risk of loss by failing to preserve administrative remedies as required by the contracts, and by failing to protect OPIC's interests as a potential successor to ITT's rights."[43] Earlier, OPIC had denied Anaconda's claim for $154 million for its Chilean copper mines. That claim is under arbitration.

Although OPIC's formal announcement was in "obscure language" on which officials refused to elaborate,[44] the agency appeared not to be accusing ITT of provoking the Chilean government into nationalizing Chiltelco, which would have been a legitimate reason for refusing the claim. ITT announced that under the terms of its contract, it would immediately submit the claim to an independent arbitration panel, which could reverse OPIC's decision. It might be noted here that internal company correspondence released by the subcommittee indicates that ITT's legal department was afraid that the company's activities in interfering in Chile's election might prejudice their claim with OPIC (Appendix B, Exhibit 6).

Many congressional observers felt that the decision from OPIC was based on political considerations. At a time when the agency was attempting to obtain an additional appropriation of $72.5 million, *The Wall Street Journal* quoted one Capitol Hill source as saying, "I think there would have been a political storm [in Congress] if they'd have approved the claim." Denying the claim, and allowing it to go to arbitration, "depoliticized" the case, the source stated.[45] OPIC denied that political considerations had affected its decision; "The reasons given for the denial didn't arise out of the [Senate] hearings," an OPIC spokesman said.[46]

43 "Federal Insurer Bars ITT's Claim for Its Chile Unit," *The Wall Street Journal,* April 11, 1973, p. 2.
44 "U.S. Won't Pay ITT for Chilean Loss," *The New York Times,* April 10, 1973, p. 2.
45 *The Wall Street Journal,* April 11, 1973, p. 2.
46 *Ibid.*

The OPIC guarantee was used in another manner that caused the sub-committee some concern. Both McCone and Ambassador Korry had used the OPIC guarantees as a reason for advising U.S. intervention in the election: "If OPIC had to compensate the companies under the guarantees, so the argument went, the cost would ultimately be borne by the U.S. taxpayer, since OPIC lacked adequate reserves to meet these potential liabilities." The report concluded: "Thus, at least in the case of Chile, OPIC insurance became an argument for American intervention 'to protect the taxpayer' " (*Report,* p. 19). This was not, the subcommittee believed, foreseen when OPIC was established, and it promised to consider the matter in later hearings on OPIC. After OPIC denied ITT's claims, the matter was submitted to an arbitration panel which subsequently upheld the validity of the claims. In January 1975 OPIC and ITT finally settled the claim at $39 million.[47]

[47] "U.S. Unit, ITT Settle Firm's Claims in Chile," *The Wall Street Journal,* January 8, 1975, p. 3.

APPENDIX A

POLITICAL ENVIRONMENT IN CHILE
IMMEDIATELY PRECEDING ALLENDE'S ELECTION

ITT consistently stated that critics of its actions in Chile took these actions out of the context of the Chilean environment, which was extremely hostile to American investment in general and ITT in particular. This appendix provides a glimpse of that environment through renderings (not literal translations) of speeches and newspaper articles from both before and after Allende was inaugurated as president. These quotations show that Allende's coalition had indeed launched an extensive propaganda campaign against foreign investment, or at least foreign control, in Chile.

The coalition that supported Allende, called the Unidad Popular (Popular Unity), consisted of the Communist, Socialist, Radical, and Social Democratic parties, along with the Military Popular Action Movement and Independent Popular Action. Their basic platform was approved on December 17, 1969, and read, in part:

1. Chile is living a profound crisis which manifests itself in social and economic stagnation, generalized poverty, and the delays of all kinds suffered by workers, peasants, and the other exploited classes. It is also seen in the growing difficulties faced by employees, professionals, small and medium-sized businessmen, and in the minimal opportunities available to women and youth.

Chile's problem can be solved. Our country has great resources, such as copper and other minerals, a great hydroelectric potential, vast expanses of forest, a long coastline rich in marine species, more than sufficient agricultural lands, and so forth. It also has the will to work and the desire for all Chileans to progress together in their professional and technical capacity.

What then has failed? What has failed in Chile is a system which does not meet the necessities of our times. Chile is a capitalistic country which depends on imperialism, is dominated by bourgeois sectors that are structurally linked to foreign capital and cannot solve the country's fundamental problems. These are the same problems that derive from class privileges, and which will never be renounced voluntarily. Furthermore, as a consequence of the development of world-wide capitalism, the surrender by the national monopolistic bourgeoisie to imperialism progressively increases and accentuates its dependence in its role as the minor partner of foreign capital.

2. In Chile, the reformist and development solutions, that the Alliance for Progress encouraged and the government of Frei made its own, have not succeeded in changing anything important.

3. The development of monopolistic capitalism denies the widening of democracy and exacerbates anti-popular violence.

4. The imperialistic exploitation of backward economies is carried out in many ways. Some are through investments in mining (copper, iron and others) and in industrial banking and commercial activities, through the technological control that obliges us to pay extremely high sums for equipment, licenses, and patents through usurious North American loans, that obliges us to spend in the United States and transport the purchased articles in North American ships, as well as others. Imperialism has snatched away from Chile large resources, equivalent to double the capital invested in our country throughout the whole of its history. The North American monopolies, with the complicity of the bourgeois government, succeeded in taking control of almost all our copper and nitrate. They control foreign trade and dictate economic policy through the International Monetary Fund and other organizations. They dominate important industrial and service sectors. They enjoy privileged laws while they impose monetary devaluation, the reduction of salaries, and distort agricultural activity through agricultural surpluses. They also interfere in education, culture, and the communications media. Taking advantage of military and political agreement, they have tried to penetrate the armed forces.

5. Chile governs and legislates in favor of the few, the big capitalists and their followers, the companies that dominate our economy, and the large landowners whose power remains almost intact. . . .

The only truly popular alternative, and consequently the fundamental chore that the government of the people has before it, is to end the dominion of the imperialists, the monopolists, and the landholding oligarchy, and to begin the construction of socialism in Chile.[1]

Throughout 1971 the leftist partisans and press continued their attacks on foreign ownership in Chile. Peter Vuskovic, director of the University of Chile's Institute of Economics, charged that between 1966 and 1968, foreign penetration in major industrial firms had increased from 38 percent of those firms to more than 50 percent. Of the 160 most important enterprises, he said, 33.8 percent were infiltrated with foreign capital, if not controlled by it, and of the 100 most important, the percentage of foreignization rose to 40. Furthermore, "in the last few years . . . a new means [of foreign penetration] has been devised, and that is technology as the means of colonization." [2]

Charges against specific companies were also made, both by the press and by the government. In August when an Anaconda executive made some disparaging remarks about the Chilean Congress, a criminal suit

[1] *El Siglo,* December 23, 1969.
[2] *Ibid.,* August 22, 1970.

was brought against him. A government investigating commission also determined that Anaconda had been supporting Alessandri's candidacy and had contributed to Andalién, a right-wing terrorist group. The outcry against Anaconda's actions was very strong and served further to connect foreign influence and investment in Chile with the right wing in Chilean politics.[3] Ford, too, came under attack during this period, when the Council for the Defense of the State accused the company's Chilean branch of fraud against the government.[4]

As the popular election drew near, attacks on foreign capital increased. A government study, it was reported, showed that foreign investment was concentrated in those sectors of the economy that had shown the greatest growth or the greatest potential for growth, which received special benefits from the government. The study also found that most of the foreign companies were monopolies and that they competed with Chilean enterprises in the same sectors, driving the Chilean companies out of the market. The study further charged that "the payment of royalties, patents, designs, technical assistance, and so on, do not seem to be any remuneration for a technological transfer, but rather an alternate way to take money out of the country." [5]

Allende himself made his position very clear. In a speech at the University of Chile, he stated:

> The Unidad Popular was born to defend Chile from capitalistic exploitation and from foreign intervention. Because Chile, as long as she remains economically dependent, and as long as her natural resources are not controlled by the government, cannot emerge from her present state of underdevelopment.[6]

In a later speech, Allende disclosed the industries that he planned to nationalize, among which was included ITT.[7]

These attacks on foreign capital were not moderated after Allende's victory in the popular election. Oscar Garreton, a member of Allende's government, accused the large corporations in Chile, most of which were foreign controlled, of fixing prices, controlling bank credit, operating arbitrarily during periods of labor fluctuations, and selling poor quality products, all to the detriment of the smaller Chilean enterprises. Furthermore, he said, the large corporations do not operate at full capacity, and their technology is advanced and automated, both of which contribute to a low employment figure.[8]

Another economist, Orlando Caputto, charged:

[3] *Ibid.*, August 26, 1970.
[4] *Ibid.*, August 29, 1970.
[5] *Ibid.*, September 2, 1970.
[6] *Ibid.*, August 4, 1970.
[7] *Ibid.*, September 3, 1970.
[8] *Plan*, October 1970.

In the year 1969, the egress of capital through profits from foreign investments, interest and payments on mortgages came to about $480 million. This figure amounts to almost half of the income for Chilean exports. In other words, Chile uses half the dollars from its exports to cover increasing needs for the importation of goods, especially capital goods, and intermediate products. The egress of capital as profit is explained basically by American investments in copper. However, the new orientation of foreign capital, located increasingly in the industrial sector, has uncovered other alternative ways to remit money. Payments for technology, for overbilling on imports (paying artificially raised prices to leave a greater quantity of dollars abroad) and for short- or long-term financial operations. Also, foreign capital operating in national industries imports a large part of its raw materials in the majority of cases. This is one of the main ways of taking out money, since the price of these imports is overbilled.

In Chile, the scandalous loss of $14 million through overbilling was undoubtedly one of the elements considered when the illegal importation of parts being done by Ford Motor was denounced.[9]

That Allende and the UP meant to fulfill these promises was made clear almost immediately after Allende's congressional confirmation, when the government moved in December to nationalize the copper-mining industry.

[9] *Ibid.*

APPENDIX B

The following exhibits are part of the background documents on ITT's involvement in Chile which columnist Jack Anderson used as the basis of his assertions in his column "Washington Merry-go-Round." The documents were submitted by ITT to the Subcommittee on Multinational Corporations of the Committee on Foreign Relations, U.S. Senate, pursuant to the hearings by the subcommittee on ITT and Chile, and were later released to the public by the subcommitteee. Many of the documents were also inserted by Senator Fred R. Harris in the *Congressional Record* (April 11, 1972), pp. S 5858–71.

EXHIBIT 1

COMPANIA DE TELEFONOS DE CHILE SANTIAGO 1

SYSTEM CONFIDENTIAL

To: Mr. J. W. Guilfoyle
From: B. W. Holmes
Date: September 10, 1970

CONFIDENTIAL

I am attaching hereto translation into English of the Basic Communications Program prepared by the Popular Unity Committee existing in Empresa Nacional de Telecomunicaciones (Entel-Chile), which, as I understand, has served as a basis for the speeches and statements of Mr. Allende as Presidential Candidate.

I am briefly stating hereunder the most important references contained in that program in relation with Companía de Teléfonos de Chile.

(a) Total restructuring of the communications area including the Direction of Post and Telegraph, Companía de Teléfonos de Chile, Entel-Chile, Superintendency of Electrical Services and other similar companies (page 1, second and last paragraphs).

(b) Criticizes most severely the telecommunications systems due to the ineptitude of the bourgeosie and the people who direct them, particularly the system of Companía de Teléfonos de Chile, with respect to which is indicated that its service is insufficient and of poor quality.

Poor distribution of services, due to the fact that the majority of the work and countrymen areas lack telephones, which is a consequence of the arbitrary management on the Company's part, of the investments it makes, and the high cost of installations and monthly rents (page 2, paragraph 3 and first part of page 3).

(c) Strongly criticizes ITT and its subsidiaries, ITTCOM and CSESAC, as well as the concession contract of January 23, 1930; the expansion convenio of January 15, 1958; the memorandum of agreement of February 6, 1965; and the convenio of October 6, 1967 based on the mentioned memorandum of agreement (pages 4, 5 and 6).

(d) Lack of fair equivalence in payment of Corfo contributions (page 7, second paragraph).

(e) Concealment of profits on the part of Companía de Teléfonos de Chile (page 8).

(f) Surreptitious operations on the part of ITT's subsidiaries in Chile (page 3, first paragraphs).

(g) Immediate nationalization of CTC and ITTCOM, prior to an exhaustive investigation to be carried out by an Intervention Commission to be appointed in this respect (page 11, last part).

(h) Immediate participation of workmen in the Companies' Board of Directors (page 13, paragraph 1).

(i) Even before nationalization, the Company will be forced to provide with telephone service the population centers and other parts of the country (page 13, paragraph 2).

cc: Mr. Stimson

EXHIBIT 2

INTERNATIONAL TELEPHONE AND TELEGRAPH CORPORATION

INTERNATIONAL HEADQUARTERS
SYSTEM CONFIDENTIAL

To: E. J. Gerrity
From: H. Hendrix/R. Berrellez
Date: September 17, 1970

CONFIDENTIAL

SUBJECT: Chile

The surface odds and foreign news media appear to indicate that Salvador Allende will be inaugurated as President November 4, but there now is a strong possibility that he will not make it.

The big push has begun in Chile to assure a congressional victory for Jorge Alessandri on October 24, as part of what has been dubbed the "Alessandri Formula" to prevent Chile from becoming a Communist state.

By this plan, following Alessandri's election by Congress, he would resign as he has announced. The Senate president (a Christian Democrat) would assume presidential power and a new election would be called for 60 days ahead.

Such an election would most likely match President Eduardo Frei, then eligible to run again, against Allende. In such a contest, Frei is considered to be an easy winner.

Late Tuesday night (September 15) Ambassador Edward Korry finally received a message from State Department giving him the green light to move in the name of President Nixon. The message gave him maximum authority to do all possible—short of a Dominican Republic-type action —to keep Allende from taking power [Emphasis added].

At this stage *the key* to whether we have a solution or a disaster is Frei—and how much pressure the U.S. and the anti-Communist movement in Chile can bring to bear upon him in the next couple of weeks.

The Mercurio newspapers are another key factor. Keeping them alive and publishing between now and October 24 is of extreme importance. They are the only remaining outspoken anti-Communist voice in Chile and under severe pressure, especially in Santiago. This may well turn out to be the Achilles heel for the Allende crowd.

Following are some significant points as we see the Chile situation on this date, plus some comment on various factors and a few basic recommendations:

1. Allende and the Marxist-Socialist coalition (Unidad Popular) are acting like he is the elected President. They are pressing hard on all fronts

to consolidate his slim September 4 election plurality into a solid victory in the congressional vote. Chile's Communist Party, a part of the UP coalition, is directing the pressure. Strategy is coordinated by the USSR. Party discipline and control thus far is extraordinary.

2. *The anti-Communist elements, with Alessandri's supporters in the forefront and Frei in the wings (both prodded by the U.S. government), are maneuvering—now rather efficiently—to capture the congressional vote and set the stage for a new national election. Given the atmosphere in Chile today, the prospect of a new election is looking more and more attractive as the future looks more and more bleak* [Emphasis added].

3. Since Allende and the UP won only a bit more than a one-third of the total national vote, it is strongly believed that in a two-man race and "democracy vs. communism" showdown, Frei would get most of the Christian Democratic vote—since this would put the party back in power —and all the rightest [*sic*] vote that supported Alessandri.

4. For the recent campaign the CD leadership was put in the hands of Radimoro [*sic*] Tomic, who has a deep-grained hatred for Frei and the U.S. The CD national committee is slated to meet early next month and it is expected Frei will regain leadership control. (Tomic already has pledged his support to Allende.)

5. Looming ominously over the successful application of the "Alessandri Formula" is the threat of an explosion of violence and civil war if Allende loses the congressional vote. Allende, the UP and the Castroite Revolutionary Movement of the Left (MIR) have made it clear they intend to fight for total victory. Thus, some degree of bloodshed seems inevitable.

6. Is the Chilean military capable of coping with nationwide violence or a civil war? Opinion is divided on this in Santiago. Korry has said he considers the armed forces a "bunch of toy soldiers." Well-informed Chileans and some U.S. advisers believe the army and national police have the capability. There are definite reservations about the air force and navy. We know that the army has been assured full material and financial assistance by the U.S. military establishment.

The Chilean military will not move unilaterally to prevent Allende from taking office. They will act only if it is in the framework of the constitution.

7. President Frei has stated privately to his closest associates, to Alessandri and to a State Department visitor last weekend in Vina del Mar that the country cannot be allowed to go Communist and that Allende must be prevented from taking office. Publicly, however, he is keeping out of the battle up to this point while feeling steadily increasing pressure from the U.S. and his own camp. Never known for displaying guts in a crunch, he is faced with a dilemma of not wanting to be charged with either turning Chile over to Communist rule or contributing to a possible civil war. A parlay of his highly inflated ego and a chance to occupy the presidency six more years may provide the necessary starch for his decision.

To help strengthen his position, efforts are being made this week to turn this weekend's observance of Chile Independence Day into a pro-Frei demonstration. Main feature of the observance will be a military parade by about 25,000 troops assembled in Santiago.

8. *Ambassador Korry, before getting a go-signal from Foggy Bottom, clearly put his head on the block with his extremely strong messages to State* [Emphasis added]. He also, to give him due credit, started to maneuver with the CD, the Radical and National parties and other Chileans —without State authorization—immediately after the election results were known. He has never let up on Frei, to the point of telling him to "put his pants on."

By the same token, last week when an emissary of Allende called at his office to pay respects and say that the "Allende government wanted to have good relations with the Ambassador and the United States," Korry responded only that he had been "so busy with consulate affairs helping to get visas for Chileans wanting to leave the country that he had not had time to think of the future." Thus ended the interview.

9. The anti-Allende effort more than likely will require some outside financial support. The degree of this assistance will be known better around October 1. We have pledged our support if needed.

10. There is no doubt among trained professional observers with experience in the U.S., Europe and Latin America that if Allende and the UP take power, Chile will be transformed quickly into a harsh and tightly-controlled Communist state, like Cuba or Czechoslovakia today. The transition would be much more rapid than Cuba's because of the long-standing organization of the Chile Communist Party. This obviously poses a serious threat to the national security of the U.S.—Sol Linowitz, Senator Church and others of the same thought notwithstanding—and several Latin American nations. It also is obvious from Allende's pronouncements that existing business and financial links with the U.S. would be strangled.

* * *

At a meeting with Arturo Matte at his residence Sunday (September 13), he seemed in a more relaxed frame of mind than on the last visit and he made these points:

A. The "Alessandri Formula" through which the way would be opened for new elections had the government's and Frei's personal approval. Once elected by Congress, Alessandri would resign, thus carrying out a preelection pledge that he would do so unless he received a plurality or majority of the votes in the regular balloting.

B. Alessandri did publicly announce his plans to resign if elected last week. It was subsequently learned Frei saw and approved the text of the announcement before it was released to the public.

C. Frei and his party (at least that wing that he commands) have a deep interest in this for two reasons: it would block the assumption of power by a Marxist and also give the Christian Democrats a new chance to regain power, this time backed by the Alessandri camp. Alessandri's announcement had the effect of alerting the Marxists and Allende that a powerful last-ditch effort was afoot to block them and it also probably may have partially checked a PDC congressional vote swing toward Allende.

D. Matte said the armed forces are agreed on the extreme danger to democracy that Allende's assumption of power involves. They agree he must be stopped. However, the armed forces leadership and Frei prefer a constitutional way out (i.e., congressional election of Alessandri) that doesn't preclude violence—spontaneous or provoked.

E. A constitutional solution, for instance, could result from massive internal disorders, strikes, urban and rural warfare. This would morally justify an armed forces intervention for an indefinite period. But it was apparent from Matte's exposition that there is little hope for this. The Marxists will not be provoked. "You can spit in their face in the street," Matte said, "and they'll say thank you." This means that the far left is aware of and taking every precaution to neutralize provocation.

F. A plan suggested to Frei, said Matte, calls for the creation of a military cabinet. This would be a form of extreme provocation since it would hint at the makings of a coup. It would have a definite psychological effect on the congressional voters who may be undecided about whom they'll vote for in the runoff. But, added Matte, Frei is reluctant to do it without some reason to justify it in the eyes of the public. We inferred from this that Frei will not act on this unless he is confronted with a severe national crisis.

G. The armed forces boss, René Schneider, is fully aware of the danger of Allende moving in. But he will not budge an inch without Frei's okay. *One retired general, Viaux, is all gung-ho about moving immediately, reason or not, but Matte said Schneider has threatened to have Viaux shot if he moves unilaterally. Although Viaux has some following after his abortive rebellion a few months ago, it is doubted he commands strength enough now to carry it off alone* [Emphasis added].

H. Frei, said Matte, is highly worried about the damage to his stature in the hemisphere; he is concerned that he may become, as the Brazilians have put it, the Kerensky of Latin America.

But he still refuses to take the reins in his hand without "moral" reasons, Matte said.

I. Could he be persuaded, Matte was asked, by assurances of fullest support from Washington? He thought that over a while and finally said he thought that would help. The distinct impression, however, was he might have felt this would have to be done with consummate skill and tact so as not to offend Chilean national dignity. (Korry's new mandate may serve this purpose.)

J. The military has contingency plans ready for whatever scope operation is necessary, Matte said.

The conclusions from this session were:

The leader we thought was missing is right there in the saddle (Frei), but he won't move unless he is provided with a constitutional threat.

That threat must be provided one way or another through provocation. At the same time, a subtle but firm enough pressure must be brought to bear on Frei so that he'll respond.

Matte did not mention money or any other needs. At the end when it was mentioned we were, as always, ready to contribute with what was necessary, he said we would be advised [Emphasis added].

* * *

We will be advised what help we can contribute as present activities develop between now and early October.

We have recommended, apart from direct assistance, the following:

1. We and other U.S. firms in Chile pump some advertising into Mercurio. (This has been started.)

2. We help with getting some propagandists working again on radio and television. There are about 20 people that the Matte and Edwards groups were supporting and we should make certain they are revived [Emphasis added]. Allende now controls two of the three TV stations in Santiago and has launched an intensive radio campaign.

3. Assist in support of a "family relocation" center in Mendoza or Baires for wives and children of key persons involved in the fight. This will involve about 50 families for a period of a month to six weeks, maybe two months.

4. Bring what pressure we can on USIS in Washington to instruct the Santiago USIS to start moving the Mercurio editorials around Latin America and into Europe. Up until I left they were under orders not to move anything out of Chile.

5. Urge the key European press, through our contacts there, to get the story of what disaster could fall on Chile if Allende & Co. win this country.

These are immediate suggestions and there will be others between now and October 24 as pressure mounts on Frei and the Christian Democrats.

cc: E. Dunnett
    K. Perkins
    E. R. Wallace

EXHIBIT 3

SYSTEM CONFIDENTIAL

To: HAL Hendrix—ITTHQNY
From: Robert Berrellez—ITTLABA
Date: September 29, 1970

CONFIDENTIAL

Subject: *Chileans*

Capsuled situationer:

It appears almost certain that marxist Salvador Allende will be confirmed by the Congress as Chile's next President. The Congressional runoff vote is scheduled October 24.

There's only a thin tendril of hope of an upset based on a sharp and unlikely switch in voting sentiment among the Christian Democrats who hold the balance of power in the runoff. The prevailing sentiment among the PDC is said to favor Allende.

A more realistic hope among those who want to block Allende is that a swiftly deteriorating economy (bank runs, plant bankruptcies etc.) will touch off a wave of violence resulting in a military coup.

President Eduardo Frei wants to stop Allende and has said so to intimates. But he wants to do it constitutionally—i.e., either through a congressional vote upset or an internal crisis requiring military intervention.

The armed forces are ready to move to block Allende—but only with Frei's consent, which does not appear to be forthcoming. In other words, Frei has passed the ball to the armed forces and the military will not act without Frei's orders unless internal conditions require their intervention.

– 0 –

Details:

1. Chances of thwarting Allende's assumption of power now are pegged mainly to an economic collapse which is being encouraged by some sectors of the business community and by President Frei himself. The next two weeks will be decisive in this respect. Cash is in short supply. But the government is printing more money. There's an active black market with the escudo moving at a 29 to US$ 1.00 rate on Monday. It had gone down to 26.50 to US$ 1.00 on Friday. The pre-election rate was 20 to 21 to US$ 1.00. Undercover efforts are being made to bring about the bankruptcy of one or two of the major savings and loans associations. This is expected to trigger a run on banks and the closure of some factories, resulting in more unemployment.

2. The pressures resulting from economic chaos could force a major segment of the Christian Democratic party to reconsider their stance in relation to Allende in the Congressional runoff vote. It will become apparent, for instance, that there's no confidence among the business community in Allende's future policies and that the health of the nation is at stake.

3. More important, massive unemployment and unrest might produce enough violence to force the military to move. The success of this maneuver rests in large measure on the reaction of the extreme and violent (Castroite, Maoist) left in Allende's camp. So far he has been able to keep these elements controlled.

4. It's certain that Allende is on to this scheme. He has referred to it in recent public statements. He is also certainly aware of the government's (and Frei's) complicity. Last week the finance minister issued a pessimistic report on the national economy, placing the blame on the results of the September 4 election. The statement was issued with Frei's blessings. Although it reads as an objective and realistic evaluation of economic conditions, the statement aroused the Allende camp which severely criticized it as provocative.

5. All previous evaluations of Frei's weaknesses in a crisis are being confirmed. Worse, it has been established beyond any doubt that he is double-dealing to preserve his own stature and image as the leader of Latin America democracy. For instance: he told some of his ministers he'd be more than willing to be removed by the military. This would absolve him from any involvement in a coup that, in turn, would upset Allende. Then, he turned right around and told the military chiefs he is totally against a coup.

6. A group of respected political and business leaders called on Frei Sunday at Viña del Mar, the beach resort, to call his attention to these lapses. I could not determine the results of this confrontation or its basic purpose. The assumption is that by confronting Frei, the group hoped to press him into a definitive move in the one desired direction.

7. As a result of all this inertia, an aura of defeat has enveloped important and influential sectors of the community. Some businessmen who seemed all gung-ho about stopping Allende are now talking in terms of trying to make some deals with him. Others have given up and are getting ready to leave the country.

8. Some Chilean businessmen have suggested we try to deal in some manner with Allende in an effort to rescue at least a portion of our investment instead of losing it all. At this writing, we have been told Allende's representatives have asked for a meeting with Sheraton representatives to discuss Allende's future policies concerning the hotels. My personal view is that we should do nothing to encourage or help the Allende team. Every care should also be exercised to insure that we are not identified with any anti-Allende move.

9. No hope should be pegged to conditions the Christian Democrats are demanding from Allende in exchange for their support in the Congressional vote. Some believe that if Allende turns them down the PDC

will not vote for him. Allende will promise anything at this stage. Furthermore, many of the conditions the PDC is making are covered by the constitution to which Allende will pay lip service for a while until he is firmly in the saddle and has consolidated his hold so that he can move toward converting Chile into a communist, self-perpetuating state.

10. It is obvious from his latest remarks, however, that Allende fears something is in the wind to deprive him of the presidency in the congressional vote. On Monday he warned that he would bring the nation to civil war if he was not voted into power.

11. Meantime, the Russians are busy helping shore up Allende's defenses. Since the September 4 election, the Russian embassy staff in Santiago added 20 new staffers.

12. An extreme rightist faction launched a series of terrorist acts Sunday (bombings mostly) in what appeared an amateurish attempt to provoke the Castroite-Maoist sector into a violent backlash that would produce the conditions conducive to a military intervention. The bombings failed to arouse anything outside of police action which resulted in the arrest of some of the bombers. This, we are told by the most authoritative sources, is the far right's last effort to provoke the far left in this particular manner.

$$- 0 -$$

The sum-up:

1. A Congressional defeat for Allende is unlikely at this stage. The defeated Christian Democratic candidate, Radomiro Tomic, is backing Allende and can take a sizable segment of the PDC vote with him.

2. Despite some pessimism, a high level effort continues toward getting Frei and/or the military to stop Allende.

3. Although its chances of success seem slender, we cannot ignore that a roadblock to Allende's assumption to power through an economic collapse has the brightest possibilities.

cc: Messrs. E. Gerrity, ITTHQNY
              E. Wallace,   ″
              K. Perkins,   ″
              E. Dunnett,   ″

EXHIBIT 4

ITT WASHINGTON OFFICE
Washington, D.C.

PERSONAL & CONFIDENTIAL

To: Mr. W. R. Merriam
From: J. D. Neal
Date: September 30, 1970

CONFIDENTIAL

Subject: Chile—A Questionable U.S. Policy

The unfortunately heavy probability that Allende will take office in November is well known to State Department and Embassy Santiago. Both believe Allende will start early and systematically attack foreign private enterprise. Thus forewarned, we should hope the Nixon Administration will be prepared to move quickly to exert pressure on Allende. However, because of our weak policy in the Hemisphere during the past two years, we cannot count on such immediate and effective action.

I fear the Department of State will convince the White House to again circumvent the Hickenlooper Amendment—as it has done in Peru, Bolivia, and Ecuador, etc. Instead, I look for the silent pressure (?) which will call for a drying-up of aid and instructions to U.S. representatives in the international banks to vote against or abstain from voting on Chilean loans.

For the past several years the State Department has been predicting an upsurge of Marxism in Chile, and foresaw the culmination of the threat in the September, 1970 elections. Knowing this, the U.S. stepped up its AID program in an attempt to help Chile remain democratic. . . .

The foregoing means the U.S. realized the danger of Marxism in Chile; so fought it with grants and loans, but did not have the extra forethought to follow its intuition by taking a more active part during the pre-election period to assure the defeat of Allende [Emphasis added].

The State Department and AID admitted in public congressional hearings that, "Chile is a country of major U.S. assistance emphasis because of its important political role in the Hemisphere." They continued the hearing by saying the liberal U.S. loan policy to Chile is justified because they were putting the money in there to fight Marxism. However, now that its program failed to prevent Allende from winning the election, the U.S. says, "This is a Chilean matter, thus, we must not interfere!"

Why should the U.S. try to be so pious and sanctimonious in September and October of 1970 when over the past few years it has been pouring the taxpayers' money into Chile, admittedly to defeat Marxism. Why can't the fight be continued now that the battle is in the homestretch and the enemy is more clearly identifiable?

EXHIBIT 5

ITT WASHINGTON OFFICE
Washington, D.C.

SYSTEM CONFIDENTIAL

To: Mr. E. J. Gerrity, Jr.
From: W. R. Merriam
Date: October 7, 1970

CONFIDENTIAL

Subject: Chile

Our man reports nothing new and "picture is not rosy." He says Prewett column exaggerated. Repeated calls to firms such as GM, Ford, and banks in California and New York have drawn no offers of help. All have some sort of excuse [Emphasis added]. English papers were delivered. His only message is that everyone should keep the pressure on because Allende should not take office with complete support and also for the weakening we might accomplish after he does take office—"there is always a chance something might happen later."

The information we are receiving from Hendrix and Berrellez is up-to-date, factual, and concise as any coming out of Chile. The State Department says it is swamped with rumors and facts; so there is no lack of information there either.

Everyone foresees an Allende victory in Congress unless some last minute miracle takes place. There is no, repeat no, solid news showing even a chance that Allende can be stopped.

The State Department says one factor which has paved the way for Allende is the failure of President Frei to take a strong position against Dr. Allende. They feel he could be stopped if Frei would stand firm for his country and quit trying to play the part of Hamlet, wishing to go down in history as the great democrat. Frei has not rallied the Christian Democrats as is believed possible.

The lack of strong political activity on the part of Chile has hampered outsiders like the U.S. and Argentina in trying to help defeat Allende.

Assistant Secretary of State Meyer leaves tomorrow for a week in Haiti and Santo Domingo (while Santiago burns)! [Emphasis added.]

EXHIBIT 6

SYSTEM CONFIDENTIAL

To: Mr. H. J. Aibel
From: R. R. Dillenbeck
Date: October 28, 1970

CONFIDENTIAL

SUBJECT: Chile/Memorandum to Geneen and Letter to Kissinger

Thank you for providing me with copies of Mr. Gerrity's memorandum to Mr. Geneen on the subject of Chile and Mr. Merriam's letter to Henry Kissinger with enclosure.

The letter to Kissinger, insofar as I can tell, was not checked with either Legal or Treasury Department representatives who are currently members of the "team" interfacing with the Department of State on the AID/Chiltelco problem. Given the magnitude of our potential problem in Chile and the care with which our relationships with the State Department must be conducted as a result, I find it almost unbelievable that a letter of this nature was delivered to State without any apparent effort to coordinate with the Chile "team."

In my judgment, the letter strikes a note which I believe the State Department will find uncongenial. The forceful approach it argues is contrary to the policy of the "low silhouette" as I understand it which is clearly the current approach of State. Putting aside whether or not the policy is correct, our leverage to effect a change in this policy is minimal. Identifying ourselves as being opposed to well-defined State Department policy at a time when it is imperative that we have the full confidence of our opposite numbers in State and at AID's successor (OPIC) seems to me possibly to jeopardize efforts which will be made to collect on the AID guarantee insurance. The State Department, and OPIC to the extent OPIC is identified with State Department policy, are almost universally opposed to the Hickenlooper Amendment. It is a continuing irritant to them that ITT supports Hickenlooper. Since I believe it highly unlikely that the Hickenlooper Amendment will be formally invoked in the Chilean context, regardless of what happens, we only can hurt ourselves by continually being identified with the Hickenlooper supporters.

I am not primarily concerned with the substance of the material delivered to Kissinger, even though I disagree with the tone of the letter and would take issue with some of the substance as well. What I am concerned with is the lack of corporate coordination which this letter indicates. On October 1, pursuant to top-level corporate instructions, Mr.

Goldman, Mr. Meyer of the Treasury Department and I attended a meeting at AID in Washington to review the status of the ITT/AID guarantees in Chile in light of political developments there. Mr. Merriam's office was notified by my secretary of this trip and the date and time and purpose of the meeting were provided. No representative of the Washington office appeared at this meeting. After the meeting, a memorandum was prepared by Mr. Goldman and was sent to you, with copies to Messrs. Gerrity, Hendrix, Merriam and Neal of the Public Relations Department. Even a hasty reading of this memorandum would cause one to realize that ITT must speak with one voice concerning the corporate attitude toward Latin America in general and toward Chile in particular. It is my understanding that it was agreed to by Messrs. Dunleavy et al. that there would be coordination on all levels concerning the handling of the Chile situation. Perhaps this message was not conveyed to the Public Relations Department but I believe Mr. Gerrity attended the meeting at which Mr. Geneen was also present where the policy was clearly stated.

In summary, I would be most appreciative if there would be anything that you could do to prevent this kind of "end run" from taking place in the future. I anticipate extremely difficult negotiations in Chile and in Washington concerning ITT's Chilean investments. Failure of the ITT personnel involved to work as a team can only complicate the lives of all of us and, more seriously, possibly jeopardize recovery of the AID insurance.

For your guidance, I have attached a copy of the October 2 memorandum.

Before I had seen the Merriam letter to Kissinger, I had a chance to see Mr. Gerrity's note to Mr. Geneen entitled "Chile: the Aftermath." At my request, Bob Crassweller prepared an analysis of this memorandum and stated his personal views with which I totally associate myself. A copy of Bob's memorandum is attached hereto and I think you will find its balance, judgment and literate nature refreshing when compared to the other effort. Should you think it appropriate, perhaps Mr. Geneen would appreciate having some exposure to an opposite view to that to which he has been exposed already.

I am sure Mr. Gerrity knows that my views differ substantially from his and those of Jack Neal with respect to Latin America and perhaps that is the reason the Legal Department is not given an opportunity to participate in advance of dispatch of material outside of ITT. I think this kind of performance is not up to the best standards of ITT where opposing views are supposedly worked out in-house and then a united front presented. End runs such as this caused by the Public Relations Department are demoralizing and eventually self-defeating to ITT's business goals.

cc: Mr. R. G. Bateson

The following observations are prompted by the attached memorandum dated October 20, 1970 from E. J. Gerrity, Jr. to Mr. Geneen:

I

Referring first to the broadest question raised by the Gerrity memorandum, I think it is correct to conclude that characteristics and directions of the Allende government are not yet marked out in full detail, although of course the country will swing sharply to the left. The exact nature of the leftist measures that it will take, however, and the speed with which these will be realized, are by no means clear.

A. Certain factors point to a quick movement leftward. The government will have all the usual incentives to produce quick results. The enthusiasm and fanaticism of some of the members of the coalition will naturally create pressure for immediate measures. If the present economic decline continues, and particularly if a mood of panic arises, the Government may be forced into harsh steps at an early moment.

B. Other factors point to the likelihood of a slower leftward movement. Allende has agreed to constitutional guarantees that will have a moderating influence. There are six members of his coalition, and the difficulties of coalition politics often make it necessary to proceed with caution. The government would have little to gain by the adverse internal and foreign reactions that would result from hasty radical action, and Allende may find it easier and more profitable to attain his ends by a gradual process, step by step, without exciting his opposition into a really strong confrontation.

II

The difficulty of appraising internal developments authoritatively at this time makes it likewise impossible to predict with any confidence the impact of the Chilean experience upon the rest of Latin America.

A. There is no reason to believe, however, that a domino effect will be created. Such a reaction has failed to materialize from the Cuban example, in spite of the fact that the Cuban government has maintained a considerably more forthright dedication to Communism and to foreign subversion than is associated with any of Dr. Allende's pronouncements. It is not realistic to say that Chile itself is an exception to this Cuban generalization; Allende is close to Castro on a personal basis, but the long and gradual leftward tendency in Chile appears to have roots that preceded the Cuban experience, and the Chilean self-image would be offended by the suggestion that this major country was dominated and led in its development by a small and remote island.

B. The situations of Chile's neighbors vary considerably from each other, and a uniform reaction is highly improbable. This is fortified by the strength of nationalism everywhere.

1. The most important neighbor is Argentina, which has long been accustomed to asserting its dignity and its stature in opposition to Chile. It is not at all realistic to think that the present state of public opinion, to say nothing of the government, would meekly turn 180 degrees and head to the Communistic left.

2. Peru has its own brand of nationalism and statism, and these are jealously regarded by the government. There is also an 80 year tradition of rivalry with Chile, and bad feelings between the two countries.

3. Bolivia is so volatile that its reaction cannot be generalized. In any event, however, from the point of view of ITT Bolivia is relatively unimportant, and whatever reaction it does show is unlikely to be more stable than previous regimes and reactions have been.

4. The other countries of South America are insulated by distance and by other differences. Brazil is too large to be heavily influenced by Chile. Venezuela and Colombia are far away and nothing that is in prospect in either one of them indicates that they would be vulnerable to the Chilean example.

III

The reaction of the Department of State (D.O.S.) will necessarily depend upon the development of the factors considered in I and II above.

A. As a generalization, however, it is unlikely that D.O.S. will jeopardize hemispheric relations by taking an extremely hostile stance vis à vis Chile, or by making what D.O.S. would consider an overly-strenuous and impolitic intervention on behalf of one or more American companies with confiscated Chilean assets. D.O.S. is likely, in other words, to do whatever can be done in a restrained and realistic manner, as was the case in Peru, but it is unlikely to make an all-out effort in circumstances over which it exerts little control or leverage. The history of the D.O.S. involvement in the oil nationalization programs in Mexico in 1938, in Bolivia in the 1950's and in 1969, and with IPC in Peru, all point in this direction. Aid and other forms of cooperation might well be reduced, but it is not likely that the Hickenlooper Amendment will be invoked, at least publicly and officially. There are at least two reasons for this. First, the Allende government would be likely to make some offer of compensation; this might be inadequate, but it would at least be arguable, and this would undercut application of the Hickenlooper doctrine. Second, in any event D.O.S. will make a determined effort to preserve its flexibility and its options by refusing if at all possible to have recourse to so rigid a sanction.

B. Specifically, with reference to particular recommendations in the Gerrity memorandum:

1. I see no reason to imagine that D.O.S. will allow itself to be "pinned down on the record in a written exchange of views so that, in effect, a formal history is set down." There are innumerable ways of avoiding this, even while maintaining correspondence, and it seems clear enough that D.O.S. will not commit itself in writing to firm policy stances for the sole purpose of satisfying ITT.

2. It is not entirely clear to me why Mr. Gerrity contends, on the one hand, that it is important that ITT establish on the record the estimate of D.O.S. as to what will happen to U.S. investment in Chile; and on the other hand comments a few paragraphs later that D.O.S. has been wrong in Chile so far and is always wrong anyway. In this connection I think it is likely (although I am not certain) that D.O.S. expected a narrow victory by Allesandri [sic], so did ITT, and most other observers. In the event, the Allende margin over Allesandri [sic] was a bit more than 1% and no one purports to be infallible to that degree in any Latin American political situation.

3. In the top paragraph on page two, it seems to me presumptuous to "demand" that the White House require U.S. representatives in international banks to take a "strong stand" against any loan to countries expropriating American companies or discriminating against foreign private capital.

4. I also think that the second paragraph on page two, recommending that ITT request members of Congress to warn the Nixon administration that mistreatment of U.S. private capital will result in terminating U.S. contributions to international lending institutions, is presumptuous.

5. The fifth paragraph on page two, suggesting that ITT urge staff reductions in the U.S. diplomatic establishments in Latin America, is naive and unrealistic, and would certainly be resented in Washington.

6. All of the points discussed in paragraphs 3, 4 and 5 above would, if implemented in the manner indicated, in the Gerrity memorandum, be counter-productive rather than helpful. They would be ideally calculated to support leftist assertions about American economic imperialism, and their tendency would be to stimulate a nationalistic backlash against foreign private investment generally.

7. The reappraisal of the ITT position in Latin America referred to in the Gerrity memorandum might be helpful, but this should come after the Chilean situation has been clarified. Although it is impossible to be dogmatic or to read the future, it is likely that a thorough and dispassionate analysis would yield a reasonably optimistic estimate of a program based on increased investment in a broad cross section of industrial and commercial fields, with greater geographical diversification.

EXHIBIT 7

COUNCIL OF THE AMERICAS
680 Park Avenue, New York, New York

November 5, 1970

His Excellency Dr. Salvador Allende
President of the Republic of Chile
Palacio Presidencial La Moneda
Santiago, Chile

My dear Mr. President: . . .

3. With regard to the past, let me stress that companies operating in Chile with U.S. capital have substantially promoted the human and economic development of the Chilean people and their country. Foreign-capitalized companies have enhanced the personal dignity and self-fulfillment of many thousands of Chileans and their families by providing them with modern skill-training and general education, rapid promotion to positions of high responsibility within these companies, much-increased income and constantly growing opportunities for service to their country. Specifically, U.S.-capitalized companies have opened rich world markets to Chilean exports, and through import-substitution activities they have helped Chile to produce at home much of what it formerly needed to buy from abroad.

4. With regard to the future, and this is what is really important to Chile and to the U.S., I feel that the following statements represent the consensus of thinking in the forward-looking managements of most U.S. companies:

(a) Enlightened private enterprise working in close cooperation with an enlightened government is today the best (I am tempted to say the only) method for development. There are many examples around the world today to prove that this cooperative effort of private sector and government will be even more essential in the future.

(b) Nationalization of private economic enterprises, with subsequent ownership and management by the state, inevitably exacts a grievous social cost from people and their countries.

Hundreds of thousands of private savers, not only foreign but also Chilean, would be forcibly deprived of their investments in those enterprises slated for nationalization by your platform. There is no evidence that the incoming Chilean government will possess, or can acquire, the resources to afford these hundreds of thousands of private savers the prompt, adequate and effective compensation for nationalization which is specified under international law.

(c) Multinational companies are the most effective element for development today and will be even more so tomorrow, as:

(1) The multinational company "goes international" primarily to

serve or develop markets. Thus, it will prosper only if the host country prospers. It is committed to the host country's prosperity. It plans for the future.

(2) The multinational company is so complex that, to survive, it must be run by an efficient technostructure with a forward-looking philosophy with regard to profits and their distribution. Being basically growth-oriented, it will generally reinvest a large percentage of its earnings.

(3) The multinational company has prestige and power in its home country and can be the best ally, where it counts, to "sell" the need for overseas development.

(4) The multinational company has the technological, financial and manpower resources and the organization needed for success. It operates by objectives, but it is generally still flexible enough to react with the required speed when considering the all important "time factor of development."

(5) The multinational company is outward-looking and export-minded. Though it recognizes the value of intelligent import-substitution programs, it does not consider these as an end in themselves.

(6) The multinational company is trying hard to learn to become a good corporate citizen throughout the world. Due to the dynamic competitive society which it supports, it knows that if it fails in this very important task, others are there to take its place. In addition, its fundamental belief in a competitive philosophy results in its accepting pluralistic situations in private/public economies without undue fear of being overwhelmed.

I reiterate, the Council of the Americas is deeply concerned about what may happen to Chilean-U.S. relations. It is concerned that many years of collaboration which, in our view, have been to the overall good of Chile and the U.S., will cease. We are, above all, concerned that—at a time when the private sector in the U.S. has become both a dynamic and innovating force internationally and has acquired the techniques and the will for development—at a time when, due to its responsiveness to what the market wants, it is becoming increasingly involved with the quality of life—the U.S. private sector may be rejected by Chile in exchange for theories which once were new but which are no longer suitable to the pressing new needs of the year 2000.

The Council of the Americas earnestly desires to maintain the historic Chilean-U.S. cooperation. Council representatives are prepared to meet at any time, in any mutually acceptable place, with representatives of your government to work out ways and means of continuing this cooperation. Indeed, the Council and the forward-looking multinational corporations of which it is composed are eager to work with all who seek to build a peaceful, integrated, world-wide economy, devoted to rapid social development.

Sincerely,
(Signed) JOSE DE CUBAS, President
Council of the Americas

EXHIBIT 8

INTERNATIONAL TELEPHONE AND
TELEGRAPH CORPORATION
1707 L Street, N.W.
Washington, D.C. 20036

William R. Merriam
Vice President
Director, Washington Relations

October 1, 1971

The Honorable
Peter G. Peterson
Assistant to the President
  for International Economic Affairs
Old Executive Office Building
Washington, D.C. 20500

Dear Pete:

When Mr. Geneen lunched with you a few weeks ago, he stated he feared ITT'S seventy percent owned Chilean Telephone Company (Chiltelco) would soon be expropriated. This has now happened! The takeover was on September 29, 1971.

As Mr. Geneen said, we anticipated this action and were attempting to delay or prevent it. However, during the past month, the Chilean government moved rapidly with its campaign of harassment which went far beyond our anticipation. The following demoralizing incidents leading to expropriation took place during September:

Bank Accounts Frozen

In early September, Allende froze Chiltelco's bank funds, thus depriving ITT of existing operating cash and blocking the daily flow of customer payments to our accounts at the banks.

Records Confiscated

A few days later, the Chilean Revenue Service entered Chiltelco's Santiago headquarters, confiscated records, and announced an immediate investigation of company accounts.

ITT Officials Jailed

Last Saturday, September 25, a sizeable group of special police surrounded the home of Senor Benjamin Holmes, the manager of Chiltelco. Aged 71, Mr. Holmes is a distinguished, highly respected and well-known native-born Chilean citizen. The police startled and arrested Holmes in his bedroom, then placed him in prison after a lengthy interrogation.

Senor Gonzalo Von Wersch, also a native-born Chilean who manages another of our companies—Guias y Publicidad—which publishes yellow page directories—also was arrested and jailed.

Dr. Fernando Eguiguren, our distinguished Chilean attorney, was taken into custody; as was Senor Leon Berstein, the manager of our tele-communication factory.

After considerable legal intervention, we were able to get three of the Chileans released on bail, but the government felt it must keep one of them under detention. Senor Von Wersch remains in jail.

The charge against the foregoing gentlemen is some trumped-up accusation termed "fraud against the government."

Management and Legal Counsel Compromised

The forementioned terror tactics against our company officials is a well-known Communist ploy but one not customarily experienced in Latin America. Chilean actions badly damaged our interest and our chances of restitution. Not only have ITT officials been intimidated and the safety of their families jeopardized, but also our top management team and legal counsel have been placed in an untenable position. In any future negotiations or dealings with the Marxist-extremist government, our Chilean officials naturally will be cautious, thus, their usefulness will be limited.

Security of American Citizens Jeopardized

After these Chilean events, and because of a recent action against our visiting U.S. officials in another Latin American country, ITT will be hesitant about sending into Chile any officials from its New York head-quarters whether they be American citizens or other nationalities.

It is inconceivable that the lack of protection to U.S. private enterprise in foreign lands has reached the stage where not only its properties are confiscated without just compensation, but also foreign citizens working for American firms are unjustly intimidated and jailed as propaganda hostages by a supposedly friendly nation with which the United States has diplomatic relations.

When events degenerate to a level where U.S. corporations must hesitate before sending American officials into a supposedly· friendly country for legitimate business reasons then the situation calls for corrective measures. We believe recent action in Chile demonstrates this low stage has been reached.

U.S. Aid Continues

While all of this action by the Marxist government against U.S. firms is taking place, money derived from the U.S. taxpayers is still flowing into Chile in the form of aid.

In a meeting with Assistant Secretary of State Charles A. Meyer and his staff only a few days ago—September 28—we were informed that up to $1 million (U.S. dollars) are going into Chile *each month* from funds in the "Aid pipeline!" We believe this U.S. taxpayer money to the Marxist government should be terminated.

Also, we were told that funds in several "Inter-American Development Bank pipelines," not previously utilized, have been reallocated into a so-called earthquake emergency fund and made available to Chile. Considering the heavy U.S. contribution to the IADB, and the lack of a real emergency, such action should not have been permitted and, if possible, should now be rescinded.

Action Suggested

Besides curtailing the above-mentioned sources of aid to Chile, we believe the U.S. government should take every action which will bring President Allende's regime to the realization that his Marxist methods are incompatible with international practices, and inform him that he is to be held responsible for action against U.S. private enterprise.

It is noted that Chile's annual exports to the U.S. are valued at $154 million (U.S. dollars). As many U.S. markets as possible should be closed to Chile. Likewise, any U.S. exports of special importance to Allende should be delayed or stopped.

The U.S. should consult with other governments which are being effected [*sic*] by Chile's Marxism. This would include countries to which Chile owes money. Allende's treasury reserve is depleting rapidly and he has already suggested a moratorium on servicing Chile's foreign debt.

There are numerous justifiable leverages which the U.S. government could use to counteract or retaliate in this instance. We believe these leverages should be utilized to the fullest.

Sincerely,

(original signed by W. R. Merriam)

APPENDIX C

U.S. FINANCIAL AID TO CHILE AND
LATIN AMERICA

During the years 1961–68, a congressional report noted that U.S. official sources had channeled over $8 billion to Latin America. More than $1 billion of this total went to Chile in an effort to offset the country's rising Marxist tendencies. The State Department and AID stated in congressional hearings that "Chile is a country of major U.S. assistance emphasis because of its important political role in the Hemisphere."[1]

Assistance to Chile was in the form of direct aid, soft loans, military assistance, and earthquake and disaster relief, totaling approximately $1.5 billion between 1961 and 1971.[2] (This figure does not include private investment in Chile, or the country's exports to the United States, valued at about $154 million annually.) Figures for the period 1961–69 (later figures not given) are as follows, in millions of U.S. dollars:

1961	$ 132.8
1962	169.5
1963	83.7
1964	127.4
1965	130.9
1966	107.7
1967	284.6
1968	99.8
	$1,136.4

Figures for 1969 and 1970 were estimated to be over $100 million.[3] In addition, in 1971 the "Aid pipeline" was channeling up to $1 million per month into Chile, and the Inter-American Development Bank had made funds available to Chile from its earthquake emergency fund (Appendix B, Exhibit 8).

SELECTED REFERENCES

GIBSON, J. DOUGLAS, "Canada's Declaration of Less Dependence," *Harvard Business Review*, September–October, 1973, pp. 69–79.

GRIFFIN, JOSEPH P., "The Power of Host Countries over the Multinational: Lifting the Veil in the European Economic Community and the United States," *Law and Policy in International Business*, 6, 2 (spring 1974), 375–436.

1 *Congressional Record,* April 11, 1972.
2 *Ibid.*
3 *Ibid.*

JAMES, DANIEL, *Mexico and the Americas* (New York: Praeger, 1963).

JOHNSON, HARRY G., *Economic Policies Toward Less Developed Countries*, (Washington, D.C.: Brookings, 1967).

LEE, SPERRY, and S. WEBLY, *Multinational Corporations in Developed Countries: A Review of Recent Research and Policy Thinking* (Washington, D.C.: National Planning Institute, March 1973, pp. 1–77.

PERERA, VICTOR, "Law and Order in Chile," *The New York Times Magazine*, April 13, 1975, p. 15.

ROSENSTEIN-RODAN, PAUL N., "Why Allende Failed," *Challenge*, May–June 1974, pp. 7–13.

SAMPSON, ANTHONY, *The Sovereign State of ITT* (New York: Stein & Day, 1973).

SETHI, S. PRAKASH, and RICHARD H. HOLTON, eds., *Management of the Multinationals: Policies, Operations, and Research* (New York: Free Press, 1974), pp. 1–37, 77–87.

———, and JAGDISH N. SHETH, eds., *Multinational Business Operations: Environmental Aspects of Operating Abroad*, Vol. 1. (Pacific Palisades, Calif.: Goodyear, 1973).

SIGMUND, PAUL E., "The 'Invisible Blockade' and the Overthrow of Allende," *Foreign Affairs*, January 1974, pp. 322–40.

STERN, SAMUEL A., "The Judicial and Administrative Procedures Involved in the Chilean Copper Expropriations," *American Journal of International Law*, 66 (September 1972), 205–13.

United Nations, *Multinational Corporation in World Development*, ST/ECA, 190 (New York: Department of Economic and Social Affairs, United Nations, 1973).

United Nations, *The Impact of Multinational Corporations on Development and International Relations*, ST/ESA/6 (New York: United Nations Publications, 1974).

U.S. Congress, Senate, *Hearings Before the Subcommittee on Multinational Corporations of the Committee on Foreign Relations, The International Telephone and Telegraph Company and Chile, 1970–71*, March 20, 21, 22, 27, 28, 29, and April 2, 1973.

U.S. Congress, Senate, *Report to the Committee on Foreign Relations by the Subcommittee on Multinational Corporations, The International Telephone and Telegraph Company and Chile, 1970–71*, June 21, 1973, p. 2.

VAGTS, DETLEV F., "The Multinational Enterprise: A New Challenge for Transnational Law," *Harvard Law Review*, 83, 4 (February 1970), 739–92.

VICUNA, F. A., "Some International Law Problems Posed by the Nationalization of the Copper Industry by Chile," *American Journal of International Law*, 67 (October 1973), 711–27.

WALLACE, DON, JR., ed., *International Control of Investment: The Dusseldorf Corporation on Multinational Corporations* (New York: Praeger, 1974).

NORTHROP CORPORATION, LOS ANGELES

CONFLICTING PRESSURES FOR ILLEGAL POLITICAL CONTRIBUTIONS AND PAYOFFS IN THE UNITED STATES AND ABROAD—AND THE NEED FOR MECHANISMS FOR SOCIAL CONTROL

> For all the blurred lines, however, there is ample evidence that illegal acts and—by even a loose definition of business morality—unethical behavior have become all too common among many U.S. companies operating at home and abroad.
> —*Newsweek*, September 1, 1975

During the investigations following the break-in at the Democratic National Committee Headquarters in Washington's Watergate complex, it was discovered that a number of large corporations had made illegal political contributions to President Richard M. Nixon's reelection campaign. Further investigations revealed that in a significant number of cases, this was not simply a one-shot violation of the laws; such practices had persisted over a number of years, and many corporations had employed ingenious and often fraudulent ways to conceal them.

The author is grateful to the following people for their assistance in preparing this case study: Mr. John Phillips, Center for Law in the Public Interest, Los Angeles; Professor Tracy Western, Director, Communications Law Program, University of California at Los Angeles; Professor Melvin A. Eisenberg, Boalt School of Law, University of California at Berkeley.

To critics of big business, the news came as no surprise and provided additional evidence of the pervasive influence of corporations on this nation's political institutions and the formulation of public policy. The defenders of the corporations pointed out that in an era of increasing government intrusion into private enterprise and business activities, it reflected the growing power of government and political leaders to exert excessive pressure on business corporations to make political contributions. Some executives succumb to these pressures to avoid what they perceive to be potentially ruinous economic consequences for their corporations if they do not make contributions. It was also pointed out that in no case had a corporate executive been shown to have gained personally from such activities.

The arguments pro and con notwithstanding, both sides agree to the need for developing new mechanisms to (1) understand and clarify the sociopolitical environment that creates the pressures for such illegal activities; and (2) prevent the occurrence of similar events in the future.

The case of Northrop Corporation (Northrop) provides a good example of how a corporation goes about making such contributions and concealing them in a labyrinth of overseas subsidiaries and intracorporate accounting practices. It also shows how the multinational character of a corporation makes it difficult, if not impossible, to detect such illegal activities.

In the area of control mechanisms, the court-imposed solution has two novel characteristics. One, it calls for the enlargement of the board of directors and election to the board of four new "outside" directors who would be subject to judicial approval, the restructuring of the executive committee of the board, and the reconstituting and strengthening of the audit committee of the board. The court action against Northrop was instituted by a person who owned only two shares of company stock and was represented by the Center for Law in the Public Interest, a nonprofit law firm based in Los Angeles.

THE ISSUES

Among the many issues raised in the case that merit serious consideration and analysis from the viewpoint of managerial decision making and public policy are these:

1. How clean and aboveboard are the operating practices of large U.S. corporations? Are payoffs, slush funds, and the like mere aberrations, or are they quite widespread and pervasive, and commonly accepted as the cost of doing business at home and abroad?
2. Even when a corporation alleges that by engaging in illegal payoffs abroad, it is simply doing what it must to secure business, and that such an act is not illegal in terms of U.S. laws, is it reasonable to

assume that a corporation can maintain a split personality and would not resort to similar practices at home?

3. If business is indeed dishonest and has indulged in illegal practices, as has been shown recently in a number of cases involving large *multinational* corporations, why do so few executives go to jail, and why are the fines for their offenses so small when compared to their own net worth or their company's? Is there, in fact, a double standard of justice at work—one for the rich and powerful, another for the poor and helpless?

In terms of understanding differences between the legal framework and reality of corporate control and the need for developing better mechanisms for social control of corporations

1. What are the rights of stockholders in terms of access to information about activities of a corporation or its top executives that might embroil the company in future litigation and adversely affect its economic performance?

2. Is there anything in the nature of a business or corporation—for example, type of activity, size, management structure, or personalities of the top officers—that makes it desirable to engage in illegal political activities?

3. How is the interference by the courts in mandating the restructuring of the board of directors and other top management committees likely to affect the discretion of management decision making in its long-range planning as well as day-to-day operations? What happens if consumers, environmentalists, and other groups seek similar restructuring of the boards through the courts?

4. How are the court-imposed "outside" directors likely to behave and where does their responsibility lie? Is this a good mechanism for making corporations and their officers more accountable for their activities? What other alternatives are worth pursuing?

5. Should the courts entertain suits by stockholders with such a minuscule stake in the corporation? Doesn't it border on harassment? What kinds of limits should be imposed on the right of a stockholder to sue the corporation?

6. If illegal contributions cannot be stopped, isn't it better to make them legal, bring them out in the open, and institute some other mechanism to control their abuse?

THE FACTS OF THE CASE

On November 23, 1974, Northrop Corporation and its officers, including Thomas V. Jones, chairman of the board, president and chief executive, and James Allen, vice-president and assistant to the president, entered into a consent agreement in settlement of a civil action brought by Jay Springer, a stockholder, individually and on behalf of all Northrop stockholders. The suit charged the defendants with illegally using company funds for political contributions, making false and fictitious entries in the company books to hide such misappropriation of funds, and making false and misleading public reports in violation of the relevant regulations of the Securities and Exchange Commission.[1]

Earlier, during the summer of 1973, in the midst of the Watergate investigations, it was discovered that Northrop executives had been donating corporate funds to Nixon's 1972 reelection campaign. It also came to light that Nixon's Committee to Re-elect the President (CREEP) was not the only beneficiary of Northrop's beneficence. For thirteen years, beginning in 1961, Jones and Allen had directed a company slush fund that donated to the campaigns of Richard Nixon, Hubert Humphrey, Pierre Salinger, George Murphy, Edmund G. Brown, Sr., Ronald Reagan, and Ed Reinecke.[2]

In May 1974, Jones and Allen pleaded guilty to contributing $150,000 to CREEP. Northrop was fined $5,000, Jones $5,000, and Allen $1,000 by United States District Court Judge George L. Hart. Jones and the company were the first ever to be brought to court for violating a 1940 law prohibiting companies that receive big government contracts from making campaign donations. Allen was fined under the statute prohibiting any company from making political contributions.

Leon Jaworski, the Watergate special prosecutor, said, however, that his office had not uncovered any evidence indicating that Northrop's political contributions were in any way connected to receiving government contracts. In a statement to the press, a Northrop official declared that "the officials involved" reimbursed the full $150,000 to the company and that Jones himself paid the company's $5,000 fine. The statement hinted that the board of directors had considered firing Jones, but decided to keep him on in the best interests of the company.[3]

A few days later, on May 7, Jones announced that he would be resigning from all outside directorships. These included seats at U.S. Steel, Times Mirror Co. (Los Angeles), and Wells Fargo. A Northrop spokesman said: "He has decided that he isn't going to serve on outside business boards so that he can devote his full business efforts to Northrop." A few days later Allen resigned as a director of Northrop and also gave up his directorship of Captech, Inc., a diversified Long Beach, California, com-

---

1 *Jay Springer et al.* v. *Thomas V. Jones, et al.*, Civil Action No. 74–1455–F. United States District Court, Central District of California.

2 For a chronological narrative of events leading up to the disclosure of campaign contributions by Northrop and the conviction of the company and its officers, see "Firm Pleads Guilty in Nixon Donations," *San Francisco Chronicle*, May 2, 1974, p. 10; "Northrop Corp., 2 Officers Fined for Nixon Gifts," *The Wall Street Journal*, May 2, 1974, p. 14; "Northrop's Jones to Quit Posts on Outside Boards," *The Wall Street Journal*, May 7, 1974, p. 3; "Northrop's Allen Quits 2 Directorships after Being Fined for Political Donation," *The Wall Street Journal*, May 10, 1974, p. 8.

3 *The Wall Street Journal*, May 2, 1974, p. 14.

pany. When asked about his resignation, he said, "I think it was proper to resign as a director, so I did that." [4]

Later, as a result of further investigations, it turned out that Northrop (1) had made in excess of $300,000 of not necessarily illegal contributions to a host of federal, state, and local candidates from 1961 to 1973, using money illegally laundered through a Paris consultant; (2) paid $450,000 intended as bribes for two Saudi Arabian generals, (3) paid other possible bribes to politicians and military officials in Indonesia and Iran; (4) and had General Paul Stehlin, vice-president of the French National Assembly, on its payroll.[5]

The Corporation

Northrop is a relatively small, California-based company in the aerospace industry. In 1972 its total assets amounted to $409.9 million, whereas the giant Boeing's were $2 billion.[6] Subsidiaries specialize in telecommunications, nuclear power plants, and navigation systems, but its main product is aircraft, especially fighter planes. Since 1965 there have been over 1,000 F–5 Freedom Fighters sold to the air forces of twenty different countries. Its new model, the F–5E Tiger II, is expected to sell just as well, if not better. Northrop also makes the main fuselage for the Boeing 747 and various components of the U.S. Army's air defense system. Forty-six percent of its 1973 sales, which totaled $700 million, were to the federal government.

The Lawsuit

The legal action was initiated in May 1974 by Jay Springer of New York, a stockholder, and the Center for Law in the Public Interest (CLPI). The defendants were Northrop; President Jones; Vice-President Allen; Vice-President, Operations, Frank W. Lloyd; and Vice-President Finance and Treasurer, James D. Willson. One of the results of this suit was the discovery of the $1.2 million secret political slush fund. Before then it was believed that the only sum in question was the $150,000 donated to Nixon's campaign. During the summer, however, CLPI attorneys had

---

4 *The Wall Street Journal,* May 10, 1974, p. 8.
5 Henry Weinstein, "Northrop: Fame in Aircraft, Shame in Politics," *The New York Times,* May 18, 1975, Sec. 3, p. 1; "Northrop Committee Admits Firm Paid $450,000 Intended to Bribe Two Saudis," *The Wall Street Journal,* June 6, 1975, p. 5; "French Official on Northrop Payroll," *San Francisco Chronicle,* June 7, 1975, p. 1; "Northrop Hired Many High-Level Agents To Help Foreign Sales," *The Wall Street Journal,* June 9, 1975, p. 4; "Northrop Aide Is Quoted as Saying Sales of Warplanes to U.S. Involve Politics," *The Wall Street Journal,* June 11, 1975, p. 10; "Agents of U.S. Firms Abroad Are Termed Influence Peddlers by Ex-Northrop Aide," *The Wall Street Journal,* June 10, 1975, p. 6.
6 Eileen Shanahan, "S.E.C. Says Northrop Kept $30 Million Secret Fund," *The New York Times,* April 17, 1975, p. 56.

obtained testimony from several Northrop executives. The depositions revealed that the contribution to CREEP was only one of many political contributions made over a span of thirteen years. This testimony was in direct contradiction to the information Northrop had released to its shareholders in May, which had implied that the CREEP contribution was "an abnormal departure from the high standards of business conduct" at Northrop.

Prior to the commencement of this action, the board of directors of the company initiated a special investigation through Ernst and Ernst (its independent auditors) and Price Waterhouse (auditors specially retained for this purpose). The purpose of the investigation was stated as follows:

(i) to identify the nature and amount of any contributions since 1961 of corporate funds for political purposes, either directly or indirectly, and whether made through employees, committees, independent contractors, or otherwise; (ii) to identify unauthorized or illegal payments by consultants, agents or other representatives of the Company; (iii) to determine the extent to which the Company has been reimbursed for the contributions that were the subject of the information filed by the Watergate Special Prosecutor and the expenses and disbursements to the Company which resulted from those contributions; and (iv) to assist in preparing and filing any required amended corporate tax returns and documents required to be submitted to the SEC and the Stock Exchange.[7]

The auditors' report showed, among other things, that corporate funds had not been used for the personal gain of any officer or director. It also showed that William Savy, a European marketing consultant, was only one of those who returned corporate funds to the company for political contributions.[8]

The SEC Suit

On April 17, 1975, the Securities and Exchange Commission filed suit against Northrop, accusing it of failing to disclose that it had created a slush fund for "unlawful political contributions" and of failing to keep track of about $30 million in payments to consultants and others. The charges stated that Northrop failed to disclose to its stockholders what it was doing with significant sums of money. Jones and Allen were also named as defendants. The SEC's complaint alleged that the fund was in existence from 1971 through 1973. The complaint also alleged that Northrop had maintained a secret fund used for illegal campaign contributions since 1961.

[7] *Springer* v. *Jones, Civil Action* No. 74–1455–F. United States District Court, Central District of California.
[8] "Northrop Tentatively Settles Class Action over Illegal Gifts to '72 Nixon Campaign," *The Wall Street Journal*, November 21, 1974, p. 22.

Although the SEC suit did not state directly that the $30 million fund had been used illegally, the company itself seemed to imply this when it said that it was making a study of "approximately $30 million paid or to be paid in sales commissions or fees" to certain "consultants or sales agents in regard to the company's foreign sales." [9] A week before, SEC cited a suit against United Brands (formerly United Fruit) for allegedly paying a $1.25 million bribe to Honduran officials.

Apparently most of the $30 million was spent abroad, where Northrop had been aggressively promoting its fighter planes. The SEC suit stated that Northrop did not adequately account for the disbursement of the $30 million. Northrop denied this, stating

> These disbursements were in all cases made to individuals and companies under contractual commitments. . . . They were made through normal disbursing and accounting procedures, and all transactions were properly recorded on the company's books.[10]

Northrop immediately agreed to a permanent injunction against "future violations of applicable laws and SEC regulations," although it did not admit to any guilt.

How the Funds Were Laundered

Attorney William Savy, a Northrop consultant based in Paris, is one of the pivotal characters in the laundering technique adopted by Northrop. Savy was overpaid for his services to the company. He converted his overpayments into cash and gave them to Stanley Simon of New York, with whom Savy had had business dealings. James Allen would then pick up the cash—in $10,000 packets—from Simon. About $500,000 was delivered in this fashion.[11] The next link in the chain was another Northrop consultant, Frank J. De Francis, based in Washington. De Francis picked the money up from Allen and carried it to John R. Blandford, a Washington lawyer who had served as chief counsel to the House Armed Services Committee. De Francis believed it "advisable" to pay Blandford $1,000 a month in order to obtain "protection" for Northrop.[12] When the text of the report prepared by Ernst and Ernst was released by the Senate Subcommittee on Multinational Corporations in June 1975, "Northrop's network of the politically prominent and the professionally obscure" was revealed.[13]

In addition to the services of Savy and De Francis in the U.S., Northrop was shown to have hired high-level contacts to help promote overseas sales,

9 "Northrop Is Accused by SEC of Failing to Disclose It Had Political Slush Fund," *The Wall Street Journal*, April 17, 1975, p. 6; see also Shanahan, "S.E.C. Says Northrop Kept $30 Million Secret Fund," p. 1.
10 "A Question of Bribery," *Newsweek*, April 28, 1975, p. 70.
11 "Northrop Asks U.S. for Secrecy on Details of $30 Million Outlays for Foreign Sales," *The Wall Street Journal*, April 18, 1975, p. 16.
12 *The Wall Street Journal*, June 9, 1975, p. 4.
13 "All the Right People," *Newsweek*, June 16, 1975, p. 65.

among them General Paul Stehlin, a former chief of the French air force; General Adolf Galland, a World War II Luftwaffe combat pilot; Hubert Weisbrod, a Swiss lawyer who had helped promote Lockheed Aircraft Corporations' foreign sales, and Franz Bach, a former member of the West German parliament.[14]

As the focus of its foreign dealings, Northrop covertly created the Economic and Development Corporation (EDC) of Zurich, Switzerland. Following a model allegedly used by Lockheed, De Francis organized the company in 1971 to work "behind the scenes through the use of the right people in the right places." [15] Since its inception, EDC had served as a conduit for more than $3 million in commissions to foreign politicians and others on the sales of F–5 fighters. But Andreas Froriep, the Zurich lawyer who runs the operation, claims EDC "was not involved in any bribing or passing of bribes." [16] Northrop's top executives also deny they knew of EDC's dealings. Jones testified before the Senate subcommittee that he had no idea what EDC did with the money, who owned the company, or why they got a 1.5% commission on all F–5 sales overseas.[17] Not limited to operating in Europe alone, Northrop hired a former CIA official, Kermit Roosevelt, who had been involved in supporting current rulers in the Middle East on behalf of the U.S. government, to "actively participate in establishing and maintaining the contacts of Northrop on the highest levels of government in the Middle East." [18]

Northrop's executive committee also admitted passing $450,000 to Adnan Khashoggi, a Saudi Arabian businessman, and his Triad Financial Establishment to be used to bribe two Saudi Arabian generals during negotiations to sell the F–5E fighter to Saudi Arabia.

How the Officers Were Treated by the Company

Allen, 68, resigned from his post on the board of directors in March 1974 and retired as vice-president the following December. Jones, still in his fifties, in agreement with the settlement of the class action suit, will step down from the presidency and will be replaced by mid-1976. He has paid to Northrop $155,000 in fines and reimbursements. At that time some believed that he would lose his titles of chairman and chief executive officer as well.[19]

Pursuant to the six-month study of the executive committee of Northrop's board of directors, which blamed Jones for the corporate "atmosphere" that led to Northrop's controversial payouts, Jones resigned as chairman, remaining at least temporarily as chief executive. A search for

14 *The Wall Street Journal,* June 9, 1975.
15 *Ibid.,* p. 4.
16 *Newsweek,* June 16, 1975.
17 "Northrop's Men Traveled about Coated in Cash," *San Francisco Sunday Examiner & Chronicle,* June 15, 1975, Sec. A, pp. 16–17.
18 *Newsweek,* June 16, 1975, p. 65.
19 "Northrop's Punishment for Campaign Giving," *Business Week,* February 24, 1975, p. 60.

"Mr. Clean"—an outsider untainted by illegal political contributions and foreign payoffs—has begun. Richard W. Miller, current chairman of the executive committee, is the interim chairman of the board.[20]

Northrop has released Jones and Allen from further liability to the company. Springer signed the release reluctantly. He might even bring another suit in order to "dump Jones—his original goal" and collect punitive damages [21] if the predictions about Jones's complete removal from Northrop prove false.

The Consent Order

The agreement between Northrop and Jay Springer and CLPI not only permanently enjoined Northrop and its executives from making illegal political gifts but also contained some novel and important provisions aimed at restructuring top management and the board of directors to prevent similar activities in the future. The important features of the agreement are as follows:

A. Actions as to Past Activities

Northrop executives are "permanently enjoined" from including false or misleading information in annual or other reports; soliciting proxies from the shareholders based on false information; making false or fictitious entries in the company books; and using any funds or facilities of the company for illegal political purposes.

Jones and Allen must pay back $50,000 and $10,000, respectively, in addition to monies already reimbursed the company by them. None of the defendants is to be reimbursed by Northrop for any expenses incurred due to this litigation.

The executive committee of the board of directors will continue and complete the investigation of Northrop begun by two sets of auditors. The purpose of the investigation is to discover the extent of all political campaign contributions and the way funds were funneled, and how Northrop has handled its foreign sales in the past, particularly the extent of any bribes made to ensure these foreign sales.

The company must make the auditors' report public and file a copy of it with the Securities and Exchange Commission. It must be completed by November 25, 1974.

Until the report is received and acted upon, there must be board approval for any new or revised contracts with consultants if total compensation will exceed $200,000 or if the contractual relationship is to be a sensitive one. If total compensation is to exceed $35,000 in a year or $50,000 on an accumulated basis, written approval of counsel and of the president (or vice-president international in the instance of a foreign consultant) is required.

---

20 "In Business This Week," *Business Week,* August 4, 1975, p. 30.
21 *Ibid.*

B. New Outside Directors and Procedures for Their Selection

The company must elect three new directors and recommend them plus one more to the shareholders at the annual meeting. The final appointments will be subject to court approval. All four directors must be "independent outside directors," that is, they must not be a Northrop officer, they must not have received in the past four years nor will they receive in the coming year more than $25,000 for services rendered or from any sales, and they must not be associated with any company that has or will receive more than 1 percent of its gross sales from Northrop. The plaintiffs will propose up to six candidates to be considered for the posts along with other candidates.

C. Reconstitution of the Executive Committee of the Board of Directors

Until the annual meeting following December 31, 1976, the executive committee membership must be changed so that five of its six members will be independent outside directors (three of whom shall be new ones); the chairman will also be an independent outside director. Only independent outside directors will vote on matters having to do with the investigation.

The size of the board will be increased to fifteen persons, 60 percent of whom must be independent outside directors. The executive committee must also be made up of 60 percent of independent outside directors. The entire membership of the audit and nominating committees must be made up of independent outside directors.

D. Reconstruction of the Audit Committee and Nominating Committee of the Board of Directors

The audit committee is to be appointed by the board of directors. It is to be composed entirely of independent outside directors.

The nominating committee is to be set up in like manner.

E. New President

Within eighteen months (by mid-1976) the company will elect a new president. It was agreed that Jones would step aside as president, although nothing was said about his retaining his positions as chairman and chief executive officer.

F. Involvement in Political Activities

The use for political purposes of any Northrop funds and facilities is to be prohibited for two years, and the good citizenship committee is to be abolished. After the two-year period, this policy can be changed but only with shareholder approval.

Proxy solicitation materials to be submitted to shareholders before the next annual meeting will be subject to prior review by the plaintiff shareholders.

It was necessary for Northrop to make several amendments to its articles and bylaws in order to comply with the conditions of the consent order. At the same time it issued these changes, the board of directors also issued a resolution concerning its political contributions policy. It denounced the illegal use of company funds as not being in the corporation's best interests and prohibited this from being done again. However, it reserved the right to use company funds for certain political, nonpartisan uses in order to promote Northrop's normal business operations.

EVALUATION OF THE SETTLEMENT AND ITS IMPLICATIONS

What the settlement will mean to Northrop and to all big corporations is still a subject of controversy. There are those like Richard W. Miller, an investment banker and Northrop director, who think that it will change nothing. Federal Judge Warren J. Ferguson, who approved the settlement, says: "This is going to have a serious impact not only on Northrop but as a precedent for all large corporations. There's no question it's a landmark." [22]

According to the consent order, Springer had the right to submit a list of names for the four new independent director positions to the nominating committee. CLPI disagreed with four of his five choices and presented its own list of possible choices to the company. Northrop accepted two of them—William F. Ballhaus, president of Beckman Instruments, Inc., and a former Northrop executive vice president; and O. Meredith Wilson, former chairman of the Federal Reserve Bank of San Francisco and former president of the University of Oregon—and chose two others: Richard J. Flamson, III, president of Security Pacific Corporation, the holding company that controls California's second largest bank; and Thomas C. Barger, retired chairman of Arabian American Oil Company (Aramco). The choices have now to be approved by Judge Ferguson.

Some Northrop officials are quite disgruntled by the amount of power Springer, who owns two shares, has been given. Springer will play the role of watchdog over the company; if he sees that the company is wandering away from any of the terms of the settlement, he can complain to Judge Ferguson, who retains jurisdiction.

Melvin A. Eisenberg, corporate reform expert and law professor at the University of California at Berkeley who worked with CLPI attorneys to draw up the settlement, responded to the bitterness expressed by Northrop vice-president Les Daly when he asked, "What right does a guy with two shares have to claim to represent all the stockholders?" by saying, "Other shareholders had the right to object in court [none did], and Northrop didn't have to settle." [23]

In Eisenberg's opinion, the impact of the settlement will have much to do with whether or not it seizes people's imaginations—whether or not, for example, a board composed of a majority of outside independent directors is an idea whose time has come. He thinks it may just be that the Northrop settlement may well become a model for other settlements and perhaps eventually a model for legislation.

He also sees the transformation of the board, its strengthening and reshaping into a powerful monitoring body, as part of a process of building several bases for control of the actual policymakers, who are management. It is an addition to the control potential of growing shareholder power and the independent accountant auditors. No one base would be able to exercise enough leverage—particularly not the shareholders alone. If, as he proposes, control of the proxy machinery on management's behalf is vested solely in independent outside directors who comprise 60 percent of the board, along with control of the audit committee, then the existing nucleus of independent directors, through the proxy machinery, would at least in form choose the new directors, who would then be beholden to them rather than to management, as is now the case. This method he sees as far more likely to achieve solid, long-term results than choosing outside independent directors in terms of constituent interest groups— for example, a consumer director or a labor director, or having the government intervene. *Business Week* magazine comments on the subject:

> A basic question raised by the entire corporate political contributions scandal is the ability of any board of directors to monitor management. Skeptics doubt, for example, that even Northrop's new "independent" board would have discovered the company's slush fund.[24]

A review of recent court cases and activities of the Securities and Exchange Commission (SEC) indicates that at least in a limited manner the courts and the regulatory agencies are imposing constraints on stockholders' rights to elect their board of directors. The constraints imposed so far have been either in the name of broader public interest or in the interest of debt holders of the corporation. Thus, in the case of *Herald Co. v. Seawell,* the court held that the directors of the Herald Company, who owned the *Denver Post,* had the discretionary power "to act in the public interest at potential financial cost to the stockholders." [25] It was the first time a court had suggested that a corporation could block a takeover

23 *Ibid.*
24 *Ibid.*
25 "Herald Co. v. Seawell: A New Corporate Social Responsibility?" *University of Pennsylvania Law Review,* 121, 5 (May 1973), 1157; see also *Herald Co. v. Seawell,* Vol. 472, F. 2d, p. 1081 (10th Cir. 1972).

bid by purchasing its own shares for reasons other than to protect business interests. It was also the first judicial assertion that corporate management had an obligation to operate its business in a socially responsible manner.[26]

In the case of Mattel, Inc., one of the country's largest makers of toys and leisure time products, the SEC charged the company with making false and misleading press releases at various times during 1972 and 1973 overestimating the company's profits in these years. Mattel entered into a consent order, without admitting any wrongdoing, whereby it agreed to: not engage in similar antifraud violations of the (SEC) provisions in the future; appoint two additional independent directors, cleared by the court and the SEC, increasing the size of the board to ten directors; establish a SEC-cleared financial control and audit committee; set up a litigation and claims committee of three SEC-approved directors to study SEC's complaint and determine if any action should be taken against current or past Mattel officers or directors.[27]

A month later, however, Mattel announced that the company's continuing investigation showed that their financial statements of previous years "inaccurately reflected in material respects the financial condition and results of operations" for the periods covered.[28] The revelations led SEC to amend its earlier consent order to require the company to name a new independent majority of eight directors to its board and appoint a special counsel to investigate misrepresentations in prior financial statements. The executive committee of the board was also required to have a majority of outside directors. Thus, the SEC took the unusual step of seeking a court order "requiring that control of a company's board be turned over to people unaffiliated with the company." [29]

---

[26] *Ibid.;* see also Phillip I. Blumberg, "Corporate Responsibility and the Social Crisis," *Boston University Law Review,* 50 (1970), pp. 157–74.

[27] "Mattel Charged with Issuing False Reports," *The Wall Street Journal,* August 6, 1974, p. 7.

[28] "Mattel Says It Has Found Possible Errors In Fiscal '71 Financial Reports," *The Wall Street Journal,* September 9, 1974, p. 14.

[29] "Mattel Told to Put Outsiders in Majority of Board Seats, Undergo Special Audit," *The Wall Street Journal,* October 3, 1974, p. 4.

APPENDIX

CENTER FOR LAW IN THE PUBLIC INTEREST

The Center for Law in the Public Interest is a nonprofit corporation based in Los Angeles. Its six attorneys provide legal aid without charge to people and groups who seek redress on issues of broad public importance. It is supported by foundation grants and public contributions and from court-awarded attorneys' fees. There is a board of trustees, which deals with policy and allocation of funds.

Presently there are three main areas of concentration for their legal efforts. These are political reform and access to information, environmental quality, and civil rights.

Political Reform and Access to Information. This area "focuses on legal methods of reforming the conduct of government officials and big business who have infringed the public's right to fair and informed elections." *Springer* v. *Jones* is one of the cases in this category. Others deal with the right to obtain birth control information and one-sided electioneering being paid for by utility ratepayers.

Environmental Quality. The CLPI has been particularly active in the field of the environment. Several of its cases involved the California Environmental Quality Act of 1970 and its key provision, the environmental impact report. The court decisions in some of these cases have helped to clarify and define the act and the report. Coastal oil drilling, land use planning, transportation planning, and energy conservation have been the subjects in cases involving this act. In addition, the CLPI's litigation has dealt with the problems of proper planning for an urban environment and its consequences for southern California in three major areas of concern—transportation and air quality, land use planning, and the development of nuclear power technology. These cases have gained national attention because California's environmental legislation is the pacesetter for the nation. The success of California's efforts to prevent further environmental abuses, and to correct present problems, will have a tremendous impact on the planning decisions of other states.

Civil Rights. The CLPI has filed more than a dozen lawsuits aimed at making a reality out of Title VII of the 1964 Civil Rights Act (it is illegal to discriminate in employment practices on the basis of race, sex, or national origin). Much of the successful litigation and negotiation has improved the employment status of blacks, Mexican-Americans, and women and has brought millions of dollars into the minority communities of Los Angeles.

SELECTED REFERENCES

BLUMBERG, PHILLIP I., E. GOLDSTON, and G. D. GIBSON, "Corporate Responsibility and the Social Crisis," *Boston Law Review*, 50 (1970), 157–210.

———, ———, and ———, "Corporate Social Responsibility Panel: The Constituencies of the Corporation and the Role of the Institutional Investor," *The Business Lawyer*, 28 (March 1973), 177–213.

———, ———, and ———, "Reflections on Proposals for Corporate Reform Through Change in the Composition of the Board of Directors: Special Interest or Public Directors," *The Unstable Ground: Corporate Social Policy in a Dynamic Society*, ed. S. Prakash Sethi (Los Angeles: Melville, 1974), pp. 112–34.

CHANDLER, MARVIN, "It's Time to Clean Up the Boardroom," *Harvard Business Review*, September–October, 1975, pp. 73–82.

EISENBERG, MELVIN A., "The Legal Roles of Shareholder and Management in Modern Corporate Decision-Making," *California Law Review*, January 1969, pp. 1–60.

———, "Access to the Corporate Proxy Machinery," *Harvard Law Review*, 83, 7 (May 1970), 1489.

———, "Megasubsidiaries: The Effect of Corporate Structure on Corporate Control," *Harvard Law Review*, 84, 7 (May 1971), 1577.

———, "Voting Membership in Publicly Held Corporations," in *The Unstable Ground: Corporate Social Policy in a Dynamic Society*, ed. S. Prakash Sethi (Los Angeles: Melville, 1974), pp. 135–50.

———, "Legal Models of Management Structure in the Modern Corporation: Officers, Directors, and Accountants," *California Law Review*, 63, 2 (March 1975), 375–439.

FLOM, JOSEPH H., and PETER A. ATKINS, "The Expanding Scope of SEC Disclosure Laws," *Harvard Business Review*, July–August, 1974, pp. 109–19.

HEATHERINGTON, J. A. C., "Fact and Legal Theory: Shareholders, Managers, and Corporate Social Responsibility," *Stanford Law Review*, 21 (January 1969), 248–92.

"Herald Co. v. Seawell: A New Corporate Social Responsibility?" *University of Pennsylvania Law Review*, 121, 5 (May 1973), 1157–69.

Herald Co. v. Seawell, Vol. 472, F.2d, p. 1081 (10th Cir. 1972).

NADER, RALPH, and MARK J. GREEN, eds., *Corporate Power in America* (New York: Grossman, 1973).

SCHWARTZ, DONALD E., "The Federal Chartering of Corporations: A Modest Proposal," in *The Unstable Ground: Corporate Social Policy in a Dynamic Society*, ed. S. Prakash Sethi (Los Angeles: Melville, 1974), pp. 152–68.

COCA-COLA
AND THE MIDDLE EAST CRISIS

TRADE DISCRIMINATION AND UNDUE PRESSURE FROM FOREIGN NATIONS AGAINST A FRIENDLY FOREIGN COUNTRY AND CONTRARY TO U.S. FOREIGN POLICY

[It is] very disturbing indeed and very mischievous—when private groups or businesses or individuals take it on themselves, by act or omission, to alter or dictate or defeat official policies of the United States Government. This amateur policy making—or policy breaking—can be accomplished by almost any group or organization endowed with the conviction that it knows more about some aspect of foreign policy than anybody else and with the will to intimidate officials or other organizations that are not very hard to intimidate. It has been done by business interests seeking a competitive advantage, by organized labor, and by those sterling patriots whose self-designed task it is to keep the rest of us in line, loyal and true to the red, white, and blue . . .

—SENATOR J. WILLIAM FULBRIGHT

Congressional hearings conducted in March 1975 by Senator Frank Church (D, Idaho), chairman of the Subcommittee on Multinational Corporations of the Senate Foreign Relations Committee, revealed that Arab pressure on U.S. and other foreign companies not to sell or invest in Israel was more widespread than had been earlier expected. As many as 1,500 American firms were listed on the Arab blacklist.[1]

What started as a feeble and largely ineffective attempt by the Arab

1 "The Furor over the Blacklist," *Newsweek*, March 10, 1975, p. 59.

league in the early 1960s seemed to have mushroomed into a widely used and quite potent weapon as a result of the 1973–74 Arab oil embargo against the United States and other industrialized nations to force them to bring pressure on Israel in order to seek a solution of the Palestinian issue and also to regain Arab territories occupied by Israel as the result of the Arab-Israel War of 1973.

Pursuant to the lifting of the embargo, Arab nations have moved boldly and openly to discriminate (or punish) those businesses, including some of the largest banks and investment companies in Western Europe and the United States, that are suspected to be pro-Israel.[2] The resultant publicity has revealed that the acquiescence of American business, including the largest of the multinational corporations, has been more pervasive than was originally anticipated and appeared to have become widespread with the increase in Arab wealth and consequent improved business prospects.[3]

The attitude of American business shows an ambivalence that is not unusual, given the complexity of the issue and the conflicting pressures brought upon it by various sources. Similarly, the U.S. government has been equally vague and ambivalent and has demonstrated a large gap between rhetoric and action. While President Ford has condemned boycotts as "totally contrary" to American principles, the Department of Commerce has shown a less than adequate commitment to discouraging American firms' compliance with Arab demands. Thus, only a handful of firms are filing the data required by federal law if an American firm has encountered boycott demands. Furthermore, the Department of Commerce has continued to circulate offers for Arab business opportunities that contain restrictive provisions against persons or companies supporting Israel, contending that its responsibility was fulfilled by affixing such offers with a "small print" rubber stamp informing exporters about U.S. policy and also stating that "exporters are 'encouraged and requested' but aren't 'legally prohibited' from actions in support of Israel."[4] It refused to provide data to the appropriate congressional committees on the names of companies that have acceded to Arab pressures, stating that this "could do 'irreparable harm' to the companies and industries involved . . . [and make them] vulnerable to domestic pressures and economic reprisals."[5]

It should be noted that the law provides for the public disclosure of information except where the Secretary of the Commerce Department determines that disclosure would be contrary to the national interest.

2 Neil Ulman, "Publicity of Arab Boycott Has Banks on Both Sides Wishing Fuss Would Fade," *The Wall Street Journal*, March 6, 1975, p. 28. See also "Blacklist: A Cowardly Attitude," *Newsweek*, February 24, 1975, p. 70.
3 See, for example, "Standard Oil Backs Arabs," *San Francisco Chronicle*, August 2, 1973, p. 1; "Big Oil Firms Tried to Shape U.S. Policy in Mideast at Arabs' Behest, Memos Show," *The Wall Street Journal*, August 7, 1974, p. 5; "Texco Claims It Was Responsible Citizen in Arab Embargo Acts," *The Wall Street Journal*, August 8, 1974, p. 7; "Boycott by Arabs Affecting Israel," *The New York Times*, April 20, 1975, p. 6.
4 "Morton Won't Yield Arab Boycott Data to Congress; Contempt Citation Possible," *The Wall Street Journal*, September 23, 1975, p. 21.
5 *Ibid.*; see also "Suit Charges U.S. Aids Arab Boycott," *The New York Times*, September 11, 1975, p. 1.

However, it is hard to argue that supporting the Arab boycott is in the national interest.

THE ISSUES

The Coca-Cola controversy, although it took place between 1964 and 1968, reveals the main ethical, social, political, and economic dilemmas involved in such a case. For the purposes of analysis, the problem can be posed in the following terms:

1. Does a company have a moral responsibility to take a stand either for or against an expressed U.S. government policy even at the cost of possible injury to its stockholders and the company's future market position?

2. What should a company do when a decision based on purely economic grounds is likely to be misinterpreted as discriminatory or racist?

3. How should a company avoid becoming involved in questions of foreign policy? What is the responsibility of a company when its decisions are likely to be interpreted in foreign countries as an expression of U.S. foreign policy?

4. Does a publicly owned company have the right to take a controversial political position and represent it as the opinion of its stockholders? In the case of Coca-Cola, management held most of the stock, but it also wanted to hold together an international network of bottlers who had a considerable economic stake in the company's actions. Considering the power of the bottlers, it would not have been wise to antagonize them.

5. What should be the decision-making process to assist a company in developing a suitable and effective response to similar problems, whose frequency is likely to increase: investment in South Africa; selling arms to poor nations; marketing of products in less developed countries that are unnecessary, or promoting theirs in a manner that is likely to misguide or harm the consumer who could afford them. Examples of the latter can be found in the manner in which infant baby formula as a substitute for mother's milk and nutritionally poor beverages and processed foods are promoted by the large multinational corporations in the less developed countries.[6]

THE INCIDENT

In late 1964 the management of Coca-Cola was faced with a crucial policy decision concerning its overseas business: whether to grant a bottling franchise in Israel to its then distributor, the Tempo Bottling

[6] For some examples of marketing practices and their unintended adverse social consequences, see S. Prakash Sethi, *Images and Products: Marketing Institutional Advertising, and the Public Interest* (Santa Barbara, Calif.: Wiley/Hamilton, 1976).

Company of Israel, thereby antagonizing its Arab customers who were, in effect, at war with Israel.[7]

In 1951, three years after the modern State of Israel was founded (May 14, 1948), the Arab nations set up an economic boycott against certain companies doing business with the Israelis.[8] In most instances the Arabs had not objected to ordinary trade with Israel but had enforced the ban when capital goods or military equipment was involved.[9]

Had Coca-Cola accepted Tempo's application for the bottling franchise, the Israeli company would have built its own bottling plant and purchased syrup but not the finished product from Coca-Cola.

In January 1965 the company decided that the potential demand for Coca-Cola in Israel did not justify a bottling plant at that time and therefore refused the franchise. Several important considerations were responsible for the company's decision.

The principal reason was profits: The potential Israeli market for Coke—some 2.5 million Israelis—was dwarfed by the 104.7 million Arab population in the Arab League countries.[10] The Arabs had been among Coke's heaviest consumers from the time the soft drink had been introduced in the Middle East during World War II. Even tiny Kuwait had a per capita consumption of 175 bottles a year—nearly double the average United States rate. The hot desert climate and the Arab taboo against alcoholic spirits combined to make Coke a widely consumed beverage in the Middle East.[11]

In contrast, early governments of Israel, to minimize their exchange problems, had yielded to local citrus fruit lobbyists and had abrogated Abraham Feinberg's contract to bottle Coke in 1949. Coca-Cola knew that American companies such as Zenith Radio Corporation and Ford Motor Company had been barred from doing business in Arab countries because they sold their products in Israel. Therefore, it seemed that Coca-Cola might be able to operate either in the Arab countries or in Israel, but not in both.[12] If business firms have an obligation to their customers as well as to their stockholders, then Coca-Cola certainly owed such an obligation to the Arabs, who had long been devoted to its products.

Moreover, in view of the competitive conditions, the danger of losing the lucrative Arab market appeared very real. The Arab countries could shut down the twenty-nine franchised Coca-Cola bottling plants because they could easily substitute Pepsi-Cola for Coca-Cola. Psychologists have tested panels of regular cola drinkers and have concluded that people cannot differentiate between colas by taste alone.[13] Pepsi competed with Coke

[7] Irving Spiegal, "Coca-Cola Refuses Israelis a Franchise," *The New York Times,* April 8, 1966, p. 1.
[8] *MSU Business Topics,* Spring 1968, p. 74.
[9] "Business in Mideast Walks on Shifting Sands," *Business Week,* July 2, 1966, pp. 26, 28.
[10] Luman H. Long, ed., *The World Almanac and Book of Facts, 1967* (New York, Newspaper Enterprise Association, 1966), p. 630.
[11] "Bottled Up," *Newsweek,* April 18, 1966, p. 78. See also Thomas Buckley, "Coca-Cola Grants Israeli Franchise," *The New York Times,* April 16, 1966, p. 1.
[12] *Business Week,* July 2, 1966, pp. 26, 28.
[13] James A. Myers and William H. Reynolds, *Consumer Behavior and Marketing Management* (Boston: Houghton-Mifflin, 1967), Chap. 2.

in the Arab market and would most probably capitalize on Coke's fall from Arab favor.

A second consideration in refusing the franchise to Tempo was the company's dissatisfaction with its Israeli distributor. In 1963 Coke filed suit in a Tel Aviv court against Tempo for infringing upon the Coca-Cola trademark. Coca-Cola was also unhappy with Tempo because it bottled other soft drinks. By custom, Coca-Cola franchises are granted in perpetuity as long as the bottlers uphold rigid quality standards specified by the company. Although many Coca-Cola bottlers also manufacture and sell other soft drinks, the company's tradition of granting franchises of indefinite duration made it necessary for them to choose only those companies with whom they could get along.[14] Obviously, Tempo's past record did not meet this criterion.

REPERCUSSIONS OF COCA-COLA'S REFUSAL TO GRANT THE FRANCHISE TO TEMPO

Tempo was not satisfied with Coca-Cola's contention of insufficient market in Israel. It averred that Coca-Cola's management had set arbitrary and unusually high quotas for Tempo, which were impossible to meet. They charged that the main reason for the refusal of the franchise was to support the Arab boycott and asked the Anti-Defamation League of B'nai B'rith to undertake an investigation.[15] If Coco-Cola were indeed supporting the boycott, it would be violating United States government foreign policy.[16]

In April 1966, after a fifteen-month investigation, the Anti-Defamation League released a report stating that Israel was one of the few countries in the free world without a Coca-Cola bottling plant. The reason for this, the report alleged, was that the Coca-Cola Export Corporation was cooperating with the Arab League boycott. The report cited the three major prerequisites Coca-Cola had for granting a bottling plant franchise: a $1 million minimum investment, a "viable market," and "practically exclusive manufacture of Coke." Tempo, which had $2.2 million in sales in 1965, had supposedly met the first two requirements and had agreed to the third.[17] The Anti-Defamation League stated that the Israeli market was potentially more profitable than that of the Arab franchise. Therefore, "The deducible facts seem strongly to indicate that, while submitting to the Arab boycott, Coca-Cola has assiduously attempted to camouflage its submission as a pure nonpolitical, economic decision."[18]

The aftermath of the report was sheer confusion. James A. Farley (former United States postmaster general), chairman of the Coca-Cola

[14] E. J. Kahn, Jr., "Profiles," *The New Yorker*, February 14, 1959, pp. 37–40ff.
[15] "Israel: Capping the Crisis," *Time*, April 22, 1966, p. 75.
[16] Spiegal, "Coca-Cola Refuses Israelis a Franchise," p. 1.
[17] *Newsweek*, April 18, 1966.
[18] Spiegal, "Coca-Cola Refuses Israelis a Franchise," p. 1.

Export Corporation, vigorously denied the charge of honoring "any boycott." He said that detailed surveys of economic and market conditions evidenced a low success potential in the Israeli market but indicated that "all decisions of this kind are constantly under assessment and reassessment." Farley also said that the Tempo Company "had been found guilty in a Tel Aviv court of infringing the Coca-Cola trademark and bottle design in the marketing of its own product, Tempo Cola." [19] Denying that the company had yielded to the threat of an Arab boycott, Robert L. Gunnels, Coca-Cola export vice-president, said that an Israeli bottling plant would not be "mutually profitable" to Tempo and Coca-Cola and added that a similar decision had been made regarding bottling franchises in Jordan and Syria.

Some of the information advanced by Coca-Cola was unknown to the Anti-Defamation League. Arnold Foster, who prepared the report, said that the league was unaware of Coca-Cola's granting Abraham Feinberg's earlier application for a franchise and also of Tempo's infringement on the Coke trademark. He said that these facts had not been mentioned when the league contacted Coca-Cola in regard to the franchise denial to Tempo.[20]

The managing director of Tempo, in turn, objected to Coca-Cola's statements, saying that Tempo had not been found guilty by the court as the case had been settled out of court and that the shape of the Tempo Cola bottle was not at issue. According to *The New York Times,* court records bore out the Tempo statement.[21]

Coca-Cola's basic position was that if it were to operate profitably at home and abroad, it must cater to everybody. A year before the Anti-Defamation League report, Coca-Cola President J. Paul Austin had received a human relations award from the American Jewish Association. The company had a record of being a goodwill ambassador for the United States. In 1949, as a result of left-wing agitation, an anti-Coke bill had become law in France. This aroused anti-France feelings in the United States, leading to several proposals of boycotts of French products. However, the company refused to exploit the anti-France feelings; and James Farley succeeded, through persuasion and diplomatic negotiations, in getting France to repeal the law.[22] The company had also begun operations in Bulgaria in response to the United States government's policy of "building bridges to the East." [23]

Coca-Cola, of course, was aware that Congress had gone on record opposing foreign-initiated boycotts in the Williams-Javits law of 1965 [24] and pointed out that its decision was solely based on economic grounds and that it was not violating the statute or the intent of Congress.

[19] Buckley, "Coca-Cola Grants Israeli Franchise," p. 1.
[20] "Coca-Cola Unit Denies Charge It Is Supporting Arab Boycott of Israel," *The Wall Street Journal,* April 13, 1966, p. 11.
[21] Buckley, "Coca-Cola Grants Israeli Franchise," p. 1.
[22] Kahn, "Profiles," pp. 37–40ff.
[23] "Thaw That Refreshes," *Time,* December 3, 1965, p. 98.
[24] Spiegal, "Coca-Cola Refuses Israelis a Franchise," p. 1.

The Anti-Defamation League had, since its founding, become a powerful force in the use of reason and moral suasion to eradicate prejudice against Jews Despite Coca-Cola's arguments and the league's admission of ignorance of some of the facts, the company stood to lose the patronage of some 5.6 million Jewish people in America—since a rumor had spread that Coca-Cola was anti-Jewish. (It should be noted, however, that the 104.7 million Arab population at that time dwarfed the 13.3 million worldwide Jewish population; so, from the standpoint of income, the Arabs appeared to be more desirable friends than the Israelis.) [25]

Mount Sinai Hospital in New York stopped taking delivery of Coca-Cola for its cafeteria. A New York theater chain and Coney Island's Nathan's Famous Hot Dog Emporium threatened to follow suit, and the New York City Human Rights Commission called for an investigation of Coca-Cola. Within a week of the league's charges, and despite Coca-Cola's denial of them, the company again issued a bottling franchise for Israel to Abraham Feinberg, now a New York banker, president of the Israel Development Corporation, and a promoter of Bonds for Israel. The Anti-Defamation League said that Coca-Cola's decision "will show other American corporations the sham that the Arab boycott really is." [26]

Actually, Feinberg had contacted Coca-Cola about his "renewed interest" a week before the league's charges were made public. Feinberg commented that he would not have accepted any franchise "if I believed Coca-Cola bows to Arab boycott threats." [27]

Now it remained to be seen what the Arabs would do. Israeli officials predictably reported that the boycott's influence had declined in recent years, since the Arab governments had not invariably backed up their threats. The Israeli Consulate General stated there were more than two hundred American companies doing business with both Israel and the Arab League nations. *Business Week* reported that although the rich nations—Saudi Arabia, Kuwait, Libya—were the strictest enforcers of the boycott, Egypt often "winks at boycotts" (Nasser was a heavy Coke drinker), and Tunisia, Algeria, and Morocco "ignore the boycott more than they observe it." [28] Despite these reassurances, however, the possibility of large sales losses was real.

The reprisals from the Arab countries were not long in coming. In July 1966 the Central Office for the Boycott of Israel of the Arab League asked the company about its plans for setting up bottling plants in Israel and warned Coca-Cola that it faced a ban on its product and that the bottling plants would be closed within three months if the Israeli plant was approved. In November the thirteen-country Arab League Boycott Conference met in Kuwait.[29] The Boycott Bureau told the conference it had received unsatisfactory replies from Coca-Cola.

[25] Long, *World Almanac,* pp. 332, 594–670.
[26] *Time,* April 22, 1966, p. 75.
[27] Buckley, "Coca-Cola Grants Israeli Franchise," p. 1.
[28] *Business Week,* July 2, 1966, pp. 22, 26.
[29] Composed of the United Arab Republic, Iraq, Jordan, Lebanon, Saudi Arabia, Syria, Morocco, Yemen, Algeria, Kuwait, Libya, Sudan, and Tunisia.

The conference then passed a resolution to stop the production and sale of Coca-Cola within Arab League countries. Enforcement of the ban, however, was left to the discretion of the individual countries.[30] The Boycott Bureau established a nine-month time limit to allow Arab bottling plants to use up Coke concentrates in stock.

The company made some belated efforts to placate Arab opinion. One month before the Arab League meeting, the company ran an advertisement in a Cairo newspaper showing the important economic and social role played by Coca-Cola in the Arab countries. However, a month was apparently not enough time for the advertisement to have any effect. In December 1966 Baghdad Radio announced that Iraq had begun its ban on Coca-Cola. The company said that it had received no official notification from Iraq but that in the three months since the ban had been announced by the Arab League, the boycott "has not manifested itself in production or sales." [31]

In September 1967, nine months after Arab League representatives had met to approve the boycott, the Boycott Bureau announced that the ban was effective. Despite the ban and the Arabs' increased hatred of Israel after the six-day war, Coke was not deterred and a Coca-Cola bottling plant opened for business in Tel Aviv in February 1968.

SELECTED REFERENCES

E. J. KAHN, JR., "Profiles," *The New Yorker,* March 7, 1959, pp. 58–60.

———, "Profiles," *The New Yorker,* February 14, 1959, pp. 37–40.

"Business in Mideast Walks on Shifting Sands," *Business Week,* July 2, 1966, pp. 26–28.

"Iraq Plans To Boycott Three U.S. Companies," *The Wall Street Journal,* December 20, 1966, p. 5.

"Pause That Nourishes" *Newsweek,* February 19, 1968, pp. 73–74.

IRVING SPIEGAL, "Coca-Cola Refuses Israelis a Franchise," *The New York Times,* April 8, 1966, p. 1.

"Israel: Capping the Crisis," *Time,* April 22, 1966, p. 75.

"Coca-Cola Unit Denies Charge It Is Supporting Arab Boycott of Israel," *The Wall Street Journal,* April 13, 1966, p. 11.

[30] Thomas F. Brady, "Arabs Vote to Bar Ford, Coca-Cola," *The New York Times,* November 21, 1966, p. 1. See also *Business Week,* November 26, 1966.

[31] "Iraq Plans to Boycott Three U.S. Companies," *The Wall Street Journal,* December 20, 1966, p. 11.

Business Lobbying and Social Goals

NATIONAL RIFLE ASSOCIATION (NRA) AND GUN CONTROL

LOBBYING ACTIVITIES AND THEIR INFLUENCE ON GOVERNMENT DECISION MAKING

> When guns are outlawed,
> only outlaws will have guns
> —*NRA-inspired and -promoted*
> *bumper sticker*

On October 22, President Lyndon Baines Johnson signed the Gun Control Act of 1968, to be effective that December 16. It was a step toward his goal but not the strong bill with licensing and registration requirements that Johnson had submitted to Congress shortly after the assassination of Senator Robert F. Kennedy in June 1968. In signing the inadequate bill—nonetheless the first major firearms legislation since 1938—Johnson voiced his dissatisfaction and his intention to pursue stiffer requirements: "The voices that blocked these safeguards were not the voices of an aroused nation. They were the voices of a powerful gun lobby that has prevailed for the moment in an election year." [1]

The unparalleled congressional nonresponse to consistent and overwhelming public support for gun control legislation is the achievement of the "gun lobby," spearheaded by the National Rifle Association. The success of the gun lobby is not due to a dearth of proposals by the forces

[1] "President Signs Second Gun Bill," *The New York Times*, October 23, 1968, p. 16.

favoring gun control legislation. There has been a steady flow of bills in federal, state, and local legislative bodies with, as might- be expected, increased activity following actual or attempted assassinations of public figures. From 1955 to 1962, for example, no fewer than 35 gun control bills were introduced in Congress, and 20 more were pending at the time of President Kennedy's assassination in 1963. In 1964 there were 189 bills in state legislatures, and between 1965 and 1967, 500 more were introduced.[2] However, with a few minor exceptions (the NRA calls them "major setbacks") none of these bills was enacted.[3] Gallup polls taken since 1934, the height of the prohibition-sparked gangster era, have shown that from 54 to over 80 percent of the American public supports some kind of restrictions on the sale and possession of guns. Indeed, the 1959 survey indicated that even gun owners, by a margin of two to one, would be willing to obtain a police permit before purchasing a gun. Table 1 indicates the public response, from 1959 to 1972, to the question, "Do you favor or oppose a law requiring a police permit to buy guns?"

TABLE 1   PUBLIC OPINION ON REQUIRING POLICE PERMITS TO BUY GUNS

	Favor	Oppose	No Opinion
August 1959	75	21	4
January 1964	78	17	5
February 1965	73	23	4
August 1966	73	23	4
September 1966	68	29	3
August 1967	73	23	4
October 1971	71	24	5
April 1972	79	18	3

Source: The Wall Street Journal, May 19, 1972, p. 10. Reprinted with permission of Dow Jones books, © Dow Jones & Company, Inc. 1972. All rights reserved.

Official pro-gun control supporters include the National Riot and National Crime Commissions, American Bar Association, National Council on Crime and Delinquency, General Association of Women's Clubs, Women's Clubs of America, National Association of Sheriffs, American Civil Liberties Union, AFL–CIO, United Auto Workers, Americans for Democratic Action, and Leadership Conference on Civil Rights (forty affiliated organizations). In addition, public opinion polls, most major newspapers, most judges, the late J. Edgar Hoover, some big-city police chiefs, and most big-city mayors favored registering all types of guns.

2 Robert Sherrill, "A Lobby on Target," *The New York Times Magazine,* October 15, 1967, p. 27.
3 Carl Bakal, *The Right to Bear Arms* (New York: McGraw-Hill, 1966), p. 213.

Why were these groups so ineffective? Although it is hard to under-emphasize the potency and effectiveness of the anti-gun control lobby, many critics argue that the congressional supporters of gun control were considerably handicapped by their chief spokesman, Senator Thomas Dodd of Connecticut, who was alleged to suffer from an inferiority complex, to be afraid of anti-gun control spokesman Senator Hruska, and to accept favors for legislative manipulation.[4]

THE ISSUES

The success of the NRA and its allies despite unequivocal popular sentiment against it raises a number of questions about its role in the legislative process. Is it, as it claims, protecting the constitutionally guaranteed freedom of millions of men, women, and children to keep and bear arms in the interests of sports, liberty, and the American way of life? Or is it working to protect the interests of arms manufacturers and other sporting goods producers who benefit from the promotion of shooting as a sport? Does its ability to prevent the enactment of legislation signal the strength of a system that enables vigilant citizens to protect their rights? Or does it point out the vulnerability of a system that can be virtually paralyzed by a small but vocal and organized minority protecting its privilege against the contrary demands of public opinion, interest, and general welfare? In either case, is it the responsibility of any special interest group to ensure that Congress does not act contrary to its own view of the public welfare? Or is it Congress's responsibility to regulate the activities of such groups to ensure that their limited definitions of the public interest do not completely override broader and more generally accepted ones? Where does the proper compromise lie between individual rights and liberties and collective or societal necessity? And is such a compromise either possible or in the public interest?

HISTORY OF REGULATION [5]

State and Local Regulation

Although legislation restricting a citizen's right to carry arms in public predates nationhood (Massachusetts, for example, enacted such a law in 1692), the concept of legislation to control the purchase and ownership of

---

[4] Robert Sherrill, *The Saturday Night Special* (New York: Charterhouse, 1973), pp. 70–75.
[5] For a historical view of gun control, see Plato's Dialogues, *Law* vii: 829 (trans. B. Jowett, 1892); NRA Annual Report 1963; Carl Bakal, *Right to Bear Arms;* "Federal Firearms Control Legislation," *Congressional Digest*, 45, 12 (1966), p. 289; "On Firearms Control," *Congressional Quarterly Weekly Report*, 24, 33 (1966), p. 1803; "King's Murder, Riots Spark Demand for Gun Controls," *Congressional Quarterly Weekly Report*, April 12, 1968, p. 814; Richard Harris, "Annals of Legislation: If You Love Your Guns,"

guns did not appear in this country until 1911. At that time New York enacted its still-controversial Sullivan Law, which requires a license to purchase or own a handgun or other concealable weapon. The other 2,000 or so state laws dealing with the manufacture, sale, and use of firearms which existed as of 1968 are much less effective in controlling or recording the rapidly proliferating possession of guns by the general public. Table 2 summarizes state laws concerning handguns (no states significantly regulated the purchase or possession of rifles and shotguns) as of 1966.

TABLE 2   STATE LAWS REGULATING HANDGUNS IN 1966

Type of Regulation	Number of States with Laws
Handgun sales prohibited	1
License or permit required for purchase	7
Waiting period between purchase and delivery	17
Handgun sales reported to police	20
License required for retail sales	24
License or permit required for possession in home or place of business	1
License or permit required to carry openly on person	11 *
Minimum age required for purchase (varies between 14 and 21)	41
License or permit required to carry concealed on person	29 †

* Plus 2 states that prohibit openly carrying weapons.
† Plus 16 states that prohibit carrying concealed weapons.

Source: Compiled from information in Carl Bakal, The Right to Bear Arms (New York: McGraw-Hill, 1966), pp. 346–51.

Since 1966, a number of states have passed more restrictive gun legislation. New Jersey, for example, passed a law in August 1966 requiring purchasers of *any* type of firearm to obtain a police permit, the application for which required fingerprints, photographs, and the serial number of the gun purchased. In 1970 Maryland prohibited handguns from being worn or carried anywhere but to or from a hunt or target shoot, made mandatory minimum sentences for offenders, and allowed police to stop

The New Yorker, April 20, 1968, p. 56; "Lobby Activities," Congressional Quarterly Weekly Report, June 14, 1968, p. 1464; "Constitutional Limitations on Firearms Regulations," Duke Law Journal, August 1969, pp. 773–95; Paul B. Wright, "The Effectiveness of Federal Firearms Control," Brooklyn Law Review 35, 3 (1969), 443; Carl Bakal, "The Failure of Federal Gun Control," Saturday Review, July 31, 1971, pp. 14–15; John Bennett, "The Gun: The Symbolic Meanings of Firearms in the U.S. Make the Debate Bitter," The Wall Street Journal, June 9, 1972, p. 1; "Tighter Gun Controls, Both Sides of the Dispute: Symposium," U. S. News and World Report, July 10, 1972, p. 68; Sherrill, The Saturday Night Special.
    Also see various hearings and court decisions cited in the section "Arguments: Pro and Con."

and frisk people "on reasonable suspicion" that they were carrying a gun.[6]

However, the enforcement of state gun laws is usually fairly lax. According to the National Commission on Violence, only New York, Massachusetts, and New Jersey have strictly enforced restrictive handgun licensing laws. To counter the lack of effective control at the state level, various municipalities have enacted their own more stringent regulations. Others have historically had requirements covering such areas as dealer registration, purchase permits, waiting periods, permits for possession, regulations on indiscriminant firing of guns, and in some cities the registration of all handguns.

Federal Regulations

Congress enacted two minor pieces of legislation during the 1920s: a 1924 excise tax on gun and ammunition sales, and a 1928 prohibition, with some exceptions, of handgun shipments by mail (easily obviated by express shipment).

These fledgling attempts at federal regulation did not come to grips with the issue of control over purchase and possession of guns. However, the attention of the increasingly crime-conscious nation in the gangster era came into abrupt focus with the February 15, 1933, attempted assassination of president-elect Franklin D. Roosevelt. In a pattern to become fearfully familiar in the ensuing forty years, national shock was soon translated into stringent gun control demands. During 1933 twelve gun control bills were introduced in Congress—seven in the House, five in the Senate. These laws, as originally proposed, required record-keeping at the time of sale of small, concealable handguns, such as pistols and revolvers, as well as such "gangster" weapons as machine guns, silencers, sawed-off shotguns, and rifles. The penalty for illegal possession was to be up to five years in prison. The twofold intent of the law was to discourage weapon use and to afford another device for arresting gangsters. The NRA bore down hard: pistols, revolvers, handguns, and semiautomatic rifles were eliminated from the list of weapons.

The final version of the law, enacted over the strenuous opposition of the NRA, was the National Firearms Act of 1934. This law, which excludes handguns, provides for a prohibitive tax on the manufacture, sale, or transfer of machine guns and other fully automatic weapons, sawed-off shotguns and rifles, mufflers and silencers. Although useless in controlling the flow of handguns to the general public, the act did eliminate the "smoking tommy gun" as the symbol of organized crime and ended much of the more open underworld warfare.

The Federal Firearms Act, a second bill enacted in 1938, makes the interstate shipment of firearms a criminal offense if a dealer knows or has reasonable cause to believe that the recipient is a criminal. Since it is one

---

[6] Richard Martin, "The Gun: New Moves to Control Firearms Won't Go Far If the Past Is a Guide," *The Wall Street Journal,* May 19, 1972, p. 1.

thing to prove that a gun was shipped to a convicted felon, but quite another thing to prove that the dealer knew that the recipient was a felon, the law was almost ineffectual. NRA justifiably claimed the victory.

That was, with a few minor exceptions (such as the Federal Aviation Act of 1958, which prohibited carrying weapons in an airplane), the state of federal gun control laws until 1968. The assassinations of Martin Luther King, Jr., in April of that year and of Senator Kennedy in June finally broke the resistance of a Congress that had refused to act following the deaths of President John F. Kennedy, Malcolm X, George Lincoln Rockwell, and Medgar Evers. On June 7, 1968, the day after Senator Kennedy's death, the House passed the 1968 Omnibus Crime Bill, Title IV of which contained restrictions on the sale and possession of handguns. The bill originally covered rifles and shotguns as well, but this coverage was deleted in the Senate, which had earlier passed the bill. In the interests of capitalizing on the national shock over Kennedy's death, Johnson urged immediate passage of this bill as a first step but not a final solution. When he signed it on June 20, he called on Congress to take more decisive action: "We must go further and stop mail order murder by rifle and shotgun. . . . What in the name of conscience will it take to pass a truly effective gun control law?" [7]

Congress complied, and in October President Johnson signed the second major federal gun control legislation of the last three decades. The Gun Control Act of 1968 bans the importation of cheap, concealable, and often inaccurate handguns by limiting imports to those weapons judged to have some sporting uses; it restricts mail order sales and shipments of firearms of all types to transactions between licensed dealers and manufacturers; it requires all dealers to keep records of the name, address, and age of the buyers of all firearms, ammunition, and ammunition components; and it limits purchases of firearms and ammunition to the purchaser's state of residence.

With the advent of the Nixon era in 1969, attitudes toward gun control legislation changed sharply. The president and Attorneys General Mitchell and Kleindienst continually reiterated their opposition to further legislation and their distaste for the 1968 act. During the 91st Congress (1969 and 1970), of the 183 bills introduced—107 to weaken and 76 to strengthen existing controls—one succeeded. The act was amended in November 1969 to repeal the recordkeeping requirements in the sale of shotgun and high-power rifle ammunition. Within the next three years both proponents and opponents were active, but little was accomplished. Of the 61 bills introduced into the first session of the 92nd Congress (1971) —37 to ease and 24 to tighten controls—none succeeded.

But pressures were building for stricter controls. The May 16, 1972, attempted assassination of Governor George Wallace brought these pressures to a head and fueled a brief spurt of positive action. A bill banning the sale and manufacture of pistols with barrels three inches or less, which

[7] "Transcript of Johnson's Statement on Signing Crime and Safety Bill," *The New York Times,* June 20, 1968, p. 23.

was then before the Senate Judiciary Committee, was promptly approved by the committee and later by the full Senate. Ironically, the Senate also voted to repeal recordkeeping requirements for .22-caliber rimfire ammunition, which can be used in many weapons, including the cheap handguns the other bill was attempting to control. The Nixon administration, however, opposed the bill, although it indicated support for the idea of controlling these cheap handguns, called "Saturday night specials." President Nixon said that Congress should pass a law to control them and that he would sign it so long as it was precisely written.[8] But the House bills that would have regulated these guns remained in committee and died on the adjournment of the 92nd Congress, as did twenty-seven other control bills introduced before it.

The 93rd Congress showed a similar pattern of activity. Opponents of gun control moved immediately: Six bills to repeal the 1968 act were introduced into the House in the first week; by May there were ten bills altogether to repeal the act, and at least four to exempt .22-caliber rimfire ammunition from the act's recordkeeping requirements. Congress also began early consideration of a bill to overhaul the entire U.S. Criminal Code. The National Commission on Reform of Criminal Laws, upon whose recommendations the bill was based, had recommended outlawing private possession of handguns and registration of all other firearms, but the bill placed before Congress in January 1973 contained no new gun legislation.

The January 30, 1973, robbery-shooting of Senator John Stennis gave considerable impetus to control efforts. A caucus of Senate Democrats voted unanimously the next day to move ahead quickly on anticrime bills, and President Nixon in a news conference stressed the necessity for more stringent controls. He tempered his support for such measures, however, by stating: "I do know that in terms of the United States Congress, what we need is a precise definition which will keep guns out of the hands of the criminals and not one that will impinge on the rights of others to have them for their own purposes in a legitimate way." [9]

Not all support for controls, however, was similarly limited. Senator Edward Kennedy introduced a bill (S. 982) in February to register all privately owned guns, to ban all "hand-held firearms" not designed for sport, and to provide stringent tests for anyone wishing to own a gun.[10] A less stringent bill, more in the spirit of the president's statement, was introduced by three pro-gun congressmen. This bill would have covered only Saturday night specials, to be identified by the melting point of their frames. According to the *American Rifleman,* the NRA membership magazine, this bill was an effort "to head off the worst of the anti-handgun bills." [11] To date Congress has not acted on any of these bills.

[8] "Transcript of President Nixon's News Conference Emphasizing Foreign Affairs," *The New York Times,* June 30, 1972, p. 2.
[9] "Transcripts of the President's News Conference on Foreign and Domestic Matters," *The New York Times,* February 1, 1973, p. 20.
[10] "Notes and Comment," *The New Yorker,* March 10, 1973, p. 29.
[11] "What the Lawmakers Are Doing," *American Rifleman,* April 1973, p. 49.

THE ARGUMENTS: PRO AND CON

For four decades the gun control debaters have held firm positions. Opinions held in the 1930s are argued with unabated fervor. Neither side has dented the arguments or the position of the other. Each side seems to hold an emotional, not factual, stance unsusceptible to compromise.[12]

Opponents to controls begin, as the *American Rifleman* repeatedly puts it, from the "bedrock stand" that everyone is entitled to have guns. Proponents begin from what they consider to be the "self-evident" proposition that "the reason guns are involved in so many acts of violence is that there are so many guns in so many hands." [13] Other arguments and facts are used to bolster these beliefs—many facts and figures are, indeed, used by both sides to prove absolutely contradictory points. The bitterness of the struggle is largely due to the fact that these positions are deeply felt beliefs, symptomatic of much larger issues.[14] It is the conflict between a frontier heritage and an urban future, between the Minutemen of Concord and Lexington and the rockets of Cape Kennedy, between a world where a gun is used to hunt food and dangerous animals and a world where it is used to kill a president.

The Constitutional Argument

The common anti-gun control argument, claiming that the Second Amendment of the Bill of Rights in the U.S. Constitution gives individuals the unlimited right to firearms, touches only one small part of the constitutional implications of firearms legislation. Although court interpretations of the Fifth Amendment have resulted in firearm legislation changes, those portions of the Second Amendment constantly quoted by gun enthusiasts have in fact been consistently defined by the courts

[12] See, for example, the following congressional hearings: U.S. Congress, House, Subcommittee on Interstate and Foreign Commerce, *Hearings on Several Bills Pending Before the Committee to Regulate the Interstate Shipment of Firearms,* 71st Cong., 2d sess., April 1930. U.S. Congress, House, Committee on Ways and Means, *Hearings on H.R. 9066 (National Firearms Act),* 73rd Cong., 2d sess., April–May 1934. U.S. Congress, Senate, Judiciary Committee, Subcommittee on Juvenile Delinquency, various hearings: *On Interstate Traffic in Mail-Order Firearms,* 1963; *On Amendments to Federal Firearms Act,* 1965; *On Amendments to Federal Firearms Act,* 1967; *On Bills to Register Firearms, Establish a National Firearms Registry, and Disarm Lawless Persons,* 1968; *On Various Senate Resolutions,* 1969; *On Amendments to 1968 Gun Control Act to Prohibit the Sale of Saturday Night Special Handguns,* 1971. U.S. Congress, House, Committee on Ways and Means, *Hearings on Proposed Amendments to Firearms Acts,* parts 1 and 2, 89th Cong., 1st sess., July 1965. U.S. Congress, House, Judiciary Committee, *Hearings on H.R. 5037, 5038 5384 5385, and 5386 (Anti-Crime Program),* 90th Cong., 1st sess., March–April 1967.
[13] Martin, "The Gun."
[14] See, for example, Bennett, "The Gun."

entirely opposite to the gun enthusiasts' usage. The Second and Fifth amendments and Articles I and IV have all affected legal judgments on gun control. Previous courts have unquestionably set the tone of the issue as not whether Congress can regulate the transfer and possession of fire-arms, but of how far such legislation can constitutionally extend.[15] Con-stitutional implications are much broader than the pro and con arguments cyclically used in Congress and journals, with the powers and limits on firearms regulation enunciated in many cases, yet still leaving a few holes.

Article II of the Bill of Rights (the Second Amendment to the Consti-tution) states: "A well regulated militia, being necessary to the security of a free State, the right of the people to keep and bear Arms, shall not be infringed." The NRA interprets this statement literally. "We prefer to believe that the simple, straightforward language means exactly what it says," editorialized the NRA in the July 1955 issue of the *American Rifleman.* "Do we, as law-abiding citizens of the United States, possess an inalienable right to bear arms comparable to our right of assembly, our freedom of speech, and our freedom of worship?" asks another editorial. The answer is immediate: "Undoubtedly there is an inalienable right to own and use private weapons for lawful purposes. This right is not cast in doubt by state laws controlling certain actions under their police power" (p. 14).

The NRA and other opponents of controls argue that gun legislation, particularly at the federal level, is an infringement of this right. According to the Statement of Policy of the National Rifle Association:

> The NRA is opposed to the registration on any level of government of the ownership of rifles, shotguns, pistols or revolvers for any purpose whatever. Regardless of professed intent, there can be only one outcome of registration, and that is to make possible the seizure of such weapons by political authorities, or by persons seeking to overthrow the government by force. Registration will not keep guns out of the hands of undesirable persons, and few people seriously claim that it will.[16]

Supreme Court cases have established two conceptual interpretations of the Second Amendment. The first is that the amendment's phrase, "shall not be infringed," applies only to the federal government. This interprets a prohibition only against Congress and not against the states with respect to the First Amendment, which states that "Congress shall make no laws" and comes from the rationale that the first ten amendments are federal restrictions only. This is not reason enough to limit the Second Amend-

15 "Constitutional Limitations . . . Regulations," *Duke Law Journal.* See also "Con-stitutional Limitations on Federal Firearms Control," *Washburn Law Journal,* Winter 1969, p. 238; "Right to Bear Arms," *South Carolina Law Review,* 19 (1967), 402; and John Brabner-Smith, "Firearms Regulations," *Law and Contemporary Problems* 1, 4 (1934), 400, 410–12.
16 Appendix V, Statement of Policy of the National Rifle Association (cited in Bakal, *Right to Bear Arms,* pp. 357–58).

ment only to the federal government, because the due process clause of the Fourteenth Amendment has made the Fifth, Sixth, and the Eighth amendments also applicable to the states. Further legal clarification is needed before it is understood against whom the prohibition applies.

In *United States* v. *Miller,* 307 U.S. 174, 178 (1939), the Supreme Court upheld the conviction of two men who transported in interstate commerce a shotgun, which came within the definition of a firearm under the National Firearms Act of 1934 and was not registered as required by the act nor covered by a stamp-affixed order. The act was challenged on constitutional grounds. The Court found that the Second Amendment did not guarantee the keeping and bearing of any weapon not having a reasonable relationship to the preservation or efficiency of a well-regulated militia. The Court stated that the obvious purpose of the amendment was to ensure the continuation and render possible the effectiveness of the militia subjected to call and organization by Congress under Article I, section 8, clauses 15 and 16 of the Constitution and that the amendment must be interpreted and applied with that end in view (at 178).

In *Presser* v. *Illinois,* 116 U.S. 252 (1886), the Supreme Court upheld an Illinois statute that forbade drilling or parading with arms in cities and towns unless authorized by law. The Supreme Court defined the well-regulated militia as a governmentally controlled body rather than a privately organized army, and this is the definition generally accepted today. It guarantees a collective right to keep and bear arms in order to preserve a militia. A question arises as to the type of arms included with the protection of the provision.

In *Commonwealth* v. *Murphy,* 44 N.E. 138 (Mass. 1896), the overwhelming majority of state cases follow the doctrine expressed in this case that "it has been almost universally held that the legislature may regulate and limit the mode of carrying arms." Therefore, a state statute regulating or sometimes prohibiting the carrying of enumerated deadly weapons is not repugnant to the Second Amendment or its counterpart in the state's constitution. No infringement would bear upon the amendment with acts barring deadly weapons or requiring licenses.

The Supreme Court, however, struck down one provision of the 1934 law on constitutional grounds. In 1968 the Court declared unconstitutional a portion of the law's registration system. The Court's decision was, however, based on the *Fifth* Amendment, not the Second: the Court held that the registration system in effect required persons to testify against themselves.[17]

The federal government has full power, under the Constitution, to control firearms in the United States. The power of Congress to regulate firearms under the taxing and commerce clause is clear. Recent Supreme Court decisions have reaffirmed congressional power to enact a broad range of regulatory legislation under the taxing provisions of the National Firearms Act as a legitimate exercise of the United States Congress' power to tax. There remains only for Congress to find that sale and possession of

---

[17] *Haynes* v. *U.S.,* 390 U.S. 85, 98 (1968).

firearms affect interstate commerce or should be taxed, and they may take whatever steps in regulation they desire.

The NRA has continued to maintain that the right to possess arms, including sawed-off shotguns for sports, in the interest of a prepared citizenry is fundamental to Americans.[18] The NRA further insists that this liberty, far from being a privilege, is a necessity for the protection of the nation from its enemies, both foreign and domestic. The *American Rifleman* states:

> Fighting in the next major war will not be confined to the battlefield alone. It is inevitable that our homeland will be attacked. . . . More than ever, the individual soldier and the individual citizen will be forced to rely on the weapon with which he is armed, and on his ability to use it effectively, if he is to survive.[19]

Thomas L. Kimball of the National Wildlife Federation, staunchly opposed to controls both individually and organizationally, testified before the Senate Commerce Committee in 1964:

> U.S. Armed Forces deployed an entire armored division from the United States to West Germany in three days. Is it so unconceivable that our enemies could perform the same feat? In my humble opinion the day will never come when war becomes so sophisticated that the occupation of land will become unnecessary. The role of the foot soldier and armed citizen fighting from hedgerow to hedgerow and from house to house can never be discarded as a significant military force if this nation is determined to protect its basic freedom.[20]

But experience contradicts this theory. Texas Senator Ralph Yarborough, an NRA member, told the same committee:

> I was on the staff of an infantry division and I saw the invasion of Germany. Hitler called on every German to die in his home, at his post, and the first time a sniper fired in a town at an Allied soldier they learned. These men were trying to be nice to the civilians, but the snipers fired. After that, the towns were simply sawed down. And pretty soon there was total surrender.
>
> As we advanced in Germany, not only towns surrendered, but every house. . . . They realized this idea of civilians sniping at soldiers is obsolete, that it is not feasible, simply because firepower is so great in modern armies.[21]

---

18 See, for example, *American Rifleman,* March 1973, "Editorial Report," pp. 17–19.
19 *American Rifleman,* May 1957.
20 U.S. Congress, Senate, Committee on Commerce hearings, January 23, 1964, pp. 79–80.
21 *Ibid.,* p. 251.

The Crime Argument

For proponents of firearms controls, the basic issue and the basic threat is crime. The late J. Edgar Hoover articulated this belief: "There is no doubt in my mind that the easy accessibility of firearms is responsible for many killings, both impulse and premeditated. The statistics are grim and realistic. Strong measures must be taken, and promptly, to protect the public." [22]

James V. Bennett, then director of the U.S. Bureau of Prisons, spoke even more forcefully when he testified before the subcommittee in 1963.

> Today, we do not have the organized bands of desperate criminals that we had in the 1930's [but] the truth, however, is that we have more bank robberies than ever and the number of kidnappings has not declined. Only the nature of the criminals committing these offenses has changed. Instead of the "professionals" like John Dillinger and "Machinegun" Kelly and ruthless desperadoes, like Wilcoxson and Nussbaum, we have now the economically desperate amateur, the emotionally disturbed, the impulsive, the unstable, and the heedless individual and juvenile.
>
> All they need is a gun and their warped ideas or mentality lead inevitably at least to violence and frequently death. Our files are full of such cases. [23]

Bennett's words were not overly pessimistic. Since 1960, figures for both crime and gun ownership have shown a steep upward climb. Figures from the *FBI Uniform Crime Report* for 1970 and 1971 show the following changes:

	Percent Increase			
	Number Committed		Crime Rate	
Kind of Crime	1966–1971	1960–1970	1966–1971	1960–1970
Overall increase in crime	83%	176%	74%	144%
Violent crime (murder, rape, robbery, aggravated assault)	90	156	80	126
Property crime (burglary, larceny over $50, auto theft)	82	180	73	147

22 Cited in U.S. Congress, Senate, Committee on the Judiciary, Subcommittee to Investigate Juvenile Delinquency, *Hearings on Federal Firearms Legislation,* June 26, 27, 28, and July 8, 9, 10, 1968, p. 20. (Hereinafter referred to as *FFL.*)
23 Cited in U.S. Congress, Senate, Committee on the Judiciary, Subcommittee to Investigate Juvenile Delinquency, *Hearings on Interstate Traffic in Mail-Order Firearms,* January 29 and 30, March 7, and May 1 and 2, 1963, p. 3368. (Hereinafter referred to as *Hearings.*)

Parallelling these increases were similar jumps in the sales of firearms. Between 1963 and 1971, annual sales of shotguns and rifles doubled, while the sale of handguns quadrupled.[24] Domestic production of all firearms increased from 1.5 million units in 1960 to 5.2 million in 1969; handgun production during that period grew from 475,000 to 2.8 million.[25] What these figures mean in terms of total gun ownership, however, is unclear, for according to a five-month study conducted by the Stanford Research Institute in 1968, *"we do not know with any precision the order of magnitude of the number of guns out in individual possession in the United States today."* [26] Estimates at that time varied between 100 and 200 million individually owned handguns, rifles, and shotguns.

The United States is the only industrialized nation that does not have strict firearms regulation on a national basis. In Britain, for example, the purchaser of any gun, even for hunting, must obtain a permit, and all sales are registered with the police. France and Italy have similar regulations, and background investigations of would-be gun purchasers in those countries may take up to six weeks. Spain imposed the additional restriction that only fifty rounds of ammunition may be purchased at one time. In West Germany, "well-reputed and trustworthy citizens" may own handguns only upon showing a specific need for personal protection, such as dangerous occupations or living quarters, and permits are required for their purchase and carrying.[27] Opponents of controls frequently point to Switzerland as an example of a country where gun ownership is universal. Virtually every male of military age is required to keep his military equipment in his home, including weapons and ammunition, but what opponents neglect to mention is that each of these guns is registered and every round of ammunition for them must be accounted for. The purchase and ownership of nonmilitary weapons is as strictly regulated in Switzerland as in other European countries.[28]

These countries, all with stricter firearms controls than the United States, also have a much lower firearms fatalities rate than does this country, as shown in Table 3.

According to the *FBI Uniform Crime Report* for 1971, the U.S. murder rate for that year was 8.5 victims per 100,000 inhabitants, an increase of 9 percent over the 7.8 rate reported in 1970. The comparison of this figure with those for other countries is, for proponents of controls, a very strong argument in their favor. A Stanford Research Institute report states:

> On an aggregate basis, the data make clear the fact that effective firearms control laws serve to reduce the amount of violence by firearms in a very effective and significant manner. In some of these countries, such as Japan, this effect is achieved by substantial reduc-

24 Bakal, "Failure of Federal Gun Control," p. 12.
25 U.S. Bureau of the Census, *Statistical Abstract of the United States—1972* (1972), p. 147.
26 *FFL,* p. 240.
27 "Strict Gun Control Practiced Abroad," *The New York Times,* June 13, 1968, p. 20.
28 Bakal, *Right to Bear Arms,* p. 284.

tion and control over the number of firearms in individual possession. In other countries, multifaceted, socioeconomic and political factors may contribute to the lower per capita violence by firearms in comparison with the United States.[29]

To opponents of controls, however, this argument is worthless. Says Harold Glassen:

Throughout the recent controversy, one of the most publicized facts has been that England had only 30 firearms homicides last year, in comparison to the 6,500 killed in the United States during the same period. Nowhere is mention made that England has for many centuries had a homogeneous population, subject to a totally different set of social conditions that the United States or that the English people for generations have accepted as a way of life that the aristocracy and large landholders are entitled to certain rights and

TABLE 3   DEATHS DUE TO FIREARMS AND EXPLOSIVES IN SELECTED COUNTRIES
(Number and rate per 100,000 population)

Country	Population * (000)	Homicide Number	Rate	Suicide Number	Rate	Accident Number	Rate
United States (1966)	195,936	6,855 †	3.5 †	10,407	5.3	2,558	1.3
Australia (1965)	11,360	57	0.5	331	2.9	94	0.8
Belgium (1965)	9,464	20	0.2	82	0.9	11	0.1
Canada (1966)	19,604	98	0.5	609	3.1	197	1.0
Denmark (1965)	4,758	6	0.1	48	1.0	4	0.1
England and Wales (1966)	54,595	27	0.1	173	0.4	53	0.1
France (1965)	48,922	132	0.3	879	1.8	252	0.5
German Federal Republic (1965)	59,041	78	0.1	484	0.9	89	0.2
Italy (1964)	51,576	243	0.5	370	0.7	175	0.3
Japan (1965)	97,960	16	0.0 ‡	68	0.1	78	0.1
Netherlands (1965)	12,292	5	0.0 ‡	11	0.1	4	0.0 ‡
Sweden (1966)	7,734	14	0.2	192	2.5	20	0.3

* Population figures are for latest year for which data are available.
† However, Table 20, *FBI Uniform Crime Reports,* 1966, shows 5,660 homicides, or a rate of 2.9 per 100,000. The HEW homicides are based on death certificates. Deaths by explosives are insignificant according to HEW.
‡ Insignificant in number.

Source: Adapted from table in *FFL,* p. 356. Data for U.S. from U.S. Department of Health, Education, and Welfare, Bureau of Vital Statistics; data for other countries from World Health Organization.

[29] *Firearms, Violence, and Civil Disorders,* p. 72, cited in *FFL,* p. 357.

privileges reserved to their class. Numbered among these privileges is the right to keep a firearm for hunting or sporting purposes. A totally different set of values and circumstances, however, prevails in America, where every man is free to choose his pleasures and interests regardless of his station in life.[30]

The gun control-crime relationship is clear. FBI figures for 1970 and 1971 show 65 of every 100 murder victims died by gunfire: 51 by handguns, 8 by shotguns, 6 by rifles. Of the 35 additional victims, 21 died by cutting or stabbing weapons, 9 by personal weapons (hands and feet), and 6 by clubs, poisons, etc.[31] Significantly, the murder rate is highest where gun controls are lowest, as in the South, where the murder rate in 1971 was 12.2 (national rate 8.5) and where 73.5 percent of the murders were by gun (national average 65 percent).[32]

These figures do not silence the debate. As Senator Tydings (D, Md.) put it, "good gun laws do reduce gun crimes," [33] but Representative John Dingell (D, Mich.), testifying before the subcommittee in 1968, stated:

I think that the first thing that this committee should consider is whether or not the legislation that is before it is going to work. I think that it is quite clear, from a fair history of firearms control laws . . . that registration legislation won't stop crime, it won't stop crimes of violence. . . . the only concrete effect of such legislation has been to strip the law-abiding citizen of a very important right and privilege, and to deny him the means and access to an instrument which in its own nature is innocent and which is wrong only because of its capacity for misuse.[34]

The then-president of the NRA, Karl T. Frederick, was even more explicit in his description of the effects of controls when he testified in 1934: "I am just as much against the gangster as any man. I am just as interested in seeing him suppressed, but I do not believe that we should burn down the barn in order to destroy the rats." [35] The opponents of gun control further argue that the percentage of illegal gun use is very small, and thus restrictions should not hamper the dominating legal uses because criminals disobey laws anyway. In 1970, only 1 percent of the estimated 24 million handguns were used to commit homicides.[36] No problems are caused by the 99 percent, and thus to prohibit all to restrict the 1 percent who are already breaking existing laws would be inadvisable. For the availability

---

[30] *FFL*, pp. 204–05.
[31] *Crime in the United States: Uniform Crime Reports, 1971* and *1970*, pp. 8–9.
[32] *Ibid.*
[33] *FFL*, p. 27.
[34] *FFL*, p. 469.
[35] U.S. Congress, House, *Hearings Before the Committee on Ways and Means on the National Firearms Act, H.R. 9066,* 73rd Cong., 2d sess., April 16, 18 and May 14, 15, 16, 1934, p. 58.
[36] "Tighter Gun Controls," *U.S. News and World Report.*

of firearms to be a significant factor in crime; as stated in Bill S.1's "Findings & Declaration," L. C. Jackson commented that "one would have to conclude that the mere possession of a gun would tempt an otherwise law-abiding citizen to commit a crime." [37] Strict laws reducing easy legal access will simply force the trade underground.[38] An attempted support of this is that in countries having strict controls, it is still possible to buy illegal guns.[39] An attempt to reduce the number of guns in certain people's hands would be a great waste of energy when only 1 percent of the total guns are the ones the restrictions are meant for. There are so many other guns around that this would not prove to be a valid solution to the crime problem.

The argument that private ownership of guns serves to keep crime rates low and to provide personal protection is frequently heard. The *New Republic* quotes the NRA more recently:

> One is forever being told, "You don't need to protect yourself; that's the job for the police." What kind of talk is this for America? Are we becoming a nation of defeatists, devoid of personal pride and content to rely entirely on our police for protection? [40]

The police, however, see the situation in a different light, and suggest that the pride that counsels armed resistance is frequently fatal. One police sergeant stated:

> Having a gun for protection only gives you a false sense of security. Many people think that if a criminal knows you're armed, he won't bother you. Well, criminals know that most liquor store owners are armed, and yet they are the ones most liable to be held up. . . . When someone comes in to commit a crime, the element of surprise is on his side.[41]

The opponents of gun controls offer another argument: that it is not the gun, but the criminals and the courts that should be our prime concern in any drive for crime abatement. Georgia's Senator Strom Thurmond states:

> The real fault of crime is criminals who today are operating in an atmosphere of permissiveness and arrogance. Supreme Court decisions have severely handicapped the police in the apprehension of criminals and diminished the power of the courts to see that the

37 Leon C. Jackson, antique dealer, before the Senate Subcommittee on Juvenile Delinquency, *Hearings on Amendments to Federal Firearms Act, 1967,* vol. 14, p. 635.
38 "King's Murder, Riots Spark Demands for Gun Controls," *Congressional Quarterly Weekly Report.*
39 S. Mosk, "Gun Control Legislation, Valid and Necessary," *New York Law Forum,* winter 1968, pp. 747–48.
40 December 14, 1963.
41 *Ibid.,* p. 259.

guilty are punished. . . . Only one lawbreaker in eight is tried and convicted; of all persons arrested in 1966, 76 percent were repeat offenders. . . .

Why not exercise stringent laws? . . . In Washington, harassed police are able to arrest only one-quarter of perpetrators of crime, whereas a decade ago they caught one-half of them.[42]

One law by which these contradictory beliefs could presumably be tested is New York's Sullivan Law, enacted in 1911, which requires a police permit for the purchase of any handgun. But this law and its effects have been the subject of some of the most bitter moments in the debate. An NRA director complained in 1964: "New York's so-called Sullivan Law is the most restrictive gun legislation on the statute books. Yet it is a complete failure, not only in keeping guns out of the hands of the criminal element but also at reducing the crime rate." [43] Leonard E. Reisman, deputy commissioner of the New York City Police Department, felt quite differently. He testified that the law enabled police to make many arrests for the illegal possession of pistols and revolvers before the possessor has had the opportunity to commit a crime of violence: "On this score, we have had a substantial degree of success. We have been able to prevent many crimes of violence by such arrests." [44]

However, as Representative Dingell stated in his testimony, the Sullivan Law has not had the desired effect either of reducing crime or of keeping guns out of the hands of criminals. Since 1930, he testified, New York police have been steadily reducing the number of pistol permits granted, with no comparable effect on crime rates in the city. And of the guns used in crimes, most are possessed illegally—a fact admitted by New York City officials as well as by officials of other localities with strict gun laws, who further stated that most of these guns were acquired through some other source, usually by mail or out of state.[45] Massachusetts, which has had strict gun laws since 1957, has a similar problem: In 1965 the Department of Public Safety revealed that nearly 87 percent of the weapons recovered from criminals during the previous eight years had been bought not in Massachusetts but in the neighboring states of Maine, New Hampshire, and Vermont, which have more lenient laws.[46] This, for the NRA and other opponents, is proof that strict gun laws will not work.[47] Glassen, the former NRA president, testified:

In 1966, 28.5 percent of all the serious crime in New York City was

42 *FFL*, pp. 55–56.
43 Harris, "Annals of Legislation," p. 73.
44 *Ibid.*, pp. 73–74.
45 *Ibid.*, p. 100.
46 *Ibid.*, p. 70.
47 For a good discussion on the interpretation of crime statistics, see John A. Webster, *Crime Statistics—Facts or Fear?*, Institute of Urban and Regional Development, Center for Planning & Development Research, University of California, Berkeley, December 1966.

committed with the aid of firearms. Unlicensed handguns accounted
for 87.16 percent of the firearms crimes. This, to me, provides ample
proof of the fact that criminals will not abide by the law, or that
strict licensing laws will not significantly reduce crime. . . . It is
often stated by gun control advocates that Dallas, with relatively
lenient gun laws, had an 11.4 homicide rate as opposed to New
York's 6.4 with strict laws, but if one compares the three main categories of crime in which firearms are involved—homicides, aggravated assaults, and robberies—New York's overall rate is much
higher than Dallas's, 434.2 per 100,000 as opposed to 291.2. The
conclusion is definitely warranted that living under strict gun laws
does not actually reduce one's chances of being the victim of a
violent crime.[48]

But proponents of controls see these facts as arguments for their own
case—that present laws are ineffective both because they are not uniform
and because mail order sales are not adequately controlled. According to
a National Crime Commission report:

On the federal level, the statutes do little to control the retail and
mail-order sales of handguns, rifles, and shotguns. . . . Only eight
states have enacted permit laws. If there are local ordinances within
a state, but no state law, the federal provision does not apply. The
prohibition against transport of firearms to, or receipt by, felons or
fugitives applies only to direct interstate shipment and does not prevent such persons from buying firearms locally after they have been
transported from another state. Despite federal laws, therefore,
practically anyone . . . can purchase firearms simply by ordering
them in those states that have few controls. . . . While information
is sparse, there are strong indications that mail-order houses and
other out-of-state sources provide a substantial number of guns to
those who commit crimes.[49]

Proponents argue that there is no adequate check on the backgrounds
of those who purchase guns. Mail order sales are particularly susceptible
to this type of abuse: Checks into shipments by one mail order firm showed
criminal records for 23 percent of their Chicago purchasers; more than 10
percent of their Hartford purchasers; and slightly less than 10 percent of
their Indianapolis purchasers. Many law enforcement officers feel that
strict requirements for licensing all gun purchasers, with an adequate
check for criminal record, mental instability, alcoholism, and certain
other characteristics would contribute mightily to keeping guns out of the
hands of those who show the highest potential to abuse them. Such an
investigation would require fingerprints and character references, as under
New York's Sullivan Law, and opponents of controls roundly object to
this as being directed at the wrong target.

[48] *FFL,* pp. 202–03.
[49] *Ibid.,* pp. 24–25.

Senator Hruska, another opponent of gun control laws, contended that "the burden of overcoming the misuse of the gun by a relatively few people will expose these many millions to harassment, to the possibility of violating the law, these stiff penalties, and this constant business of living in a straitjacket every time they move, every time they do anything—the renewal of a license." [50] Attorney General Clark replied:

> Senator, I hope we would never weigh murder and suicide and armed robbery and tens of thousands of assaults with firearms against mere inconvenience. We are a highly urbanized and highly interdependent people. We have to be willing to make some sacrifices for our own safety and for the safety of others. . . . And if this involves some small inconvenience, we should proudly pay that price. . . . The risks are minimal to any law-abiding citizen. His right to have a gun will not be challenged. His life will be safer because of it.[51]

THE GUN LOBBY: STRATEGIES AND TACTICS OF ANTI-GUN CONTROL FORCES

In a democratic society, laws invariably reflect lawmakers' perceptions of the long-run public interest—perceptions often tempered by lobbyists for special interests. Therefore, the fate of gun control efforts must be analyzed not only by the rationale of various sociopolitical, or legal, or economic arguments pertaining to society overall, but also on the strengths, weaknesses, and influence of vested interests, here most notably the NRA. The gun lobby, spearheaded by the National Rifle Association, includes manufacturers of guns and related equipment (including clothing), sportsmen, target shooters, conservation groups, and right-wing extremist groups.

The National Rifle Association (NRA)

Of the powerful NRA, Representative Abner Mikva remarked that "There's nobody even second to the NRA as a lobby." [52] And one western senator stated: "I'd rather be a deer in hunting season than a politician who has run afoul of the NRA crowd. . . . they don't want *anyone* to tell them *anything* about what to do with their guns, and they *mean* it." [53]

The National Rifle Association was organized in 1871 by a few National Guard officers to enhance the peaceful and safe use of firearms. It gained tax exemption at its founding and is not a registered lobby group, since

[50] *FFL*, p. 617.
[51] *Ibid.*
[52] Robert Sherrill, "The Saturday Night Special and Other Hardware," *The New York Times Magazine*, October 10, 1971, p. 60.
[53] Harris, "Annals of Legislation," p. 57.

only a small part of its funds go to legislative work. By 1972, the nearly million-member organization operated from its own $3 million office building in Washington with a $7.7 million annual budget, a paid staff of 250, 12,000 affiliated clubs around the country, and a 150-member affiliate club operating from the office of the Secretary of Defense.[54]

As the organization grew and broadened its membership, its goals also broadened. These restated aims are: To promote social welfare and public safety, law and order, and the national defense; to educate and train citizens of good repute in the safe and efficient handling of small arms and in the technique of design, production, and group instruction; to increase the knowledge of small arms and promote efficiency in the use of such arms on the part of members of law enforcement agencies, of the Armed Forces, and of citizens who would be subject to service in the event of war; and generally to encourage the lawful ownership and use of small arms by citizens of good repute.[55] In pursuit of these goals, the NRA sponsors fire-arms safety and marksmanship courses, as well as thousands of shooting matches each year. It also selects the rifle and pistol teams that represent the United States in the Olympics and other international competitions.

One of its great membership recruiting strengths was the 1903 law that limited the Pentagon's disposal of surplus firearms and ammunition at discount prices strictly to NRA members. This finally ended in 1967, when the government forced the Pentagon to stop supporting NRA-sponsored National Rifle Matches.[56] A very interesting membership phenomenon occurred between 1964 and 1966 during the civil rights action in the South.[57] NRA membership grew 54 percent in Alabama and 50 percent in Mississippi, the first and second highest rates in the nation, and Alabama's 1965 homicide rate was also the nation's highest. Any conclusions from these correlations are both speculative and horrifying. The most recent membership figures from the NRA's long years of supporting and pro-tecting gun lovers is about 900,000.[58] Furthermore, according to the *Congressional Quarterly,*

> A major source of strength in recruiting membership is a 1903 law (establishing the National Board), and its subsequent amendments, which gives the Pentagon only two days to rid itself of surplus fire-arms and ammunition. It can sell the surplus for scrap. Or it can sell it to NRA members at a bargain price. In 1967 after the Detroit riot, 400 members of the Detroit police force were required to pay a $5 membership fee to the NRA before they could purchase surplus carbines for use in riot control.[59]

54 Stanford N. Sesser, "The Gun: Kingpin of 'Gun Lobby' Has a Million Members, Much Clout in Congress," *The Wall Street Journal,* May 24, 1971, p. 1.
55 Bakal, *Right to Bear Arms,* pp. 131–32.
56 "King's Murder, Riots Spark Demand for Gun Controls," *Congressional Quarterly Weekly Report,* p. 806.
57 Sherrill, *New York Times Magazine,* October 15, 1967, p. 124.
58 An excerpt from a June 15, 1968, letter by Harold W. Glassen, president of the NRA, "Gun Control," *Congressional Quarterly Weekly Report,* June 21, 1968, p. 1558.
59 *FFL,* p. 450.

The National Board is also authorized to provide free ammunition and to lend guns to NRA-affiliated clubs in support of the civilian marksmanship training program. According to Bakal, the cost of these programs for the five-year period ending in 1964 was at least $12.0 million, of which $7.2 million was for free ammunition and $2.3 million was for guns and other equipment on loan. Accounting for the rest of these costs were such items as transportation for rifle teams, and badges, medals, and trophies. The importance of these funds to the organization may be judged by the fact that when in 1948 no appropriations for these programs were granted, the NRA immediately raised its membership fee and canceled that year's national matches. And without the inducement of free guns and ammunition, membership dropped from its then all-time high of nearly 300,000 in 1948 to 230,000 in 1950.[60]

NRA activities are governed by a seventy-five-member board of directors, who are elected by life members *only* (those who have paid $150 for their membership instead of the $7.50 annual dues). Thus it appears that the large body of rank and file members have little control over the policies of NRA or its day-to-day activities, and officials admit that they have never attempted to question the membership about their opinions on gun legislation. "We have never felt the need to take a poll," said past president Harold Glassen.[61]

NRA, the Congress, and the Executive Branch

NRA has well-established links in Congress and boasts at least thirty-five congressmen as members, and a number of sympathizers in the White House and the executive branch.[62] Among the more notable supporters of NRA in Congress are Senators Carl Hayden, John Flynt, Bourke Hickenlooper, Barry Goldwater, Warren Magnusen, and Roman Hruska; and Congressmen Wilbur Mills, Cecil R. King (an NRA director), John D. Dingell, and Robert L. F. Sikes (an NRA director). President Nixon became an NRA life member in 1957.[63]

NRA's relationships with various government agencies were cooled during the Johnson era, which followed on the heels of President Kennedy's assassination, riots, increase in crime rates, and the big move for a gun control law, but during the Nixon administration the NRA had the executive branch as an ally. In July 1971, Carl Bakal wrote that an NRA-affiliated gun club was working out of Defense Secretary Melvin Laird's office and was acting as the focal point for anti-gun control lobbying. Bakal also heard of a January 1971 White House meeting between three top NRA officials, the administration's staff, and gun lobby representatives. One of the apparent outcomes was an announcement at the April 1971 centennial convention of the NRA by their president, Woodson

60 Bakal, pp. 141–42.
61 "Lobby on Target," p. 122.
62 Sesser, "The Gun," p. 1.
63 *Ibid.*

Scott: He said that the NRA had been assured by "important members of the administration" that there would be no further effort to limit gun traffic.[64]

NRA and the Treasury and State Departments

The loopholes in the gun control laws are more than matched by the lackadaisical attitude of the federal bureaucracy charged with the responsibility of enforcing federal laws. For example, although the authority existed under the 1930 and 1934 laws, the Treasury Department did not collect any figures on the production of different types of guns in the United States. In 1968, the only figures available were those collected by the Bureau of Census for 1963. The State and Treasury departments have not done enough to execute the gun control laws of which they are the chief custodians. Specifically, this is the fault of particular bureaucrats. More generally, it is a reflection of governmental nonchalance toward gun control measures.

Existing gun control laws are peppered with loopholes and laxly enforced. Specifically, such laxity is the fault of particular bureaucrats; generally, it reflects government apathy toward gun control measures. The pervasive attitude is summed up in Acting Assistant Secretary William Dickey's comment that "there was no requirement" for his office to collect information legitimately requested by a senator and that he didn't intend to collect it.[65] For more than thirty years, bureaucratic neglect of gun control duties has increased on two fronts: gun dealer supervision and State Department attitude toward gun imports.[66]

The attitude toward the importation of guns seems to be reflected in the words of John Sipes, director of the Office of Munitions Control (OMC) of the State Department. He admitted that his agency was authorized to keep out arms it felt to be detrimental to the security of the United States, but held it did not have the authority to ban firearms for which there is a legitimate commercial market, just because there is the possibility that these guns may end up in the hands of dangerous people. Sipes's statement demonstrates that Congress's interest in passing the Mutual Security Act was only in *how to unload millions of dollars worth of United States arms and ammunition onto other countries.*[67]

NRA Strategies and Tactics

The basic strength of NRA lies in its ability to mobilize and coordinate the efforts of a million members in more than 12,000 affiliated local and state gun clubs.

64 Bakal, *The Right to Bear Arms,* p. 49.
65 Sherrill, *The Saturday Night Special,* p. 142.
66 *Ibid.,* p. 143.
67 *Ibid.,* p. 147.

Strategy. NRA's overall strategy has been initial total opposition to any gun control legislation, to be modified later only if the government submitted to NRA-demanded changes, thereby rendering such legislation effectively useless.[68]

NRA denies this: "Our critics and adversaries often proclaim by word of mouth and on the printed page that the NRA is for minimum firearms controls or no gun regulation at all. This is, of course, completely untrue," said the late executive vice-president Franklin Orth. But NRA "looks on the vast majority of bills for firearms legislation as the misdirected efforts of social reformers, do-gooders and/or the completely uninformed who would accomplish miracles by the passage of another law." [69] In their opposition to the 1968 gun control law, Frank C. Daniel, NRA's secretary, explained that the organization had been unable to support a specific bill, because no one had been able to come up with a definition of a Saturday night special that was agreeable to the organization.[70]

The association frequently cites its support for the 1934 and 1938 federal firearms laws. It should be noted, however, that this support was given only after fighting the government to a standstill, and after provisions in the laws making it illegal to sell handguns in interstate commerce were dropped. Since then, the association has supported only those bills that would weaken existing laws or would impose harsh criminal penalties.

NRA's opposition and pressure tactics enrage gun control proponents less than the strong conviction that NRA garners support by statements calculated to mislead its members. Former Senator Tydings, for whose recent defeat the NRA likes to take credit, described the effects of the association's activities:

> The NRA has convinced outdoor people . . . that the gun bill would deprive them of their right to hunt, or to shoot a marauding coyote or a human predator. In their minds, this is only the first step in a conspiracy to disarm them altogether. The NRA's lies have had a very great effect—so great that I don't know if we can ever reverse it.[71]

Tactics. The main tactic employed by NRA is to exhort members to write to their senators and representatives and register their opposition to any pending gun control legislation. Members are reached via two channels: the well-edited and widely circulated *American Rifleman,* the official organ of the NRA sent free to all dues-paying members; and legislative bulletins sent to members in localities considering firearm legislation. Other tactics include editorials in the *Rifleman* and assistance in the election or defeat of candidates based on their gun control position.

The *Rifleman,* besides carrying articles of interest to the gun enthusiast,

[68] Sherrill, *Saturday Night Special,* p. 60.
[69] "Lobby on Target," p. 112.
[70] Sesser, "The Gun," p. 1.
[71] Harris, "Annals of Legislation," p. 152.

fills two important and related functions for the NRA: it provides a major revenue source through advertising sales (22 percent of the NRA's 1971 income, with the balance primarily from dues); [72] and it promotes gun use and ownership by providing NRA members with prompt notification of any attempt to limit the right to buy, own, use, or sell guns. In a monthly column called "What the Lawmakers Are Doing," the magazine carries "a concise bill-by-bill summary of firearms proposals and legislative action at both the federal and state levels." [73]

Although the *Rifleman* gets the lion's share of advertising revenue, other magazines receiving a share reflect their concern over restrictions on the availability of firearms. The three largest and most prestigious are *Field and Stream*, *Outdoor Life*, and *Sports Afield*. As of 1966, each of these magazines had net receipts of about $500,000 annually from arms and ammunition advertising (about one-sixth of their total advertising income), and each had a circulation of about 1.3 million. All three of the magazines vehemently oppose firearms controls and follow the general lead of NRA.[74] Approximately fifteen additional magazines are devoted exclusively to guns. They reflect a smaller, more homogeneous audience (total 1966 circulation less than 1.5 million), are dependent on a single source for revenue and readership, and are even more vehement and sensational in their gun control opposition.

In the traditional sense of lobbying activities, NRA officers are seldom in direct contact with members of Congress. Instead, they exert pressure through NRA members writing to their representatives. The NRA in 1964 published fifty-seven magazine columns on legislative matters and sent twenty-six legislative bulletins to 141,000 members and clubs in eleven states. "NRA members reacted promptly, firmly, and in force," said the 1964 NRA Operating Report. "As a result, no severe legislation was enacted." [75] Neither the costs of producing the *Rifleman* and the bulletins nor the salaries of the executives whose duties relate to NRA's legislative activities are considered lobbying expenditures. In 1964, the editorial division of the NRA spent a total of $1,617,303, largely on publication and distribution of the *Rifleman*, and the executive staff budget for that year (which includes the salaries of the top officials and four field representatives) was $392,672.[76] In 1965, its expenditures for "legislative and public affairs" were $171,485.86.

> That figure did not include the salaries of officers who, like [then executive vice-president Franklin] Orth, spent much of their time directly or indirectly opposing gun legislation, nor did it include the expenses that the *American Rifleman* incurred in printing sixty-six pages of editorial material that year, or the cost of running the maga-

[72] David Gumpert, "The Gun: To the Arms Industry, Control Controversy Is a Business Problem," *The Wall Street Journal*, May 31, 1972, p. 21.
[73] Bakal, *Right to Bear Arms*, p. 112.
[74] *Ibid.*, pp. 109–11.
[75] Cited in *FFL*, p. 445.
[76] Bakal, *Right to Bear Arms*, p. 138.

zine and the publicity department. . . . According to the sub-committee staff, if all these expenses were totted up they would come to more than two million dollars a year.[77]

What is the content of the materials that the NRA sends to its members, which it says do not constitute lobbying but merely information? If it were true that the organization provided its members with accurate information on pending legislation and that it attempted to educate them in the issues involved in control legislation, its activities would probably generate little controversy. Such, however, is not the case. Members of Congress, presidents, law enforcement officers, and others who support control legislation continually accuse the NRA of misrepresentation and distortion, of capitalizing on and at times promoting irrational public fears and prejudices, and of opposing any and all approaches to the issue of controls. They further point out that the organization receives considerable public largesse in support of its activities, both directly in terms of benefits through its relationship with the Pentagon and indirectly in terms of its tax-exempt status.

In its legislative bulletins, for example, the association is sometimes incorrect in its descriptions of the provisions in a given bill. In 1965 the Johnson administration, riding high on its landslide victory, introduced a bill that would have limited interstate mail order sales to individuals (as opposed to dealers), prohibited sales of handguns to minors and nonresidents of the state in which the sale was made, and prohibited sales of rifles and shotguns to those under eighteen. Other provisions prohibited the importation of foreign surplus weapons not suitable for sporting purposes and of "destructive devices" such as bazookas and mortars. The bill required that dealers keep records of their sales to aid in prosecution of violations of federal and local laws, and raised the fees for various manufacturers' and dealers' licenses. "The purpose of this measure is simple," said Attorney General Katzenbach in support of the bill. "It is merely to help states protect themselves against the unchecked flood of mail-order weapons to residents whose purposes might not be responsible, or even lawful." [78] The NRA sent an analysis of the bill to its members attacking the bill on nine grounds—all of which, according to a Treasury rebuttal, were false, misleading, or meaningless.

If response to the NRA's pleas for communication with legislators is an indication of membership support for its policies, there may indeed be no need to poll the members. The organization suggests that its appeals can generate as many as a half-million letters to Congress, and members of Congress tend to agree. In 1965, for example, opposition to then-pending legislation reached epic proportions: "I have received an enormous amount of mail, really enormous, almost unbelievable . . . expressing opposition to this bill," said Senator Jacob Javits. And Senator Roman Hruska stated that "By actual count, only three letters supporting

[77] Harris, "Annals of Legislation," p. 108.
[78] *Ibid.*, p. 90.

the bill have been received so far out of more than three thousand." [79] Some supporters of control legislation, however, have little doubt about whose opinions these letters express. William Mooney, Jr., a field investigator on the subcommittee staff, remarked:

> These sportsmen are mostly ordinary, decent fellows. They have no idea that they have been intentionally misled for someone else's personal gain, and that they are indirectly responsible for thousands and thousands of unnecessary deaths and injuries every year. If we could only get the truth across to them, they'd back us all the way.[80]

The most interesting part of the NRA's success is that it has always supported the side directly opposite to the national feeling favoring gun control. The polls have covered different issues, but the basic question has been the requirement of police permits or the registration of firearms.[81] The surveys showed the following percentages favoring registration: 1938— 84 percent; 1940—80 percent; 1958—75 percent; 1963—73 percent; 1964— 78 percent; 1965—73 percent; 1966—68 percent; 1967—70–73 percent; and 1968—71–81 percent. Against such overwhelming public opposition, the NRA has succeeded by arousing in its membership the feeling of being threatened, causing protective letter-writing barrages, while the complacent public majority is aroused sporadically by assassinations and then only for a very short period.

The Industry

While the gun and ammunitions companies try to keep a low profile in the struggle between anti-gun control forces and the gun lobby, their economic stake is significant. According to *The Wall Street Journal*:

> Gun manufacturers play an important part in bankrolling the thus-far largely successful fight to minimize gun legislation. Money from gun makers and sellers, either through outright subsidy or indirectly in the form of advertising in membership journals and the like, helps finance such leaders in the antigun fight as the National Rifle Association and the National Shooting Sports Foundation.[82]

The NRA would doubtless have gone out of business—in fact, it did suspend operations for eight years from 1892 to 1900—if the gun and ammunition industry hadn't seen it as a beautiful quasi-official flag to march under. Operational expenses for many of the early NRA matches were subsidized by DuPont Powder Company, U.S. Cartridge Company

[79] *Ibid.*, p. 128.
[80] *Ibid.*, p. 130.
[81] G. H. Gallup, *The Gallup Poll: Public Opinion 1935–1971* (1972), pp. 99–100, 1625–27, 1858–59, 1922–33, 2026–27, 2077; Hadley Cantril, ed., *Public Opinion, 1935–1946* (Princeton: Princeton University Press, 1951), p. 214; note 16, p. 805.
[82] Gumpert, "The Gun," p. 1.

of Massachusetts, and Union Metallic Cartridge Company, to name a few members of the industry.[83]

Economic fallout from the gun industry and the promotion of shooting sports affects a large and diverse group of interests, from actual gun manufacturers to producers of related sporting goods (specialty clothing, camping gear and vehicles, leather gun cases, and other accessories), sporting magazines, shooting clubs, and wildlife organizations. The economic base of the industry is not small. In 1968, *The New York Times* estimated the dollar volume of nonmilitary gun sales (including ammunition and less than $100 million in sales of imported weapons) at $400 million annually.[84] By 1971, sales had grown to $553.8 million.[85] These figures are, however, only the beginning. Guns are also advertised: In 1967, according to the Publisher's Information Bureau, $3.85 million was spent in retail advertising of guns.[86] Related sporting equipment sales and advertising, gun club memberships, magazine subscriptions—all these add to the basic figures for the industry and combine to form a powerful economic interest in the continuing easy accessibility of guns.

The industry is highly competitive; production statistics are closely guarded, and publicity is avoided at every level. The one issue unifying the more traditional members of the industry is opposition to the manufacturers of cheap handguns. They argue that criminals are attracted to the low price of the Saturday night special. They feel that these guns are dangerous because they are poorly made, but more important, they feel that their sale provides pro-gun control forces with that much more ammunition in seeking restrictive gun laws. The National Shooting Sports Foundation (NSSF), a trade group of arms makers, says that none of its members produce such guns. Its president, Warren Page, adds that the group views their existence as a "great, grave problem." [87]

One of the two main organs of the industry's public relations effort is the NSSF, established in 1960 to coordinate the efforts of many public and industrial groups "to monitor vigilantly the yearly torrent of bills in Congress, legislatures and city councils aimed at the regulation of firearms." [88]

A member of the board of governors of NSSF, testifying in 1963 in opposition to restrictive controls, stated that NSSF had been established "to foster in the American public a better understanding and a more active appreciation of all shooting sports." [89] At that time the foundation had ninety members—manufacturers, retailers, publishers, importers, manufacturers and dealers in accessories, and the National Wildlife Federation. According to a report by the *Congressional Quarterly*:

---

[83] Sherrill, *The Saturday Night Special,* p. 212.
[84] "Many Retailers Are Ending or Playing Down Sales of Guns and Ammunition," June 23, 1968, Sec. 3, p. 14.
[85] Gumpert, "The Gun," p. 1.
[86] "Advertising: Of Guns and Media for Guns," *The New York Times,* June 7, 1968, p. 63.
[87] Gumpert, "The Gun," p. 22.
[88] Bakal, *Right to Bear Arms,* p. 120.
[89] *Hearings,* p. 3495.

The organization spends large sums of money on advertising and promotion ($200,000 in 1963, according to Bakal), and some of the ads are concerned with legislation. For instance, one which ran in outdoor magazines went: "Lawmakers who know the feel of the field can become great marksmen. Good enough to shoot holes in the anti-firearms argument." The NSSF has never registered as a lobbyist.[90]

In addition to NSSF, nine of the largest makers of guns and ammunition belong to a trade association, the Sporting Arms and Ammunition Manufacturers' Institute (SAAMI), founded in 1926. Its principal purpose does not seem to be fostering opposition to control legislation. According to Bakal, "A promotional program of the institute conducted by its Sportsmen's Service Bureau was incorporated together with the bureau itself into the National Shooting Sports Foundation in January 1963." [91] The *Congressional Quarterly,* however, reported that SAAMI has opposed gun control legislation.

The rapid escalation of violence in America may be changing opinions even among manufacturers. In 1968 five major firms submitted a statement to the subcommittee in which they supported a number of restrictions on firearms, including licensing of gun owners:

> While recognizing the inconveniences such legislation will cause sportsmen and hunters, the above-named manufacturers believe that the national interest demands effective legislative deterrents to the misuse of guns. The inconveniences can be minimized, and the proper use of guns for sporting purposes protected if the gun industry, sportsmen and conservation groups cooperate with the Congress and state legislatures in support of a system to license gun owners and users.[92]

In addition, Remington and Winchester-Western (two of the five) offered their support to the National Advisory Commission on Civil Disorders for an independent and objective appraisal of just how significant firearms were in the overall disorder situation in 1968. That offer resulted in a five-month study by the Stanford Research Institute. In its report, *Firearms, Violence and Civil Disorder,* SRI stated:

> The research found Winchester and Remington quite earnest in their desire to identify and follow through on measures to protect the public in future disorders. Working with the International Association of Chiefs of Police, they have instituted provisions, through Project Secure, for public safety measures in anticipation of the possibility of riots or during riots. . . . Stanford Research Institute believes such steps to be quite significant and helpful.[93]

---

[90] *FFL,* p. 450.
[91] Bakal, *Right to Bear Arms,* p. 119.
[92] *FFL,* p. 903.
[93] *Ibid.,* pp. 237–38.

Conservation Groups

Conservation groups make strange bedfellows with gun control opponents, but they depend heavily on the financial support of the firearms
and ammunitions industry. Furthermore, a sizable portion of the federal
funds earmarked for wildlife and conservation are directly related to gun
and ammunition manufacturing. Under the Pittman-Robertson Act (the
Federal Aid in Wildlife Restoration Act) of 1937, which was supported by
the gun industry, an 11 percent excise tax on the manufacture of sporting
arms and ammunition is used for aiding state fish and game agencies. In
1967, this excise tax generated $28 million for the states.[94]

Further cementing the relationship between conservation activities and
anti-gun control sentiment is the fact that hunting license revenues are
also applied to state and local wildlife programs. The Virginia Commission of Game and Inland Fisheries wrote to the subcommittee in 1968 in
opposition to controls, stating that if it became more difficult to legally
obtain, possess, transport, and use firearms for legitimate purposes, there
would be less and less participation in hunting and other shooting sports.
Since hunting licenses and taxes on sporting arms and ammunition support virtually all government programs for wildlife protection and management, the wildlife resources of the nation would be endangered to the
same degree that interest in shooting sports would wane.[95]

Not all conservationists share either in the gun industry's financial
support nor in the concept of managing wildlife for the benefit of hunting
activities. But the National Wildlife Federation and the Wildlife Management Institute, two of the largest beneficiaries of industry support,
were created with the help of the industry and have numerous industry
representatives as officers and directors. The current president of the
World Wildlife Fund's American chapter and the honorary president of
World Wildlife, C. R. Gutermuth, is the second-ranking officer of NRA.
John Olin, retired chairman of Olin Corporation (a manufacturer of arms
and ammunition), is a director of World Wildlife. Critics also say that
World Wildlife has accepted large contributions from oil company execu-
tives, which may account for its support of the controversial Alaskan
Pipeline.[96] They are, like many state and local wildlife agencies, staunchly
opposed to firearms controls. Thomas Kimball, executive director of the
National Wildlife Federation, testified in 1968:

> The reason a wildlife conservation organization such as ours is in-
> terested in gun legislation revolves around the fact that hunters
> contribute materially to the wildlife management programs of this
> country through their license fees, and that they are quite interested

94 *Congressional Quarterly,* April 12, 1968, cited in *FFL,* p. 450.
95 *FFL,* p. 773.
96 John Kwitny, "Who's the Real Conservationist? That's An Issue in a Big Inter-
necine Quarrel," *The Wall Street Journal,* November 26, 1973, p. 9.

in seeing that legislation that is considered by the Congress does not materially and adversely affect this interest. . . .

For this reason, the federation is vitally interested in preventing any unnecessary discouragement of law-abiding citizens desiring to purchase, possess, and transport arms for hunting purposes, while at the same time anxious to be helpful in reducing the crime rate.[97]

Extremist Groups

One final component, and probably the least savory, of the lobby must be mentioned. Various extremist and paramilitary groups, such as the Minutemen, Ku Klux Klan, Breakthrough, and Revolutionary Action Movement, have more of an ideological than an economic interest in protecting their freedom of access to firearms. They nonetheless are able to benefit from the economic and political muscle of the rest of the lobby, and are equally vociferous in protecting their right to own guns. These groups frequently form or join organizations which through NRA affiliation are eligible for special discount rates on surplus military weapons and ammunition. The NRA repudiates these groups and does not knowingly allow them to join the association, but lacks screening procedures to identify individuals.

WHAT LIES AHEAD?

Five years after enactment of the 1968 law, one thing is clear: The flow of guns to criminal elements has not been cut. As opponents of gun control had predicted, when legitimate purchase became difficult, criminals began to steal guns. Gun thefts have skyrocketed since the passage of the law. The National Crime Center has reports of 669,549 stolen guns, and its files are expanding at a rate of over 100,000 a year.[98]

Proponents of gun control find this argument illogical. The question is not further relaxation of the law but tighter security to minimize thefts. Proponents also argue in favor of closing certain loopholes in the 1968 law as a further deterrent to criminal gun use. That law banned the import of cheap handguns, but the import of their parts was unaffected. Result: parts imports from 1968 to 1972 were sufficient to produce 4,072,-111 Saturday night specials.[99]

Although the law ended the mail order gun business, another loophole made this provision ineffective. The efforts of the pro-gun control forces to close this loophole have been unsuccessful so far. On the other hand,

[97] *FFL,* pp. 539–40.
[98] William M. Bulkeley, "Thefts of Firearms Are Skyrocketing in the U.S. in Apparent Bid to Circumvent 1968 Control Law," *The Wall Street Journal,* January 3, 1974, p. 26.
[99] "Gun Controls—Reforms Fall Short of Mark," *San Francisco Chronicle,* November 23, 1973, p. 20.

anti-gun control forces have succeeded in gradually eliminating some of the more restrictive provisions of the law. If the past is any guide, the prognosis for the future for the proponents of gun control is not encouraging.

SELECTED REFERENCES

BAKAL, CARL, *The Right to Bear Arms* (New York: McGraw-Hill, 1966).

———, "The Failure of Federal Gun Control," *Saturday Review,* July 3, 1971.

BRABNER-SMITH, JOHN, "Firearms Regulations," *Law and Contemporary Problems,* 1, 4 (1934).

CAMPBELL, JAMES S., "Violence in America," *New York Times Encyclopedic Almanac,* 1971.

"Constitutional Limitations on Federal Firearms Control," *Washburn Law Journal,* winter 1969.

"Constitutional Limitations on Firearms Regulations," *Duke Law Journal,* August 1969.

"Defying the Gun Lobby," *Nation,* September 28, 1970, p. 262.

"Firearms: Problems of Controls," *Harvard Law Review,* 80 (April 1967), 1328–46.

HALEY, MARTIN R., and JAMES M. KISS, "Larger Stakes in Statehouse Lobbying," *Harvard Business Review,* January–February, 1974, pp. 125–35.

HARRIS, RICHARD, "Annals of Legislation: If You Love Your Guns," *The New Yorker,* April 20, 1968.

KEY, V. O. JR., *Politics, Parties, and Pressure Groups,* 5th ed. (New York: Crowell, 1968).

"Model N.Y. Lobbying Statute," *Columbia Journal of Law and Social Problems,* 4 (March 1968), 69.

MOSK, S., "Gun Control Legislation: Valid and Necessary," *New York Law Forum,* winter 1968.

"Public Disclosure of Lobbying Activities," *Fordham Law Review,* 38 (March 1970), 524.

Report of the Senate Committee on the Judiciary, Omnibus Crime Control and Safe Streets Act of 1968. S. Rep. No. 1097, 90th Cong., 2d sess., 1968.

RICHARDSON, M. E., "Lobbying and Public Relations—Sensitive, Suspect or Worse?" *Antitrust Bulletin,* 10 (July–August 1965), 507–18.

"Right to Bear Arms," *South Carolina Law Review,* 19 (1967).

SHERRILL, ROBERT, "A Lobby on Target," *The New York Times Magazine,* October 15, 1967.

———, "The Saturday Night Special and Other Hardware," *The New York Times Magazine,* October 10, 1971.

———, *The Saturday Night Special* (New York: Charterhouse, 1973).

SMITH, JUDITH G., *Political Brokers* (New York: Liveright, 1972).

U.S. Congress, House, Subcommittee on Interstate and Foreign Commerce, *Hearings on Several Bills Pending Before the Committee to Regulate the Interstate Shipment of Firearms,* 71st Cong., 2d sess., April 1930.

U.S. Congress, House, Subcommittee on Ways and Means, *Hearings on H.R. 9066 (National Firearms Act)*, 73rd Cong., 2d sess., April–May 1934.

U.S. Congress, Senate, Judiciary Committee, Subcommittee on Juvenile Delinquency, various hearings: *On Interstate Traffic in Mail-Order Firearms*, 1963; *On Amendments to Federal Firearms Act*, 1965; *On Amendments to Federal Firearms Act*, 1967; *On Bills to Register Firearms, Establish a National Firearms Registry, and Disarm Lawless Persons*, 1968; *On Various Senate Resolutions*, 1969; *On Amendments to 1968 Gun Control Act to Prohibit the Sale of Saturday Night Special Handguns*, 1971.

U.S. Congress, House, Committee on Ways and Means, *Hearings on Proposed Amendments to Firearms Acts*, Parts 1 and 2, 89th Cong., 1st sess., July 1965.

U.S. Congress, House, Judiciary Committee, *Hearings on H.R. 5037, 5038, 5384, 5385, and 5386 (Anti-Crime Program)*, 90th Cong., 1st sess., March–April 1967.

WOLFGANG, MARVIN E., "Patterns in Criminal Homicide," in *Homicide in the United States*, ed. H. C. Brearley (Montclair, N.J.: Patterson Smith, 1969).

WRIGHT, PAUL B., "The Effectiveness of Federal Firearms Control," *Brooklyn Law Review 35, 3* (1969).

ZIEGLER, L. HARMON, and G. WAYNE PEAK, *Interest Groups in American Society* (Englewood Cliffs, N.J.: Prentice-Hall, 1964).

ZIMRING, F., "Is Gun Control Likely to Reduce Violent Killings?" *University of Chicago Law Review*, summer 1968.

Cases:

Commonwealth v. *Murphy*, 44 N.E. 138 (Mass. 1896).

Haynes v. *U.S.*, 390 U.S. 85, 98 (1968).

Presser v. *Illinois*, 116 U.S. 252 (1886).

U.S. v. *Miller* 307 U.S. 174, 178 (1939).

Indirect/Direct Use
of the President's
Executive Authority

THE STEEL PRICE CONTROVERSY

KENNEDY-JOHNSON AND THE DISCRETIONARY
USE OF PRESIDENTIAL POWER

> Sometime ago I asked each American to consider what he would do for his country, and I asked steel companies. In the last twenty-four hours we had their answer.
>   My father always told me that all businessmen were sons of bitches, but I never believed it until now.
>   ——President JOHN F. KENNEDY

> The steel controversy was the result of a power struggle in which—either by accident or design—U.S. Steel openly challenged the office of the Presidency, and the President chose to meet that challenge with the full powers of the office of the Presidency—but . . . he paid a tremendous price for his "victory."
>   —ROY HOOPES
>   in *The Steel Crisis*

We have traveled quite some distance in the area of presidential "persuasion" and business "cooperation" since the classic confrontation between President Kennedy and Roger Blough of U.S. Steel. There have been "voluntary" restraints on foreign investments, which were not so voluntary to begin with but eventually became compulsory restraints during President Johnson's term. In the Nixon administration various "game plans" and a series of "phases" of varying degrees of voluntariness emerged to direct the nation's economy. It is surprising to realize the extent to which businessmen have reconciled themselves to the inevitability of such persuasion. The dissent, if there is any, is so muted as to be ineffective.

THE ISSUES

Two basic questions raised by the steel price controversy still remain unanswered: How appropriate is the discretionary use of presidential power through the prestige of the office, and what is the sociopolitical environment that makes it possible? What are its consequences on the economy and society? More recently, we have become aware of even more serious side effects that need careful study and analysis, among them those caused by the Watergate scandal and ITT's alleged use of political pressure and campaign contributions to gain a favorable settlement of its antitrust case and its interference in Chilean internal political affairs.

The primary focus of this study is the social and political environment in the United States as it affects vital industrial enterprises—the concepts of free market, competitive economy, and freedom of private enterprise notwithstanding—and the obligation of the government to protect the public interest as it sees it. What happens when the delicate balance between government and business spheres of activity is upset by changes in economic circumstances or by the outlook, beliefs, and actions of those who control these institutions? The ensuing struggle and the outcome are never confined to the immediate issues but have a lasting effect on all social institutions. The steel price controversy provides us with a classic example. Brewing since the Eisenhower days, it exploded with tremendous impact on the national horizon when, despite President Kennedy's urging, the U.S. Steel Corporation defied him and announced an across-the-board price increase on April 10, 1962. As one observer pointed out, the issues surrounding the price of steel were not of economics, but of power.[1] The complicated and controversial economics of steel pricing cannot be treated exhaustively here. Treatment of economic issues is limited to providing an understanding of some of the motivations of the parties involved in the controversy and the use or misuse of statistics to support various viewpoints.[2]

More specifically, one might ask:

[1] Roy Hoopes, *The Steel Crisis* (New York: John Day, 1963), p. 243.
[2] Some sources concerned with the economics of steel prices are Charles L. Schultze, "Study Paper No. 1, Recent Inflation in the United States," for the Joint Economic Committee's "Study of Employment, Growth, and Price Levels," United States Congress, September 1959; "Employment, Growth, and Price Levels: Report of the Joint Economic Committee," Congress of the United States, January 26, 1960; "Administered Prices: A Compendium on Public Policy," Subcommittee on Antitrust and Monopoly of the Committee on the Judiciary, U.S. Senate, 88th Cong., 1st sess., March 11, 1963; G. J. McManus, "Has Steel Turned Profit Corner?" *Iron Age,* November 7, 1968, pp. 57–58; Robert R. Miller, "Price Stability, Market Control, and Imports in the Steel Industry," *Journal of Marketing,* April 1968, pp. 16–20; Gertrude Shirk, "The 5.94-Year Cycle in Steel Production," *Cycles,* May 1968, pp. 54–60; Richard S. Thorn, "The Trouble with Steel," *Challenge,* July–August 1967, pp. 8–13.

1. What are the social and political consequences of the use of the Presidential office to intervene in the marketplace?

2. If it is in the nation's interest that the behavior of certain industries be restrained in some way, should it not be done through specific legislation that grants the President authority to do so?

3. To the extent that such interest and authority are not clearly defined, who should define them? When, as in the current case, the President takes it upon himself to do so, should there be limits on his authority?

4. Assuming that the authority to take action is implied in the President's responsibility for the nation's economic health, questions of specific tactics arise. For example:

   a. How should one distinguish between "persuasion" and "coercion" when the President asks corporations to roll back prices?

   b. When a President enters into an economic dispute, does he raise the level of dispute to unreasonable proportions and make a rational solution difficult or impossible?

   c. What are the likely effects of continuous Presidential intervention or jawboning on the prestige and efficacy of the office of the President?

   d. How does jawboning affect the lawmaking powers of the U.S. Congress? Does it mean "government by fiat"?

   e. What are the inherent dangers in the use or abuse of public opinion by a President against the actions of a special-interest group acting within their legal rights but allegedly not in the public interest as seen by the President?

5. Is the big corporation immune to the discipline of the marketplace as Galbraith and others have argued and does it therefore require other types of social discipline, such as government intervention?

BACKGROUND

The Eisenhower Legacy

In June 1959 the United Steelworkers Union called for a strike against the steel industry, and in the same month the Eisenhower administration, acting through Vice-President Richard M. Nixon and Secretary of Labor James P. Mitchell, began participating in the negotiations between industry and union. To both parties in the negotiations, who had been preparing for the talks for nine months, the government intervention came as a surprise. The government, calling for an agreement that would not necessitate a price increase in steel, said any wage increases should be justified on the basis of increased worker productivity alone. The contract not only did not prevent a price increase but the increase was rather long lasting.

The contract, to extend until mid-1962, called for periodic wage increases —the final one being in October 1961.

By July 1961 both industry and union were planning ahead for the 1962 talks. According to *Business Week,* "the industry is uncomfortably aware that its every move will be under the close scrutiny of the Administration." In fact, these feelings began when John F. Kennedy was elected to the presidency the previous November, for "both his position as a senator and his labor policies as a presidential candidate left no doubts about a quick end of any hands-off policy in disputes." The steel industry became even more uneasy in July 1961 when Kennedy's advisory committee on labor-management relations began a study of "free and responsible collective bargaining and industrial peace." [3]

Steel Prices and the Liberal Democrats

Inflation was a key concern of the 1961 Congress. The Democratic majority, determined to control it, was sure of sympathetic understanding in the New Frontier activism of the Kennedy administration. Therefore, when the steel industry publications speculated about a price increase of $4 to $5 per ton to compensate for the union pay raise, there was a flurry of debate and activity in the Senate.[4] On August 22, 1961, Senator Frank E. Moss (D, Utah) contended that between 1947 and 1958, 40 percent of the rise in the wholesale price index stemmed from steel prices being pushed up faster and further than the average of all other commodity prices. He felt that steel's importance in the United States price structure could scarcely be overestimated as it was not only a truly basic commodity, upon which most of our industrial capability depended, but its price had an enormous psychological effect on the price-setting process in other industries and was traditionally a bellwether of the economy. Through pyramiding, a $6 per ton rise in the price of steel in 1958 raised the cost of a tractor using only half a ton of steel as much as $97!

Senator Albert Gore (D, Tenn.), by far the most vociferous Senate opponent of steel's pricing policies, charged that the steel industry administered prices—prices set without regard to economic laws of supply and demand. He cited a study by the Joint Economic Committee of the Congress [5] which "proved beyond reasonable doubt that administered prices played the key role in the inflation of recent years." According to Gore, the industry had "established something of a ritual when the time for administered price increase is upon them." He further contended that "market forces will not bring about, nor will they justify, this increase," since the industry was earning a "good rate of return on low levels of

---

[3] "Steel Has Eye on Washington," *Business Week,* July 22, 1961, pp. 102–3.
[4] For documentation of senators' statements, see the *Congressional Record* for the 87th Cong., 1st sess., 1961, August 22, pp. 16679–88, 16694–708, 16710–14; August 29, pp. 17324–25; September 7, pp. 18519–64.
[5] John F. Kennedy, while still a senator, was a member of this committee in 1959.

production." The senator concluded that public welfare demands prevented a price rise and "the real question is how to prevent such a rise
within the framework of our free enterprise system." This prevention
would have to be the government's job, and Gore indicated several ways
it could act:

1. The president of the United States should use his great legal and
   moral powers in which he would be backed by the majority of the
   Congress. Should the steel industry show any recalcitrance, he
   should not hesitate to pursue many options open to him, including
   "bringing to bear the vast weight of public opinion."
2. The Federal Trade Commission could move to police the steel industry according to the mandate laid down for it by Congress.
3. The Department of Justice, Antitrust Division, could investigate the
   steel industry in light of administered prices.

Gore made one of the more controversial statements of the debate when
he said that large steel companies should possibly be divided into smaller
units to restore true competition and free enterprise to the steel industry.
And, if all else failed, steel prices could be brought under utility-type
regulations. Few would favor this, but it might be necessary. The public
and the government must not be victimized by either big business or big
labor, or both.

Senator Estes Kefauver (D, Tenn.), chairman of the Subcommittee on
Antitrust and Monopoly which investigated the steel industry after the
1959 strike, also felt that the steel price rise was unjustified. He noted that
between 1947 and 1959, according to the Bureau of Labor Statistics,
average hourly earnings in the steel industry rose 113 percent while man-
hour productivity increased only 43 percent. Thus the unit labor cost
grew, but by only 70 percent, while steel prices jumped 109.7 percent.
Kefauver added that there was no basis for the industry's frequent claim
that an increase in employment costs was accompanied by increases in
nonemployment costs, since the industry had failed to show any such nonemployment cost increases.

Kefauver contended that a price hike in the face of unused capacity was
"a violation of the consent order entered into in 1951 by the steel industry
under Section 5 of the Federal Trade Commission Act," under which the
industry was "ordered to cease and desist from entering into any 'planned
common course of action, understanding or agreement' to adopt, establish,
fix, or maintain prices." [6]

Kefauver began his argument by noting that when one steel company
lowered its prices, competing companies also lowered theirs. However,

[6] In 1948 the Federal Trade Commission issued a complaint against virtually all members of the steel industry, charging that there had been a conspiracy to fix prices in
violation of Section 5 of the Federal Trade Commission Act. It was a major antitrust
case. There were 1,237 exhibits and 5,458 pages of testimony. Finally, on June 15, 1951,
the steel companies voluntarily entered into a consent decree which they themselves
had proposed to the commission.

illogically, the same rationale was used for price increases: prices were *raised* to meet competition! Why, Kefauver asked, did firms with equal or greater efficiency invariably feel it necessary to go along with U.S. Steel's increases? And why, in view of the relationship between operating rate, as a percentage of capacity, and return on investment, did no major steel producer adopt a *smaller* price increase than the leader's?

A final economic point presented by Senators Albert Gore and Hubert H. Humphrey (D, Minn.) was the impact any steel price increase might have on the industry's talks with the United Steelworkers Union. "If steel prices rise in October it would be naive of the steel companies to believe that the advance in profit margins which results will last much longer than the end of the next series of labor-management negotiations in mid-1962."

The Republican Reply

The widespread and generally negative press reaction to the Democratic attack on the steel industry was variously used by the Republican senators to support their arguments. The press comments were divided into three main areas: The attack on the steel industry was also an attack on the free enterprise system, the attack was well planned, and the tactics used were those of intimidation and fear and were unworthy of the representatives of the people in a democratic society. The following comments were perhaps typical of those expressed by the news media in general.

A *New York Times* editorial attacked Gore's "threats" to break up the steel industry:

> The private enterprise system operates on the assumption that prices should be set in the marketplace, and reflect the force of competition among buyers and sellers. The Senate floor is not the marketplace. . . . Competition is probably a much more real force in the American economy than Senator Gore believes. . . .
>
> In the case of steel, for example, there is not only the elementary competition of different producers and sellers, but also the competition to steel from other metals and plastics, and the significant competition given domestic steel by imports of foreign steel.[7]

The August 31 issue of *Iron Age,* a steel industry trade publication, said of the Democrats who led the attack on steel that the timing of "this well-planned attack" had a definite purpose. It added up like this:

> Although this type of moral suasion is not direct control, it can have the same effect. The importance of the group attack can not be over-emphasized. This group represents the Senate majority, the Administration, and the forces of trustbusting, small business, the consumer,

7 "Price Fixing in Congress," *The New York Times,* August 24, 1961.

and labor. Like a single voice, they agreed the nation's steel companies could not justify price increases this fall.[8]

On September 7, 1961, the Republican minority in the Senate responded to the Democratic attacks on a possible steel price increase. Senator Everett Dirksen (R, Ill.) said:

> This appears, so far as I know, to be the first attempt at psychological price control by using threats, and by using persuasion, as weapons and as appeals to a kind of fear instinct. . . . One has no business trying, through the powers of government and through threats, to tell the producers what the price shall be unless they have had an opportunity to present their case. . . .

Republican senators criticized the Democrats' economic reasoning. Senator Barry Goldwater gave the most complete and detailed answer to the attacks on the steel industry.

Strategy. Of the Democrats' strategy, Goldwater said that by attacking the industry before it had made any price increases, the Democrats were "laying the groundwork for controls," and they should "explain why they have not [also] taken vigorous anti-inflation action on unnecessary government spending, or have not exerted equal pressure on current wage demands which, in the past, have proved to be the most contributory factor behind 'cost-push' inflation."

Causes of Inflation. Inflation, said Goldwater, must be attributed to three broad influences "far beyond the confines of a single company or industry" such as steel: government deficit spending; cost-push inflation; and "better business conditions," or "the reemployment of production resources which have been idle for the past year and a half."

When government blamed the wrong sources for inflation, it put the steel industry "in an economic-political dilemma." Economics prevented raising prices during bad market periods (although costs continued to rise), but in good periods the government tried to prevent a price-cost adjustment.

Competition in the Steel Industry

Goldwater contended that there *was* competition in the steel industry, that many large steel buyers frequently divided their orders, playing one steel company against another, and cited specific voluntary price cuts:

> The Senators are really saying that free enterprise—the competitive marketplace—is not the proper place to set prices. They are also say-

---

[8] R. W. Crosby, "Senators Launch Attack Against 'Phantom' Steel Price Hikes," *Iron Age*, August 31, 1961, pp. 55–57.

ing that American business is not public-interest minded, but is avaricious to the point where it must be broken into little pieces or completely regulated by a political body.

This, by any other name, is socialism.

Statistics. Goldwater attacked the Democratic senators' use of statistics. The base years for their statistics, the senator said, were designed to favor their argument and were "nontypical."

As an example of what changing the base year would do for statistics, Senator Wallace F. Bennett (R, Utah) later noted that if 1940 were used as a base year, employment costs from 1940 to 1960 increased 322 percent and output per man-hour increased 40 percent. "This represents an inflationary gap of 282 percentage points. Prices were bound to increase under such pressures. And this they did, to the extent of 174 percent."

Iron Age criticized using 1947 as a base year as a "setup to prove one point alone—what the White House wanted to prove." During the Depression steel prices were "among the lowest in the century" due to a "bloodletting spate of price cutting" from 1932 to 1939. The fast pace of wartime production resulted in an industry "hard up for money to expand its capacity, to repair its plants and equipment." [9] Steel began to raise its prices after the war, not to gouge the consumer but rather, in the words of *Business Week,* to "recover profitability and generate heavy retained earnings to help finance massive plant rehabilitation and expansion." Thus began a price spiral lasting until 1955. In 1958, however, U.S. Steel, feeling that it "might be pricing its product too high," refused to lead in any price increase after the labor settlement and "forced its competitors to take the initiative. . . . Thus began the price stability of the past 37 months." [10]

Balance of Payments. Goldwater accused the Democratic senators of implying that the country's balance-of-payments problems were due solely to the excess of steel imports over exports when in fact the trend was paralleled by almost all of American industry. The American steel industry could not compete because employment costs had risen faster than the productivity level, but to compete and produce, industry needed the best of equipment, and that came only from private investment. Therefore, the profit incentive must be kept alive if the United States steel industry was to be competitive. Finally, Goldwater argued that

If the steel companies charged too much, they must have made too much money. Yet, every investment yardstick shows just the opposite. . . . If it [the steel industry] has that kind of power—and ended up with that kind of result—it is the most public spirited private

[9] Tom Campbell, "Steel Men Hot Under the Collar at President's Price Attack," *Iron Age,* September 14, 1961, pp. 143–44.
[10] "Steel Price Increase Hopes Are Dashed," *Business Week,* September 16, 1961, p. 25.

enterprise in the history of this country. Certainly no amount of public control and regulation could do as well.

The President Acts

On September 6, 1961, the day before the Republican rebuttal in the Senate, President Kennedy sent telegrams to the chief executive officers of the twelve [11] largest steel companies, saying: "I am taking this means of communicating to you, and to the chief executive offices of 11 other steel companies, my concern for stability of steel prices. . . ."

Using 1947 as the base period, he contended that between 1947 and 1958 steel prices rose by 120 percent—during the same period industrial prices as a whole rose by 39 percent, and employment costs in the steel industry rose by 85 percent—providing much of the inflationary impetus in the American economy and adversely affecting steel exports and United States balance of payments. He went on to say that although since 1958 the general price level and steel prices had stabilized, this was accomplished at the cost of persistent unemployment and underutilized productive capacity, including that of the steel industry, whose utilization rate during the preceding three years had averaged 65 percent. In consequence

> Many persons have come to the conclusion that the United States can achieve price stability only by maintaining a substantial margin of unemployment and excess capacity and by accepting a slow rate of economic growth. This is a counsel of despair which we cannot accept. . . .
>
> The amount of the increase in employment cost per man-hour [on October 1] will be difficult to measure in advance with precision. But it appears almost certain to be outweighed by the advance in productivity resulting from a combination of two factors—the steady long-term growth of output per man-hour, and the increasing rate of operations foreseen for the steel industry in the months ahead.
>
> The Council of Economic Advisors has supplied me with estimates of steel industry profits after October 1, . . . and the steel industry, in short, can look forward to good profits without an increase in prices.
>
> The owners of the iron and steel companies have fared well in recent years.
>
> A steel price increase in the months ahead could shatter the price stability which the country has now enjoyed for some time. In a letter to me on the impact of steel prices on defense costs, Secretary of

[11] Armco Steel Corporation, Bethlehem Steel Corporation, Colorado Fuel & Iron Corporation, Inland Steel Company, Jones & Laughlin Steel Corporation, Kaiser Steel Corporation, McLouth Steel Corporation, National Steel Corporation, Republic Steel Corporation, United States Steel Corporation, Wheeling Steel Corporation, and Youngstown Sheet & Tube Company.

Defense McNamara states: "A steel price increase of the order of $4 to $5 a ton, once its effects fanned out through the economy, would probably raise the military procurement costs by $500 million per year or more. . . ."

In emphasizing the vital importance of steel prices to the strength of our economy, I do not wish to minimize the urgency of preventing inflationary movements in steel wages. I recognize, too, that the steel industry, by absorbing increases in employment costs since 1958, has demonstrated a will to halt the price-wage spiral in steel. If the industry were now to forego a price increase, it would enter collective bargaining negotiations next spring with a record of three and one-half years of price stability. The moral position of the steel industry next spring—and its claim to the support of public opinion—will be strengthened by the exercise of price restraint now.

I have written you at length because I believe that price stability in steel is essential if we are to maintain the economic vitality necessary to face confidently the trials and crises of our perilous world. Our economy has flourished in freedom; let us now demonstrate again that the responsible exercise of economic freedom serves the national welfare.

I am sure that the owners and managers of our nation's major steel companies share my conviction that the clear call of national interest must be heeded.

Sincerely,
JOHN F. KENNEDY

Response to the President's letter

According to *Iron Age*,[12] Kennedy's letter stunned the industry. The steel executives thought that by refraining from a price rise for three years, despite employment cost boosts, they were already acting in the national interest and being competitive with foreign steel and domestic substitute materials.

Business Week said the response to the letter was "immediate anger and long-term alarm." [13] The steel industry scorned Kennedy's reasoning, resented his motivation, and the list of United States presidents it did not trust now read: Harry Truman, Dwight Eisenhower, John Kennedy. Compounding the resentment was the widespread belief that Kennedy would not act against any excessive wage demands by the United Steelworkers.

The recipients of the president's letter—who were generally critical of the steel industry's being singled out while other causes of inflation were ignored—were largely noncommittal in regard to steel prices. The most publicized reply came from Roger Blough, chairman of U.S. Steel:

---

12 Campbell, "Steel Men Hot Under the Collar," pp. 143–44.
13 *Business Week,* September 16, 1961, p. 25.

I am certain, Mr. President, that your concern regarding inflation is shared by every thinking American who has experienced its serious effects during the past 20 years . . . First, let me assure you that if you seek the causes of inflation in the United States, present or future, you will not find them in the levels of steel prices or steel profits.

Blough then used 1940 as a base year and noted that although steel prices had risen 174 percent since that time, employment costs had risen 322 percent. Wage-earner costs had increased and "far exceeded any productivity gains that could be achieved," despite new investment. Blough continued:

So far as profits are concerned, your advisers have chosen to measure them in terms of the return on reported net worth; and again I am afraid that this does more to confuse than to clarify the issue in the light of the eroding effects of inflation on investments in steel-making facilities over the past 20 years. If we compare the 50-cent profit dollars of today to the 100-cent dollars that were invested in our business 20 years ago, the resulting profit ratio can hardly be said to have any validity. . . .

The most useful measurement of the profit trend in a single industry over an inflationary period, is, of course, profit as a percentage of sales. On this basis . . . profits in the steel industry have only once in the past 20 years equaled the 8% level at which they stood in 1940, and have averaged only $6\frac{1}{2}\%$ in the past five years. . . . [Moreover] averages can be dangerously misleading. Some companies will earn more than the average, while some may be suffering losses which they cannot sustain indefinitely.

Whatever figures your advisers may elect to use, however, the simple fact is that the profit left in any company, after it pays all costs, is all that there is out of which to make up for the serious inadequacy in depreciation to repay borrowings, to pay dividends and to provide for added equipment. If the profit is not good enough to do these things, they cannot and will not be done; and that would not be in the national interest.

So reviewing the whole picture, I cannot quite see how steel profits could be responsible for inflation—especially when their portion of the sales dollar over the last 20 years has never exceeded 8 cents and is lower than that today.

As for the admittedly hazardous task which your economic advisers have undertaken in forecasting steel industry profits at varying rates of operation . . . it might reasonably appear to some—as frankly, it does to me—that they seem to be assuming the role of informal price-setters for steel—psychological or otherwise. But if for steel, what then for automobiles, or rubber, or machinery or electric products, or food, or paper, or chemicals—or a thousand other products? Do we thus head into unworkable, stifling peacetime controls of prices? . . .

THE EVENTS OF 1962

The Administration and the Steel Talks [14]

That steel prices were not raised in October was attributed to economic forces and not to the president's letter. Kennedy's letter was not the final involvement of the government in the industry's affairs, however, for—although the United Steel Workers' contract was to expire on July 1, 1962—in November 1961 Labor Secretary Arthur Goldberg pointed out that the administration was willing to use its good offices to achieve an early settlement not only to prevent steel users from stockpiling but also to achieve a modest contract and thus prevent another wage-price spiral.

In January several union and industry officials met at the White House to discuss with the president the importance of an early settlement. Goldberg later contacted both union and industry and they began negotiating in early February—the first time since World War II that the two parties had met so early in the year. By discussing the new contract at this time, the union was setting aside its strongest weapon—the threat of a strike at the last minute if its demands were not met. The union also limited its demands to a seventeen-cents-per-hour job security package, forgoing a wage increase.

Apparently, after pressuring the industry, the administration was now pressuring the union (even on national television). Renewed negotiations fell flat on March 2, industry saying the benefit package cost was too high. Secretary Goldberg then talked to Roger Blough, who said that the union proposal was inflationary but agreed to resume talks if the union would lower its proposals. Upon Goldberg's intervention, David J. McDonald, president of the United Steelworkers Union, agreed to lower the demands.

Toward the end of March, agreement was reached for a contract that would add ten to eleven cents an hour in a job security package. The contract, signed on April 6, was to be effective at least until April 1963. President Kennedy said the settlement was "obviously noninflationary and should provide a solid base for continued price stability." Even the business community praised the contract.

The Shattered Masterpiece [15]

With the strike threat averted, most executives were optimistic about the near future. On April 9, 1962, *The Wall Street Journal* reported that

[14] Documentation for this section appears in Hoopes, *The Steel Crisis*, especially pp. 45–52, which is a complete, almost moment-by-moment account of the administration's activities in regard to steel from fall 1961 to fall 1962. A shorter book of the same nature is Grant McConnell's *Steel and the Presidency, 1962* (New York: Norton, 1963).

[15] All statements in the ensuing discussion not otherwise specifically documented can be found in Hoopes, *The Steel Crisis* (page reference shown).

most producers of steel doubted there would be a general rise in steel prices in 1962 (p. 14). However, on Friday, April 6, U.S. Steel's operations policy committee—the company's top ten executives—unanimously decided to raise base steel prices about 3.5 percent. On the following Tuesday, the executive committee of the board of directors approved the decision. The Public Relations Department prepared a press release announcing the "catch-up" price as "adjustment."

The reason given for the price increase was the profit squeeze facing the company. The company had spent $1.2 billion for modernization and replacement of plant and equipment since 1958, of which the two sources of money for this investment—depreciation and reinvested profit—contributed only two-thirds. The rest of the money had to be borrowed and "must be repaid out of profits that have not yet been earned and will not be earned for some years to come." The release concluded that the new resources that would be generated by the price increase would improve the company's products and would be "vital not alone to the company and its employees, but to our international balance of payments, the value of our dollar, and to the strength and security of the nation as well" (p. 293).

When the board meeting broke up at 3 P.M., Roger Blough phoned for an appointment with Kennedy and after flying to Washington was admitted to see the president at 5:45 P.M. on his as yet unannounced business (p. 220). With a minimum of amenities, Blough handed Kennedy the company press release, which was at that moment being sent to newspapers in Pittsburgh and New York, explaining that it was a matter of courtesy to inform the president personally. Kennedy is reported to have said, "I think you have made a terrible mistake." Forthwith he summoned Labor Secretary Arthur Goldberg, who raced to the White House and angrily lectured Blough on the effect of the company's decision on the administration's economic policy, and the effect of the decision on Goldberg's, indeed the whole administration's, credibility in its pleas to unions to restrain their wage demands.

Blough quietly defended U.S. Steel's price increase and left the president's office in less than an hour. Neither Goldberg nor the president asked him to rescind the increase.

As soon as Blough left, Kennedy was reported to have "exploded" with anger and called together high-level administration officials and the Council of Economic Advisers. During the meeting the president found that only a "gentlemen's agreement" and never a firm price commitment had been made during the negotiations. Indeed, a request for such a pledge might have violated antitrust laws. As the meeting progressed, the president called his brother, Attorney General Robert F. Kennedy, who later released the announcement that "because of past price behavior in the steel industry, the Department of Justice will take an immediate and close look at the current situation and any further developments." The president also called Senator Kefauver, who agreed to issue a statement of "dismay" at U.S Steel's action and to say that "I have ordered the staff of [my] subcommittee to begin an immediate inquiry into the matter" (pp. 22–26). Thus ended the opening moves of the war to hold steel prices.

The Wall Street Journal said of the day's events, "Wage-price stability in steel was intended as the graven image of a total program of stability; the Kennedy sculptors unveiled it as a finished masterpiece—and then suddenly it was shattered" (p. 53).

Reaction to the Price Hike

At the very least, U.S. Steel's timing was extremely poor and clearly embarrassed the White House for, as expected, the United Steelworkers were later to say that they would have upped their demands if they had known prices would be raised. The business community was surprised at the move, since the early settlement meant that steel users had not stockpiled and that demand was expected to be low until fall. Even so, any price increases were expected to be selective—not across the board—and to occur *after* the union security package took effect on July 1.

Regardless of Blough's actual reasons, it appeared to the White House as either of two things: (1) a challenge to the administration on the broad issue of government intervention in labor-management disputes, or (2) a personal affront to Democratic President John F. Kennedy designed to demonstrate that American industry could be as tough as the much publicized New Frontiersmen. The president accepted the challenge. Rumors soon circulated in Washington that both the Justice Department and the FTC would be conducting antitrust investigations, that the Treasury Department would abandon plans to relax tax depreciation rules, and that the IRS was checking up on U.S. Steel's stock option plan. In the Congress the Democrats attacked U.S. Steel's action and Speaker John McCormack called it "shocking, arrogant, irresponsible." Most Republicans were cautiously silent, as the price hike had taken them by surprise.

The First Day of Battle

On Wednesday morning, April 11, the president met with members of his administration. The decision was to concentrate on persuading a select group of the large steel companies to hold the price line. Industry sources friendly to the administration had told the White House that if companies producing 16 percent of the industry's output were to hold the line, they would soon capture 25 percent of the market. Everyone in the administration who knew anyone in the business world—especially in the steel industry—was urged to telephone him to explain the president's point of view. These calls were "an organized, strategic, integral part of the Administration's campaign." In none of the calls was there an attempt to coax or to threaten—the approach was to explain the government's position, nothing more. The callers discovered that important segments of the business community were far more opposed to the increase than they had been willing to admit publicly.

Inland Steel was deemed to be the key company in the dispute because of its close ties with the government through its board chairman, Joseph L. Block, and because it was probably the most profitable of the large steel companies. But Block was vacationing in Japan at the time. The administration learned that if Inland or Armco Steel were to raise prices they would wait at least one or two days, but Bethlehem Steel did not wait. By noon Wednesday Bethlehem announced a raise of $6 a ton, although less than a day before—at its annual meeting and before U.S. Steel raised its prices—its president had told reporters that Bethlehem would *not* increase prices.

According to *Business Week,* after Bethlehem's announcement, "it looked like a race against time for other producers to get themselves on record before Kennedy's press conference at 3:30 P.M. Most of them made it." [16] These were Republic, Wheeling, Youngstown, and Jones & Laughlin —half of the twelve largest companies had announced higher prices. The president felt that the steel company actions had blatantly and openly challenged the antitrust laws in the noon to 3:30 P.M. rush. Of the six large companies that had not yet raised prices, five had not reached a decision. The combined volume of these five was 14 percent of the market— close to the 16 percent the administration thought necessary to hold the price line.

That afternoon, as Kennedy rode to the State Department where he usually held his weekly press conferences, he put the finishing touches on his statement.

Good afternoon, I have several announcements to make.

The simultaneous and identical actions of United States Steel and other leading steel corporations increasing steel prices by some six dollars a ton constitute a wholly unjustifiable and irresponsible defiance of the public interest.

In this serious hour in our nation's history when we are confronted with grave crises in Berlin and Southeast Asia, when we are devoting our energies to economic recovery and stability, when we are asking reservists to leave their homes and families . . . to risk their lives— and four were killed in the last two days in Vietnam—and asking union members to hold down their wage requests . . . the American people will find it hard, as I do, to accept a situation in which a tiny handful of steel executives whose pursuit of private power and profit exceeds their sense of public responsibility, can show such utter contempt for the interest of one hundred and eighty-five million Americans. . . .

In short, at a time when they could be exploring how more efficiency and better prices could be obtained, reducing prices in this industry in recognition of lower costs, their unusually good labor contract,

[16] "The Storm over Steel," *Business Week,* April 14, 1962, pp. 31–33.

their foreign competition and their increase in production and profits which are coming this year, a few gigantic corporations have decided to increase prices in ruthless disregard of their public responsibility.

Kennedy then praised the steelworkers' union for abiding by its responsibilities; announced that the FTC would conduct an "informal inquiry" into the possibility that its 1951 consent order with the steel industry had been violated; hinted that the Department of Defense might shift its contracts for steel to companies holding the price line; and mentioned that proposed tax benefits to the steel industry through liberalized depreciation schedules were being reviewed (pp. 77–86).

In response to the president's accusation that U.S. Steel had not acted in the public interest, Roger Blough declared: "I feel that a lack of proper cost-price relationship is one of the most damaging things to the public interest." Blough announced that he would be giving his own news conference the next afternoon, Thursday, April 12.

The Second Day, April 12

The Justice Department, considering a possible antitrust suit against various members of the steel industry, was much interested in the reported Tuesday afternoon statement by Bethlehem's President Martin that his company would not raise prices. But when U.S. Steel raised its prices, Bethlehem was the first to follow suit. There were antitrust implications here—U.S. Steel, because of its immense size, might exercise undue influence over other steel producers—so at 6 P.M. Wednesday, Attorney General Kennedy ordered his department to proceed with all possible speed in gathering necessary information. Apparently the FBI overreacted to this order, and between 3 A.M. and 4 A.M. Thursday phoned several reporters who had been present at Martin's press conference and announced their intention to come calling immediately.

On Thursday morning, Kennedy asked every cabinet member to hold press conferences in the next few days to outline the effect the price increase would have on each department and on every citizen of the land. The Justice Department, instead of the FTC, was given the principal responsibility for investigating the steel industry. The investigation was to include possible price collusion and the extent to which U.S. Steel had monopoly powers dangerous to the national interest.

Also on Thursday two more steel companies, one in the top twelve, announced price increases. On Wall Street the stock market dropped to a new low for 1962, with steel leading the retreat. FBI agents showed up at eight steel companies with subpoenas requesting information and a look at their files. Talk from the Pentagon was that exceptions to the Buy America Act might allow the Pentagon to increase its purchases of foreign steel (pp. 109–10).

Thursday Afternoon—Blough's Press Conference

On Thursday afternoon Blough held his news conference:

> . . . We have no wish to add to acrimony or to misunderstanding. We do not question the sincerity of anyone who disagrees with the action we have taken. Neither do we believe that anyone can properly assume that we are less deeply concerned with the welfare, the strength, and the vitality of this nation than are those who have criticized our action. . . .
>
> The President said, when questioned regarding any understanding not to increase prices, "We did not ask either side to give us any assurances, because there is a very proper limitation to the power of the Government in this free economy." Both aspects of this statement are quite right. . . . [pp. 118–20]
>
> Our problem in this country is not the problem with respect to prices; our problem is with respect to costs. If you can take care of the costs in this country, you will have no problem taking care of the prices. The prices will take care of themselves. [p. 133]

Blough also denied that U.S. Steel was in any way defying the president by its decision, which it had a right to make, and on the White House role in labor negotiations said, "I have no criticism. I do believe that when the air clears a little bit, I think we will all realize that this type of, shall I say—assistance?—has some limitations."

Blough denied having an understanding with other companies about prices. That prices were raised in a Democratic administration but had been kept level during a Republican one was not significant. Blough denied any political motivation. He did mention, though, that if other companies did not raise their prices, U.S. Steel would be obliged to reconsider. All in all, industry sources felt that Blough did not present the best possible case.

The Turning Point

At seven o'clock Thursday evening Attorney General Kennedy announced that he had authorized the grand jury to investigate the steel price increases and to find out if U.S. Steel "so dominated the industry that it controls prices and should be broken up." Later in the evening Tyson (chairman of the Finance Committee of U.S. Steel's board of directors) and several other U.S. Steel executives met in New York. According to Hoopes, "If there was any single turning point in the steel crisis, it probably came at this meeting." The executives were "convinced that the

Administration men meant business." The executives had noticed that Inland had not gone along with the increase, and if it did not soon, Bethlehem would rescind its price and others would naturally follow (p. 145).

The Third Day

Early in the morning of Friday the thirteenth, Kennedy talked to Roger Blough, who suggested that communications should be maintained. Seeing this as a hopeful sign, Kennedy then moved to restrain members of his administration and to preserve a mood of conciliation. Also on Friday morning, Inland's late-Thursday decision not to raise prices was made public. Attention now turned to Armco Steel, which had led off the price increase in 1958 when U.S. Steel refused and had a reputation for unpredictability. The real maverick of the industry, Kaiser Steel, had also not yet raised its prices. Meanwhile rumors circulated that Roger Blough would resign; Inland's stock prices rose; other steel stocks fell. At 10:00 A.M. Defense Secretary Robert S. McNamara stated that "where possible, procurement of steel for defense production will be shifted to those companies which have not increased prices."

All during the battle between steel and the administration, public opinion was firmly behind the president, as was shown by a number of newspaper polls and by telegrams received by the White House. According to Roy Hoopes, "the majority of the nation's most influential newspapers [were] critical of the steel companies' action, [and] the business community [was] only lukewarm in its support of the steel industry. . . ."

The Final Battle

Blough's telephone conversation with Kennedy on Friday resulted in a meeting the same afternoon of Clifford and Goldberg, and Blough, Tyson, and Worthington (president of U.S. Steel). According to reports, Clifford (a Washington attorney who was friendly to the Kennedy administration) explained that many continuing investigations of steel would be very uncomfortable, especially since Kennedy would be in office for a number of years and doing business in Washington might be difficult. Clifford and Goldberg also explored ways U.S. Steel could roll back its prices and still save face. During the meeting the various members were kept informed of events as they occurred outside: one in particular came at 3:25 P.M. announcing that Bethlehem had rescinded its price increase in order to remain competitive. This was the final blow to the company, and before the meeting was over, Blough and his fellow executives told Clifford and Goldberg that they too would later be announcing a rollback (p. 164).

Within a few hours, in the words of *Time* magazine, there was a "precipitous rush to surrender" as the other steel producers rolled back their prices. The reason given for the rollbacks was "to remain competitive" in spite of poor profit conditions.

AFTERMATH: THE KENNEDY YEARS

Grant at Appomattox

Naturally the administration's plans for further attacks on the steel industry and proposed legislation were canceled or filed away and, for once, the administration was not crowing about its victory. As *Business Week* aptly said, "The President went out of his way to assure there will be no public recriminations now that the mistake has been retracted. Like Grant at Appomattox, he is letting the vanquished forces keep their horses and sidearms." The relationship between the White House and U.S. Steel returned to normal, and Roger Blough agreed to stay on the president's business advisory committee.

The Kennedy Antibusiness Crusade

Most of the steel companies held their annual meetings soon after the "price fiasco." All those that had originally raised prices and then backed down maintained they were forced to do so because the competition did not follow. One element of agreement among all steel spokesmen was that the need for a price increase had not passed—even Joseph Block agreed on this point and said Inland had refused to raise its prices only as a concession to the national interest (pp. 224–25).

Despite its campaign of conciliation, the administration persisted in its economic policies and announced that it might act to prevent a price hike in the aluminum industry. There then began to emerge a "growing hostility" by the business community toward Kennedy, and a stock market crash in the summer of 1962 was attributed by many businessmen to the "Kennedy crowd." The animosity collapsed, however, by mid-autumn, perhaps because the administration's attempts at dialogue eventually got through or because a number of business leaders (including Blough and Block) helped to restore the peace. During the summer the Congress passed an administration-backed investment tax credit law and the Treasury Department announced revised tax depreciation schedules.

Kennedy's Last Year with Steel

A year passed without steel's making any price increases, but in April 1963 Wheeling Steel Corporation, with less than 2 percent of the United States market, announced a selective price increase of $4.50–$10.00 per ton on six items. The president's formal reply to the hike was a surprise:

I realize that price and wage controls in this one industry, while all others are unrestrained, would be unfair and inconsistent with our free competitive market . . . and that selective price adjustments up or down—as prompted by changes in supply and demand as opposed to across-the-board increases—are not incompatible within a framework of general stability and steel-price stability and are characteristic of any healthy economy.[17]

Actually, throughout 1963 the government allowed increases on 75 percent of the industry's product mix—all without protest.[18]

LYNDON B. JOHNSON AND STEEL

After President Johnson took office, government-industry crises took longer to reach the confrontation stage. The Johnson administration's actions were less visible than Kennedy's, but its victory was also less clearcut. The government criticized Bethlehem Steel's small ($5 a ton) increase in structural steel and piling prices on New Year's Day 1966. U.S. Steel, on the other hand, deliberated about a week before raising prices on the products $2.75 a ton and drew praise from Washington. Bethlehem thereupon trimmed back its announced increase. However, the industry's later increases in large-volume steel and strip received "only a mild comment of displeasure," and the government "only privately urged stainless steel makers to eschew any price boosts" in the fall, although prices were raised anyway.[19]

The government said nothing publicly about price increases until late August 1967, when Republic Steel hiked its prices 1.8 percent on carbon and alloy steel bars and the administration finally began to move to head off another increase.[20]

1967: The Biggest Binge in Four Years

In response to Republic's boost, Gardner Ackley, chairman of the Council of Economic Advisers, called on the rest of the industry not to follow suit, but U.S. Steel, Bethlehem, Armco, Inland, Jones & Laughlin, and Kaiser raised prices anyway.

The Wall Street Journal, analyzing the significance of steel's move, said that the steel industry had just treated itself to the biggest price-raising binge in four years and that the government had even encouraged steelmakers by allowing the previous increases:

The increases so far this year covered 42% of the industry's volume. By contrast, once it became clear that the mills wouldn't back down

---

[17] *Ibid.,* p. 37.
[18] "Inflation Hassle," *The Wall Street Journal,* October 4, 1967, p. 16.
[19] *Ibid.*
[20] "What's News—Business and Finance," *The Wall Street Journal,* September 1, 1967, p. 1.

on sheet and strip in August 1966, Johnson Cabinet members began to describe the increases as covering "only a small fraction" of industry sales and as being "within bounds." [21]

The *Journal* then went on to criticize the administration's fiscal attempts to control the inflation [tax surcharge and investment tax credit] as being too late or too little.

In the first week of December, U.S. Steel raised its base price for cold rolled sheet, the prime steel product by volume, $5 a ton. Ackley's response to U.S. Steel's move was to urge the other companies to "consider carefully" the "interests of the industry and the nation" before following suit.

The President's Response: Verbal Power

President Johnson's simple response to the increase was that "we have exercised such rights as we had" to keep prices on cold rolled sheet steel down. A *Wall Street Journal* editorial complimented Ackley for not blaming inflation on steel and also for criticizing the auto union settlement. The editorial pointed out that the administration's pressure on the industry seemed to have been "largely verbal—so far, anyway," and noted the contrast with actions Kennedy took, saying, "At least this time they didn't try to hang Roger Blough from the nearest lamppost." [22]

Wednesday, July 31, 1968:
Time of "Dire Consequences"

In May 1968, according to *The Wall Street Journal,* U.S. Steel began to cut prices in areas subject to foreign competition and attempted to keep these "reductions quiet, hoping to prevent them from leading to any general break in steel prices." Big Steel's actions broke with industry precedent which said that importers, backed up with lower labor costs, could easily win a price war, and indeed the price cut occurred as American industry was stocking up for a possible steel strike on August 1.

No strike occurred, however, and on July 30 labor won a rather hefty settlement—one union estimate was that it represented a 6.1 percent increase in employment costs to the industry, the largest since the 7.5 percent increase in 1958.

Less than a day after eleven companies signed the contract several increased their prices, led by U.S. Steel, which announced a limited hike on can-making steel. An hour later, Bethlehem brought on yet another crisis by raising its prices *across the board* by nearly 5 percent, citing the extra labor costs of the new contract.

At a hastily called press conference, the president labeled Bethlehem's

---

[21] "Inflation Hassle," p. 16.
[22] "The High Price of Inflating," *The Wall Street Journal,* December 12, 1967, p. 16.

hike as "unreasonable" and said it "just shouldn't be permitted to stand." Johnson added that he was "very hopeful that other steel companies wouldn't join the parade"; he had singled out Bethlehem because its increases were "across the board," and he said that he was not opposed to "selective increases that individual companies have made gradually." He noted that if the industry did not follow Bethlehem's lead, "competitive factors would, as they have in the past, bring about a readjustment," but if followed "it will have dire consequences for our nation." Furthermore, Bethlehem did not need a price increase, since it had increased its first half earnings by 41 percent over the previous year.

Bethlehem's Chairman Edmund F. Martin responded to the president by saying, "Our announcement this morning speaks for itself. In our opinion our price increase is absolutely necessary, and we don't intend to withdraw it." The general feeling was that if other producers were to follow Bethlehem's lead, the increases would stick—as they had before even in times of decreased demand.

Thursday: No FBI Agents This Time

On Thursday, August 1, the administration continued its quick response to the steel price increases: The chairman of the president's Council of Economic Advisers sent telegrams to twelve steel companies that had not raised their prices asking that they consult him before doing so, and the president wrote to both the Speaker of the House of Representatives and the Senate Majority Leader repeating his warning of the "dire" consequences that would result if Republic's and Bethlehem's increases were followed by the rest of the industry. The letters, however, did not make any specific requests for congressional action.[23]

At this juncture the administration felt that U.S. Steel was the key factor in preventing across-the-board hikes from spreading throughout the industry, although later in the day both Inland and Pittsburgh announced general increases of nearly 5 percent, matching Bethlehem's move the day before. By evening the flurry of activity reached its peak, for "all within a matter of minutes" U.S. Steel again raised its prices, the government acted to buy steel only from firms not going along with the price hike, and the president called for a meeting with twenty congressional leaders. The U.S. Steel price boost, the second in two days, increased prices an average of more than 5 percent on items that, industry wide, accounted for 14 percent of all shipments. The company said that further increases on other products would be made soon.

Since industry requested and Congress considered import quotas, one high government official thought the price boosts were "incredible" and said, "It seems the American consumer is the one who needs protection" from the steel industry.

---

23 "Government, Steel Industry Escalate War over Prices; U.S. Steel Posts Second Rise, Says More Are Likely," *The Wall Street Journal*, August 2, 1968, p. 3.

Over the Weekend: "Doubtful Tactics"

Other companies raised their prices over the weekend and said the increase might mean employee layoffs because of declining demand. The president applied his order to buy steel "at the lowest possible price" to all government agencies. Their combined civilian requirements for steel totaled $700 million per year.

The Wall Street Journal said that the government's punishment of "those nasty firms for spurring inflation" was "surely pretty stupid; if anyone deserves punishment for spurring inflation it's the government. . . . Washington, after all, is spending the taxpayer's money with considerable abandon." [24]

Also over the weekend Senator Philip A. Hart, chairman of the Senate Antitrust Committee, wrote to the chairman of the FTC, Paul Dixon, asking for an investigation "in light of the [steel] industry's pricing practices."

Monday: Seeming Contradictions

On Monday morning the FTC commissioners decided to gather information on Senator Hart's request before going ahead with an investigation. Congressman Joe L. Evins, chairman of the House Small Business Committee, ordered a staff investigation preliminary to a "full inquiry" on steel price hikes and their effect on small businesses which would "square up to the dangers posed by the greedy actions of the steel industry." Meanwhile the Department of Transportation, the General Services Administration, and HUD (Housing and Urban Development) took steps to ensure that steel orders—direct and indirect through contractors—went to lower-priced steel.

On Monday it was clear that the administration was still hoping to force a partial rollback through competitive pressures by keeping U.S. Steel and others who had announced selective increases from extending them across the board. Republic Steel promised not to increase prices on steel used to make items for the Vietnam war; Armco said its hike would not apply on two of the three items it sold to the department; Bethlehem said its increases did not include certain military items. However, Pittsburgh Steel stood firm on its hike, and Inland Steel said nothing—but its Defense Department shipments were less than 2 percent of its total sales.

Wednesday: The Boost's Broken Back

On Wednesday, August 7, U.S. Steel raised some of its prices 2.5 percent on the average—not much above the 2 percent government guidepost —and thus "broke the back" of the Bethlehem-led 5 percent general in-

[24] "What's Going On Here?" *The Wall Street Journal,* editorial, August 5, 1968, p. 12.

crease. "Within minutes" Bethlehem and others (Inland, Armco, Youngstown Sheet and Tube, Pittsburgh, Jones & Laughlin) compared their prices to U.S. Steel's levels and rescinded increases on prices U.S. Steel "had omitted from its boosts."

White House Press Secretary George Christian said the president welcomed the move by U.S. Steel, and Arthur M. Okun, chairman of the president's Council of Economic Advisers, found the developments "gratifying"; "taking account of all recent developments in steel prices and costs, the nation has a right to expect renewed price stability in this basic product in the months ahead." [25]

"No One Now Will Ever Know"

A *Wall Street Journal* editorial said the administration's claim to victory in the war over steel prices was "strange" under the circumstances and expressed regret at its price-holding actions.

In our supposedly free economy companies naturally try to set prices high enough to cover their costs and provide them with a reasonable profit. That, essentially, is what the steel companies did in the wake of the costly contract settlement with the United Steelworkers.

[The Government's] extra-legal price control naturally distorts the workings of competition. With imports sizable and with steel users working off inventories built up in fear of a strike, it's more than possible that the original price increases would not have held for very long even if the Government had not said a word.

Unfortunately, no one now will ever know.[26]

But the editor lamented too soon, for reports in October were that "a price war has broken out in the domestic steel industry," as some high-volume products had their prices slashed as much as 20 percent. According to *The Wall Street Journal*:

The price cutting has taken much of the significance from President Johnson's success two months ago. . . . But current selling prices, in many cases, are considerably below even the pre-August list prices.[27]

One novel twist to the price war was that most mills were denying the price cuts, which went only to large-volume customers, while insisting that everyone else was cutting prices! In November the whole industry was jolted when Bethlehem "cut its price of hot rolled steel—the in-

[25] "U.S. Steel Increases Prices 2.5%, Spurs Partial Rollback," *The Wall Street Journal,* August 8, 1968, p. 3.
[26] "A Peculiar Price Victory," *The Wall Street Journal,* August 9, 1968, p. 6.
[27] "Makers Quietly Cutting Prices as Much as 20% in Bid to Unload Surplus," *The Wall Street Journal,* October 7, 1968, p. 1.

dustry's second largest tonnage product—by 22 percent. . . . Bethlehem stressed that it acted to meet domestic competition. Steel executives translate this into retaliation against covert price cutting by U.S. Steel." [28] The rest of the industry soon fell into line with Bethlehem's cuts. According to *Business Week,* "Steel executives couldn't recall a more drastic price cut since the rampant competition of the early 1930s, nor could they recall a more direct challenge to the industry's leader, U.S. Steel Corp." [29] Indeed, "Price cutting has pushed the industry's traditionally stable pricing structure close to chaos." [30]

SELECTED REFERENCES

"Administered Prices: A Compendium on Public Policy," Subcommittee on Antitrust and Monopoly of the Committee on the Judiciary, U.S. Senate, 88th Cong., 1st sess., March 11, 1963.

CANNON, JAMES, and JEAN HALLORAN, "Steel and the Environment: A Long Way to Go," *Business and Society Review/Innovation,* winter 1972–73, pp. 56–61.

"Employment, Growth and Price Levels: Report of the Joint Economic Committee, Congress of the United States, January 26, 1960.

GALBRAITH, J. K., *The New Industrial State* (Boston: Houghton Mifflin, 1967).

GOLDEN, L. L. L., *Only by Public Consent* (New York: Hawthorne, 1968).

HOOPES, ROY, *The Steel Crisis* (New York: John Day, 1968).

McCONNELL, GRANT, *Steel and the Presidency* (New York: Norton, 1963).

SCHLESINGER, ARTHUR M., JR., *A Thousand Days* (Boston: Houghton Mifflin, 1963).

SCHULTZE, CHARLES L., "Study Paper No. 1, Recent Inflation in the United States," for the Joint Economic Committee's "Study of Employment, Growth and Price Levels," United States Congress, September 1959.

SMITH, RICHARD A., *Corporation in Crisis* (Garden City, N.Y.: Doubleday, 1963).

SORENSEN, THEODORE C., *Kennedy* (New York: Harper & Row, 1965).

28 *Ibid.*
29 "Revolution in Steel Pricing?" *Business Week,* December 14, 1968.
30 "Pittsburgh Expects to Be Happier," *Business Week,* December 14, 1968, p. 40.

Government and Business as Partners

THE SUPERSONIC TRANSPORT (SST)

A CASE STUDY IN GOVERNMENT-INDUSTRY COOPERATION AND THE DETERMINATION OF NATIONAL PRIORITIES

You're darn right. It's a patriotic program.
—WILLIAM MAGRUDER
Director, SST Development, Nixon administration

The federal government is guaranteeing everything. . . . Would not a businessman fight for this kind of opportunity? . . . What would he have to lose? . . . And the taxpayer is the pigeon, the fall guy—as Texas Guinan or P. T. Barnum would put it, the sucker.
—SENATOR WILLIAM PROXMIRE

The supersonic transport program, one of the most fateful and controversial in American history, sprang from a union of patriotic fervor, an unshaken belief in America's greatness, and a desire to be Number 1, especially to be ahead of the Russians. The program died ignominiously. Contributing causes of death were its environmental hazards, technological uncertainties, and changing social priorities.

After the burial there emerged a realization that there are no technological answers to many social problems and that technological innovations, for their own sake, are not necessarily desirable. The aspirations of three United States presidents for American preeminence in supersonic transport were quashed less than eight years after the big dream was first announced. The frantic activity preceding the congressional vote and the debate leading to the defeat of the SST appropriations reveal all the agonies of a nation whose conscience was pricked, whose accepted values were challenged, and whose directions were forcibly changed.

The Congressional decision to scrap the SST program marks a milestone in modern American history. This highly technologically oriented nation, whose past exploits range from building the first atomic bomb and the first electronic computer to landing the first man on the moon, has—after long argument and careful consideration—decided to bow out of the competition to make the fastest passenger plane in the world. . . . Far from being an expression of an irrational flight from the machine, the decision to kill the SST was, we believe, testimony to the new technological sophistication of the American people and of their representatives in Congress.

It is a sophistication which refuses to believe that man is subordinate to technology. . . . On the contrary, the attitude reflected in the anti-SST vote was that technology exists to serve man; and that proposals to move it ahead at great expense must be judged on the basis of cost-benefit analysis of the widest and most comprehensive sort. . . .

What Americans want is more and better technology which will help meet the urgent problems of the day. An automobile that can provide adequate personal transportation at reasonable cost without poisoning the atmosphere would be welcomed enthusiastically by all Americans. The same is true of a new technology that would generate power at competitive prices without exacting the environmental costs of existing fuels, including fissionable plutonium and uranium.[1]

The death of the program was almost anticlimactic, following as it did the frenetic and often acrimonious debate between the supporters and opponents.

THE ISSUES

This case is an excellent example of the value of the arguments—economic, environment, political, and philosophical—that emerge whenever a new technology with vast and unpredictable consequences is about to be introduced into the social system. An analysis of these arguments should lead one to a better understanding of the interrelatedness of economic considerations with environmental, social, and political considerations; and of how different groups tend to define their goals and claim to represent the broad interests not only of the society, but of future generations as well. Critical to the whole analysis is an appraisal of the criteria by which new technology of vast national import is currently

[1] *The New York Times,* Editorial, March 29, 1971, Sec. 4, p. 14.

introduced into the society—that is, the immediate interests of the micro economic unit possessing that technology, whether or not .there was a need for developing broader criteria, and if so, how such criteria might be developed.

THE BIRTH OF AN IDEA

President John F. Kennedy startled the world on June 5, 1963, with the announcement at commencement exercises at the United States Air Force Academy that

> As a testament to our strong faith in the future of airpower, and the manned airplane, I'm announcing today that the United States will commit itself to an important new program in civilian aviation. Civilian aviation, long both the beneficiary and the benefactor of military aviation, is of necessity equally dynamic.

> Neither the economics nor the politics of international air competition permit us to stand still in this area. Today the challenging new frontier in commercial aviation and in military aviation is a frontier already crossed by the military—supersonic transport.

> [After reviewing the recommendations of the leading members of this Administration] it is my judgment that this government should immediately commence a new program in partnership with private industry to develop at the earliest practical date the prototype of a commercially successful supersonic transport superior to that being built in any other country in the world. . . .

> An open preliminary design competition will be initiated immediately among American airframe and powerplant manufacturers with a detailed phase to follow. *If these initial phases do not produce an aircraft capable of transporting people and goods safely, swiftly, and at prices the traveler can afford and the airlines find profitable, we shall not go further.*

> . . . Spurred by competition from across the Atlantic and by the productivity of our own companies, the Federal Government must pledge funds to supplement the risk capital to be contributed by private companies. It must then rely heavily on the flexibility and ingenuity of private enterprise to make the detailed decisions and to introduce successfully this new jet age transport into world-wide service. . . . This commitment, I believe, is essential to a strong and forward-looking nation. . . .[2]

The program was launched amid the greatest fanfare, images of national glory, and technical might. The Kennedy administration, sup-

[2] *The New York Times,* June 6, 1963, p. 25. Emphasis added.

ported consecutively and actively by those of Lyndon Johnson and Richard Nixon, all wanting America to be first in commercial supersonic flight, could not brook the thought of being beaten to the post by the Russians or the French. The United States populace, despite the flourishing of verbal trumpets, did not wave the flag in line with the leaders. The ecology movement, with its emphasis on air and noise pollution, swept the land. The economy took a downturn. Technology lost some of its clout. And not least, the government's first commitment not to invest more than $750 million for SST research had escalated geometrically. More than that, the original plan called for a government/industry investment ratio of 3:1. It rose instead to 9:1, and the government had spent more than a *billion* dollars on the project.

The more than 99.5 percent of the taxpaying population who would never have purchased tickets on the luxury-fare SST had had enough of underwriting the program for the less than half of one percent of the population who might have one day flown faster than sound. The feeling was also strong that

> With its commitment to the SST, the government had pledged to preserve the aircraft manufacturing industry. And this is why SST is such a sharp break with the past. It does not increase competition. It is not necessary. It is not a humanitarian expenditure. It is not needed for defense. The purpose of the SST is to guarantee the future of the aircraft industry.[3]

In the matter of national priorities, super speed in the sky ranked far below clean air and water, solid waste disposal, safe automobiles, efficient rapid transit, the end of bitter poverty, and so on. And the "America First" thrust had lost its edge. As Senator Percy (R, Ill.) noted, Russia's TU–144, the first supersonic civilian plane to fly—and to crash, at the Paris Air Show on June 3, 1973—would fly from Moscow, where the waiting time for new automobiles is between five and ten years, to Calcutta, where oxcarts are still status symbols. "To be stampeded into competing with the Russians would be foolish and irrational."[4]

The idea of a civilian SST has been around since the early fifties, but there were serious doubts about its economic and technical feasibility. In 1956 the National Advisory Committee for Aeronautics, precursor of the National Aeronautics and Space Administration (NASA), launched a research program to explore the possibility of developing an engine capable of flying airplanes at speeds of near Mach 3.[5] This was a prelude to the B–70 bomber program, the contract for which was awarded to North American Aviation Corporation in February 1958. Quite a bit of research work had already gone into the various aspects of the program, and the nation's aircraft industry hoped to rely heavily on the technology devel-

3 Leonard Baker, *The Guaranteed Society* (New York: Macmillan, 1968), p. 11.
4 "The Public Cast the Deciding Vote," *The New York Times*, March 28, 1971, p. 2.
5 *National Aeronautics*, June 1966, p. 24.

oped in the B–70 program for later exploitation in a civilian version of SST. However, by the end of 1959—and after spending more than $330 million—the B–70 program was on the verge of being scrapped, along with the hopes of aircraft manufacturers. In the interest of economy, the Eisenhower administration had decided to terminate the program when Dr. George Kistiakowsky, the president's scientific adviser, predicted that intercontinental ballistic missiles would make the development of manned bombers needless.

There were strong supporters of the SST program who advocated the development of the B–70 for both its military use and its benefits to the civilian SST program. These included Senator Lyndon B. Johnson, chairman of the Preparedness Investigating Subcommittee of the Senate's powerful Committee on Armed Services, Air Force Chief of Staff Thomas White, Senator A. S. (Mike) Monroney, and General Elmwood R. (Pete) Quesada, President Eisenhower's appointee to run the new Federal Aviation Administration (FAA), who subsequently developed highly unfavorable views of the SST program.

As Quesada saw it, the United States could ill afford to lose face or market dominance by letting the Russians or the Anglo-French win the SST race. In November 1960, shortly before his resignation because of the change in the administration, Quesada recommended to President Eisenhower an initial funding of $17.5 million for fiscal year 1961. The Bureau of the Budget, however, reduced this figure to $5 million. At the same time, Quesada awarded the first SST engine-design research contracts to General Electric and Pratt & Whitney.[6] President-elect Kennedy's appointee to succeed Quesada as chief of FAA was Najeeb Halaby, who recommended that Congress spend $12 million a year for SST studies. Despite President Kennedy's support, the Senate only narrowly defeated amendments to the administration's appropriation bills that would have eliminated the SST studies.

In March 1961 President Kennedy asked Halaby to develop a program of national priorities to give the nation the "safest, most efficient and most economical national aviation system attainable."[7] The Halaby report, titled *Project Horizon,* was submitted to President Kennedy on September 5, 1961. It painted a picture of a fast-growing and changing world in glorious terms and described the role of air travel in it. "Faster, bigger aircraft have shrunk the globe to the point where the capitals of the world are almost as accessible to an American as the county seat of a few decades ago. . . ."[8] Recommending government participation in the SST program, the report said: "Government funds should be utilized through the research, design, development, prototype and probably production stages. Every effort must be made to recoup the Government's

[6] *United States Supersonic Transport Program Summary,* Federal Aviation Agency, Washington, D.C., July 1965, p. 1.
[7] *Supplementary Report to the Supersonic Transport Steering Group,* Federal Aviation Agency, Washington, D.C., May 14, 1963, p. 8.
[8] *Report of the Task Force on National Aviation Goals—Project Horizon,* Federal Aviation Agency, Washington, D.C., September 1961.

financial investment through some type of royalty system to be paid by the operators." [9]

THE POTENTIAL THREAT OF BRITISH-FRENCH
AND RUSSIAN SSTs

Since the early fifties both British and French aircraft and engine manufacturers had been working separately on a commercial SST for the world markets, the British to develop a long-range and the French a medium- and short-range version. However, the tremendous financial costs and the fear of American and Russian domination brought the British and French governments together. On November 29, 1962, the two countries agreed to establish a consortium of British and French interests (Concorde) to develop an SST jointly. The Anglo-French SST, to have a top speed of Mach 2.2 (1,450 mph), depended heavily on financial subsidies from the French and British governments.

The goal of the program was to get the Concorde into airline service by 1971, thus giving it a three- to four-year time lead over the United States SST. Despite various doubts as to its economic feasibility, several airlines ordered Concordes. BOAC and Air France were first, with orders of eight each, Pan American World Airways was next with six, and by 1967 orders for seventy-four Concordes worth $1 billion had been placed. The market projections were for two hundred to three hundred Concordes by 1980, with most of the sales coming in the early years.

The rising costs of the program, the unfavorable balance of payments, and other domestic problems caused England to review her commitment to the Concorde when a Labour government came into power in the fall of 1964. Fearing a jettisoning of the program, BOAC reserved a position for six US/SSTs. Air France immediately followed suit. However, by January 1965, when the British government discovered that the agreement with the French was irrevocable, estimates for the British share of the cost had gone from the original estimate of £50 million to £165 million.[10] The cost estimates for the Concorde kept rising, and in November 1966 it was estimated that the program would cost $1.4 billion—up from the original estimate of $400 million—and that eventual costs might go as high as $2.4 billion! [11]

The first Concorde 001 (the French version) was test flown on March 2, 1969. Concorde 002 (the British version) was flown a few weeks later. Neither was flown at supersonic speeds, for the requisite more-powerful engines were not slated to be completed until late 1970 or early 1971. A model of the Russian SST TU–144 was first shown to the West at the Paris Air Show in 1955 and was test flown in Russia on December 31,

9 *Ibid.*
10 *Los Angeles Times,* January 20, 1965.
11 "Race for a Superjet—Can U.S. Catch Up?" *U.S. News and World Report,* March 17, 1969, pp. 38–39.

1968.[12] The Soviet plane was designed to operate at 1,550 mph and carry more than 90 passengers (Concorde's estimates were 126 passengers for short to medium range and 112 for distances of 4,000 miles). TU–144 was expected to cost about $20 million, or the same as Concorde. Most aviation officials in the West, however, believed that TU–144 would not offer much competition because in the past Soviet planes had proved uneconomical.[13]

PROGRESS OF THE US/SST—
THE KENNEDY–JOHNSON ERA

Nine days after his Air Force Academy announcement, President Kennedy sent a message to Congress in which he flatly stated that "in no event will the Government investment be permitted to exceed $750 million [and] the Government does not intend to pay any production, purchase or operating subsidies to manufacturers or airlines." [14] The development costs of the program were estimated as approximately $1 billion over the next six years, of which the manufacturers were expected to repay a portion of the government's development costs through royalties.[15]

President Kennedy's request for a $60 million appropriation to fund the government's share of SST design, although subsequently approved, ran into some sharp congressional criticism. One of the critics, Senator Fulbright, remarked:

> This Congress has been asked to demonstrate that a "democratic, free enterprise system" in the President's words, can compete with Britain and France. . . . I had always thought that the outstanding virtue of our free enterprise system was that it was free and that it rested on the enterprise of individuals. Thus, I fail to see how a Government subsidy of three-quarters of a billion dollars to the airplane builders is going to represent a triumphant vindication of free enterprise.[16]

In January 1964 three airframe and three engine companies submitted initial design proposals. The proposals were evaluated independently both by the government and by a panel of ten airlines. The government's evaluation found that none of the airframe designs met range-payload economic requirements. In May the president directed the FAA to award contracts for further design to two airframe companies (Boeing and Lockheed) and two engine companies (General Electric and Pratt & Whitney, a division of United Aircraft), which ranked best in the evalua-

---

12 *Ibid.*
13 *Ibid.*
14 *Congressional Record*, July 9, 1963, pp. 12283–84.
15 *Ibid.*
16 *Congressional Record*, June 26, 1963, pp. 11706–7.

tion. The president also asked the Department of Commerce to conduct economic studies and the National Academy of Sciences to continue its supervision of the sonic boom studies. The selected airframe designs were these: (1) Boeing proposed a swing-wing (which would fold back during supersonic flight) and would carry 150 passengers at Mach 2.7 for 4,000 miles; and (2) Lockheed proposed a double delta wing design and would carry 218 passengers at Mach 3.0 for 4,000 miles. In November the airframe and engine competitors submitted their revised designs. After more than six months of review by various technical committees and the President's Advisory Committee on Supersonic Transport, in July 1965 President Johnson announced an eighteen-month design program running to the end of 1966. He also requested that Congress appropriate $140 million for the program for fiscal 1966.

Criticism in Congress became more severe and the public arguments both for and against the program more vocal. President Johnson's request for $140 million to get the eighteen-month phase II of the program finished in only eleven months raised eyebrows in Congress. Was this only a "speed-up," or was it an indirect way of committing the government to the program? To secure congressional approval, and also to put the program in more favorable hands, the administration did two things: Considerable pressure was exerted on various senators and representatives to vote for the appropriation, and the president nominated, and the Senate approved, General Seth J. McKee as FAA administrator to replace Najeeb Halaby, who was retiring. To do this, the FAA act which specified that the FAA administrator must be a civilian had to be amended. This was done at a time when the FAA was already top-heavy with military personnel, with ninety-four retired and active officers holding down key jobs.[17]

On December 31, 1966, the FAA announced that Boeing and General Electric had been selected to construct the SST airframe and engine, respectively. Thus, after a government commitment of $311 million and expenditure of $244 million, in addition to $70 million spent by the plane manufacturers, the program was finally on the go. In the process, it had been reviewed by three presidential committees, the National Academy of Sciences, seven congressional committees, and thirteen federal agencies and departments.[18] It had also been analyzed and pronounced ill-advised and uneconomical by a host of other profit and nonprofit consulting organizations, and by Stanford Research Institute (SRI), which concluded that there was "no economic justification for an SST program." [19]

Construction contracts were signed on May 1, 1967, at which time Congress was also requested to appropriate $198 million for the fiscal year 1968 to help finance the prototype construction phase of the pro-

17 *Los Angeles Times,* July 12, 1965.
18 *Newsweek,* August 29, 1966, p. 48.
19 *Final Report: An Economic Analysis of the Supersonic Transport,* SRI Project No. ISU–4266, p. 1.

gram. It was, however, still not clear how the $4.5 billion program would eventually be paid for.

President Johnson and the other supporters of the program notwithstanding, the SST program kept encountering new technological problems. In the fall of 1968, after a year and a half and millions of dollars had gone into the swing-wing design, Boeing announced that its design would have to be scrapped. The corporation said it had found that the swing-wing, and especially its pivots, had made their plane too fat by 25 tons. Thus, the design would have to be rejected in favor of a fixed-wing after all. Unfortunately, Boeing's design was now even less well along than Lockheed's had been a year and a half earlier, *before the contract had even been awarded!* Had Lockheed's more realistic fixed-wing design been awarded the contract, it is safe to say that much time and money would have been saved. This, however, is only one of the unforeseen technical problems that constantly blocked progress on the SST.

THE NIXON ERA

When Richard Nixon was elected president in November 1968, the future of the program became clouded again as both friends and foes vied for favorable positions with the new administration. Both groups were obliged. Soon after his inauguration, on February 19, 1969, President Nixon announced yet another ad hoc committee of high-ranking officials to review the SST program and to "investigate the national interest questions associated with the pending SST decision." [20] The presidential guidance was that the "SST must be safe for the passenger, profitable for the manufacturers and airlines, and superior to any other aircraft." [21] The committee, after hearing expert testimony in February and March 1969, turned in a report highly critical of the SST program. Consequently, the Department of Transportation, which had consistently advocated continuance of the SST program, kept the report secret until October 31, 1969, when it was released at the request of Congressman Henry S. Reuss (D, Wis.).[22]

REPORT OF THE AD HOC COMMITTEE

The committee created four panels to examine the impact of the SST program in four specific areas: balance of payments and international relations, economics, environmental and sociological impact, and technological fallout. A summary of their findings follows.[23]

[20] *Congressional Record,* October 31, 1969, H10432.
[21] *Congressional Record,* November 17, 1969, H10950.
[22] "Reuss Bill Would Ban Commercial Supersonic Flights in U.S.," press release from the office of Congressman Henry S. Reuss, November 11, 1969, p. 2.
[23] *Congressional Record,* October 31, 1969.

Balance of Payments and International Relations

The SST's balance of payments effect (BOP) was analyzed in terms of its overall impact on the United States BOP. This included both import and export of aircraft and increase in international air travel and its distribution between United States and foreign carriers. (The Commerce Department wanted to consider only the aircraft account; the Treasury and State departments wanted to include all aspects of BOP.) The panel observed that on aircraft sales alone the United States BOP was likely to improve by between $11 and $18 billion (depending on competition from a commercially viable Concorde) from introduction in 1978 through 1990. The committee then analyzed the effect of SST on air travel expenditure. The current United States deficit in this category was estimated at $1.6 billion, and "even in the absence of any commercial supersonic aircraft, it is expected to increase in absolute amount . . . totalling around $70 billion for the period 1970 through 1990." After taking the impact of the SST into account and even revising estimates of deficit downward, the committee concluded that "an adverse impact of speed-induced supersonic travel on the U.S. travel account [was likely to be] considerably greater than the estimated beneficial impact of supersonic aircraft sales on the U.S. aircraft account."

In terms of foreign relations impact, the committee observed that the United Kingdom and France would frown at hasty action on the SST as designed to scuttle the Concorde. Similarly, strict noise standards could bar the Concorde from major United States airports. The committee recommended that both the UK and France be kept advised of "U.S. noise developments to ensure their full understanding if not acceptance of the U.S. position on noise."

Economics

The economic subcommittee expressed deep concern over the grave uncertainty associated with all economic aspects of the program: development and production costs, financing costs, and employment potential. The subcommittee observed that "almost every economic aspect of the program reflects unverifiable matters of judgment with great variance in the opinion of experts. Probably the single most uncertain aspect of the whole program relates to the uncertainty as to whether an SST can be built in the given time that will meet the specifications of being efficient, safe, and economical." [24]

The subcommittee did not put much faith in the assurances given by the manufacturers, FAA, and other interested government agencies and private business interests in view of similar assurances given to earlier investigating committees and also past experience with plane develop-

24 *Ibid.*

ments. It noted that even where commercial plane development, such as the Boeing 707, was based on well-established military technology, "production costs have often been more than three times what they were predicted to be." The SST represented a jump of unprecedented magnitude in new technology, and even if all technical problems were solved, there was little doubt that costs would escalate considerably.

Demand for the SST was another uncertain area. The FAA, assuming that consumers valued their flight time at 1.5 times their hourly earnings, projected that 500 SSTs would be sold. The Institute of Defense Analysis (IDA), assuming passenger valuation of flight time as equal to hourly earnings, estimated sales of 350 SSTs. Ruben Grunau, in his 1967 Columbia Ph.D. study, "concluded on the basis of a very detailed statistical study of air travel time from New York City to other points that businessmen value their time in air travel at 0.4 times their average hourly family income and that pleasure travellers valued their time in aircraft travel at zero."

The FAA in its base case assumed that supersonic transport would have a 25 percent passenger fare premium over subsonic planes. It estimated that 1978 SST fares would equal 1965 subsonic fares and that subsonic fares would decline 25 percent in real terms between 1965 and 1978, thus producing the rate differential. However, subsonic fares declined 18 percent between 1965 and 1968, so—if we accept the IDA and FAA estimates of 1.8 percent per year fare decline—the relative difference between supersonic and subsonic fares would increase to 36 percent, thus reducing SST sales estimates to 200.

These highly speculative estimates were based on an untenable assumption—that American SSTs and British-French Concordes would not compete in the same markets. Further, Concorde, scheduled to be introduced five years before SST, might secure a considerable foothold in the market, and SST, despite its lower operating costs, might not be able to lower fares and obtain a greater market share. (We might recall here that Boeing 707 was more than two years behind the British turboprop Electra in coming into the market. Electra was a combination prop-jet; Boeing was a pure jet. Despite its delay in entering the market, Boeing was successful in capturing the world markets for its plane because of a superior product and lower operating costs.)

The subcommittee noted:

International fares are set by unanimous agreement of IATA in which each airline has a vote. With many airlines having the Concorde and with two airlines being intimately connected with its production—BOAC and Air France—it seems unlikely that the SST will force supersonic fares below those that are economical for the Concorde and drive the Concorde out of the market—the FAA assumption. The Concorde will be sold for about half the price and will have the seating capacity of an SST. Thus, two Concordes can be secured for each SST, giving airlines an additional flexibility in scheduling. If fares are kept high enough to protect the Concorde so that both types of supersonic planes operate in the same markets at the same price, then they may split the market which will reduce SST sales from 500 to 250.

In terms of rate of return on investment to the United States government, the subcommittee observed:

> By the terms of the FAA-Boeing contract, Boeing establishes the price of the plane. Given the demand model specified, Boeing . . . could make more money at a price of $40 million than at a price of $37 million. In fact, Boeing could maximize its profits if it charged about $48 million. Such a price would reduce sales of planes to something under 350. This would in turn reduce government royalties to the point that the government barely got its money back.

The return on investment (ROI) for the airlines was based on an unrealistically high load factor of 58 percent. (The industry average was 52.6 percent in 1968 and 50 percent in 1969.) [25] Even assuming the somewhat more realistic 55 percent load factor, it was estimated that airlines would earn a ROI of 25.2 percent before taxes. With after-tax profits declining steadily from 1966 on, it is likely that the airline industry was already overcapitalized and continuing declining ratios would have made the problem of financing the purchase of SSTs quite difficult.

The subcommittee also questioned the FAA estimates of additional direct and indirect employment of more than 100,000 workers. First, an unknown proportion of this number was to result from relative declines in other parts of the aerospace industry. Second, this employment would have been concentrated in highly skilled and semiskilled managerial and professional occupations which were in short supply and in periods of full employment might have proved inflationary. "The net employment increase from SST would likely be negligible and . . . the project would have practically no employment benefits for the disadvantaged hard-core unemployed with low skill levels."

After considering all the evidence, the subcommittee recommended that

> no funds for prototype construction be included in the 1970 budget. The funds still available under the old design contract, and possibly some additional funds for research, should be used to clarify the characteristics of the SST. . . . We would also suggest that any further research on this plane be done under the responsibility of an agency other than FAA. While we do not wish to suggest that the role of FAA in the development of the aircraft has been improper in any way, we are concerned about possible conflicts of interest in the future.

[25] The load factor for domestic airlines in the U.S. was reduced to 50 percent in 1969. *The New York Times,* January 11, 1970, Sec. 12, p. 17.

Environmental and Sociological Impact

The subcommittee considered four areas of environmental and socio-logical impact of SST to be its main concern. These were sonic boom, airport noise, hazards to passengers and crew, and effects of water vapor in the stratosphere. On all these counts it was concluded that major problems remained to be solved and "should be the subject of further intensive research before proceeding with prototype construction."

Technological Fallout

The subcommittee considering the effects of technological fallout from the SST program concluded as follows:

The SST program will advance many areas of technology and will result in technological fallout both to the aircraft industry in general and to other industrial and military applications. The magnitude of this effect is very difficult to assess, but it appears to be small. Nevertheless, there are a number of areas which can be identified as having a high probability of potential benefit, such as: flight control systems, structures, materials, aircraft engines, aerodynamics.

While technological fallout will inevitably result from a complex, high technology program such as the SST development, the value of this benefit appears to be limited. We believe technological fallout to be of relatively minor importance in this program and therefore should not be considered either wholly or in part as a basis for justifying the program. In the SST program, fallout or technological advances should be considered as a bonus or additional benefit from a program which must depend upon other reasons for its continuation.

Following the deliberations of the Ad Hoc Committee and its subcommittees, Chairman James Beggs prepared a draft report purportedly summarizing the views of the members of the committee. This draft report was later to be submitted to the secretary of transportation and President Nixon. The draft was highly biased in favor of the SST program; it completely ignored or sharply toned down the criticism leveled at the program by various panels and greatly exaggerated the positive findings. The reaction of the committee members, although couched in gentlemanly language, was scathing denunciation.

The differences between the conclusions in Chairman Begg's draft summary report and those of the individual members were so strong that a meeting of the full committee was called. When reconciliation proved impossible, it was decided that the entire record of the proceedings should be sent to the president for his consideration.

Despite the highly critical and unfavorable findings of his own committee, on September 23, 1969, President Nixon announced that he would ask Congress for a $96 million appropriation for the fiscal year ending June 30, 1970, for the "start of construction of two prototype SST aircraft." [26] Mr. Nixon said the decision was "based on need to keep the U.S. as world leader in air transport and to shorten flying times" [27] between the United States and the rest of the world. "The Transportation Secretary and other department officials said *the SST won't be permitted to fly over the U.S. mainland because of the sonic booms.*" [28] There were also indications that the project would be removed from FAA jurisdiction and be placed directly under Transportation Secretary Volpe. The government, which had already spent $600 million, estimated that its cost burden for the development phase would be $1.29 billion of a total estimate of $1.51 billion, the remainder to come from the manufacturers and the airlines. Recall here that when President Kennedy launched the SST project he said: "In no event will the government investment be permitted to exceed $750 million." [29] The $96 million funding was approved, but not without opposition. A motion by Congressman Yates (D, Ill.) to delete the SST appropriation from the Transportation Department budget was defeated 26 to 13.[30]

During the debate on the House floor it further appeared that the Department of Transportation (DOT) had tried to keep from Congress the highly unfavorable views of the former head of the FAA, Lt. Gen. Elmwood L. Quesada, a director of American Airlines. Congressman Reuss reported to the House that he had tried to obtain from DOT a copy of General Quesada's testimony before the SST Ad Hoc Review Committee in March 1969. According to Reuss, "DOT at first told me that no transcript of the General's testimony even existed, but finally, after repeated requests, they were able to produce one copy. It had been found in a safe in the office of the Under Secretary of Transportation." [31]

In his testimony, General Quesada stated that the SST program as originally conceived was never intended to develop an entirely new technology but to adapt commercially the knowhow that was being developed for the B–70 program. "It was anticipated that a major sponsor of the supersonic transport would be economic demand [not the Federal Government] and when economically feasible a supersonic transport program would proceed, hopefully helped by the government." [32] As it turned out, the B–70 program was later scrapped.

In terms of world competition, Quesada stated that our competition

---

[26] "SST Faces Hard Fight in Congress but Chances of Funding Seem Good," *The Wall Street Journal,* September 24, 1969, p. 3.
[27] *Ibid.*
[28] *Ibid.* Emphasis added.
[29] *Congressional Record,* July 9, 1963, pp. 12283–84.
[30] "House Panel Approves $96 Million SST Sum for This Fiscal Year," *The Wall Street Journal,* November 14, 1969, p. 21.
[31] *Congressional Record,* November 17, 1969, H10947.
[32] *Ibid.,* H10948.

with the Anglo-French Concorde or the Russian TU–144 must be on the basis of product quality and economic feasibility alone. Finally, he urged a more judicious use of the country's scarce economic resources while continuing the SST program on a more orderly basis, adding that "It would be a great tragedy if this program were ever eliminated."

THE AIRLINE REPORT ON SST

The FAA also sought the views of nine major American airlines holding positions on the reservation list for the SSTs. All agreed that a prototype should be built, but none was enthusiastic about the current design, timing of delivery, and sharing of development costs. Examples of the early 1969 comments follow:

Airline 1

The recent SST review along with an assessment of the environment in which we are currently operating has led us to take a different posture than has been the case to date. The factors influencing this change are:

First, the operating economics of the presently proposed SST indicate that a substantial fare premium undoubtedly will be required to match the economic performance of the present generation of subsonic jets.

Second, there appears to be serious doubt that the proposed SST can meet existing or proposed airport noise criteria.

Third, the SST undoubtedly will be limited to overwater operation because of the sonic boom problem.

Fourth, the final cost per airplane will undoubtedly fall in the $40–50 million area representing an enormous risk per single vehicle.

Fifth, important and costly improvements are immediately required to bring both our airways and airports up to a capacity compatible with the current and future traffic demand.

There are other factors which weigh against unqualified commitment to the SST development schedule, but the above are the most important ones in my view. . . .

If our government's assessment of this program indicates that the United States must retain its dominant position in the aircraft manufacturing industry for national reasons, then it is my opinion that the development cost risks must be assumed by the government . . .

In summation, the provision of completely adequate airways and airports in this country must take precedence over any other consideration if the vigor of our economy is to be maintained. If there are funds available after the above need is satisfied, then these funds should go toward the orderly development of an SST at whatever rate of progress is possible.

Airline 2

It is obvious that there are still some serious problems in the areas of community noise and economics. It also appears certain that the operation of the SST will be restricted to subsonic speeds over inhabited areas because of sonic boom. This will limit utilization and place an arbitrary ceiling on the total market for supersonic aircraft, increasing the unit cost.

Airline 3

We continue to be concerned about many of the technical aspects of the program, including weight and balance, flutter and dynamics, engine inlet design, and airport and community noise. Experience has indicated that solutions to problems of this type invariably add complexity and weight to an aircraft. Since the design payload-range characteristics already appear marginal, we question whether an economically viable airplane can be produced until these solutions are accurately defined.

Airline 4

Present indications are that the SST program will not produce a vehicle as economically viable for airline use as formerly was believed to be the case. Nevertheless, in view of the efforts of other nations in the SST field . . . we remain convinced that national interest considerations, relating to the balance of payments and the competitive position of our aeronautics manufacturing industry, would be served by development and production of U.S. SSTs at an early date.[33]

Boeing's Representation to the Ad Hoc Committee

The Boeing Company also submitted its views [34] to the Ad Hoc Committee, supporting the continuation of the SST program and government participation in it, and has since then continuously defended its position in the news media and before various public and private bodies. A summary of Boeing's position follows:

1. Traffic forecasts by various independent analysts indicate that revenue passenger miles in the free world will increase at least

---

[33] *Congressional Record,* October 31, 1969, H10444–45.
[34] *The SST Program and Related National Benefits* [*The Boeing Report*], Boeing Company, Seattle, Washington, February 12, 1969.

sixfold between 1968 and 1990, and $125 billion of new aircraft will be needed to carry this traffic.

2. Supersonic transports will constitute a significant part of this $125 billion market. A comprehensive analysis of operating costs, competing equipment, and appropriateness to various routes shows that even without flying over populated areas to avoid sonic boom effects, the SST market will total $25 billion by 1990.

3. SSTs will be built whether we like it or not. Because of our technical capacity, the United States is now in a position to obtain $20 billion of this $25 billion market through the sale of an estimated 500 SSTs, 270 of them to foreign airlines.

4. In terms of balance of payments, the SST program (aircraft account) would bring in an additional $11.9 billion between 1975 and 1990. Conversely, if a timely US/SST is not introduced, the negative effect on the aircraft account in the balance of payments could reach $16 billion by 1990. To counteract the argument of balance of payments deficits in travel account, Boeing argued that "if so inclined, U.S. tourists will travel overseas in Concordes (or even TU–144s) to spend their money. Actually, the foreign tourist coming *to* the U.S. also spends money, and the number of foreign visitors coming to the U.S. has been increasing in recent years." [35]

5. On a direct business venture basis, the government will be paid royalties on the sale of production airplanes in an amount returning the original investment of $1.2 billion by approximately the three hundredth plane and producing in excess of investment by the five hundredth delivery. In addition, it will bring in an additional $5.4 billion to the federal government and $1.3 billion to various state and local governments through corporate and personal income taxes of program participants and secondary employment through the "multiplier" effect. [36]

6. The production phase will yield prospective employment of approximately 500,000 highly skilled, high-wage persons at peak production. It will also provide secondary employment of over 100,000 in trades and professions including substantial numbers in semiskilled and unskilled categories.

7. There are impressive technological effects of the program for the nation which alone could justify the development of the prototypes. The benefits will, furthermore, not be confined to the transport industry but will be spread in all phases of industry through the development of new materials, manufacturing techniques, and electronic equipment.

8. The program will relieve congestion both at the airports and in the air by providing speedier movement at higher altitudes not presently used and quicker turnaround.

[35] Communication to the author by the Boeing Company, November 12, 1969.
[36] *Development of a National Asset—The American SST*, Boeing Company, Seattle, Washington, October 1969, p. 9.

Boeing argued against the need for additional expenditure for airport modifications because of SSTs by stating that the SST was designed for operation from existing international airports. No modifications to runways would be necessary. By the time it entered commercial service in 1978, airports and loading docks would have been developed to take care of the 747 and the other large-capacity subsonic jets. The SST would use these same facilities.[37]

THE HOME STRETCH—
DEFEAT OF THE SST PROGRAM

The SST became the fulcrum of a vigorous seesaw. Its opponents gained considerable strength from the mushrooming ecology movement—environmentalists came out in force against the SST. Its backers, in an ameliorative move, transferred program responsibilities from the FAA to the Secretary of Transportation. President Nixon put his weight behind the SST; several opinion surveys showed a majority of the public opposed it. Many congressional candidates pledged future votes against the project. William Magruder, a former Lockheed test pilot appointed by Nixon to head the SST program, barnstormed the country touting the SST as so important to the nation's economy, future, and prestige abroad that it would be unpatriotic to vote against it.

In the midst of the polemical crossfire, the Senate—on December 1, 1970—voted 52 to 41 to deny SST prototype funding through June 30, 1971. But seven days later the House voted to appropriate the full $290 million President Nixon had requested. With the funding question stalemated, the bill went to the Joint Economic Committee, where it faced four pro and three anti senators. Senator Proxmire, the Senate's SST-opposition leader, reluctantly agreed to stop his filibuster—after the committee agreed to fund the project with $210 million—by extracting a commitment from the pro-SST forces that allowed for a vote solely on the SST in March in return for three months' additional funding for the SST during that time ($52.5 million). An end to the filibuster was imperative. It had been holding up the entire Department of Transportation budget.

But the SST fight wasn't finished. Magruder, continuing to push hard, launched an industry-union group—the National Committee on an American SST—to promote a grass-roots letter-writing campaign urging members of Congress to vote for the plane.[38] Committee members ranged from twenty-two big corporations, such as Boeing, other aerospace companies, and defense contractors, to thirty-one unions, notably excluding the United Auto Workers Union, which refused to join. The drive started with full-page ads focused at Congress in three Washington, D.C., daily newspapers. The follow-up was a massive advertising campaign in the

---

[37] Communication to the author by the Boeing Company, November 12, 1969.
[38] "A New Drive for SST Support," *San Francisco Chronicle*, February 23, 1971, p. 10.

nation's other newspapers and in labor publications. The campaign failed. The House voted 215 to 204, and the Senate, on March 25, 1971, voted 51 to 46 to deny further SST funding. Officially, it was dead.

Death of the SST does not preclude a possible resurrection, and the Nixon administration continued to try to revive it. The opposition, spearheaded by Senator Proxmire, continued all efforts to keep it buried, in particular by ensuring that SST funds were not hidden in some other program. A flurry of bills was introduced in Congress to control aircraft engine noise. The Coalition Against the SST opened a permanent office in Washington. Reportedly, thirty groups formed an anti-SST lobby in Washington. Jurisdiction over aircraft noise standards was transferred from FAA to the Environmental Protection Agency.[39] Research on the various aspects of supersonic flight continues: in the Climatic Impact Assessment Program overseen by the National Academy of Sciences and the National Academy of Engineering; in NASA's study on wing designs, fuselage shapes, airframe and engine metals, and a "variable cycle" engine related to supersonic transport; in studies of the economics, potential stratosphere pollution, and noise effects of supersonic transport. The SST may be dead officially, but it's an uneasy corpse.

The competition is still alive, the Concorde and the TU–144, but its health is waning. Estimates of the Concorde sales price kept going up as the financial health of U.S. airlines was going down. The first blow came on January 31, 1973, when Pan Am, citing cost as the major factor, dropped its options for eight Concordes. That opened the floodgates, and in short order TWA, American, and Eastern Airlines each canceled options for six, Continental and Japan for three, Sabena for two, and El Al for one.[40] As of July 1973, Concorde had firm orders for only nine aircraft—five for BOAC and four for Air France—and options for another fourteen.

Regardless of the dampened outlook for supersonic craft, Concorde manufacturers are pushing ahead on their manufacturing plans and the flight testing necessary for certification from various governments. TU–144 is also making progress, with domestic commercial service scheduled for 1975. Aeroflot has ordered thirty planes and expects eventual requirements to be between sixty and seventy-five.[41]

It would be presumptuous to say either that supersonic transport is permanently blocked in the United States or that all opposition has been futile and purposeless. Both industry and government have been forced to consider the environmental and socioeconomic aspects of introducing new technology into the lives of people after basing their decisions only on the narrow economic and technological considerations of the companies involved. If and when the SST comes, it is likely to be a better

39 *Aviation Week & Space Technology*, November 20, 1972, p. 63.
40 "Slowdown of Concorde Production Seen," *Aviation Week & Space Technology*, February 5, 1973, p. 30; "Three More Airlines Drop Concorde Options," *Aviation Week & Space Technology*, February 19, 1973, p. 19.
41 "Top Priority Speeds TU–144 Production," *Aviation Week & Space Technology*, June 25, 1973, p. 12.

aircraft, and it will be introduced with the voluntary approval not only of its users but of the affected public. If the SST is indeed to be the aircraft of the future, the question remains: Why doesn't the *industry* build it?

SELECTED REFERENCES

BAKER, LEONARD, *The Guaranteed Society* (New York: Macmillan, 1970), section on SST.

CHATHAM, GEORGE N., and FRANKLIN P. HUDDLE, *The Supersonic Transport* (Washington, D.C.: Library of Congress, February 26, 1971), pp. 71–78.

"Controversy over the Supersonic Transport," *Congressional Digest,* December 1970.

Development of a National Asset—The American SST, Boeing Company, Seattle, Washington, October 1969.

DUPRE, T. STEFAN, and W. ERIC GUSTAFSON, "Contracting for Defense: Private Firms and the Public Interest," *Political Science Quarterly,* 57 (June 1962), 161–77.

ENKE, STEPHEN, "Government-Industry Development of a Supersonic Transport," *American Economic Review,* May 1967, pp. 71–79.

Federal Aviation Agency, *Report of the Task Force on National Aviation Goals— Project Horizon,* September, 1961.

———, *Supplementary Report to the Supersonic Transport Steering Group,* May 14, 1963.

———, *United States Supersonic Transport Program Summary* (Washington, D.C.: July 1965).

Final Report: An Economic Analysis of the Supersonic Transport, Stanford Research Institute Project No. ISU–4266.

HILTON, GEORGE W., "Federal Participation in the Supersonic Transport Program," *Business Horizons,* 10, 2 (summer 1967), 21–26.

U.S. Congress, House, Committee on Appropriations, *Department of Transportation and Related Agencies Appropriations for 1970: Hearings before Subcommittee,* Part 3, 91st Cong., 1st sess., 1969, pp. 216–348.

MEREWITZ, LEONARD, and H. SOSNICK, *The Budget's New Clothes: A Critique of Planning—Programming—Budgeting and Benefit-Cost Analysis* (Chicago: Markham, 1971).

RUSSETT, BRUCE M., "Who Pays for Defense?" *American Political Science Review,* 63 (June 1969), 412–26.

SHURCLIFF, WILLIAM A., *SST and Sonic Boom Handbook* (New York: Ballantine, 1970).

STOCKFISH, J. A., and D. J. EDWARDS, "The Blending of Public and Private Enterprise—The SST as a Case in Point," *Public Interest,* winter 1969, pp. 108–17.

The SST Program and Related National Benefits (The Boeing Report), Boeing Company, Seattle, Washington, February 12, 1969.

CORPORATIONS, THEIR DEPENDENCIES, AND OTHER SOCIAL INSTITUTIONS

Corporations
and
the Stockholders

SECURITIES AND EXCHANGE COMMISSION
VERSUS
TEXAS GULF SULPHUR COMPANY*

USE OF MATERIAL INFORMATION BY CORPORATE EXECUTIVES
AND OTHER "INSIDERS" IN THE SALE AND PURCHASE
OF COMPANY STOCK FOR PERSONAL GAIN

When the history books are written, the Texas Gulf case may turn out to be
a landmark in the evolution of capitalism from the original "public-be-damned"
to capitalism as a public trust.

—*Business Week*

This is not regulation—it is bureaucracy run wild. . . . At each fresh aggran-
dizement of the agency's power, each assault on personal freedom, brokers and
businessmen have beat a retreat under the ignoble standard, "we can live with it."
Gentlemen, can you live with the police state?

—*Barron's*

At 10 A.M. on April 16, 1964, Texas Gulf Sulphur Company (TGS)
issued a press release announcing a major strike of zinc, copper, and silver
on its properties in the Timmins area of Ontario, Canada. The news culminated in the confirmation of a long-circulating, but recently intensified,

---

* This case was co-authored with Professor John Hogel, Golden Gate University, San
Francisco, California.

rumor of the presence and discovery of sizable ore deposits by TGS on the Timmins property. The press release stated, in part:

> Texas Gulf Sulphur Company has made a major strike of zinc, copper and silver in the Timmins area of Ontario, Canada. . . .
>
> Seven drill holes are now essentially complete and indicate an ore body of at least 800 feet in length, 300 feet in width and having a vertical depth of more than 800 feet. . . .
>
> This is a major discovery. The preliminary data indicate a reserve of more than 25 million tons of ore. The only hole assayed so far represented over 600 feet of ore, indicating a true ore thickness of nearly 400 feet. . . .
>
> The ore body is shallow, having only some 20 feet of overburden. This means that it can easily be mined initially by the open pit method.[1]

The events that led to the press release started in 1957. At the time of the press release none of the participants knew that these events were but the beginning of a long, arduous travail that would expand the fiduciary responsibilities of the corporate management and those who might have access to inside information in exploiting that information for their personal gain.

THE ISSUES

From all accounts, the Texas Gulf Sulphur case was a landmark decision whose reverberations are likely to be felt for a long time. It may have significant influence on many aspects of corporate management and investing public relationships, and on the nature and direction of SEC regulation over the financial handling and reporting aspects of corporate affairs.

The facts in the case were clearly established and were accepted by all parties concerned. It must be understood, however, that facts themselves do not have any future relevance. The crucial point, therefore, is not the "facts" as such, but their interpretation. It is this interpretation that provides the connecting link between two seemingly unrelated events. It is this generalization effect that is important because, when converted into an operational principle, it provides continuity in the understanding of a phenomenon, thereby giving it stability and order.

Thus, a critical evaluation of the logic applied in the decisions of the lower court and appeals court in interpreting the data should provide valuable understanding on such broad questions as these:

[1] "Major Ore Lode Hit by TGS in Canada," *The Wall Street Journal*, April 17, 1964, p. 2.

1. What are the principles of materiality and disclosure? What are the grounds on which one piece of information becomes material, and how it should be evaluated?

2. When is information considered to have been properly disseminated and, therefore, in the public domain? What are the implications of constructing a set of broader or narrower limits, in terms of time and channels of communication, for the dissemination of information?

3. Who can be defined an insider and under what circumstances? What are the implications of a narrower or broader definition of insider for the financial markets, corporations, large and small stockholders, and the maintenance of general investor confidence in the fairness of trading in stocks?

4. What are the responsibilities of an insider in terms of (a) exercising stock options, and (b) purchase or sale of a company's stock?

5. What is the proper role of the SEC in preventing abuse of inside information for personal gain by insiders? Has the SEC been effective in achieving this goal? What is the evidence of the marketplace since the TGS case?

6. Can we propose or devise other measures that would curtail or prevent the misuse of inside information, if such a course of action is called for?

BACKGROUND

TGS, which was incorporated in 1909, is the world's major supplier of sulphur. However, in 1963 the company's annual earnings ($9 million) showed a dramatic decline from 1955 ($32 million).[2] TGS attributed this decline in earnings (as well as sales of $93 million in 1955 against $62 million in 1963) to an oversupply of sulphur on the world markets, with the resulting implications of declining prices ($28 per ton in 1956 against $20 per ton in 1963). However, in late 1963 the price decline was reversed, so that by April 1, 1964, TGS announced an increase of $2 per ton. This announcement followed the disclosure on February 8, 1964, of the company's increased production plans.

As part of its worldwide exploration for increased supply, in 1957 TGS initiated a search for sulphides [3] on the Canadian Shield, the vast, flat, and mostly barren area of eastern Canada, which is composed of Precam-

[2] Earnings per share 1960—$1.27, 1961—$1.26, 1962—$1.21, 1963—$0.93, 1964—$1.15. The large decline in 1963 was due to extraordinary loss of one of TGS's seagoing tankers.

[3] Certain minerals combine with sulphur, some of which, such as copper sulphide and zinc sulphide, may be mined commercially if found in quantity. Sulphides conduct electricity better than most other rock types and thus can be detected by aerial survey if in sufficient quantity and not buried too deeply.

brian (very complex and distorted) rock formations. After the initial surveys, an aerial geophysical survey was begun in March 1959. This survey, conducted by an exploration group consisting of Richard D. Mollison, Walter Holyk, Richard H. Clayton, and Kenneth H. Darke (see cast of characters), detected several thousand anomalies (unusual variations in the conductivity of the rock). These were reduced to several hundred that merited further study. One of these anomalies was located in Kidd Township, near Timmins, Ontario (hereafter referred to as Kidd 55).

CAST OF CHARACTERS

Name	Position
Claude O. Stephens	President and director
Charles F. Fogarty	Executive vice-president [a] and director
Thomas S. Lamont	Director
Francis G. Coates	Director
Harold B. Kline	Vice-president and general counsel [b]
Richard D. Mollison	Vice-president
David M. Crawford	Secretary [c]
Richard H. Clayton	Engineer
Walter Holyk	Chief geologist
Kenneth H. Darke	Geologist
Earl L. Huntington	Attorney
John A. Murray	Office manager

[a] Prior to February 20, 1964, was senior vice-president.
[b] Prior to January 31, 1964, was vice-president—administration, and secretary.
[c] Employed by TGS in January 1964 and became secretary on February 20, 1964.

Source: Securities and Exchange Commission v. Texas Gulf Sulphur Company, S.D. N.Y. 258 F. Supp. 262 (1966), 269.

Kidd 55 Segment

As a result of the aerial survey of the Kidd 55 segment, on June 6, 1963, TGS acquired an option to buy the northeastern quarter section of 160 acres for $500. Clayton, in conducting a ground survey on October 29 and 30, 1963, confirmed the indicated presence of conductive subsoil material. After consultation with Holyk and Darke, a drill site, K–55–1, was chosen, and drilling operations began November 8, 1963.[4] Darke telephoned Holyk on November 11 at his home in Stamford, Connecticut, to report findings of a strong initial evidence of mineralization in the core sample. Holyk left for Timmins the same day. Prior to his departure

---

[4] *Securities and Exchange Commission* v. *Texas Gulf Sulphur Company*, S.D.N.Y. 258 F. Supp. 262 (1966), 288. All subsequent references in the text to this citation will be shown as (1. page number).

he called Mollison, who passed on the findings to Charles F. Fogarty, the company's executive vice-president. Fogarty in turn called Claude O. Stephens, the company's president. The drilling was terminated the following day after work had been done on a core section 655 feet in length. In a visual mineralization estimate, Holyk predicted an average copper content of 1.15 percent and a zinc content of 8.64 percent over a length of 599 feet. On November 13 Mollison and Fogarty flew into Timmins for consultation with the exploration group. The following morning they returned to New York with Holyk. For confirmation, a split core sample was flown by TGS to the Union Assay House in Salt Lake City for a detailed chemical analysis. The results of this analysis later indicated (mid-December) a copper content of 1.18 percent, a zinc content of 8.26 percent, and a silver content of 3.94 ounces per ton over a length of 602 feet (1,271).

Secrecy of Drilling Operations

The company instituted standard exploratory security measures to insure that its findings remained secret. The drilling crew was told to keep the results and the site confidential. Drilling on the K–55–1 anomaly was terminated, and the drilling rig was moved to a new drill site, K–55–2, located off the anomaly (Figure 1). Drilling was begun on November 20 and was completed ten days later. The rig was then moved out, leaving behind an obvious drill site, but a barren core. Small saplings were planted in the core area of K–55–1 to conceal its location. A convenient snowfall completed the concealment of drilling activities. During this time and in subsequent months, strong rumors of a major nickel find by TGS began to circulate.

Land Acquisition

Based on Holyk's estimates, and without the confirming analysis of the official assay, TGS decided to acquire the three remaining quarter sections of K–55. Under the direction of Darke, TGS began to stake claims in the area surrounding the Kidd site. This work was completed on March 27, 1964. Three days later a TGS legal team, including Harold B. Kline, vice-president, consummated the purchase of the remaining Kidd–55 sections.[5] Because of TGS's drilling activity, the growing rumors, and the claim-staking activity, there was increased trading in mining claims and stocks on the Toronto Stock Exchange. Many of the worthless claims in the area surrounding Timmins and the Kidd site were bought up by a Timmins partnership, including Darke, which began to sell them off. Worthless or not, a "traditional" Canadian mining frenzy was on.

After obtaining the rights to the full Kidd Township section, drilling

[5] Morton Shulman, *The Billion Dollar Windfall* (New York: William Morrow, 1970), p. 107.

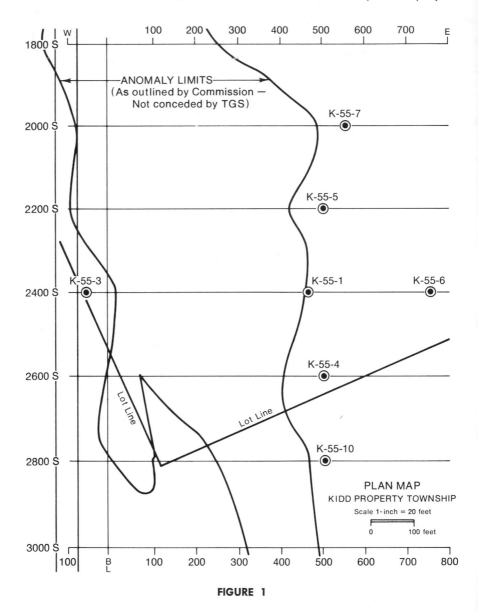

FIGURE 1

was resumed on March 31, 1964, at the K–55–3 drill site. That same day in New York, TGS announced a $2 per ton increase in the price of sulphur. The drilling operation was completed on the evening of April 7 at a length of 876 feet. The visual estimates showed an average copper content of 1.12 percent and a zinc content of 7.93 percent over 641 feet. Throughout the drilling operation, Mollison and Holyk gave daily progress reports to Stephens and Fogarty in New York.

TGS brought in additional rigs so that test drilling could proceed at a faster pace. Drilling at the K–55–4 site was begun on April 7. Two days later, the visual estimates showed a copper content of 1.14 percent and a zinc content of 8.24 percent over 366 feet. Combined with the results of K–55–1 and K–55–3, the evidence to date showed the existence of substantial mineralization on the eastern edge of the K–55 anomaly, which was the first time TGS had a firm indication, if not solid geophysical proof, that the discovery was minable (i.e., was three-dimensional in sufficient size). (See Figure 1.)

Drill site K–55–6 was begun on April 8, and by April 10 it was evident that substantial copper mineralization existed over the last 127 feet of the total 569-foot length. No visual estimates were made, as none of the geologists were on the site. Drill site K–55–5 was begun on April 10, and by that evening evidence of strong mineralization was apparent over the last 42 feet of the 97-foot core length (1,272).

Rumors and Reality

On April 9, 1964, several Toronto newspapers reported that TGS had discovered what was termed "one of the largest copper deposits in North America, [and] a major copper strike" (1,293). Similar stories circulated in the *Northern Miner* and the *Toronto Star*. Alerted to the Toronto news stories, Stephens telephoned Thomas S. Lamont, a company director, on the tenth for advice on handling the Canadian rumors. Lamont recommended that TGS take no action as long as the rumors remained solely in Canada or at least until TGS had enough information about the implications of the drilling results to issue an appropriate statement to the press. However, he said, should the rumors reach New York, a press release would be necessary.

The following day, April 11, Stephens read the articles that appeared in *The New York Times* and the *New York Herald Tribune*. The *Herald Tribune* stated in part that the K–55 discovery was "the biggest ore strike since gold was discovered more than 60 years ago in Canada. . . . A bed of copper sulphide 600 feet wide with a possible over-all copper return of 2.87% through most of its width" (1,293). The article also stated that TGS had four drilling rigs in operation on the K–55 site and that the cores' richness was such that they had to be flown out of Canada for assay.

Immediately after reading the articles in the New York papers, Stephens phoned Fogarty at his home in Rye, New York, and asked Fogarty to read the articles and call him back. Later Fogarty called Stephens at his home in Greenwich, Connecticut, and told him that he was "quite upset . . . because certainly they [the articles] were full of exaggerations and what I considered to be erroneous statements" (1,294). Stephens indicated that TGS should issue, as soon as possible, a press release to clarify the situation and to dispel the rumors. Fogarty then contacted Carroll of TGS's public relations firm, Doremus and Company, and Carroll agreed that a press release was necessary.

That evening Fogarty went to Greenwich to discuss the situation at the drill site with Mollison, who had flown in from Timmins to spend the weekend at home. Mollison advised that, based on the information he had up to the time he left Timmins on the morning of April 10, it was too early to determine what type of discovery TGS had made. He said that "it was impossible at that time . . . to understand the structure [of the discovery or] . . . to make projections from one hole to another" (1,294).

Fogarty returned to New York City, and with the help of Carroll and David M. Crawford, the company's secretary, drafted a statement for release to the press on April 12. The draft was given to Earl L. Huntington, the company's attorney, to verify the legalities of the press release.

The April 12 Press Release

On the morning of April 12, Fogarty called Mollison at his home and told him to return as soon as possible to Timmons, along with Holyk (who had also returned to New York for the weekend), to "move things along" (1,294). Fogarty then called Stephens and read the statement to be released at three o'clock that afternoon for publication Monday morning:

> During the past few days, the exploration activities of Texas Gulf Sulphur in the area of Timmons, Ontario, have been widely reported in the press, coupled with rumors of a substantial copper discovery there. These reports exaggerate the scale of operations, and mention plans and statistics of size and grade of ore that are without factual basis and have evidently originated by speculation of people not connected with TGS.
>
> The facts are as follows. TGS has been exploring in the Timmins area for six years as part of its overall search in Canada and elsewhere for various minerals—lead, copper, zinc, etc. During the course of this work, in Timmins as well as in Eastern Canada, TGS has conducted exploration entirely on its own, without the participation by others. Numerous prospects have been investigated by geophysical means and a large number of selected ones have been core-drilled. These cores are sent to the United States for assay and detailed examination as a matter of routine and on advice of expert Canadian legal counsel. No inferences as to grade can be drawn from this procedure.
>
> Most of the areas drilled in Eastern Canada have revealed either barren pyrite or graphite without value; a few have resulted in discoveries of small or marginal sulphide ore bodies.
>
> Recent drilling on one property near Timmins has led to preliminary indications that more drilling would be required for proper evaluation of this prospect. The drilling done to date has not been conclusive, but the statements made by many outside quarters are

unreliable and include information and figures that are not available to TGS.

The work done to date has not been sufficient to reach definite conclusions and any statement as to size and grade of ore would be premature and possibly misleading. When we have progressed to the point where reasonable and logical conclusions can be made, TGS will issue a definite statement to its stockholders and to the public in order to clarify the Timmins project.[6]

K—55 Revisited

When Mollison left Timmins for New York on the morning of April 10, he had the up-to-date results of the drilling operations. However, drilling did not stop while he and Holyk were absent. Rather, operations had intensified.

At site K–55–5 drilling resumed on the evening of April 10 and was completed on April 13. The core sample indicated mineralization to the 580-foot level, and the visual estimates over a 525-foot section indicated an average copper content of 0.82 percent and a zinc content of 4.2 percent. At site K–55–6 drilling also resumed on April 10 and was completed at 7 A.M. on April 13. The visual estimates showed mineralization over 504 feet of the 946-foot core, with a copper content of 1.72 percent and a zinc content of 6.60 percent (1,272).

On April 11 drilling on K–55–8 was begun. This particular site differed from the others in that it was a mill test hole.[7] The bore was completed on April 13. No visual estimates or other geological evidence was available or reported prior to April 16 because a mill test requires more detailed analysis (1,273).

A new site, K–55–7, was begun on April 12 and by the following day had encountered mineralization of 50 feet over its 137-foot length. By April 15 the core had been drilled to 707 feet, but with only an additional 26 feet of mineralization between the 425- to 451-foot level. The last site drilled by the exploration group, K–55–10, was begun on April 14. By 7 P.M. the following day, substantial mineralization was evident over the last 231 feet of the 249 feet of drilling (1,273).

The Northern Miner

Because of the rumors sweeping Canada in early April, the *Northern Miner*, a weekly mining trade journal published in Toronto, asked TGS

---

6 "TGS Calls Talk 'Premature' on Canada Copper Lode," *The Wall Street Journal*, April 13, 1964, p. 12.

7 A mill test hole differs from the others in that the diameter is twice the normal drill core size ($2\frac{1}{4}$" vs. $1\frac{1}{8}$"). It is used to determine the amenability of the mineral material to routine mill processing.

for an inspection tour of the Kidd site and interviews with the exploration team so that it could gather information for an article that might clarify the rumors. The circulation of the journal in the United States was very small (7,400 subscribers, of whom, 1,412 were in New York, plus a small newsstand circulation) (1,285). TGS agreed and made arrangements to have one of the paper's reporters, Graham Ackerley, visit the site on April 12. However, because of the printing of the articles in the Toronto press, Stephens and Fogarty on April 11 asked that Ackerley's visit be postponed to April 13 so that it would not coincide with the April 12 press release.

Ackerley visited the Kidd site and inspected the drilling records to date and the core samples, and he interviewed Mollison and Holyk (both of whom had returned to Timmins from New York), and Darke. While at the site Ackerley wrote the draft of his article, which he submitted to Mollison for clearance. Both Mollison and Holyk read the proposed article and decided that "some conclusions were too optimistic. . . ." (1,285). However, they did not require any major revisions. The article stated, in part, *"The Northern Miner* can say that a major zinc-copper-silver mine is definitely in the making, one that has all the earmarks of shaping into a substantial open pit operation . . . something in excess of 10 million tons of ore is indicated." [8]

Mollison returned the draft to Ackerley on the evening of April 15 with his clearance for publication. The article was published in the paper's April 16 morning edition. The paper hit the streets in Toronto between 7 and 8 A.M. Reports of the article were telephoned and telexed to New York City from Toronto prior to the opening of the New York Stock Exchange (10 A.M.) on April 16, 1964 (1,285). By 9:15 A.M. the TGS discovery was the talk of the financial community in New York.[9]

Ontario Minister of Mines

During the period between the two press releases, the Canadian Institute of Mining and Metallurgy held its annual convention in Montreal (April 13–15). The main subject of conversation throughout the meeting was the rumors of the TGS discovery which were sweeping the Canadian mining and business communities. One of the participants at the convention was Ontario Minister of Mines George Wardrope.

First contacted by Holyk in Montreal, Wardrope arranged a meeting for Tuesday, April 14. Mollison and Holyk arrived for the meeting to find themselves celebrities, with a press conference waiting. Since they had no authorization to make a public statement, they went back to their hotel. It was then agreed that they would fly the minister and his deputy to Toronto the following day (9:30 A.M.). During the flight Wardrope was informed of the current developments at the Kidd drilling site. He

[8] "TGS Comes Up with Major Find Carrying Important Copper, Zinc, Silver Values," *Northern Miner,* April 16, 1964, p. 1.
[9] John Brooks, "Annals of Finance: A Reasonable Amount of Time," *New Yorker,* November 9, 1968, p. 174.

was enthusiastic over the scope of the discovery and expressed a desire to make a public statement concerning the exploration operation, and both Mollison and Holyk agreed that such a statement was desirable.

With the assistance of Mollison, Wardrope drafted a statement which concluded: "The information in hand . . . gives the company confidence to allow me [the minister] to announce that Texas Gulf Sulphur has a minable body of zinc, copper, and silver ore of substantial dimensions that will be developed and brought to production as rapidly as possible" (1,285–86).

It was decided that the minister would issue the statement in Toronto on radio and television at 11 P.M. (April 15). Mollison phoned Stephens and Fogarty in New York about the timing of the statement's release. Mollison and Holyk went on to Timmins, took a quick look around (by this time Timmins was a boomtown), conferred with John A. Murray, the company's office manager, and then returned to New York, arriving late that evening. For some undisclosed reason, the minister's statement was not made that evening, but instead was given the following morning (April 16) at 9:40 at the Ontario Parliament in Toronto.

April 16 Press Release

At 9 A.M. on April 16, the TGS board of directors held its regularly scheduled monthly meeting at its offices in the Pan American building in New York. Copies of the press release were distributed and read to the members of the board (all fifteen of whom were present). For most of them this was the first confirmation of the rumors that had appeared in the Canadian and the New York press. Stephens also told the board that the Ontario minister had made a statement the previous evening (this had not been confirmed by TGS). They were then briefed by Holyk and Mollison on the Kidd operations. After a short meeting, Stephens called the reporters into the boardroom at 10 A.M. and then read the press release (see pp. 281–82 of this book).

The reporters rushed from the room to call in the story to their respective services. The first summary of the release was carried over the internal wires of the brokerage house Merrill Lynch, Pierce, Fenner and Smith at 10:29 A.M. The Dow-Jones broad tape carried parts of the release between 10:45 and 11:02 A.M. (1,289).

Purchase of Stocks Options and Calls

In March 1961 TGS instituted the Restricted Stock Opinion Incentive Plan, which was for management personnel making an annual salary of over $24,000. On February 20, 1964, the board of directors voted to grant stock options to twenty-six members of TGS. This was done on the recommendation of a committee composed of J. H. Hill, chairman of the board of Air Reduction and other companies, and Francis G. Coates—

the third member, L. M. Cassidy, was not present. Twenty-one of the options were granted to personnel making more than $24,000 (which included Stephens, Fogarty, Kline, and Mollison). The other five options were granted to personnel making between $15,000 and $21,000 (which included Holyk). The plan stated that the options would be granted at a minimum of 95 percent of the fair market price of the shares on the day of their approval. The options were to be based on the average of the high and the low quote for TGS stock on February 20, 1964—$23.81 per share (1,290–91).

In making the stock options, neither the committee nor the board of directors asked, or were they told, if any of the prospective recipients had any special knowledge that might affect the market performance of TGS shares. However, each of the named recipients was aware of the developments to that point at the Kidd site.

Individual Actions of the Principal Characters

1. *Thomas S. Lamont.* Lamont first heard of the Kidd operations on April 10 when Stephens called to ask him for advice on handling the Canadian rumors. Lamont recommended that nothing be done at that stage. On April 13 and 14 Lamont talked with Executive Vice-President Hinton of Morgan Guaranty about the articles in the press and TGS's public statement that Lamont knew "nothing more than what was in the papers." On April 15 Stephens phoned Lamont and informed him of the press release to be issued the following day. At 10:40 A.M. he called Hinton at Morgan Guaranty and advised him of impending good news on the "tape." Hinton immediately called the bank's trading department and was told that the market for TGS was active and up three points. He then placed orders for 12,000 shares for various bank customers. At approximately 12:30 P.M. Lamont placed a buy order for 3,000 shares for himself and his family.

2. *Francis G. Coates.* Coates, who was in Houston, Texas, telephoned Stephens in New York after reading the April 11 article in the *Herald Tribune.* He was informed of the TGS position with regard to the rumors and of the press release scheduled for the following day. On April 15 Coates flew to New York and saw a draft of the April 16 press release. He attended the directors' meeting on the sixteenth. At 10:20 A.M. he left the room and called his son-in-law, H. Fred Haemisegger, a stockbroker in Houston, and after informing him of the TGS discovery, placed an order for 2,000 shares for the accounts of four family trusts of which he was a trustee. Haemisegger told four of his customers of the TGS announcement, and they bought 1,500 shares of TGS.

3. *David M. Crawford.* Crawford read the April 11 article in the *Herald Tribune* on the way to Houston to prepare for the annual stockholders' meeting scheduled for April 23. He returned to New York either late on April 14 or early on April 15. Along with Fogarty and Orlando of Doremus and Company—TGS's public relations firm—he helped to

draft the press release on the afternoon of April 15. This was the first time that he was made aware of the developments at the Kidd site.

Crawford spent that night in New York. At midnight he telephoned his broker in Chicago and ordered three hundred shares for himself and his wife to be bought at the opening of the exchange. In the morning, at 8:30, he called Chicago again and increased his order to six hundred shares.

4. *Richard H. Clayton.* In Timmins on April 12 and 13, Clayton returned to New York on April 14. He spent April 15 in TGS's offices. That day he called his broker in Toronto and ordered two hundred shares.

Reaction to the Press Release of April 16

The public reaction to the confirmation of the rumors about the Kidd discovery caused the price of TGS shares on the New York Stock Exchange to soar "$7 to close at $36.375 a share. It was the most active Big Board Stock, with 444,200 shares traded." [10] Between April 16 and 29, the TGS stock rose from $36.375 to $56.750.

Public reaction to the April 12 announcement and the company's negation of the "premature and possibly misleading" [11] rumors came under public criticism. Fogarty stated in an interview that the April 12 press release was issued because so much information was coming out about the company that the situation had to be clarified in the public interest. The April 16 press release followed as soon as the company had, some substantive information.[12]

On Monday, April 20, the NYSE announced that it "was barring stop orders in Texas Gulf Sulphur . . . effective at today's market opening [Tuesday, April 21]." [13] The same day TGS announced an increase of 19 percent in its first-quarter earnings. Sales climbed to $15,237,000 for the quarter, from $14,723,000. It stated that the improved earnings "resulted mainly from economies in the delivery of sulphur and in the operation of the Texas Gulf facilities and in some price improvement abroad." [14] Fogarty also said that TGS expected a continued favorable trend.

Two days later, Fogarty announced that "Texas Gulf Sulphur Company's mineral discovery in Canada won't benefit the company's earnings

[10] *The Wall Street Journal,* April 17, 1964, p. 2.
[11] *The Wall Street Journal,* April 13, 1964, p. 12.
[12] "Texas Gulf Sulphur Ore Discovery Still Has Mine Stocks, Claims Flying," *The Wall Street Journal,* April 20, 1964, p. 32.
[13] A *stop order* is an order an investor places with his broker to buy a specified number of shares of a stock if the price of the stock rises above a specified level or to sell if it falls below a specified level. When the stop price is reached, a stop order becomes a market order, or an order for the broker to get the best possible price. Stop orders tend to increase the price fluctuations of a volatile stock.
[14] "Texas Gulf Sulphur and Curtis Stock Prices Climb Again in Wake of Ore Find in Canada," *The Wall Street Journal,* April 21, 1964, p. 6.

this year [1964]," adding that any increased earnings would "probably start in 1965." [15]

At the annual stockholders' meeting in Houston, Stephens announced that it would be another six months before the company's copper, zinc, and silver discovery in Canada could be fully evaluated. He also indicated that the initial announcement of the discovery's size on April 16 was a conservative one.

Public Disclosure of Stock Purchases by Insiders

Approximately one month after the public announcement of the TGS discovery, news began to surface that executives of TGS had purchased shares in the company on the open market on or about the date of the announcement. On May 14, 1964, an article in *The Wall Street Journal*, quoting NYSE sources, reported that two officers and a director of TGS had purchased a total of 3,730 shares of TGS common in April 1964. The officers named were Crawford (530 shares) and Lamont (3,200 shares).[16]

Lamont informed the *Journal* that his purchase on April 16 had been made "in the afternoon long after the public announcement" and that "for obvious reasons I wouldn't dream of buying stock before the news got out." The same article stated that Fogarty had purchased TGS shares on April 1, on April 6, and on April 22. When reached for comment, Fogarty stated that his purchases at the beginning of April had been made "after public announcements of other Texas Gulf Sulphur activities that have been overlooked amid the recent attention focused on the ore discovery." This reference was to TGS announcements at the beginning of April that the company was undertaking a major potash development in Utah, that a $2 per ton price increase for sulphur was being introduced, and that a $45 million phosphate development was being initiated in North Carolina.[17]

The next day, May 15, it was further revealed that another TGS employee, Francis G. Coates, of Baker, Botts, Shepherd, and Coates, a Houston law firm representing TGS, and a TGS director, had purchased 2,000 shares of TGS common on April 16. The NYSE further stated that the purchases were executed after the public announcement.[18]

On June 18, 1964, TGS announced its plans for developing the Kidd site and stated that the ore body appeared to be twice the size of the original estimate. The announcement set off such a flurry of trading on the NYSE that activity had to be halted briefly.

---

[15] "Texas Gulf Believes Find Won't Lift Net Until '65," *The Wall Street Journal*, April 23, 1964, p. 32.
[16] "Texas Gulf Sulphur Co. Stock Bought in April by Two Officers, Directors," *The Wall Street Journal*, May 14, 1964, p. 15.
[17] *Ibid.*
[18] "Another Texas Gulf Sulphur Aide Bought Stock April 16," *The Wall Street Journal*, May 15, 1964, p. 4.

SECURITIES AND EXCHANGE COMMISSION SUIT

On April 19, 1965, the SEC filed a thirty-four-page civil suit against TGS and thirteen "insiders" (see cast of characters) in the United States Court for the Southern District of New York.[19] The complaint alleged that twelve of the defendants used inside information about the discovery on the Kidd site to make illegal gains in market activity in TGS common stock before word of the find was made public. The other defendant, Thomas S. Lamont, was accused of giving the Morgan Guaranty Trust Company advance knowledge of the ore discovery on April 16. The complaint covered the period between November 12, 1963, when drilling first indicated an ore find, and April 16, 1964, when the find was made public.[20]

The defendants were alleged to have made outright purchases of 9,100 TGS shares and to have bought call options on an additional 5,200 shares. They were also alleged to have received stock options on 31,200 shares. Additionally, the complaint charged that TGS personnel tipped off other individuals who bought 14,700 shares outright and calls on another 14,100 shares.[21] Furthermore, the suit was supposed to alert investors who had sold TGS stock to insiders that they had the right to sue the TGS insiders for their losses.[22] By the middle of June 1965, at least fifteen major stockholder damage suits had been filed naming TGS and various company officials. The total damages demanded in the various actions ran into the millions of dollars.[23]

Offer To Return Profit to the Company

During the last week of April 1965, TGS again held its annual stockholders' meeting in Houston. Frequently interrupted by applause, TGS President Stephens addressed the meeting and said that the company was satisfied that no element of bad faith or overreaching was involved in any purchases by officers or directors. However, he recognized that others, influenced by hindsight and the magnitude of the Timmins discovery, might be concerned. Stephens also revealed that officials of the company had offered to return to the company any profits made on stock purchases since the ore discovery on the Kidd site, but that these offers had been summarily rejected by the SEC. In a press interview, Fogarty suggested

[19] The case was heard only against twelve defendants. One defendant, Thomas P. O'Neill, an accountant with TGS, was served with a summons but failed to appear. His case was separated from the rest of the defendants.
[20] "Texas Gulf Sulphur Officers Accused by SEC of Profiting by Inside Data," *The Wall Street Journal,* April 20, 1965, p. 3.
[21] "Texas Gulf Suit Opens New Door for SEC," *Business Week,* April 24, 1965, pp. 24–25.
[22] "Offer Declined," *Forbes,* May 1, 1965, p. 16.
[23] "Stock Suits Pile Up," *Chemical Week,* June 12, 1965, p. 38.

that this refusal was part of an attempt "to strengthen their [the SEC's] policing powers. They are interested in getting broad legislation to prevent anyone in a company from buying that company's stock." A spokesman for the SEC promptly denied the charge, stating that "present legislation completely covers this kind of situation." [24]

Summary of SEC Complaint

The SEC complaint charged each of the defendants with violations of Section 10b of the Securities and Exchange Commission Act of 1934 (15 U.S.C. § 78j(b)) and Rule 10b–5 promulgated thereunder by the commission. Section 10 of the act reads, in pertinent parts, as follows:

> It shall be unlawful for any person, directly or indirectly, by the use of any means or instrumentality of interstate commerce or of the mails or of any facility of any national securities exchange . . .
>
> (b) To use or employ, in connection with the purchase or sale of any security registered on a national securities exchange or any security not so registered, any manipulating or deceptive device or contrivance in contravention of such rules and regulations as the Commission may prescribe as necessary or appropriate in the public interest or for the protection of investors.

Rule 10b (17 C.F.R. 240) provides that

> it shall be unlawful for any person, directly or indirectly, by use of any means or instrumentality of interstate commerce, or of the mails, or any facility of any national securities exchange,
>
> (1) to employ any device, scheme or artifice to defraud,
>
> (2) to make any untrue statement of a material fact or to omit to state a material fact necessary in order to make the statements made, in the light of the circumstances under which they were made, not misleading, or
>
> (3) to engage in any act, practice, or course of business which operates or would operate as a fraud or deceit upon any person, in connection with the purchase or sale of any security.

The commission specifically charged that:

> 1. TGS violated Section 10b and Rule 10b–5 by issuing a false press release on April 12, 1964, concerning its exploratory activities on the Kidd 55 segment near Timmins, Ontario, between November 12, 1963, and April 16, 1964.

---

[24] "Texas Gulf Says SEC Rejected Profit Turnback," *The Wall Street Journal*, April 23, 1965, p. 3.

2. Each defendant was charged with similar violations, for purchasing stocks or calls on TGS stock or recommending such purchases to others between November 12, 1963, and April 16, 1964, on the grounds that defendants used to their own advantage *material information,* which they possessed, as to TGS's exploratory activities, which material information *had not been disclosed to or absorbed by the stockholders or the public.*

3. Five of the defendants were further charged with similar violations for accepting stock options granted by TGS on February 20, 1964, on the grounds that they used *material information* in their possession to their own advantage by failing to disclose it to the directors' committee that granted the stock options.

In seeking remedy against these violations, the SEC sought to have the court decree:

1. Cancellation of stock purchases made by the thirteen defendants
2. Cancellation of the stock options
3. An injunction against further insider transactions based on inside information
4. An injunction against issuing misleading press releases
5. Additional relief not yet specified

The central precedent for SEC's suit of the alleged violation of Rule 10b–5 was the 1961 *Cady, Roberts* case, in which a representative of that brokerage house, who was also a director of Curtis-Wright Publishing Company, told an associate, thirty minutes before public release of the information, that Curtis-Wright was reducing its dividend rate. The associate used this information to make a financial gain. The decision, written by the then SEC Chairman William L. Cary, found this to be a violation of Rule 10b–5, stating that insiders must disclose material facts known to them by virtue of their positions but not known to persons with whom they deal and that, if known, would affect their investment judgment. Failure to make disclosure in these circumstances constitutes a violation of the antifraud provisions.[25]

The SEC provided evidence to show that all the individual defendants purchased shares of TGS or calls on TGS stock between November 12, 1963, and April 16, 1964. Evidence also showed that certain persons, called "tippees" by the SEC counsel at the trial, purchased shares of TGS or calls on TGS stock on the basis of advice received directly or indirectly from defendants Darke, Coates, and Lamont (Table 1).

The SEC suit charged that the defendants had failed to disclose "material facts" in the sale or purchase of TGS securities and asked the defendants to reimburse for their losses those individuals who sold TGS stock based upon the "false and misleading" April 12, 1964, press release

[25] *SEC* v. *Cady, Roberts & Co.* (S.D.N.Y. 1962).

TABLE 1 ESTIMATED PROFITS OF DEFENDANTS AND THEIR "TIPPEES" ON THE PURCHASE OF SHARES AND/OR CALLS OF TEXAS GULF SULPHUR STOCK FROM NOVEMBER 12, 1963, TO CLOSE OF BUSINESS APRIL 16, 1964

Defendants (and associates)	*Estimated Dollar Profits*			
	From 11/12/63 to 7 P.M., 4/9/64	*From 7 P.M., 4/9/64 to 10 A.M., 4/16/64*	*From 10 A.M., 4/16/64 to close of business 4/16/64*	*Total*
Charles F. Fogarty	39,384			39,384
Thomas S. Lamont			41,150	41,150
Francis G. Coates			15,086	15,086
Richard D. Mollison	4,200			4,200
David M. Crawford		3,712		3,712
Richard H. Clayton	13,953	1,400		15,353
Walter Holyk	21,154			21,154
Kenneth H. Darke	127,205			127,205
Earl L. Huntington	2,562			2,562
John A. Murray	4,086			4,086
Total	$212,544	$5,112	$56,236	$273,892

concerning the Kidd discovery. The SEC contended that the defendants had engaged in a "course of business" that operated "as a fraud or deceit" on the stockholders. The suit would require the defendants to either sell back stock at the original prices or make up the difference in cash for those who sold their holdings in TGS based on the April 12 statement. It was this aspect of the suit that generated the most interest in the financial and legal community because, for the first time, the SEC was levying damages against "insiders." The suit also tended to break new ground in four major aspects, namely: (1) What is material information? (2) What is false and misleading information? (3) Who are the insiders? (4) What is a reasonable time that must elapse before a piece of information can be said to have become public knowledge?

In its briefs and at the trial, the commission made no distinction among the three sections of Rule 10b–5 as to violations, relying on precedents which noted that as long as a violation of the rule was alleged, it was immaterial which section of the rule was invoked (1,276).

Summary of Defendants' Response

By the middle of July, TGS filed an answer to the SEC complaint, denying that the purchases made by the defendants were made "with knowledge and information or material facts that were not disclosed to sellers of stock . . . or that the company issued a misleading press release concerning the extent of the copper and zinc minerals strike at Timmins, Ontario." TGS further spelled out the history of the Kidd site, specifically stating that K–55–1 "could not indicate that there was a mineable body of ore, much less that there was a major sulphide deposit . . . in that the core sample . . . didn't show whether mineralization occurred in thin, intermediate, or wide zones, or discontinuous zones." The company also stated that the unsubstantiated "rumors compelled TGS to make an immediate public statement [April 12] . . . indicating that it was not the source of these rumors." [26]

In addition to the company's answer to the SEC complaint, each defendant filed a separate answer. The defendants further asserted that:

1. The commission must first "establish the elements of common law fraud—misrepresentation or nondisclosure, materiality, scienter, intent to deceive, reliance, and causation citing decisions in private actions brought under Section 10(b) requiring proof of one or more of these traditional elements as a condition precedent to relief" (1,277).
2. The commission cannot broaden the definition of "insiders" or the limits of their liabilities to the sanctions beyond what Section 16 of the Act (15 U.S.C. 78p) specifies relating to directors, officers, and principal stockholders (1,278).
3. The facts do not prove the commission's allegations.

SUMMARY OF THE LOWER COURT'S DECISION

District Court Judge Dudley B. Bonsal rendered the lower court's decision on August 19, 1966. For easier understanding, the decision is divided into two parts—questions of law and questions of the facts in the case.

Questions of Law

The court held that in a regulatory or enforcement proceeding, the commission was not required to prove common law elements. "It is only necessary to prove one of the prohibited actions such as the material statement of fact or the omission to state a material fact" (1,277). Furthermore, the court cited the following Supreme Court decision:

It would defeat the manifest purpose of the Investment Advisers Act of 1940 for us to hold, therefore, that Congress, in empowering the courts to enjoin any practice which operates "as a fraud or deceit," intended to require proof of intent to injure and actual injury to clients (375 U.S., at 192, 84 S. Ct., at 283). . . .

26 "TGS Fights Back," *Chemical Week,* July 17, 1965, p. 28.

Congress intended the Investment Advisers Act of 1940 to be *construed like other securities legislation* "enacted for the purpose of avoiding frauds," not technically and restrictively, but flexibly to effectuate its remedial purposes (375 U.S., at 195, 84 S. Ct., at 284). [1,277]

The court also rejected the defendants' arguments regarding the definition of insiders and the limits of their liability under Section 16 of the act, citing various legal precedents that the scope of Section 16 was narrower and was intended only as a "crude rule of thumb" to make unprofitable all short-swing speculation by a *specifically defined group of insiders* (1,278). Section 10b, on the other hand, applied to "any person" claiming to have been defrauded and was *not* limited to the purchase or sale of a listed security as in Section 16. Therefore, Section 16 imposed no limitations on the enforcement of Section 10b.

To establish violations of Section 10b and Rule 10b–5(3), the commission had to prove that the defendants engaged in a course of business that operated as fraud or deceit in connection with the purchase or sale of any security. The court then turned its attention to the question of whether insider purchases based on material undisclosed information did indeed constitute such violations. If such a contention were granted, then it must be decided as to who the insiders were, whether the act and the rule were limited to "face-to-face" transactions, and what constituted material information (1,278).

After citing various legal precedents and earlier court decisions, the court concluded:

1. The failure of the director and general manager of a corporation to disclose special facts in purchasing its securities operated as a fraud on the seller. The U.S. Supreme Court had stated in a decision:

   If it were conceded, for the purpose of the argument, that the ordinary relations between director and shareholders in a business corporation are not of such a fiduciary nature as to make it the duty of a director to disclose to a shareholder the general knowledge which he may possess regarding the value of the shares of the company before he purchases any from a shareholder, yet there are cases where, by reason of the special facts, such duty exists (213 U.S., at 431, 29 S. Ct., at 525). [1,278]

   The court applied this "special facts" doctrine to Section 10b and Rule 10b–5 and declared that trading by an insider on the basis of undisclosed information was indeed a violation of the act and the rule.

2. *Insiders* might include employees of a company as well as directors, officers, and major stockholders who were in possession of material undisclosed information obtained in the course of their employment or engagement with the company.

3. As far as the court was concerned, *material information* was any "important development which might affect security values or in-

fluence investment decisions [of] reasonable and objective" investors.

4. The obligation to *disclose* material information rested on two grounds:

   (a) there must exist some basis for access to information intended for corporate purposes only and not for the personal gain of anyone; and

   (b) there must be some "inherent unfairness" involved where one party takes advantage of such information, knowing that it is not available to those with whom he is dealing.

5. An insider's *liability* for failure to disclose material information that he used to his advantage in the purchase of securities extended to purchases made on national securities exchanges, as well as to face-to-face transactions.

6. *Fraud* might be accomplished by false statements, by failure to correct a misleading impression left by statements already made, or, as in the present case, by not stating anything at all when there was a duty to come forward and speak.

7. The court also rejected the defendants' argument that it would be impossible for an insider trading on a national exchange to locate the buyers or sellers to disclose material information to them. The court maintained that there were other ways to disclose significant corporate developments. For example, the New York Stock Exchange stated in its *Company Manual* that important developments that might affect security values or influence investments should be promptly disclosed. However, where material information was available to the employees of the corporation that was only for corporate use and could not be disclosed, even to stockholders, then the employee must avoid using it to his own advantage. However, to establish a violation of Section 10 and Rule 10b–5, the undisclosed information must be material. Nothing in the act would prevent insiders from buying their company's stock or benefiting from the company's incentive stock option plan:

   On the contrary, it is important under our free enterprise system that insiders, including directors, officers, and employees, be encouraged to own securities in their company. The incentive that comes with stock ownership benefits both the company and its stockholders.

   Moreover, it is obvious that any director, officer, or employee will know more about his company or have more specialized knowledge as to at least some phase of its business than an outside stockholder can have or expect to have. Often this specialized knowledge may whet the speculative interest of the insider, particularly if he believes in the future of his company, and may lead him to purchase stock. Purchases under such circumstances are not encompassed by Section 10(b) and Rule 10b–5. [1,280]

Nevertheless, the court maintained that where an insider came into possession of material information that he used to his own advantage by purchasing stock of his company prior to public disclosure, he was indeed violating Section 10b and Rule 10b–5.

Information is not material merely because it would be of interest to the speculator on Bay Street or Wall Street. Material information has been defined as information which in reasonable and objective contemplation might affect the value of the corporation's stock or securities. . . .

Material information need not be limited to information which is translatable into earnings, as suggested by defendants. But the test of materiality must necessarily be a conservative one, particularly since many actions under Section 10(b) are brought on the basis of hindsight.

The court therefore decided that all the defendants were indeed subject to the jurisdictional requirements of Section 10b and Rule 10b-5.

Questions as to Facts

The court then turned its attention to the issue of whether any of the defendants, in purchasing TGS stock or calls, were using, to their own advantage, material information as to the drilling on the Kidd–55 segment not disclosed to the public. To analyze this issue, the court divided the total time period into the following three segments:

1. From November 12, 1963, to 7 P.M., April 9, 1964
2. From 7 P.M., April 9, 1964, to 10 A.M., April 16, 1964
3. From 10 A.M., April 16, 1964, to the close of business on that day

November 12, 1963, to 7 P.M., April 9, 1964.   Regarding the materiality of information on Kidd–55–1, there was no doubt that the drill core was unusually good. However, all the experts agreed that one drill core does not establish an ore body, much less a mine. The SEC contended that the results of K–55–1 were material because of the significance certain defendants attached to those results. Between the completion of K–55–1 on November 12, 1963, and the completion of K–55–3 on April 7, 1964, defendants Fogarty, Mollison, Holyk, Clayton, and Darke spent more than $100,000 in purchasing stocks and calls on the stock of TGS. However, the court maintained that those purchases were made on the basis of educated guesses, which were not proscribed under Section 10 or Rule 10b–5.

As to K–55–3, the court stated that its results, added to the information previously known but did not constitute material information.

The court concluded that there was strong evidence that TGS had a commercially minable area, since the drilling of K–55–4 to 7 P.M. on April 9, 1964, had indicated that the mineralization encountered on the vertical plane between K–55–1 and K–55–3 extended southward 200 feet (Figure 2). But the court felt that the total drilling results up to 7 P.M. on April 9, 1964, did not provide material information that, if disclosed,

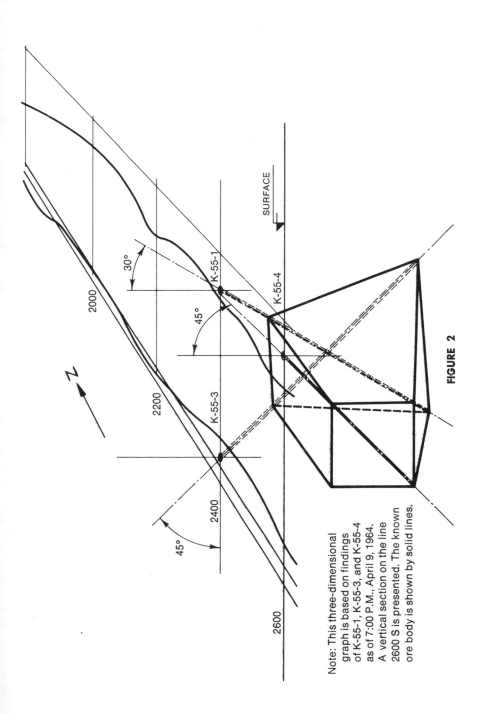

2000

2000

N

30°

45°

K-55-1

SURFACE

K-55-4

2200

K-55-3

2400

45°

2600

Note: This three-dimensional
graph is based on findings
of K-55-1, K-55-3, and K-55-4
as of 7:00 P.M., April 9, 1964.
A vertical section on the line
2600 S is presented. The known
ore body is shown by solid lines.

FIGURE 2

303

would have had a substantial impact on the market price of the company's stock.

Accordingly, the purchases made by certain defendants prior to 7 P.M. on April 9, 1964, were not based on material information. The fact that subsequent drilling established a major ore body was immaterial (1,285).

7 P.M., April 9, 1964, to 10 A.M., April 16, 1964. This period starts with the completion of K–55–4 and the firm establishment of the availability of commercially exploitable ore. The SEC's experts contended that K–55–4 established the third dimension to the mineralization zone. Therefore, on the basis of work done up to 7 P.M., April 9, 1964, TGS should have realized a mine, and, furthermore, TGS could have calculated the ore reserves up to 7.7 million tons with a gross assay value of $204.2 million.

The court rejected the defendants' argument that if the information were indeed true, it had already become public knowledge through the story in the *Northern Miner,* the rumors in Canada, and the pending announcement by the Canadian minister of mines. The court maintained that if TGS officials did believe that the news had already become public, there was "little purpose in making the arrangements for a press conference and issuing a detailed announcement on April 16" (1,286).

Therefore, the court held that information on the Kidd property during this period was *material undisclosed information,* and hence its use by any of the defendants for their personal gain would constitute a violation of Section 10b and Rule 10b–5.

10 A.M., April 16, 1964, to Close of Business on That Day. The court held that any material information became public knowledge *as soon as* the announcement had been made: "It is the making of the announcement that controls" (1,288). The court rejected the SEC's contention that although the information was announced it was not absorbed by the public for some time. First, if the commission's argument were to be accepted, its application should be extended beyond corporate insiders to those people who might be in a position to take unfair advantage of the stockholders—for example, brokers, press reporters, or telephone operators who received the news in the course of their work before the general public did. Second, if the courts were to decide what was a reasonable elapsed time after the fact, to take into consideration specific circumstances in individual cases, it would lead to uncertainty because no insider would know if he had waited long enough after an announcement had been made.

Therefore, the court held, purchases of TGS stock by any of the defendants after the press announcement had been made did not constitute a violation of Section 10b or Rule 10b–5.

The Issue of Stock Options

Five of the defendants—Stephens, Fogarty, Kline, Mollison, and Holyk —were charged with violation of Section 10b and Rule 10b–5 by accepting stock options voted to them on February 20, 1964, by the directors' committee. The SEC contended that these defendants violated the section and the rule because they had knowledge of K–55–1 and its results, which they failed to disclose to the committee or to the board of directors prior to accepting the options.

The court agreed that the committee necessarily relied on information furnished it by the higher echelon of TGS's management (which would include defendants Stephens and Fogarty, but not Kline, Mollison, or Holyk). The court agreed that Mollison and Holyk knew the results of K–55–1 and reported these results to their superior, defendant Fogarty. Kline, Mollison, and Holyk had no duty to inform the committee of information already known to their superiors, since they could assume that such information would be reported to the committee by the management. However, defendants Stephens and Fogarty *were* management and therefore were under an obligation to inform the committee of material information affecting the issuance of the stock options.

Notwithstanding, the court held that since this information was not material, the defendants did not violate Section 10b and Rule 10b–5 in accepting the stock options.

The Press Release of April 12

The SEC charged that the press release was materially misleading in characterizing the Kidd discovery as a prospect and in saying that any statement as to size and grade of ore would be premature and therefore in violation of the section and the rule. TGS denied this charge, further contending that no violation had occurred, since the press release had not been issued "in connection with the purchase or sale of any security" (1,293).

In reviewing the circumstances surrounding the press release, the court noted that the purpose of the April 12 press release was an attempt by TGS to meet the rumors that were circulating with respect to the Kidd–55 segment. There was no evidence that TGS derived any direct benefit from the issuance of the press release or that any of the defendants who participated in its preparation used it to their personal advantage.

Consequently, the court held that in the absence of any evidence that the April 12 press release was deliberately deceptive or misleading or was intended to affect the market price of TGS stock to the advantage of TGS or its insiders, the issuance of the press release by TGS did not violate Section 10b or Rule 10b–5.

Conclusion

The court dismissed the SEC complaint against defendants Texas Gulf Sulphur Company, Charles F. Fogarty, Richard D. Mollison, Walter Holyk, Kenneth H. Darke, Thomas S. Lamont, Francis G. Coates, Claude O. Stephens, John A. Murray, Earl L. Huntington, and Harold B. Kline. Defendants Richard H. Clayton and David M. Crawford were found to have violated Section 10b and Rule 10b–5 by purchasing TGS stock or calls during the period between 7 P.M., April 9, 1964, and 10 A.M., April 16, 1964.

NOBODY IS HAPPY WITH THE DECISION— EVERYBODY APPEALS

The SEC immediately began to plan its appeal to the U.S. Court of Appeals, Second District (New York). Although disappointed with the findings of the district court, the SEC actually had many of the basic principles of its case accepted in Judge Bonsal's decision. For the first time, explicit rules were established for management decision making concerning the public release of major corporate developments and the operation of corporate stock-option and investment programs.

The SEC filed its briefs in the court of appeals during the first week of December 1966. The first brief was against TGS and the ten exonerated individual defendants. The second was in response to the appeals of Clayton and Crawford. The appeals were argued before a panel of three circuit court judges, Waterman, Moore, and Mays, on March 20, 1967. It was then ordered that the case be submitted to the court in banc (all other judges of the appeals court review the evidence and arguments and then submit individual opinions).

The Appeals Court Decision

On August 13, 1968, the appeals court handed down its decision.[27] By a seven-to-two majority, the court affirmed the decision of the lower court in the cases of Clayton and Crawford. The court also affirmed the dismissal of charges against Murray. However, in the remaining cases, the court reversed the decision of the lower court and found TGS and the remaining eight defendants (Lamont having recently died) in viola-

---

[27] *Securities and Exchange Commission* v. *Texas Gulf Sulphur Co.; Securities and Exchange Commission* v. *Crawford and Clayton*. United States Court of Appeals, Second Circuit, No. 30882, August 13, 1968. Appeal from the United States District Court, Southern District of New York (Federal Securities Law Reports) No. 214–15, 8-16-68. Unless otherwise specified, all references to this citation in the text will be shown as (2. page number).

tion of Rule 10b. All the defendants, with the exception of Murray, were remanded to the district court for determination of appropriate penalties.

In arriving at its decision, the appeals court considered the following questions:

1. Whether or not the drilling results prior to 7 P.M., April 9, 1964, were "material." Note that Judge Bonsal had decided that the drilling results during the remaining two periods—that is, 7 P.M., April 9, 1964, to 10 A.M., April 16, 1964; and 10 A.M., April 16, 1964, to the close of business that day—were material information. The appeals court concurred with the lower court's findings on this issue.

2. Whether the issuance of the press release of April 12 was lawful (as decided by the lower court) because it was not issued for the purpose of benefiting the corporation; there was no evidence that any insider used the release to his personal advantage, and it was not misleading or deceptive on the basis of the facts then known.

3. Whether or not information becomes public knowledge *immediately* on announcement to the press.

The court analyzed the activities of the defendants and the movements in TGS stock prices during the period under question. Between November 12, 1963, when K–55–1 was completed, and March 31, 1964, some of the defendants and their "tippees" increased their stock holdings from 1,135 to 8,135 shares and from 0 to 11,300 calls. The court noted that the drilling results of K–55–1 (the first hole) were "so remarkable that neither Clayton, an experienced geophysicist, nor four other TGS expert witnesses, had ever seen or heard of a comparable initial exploratory drill hole in a base metal deposit."

Based on the evidence presented, the trial court had also concluded "that the vertical plane created by the intersection of K–55–1 and K–55–3, which measured at least 350 feet wide by 500 feet deep, extended southward 200 feet to its intersection with K–55–4, and that there was real evidence that a body of commercially minable ore might exist" (299,174). (See Figure 2.)

The appeals court contended that, under the rule, the term *insider* applied not only to the officers, directors, and employees of the company but also to others who might possess inside material information and who might not be strictly termed *insiders* within the meaning of Section 10b of the SEC act. Thus, anyone so termed possessing material information must either disclose it to the public or refrain from using it to his own advantage.

So, it is here no justification for insider activity that disclosure was forbidden by the legitimate corporate objective of acquiring options to purchase the land surrounding the exploration site; if the information was, as the SEC contends, material, its possessors should have kept out of the market until disclosure was accomplished [297,178].

The appeals court agreed with the lower court that the insiders' regulatory obligation to disclose material information was that it must be enjoyed equally, so that outsiders might draw their own conclusions based on knowledge equal to that of the insiders. However, the appeals court disagreed with the lower court that "the test of materiality must be a conservative one" (1,280) but stated:

> The basic test of materiality . . . is whether a *reasonable* man would attach importance . . . in determining his choice of action in the transaction in question. This, of course, encompasses any fact . . . which in reasonable and objective contemplation *might* affect the value of the corporation's stock or securities. . . . Such a fact is a material fact and must be effectively disclosed to the investing public prior to the commencement of insider trading in the corporation's securities. The speculators and chartists of Wall and Bay Streets are also "reasonable" investors entitled to the same legal protection afforded conservative traders [299,178].

Notwithstanding the trial court's conclusions that the results of the first drill core, K–55–1, were "too remote" to have had any material impact on the market, knowledge of the possibility of the existence of a mine was surely more than marginal. This might well have affected the price of TGS stock and would certainly have been an important fact to a reasonable, if speculative, investor in deciding whether to buy, sell, or hold.

The appeals court stated that its disagreement with the district judge was not as to his findings of basic fact, but as to the application of a "clearly erroneous" rule to test the materiality of information.

A major consideration in determining whether the K–55–1 discovery was a material fact is the importance attached to the drilling results by those who knew about it. Stock purchases and purchases of short-term calls—in some instances by individuals who had never before purchased calls or even TGS stock—virtually compels the inference that the insiders were influenced by the drilling results. This insider trading activity, which surely constitutes highly pertinent evidence and the only truly objective evidence of the materiality of the K–55–1 discovery, should not have been disregarded by the lower court in favor of the testimony of the defendants' expert witnesses, all of whom "agreed that one drill core does not establish an ore body, much less a mine" (1,282–83).

Therefore, the appeals court held that all transactions in TGS stock or calls by individuals with knowledge of the drilling results of K–55–1 were made in violation of Rule 10b–5. It further stated:

> Our decision to expand the limited protection afforded outside investors by the trial court's narrow definition of materiality is not at all shaken by fears that the elimination of insider trading benefits will deplete the ranks of capable corporate managers by taking away an incentive to accept such employment [297,180].

When May an Insider Act?

The appeals court contended that the effective protection of the public from insider exploitation of advance notice of material information required that the time that an insider placed an order, rather than the time of its ultimate execution, be determinative for Rule 10b–5 purposes. Otherwise, insiders would be able to "beat the news." Before insiders may act upon material information, such information must have been effectively disclosed in a manner sufficient to ensure its availability to the investing public. Particularly here, where a formal announcement to the entire financial news media had been promised in a prior official release known to the media, all insider activity must await dissemination of the promised official announcement.

In the *Cady, Roberts* case, SEC set the standard by instructing insiders to "keep out of the market until the . . . public release of the information . . . is carried out instead of hastening to execute transactions in advance of, and in frustration of, the objectives of the release." The reading of a news release to the press was merely the first step in the process of dissemination required for compliance with the regulatory objective of providing all investors with an equal opportunity to make informed investment judgments. Assuming that the contents of the official release could instantaneously be acted upon, at the minimum the insiders should wait until the news could reasonably be expected to appear over the medium of widest circulation, the Dow-Jones broad tape, before entering the market to purchase shares in their company (297,181–82).

The appeals court also rejected the arguments of "good faith" on the part of the defendants when they stated that their purchases before the April 16, 1964, news release were justified because they "honestly believed that the news of the strike had become public at the time they placed their orders" (299,182). Moreover, a review of other sections of the act, from which Rule 10b–5 seemed to have been drawn, suggested that the implementation of a standard of conduct that encompassed negligence as well as active fraud comported with the administrative and the legislative purposes underlying the rule. The court also held that "in an enforcement proceeding for equitable or prophylactic relief, the common law standard of deceptive conduct has been modified in the interests of broader protection for the investing public so that negligent insider conduct has become unlawful."

Insiders' Acceptance of Stock Options

The appeals court concluded that contrary to the lower court's findings, Kline (in addition to Stephens and Fogarty, directors of the corporation) also had a duty to disclose to the directors' committee his knowledge of the Kidd discovery before accepting stock options. Kline, a vice-president who had become the general counsel of TGS in January 1964, had been secretary of the corporation since January 1961. As such, he was a member of top management and was under an obligation, before accepting his option, to disclose any material information he may have possessed. Therefore, he was also in violation of Section 10b and Rule 10b–5.

TGS and the April 12, 1964, Press Release

TGS defended its actions by asserting that (1) the issuance of press release produced no unusual market action; (2) no proof was offered by the SEC that the purpose of the press release was to affect the market price of the TGS stock for the benefit of TGS or its insiders; and (3) the issuance of the press release did not constitute a violation of Section 10b or Rule 10b–5, since it was not issued "in connection with the purchase or sale of any security" (297,185).

The appeals court first took issue with the defendants' interpretation of the "in connection with" of the act. According to the court, a review of the congressional intent in passing the Securities and Exchange Act of 1934 would indicate that the dominant purposes underlying the act were to promote free and open public securities markets and to protect the investing public from suffering inequities in trading that follow from trading stimulated by the publication of false or misleading corporate information releases. The relevant congressional committee report on the bill stated:

> The idea of a free and open public market is built upon the theory that competing judgments of buyers and sellers as to the fair price of a security brings about a situation where the market price reflects as nearly as possible a just price. Just as artificial manipulation tends to upset the true function of an open market, so the hiding and secreting of important information obstructs the operation of the markets as indices of real value. *There cannot be honest markets without honest publicity* . . .
>
> Delayed, inaccurate, and misleading reports are the tools of the unconscionable market operator and the recreant corporate official who speculate on inside information [297,186].

Indeed, from its very inception, 10b was always acknowledged as a catchall and not to be narrowly construed. Accordingly, the court held that Rule 10b–5 is violated whenever assertions are made, as here, in a manner reasonably calculated to influence the investing public, that is, by means of the financial media. However, if corporate management "demonstrates that it was diligent that the information it published was the whole truth" and that such information "was disseminated in good faith, Rule 10b–5 would not have been violated" (297,188).

As to the specific action of TGS in issuing the April 12 statement, the court held that TGS either should have made the statement on the basis of the facts known to it or should have delayed the presentation a bit until an accurate report of a rapidly changing situation was possible. According to the court, the choice of an ambiguous general statement rather than a summary of the specific facts could not reasonably be justified by any claimed urgency. Thus, the court concluded that the release was issued in a manner reasonably calculated to affect the market price of TGS stock and to influence the investing public, and it remanded to the district court to decide whether the release was misleading to the reasonable investor, and if so, whether the court in its discretion should issue the injunction sought by the SEC (297,190).

REACTION TO THE DECISION OF THE APPEALS COURT

The reaction to the decision and its implied expansion of the interpretation of Rule 10b was remarkable in its sedateness. Texas Gulf shares on the NYSE showed almost no effect from the decision. A Dow-Jones midweek financial news summary found relatively little concern among corporate executives questioned. Typical of the comments were the following: "This decision will do no more to us than to confirm our previous policy of care and scrupulousness in the dissemination of information. . . ." "We don't live on tips." However, the official reaction of the influential financial weekly, *Barron's,* was immediate and vociferous. In an article published on August 19, it found Wall Street's lack of concern disquieting. "Like other disaster victims, neither business nor financial circles seem to realize what has hit them." Predicting a stopping of the flow of corporate information to the public, the article stated that "in the end, as the flow of information, 'inside' and out, inevitably slows down, the chief victims will be the investors whom SEC is sworn to protect." It then took the court to task:

> Only by riding roughshod over legislative history, legal precedent, simple logic and common sense could the court majority have reached its conclusions. . . . The restraint constitutes not "double" jeopardy but "perpetual" jeopardy. What about a businessman's civil rights? . . . This is not regulation—it is bureaucracy run wild.[28]

Forbes, another weekly business periodical, saw the TGS court decision in an entirely different light:

> The Texas Gulf ruling is not isolated: It is part of a growing trend on the part of the courts and of the laws to be increasingly strict and precise as to the nature of the relationship between a corporate management and its scattered and relatively powerless public stock-

---

28 "Perpetual Jeopardy," *Barron's,* August 19, 1968, p. 1.

holders. The issues raised in the Texas Gulf case go far beyond that company.[29]

Although stating that "the limits of the law have yet to be reached," *Forbes* concluded by finding that "it adds up to one more illustration of how capitalism is capable of becoming more democratic—and hence more durable." [30]

On October 30, 1968, TGS filed a motion in the U.S. District Court, in connection with a stockholder's suit, that its constitutional right of free speech was being abridged by the appeals court decision. This motion was seen as the foundation work for an appeal to the U.S. Supreme Court.[31]

Legal "Remedies" for the Defendants

Beginning in October 1969 and lasting through part of February 1970, Judge Bonsal of the U.S. District Court imposed "remedies" upon the defendants, as outlined by the appeals court, finding the April 12, 1964, press release misleading to reasonable investors using due care and ruling that the framers did not exercise due diligence in its issuance. The judge denied the SEC's request that TGS, as a corporation, be enjoined from issuing or otherwise disseminating false, misleading, or inadequate information in that "no proper showing of any reasonable likelihood of future violations was evident." Judge Bonsal refused to issue injunctions against future illegal trading against Darke, Holyk, Huntington, Fogarty, and Mollison. However, the judge did enjoin Clayton and Crawford from future illegal trading "because they purchased during a period of nondisclosure, knowing beyond doubt that Texas Gulf had made a very important mineral discovery." [32]

The remaining defendant, Coates, had reached a court settlement in October, which became the guideline for the remedies imposed by Judge Bonsal. Coates paid $26,250 into a 6 percent escrow fund, $9,675 of which was the profit gained by his tippees. The formulation of the settlement was based on the difference between the purchase price of the stock and its price on April 17, 1964, plus bank rate interest.

In February the other defendants were ordered to make the following payments into the escrow fund (to be used for settlements in other suits against TGS): Darke—$41,794, plus $48,404 for the profits of his tippees; Holyk—$35,663; Huntington—$2,300; and Clayton—$20,010. Crawford had already surrendered to the company, at his cost, the stock he purchased, making any other penalty unnecessary.[33] Fogarty and Mollison surrendered to TGS, at their cost, the shares that they purchased.

At the time of the settlement of the SEC charges (and TGS was plan-

29 "The Law: Trouble for the Top," *Forbes*, September 1, 1968, p. 23.
30 *Ibid.*
31 "Abreast of the Market," *The Wall Street Journal*, October 29, 1968.
32 "Texas Gulf Ruled to Lack Diligence in Minerals Case," *The Wall Street Journal*, February 9, 1970, p. 26.
33 *Ibid.*

ning to appeal the decision), there were more than sixty stockholders' suits pending. In the second week of February 1970, TGS filed an appeal to a Utah civil decision in which TGS was found guilty of issuing a misleading press release and ordered to pay $22,000 in damages to former shareholders.[34]

During early June 1971, the U.S. Court of Appeals for the Second Circuit upheld, under a TGS appeal, Judge Bonsal's penalties for all the defendants with the exception of Kline. The court stated that the district court had erred in ordering Kline's option canceled without giving him a chance to be heard on the matter.[35]

Eight years to the day after TGS's initial press release, Judge Bonsal upheld a proposed settlement of stockholder claims against TGS in the New York District Court as being "fair, reasonable and adequate." Under the terms, TGS agreed to pay $2.7 million to former stockholders who sold their stock on the basis of the April 12, 1964, press release. The judge concluded the case by stating that "the settlement is in the best interests of all parties."[36]

EPILOGUE

Early in August 1973, Canadian Development Corporation (CDC), a government-controlled corporation, made a tender offer of $290 million for the purchase of 10 million shares of Texasgulf, Inc. (the new name for Texas Gulf Sulphur Company). These shares together with the ones already owned by CDC and its associates would give CDC an effective controlling interest in Texasgulf (35 percent of the outstanding stock). CDC was formed by the Canadian government with the avowed purpose of assisting Canadian investments "into areas where they might better serve Canada's rather than someone else's national interests."[37] CDC's choice of Texasgulf was based on the latter's healthy profit margins "plus the fact that controlling Texasgulf provides easy entry into mining-smelting, one of Canada's main growth factors."[38]

The management of Texasgulf reacted bitterly against the proposal and went to court to enjoin CDC from proceeding with its tender offer. The complaint alleged violation of federal antitrust laws and conspiracy to violate federal securities laws by CDC and its associates. Trying to generate publicity against the takeover bid, Texasgulf had Senator Lloyd M. Bentsen (D, Tex.) testify that "the CDC takeover bid was a matter of national concern."[39]

[34] "Texas Gulf Tangle Unwinds—A Little," *Business Week*, February 14, 1970, p. 29.
[35] "Findings Upheld on Texas Gulf," *The New York Times*, June 19, 1971, p. 33.
[36] "TGS Terms of Settlement Called Fair by Court," *The Wall Street Journal*, April 12, 1972, p. 16.
[37] Peter Newman, "Why Canada Wants Texasgulf," *The New York Times*, August 5, 1973, Sec. 3, p. 3.
[38] *Ibid.*
[39] "Texasgulf Fights a Canadian Takeover," *Business Week*, August 18, 1973, p. 22.

The court, however, denied the Texasgulf petition, stating that the court's findings made it "abundantly clear . . . that no violation of laws has occurred or will occur."[40] In December 1973, Texasgulf suddenly announced that it had resolved its differences with CDC and had agreed to appoint four CDC members to its board.[41]

SELECTED REFERENCES

BRILOFF, ABRAHAM J., *Unaccountable Accounting* (New York: Harper & Row, 1972).

BROMBERG, ALAN R., "Securities Law—Fraud," *Financial Analysts Journal,* March 1968, p. 35.

"Corporate Reports Open Wider," *Business Week,* March 29, 1969, p. 53.

ESSLEN, RAINER, "Material News for Timely Disclosure," *Financial Executive,* January 1969, pp. 25–28.

FAMA, E. F., "Random Walks in Stock Market Prices," *Financial Analysts Journal,* 21 (September–October 1965), 55.

FARNER, JAMES, et al., "Insider Trading in Stocks," *The Business Lawyer,* 21 (July 1966), 1014.

FLEISCHER, ARTHUR, JR., and JOSEPH H. FLOM, *Texas Gulf Sulphur: Disclosure and Insiders* (New York: Practicing Law Institute, 1968).

FLOM, JOSEPH H., and PETER A. ATKINS, "The Expanding Scope of SEC Disclosure Laws," *Harvard Business Review,* July–August 1974, pp. 109–19.

GILLIS, JOHN G., "A Disclosure Dilemma," *Financial Analysts Journal,* November–December 1972, pp. 6–12.

HAACK, ROBERT W., "Viewpoints in Corporate Disclosure," *Financial Executive,* February 1969, p. 21.

KELLER, THOMAS F., "Another Look at Financial Disclosure," *Management Accounting,* February, 1969, pp. 19–22.

"The Law: Trouble for the Top," *Forbes,* September 1, 1968.

LOSS, LOUIS, *Securities Regulation* (Boston: Little, Brown, 1961).

MANNE, HENRY, *Insider Trading and the Stock Market* (New York: Free Press, 1966).

PATRICK, KENNETH G., *Perpetual Jeopardy: The Texas Gulf Sulphur Affair: A Chronicle of Achievement and Misadventure* (New York: Macmillan, 1972).

"The SEC Wants More Disclosure," *Business Week,* May 8, 1971, p. 21.

Securities Exchange Act Release, No. 8459 (New York: Commerce Clearing House, 1968), Sec. 6.

Securities and Exchange Commission v. Cady, Roberts & Company (S.D.N.Y. 1962).

Securities and Exchange Commission v. Texas Gulf Sulphur Company. S.D.N.Y. 258 F. Supp. 262 (1966), 288.

---

[40] "Texasgulf Loses Bid to Block Tender Offer By Canada Development," *The Wall Street Journal,* September 6, 1973, p. 10.
[41] "Life With New Partners—Canada Has One-Third Interest in Texasgulf," *The New York Times,* January 20, 1974, Sec. 3, p. 7.

Securities and Exchange Commission v. *Texas Gulf Sulphur Company; Securities and Exchange Commission* v. *Crawford and Clayton.* United States Court of Appeals, Second Circuit, No. 30882, August 13, 1968. Appeal from the United States District Court, Southern District of New York (Federal Securities Law Reports) No. 214–15, August 16, 1968.

SHANK, JOHN K., "Case of the Disclosure Debate," *Harvard Business Review,* January–February 1972, pp. 142–58.

The Wheat Report—Disclosure to Investors: A Reappraisal of Federal Administrative Policies Under the "33" Acts (New York: Commerce Clearing House, 1972).

WEISS, HERMAN L., "Why Business and Government Change Executives," *Harvard Business Review,* July–August 1974, pp. 129–40.

WISE, T. A., *The Insiders* (New York: McGraw Hill, 1969).

Corporations and Their Employees

U.S. DEPARTMENT OF LABOR VERSUS STANDARD OIL OF CALIFORNIA

A CASE OF AGE DISCRIMINATION

To age with dignity and with courage cuts close to what it is to be a man.
—ROGER KAHN, *The Boys of Summer*

On May 15, 1974, Standard Oil Company of California (SOCAL) signed a consent decree (Appendix A) with the U.S. Department of Labor settling a pending civil action for age discrimination against one of the company's divisions, Western Operations, Inc. The decree covered those employees whose jobs were terminated between December 1, 1970 and December 31, 1973. December 1, 1970, was the cut-off date of the statute of limitations. December 31, 1973, was the end date settled upon in early January 1974 when it became apparent that settlement was possible. Among the provisions of the consent decree to which SOCAL, while denying any wrongdoing, agreed were the following:

1. SOCAL was permanently enjoined and restrained from violating

The author is grateful to Mr. Daniel W. Teehan, deputy regional solicitor, Mr. John Almerico, area director, Wage and Hour Division, United States Department of Labor, San Francisco; and M. H. T. Tupper, manager, Employee and Placement Division and Mr. Robert E. Rodman, manager, Personnel Department, Standard Oil of California, San Francisco, for their assistance in preparing this study.

the existing provisions of section 4 of the Age Discrimination in Employment Act (ADEA) of 1967 and the existing provisions of section 15 of the Fair Labor Standards Act of 1938 as amended (Appendix B). In particular, SOCAL agreed not to discharge or otherwise discriminate against a person with respect to his compensation, terms, conditions, or privileges of employment because of that person's age.

2. SOCAL agreed to make offers for reinstatement, within a mutually agreed upon period, to 120 of its previously terminated employees. Those accepting this offer were to be given jobs equal to or closely comparable in status and compensation and in the same geographical area as the jobs from which they were terminated. Further, their pensions and other benefits were adjusted so that it was as if they had never left SOCAL's employment.

3. Those employees who did not choose to accept reinstatement would have their benefits—pensions, annuities, and SOCAL stock—adjusted so as to include the time between the date of their termination of employment from SOCAL and May 15, 1974.

4. Ex-employees over sixty-four years of age were paid additional restitution in lieu of reinstatement.

5. SOCAL agreed to provide up to $2 million for distribution to approximately 160 persons to compensate them, less mitigation, for 75 percent of their lost wages and benefits during the period from their date of termination to the date of the consent decree, May 15, 1974.

ISSUES

It should be apparent to any observer of the business scene that traditional business practices which result, whether intentionally or not, in discriminating against a particular group of persons are not going to be tolerated legally, socially, or politically. Therefore, business corporations and other institutions must develop practices that correct past injustices and at the same time prevent the occurrence of similar situations in the future. However, this is not as simple as it might appear. At the general public policy level, it raises two major questions:

1. Under what circumstances and to what extent law and legal procedures can be used as instruments of public policy
2. To what extent the current law against age discrimination is likely to be effective in fulfilling changing societal expectations

An analysis of the case should also lead to an understanding of the nature of the age discrimination problem for business corporations, and how business and government might cope with it. In particular

1. What are the problems in dealing with real or alleged age discrimination in employment by corporations? This should include the

problems of identification, measurement, recordkeeping, and—most important—interpretation.

2. What were the strengths and weaknesses of the performance evaluation system prevailing at SOCAL prior to the company's job-reduction action in 1970? What are the dangers of using only *current* performance, regardless of past evaluation or length of service, in determining who should be fired?

3. Is the present system of employee performance appraisal based on relative performance criteria and forced ranking of employees in similar job categories adequate to meet the needs of the company and also the requirements of the law? What are some of the problems that might arise through the use of this system?

4. What are the problems in dealing with real or alleged age discrimination from the government's viewpoint? Are the current laws sufficient both in terms of definition and enforcement? What is needed to eliminate job discrimination and yet leave companies with significant flexibility to eliminate inefficient workers regardless of age?

SEQUENCE OF EVENTS

It began with a simple age discrimination complaint. In May 1972, John Doe [1] walked into the San Francisco office of the U.S. Department of Labor, Wage and Hour Division, and stated that he had been fired from his job in the marketing department of Western Operations, Inc., a division of Standard Oil of California located in San Francisco. He further alleged that he was fired because of his age. The case was assigned to a compliance officer, or investigator.

Earlier in the year there had been other reports of age discrimination complaints against SOCAL in Long Beach, California. The investigator had suspected that there might be cause for action under the ADEA, but could not do much about it for lack of evidence. When he heard that the San Francisco office was starting an investigation, he passed on the results of his investigation to that office. Around the same time, Clyde A. Shearer,[2] a truck driver with Western Operations, lodged a complaint with the Sacramento office of the Department of Labor which stated that five of his colleagues were fired from their jobs because of their age.

The Investigation

The compliance officer assigned to the case started his investigation by asking SOCAL's home office executives for information on the number of people whose services had been terminated. He was told that the termina-

[1] Name withheld by the U.S. Department of Labor.
[2] Communication from Mr. Teehan to the author.

tions had started in 1969 and had continued through 1970 and 1971 and that they were the result of the two major reorganizations.

In October 1969, Western Operations decided to reorganize and stream-line its operation in an effort to improve efficiency and reduce overhead.[3] The reorganization called for the consolidation of a great number of districts into seventeen divisions. Another reorganization took place in April 1971 when the seventeen divisions were further reduced to twelve. About 1,200 people left of their own volition under amicable arrangements with the company. About 90 percent of them were under the age of forty. However, there was still a need to reduce the payroll by another 500 or 600 employees.

Mr. Tupper, who was the personnel manager in the marketing department of the Western Operations Division during these years, described the situation this way:

During 1969–74, the marketing department of Western Operations was in serious trouble. In the present state of energy shortages, it is very hard for people to remember back to the days of price wars. In 1970–71 gas was being sold at 20 cents a gallon at the pump, which was less than what it cost to make. Western was showing a very low profit. Our analysis showed that the biggest losses were taking place in the marketing area—the biggest marketing costs are people.

Something had to be done. In a series of three major reorganizations we eliminated 1,600 positions, or 40% of the total employment. The majority of these jobs and the people who were in them left voluntarily for one reason or another. We also stopped hiring. However, some reductions were necessary. In retrenching, we followed the following rules:

1. The people that have the worst performance had to go. Often it would be someone just on the job or someone in the job for 35 years who was not putting out enough.

2. The evaluation system was based on a sort of report card that had few, if any, quantitative criteria. However, if a person was just marked "good" (most of them were marked "very good"), he was in serious trouble. In 1969 we recognized that in 1970 we were going to consider many actions about people. Very reluctantly management resorted to ranking people. We used this performance ranking list in deciding who should go.

3. No system, however, could be used blindly where people were involved. We had no trouble letting people go where their performance was clearly unsatisfactory. The problem arose where there were two people with essentially similar performance but one stood to lose a great deal more than the other in financial and psychological grounds. In these circumstances—and there were

[3] "A Report to SOCAL Employees on the Age Discrimination Issue," from N. T. Bogard, vice president Industrial Relations, Standard Oil of California, San Francisco. Undated.

very few cases of this type—the decisions were sometimes made on compassionate grounds whereby the person with the least to lose was let go.

The following hypothetical case would show what I have in mind. Consider the case of two people who ranked 9 and 10 in comparative performance ranking. One of these two positions has to be eliminated:

Employee—Career Variables	Performance Ranking 9	Performance Ranking 10
Age	62	42
Pension Plan	no age discount	large discount
Savings Plan	fully vested	35% vested
Medical Plan	covered	loses coverage
Family	no dependents	dependents
House	paid	mortgage
Future	golf	find employment

Under these circumstances, we would have decided to keep the man who was 42 years of age and ranked 10, and let the man go who was 62 and ranked 9.

Between July 1969 and December 1973, 562 employees were early-retired or terminated. It was not clear to those whose services were so terminated how such decisions were made by SOCAL. There was a feeling that the decision as to who would be terminated was made in secrecy by a small group of people. This created an environment of uncertainty, insecurity, and fear.

Mr. Robert E. Rodman, general manager, Personnel Department of SOCAL, strongly denies this interpretation. According to Mr. Rodman:

Personnel decisions are never made publicly. If the word "secret" suggests a sinister conspiracy by a small group of management, it is inaccurate in describing what actually happened.

Faced with competitive business necessity to reduce the work force, the decision as to who would be terminated was made by the appropriate level of management. For exempt, non-management jobs the decision was made by Division Managers at the local level. For management jobs the decisions were made by the highest level of functional management in San Francisco. For non-exempt jobs the effective decision was made by first line supervisors and approved by Division Managers. There was nothing secret about the decision making *process*. It corresponded to normal line management channels on all operating decisions. The *decisions* were not made public until all actions had been reviewed by top management.

Many layers and numbers of company people were involved in this process consistent with our normal ways of making line operating decisions. In all of these actions, selection of least-effective performers was the established criterion of evaluation.

SOCAL seems to have made genuine efforts to make the terminations as painless as possible. To induce people to retire voluntarily, the company provided generous severance pay and transitional payment even where the employees were not technically entitled to it. SOCAL also took pains to get these people into categories where they would get more annuity, pension, and higher vesting in the stock plan.

According to Daniel W. Teehan, deputy regional solicitor in the San Francisco office of the Department of Labor, who was in charge of arguing the government's case:

I don't think that money was the prime consideration. They (SOCAL) just wanted young people in the marketing department.

Standard wanted to change things and thought that younger people would be more flexible. Older people would rebel; they were more set in their ways. The resistance to change seemed to have been greater in smaller towns than in the larger metropolitan areas.

Standard appeared to be dead set to get these [older] people out but they were willing to make it easier for them.

However, "inducement" also carried with it the threat of dismissal if a person did not choose to retire within a certain time period. Later investigation bore this out. That the company was trying to be generous did not negate the fact that the Department of Labor felt people's rights, as well as the law itself, were being violated. According to Mr. Rodman, the severance payment was given only to reduce the impact of termination, *not* to pay for violating people's rights. There was the charge made by Teehan and others during the investigation that SOCAL might call an employee in and tell him that if he volunteered there would be a severance allowance, but that it would be available for only three months; after that, the severance might not be available. The company was trying to reduce its work force within a finite period of time and may have used severance pay as inducement in a few cases. Rodman maintained, however, that this was not a common practice.

Based on the data furnished by SOCAL, the compliance officer conducted an analysis that consumed the better part of three months. The enormity of the job, the difficult circumstances of the investigation, and the inadequate manpower and material resources available for the task at the time make it amazing that such an investigation was not only completed but also that a *prima facie* case leading to a significant settlement was built.

The compliance officer did not have at his disposal a large computer or an army of personnel to analyze the data. He resorted to old-fashioned pencil and paper, a lot of patience, and what appeared to this author to be a missionary zeal. He painstakingly broke down data from the reams of computer printouts furnished by the company into different age categories according to division, job classification, retention, and termination. His analysis established a systematic pattern of involuntary retirements and job terminations spread through all white collar job categories in all twelve divisions. This pattern had an upward bias in terms of age. A majority of people so released were in the age group of fifty and above, and the proportion of older people fired was far greater than the proportion of younger people. Nevertheless, the company presented statistical evidence that the proportion of employees in the protected forty to sixty-five age group actually increased during the reduction in force, and that the average age actually increased. The investigation led the compliance officer to conclude that there was a big difference between the company's policy statement and its actual practices. His conclusions were based on the following findings of fact:

1. In a large and statistically significant number of job classifications *by division,* it was found the oldest employees were involuntarily terminated while the youngest were retained. Because this occurred in case after case, there was little doubt in the investigator's mind that age was a critical factor in deciding who was to be let go. Subsequently, the company was unable to prove to the Department of Labor's satisfaction that an acceptable factor other than age led to the action in many individual situations. Company representatives contended that "termination" decisions were based upon best judgment of relative performance, whether or not an acceptable level of documented evidence was always available.

2. The company initiated measuring employees on the "relative performance criteria (RPC)" only after beginning the reduction in force in 1970. According to Mr. Rodman, however, this is not strictly true. Performance ranking was started before the 1970 cutbacks, but only by a few months. The implication that performance ranking was started to justify decisions already made is incorrect. It was started as an internal device to assist management in arriving at better decisions on who would have to be released to meet required manpower levels. Prior to that, the company's employee evaluations were based on individual assessments and did not relate to across-the-board comparisons with other employees in a given job category.

3. At the same time, in at least some job classifications in central California, the company started ranking employees not only on performance but also separately on potential. In general, the potential rankings were found to be inversely related to age. In other words, the older a person was, the lower his potential—a major indication that age was an important factor in the ranking for potential. SOCAL, however, contends that potential rankings were not used to decide on terminations.

4. A large number of individual performance appraisals were found to be haphazard and unsystematic. In an extreme example, two appraisals were carried out on one employee within one week. The first was favorable to the employee. The second was unfavorable and was used as the basis for involuntary termination.

5. In many cases, there was a sudden decline in an older employee's performance appraisal and/or rating before he was let go. According to Mr. Rodman, this may have been true in a few isolated cases, but this was certainly not the general practice. Furthermore, because past performance appraisals were often inflated, the sudden decline most often reflected a more realistic, accurate appraisal.

6. In other cases, employees who refused to accept voluntary retirement were transferred to other jobs for which they were apparently unsuited by background and experience. After a very short stay on the new jobs, their relative performance was found to be low and they were made to go. Mr. Rodman denies this accusation. He states that the company tried to find jobs for people where it could, but that in a shrinking work force the jobs available were not always what the company or the individual would prefer.

7. In one division all the previous employee appraisals of discharged employees were missing and were unavailable for inspection by the Labor Department. Mr. Rodman concedes that this was factually correct and unfortunate. However, it was not indicative of a general "coverup." It affected only a fraction (about 50) of the 500 cases investigated. No one knows whether or not there would have been better or worse documentation if these files had been complete.

SOCAL's Response

The company claimed that the guiding principle in terminations was that of performance. Each employee's current performance (not his record) was carefully evaluated within a group and those employees whose relative performances were superior to that of the others in the group were retained. Those retained were most effective in meeting the performance requirements of their jobs. Those whose employment was terminated, in addition to having lower relative performance, also could not be placed in other jobs suitable to their background and work experience. The company futher maintained that length of service and age were not the criteria for termination and that, all things being equal, preference was given to seniority. Also, regardless of the fact of inconsistent and inaccurate appraisals, the company contended that the intent indeed was to identify the least effective performers at the time of the cutback.

The Legal Negotiations

Having satisfied himself that a *prima facie* case existed, the compliance officer handed over the case and all relevant material to the legal department in the San Francisco office of the Department of Labor, where Mr. Teehan took charge. Teehan informed the company of the department's intention of proceeding with the case and invited SOCAL's attorneys to discuss it with him. Time was crucial because the statute of limitations would have made a major portion of the case moot had it continued to run. The first meeting took place on November 22, 1972, between Teehan and company representatives and their counsel. Teehan outlined the case in general terms and asked the company to waive the statute of limitations. SOCAL agreed to do so on December 1, 1972.

There followed a tortuous year-long process of negotiations between the company and the Labor Department. Each and every individual case under contention was examined and argued over. The company maintained that a large number of "involuntary retirements" were in fact "voluntary." They were listed as involuntary in order to make the employees eligible for severance pay.

The Department of Labor checked the company's claims by sending a questionnaire to almost 200 people identified by the company. Two-thirds responded that they had left voluntarily.

WHY DID THE LABOR DEPARTMENT AGREE TO A CONSENT DECREE?

Mr. Teehan recognized that this could become a landmark case and set a precedent for similar cases being filed all across the country. There was a noticeable shift in discrimination cases away from minority and sex discrimination to age discrimination. This was due to the fact that in the former areas the legal issues had been clearly established; there was greater awareness of legal penalties for violation of laws because of large settlements granted in cases already settled (AT&T, the steel industry), and many voluntary public interest groups were providing watchdog services, thereby ensuring a high level of voluntary compliance.[4]

The issues in age discrimination cases, on the other hand, were less clear-cut and difficult to delineate or enforce. For example, in the absence of such identifying characteristics as sex or color of skin, how could one say whether a person was really fired because of age or poor performance? Further, while there is no evidence that SOCAL did so, a company bent on discriminating because of age can so build its personnel files and employee evaluation reports that it would be extremely difficult if not well-nigh impossible to establish evidence of wrongdoing that would stand up in a court of law. Another related factor may be that older workers have not yet identified their problem as a common problem which they should organize against in order to counteract.

There are indications that the problem of age discrimination is quite widespread and may involve numbers far greater than those in cases of minority or sex discrimination. The simple reason for this is that one gets old. Estimates are that currently more than 41 percent of the United States work force is forty years old and older and therefore potentially subject to age discrimination both at the hiring and the termination point

4 "AT&T Ends Pay Inequity for Managerial Employees," *The New York Times,* May 31, 1974, p. 1; "Steel Workers Bias Cases May Be Linked to Suits Filed by U.S. Agencies," *The Wall Street Journal,* May 22, 1974, p. 30; Lawrence Stessin, "The Ax and Older Workers," *The New York Times,* June 23, 1974, sec. 3, p. 3.

of the job life cycle. Age discrimination complaints are increasing. Between July and September 1971, subsequent to the close of the SOCAL case, the Labor Department received 1,200 complaints. According to one official, the increase is due to the state of the economy and the higher number of layoffs. More than 200 lawsuits in which age discrimination has been alleged have been filed since 1968.[5] About 100 cases are currently pending in the federal courts. The number of complaints and awards in age bias cases has increased dramatically during the last three years (see Table 1).

TABLE 1   INCREASE IN AGE-RELATED JOB DISCRIMINATION CASES

Fiscal Year	Number of Complaints	Employees Awarded Damages	Total Amounts Paid
1972	1,862	964	$1,650,000
1973	2,208	1,031	1,866,226
1974	3,040	1,648	6,315,484*

* Includes the $1.6 million paid by SOCAL.
Source: "The Courts Reinterpret Old-Age Discrimination." Reprinted from the February 24, 1975, issue of *Business Week* by special permission. © 1975 by McGraw-Hill, Inc.

The Supreme Court has not yet decided on an age discrimination case. However, the case of Phillip W. Houghton and the Department of Labor v. McDonnell Douglas Co. is working its way through the lower courts and may reach the Supreme Court in the next few months. Mr. Houghton was fired from his job at McDonnell Douglas as a test pilot at age fifty-two "because—among other reasons—he was too old for his job." However, according to medical testimony, he "is healthier today than he was 10 years ago." [6] The most notable case is that against the Baltimore and Ohio and the Chesapeake and Ohio railroads. They are being sued by the Labor Department for $20 million in back wages.[7]

In one of the more dramatic cases a federal jury in Newark, New Jersey, ordered Exxon Corporation to pay $750,000 to Mrs. Gladys Rogers, the widow of a former employee who was forced to retire because of his age. The evidence at the trial showed that it was part of the company's policy to ease out older, higher-paid executives and replace them with younger men.[8] Not included in this award is the $30,000 that Exxon had already agreed to pay in benefits that Mr. Rogers would have earned if he had

---

[5] "The Courts Reinterpret Old Age Discrimination," *Business Week*, February 24, 1975, p. 91.
[6] *Ibid.*
[7] Lawrence Stessin, "The Ax and Older Workers," p. 30.
[8] "Exxon Unit to Appeal Verdict of Age Bias," *The Wall Street Journal*, February 10, 1975, p. 24.

stayed on the job until the time of his normal retirement. The company is appealing the jury's verdict.[9]

Age discrimination, more widespread and pervasive than appears on the surface, raises serious questions of economic efficiency, morality, and social justice that are not easily resolved. Employees believe they have vested property rights in their jobs earned for providing years of faithful service. They did not quit for higher wages during their younger days in order to build such rights in their jobs. Their experience is valuable to the employer and should be rewarded. And as long as they are physically fit and able to meet job requirements, they should not be discriminated against. The employer feels that employees were paid market wages for their work, that years of service have been recognized in terms of a mutually agreed upon pension and other retirement benefits, and that he (the employer) must have flexibility in maintaining a labor force in accordance with the long-run survival and well-being of the organization. The issues become especially acrimonious in times of general economic downturn or when a firm is not making profits and must resort to cost-cutting measures. The automobile industry is a case in point. Faced by a severe decline in sales and profits, it has launched a program of reducing its total employment and has been pushing to get rid of older white collar workers and even executives through early retirement and similar measures.[10]

Teehan felt that pushing the SOCAL case through the courts might not have been the best course of action for the following reasons:

1. He was concerned about getting the people some money as quickly as possible to alleviate their financial problems.
2. A significant number of people may die if the case drags on for a long time, which was considered quite likely.
3. The psychological impact of termination was found to be quite devastating in many cases. Teehan said, "Our conscience was bothering us. Should we attempt to establish legal precedent or should we get these people some help now?"

Evidently compassion won over the logic of long-run gains in terms of establishing precedent, for Teehan decided to settle with the company.

WHY DID SOCAL AGREE TO A CONSENT ORDER?

SOCAL spokesmen offered the following reasons for agreeing to a consent decree:

1. The company maintained that it was not guilty of age discrimination and that the problem primarily resulted from the maintenance

9 *Business Week*, February 24, 1975.
10 "Auto Makers Pushing Early Retirement for Some Executives, Others 55 and Over," *The Wall Street Journal*, February 14, 1975, p. 2.

of inadequate records, and a system of performance evaluation that on reflection turned out to be archaic, and didn't always support the severance actions which were taken (Appendix C).

2. In each case, the terminations were based on relative performance rather than on considerations of age or seniority.

3. The Labor Department's case was based on the insufficiency of the company's documentation rather than on proof of wrongdoing on the part of the company. This pointed to the need for keeping detailed and accurate records. The company also implied that some inadequate recordkeeping may have been due to the desire on the part of certain supervisors to "protect" their employees by not putting adverse reports in their files.

4. Where terminations did take place, the company made generous settlements in terms of severance pay and made the utmost effort to make the transition to retirement as painless as possible.

5. In deciding to settle the case rather than litigate, the company felt that it had to balance its obligation to the shareholders to use the company's resources in the wisest way against the probability that they could win most of the cases in court, but at great expense. After all, the consent decree provided relief to only 160 of the more than 500 cases reviewed.

6. Although the scope and applicability of the ADEA was not clearly determined, the company was reluctant to become the test case and establish the case law. The company recognized that the litigation might have an adverse effect on the company's image. According to Rodman, "based on our analysis of the overall economic and legal aspects of the case, we decided on an out of court settlement."

In response to the question of whether or not it occurred to management that their termination procedures might be in violation of ADEA, Rodman states that this possibility did not occur at the time, since the basis for all severances, both then and now, was relative performance and not age. The impact of the law had never really been emphasized. It had been on the books for several years but had never been enforced. There had been occasional cases (e.g., some airline pilots had charged their employers with age discrimination), but prior to the SOCAL case, there had never been a broad-scale attempt to investigate a major company for alleged age discrimination. ADEA was a law whose time had not yet come. The SOCAL case appeared to be a good example of the government's feeling that a test case could be built to clarify legal and procedural issues.

IMPLEMENTATION OF THE CONSENT DECREE

Of the 120 persons who were offered reinstatement, only 26 took it. Of the 165 affected in terms of lost wages and retirements benefits, 50 did not receive any additional funds because the total amounts already paid them as severance pay and other benefits and earnings exceeded those due them under the plan. The remaining 115 received back wages and benefits totaling $1.6 million, with individual settlements ranging from $600 to over $57,000. Annuities were raised for 114 people, which was likely to cost the company millions in increased pension payments.

ENTER CLYDE SHEARER AGAIN

SOCAL's problems were not over, however. At the time Clyde Shearer lodged a complaint for age discrimination against SOCAL on behalf of his friends, he was working as a truck driver. Soon after, he was transferred to a desk job, where he was given the responsibility of analyzing sales data—a job for which he seemingly was not well suited. He lasted on the job for approximately one and a half years. On January 31, 1974, he was fired because of "poor performance." This was exactly one month after the terminal date instituted in the consent decree for including persons allegedly fired for age discrimination.

The efforts by the Department of Labor to seek restitution or settlement for him were unsuccessful. Finally, on November 27, 1974, the Department of Labor filed a complaint in the United States District Court against SOCAL, alleging age discrimination in the case of Clyde Shearer. Before the case could go to trial, SOCAL made an out of court settlement that paid Mr. Shearer $10,000.

A NOTE ON INVESTIGATION
AND ENFORCEMENT PROCEDURES

This case would not be complete without a comment on the wide gap that exists between the magnitude of the problem and the resources allocated by the government to enforce the law. Consider, for example, the present case, which involved only a small part of one of the many units of Standard Oil of California—yet it took almost half a man-year to investigate it. Imagine the resources needed to do an adequate job in the San Francisco area alone. Yet there are currently only twelve people on the investigative staff of the Department of Labor's San Francisco office, which has jurisdiction over sixteen northern California counties. This office is responsible for enforcing not only the Age Discrimination in Employment Act but also the Fair Labor Standards Act, the Equal Pay Act, the Public Contracts Act, the Service Contract Act, the Davis-Bacon Act, and the garnishment law. The limited staff is therefore spread very thin. In addition, there is a heavy load of complaints.

When an investigation is initiated, the department is handicapped in getting information from the company involved. Investigators do not always know what pertinent information is available and in what form.

Quite often they have to depend on information obtained from employee interviews to find out. The company can claim that such information does not exist or that the request is too ambiguous or broad to be complied with. Rodman of SOCAL states that "this was not true in the SOCAL case. No request from the Department of Labor was evaded. Uncounted numbers of man-hours were devoted to satisfying their information requests." The government can and indeed does devote large resources in pretrial discovery cases such as the pending antitrust case against IBM. However, in all but a few cases, such an ad hoc approach is impossible and would drain the department's resources as well as the courts if a significant number of large companies chose to fight the cases all the way. The resource allocation problem becomes so serious that it is highly unlikely that any small- or medium-sized company will be apprehended or prosecuted in cases involving some kind of discrimination. And therein lies the futility of the law and the frustration of those who can be injured and have their rights denied.

EPILOGUE: SOCAL'S NEW PERFORMANCE APPRAISAL SYSTEM

As the case indicated, the company initiated a new program of performance appraisal almost simultaneously with its plan for reduction in the work force. Rodman describes the new system as a "forced ranking type." Under this system, managers are asked to document critical incidents and positive and negative points about an employee as soon as they occur so that they can provide a more valid criteria for making performance-related judgments. At the time of periodical reviews, the supervisors for all regions get together and force-rank individual employees. Every attempt is made to establish criteria common to the work group under investigation in advance. This type of data is being used for salary adjustments, promotions, selection for training and development, and also for laying off people when a reduction in work force is called for. Supervisors are asked that these forced-ranking discussions be documented in the files.

In a great number of cases, the employees being appraised would have worked under more than one supervisor, and the supervisor, therefore can give honest and impartial judgments on employee performance based on a one-to-one working relationship. In most cases, the criteria for appraisal are objective. But when it comes to management level positions, it is very hard to develop objective criteria, and the supervisors do the best they can to be fair and objective.

APPENDIX A *

5-16-74 (DLR)   FULL TEXT SECTION   (No. 96) G-1
CONSENT DECREE PROVIDING FOR REINSTATEMENT AND
BACK PAY FOR STANDARD OIL EMPLOYEES FOR
AGE DISCRIMINATION
(TEXT)

IN THE UNITED STATES DISTRICT COURT
FOR THE NORTHERN DISTRICT OF CALIFORNIA
PETER J. BRENNAN, SECRETARY OF LABOR,
UNITED STATES DEPARTMENT OF LABOR,
Plaintiff,

v.

WESTERN OPERATIONS, INC., a division   CIVIL ACTION
of Standard Oil Company of California,
a corporation,   File No.

Defendant.   *JUDGMENT*

Plaintiff has filed his complaint herein, and defendant has answered denying the material allegations of the complaint, and, without admitting any violations of the Age Discrimination in Employment Act as alleged, agrees to the entry of this Judgment without contest. It is, therefore, upon motion of the attorneys for plaintiff, and for cause shown, ORDERED, ADJUDGED AND DECREED that:

(1) Defendant Western Operations, Inc., its officers, servants and employees, and all persons acting or claiming to act in its behalf and interest, be, and they hereby are, permanently enjoined and restrained from violating the existing provisions of Section 4 of the Age Discrimination in Employment Act of 1967 (29 U.S.C. § 621 *et Sec.*), and of the existing provisions of Section 15 of the Fair Labor Standards Act of 1938, as amended (29 U.S.C. § 201, *et Sec.*), at any of its establishments, and in particular defendant shall not, contrary to Section 4(a)(1) of the Age Discrimination in Employment Act and Section 15 of the Fair Labor Standards Act discharge any individual or otherwise discriminate against any individual with respect to his compensation, terms, condition, or privileges of employment, because of such individual's age.

(2) The defendant shall, within the period of time set forth in the "Supplemental Agreement of Parties," attached hereto as Exhibit A (hereinafter "Supplemental Agreement"), make offers of reinstatement to 120 of its previously terminated employees, as listed on Exhibit B attached hereto, and within the period of time set forth in the aforesaid "Supple-

---

* Published by the Bureau of National Affairs, Inc., Washington, D.C.

mental Agreement" reinstate those who desire reemployment to their former job or to one of similar status, pay and location.

(3) The defendant shall, within the period of time set forth in the aforesaid "Supplemental Agreement," pay a total amount of $2,000,000, which amount shall be distributed to approximately 160 persons listed on Exhibit C in the amounts there specified (which exhibit shall be filed within 45 days of the date of this Judgment) to compensate them for their lost wages and benefits during the period from their date of termination to the date of Judgment, May 15, 1974. The total amount of $2,000,000 shall only be reduced by the amount, if any, which the wages earned during this period by the persons receiving such restitution exceeds $500,000, as specified in the aforesaid "Supplemental Agreement."

(4) Any money which remains undistributed within one year after entry of this Judgment because of the refusal of the persons listed on Exhibit C or, if deceased, their proper heirs to accept such sums or because of an inability to locate the said recipients will be deposited with the Clerk of the Court who shall forthwith deposit such money with the Treasurer of the United States pursuant to the provisions of 28 U.S.C. §§ 2041 and 2042 (1964).

(5) Additionally, defendant shall adjust upward the monthly pension payment to be paid to those persons listed on Exhibit C to reflect the amount they would receive had they remained on defendant's payroll through May 15, 1974, in accord with the "Supplemental Agreement."

(6) This Judgment, except for paragraph 1 above, is limited to all employees of the marketing department of Western Operations, Inc., a division of Standard Oil Company of California, and to terminations by defendant in said department up to and including December 31, 1973.

FURTHER ORDERED that each party bear his own costs.

DATED: May 15, 1974.

United States District Judge

CONSENT IS HEREBY GIVEN TO
THE ENTRY OF THIS JUDGMENT:

Western Operations, Inc., a division of
Standard Oil Company of California, a
Corporation
By

William J. Kilberg
Solicitor of Labor

_____
Bruce A. Nelson
for
Pillsbury, Madison & Sutro
Attorneys for Defendant

_____
Daniel W. Teehan
Deputy Regional Director
UNITED STATES
DEPARTMENT OF
LABOR
Attorneys for Plaintiff

EXHIBIT A
SUPPLEMENTAL AGREEMENT OF THE PARTIES

It is further agreed by the parties herein as set forth below, which is to be attached to and made a part of the Judgment entered in this matter, that:

1. The gross amount due each terminated employee involved in this Judgment, prior to mitigation or any percentage reduction applied, will include the following:

a. His total lost wages from the date of his discharge to the date of the Judgment, May 15, 1974, or to his sixty-fifth birthday, whichever occurs first, based on his average monthly salary, including normal increases in the aforementioned period, times the number of months involved; and

b. The amount normally contributed by the Company to the stock plan per month based on the aforementioned average salary times the number of months in the period; and

c. The market cost of purchasing the amount of life insurance, in term, lost by the employer as a result of his termination; and

d. For employees who reached sixty-five years of age prior to May 15, 1974, the increase in the monthly pension amount, which would have resulted had the employee remained on the payroll during the applicable period, from the employee's sixty-fifth birthday to May 15, 1974; and

e. The remaining percentage of stock shares in employee's name at the time of termination that he did not receive when terminated.

2. From this total amount, as computed in paragraph 1 above, will be deducted as mitigation the severance payment paid to terminated employees, pensions paid to terminated employees in the aforementioned period, and any unemployment benefits and earnings from their employment or their own business during the period from termination to May 15, 1974.

3. Each employee listed on Exhibit C will receive approximately 75% of the sum equal to his total lost earnings and benefits minus his total mitigation, subject to the limitation of paragraph 3 of the Judgment, if applicable.

4. Those employees to be offered reinstatement, as listed on Exhibit B attached hereto, and who desire same, will be offered re-employment in their former position or one of equal status and pay in the same approximate geographical area. If there are no such jobs in existence in the appropriate area or if a job has been eliminated, the reinstatement offer will be for the most comparable job or the job now held by most persons incumbent in the prior job when eliminated, as applicable.

5. Immediately subsequent to the entry of Judgment plaintiff will inquire by certified mail of those persons listed on Exhibit D of their desires to return to employment with Standard Oil.

6. Employees responding affirmatively to the letter specified in paragraph 5 above will be contacted by the defendant, within 10 working days of being informed by plaintiff of their desires to return to work, with offers of re-employment described in paragraph 4 above. Employees will

be rehired as promptly as possible at a mutually agreed time, but no later than August 1, 1974.

7. The actual pension increases will be in accord with the following procedure:

a. Those employees who are reinstated will be treated as if they had never left the employment, and Company contributions to their pension during the period of absence will be brought up to date, and continued. In regard to these employees, they will be required to make up their own regular employee contribution for the period of their absence.

b. Those employees who refuse reinstatement will have their pension adjusted upward to reflect what it would have been had they been on the payroll of the Company through May 15, 1974. This will be so in regard to this group regardless of the fact that they may not have received 100% restitution.

c. Those who are not designated by Exhibit B to receive offers of reinstatement will have their pensions adjusted as if they had been on the payroll through May 15, 1974 except that the adjustment will be in the same percentage as the restitution specified in paragraph 3 above.

8. Payment of the sums due employees per paragraphs 1 and 2 of this agreement will be made within 15 days of receipt by defendant of substantially all mitigation information. If the necessary mitigation information is not promptly received, partial payments may be made as subsequently agreed by the parties.

9. Within 60 days of the date of Judgment, Standard will provide the Department of Labor with a precise listing of the names, gross and net amount to be paid each employee listed on Exhibit C to be filed subsequent to the Judgment. Within 90 days of the entry of Judgment, Standard will provide the Department of Labor with a list of all employees reinstated and their position and location. Within approximately 150 days of Judgment, Standard will advise the Department of Labor of pension adjustments made by name and monthly amount.

DATED: May 15, 1974

Western Operations, Inc., a division of Standard Oil Company of California, a Corporation	William J. Kilberg Solicitor of Labor

By

_____ Bruce A. Nelson for Pillsbury, Madison & Sutro Attorneys for Defendant	_____ Daniel W. Teehan Deputy Regional Solicitor UNITED STATES DEPARTMENT OF LABOR Attorneys for Plaintiff

End of Text

End of Section G

APPENDIX B

AGE DISCRIMINATION
IN EMPLOYMENT ACT OF 1967

Text of the Age Discrimination in Employment Act of 1967, P.L. 90–202, effective June 12, 1968. The Act reads as last amended by P.L. 93–259, effective May 1, 1974.

PROHIBITION OF AGE DISCRIMINATION

Sec. 4. (a) It shall be unlawful for an employer—

(1) to fail or refuse to hire or to discharge any individual or otherwise discriminate against any individual with respect to his compensation, terms, conditions, or privileges of employment, because of such individual's age;

(2) to limit, segregate, or classify his employees in any way which would deprive or tend to deprive any individual of employment opportunities or otherwise adversely affect his status as an employee, because of such individual's age; or

(3) to reduce the wage rate of any employee in order to comply with this Act.

(b) It shall be unlawful for an employment agency to fail or refuse to refer for employment, or otherwise to discriminate against, any individual because of such individual's age, or to classify or refer for employment any individual on the basis of such individual's age.

(c) It shall be unlawful for a labor organization—

(1) to exclude or to expel from its membership, or otherwise to discriminate against, any individual because of his age;

(2) to limit, segregate, or classify its membership, or to classify or fail or refuse to refer for employment any individual, in any way which would deprive or tend to deprive any individual of employment opportunities, or would limit such employment opportunities or otherwise adversely affect his status as an employee or as an applicant for employment, because of such individual's age;

(3) to cause or attempt to cause an employer to discriminate against an individual in violation of this section.

(d) It shall be unlawful for an employer to discriminate against any of his employees or applicants for employment, for an employment agency to discriminate against any individual, or for a labor organization to discriminate against any member thereof or applicant for membership, because such individual member, or applicant for membership, has opposed any practice made unlawful by this section, or because such individual, member, or applicant for membership has made a charge, testified, assisted, or participated in any manner in an investigation, proceeding, or litigation under this Act.

(e) It shall be unlawful for an employer, labor organization or employment agency to print or publish, or cause to be printed or published, any notice or advertisement relating to employment by such an employee or membership in or any classification or referral for employment by such a labor organization, or relating to any classification or referral for employment by such an employment agency, indicating any preference, limitation, specification, or discrimination, based on age.

(f) It shall not be unlawful for an employer, employment agency, or labor organization—

(1) to take any action otherwise prohibited under subsection (a), (b), (c), or (e) of this section where age is a bona fide occupational qualification reasonably necessary to the normal operation of the particular business, or where the differentiation is based on reasonable factors other than age;

(2) to observe the terms of a bona fide seniority system or any bona fide employee benefit plan such as retirement, pension, or insurance plan, which is not a subterfuge to evade the purpose of this Act, except that no such employee benefit plan shall excuse the failure to hire any individual; or

(3) to discharge or otherwise discipline an individual for good cause.

FAIR LABOR STANDARDS ACT OF 1938
(AS AMENDED BY THE FAIR LABOR STANDARDS
AMENDMENTS OF 1974)

Sec. 15. (a) After the expiration of one hundred and twenty days from the date of enactment of this Act, it shall be unlawful for any person—

(1) to transport, offer for transportation, ship, deliver, or sell in commerce, or to ship, deliver, or sell with knowledge that shipment or delivery or sale thereof in commerce is intended, any goods in the production of which any employee was employed in violation of section 6 or section 7, or in violation of any regulation or order of the Secretary of Labor issued under section 14; except that no provision of this Act shall impose any liability upon any common carrier for the transportation in commerce in the regular course of its business of any goods not produced by such common carrier, and no provision of this Act shall excuse any common carrier from its obligation to accept any goods for transportation; and except that any such transportation, offer, shipment, delivery, or sale of such goods by a purchaser who acquired them in good faith in reliance on written assurance from the producer that the goods were produced in compliance with the requirements of the Act, and who acquired such goods for value without notice of any such violation, shall not be deemed unlawful;

(2) to violate any of the provisions of section 6 or section 7, or any of the provisions of any regulation or order of the Secretary issued under section 14;

(3) to discharge or in any other manner discriminate against any employee because such employee has filed any complaint or instituted or caused to be instituted any proceeding under or related to this Act, or has testified or is about to testify in any such proceeding, or has served or is about to serve on an industry committee;

(4) to violate any of the provisions of section 12;

(5) to violate any of the provisions of section 11(c) or any regulation or order made or continued in effect under the provisions of section 11(d), or to make any statement, report, or record filed or kept pursuant to the provisions of such section or of any regulation or order thereunder, knowing such statement, report, or record to be false in a material respect.

(b) For the purpose of subsection (a)(1) proof that any employee was employed in any place of employment where goods shipped or sold in commerce were produced, within ninety days prior to the removal of the goods from such place of employment, shall be prima facie evidence that such employee was engaged in the production of such goods.

APPENDIX C

A REPORT TO SOCAL EMPLOYEES ON THE AGE-DISCRIMINATION ISSUE FROM N. T. BOGART, VICE-PRESIDENT, INDUSTRIAL RELATIONS, STANDARD OIL COMPANY OF CALIFORNIA

A U.S. Labor Department investigation of possible age discrimination in a series of job terminations by the Marketing Department of Western Operations has been concluded with the filing of a consent judgment.

The judgment specifically states that there has been no finding that the company in any way violated the Federal Age Discrimination Act. Standard has agreed to provide monetary payments and offer job reinstatement to terminated employees in those cases in which the Labor Department believed the company's documentation for the basis of termination was insufficient.

The reports of the settlement in the public media may raise more questions than they answer in the minds of SOCAL people. So, this report to employees is offered to provide a broader understanding of the issues involved. In the next several paragraphs, we will discuss the basic problem, how management tried to solve the problem, the new problems these solutions created with the Department of Labor, and how we're settling the matter.

THE BASIC PROBLEM

The necessity for a large number of job terminations was created by a basic problem of economics: Western Operations was experiencing a declining rate of return. Costs of doing business were continuing to go up, while intense competition kept a lid on prices. To remain competitive, Western Operations Marketing combined many functions, eliminated facilities and streamlined the organization, including a substantial reduction in manpower. When the product shortage hit last year, it made additional jobs surplus.

During a four-year period of 1970 to 1973, approximately 1,600 jobs were eliminated (exclusive of Standard Stations salesmen). The posts that were cut out included management, supervision, sales contact positions, administrative and clerical staff, and mechanical and operating jobs.

THE TERMINATIONS

Two-thirds of the surplus manpower problem was taken care of by normal attrition. However, there still remained about 500 more employees than there were jobs available.

Terminating people is the most difficult decision any manager has to make, and we know of no way to carry out such a program without disappointment to some individuals. But we do try to be fair. When terminations are unavoidable, it is our intent to carefully evaluate the relative performance of employees in the group, and retain those who are most effective in meeting the performance requirements of their jobs, or most capable of being reassigned to other jobs. This isn't to say that all those terminated were ineffective workers. Some good performers were affected. Rather, it was a relative matter; they were evaluated as less effective in meeting performance requirements than were those employees retained. There were simply too few jobs to go around. Employees of all ages were affected in the marketing cutback. We are aware of no employee being terminated because of his or her age.

The case of each employee to be terminated was carefully reviewed. Those with enough service for a vested interest in the Annuity Plan and those participating in the Employee Stock Plan received their vested shares, of course. In addition, the affected employees were given an adjustment payment to ease the financial transition. The size of this transitional payment varied according to salary, length of service, and the amount of vesting in the Annuity and Stock plans. The payment by itself averaged $10,000 per person.

THE DEPARTMENT OF LABOR INVESTIGATION

About two years ago, U.S. Department of Labor representatives began to review the termination of our marketing people between the ages of 40 to 65, under the provisions of the Age Discrimination in Employment Act of 1967. The Department of Labor recognizes the fact that changing economic conditions will sometimes require a cutback in a company's work force. And, the department does not find fault with terminations based on comparative job performance of employees. In the majority of these cases, the company's records of terminations on the basis of job performance review were sufficient to support the action taken. In the other cases, the Department of Labor was not satisfied with the evidence.

During this period of terminations, the average age of employees in Western Operations Marketing actually increased. But the Labor people argued that a larger percentage of people were terminated in the upper-age brackets than one might expect given their percentage in the work force. In such situations, the Labor people contended that the burden of proof fell upon the company to show that there had been no age discrimination, that these persons had in fact been terminated on the basis of relative performance.

In reviewing its job appraisal files in some of these cases, the company found that it lacked written proof that the performance of all of the employees had been properly appraised and ranked. Many of the files involved were now several years old. Some of them lacked absolute, measurable statements on an individual's performance. In this review process, we found that we could not convince the Department of Labor that every layoff was based on relative performance. So, the decision was made not to contest the matter in court if a fair settlement could be negotiated with the Department of Labor. Such a settlement was negotiated. The company and the Labor Department agreed that the company would make payments of about $2 million and offer job reinstatement to approximately 120 people.

While we feel sure that our supervisors did not discriminate against older employees, we believe these settlements are appropriate. Considering the difficulties of proof in many cases, due to the passage of time and the lack of documentation, and the cost and time of litigation, we believe that paying back wages and offering job reinstatement is the fairest and wisest course to take.

WHAT THE SETTLEMENT MEANS AND DOESN'T MEAN

First, it doesn't mean that the company is insensitive to older employees. Obviously, large numbers of employees in older age groups work for SOCAL. They receive merit increases and promotions on the basis of performance, and without regard to age. For the most highly placed jobs, the largest number of appointments are made from among people over 45.

Second, it doesn't mean the company acted to save money in salaries by laying off older, highly paid employees and retaining younger, lesser-paid people. It is true that some of the terminated individuals were high-salaried employees. But the selection of employees to be laid off is certainly not based on salary. Since the program retained people on the basis of high performance, the retained people are normally going to be rapidly moving up through the salary ranks themselves. In fact, the average salary in marketing has increased during this period, just as it has in the rest of the company.

Third, any suggestion that the company has terminated older employees before normal retirement age in order to "save money" on their retirement benefits is also untrue. The two chief sources of retirement benefits for Standard of California employees are the company's Employee Stock Plan and the Annuity Plan. The company has contributed the same percentage of profits to the Employee Stock Plan each year regardless of the number of employees participating. The termination of employees in no way lessens the size of the company contribution to the plan. And the Annuity Plan monies are placed in trust and do not revert to the company. A statistician might show that there is a potential saving in future contributions, but this is not and has never been a motivation for terminating SOCAL employees.

We have learned something from this case which should improve our appraisals in the future. The appraisal files of many terminated employees show that attempts to "protect" employees "got us into trouble" with the Department of Labor. A supervisor might be aware that an employee is doing some of his work poorly. All too often, such a supervisor would reason, "I'll tell Joe about the problem, but I won't write it down in his appraisal, and possibly hurt his chances for future opportunities."

Thus, the company had appraisal files which did not always truly reflect performance and, as a result, did not always support the decision to terminate the individual in the opinion of the Department of Labor.

However well intentioned, such attempts to withhold accurate appraisal information from the record may make it difficult to defend charges of discrimination. A company is free to use comparative job performance as a fair method of handling terminations, but it should have full written data to back up its actions regarding employees. The statistical approach taken by the Labor Department can only be met by accurate and comprehensive information. Periodic performance reviews of employees' work must therefore include more specific information than many appraisal summaries did in the past. Only then can the company be absolutely fair to all employees when faced with the necessity of a work-force reduction, and prove the propriety of its actions if questioned.

But in contrast to the problem of surplus employees is the goal of stable employment. Of course, job security cannot be guaranteed in the face of changes in competitive conditions. However, the company strives to maintain as stable an employment level as possible. This is achieved by accurate planning of management and by employees working productively. Together, management and employees can maximize this stability and minimize the necessity of work-force reduction.

SELECTED REFERENCES

"Age Discrimination Moves into the Limelight," *Business Week,* June 15, 1974. p. 104.

BARTNOFF, JUDITH, "Title VII and Employment Discrimination in Upper Level Jobs," *Columbia Law Review,* 73 (December 1973), p. 1614.

BERNSTEIN, L. S., "How to Discriminate in Hiring," *Dun's* 100 (October 1972), p. 105.

BOGLIETTI, G., "Discrimination Against Older Workers and the Promotion of Equality of Opportunity," *International Labour Review,* 110 (October 1974), p. 351.

BRENNAN, P. J., "Older Employees Have a Government Ally," *Management Review,* 63 (August 1974), p. 42.

CROTTY, P. T., and J. A. TIMMONS, "Older Minorities—Roadblocked in the Organization," *Business Horizons,* 17 (June 1974), p. 27.

"Discrimination Against the Elderly: A Prospectus of the Problem," *Suffolk University Law Review,* VII (1973), p. 917.

FOEGEN, J. H., "Time to Be Honest with Older Employees," *Public Personnel Management,* 2 (September 1973), p. 320.

HEALY, J., "Executive Life After 45," *Dun's,* 103 (March 1974), p. 99.

"More Age Bias Settlements to Come, Says Labor Department," *Industry Week,* 181 (June 17, 1974), p. 28.

SAFREN, M. A., "Title VII and Employee Selection Techniques," *Personnel,* 50 (January 1973), p. 26.

SANDERSON, G., "Job Discrimination Against the Over-40's," *Labour Gazette,* 74 (April 1974), p. 284.

SKOTZKO, E., "Arbitration and Title VII Rights," *Monthly Labor Review,* 96 (February 1973), p. 58.

SLATER, R., "End of the Road at Forty?" *Personnel Management,* 5 (May 1973), p. 31.

"Title VII and NLRA: Protection of Extra-Union Opposition to Employment Discrimination," *Michigan Law Review,* 72 (December 1973), p. 313.

"United States: Combating Age Discrimination in Employment," *International Labour Review,"* 107 (January 1973), p. 83.

BETHLEHEM STEEL COMPANY
AND
THE WOODROOFE INCIDENT

TO WHAT EXTENT CAN A CORPORATION CONTROL
AN EMPLOYEE'S SOCIAL AND POLITICAL ACTIVITIES?

> The fundamental tendency of the bureaucratic mind is to turn all problems of politics into problems of administration.
>
> —KARL MANNHEIM

On March 16, 1964, the Bethlehem Steel Company fired Philip B. Woodroofe, supervisor of municipal services at the Bethlehem, Pennsylvania, home office. The charge was that Woodroofe and his wife refused to comply with a company demand to resign from the Community Civic League, an organization to improve interracial relations. Woodroofe was a founder of the organization.

When pressed for an explanation, the company simply stated that Woodroofe had resigned and that it was not company policy to make statements on an individual employee's resignation. Woodroofe himself denied having resigned:

> I have never submitted my resignation, nor have I been asked to submit one. . . . I was told I was through. . . . I was told I couldn't act as a private citizen, nor could my wife.[1]

[1] Joseph A. Loftus, "Bethlehem Puzzled by Dismissal of Steel Aide over Racial Stand," *The New York Times*, March 22, 1964, p. 10.

This incident, which for a short time received national attention, brought into sharp focus the contradictions between a company's public posture and its private philosophy; the vulnerability of professional junior and middle-level managers—unprotected by unions or internal company due process against the arbitrary exercise of power by large corporations; and, still more important, the infringement of an individual's rights by the extension of the corporation's control over his actions in areas not directly connected with corporate activities.

THE ISSUES

The Bethlehem Steel case presents an excellent framework within which the issue of the individual versus the organization can be discussed and its various facets carefully examined. Corporate control over employees' noncorporate activities is not new. In a sense it is akin to similar issues found in all large, established public or private bureaucracies. However, in recent years the topic has become more controversial and has generated much public discussion as corporations have been increasingly subjected to public criticism over their social role and modus operandi. Our areas of concern deal with the broader issues of public policy and those relating to the actions of Bethlehem Steel. The general questions for analysis might include these:

1. What is the legal position concerning an employer's right to fire an employee? How does it apply to the Bethlehem case?
2. To what extent should a corporation or any other institution be allowed to restrict the activities of individuals—employees or non-employees—to protect its own interests?
3. What happens when the individual's activities are in the larger national or public interest?
4. How should corporate self-interest be defined?

The particular questions relating to Bethlehem Steel are these:

1. What were the environmental conditions that gave rise to the conflict between Bethlehem Steel and Mr. Woodroofe?
2. Were there any unique characteristics associated with Bethlehem Steel or Philip Woodroofe that made this a special situation, and therefore of limited applicability?
3. Could Bethlehem's position and actions be justified in view of the circumstances of the case?

THE COMPANY

Bethlehem Steel, the second largest steel company in the United States, dominates the economic and social life of the Lehigh Valley and the city of Bethlehem, Pennsylvania. It furnishes nearly 50 percent of the entire payroll of the town. Of Bethlehem's population of 77,000, about 1,000 are blacks, and a very small number are Puerto Ricans. (In the Lehigh Valley as a whole, with a population of 250,000, about 2,500 are blacks.) Schools have not been segregated, and there have been no civil rights demonstrations. There has been a problem of inadequate housing for the poor and a high rate of Negro school dropouts.[2]

> Over the years [Bethlehem Steel] has demonstrated its consciousness of the civic well-being of its home office city in many ways. It has invested heavily, without any prodding, in air pollution controls, in neutralizing the manufacturing effluents which it dumps into the Lehigh River, and in expending heavy sums to beautify the city by buying up eyesores and staving off blight along approaches or property not used for steel manufacturing. Besides, it has increasingly encouraged its people to participate in a wide range of civic activity, even to the point of giving one of its junior executives a leave of absence to run for Congress last year.[3]

In its management policies, however, the company has long been regarded as one of the "most withdrawn and individualistic companies in a conservative industry." [4]

Bethlehem Steel is run by a board of directors made up entirely of company officers, without a single outsider. Situated far from the big steel centers, the "inbred and stratified social life" of the company executives centers on the Saucon Valley Country Club. To an outsider, the company "offers a cautious austere facade." [5]

> Bethlehem is noted for being stingy with titles but generous with salaries. With $2.1 billion in sales, it has only 10 vice presidents. United States Steel, with $3.6 billion in sales, has 77.

> The lowest-paid Bethlehem vice presidents received $113,866 last year, and the highest paid, John E. Jacobs, vice president for steel operations, drew $218,358. Mr. Cort, who was president and a director for five months, received $79,167 for the period, or payment at an annual rate of $145,000.

> Mr. Martin, in his capacities as president and vice chairman, drew $251,726, and Mr. Homer, as chairman, received $301,860.[6]

The style of management has been strictly individual and authority has clearly been centralized at the top. In its fifty-nine-year history the company has had only three chief executives. The first died in office at the age

2 *Ibid.*

3 "The Woodroofe Incident," *Bethlehem Globe-Times,* March 20, 1964, p. 6.

4 John M. Lee, "1964: Year of Change for Bethlehem Steel," *The New York Times,* April 12, 1964, Sec. 3, pp. 1, 5.

5 *Ibid.*

6 *Ibid.*

of seventy-seven. The other two retired after serving for eighteen and for seven years at the ages of eighty-one and sixty-eight, respectively. The fourth chief executive officer, Edmund F. Martin, took over on March 17, 1964, at the age of sixty-one, moving up from his former position as the vice-chairman.

Arthur Homer, the retiring chairman, has been regarded as one of the most commanding figures in the steel industry:

> He is a tall, lean simply-spoken man, whose demeanor has been described as that of an affable New England preacher. He enjoys a pipe and occasionally indulges in a little wit or whimsy. . . .

> At his quarterly press conferences in New York he stood at the door to the 15th floor conference room greeting reporters as they entered. He then took a seat alone on one side of a 30-foot table and fielded questions from the newsmen arrayed opposite him.

> Behind Mr. Homer, against the wall, sit all the directors. Only occasionally did Mr. Homer ask any of them to comment. During the conference, the directors' expressions seldom changed except to laugh at a Homer quip. There was no question of who spoke for Bethlehem.[7]

PHILIP B. WOODROOFE

Woodroofe, forty-five at the time of the incident, is the son of an Episcopal minister. He interrupted his studies at Lehigh University to enter the United States Air Force shortly after Pearl Harbor. He served in World War II and in the Korean conflict as a B-29 pilot and instructor. He left the service as a lieutenant colonel in the Air Force Reserve.[8]

In 1957, when he was director of residence halls at Lehigh University, he was hired to be Bethlehem's supervisor of municipal services. His duties at the company called for, among other things, cooperation in city planning.[9]

COMMUNITY CIVIC LEAGUE

In May 1963 the Right Reverend Arthur Lichtenberger, presiding bishop of the Protestant Episcopal Church in the United States, appealed to his church members to take positive action and assume responsibility in solving this country's racial problems. Woodroofe, an Episcopalian, took this appeal seriously and initiated informal meetings between local white

---

[7] *Ibid.*
[8] "Steel Company Ousts Municipal Aide," *Bethlehem Globe-Times*, March 17, 1964, p. 7.
[9] Loftus, "Bethlehem Puzzled by Dismissal of Steel Aide."

and black leaders to develop the framework for an organization that could provide a forum where community problems could be brought into the open and discussed, thus avoiding the possibility of violent confrontation between various groups. Woodroofe took a leading role in mobilizing community support. As a result, the Community Civic League was formally organized on March 15, 1964, at the local YWCA. Participating were more than two hundred local citizens, including Bethlehem's mayor, H. Gordon Payrow, and a number of clergymen.

WOODROOFE'S TROUBLES WITH THE COMPANY

Two days before the organizational meeting of the league, Woodroofe was informed that his superiors were displeased with his involvement in league activities. According to a story in *The New York Times:*

> On Friday, March 13, F. C. Rabold, manager of general services for Bethlehem Steel, said it had come to his attention through his superiors that Mr. Woodroofe was involved in the league. The instructions to Mr. Rabold were to "get me out" of the league, Mr. Woodroofe said.
>
> One of Mr. Rabold's superiors is Russell K. Branscom, vice president for industrial and public relations. Nebraska-born, Mr. Branscom was graduated from the University of Alabama with the interfraternity award for outstanding service to the university. That was in 1935. He has been in Bethlehem since then.
>
> Mr. Woodroofe was given until Sunday noon to make his decision. He talked with Mr. Rabold Saturday and was cautioned about the consequences of a wrong decision.
>
> "Helen and I talked about exchanging places," she to go on the board of the league and he to be a rank-and-file member. "The company told me that wouldn't do," he said.
>
> Mr. Woodroofe won an extension of the deadline until 4 P.M. Sunday so that he could talk to his friend, Bishop Frederick Warneke. The Bishop was away and Mr. Woodroofe gave his answer without that counsel. The answer was:
>
> "Neither I nor Helen will disassociate ourselves from the Community League. What we started here is good. We must continue it."
>
> Mr. Woodroofe said his superior's reply was: "I think you've made a mistake."
>
> The company's view that the league would worsen rather than help the situation was conveyed to Mr. Woodroofe.
>
> When Mr. Woodroofe reported for work Monday morning, Mr. Rabold told him, "I'm surprised that you are here."

"Do you mean to say really I'm through?" Mr. Woodroofe asked.

"Yes, you're through," was the reply.

"So I went to the board and punched my time card," Mr. Woodroofe said. He was through at 10:15 and left without cleaning out his desk.[10]

The town was shocked and dismayed. The story made the national newspapers. The local papers during the next few days were full of angry letters from readers and editorials condemning Bethlehem Steel's action. Not a single word could be found in either the local or the national news media justifying or supporting the company's action.[11]

THE COMPANY'S POSTURE IN THE AFTERMATH

Bethlehem's press statement that Woodroofe had resigned was clearly unsatisfactory to the community. It refused to accept the company's statement in view of Woodroofe's charge that he was indeed fired. Consequently, in response to local inquiries, the company issued two statements denying that it was against employee participation in community affairs and insisting that Woodroofe's dismissal was based on a clear case of conflict of interest.

The first statement was issued on March 24, 1964:

[As far back as] in 1955, for example, our Chairman and Chief Executive Officer, Arthur B. Homer, addressing the Bethlehem Chamber of Commerce, emphasized that "our employees are encouraged to participate as fully as they can in the life of the community, as citizens, irrespective of their status with the company."

This continuing policy was re-emphasized in a speech on March 16, 1960, by James V. Robertson, Manager of Community Relations, who said:

". . . Part of that job is encouraging employees—and I quote Mr. Homer on this—'to participate as fully as they can in the life of the community, irrespective of their status with the company.'"

Also, in 1961, in management conferences held in all the steel plants, employees were again encouraged to participate as fully as they cared to in the life of the community, as citizens, irrespective of whether or not the company provides financial support for a particular organization's activities. That policy has continued without change to the present time.[12]

---

[10] *Ibid.*, p. 10.
[11] See *Bethlehem Globe-Times*, March 18, 20, 23–25, 27, 30, April 10, 1964; and *Allentown Morning Call*, March 27, 1964.
[12] "Company Says No Bar on Civic Activity," *Bethlehem Globe-Times*, March 25, 1964.

A company spokesman also said that "the company would be glad, if invited, to designate an official representative to participate in the activities of the committee." [13]

The second statement, issued on March 25, 1964, dealt specifically with Woodroofe's dismissal:

> As supervisor of municipal services of this company, Mr. Woodroofe participated as the official representative of the company in certain municipal activities. When he became identified with the Community Civic League, it was the company's belief that his position on matters coming before that organization would be viewed as an expression of the official position of the company. This type of activity did not represent an area related to his responsibilities with the company and the company believed it inescapable that misunderstandings would result.

> Therefore, although the company does encourage employees to participate in affairs of their local communities, the circumstances in this case were such—and Mr. Woodroofe was so advised—that there was a clear conflict between his official representation of the company in certain community activities and his participation in the League. Mr. Woodroofe chose to resign from the company.[14]

In a later announcement, the company stated that Woodroofe was offered two other jobs with the company prior to his dismissal but that he refused to accept either of them.[15]

When asked to comment, Mr. Woodroofe said that he found it difficult to accept the company's statement at face value since it demanded that his wife also resign from the Community Civic League.[16] Mrs. Woodroofe added, "And I am on the Red Cross Board. I don't speak for the company there." [17]

COMMUNITY CIVIC LEAGUE'S RESPONSE

A league spokesman considered it an encouraging sign when Bethlehem Steel indicated interest in participating in the league's affairs. The Reverend R. Wakefield Roberts, the pastor of Saint John Zion Methodist Church and a member of the league's board of directors, said that he was positive that the league would extend an invitation to the company to

[13] "Steel Company Invites Bid to Interracial League," *Bethlehem Globe-Times,* March 24, 1964, p. 12.
[14] "Steel Blames 'Conflict' in Woodroofe Case," *Bethlehem Globe-Times,* March 26, 1964.
[15] "Woodroofe Vetoed Two Other Jobs," *Bethlehem Globe-Times,* April 15, 1964, p. 1.
[16] *Bethlehem Globe-Times,* March 26, 1964.
[17] Loftus, "Bethlehem Puzzled by Dismissal of Steel Aide."

join. He also stated that the board would adopt an official position on the Woodroofe incident.[18]

The meeting took place on the evening of March 24, 1964. At the meeting the board turned down the company's bid to send an official representative to participate in the league's activities. In declining the company's request, the board cited a provision of its constitution which limited the membership in the league to persons who were "willing to work as individuals towards improving conditions of minority groups in Bethlehem, rather than as representatives of any church, industry, business or profession." [19]

The board also unanimously decided not to take any official position on the Woodroofe incident. This was done at the suggestion of Woodroofe, who requested that the board make no statement "public or private" as this "would not serve the league's purpose." [20]

On June 30, 1964, Philip Woodroofe resigned from the board of directors of the league, as he planned to move to New York where he had reportedly accepted a real estate job. However, he retained his membership in the league.[21]

EPILOGUE

On October 16, 1975, at the invitation of Bethlehem Steel, the author met with four company executives from the Industrial Relations and Public Affairs Departments to review company policies during the ten years since the Woodroofe incident occurred. A summary of their remarks follows:

1. The executives agreed that perhaps there was overreaction to Woodroofe's participation in the Community Civic League and that it should have been handled differently.[22] However, they also maintained that it was not Woodroofe per se, but the political visibility of the minority-related issues at that time which attracted the attention of the national news media and turned the case into a *cause célèbre*.

2. There was indeed a potential conflict of interest situation which the company sought to avoid; even now, if an executive's outside activity runs counter to the company policy of which that executive is in charge, he will have to withdraw from such outside activity. Furthermore, the company would not want a high-level executive to make any public statements, which are clearly outside the area of his or her expertise and job in the company, that ran counter to the company's publicly stated position.

[18] "Steel Co. Bid to Interracial League," *Bethlehem Globe-Times*, p. 12.
[19] "Civic League Fails to Offer Steel Bid," *Bethlehem Globe-Times*, March 25, 1969.
[20] *Ibid.*
[21] "Woodroofe Resigns Seat on Civic League Board," *Allentown Morning Call*, July 1, 1964.
[22] None of the executives participating in this meeting were directly involved in the Woodroofe incident.

3. Notwithstanding, there have been tremendous changes in the last ten years that make Bethlehem a very different company. These changes have evolved gradually as a result of economic, social, and political pressures, both from within and without, and as a result of changes in top management and its philosophy. Some of these changes are:

A. The company's board of directors no longer consists only of insiders.

B. There is a mandatory retirement age of sixty-five which is strictly enforced in all cases, including the top management.

C. The operating climate has changed: "We are a cosmopolitan company now." There is a great emphasis on management training and development. "Each year we send a number of our executives to Harvard Business School—and other places. We also conduct in-house advanced management courses with faculty drawn from various schools."

D. There is more open communication between management and employees. "We publish 26 separate newsletters in different locations where none existed ten years ago. Moreover, these newsletters came about at the request of employees."

E. Bethlehem has always encouraged its executives and employees to be active in the civic affairs in the community where they live and work. However, because of its sheer size, the company often tends to be a large part of the community where its operations are located. "Therefore, we have to tread a very fine line for fear that we may be accused of dominating the town's life. For example, in one town, the company applied for a re-zoning permit before the local Planning Board. One of the members of the Planning Board was a Bethlehem Steel executive. The Planning Board voted 2–1 in favor of the Company, with one of the two favorable votes cast by a Bethlehem Steel employee. We believe that in casting the favorable vote, the Bethlehem employee acted as a private citizen and not as a Bethlehem employee. Furthermore, our view toward his vote would not have changed had his vote gone against the Company."

F. Bethlehem's written policy defining areas of conflict of interest does not precisely cover the Woodroofe case. However, in most cases conflict situations are pretty clear. "In gray areas we tend to be conservative, i.e., when in doubt, even a possible or potential conflict of interest situation should be avoided."

G. The company has instituted wide-ranging programs in minority and female hiring and purchasing from minority vendors, and has even gone to the extent of developing minority suppliers and helping them to set up facilities to supply the company.

H. Bethlehem has taken vigorous steps to eliminate job discrimination based on race, sex, and age. Any infractions of company policies are swiftly punished and corrections made.

SELECTED REFERENCES

ADELL, B. L., "Labour Law—Collective Agreement—Right of Individual Employee to Sue Employer," *Canadian Bar Review,* 45 (May 1967), 354.

ALBERTS, DAVID S., and JOHN MARSHALL DAVIS, "Decision-Making Criteria for Environmental Protection and Control," paper presented at the 12th American Meeting of the Institute of Management Science, Detroit, October 1971.

ATLESON, JAMES B., "A Union Member's Right of Free Speech and Assembly: Institutional Interests and Individual Rights," *Minnesota Law Review,* 51 (1967), 403–90.

BACKRACH, PETER, "Corporate Authority and Democratic Theory," in *Political Theory and Social Change,* ed. David Spitz (New York: Atherton Press, 1967), pp. 257–73.

BLADES, LAWRENCE E., "Employment at Will vs. Individual Freedom: On Limiting the Abusive Exercise of Employer Power," *Columbia Law Review,* 67, 140 (1967), 1404–35.

BLUMBERG, PHILLIP I., "Corporate Responsibility and the Employee's Duty of Loyalty and Obedience: A Preliminary Inquiry," *Oklahoma Law Review,* August 1971, pp. 270–318.

BRUFF, HAROLD H., "Unconstitutional Conditions upon Public Employment: New Departures in the Protection of First Amendment," *Hastings Law Journal,* 21 (November 1969), 129–73.

BUCKLEY, DONALD H., "Political Rights of Government Employees," *Cleveland State Law Review,* 19 (September 1970), 568–78.

"Constitutional Law—Freedom of Speech—Statute Prohibiting Political Activity by Public Employees Held Unconstitutional for Over-breadth," *New York University Law Review,* 42 (October 1967), 750–55.

"Constitutional Law—Public Employees—'Freedom of Association' Guarantees the Right to Unionize But Not the Right to Bargain Collectively," *Tulane Law Review,* 44 (April 1970), 568–75.

"Corporations—Liability of Employees—Corporations May Seek Indemnity for Civil or for Criminal Liability Incurred by Employee's Violation of Antitrust Law Without Corporation's Knowledge or Consent," *Harvard Law Review,* 83 (February 1970), 943–50.

CREECH, W. A., "Privacy of Public Employees," *Law and Contemporary Problems,* 31, 2 (spring 1966), 413–35.

"Discharge from Private Employment on Ground of Political Views or Conduct," *American Law Reports,* Annotated, 51 (1957), 742–62.

"Dismissals of Public Employees for Petitioning Congress: Administrative Discipline and 5 U.S.C. Section 652 (d)," *Yale Law Journal,* 74 (May 1965), 1156.

FITZGERALD, A. ERNEST, *The High Priests of Waste* (New York: Norton, 1972).

FRIEDMANN, WOLFGANG, "Corporate Power, Government by Private Groups, and the Law," *Columbia Law Review* (1957).

"The First Amendment and Public Employees," *Georgetown Law Journal,* 57 (1968), 134–61.

HENNER, SIONAG M., "California's Controls on Employer Abuse of Employee Political Rights," *Stanford Law Review,* 22 (May 1970), 1015–58.

INGRAM, TIMOTHY, "On Muckrakers and Whistle Blowers," *Business and Society Review,* autumn 1972, pp. 21–30.

KUHN, JAMES, and IVAR BERG, *Values in a Business Society* (New York: Harcourt, Brace & World, 1968)

MASON, EDWARD S., *The Corporation in Modern Society* (New York: Atheneum, 1966).

NADER, RALPH, PETER J. PETKAS, and KATE BLACKWELL, eds., *Whistle Blowing, the Report of the Conference on Professional Responsibility* (New York: Grossman, 1972).

PETERS, CHARLES, and TAYLOR BRANCH, *Blowing the Whistle: Dissent in the Public Interest* (New York: Praeger, 1972).

"Political Activity and the Public Employee: A Sufficient Cause for Dismissal?" *Northwestern University Law Review,* November–December 1969, pp. 636–49.

"Professional Associations and the Right to Free Expression: Constitutional Limitations on Control of Members," *Firestone* v. *District Dental Society* (New York, 1969), *Georgetown Law Journal,* 58 (1970), 646–56.

REICH, CHARLES A., "The New Property," *Yale Law Journal,* 73 (April 1964).

———, "Individual Rights and Social Welfare: The Emerging Social Issues," *Yale Law Journal,* 74 (June 1965), 1245–57.

"Restraint of Individual Liberty in Contracts of Employment," *McGill Law Journal,* 13 (1967), 521.

SAYLES, LEONARD R., *Individualism and Big Business* (New York: McGraw-Hill, 1963).

SCHWARTZ, LOUIS B., "Institutional Size and Individual Liberty: Authoritarian Aspects of Business," *Northwestern University Law Review,* March–April 1960, pp. 4–20.

TROBINER, MATTHER O., and JOSEPH R. GRODIN, "The Individual and the Public Service Enterprise in the New Industrial State," *California Law Review,* 55 (November 1967), 1247–83.

WALTERS, KENNETH A., "Your Employee's Right to Blow the Whistle," *Harvard Business Review,* July–August, 1975.

WALTERS, KENNETH DALE, "Freedom of Speech in Modern Corporations." Unpublished doctoral dissertation, University of California, Berkeley, 1972.

Corporations and the Citizen-At-Large

GENERAL MOTORS' NADIR, RALPH NADER

CORPORATE ECONOMIC INTERESTS
AND ENCROACHMENT ON AN INDIVIDUAL'S PRIVACY

> When a trout rising to a fly gets hooked on a line and finds himself unable to swim freely, he begins with a fight, which results in struggles and splashes and sometimes an escape. Often, of course, the situation is too tough for him.
>
> In the same way the human being struggles with his environment and the hooks that catch him. Sometimes he masters his difficulties, sometimes they are too much for him. His struggles are all that the world sees and it naturally misunderstands them. It is hard for a free fish to understand what is happening to a hooked one.
>
> —KARL A. MENNINGER

An emotionally publicized business-society controversy reached its finale on August 13, 1970, when General Motors settled out of court for $425,000 Ralph Nader's $26 million invasion-of-privacy suit against it. Nader made no personal gain—the award went to the cause of auto safety and, after deducting legal fees and expenses, was to be used to establish a "continuous legal monitoring of General Motors' activities in the safety, pollution, and consumer relations area." [1] Because the case now lies in the realm of well-documented history, there is scant reason to detail all its ramifications here. Nonetheless, the high points of these cloak-and-dagger polemics are worth relating briefly. One man, committed to the

---

[1] *The Wall Street Journal,* August 14, 1970, p. 4.

cause of the consumer, the public interest in general, and automobile safety in particular, had successfully stood his ground against the forces and resources of the world's largest corporation.

In Ralph Nader's book, *Unsafe at Any Speed*, published on the last day of November 1965, he called attention to Detroit's carelessness with public safety and singled out for specific emphasis General Motor's safety defects in their early Corvairs. Within weeks of publication, Nader was testifying about traffic and automotive safety on both local and national witness stands, first in Des Moines, Iowa, before the state attorney general, then on February 19, 1966, and subsequently before the Senate's subcommittee on auto safety. As his testimony began to pile up statistics damning to the automobile industry and General Motors in particular, his purported harassment began. It soon increased. (The entire account of the undercover investigation of Ralph Nader, which reads like a fiction thriller, is worth perusing.[2])

At first someone followed him. Then came annoying and unidentified calls on his unlisted telephone, many in the small hours of the night before he was to testify before Senator Ribicoff's auto safety subcommittee. According to Ridgeway's account in "The Dick," ". . . on the evening of February 9, when he was trying to put the finishing touches on a prepared statement, Nader got half-a-dozen phone calls. A voice would say, 'Mr. Nader, this is Pan American,' and then hang up. Or, 'Mr. Nader, please pick up the parcel at Railway Express.' And finally, 'Why don't you go back to Connecticut, buddy-boy.' "

His friends and associates, even his landlady, were quizzed about everything from his political affiliations to his promptness in paying bills, to his racial feelings (with emphasis on any possible anti-Semitism) to his sex life—no facet of Nader's habits and actions was outside the scope of the investigation. Girls he knew scarcely or not at all suddenly asked him to their apartments to discuss foreign affairs or to help move furniture. Two men followed him from an airport. His old law school friend, Frederick Condon, was asked questions by an investigator supposedly representing a client who was thinking of hiring Nader. Other friends and associates were asked all kinds of questions by investigators from different agencies.[3] Nader's conviction grew that he was being checked out thoroughly for the purpose of discrediting him as a witness. As the harassment intensified, his suspicions focused on the automobile industry he had attacked so tellingly.

---

[2] Among the accounts detailing the investigation of Mr. Nader's character are the following: James Ridgeway, "The Dick," *New Republic,* March 12, 1966, pp. 11–13; Elizabeth Brenner Drew, "The Politics of Auto Safety," *Atlantic,* October 1966, p. 95. *Newsweek:* "The Nader Caper," March 21, 1966, p. 83; "Meet Ralph Nader, Everyman's Lobbyist and His Consumer Crusader," January 22, 1968, pp. 65–73. *The New York Times:* "Critic of Auto Industry's Safety Standards Says He Was Tailed and Harassed: Charges Called Absurd," March 6, 1966, p. 94; "Investigation Asked," March 9, 1966, p. 38; "Ribicoff Summons GM on Its Inquiry of Critic," March 11, 1966, p. 18.
[3] *The New York Times,* March 11, 1966, p. 18.

ISSUES FOR ANALYSIS

This case offers two major areas for analysis and exploration: specific issues relating to the behavior of General Motors, and broader questions of public interest in the face of corporate power.

With regard to General Motors, to what extent is a corporation, and especially its chief executive, responsible for the actions of all its employees? Once this is agreed upon, we can then make judgments about the morality of these actions. An analysis of GM's actions leading to an investigation of Ralph Nader and pursuant to the disclosure of such an investigation should be useful in understanding the motives and workings of large bureaucracies—private and public. As the case study will show, GM's behavior can be traced to the legal department's freedom of action and lack of accountability, GM's tradition of unconcern about anything but economic efficiency, the attitude of its top officials, and finally, to the organizational structure of the company.

One question of broad public interest is the government's role in investigating and controlling corporate behavior when it conflicts with individual rights. There were a number of "loose ends" in GM's explanation of its investigation. Did Ribicoff's subcommittee or the Justice Department have the responsibility to pursue them fully? Perhaps the most important issues of the case involve invasion of privacy and corporate responsibility. What constitutes an individual's privacy? Does an individual have a legally recognized right to this privacy? Also, are corporations responsible for their behavior? If so, how can this responsibility be enforced?

RESPONSE BY THE AUTOMOBILE COMPANIES

After Ford, Chrysler, and American Motors executives had denied any knowledge of or connection with the investigation or harassment, suddenly and belatedly, General Motors admitted that its legal department had instigated the search (without the knowledge or approval of James Roche, president of the corporation). The GM admission of responsibility had been ordered personally by Roche, who had not learned of GM's involvement until late the previous day and who was hard at work on the press release as the Ford, Chrysler, and American Motors denials were being published. Nonetheless, although Roche admitted GM's responsibility for instigating the investigation, he did not admit any GM responsibility for the incidents or harassment mentioned in newspaper stories:

Following the publication of Mr. Ralph Nader's criticisms of the Corvair in writings and public appearances in support of his book

. . . the office of its general counsel initiated a routine investigation through a reputable law firm to determine whether Ralph Nader was acting on behalf of litigants or their attorneys in Corvair design cases pending against General Motors. The investigation was prompted by Mr. Nader's extreme criticisms of the Corvair. . . . Mr. Nader's statements coincided with similar publicity by some attorneys handling such litigation. . . .

The investigation was limited only to Mr. Nader's qualifications, background, expertise and association with such attorneys. It did not include any of the alleged harassment or intimidation recently reported in the press. If Mr. Nader had been subjected to any of the incidents and harassment mentioned by him in newspaper stories, such incidents were in no way associated with General Motors' legitimate investigation of his interest in pending litigation.

At General Motors' invitation, Mr. Nader spent a day at the GM Technical Center . . . early in January visiting with General Motors executives and engineers. . . .

Mr. Nader expressed appreciation for the courtesy in providing him with detailed information, but he nevertheless continued the same line of attack on the design of the Corvair. . . . This behavior lends support to General Motors' belief that there is a connection between Mr. Nader and Plaintiff's counsel in pending Corvair design litigation.[4]

Nader told *The New York Times* that he had not represented clients involved in Corvair litigations. A number of lawyers had asked him for Corvair information, but he had never been paid for it and had left his law practice "to pursue the cause of safer designed automobiles for the motoring public." Therefore, he asked GM to admit that it could not have evidence linking him with the Corvair lawyers.[5] GM implied in a *New York Times* story [6] that it could prove the case against Nader and that the proof would be presented before the Ribicoff committee.

THE HEARING

Senator Ribicoff said he would invite Roche, Nader, and the private detectives to testify before his auto safety subcommittee on March 22:

I have not discussed this matter with any of the parties concerned,

---

4 U.S. Congress, Senate, "Federal Role in Traffic Safety," *Hearings Before the Subcommittee on Executive Reorganization of the Committee on Government Operations,* 89th Cong., 2d sess., March 22, 1966. Henceforth cited parenthetically by page numbers within the text.
5 "GM Acknowledges Investigating Critic," *The New York Times,* March 10, 1966, p. 1.
6 *The New York Times,* March 11, 1966, p. 18.

but I suggest that they come before the committee to discuss the entire matter.

The safety of the American driving public is the basic issue before the committee. To this must now be added the additional issue of a witness's right to testify before a committee of the United States Congress without fear of character assassination or intimidation.[7]

On March 22, thereupon, Senator Ribicoff conducted hearings into the investigation of Nader and, in spite of the confidence GM had displayed earlier, the only case it proved was Nader's. According to *Newsweek:*

> The scene had all the fascination of a public whipping, and the huge old Caucus Room of the Senate Office Building was appropriately jammed with reporters, cameramen, television crews and Washington citizens. In the seats of power, ranged against a white marble wall, were a tribunal of Sen. Abraham Ribicoff's traffic-safety subcommittee. At the witness table was the president of the world's largest manufacturing company.[8]

In his role as a witness, Nader made a great impression on the members of the subcommittee. According to one staff member, Nader "was a Congressional staffer's dream. . . . Nader wasn't selling anything . . . [and] he had the data—the names and phone numbers to substantiate everything." [9]

At issue was more than the discomfort and invaded privacy of a single human being. That one human being had taken up the common cause of society as it was influenced, capriciously and dangerously as he saw it, by big business. More than that, he was testifying before Senator Ribicoff's subcommittee, and federal laws provide penalties of up to five years in jail and a $5,000 fine for apparent attempts to harass or intimidate government witnesses. Thus the federal government had an interest in Nader's allegations that he was being badgered and in exposing the basis of whatever investigation had been undertaken.

Therefore, on March 8 Senators Gaylord Nelson (D, Wis.) and Abraham Ribicoff (D, Conn.) asked the Justice Department to look into Nader's being "investigated by private detectives" and the late telephone calls since his appearance before a Senate hearing. Nader was scheduled to appear before the subcommittee again and Nelson said that "the clear implication of everything reported so far is that the automobile industry has hired at least three different firms of private detectives to shadow and investigate . . . a witness before a Congressional committee." [10]

When Ribicoff convened the March 22 committee meeting, his opening words were stern:

7 *Ibid.*
8 "Private Eyes and Public Hearings," *Newsweek,* April 4, 1966, pp. 77–78.
9 *Newsweek,* January 22, 1968, p. 65.
10 "Investigation Asked," *The New York Times,* March 9, 1966, p. 38.

There is no law which bars a corporation from hiring detectives to investigate a private citizen, however distasteful the idea may seem to some of us. There is a law, however, which makes it a crime to harass or intimidate a witness before a congressional committee.

. . . [the] right to testify freely without fear of intimidation is one of the cornerstones of a free and democratic society. Any attempt to jeopardize this right is a serious matter.

I have called this special meeting today to look into the circumstances surrounding what appeared to be an attempt by General Motors Corp. to discredit Mr. Ralph Nader, a recent witness before the subcommittee. . . . [GM] has admitted responsibility for undertaking a determined and exhaustive investigation of a private citizen who has criticized the auto industry verbally and in print. (p. 1380)

GM'S POSITION

Mr. Roche said that the investigation was initiated before Nader became a congressional witness, that it was wholly unrelated to the proceedings of the subcommittee and Mr. Nader's connections with them (p. 1382), and that no "derogatory information of any kind along any of these lines turned up in this investigation" (p. 1383).

In his testimony Roche emphasized that GM had the legal right and duty to protect its stockholders' interests by making an investigation within the framework of three points:

First, to ascertain whether any actions for libel . . . should be instituted against members of the bar (including Mr. Nader) who publicly discussed pending or anticipated litigation; *second,* to ascertain whether any witness, or author of any book or article which might be offered as evidence in any court (including Mr. Nader) was entitled to the legal definition of "expert"; and *third,* to ascertain whether [these individuals] . . . show bias, lack of reliability or credibility, [or] . . . if . . . they had a self interest in the litigation or had been attempting deliberately to influence public opinion. (p. 1384)

These three points were augmented by several members of GM's legal staff who in their testimony before the subcommittee explained in greater detail the necessity GM felt to investigate Nader.

Aloysius Power, GM's general counsel, held that pretrial investigation was crucial if GM were to fight effectively the more than one hundred suits alleging injuries arising from Corvair failures due to basic design defects. It was essential that GM know the validity of Nader's claim to be an "expert," since expert testimony was vital in such cases.

INVESTIGATION STORY: GM'S VERSION

General Motors introduced its rear-engine compact car, the Corvair, in the fall of 1959, and by the time *Unsafe at Any Speed* was published in November 1965 the company was plagued with suits alleging Corvair-attributable injuries. Although GM had won two Corvair design suits, it settled another out of court (without admitting legal liability) because the jury's emotions had been aroused by gruesome photographs of the plaintiff's injury (pp. 1509–10).[11] This settlement further aggravated the situation, as it was heralded in various news media "as a victory for the plaintiffs" (p. 1408). It was followed by a flood of letters from Corvair owners and GM stockholders. Thus the company became apprehensive that "false" publicity might adversely influence future cases.

By 1962 various attorneys and law firms (many of whom were handling Corvair cases) began exchanging information, and by 1965 they were speaking publicly about Corvair's design defects. In June and July 1965 Thomas F. Lambert, Jr., of ATLA (American Trial Lawyers' Association) suggested to those seeking more information about Corvair design that they contact a then-unknown Ralph Nader:

> We also suggest that you write to Ralph Nader, . . . Winsted, Connecticut. Ralph is a lawyer who has developed expertise in the area of automobile manufacturers' liability. Ralph has a substantial amount of information on the Corvair. (p. 1416)

According to Aloysius Power, GM wanted to know who the "lawyer" was whom the ATLA editor called by his first name, how he had obtained information on the Corvair, and how he had developed the status of auto safety "expert." Further, had Nader violated Canon 20 of the Canons of Professional Ethics of the American Bar Association, which "condemns public discussion or statement by a lawyer concerning pending or anticipated litigation" (p. 1404)?

On November 18, 1965, GM's legal department asked its product liability insurer, the Royal-Globe Insurance Company, if it had ever employed any private investigators in Connecticut who might have looked into Nader's qualifications. Although Royal-Globe had not, it commissioned a Mr. O'Neill of Hartford, Connecticut, to "obtain whatever information he could with respect to [Nader's] qualifications and whether or not he was a trial lawyer in Winsted, Conn." The report stated that Nader had only briefly practiced law in Hartford, that his family lived in nearby Winsted, and that he might be in Washington, D.C., although

---

11 Ralph Nader's version of the reason GM settled is somewhat different from the company's version. GM discontinued the manufacture of the Corvair in May 1969. "The Last of the Troubled Corvairs," *San Francisco Chronicle*, May 13, 1969, p. 10.

no legal directory listed him there. No information as to his technical competence was uncovered (p. 1439).

On December 22, 1965, Miss Eileen Murphy, who was working in GM's law library and who had earlier worked in Washington, phoned Richard Danner of Alvord and Alvord, a Washington law firm, to ask if he could recommend a good investigating agency for some "background information" on Nader. Danner in turn called Vincent Gillen, president of Vincent Gillen Associates, Inc., in New York, to ask if he could handle an investigation covering several Eastern states. On January 11, 1965, Miss Murphy came to Washington and gave Danner what little information GM had obtained on Nader, reiterating GM's suspicions but adding that no compelling proof had been found (pp. 1515–16, 1524). According to Counsel Power, Miss Murphy said the investigation should cover these areas:

> Where does Mr. Nader live and where does he practice law if he is practicing? Had he been employed by the Federal Government? What other employment? Where is the source of his income? What were the details of his background that might affect his writings? Especially does he have any engineering background. . . .

> What would account for the absence of objectivity unusual in a lawyer writing about the Corvair? Does he have any connection at all with ATLA or ATLA attorneys? Are there any indications that he might be working as a consultant to lawyers handling Corvair cases against General Motors? (pp. 1440–1516)

According to Danner, however, Miss Murphy also requested "a complete background investigation of Mr. Nader's activities." The instructions given were described by those agents who actually investigated Nader: ". . . our job is to check his life, and current activities to determine 'what makes him tick,' such as his real interest in safety, his supporters, if any, his politics, his marital status, his friends, his women, boys, etc., drinking, dope, jobs—in fact, all facets of his life" (p. 1506).

Since it was necessary to conceal the nature of the investigation and the identity of the client, it was agreed that all information would be collected under the pretext of a preemployment type of inquiry instigated by a company of a prospective employee and that all reports submitted by Gillen's agency were to be sent to Danner for transmittal to GM (pp. 1440–42, 1516, 1524). Gillen told Danner that if he were to ask questions about Nader's connection with Corvair cases, his expertise in safety, and his associates in the legal profession:

> . . . the implication would be immediate, the onus would immediately be on General Motors if Nader heard of this, and I tried to dissuade them or told them "Are you prepared for what may happen, because you cannot investigate someone without their hearing about it talking to their friends." I told them right from the beginning.

Danner said, "Don't worry about it." So I did it as gently and discreetly and fairly to Nader as could possibly be done. [p. 1549]

Neither Danner nor Gillen had ever heard of Nader before Miss Murphy brought up his name, neither knew that he had been called to testify, and Gillen averred that had he known, the investigation would never have been initiated. Both Danner and Gillen agreed that Nader was not to be placed under surveillance unless it became absolutely necessary (p. 1517).

On January 17 Senator Ribicoff officially announced that Nader would be a witness at one of the subcommittee hearings on February 10.

On January 20 Gillen requested his Washington associate, D. David Shatraw, president of Arundel Investigative Agency of Severinia Park, Maryland, to investigate Nader, warning him "not to arouse the ire of Nader . . . it is important that interviews be handled with great discretion and under a suitable pretext" (p. 1525).

From January 25 to January 27, Gillen's men conducted their investigation in the Winsted-Hartford, Connecticut, area. Gillen later said that all his men used their own names and identified Gillen as their employer (they didn't know who the real client was). Little was discovered as to Nader's sources of income or activities, so it was decided on January 26 that surveillance would be necessary. Shatraw began his end of the investigation on February 3, which according to Gillen showed that Nader's assertions to the press that he was harassed in January, if true, were not the result of Gillen's or Shatraw's work. One of Shatraw's men called at an address Nader had given many months before to "ascertain if anything was known of Mr. Nader. To his surprise, the landlady said he was rooming there but was not in" (pp. 1525–26).

On Friday, February 4, two Arundel agents began watching Nader, but because of a heavy workload, stopped Saturday morning. At 4 p.m. Sunday, Gillen's own men resumed surveillance in Washington only (p. 1527). Three days later Danner substituted "spot checks" for the unproductive and expensive surveillance. On February 14, GM's Power, ex post facto, ordered the surveillance stopped (pp. 1543–44), and on February 28 instructed Danner to cease the entire investigation. This entire episode, then, had transpired many days before Roche first heard of it. Danner forwarded Gillen's final report to Miss Murphy on March 14. The final note was the bill for the investigation—$6,700 (p. 1539).

According to the testimony given at the hearings, Nader was investigated by various agencies for five or six days in mid-November 1965, and between January 25 and February 28, 1966. People from all walks of life who were even remotely connected with Nader were questioned. Frederick Condon and Thomas F. Lambert, Jr., wrote letters to the subcommittee and gave details of their interviews.

Condon, who had gone to law school with Nader, and to whom *Unsafe at Any Speed* was dedicated, was at that time assistant counsel for the United Life and Accident Insurance Company of Concord, New Hampshire. According to Condon, he suspected that Gillen was investigating

Nader on behalf of some automobile company, not for preemployment. Gillen asked questions slanted toward finding out if Nader was a homosexual. Gillen also inquired if Nader was anti-Semitic because of his "Syrian" ancestry (Nader is of Lebanese descent) or had participated in or belonged to any left-wing organization. Condon thought that Gillen had a tape recorder in his attaché case, as he was taking hardly any notes. Gillen in his testimony, however, denied having any tape recorder with him and gave a different view of his questioning of Condon. Gillen said that the sole purpose of his interview with Condon was to find out if Nader had ever had a driver's license, as official Connecticut records contained conflicting information and no one had ever seen him driving a car (pp. 1521–47).

Thomas F. Lambert, Jr., of ATLA publications, wrote to Senator Ribicoff and described his interview with Mr. Dwyer of "Management Consultants." Gillen said that he had sent Dwyer on the interview. Responding to questions, Lambert told Dwyer of his belief that Nader's writing on unsafe automobile design was the best he knew, suggested that Nader may have served as a consultant to three very able trial lawyers who were working on Corvair cases, and even supplied Dwyer with the three names.

GILLEN'S PRETEXT: WAS IT ETHICAL?

Much of the subcommittee's attention was concerned with the questions asked Nader's friends and associates. A preemployment pretext was used, but the investigators asked questions apparently irrelevant to an automobile manufacturer. Gillen, stoutly defending his investigative technique and denying any unethical practice or moral wrongdoing, said "I submit my integrity to the scrutiny of all" (p. 1532).

Senator Robert F. Kennedy, a member of the subcommittee, questioned Gillen persistently on the use of the preemployment pretext, false names, and personal questions when Nader wasn't really being considered for a job. He was further concerned about harassing Nader. Gillen's position was that the objectives might differ but that investigative methods for either objective were identical and did not constitute harassment. After all, Gillen said, pretexts "are used all the time. I know the government uses pretexts in connection with applicant investigations" (pp. 1519–20).

Gillen maintained that others were also investigating Nader a month before the subcommittee met. He suggested that the subcommittee find out who did vex Nader with phone calls, use girls as sex lures, and follow him in Iowa and Philadelphia. These were the real harassing agents (pp. 1550–51).[12]

Furthermore, our investigation uncovered absolutely no indication

---

[12] *The New York Times,* March 6, 1966, p. 94.

of any abnormality on the part of Ralph Nader. On the contrary, he obviously is an intelligent, personable young man.

The same thing applied to the questions regarding anti-Semitism. Virtually everyone we talked with in Winsted cautioned us not to attribute to Ralph the attitude and obvious feelings of some members of his family. In fairness to Ralph, we had to ask that question of all those with whom he associated during his adult life. I am happy to state that none of the people we interviewed believes Ralph Nader is anti-Semitic. (p. 1532)

The possibility of anti-Semitism was not the only thing Gillen felt it necessary to pursue "in fairness to Ralph." Nader's high school principal showed Gillen's men a yearbook which said, "Ralph Nader—women hater." He said:

Now some people get the wrong impression about Ralph and this stuff. Do not pay any attention to it.

According to Gillen, "There is where it first raised its head and we pursue it in fairness to Ralph." (p. 1549)

"What the hell's this 'fairness to Ralph'? Kennedy barked. You have to keep running around the country proving he's not anti-Semitic or not queer? Ralph's doing all right." [13]

Nader was not the only one to fall under the vast network of Gillen's operatives. Even Senator Ribicoff himself was checked to verify that he had never met Nader before he testified, as some members of GM's legal department thought Ribicoff and Nader had "some fairly close relationships" and they found it difficult to believe Ribicoff's statement that he saw Nader for the first time on February 10, 1966. Thus, Gillen was told to investigate the senator's "credibility." In fact, when Gillen visited Detroit before the hearings, a GM lawyer "attempted to convince" him that he should deny any charges of investigating Ribicoff.[14]

GENERAL MOTORS' MARCH 9 PRESS RELEASE: WAS IT DELIBERATELY MISLEADING?

Another issue raised by the subcommittee hearing was the statement released by General Motors on March 9, in which the company admitted responsibility for an investigation limited to Mr. Nader's qualifications, background, expertise in car safety, and possible association with those handling Corvair cases against GM. Senator Kennedy, however, maintained that GM denied things that they were indeed responsible for and the statement "misled and in fact, was really, I might say, false" (p. 1398).

[13] *Newsweek*, April 4, 1966, pp. 77–78.
[14] *Ibid.*

In New York on March 6 Roche saw the *New York Times* article describing Gillen's admission of the investigation. He called his legal department to ask them to deny any GM involvement. It was then he first learned of GM's responsibility. Immediately he flew back to Detroit and with his legal staff—minus Power who was out of town—hammered out the now-famous press release. After hearing the draft read over the telephone, Power, who had ordered the investigation and received the reports, made no objection. It was left to Roche to admit to the subcommittee that the statement might be somewhat misleading and that he had subsequently learned a great deal about the investigation of Nader: ". . . were I writing this statement, this press release, today, I think it would be in different language" (p. 1392).

Senator Kennedy, far from satisfied, thought it "terribly serious . . . that General Motors permitted this statement to go out on March 9 which so misled the general public and misled members of Congress and the press of the United States . . ." (pp. 1399–1400). He relentlessly pursued his line of questioning with both General Counsel Power and Assistant Counsel Louis H. Bridenstine, finally getting Power to admit that GM was wrong in having Nader followed and that maybe GM should have added after "initiate a routine investigation" the words "which developed into an intensive investigation" (p. 1453). Bridenstine held that the purpose of the statement was to admit GM's initiating an investigation but to disclaim instances reported by the press for which GM was *not* responsible (pp. 1457–60). When pressed by Senator Kennedy, however, he said ". . . if it will help us any, I will agree that it was misleading, but I will say it wasn't intended as such" (p. 1460).

Significantly, neither Power nor Bridenstine had had time to read Gillen's reports carefully. Thus, the staff members at GM who initiated the investigation and who were responsible for it were not aware of its extent. The first report Gillen sent to GM via Danner stating that surveillance had taken place was on March 3. Power had heard about it on February 14, some eight days after it started, and ordered it stopped, but by then it was too late. But the very first report sent to GM, received midway during the surveillance, mentioned the possibility of surveillance as per Gillen and Danner's discussion, yet GM took no immediate action (pp. 1446, 1449, 1463).

Senator Ribicoff was curious why GM couldn't hire its own investigative agency directly. Danner, who had never handled investigative work before (p. 1518), was an intermediary in the truest sense—he was the connecting pipeline through which Miss Murphy and Gillen exchanged requests and reports. Gillen's reports were certainly detailed, but no one high in GM's legal hierarchy read them carefully. The multiplicity of links between Gillen and Roche made for an enormous gap of ignorance (p. 1521).

**THE ISSUE OF INDIVIDUAL PRIVACY
VS. CORPORATE POWER: NADER'S POSITION**

The price paid for an environment that required an act of courage for a statement of truth has been needless death, needless injury and inestimable sorrow.

How much has this Nation lost because there are men walking around today with invisible chains?

The trademark of modern society may be the organization, but its inspiring and elevating contributions still flow from individual initiatives. Unless multiple sources of initiative and expression are kept open and asserted, the creative and humanizing infusions of a peoples' energies will atrophy.

Yet in a confrontation between an individual and a corporate organization, between myself and General Motors, if you will, the systematic immunities accrue to the corporation which has outstripped the law that created it. This problem of legal control over corporate action is one of increasing interest to a number of legal and economic scholars. I am responsible for my actions, but who is responsible for those of General Motors? An individual's capital is basically his integrity. He can lose only once. A corporation can lose many times, and not be affected. This unequal contest between the individual and any complex organization, whether it is a corporation, a union, government, or other group, is something which bears the closest scrutiny in order to try to protect the individual from such invasions.

The requirement of a just social order is that responsibility shall lie where the power of decision rests. But the law has never caught up with the development of the large corporate unit. Deliberate acts emanate from the sprawling and indeterminable shelter of the corporate organization. Too often the responsibility for an act is not imputable to those whose decisions enable it to be set in motion. The president of General Motors can say he did not know of the specific decision to launch such an investigation. But is he not responsible in some way for the general corporate policy which permits such investigations to be launched by lower-level management without proper guidelines? The office of the general counsel can put forth a document outlining the limits of a "routine" investigation merely to protect the interest of the company's shareholders. A second shield in front of the corporate shield comes in the form of a law firm commissioned in the nonlegal task of hiring a private detective agency. In this case, apparently, GM did not wish to hire agents directly. The enthusiasms of their detectives, the law firm would have us believe, were unauthorized frolics and detours. Besides, the law firm could assume responsibility in the last analysis since there was little burden to such an assumption. Aside from the Federal statute under which this subcommittee is proceeding in this matter, there are few sanctions to protect the principle of privacy in American society against such new challenges largely unforeseen by the Founding Fathers. (pp. 1466–67)

Nader said the investigation was indeed a harassment, to his family and to himself, for it sought "to obtain lurid details and grist for invidious use," [15] and

It certainly took up a lot of my time and concern, and particularly concern over where was it going to end. One can possibly take harassing phone calls. One can take surveillance. But what is quite intolerable is the probings and what possibly might be done with these probings. One never has a chance to confront the adversary in a sense. It is faceless, it is insidious, and individuals, not only myself, can be destroyed in this manner, quite apart from discomfort. And so I was quite fearful of what was going to be the end of this. How was this information going to be used, and whether there was going to be even more overt foul play, perhaps of a physical nature.

I am not particularly sensitive to criticism at all. In fact, I probably have an armor like a turtle when it comes to that. I like to give and take. As an attorney, one is used to it. I don't intimidate easily, but I must confess that one begins to have second thoughts of the penalties and the pain which must be incurred in working in this area.

I think the thing that has persuaded me to continue in this area is that I cannot accept a climate in this country where one has to have an ascetic existence and steely determination in order to speak truthfully, candidly, and critically of American industry, and the auto industry. I think if it takes that much stamina, something is wrong with the enabling climate for expression in our country. I don't think it is generally wrong, but I think that we need to look into these areas and see how we can continually improve this climate. And it goes way beyond ideological considerations. This is not an ideological problem. This is a problem of individuals confronting complex organizations, whether they are complex organizations in the United States—corporations, labor unions or what not— or whether they are complex organizations in other countries of the world. (p. 1512)

The complex organization need not have the upper hand against the individual, Nader said. Improvement of public education in this regard

[15] "GM Apologizes for Harassment of Critic," *The New York Times,* March 23, 1966, p. 1.

can become "a built-in check" against invasion of privacy. According to Nader, protection of privacy involves social sanctions as well as legal penalties so that

> when somebody comes in and probes, and just flashes a badge without even showing it, people don't surrender and say, "I'll tell you everything." They will say, "Who are you? Who do you represent? Who is your client? Why are you asking these questions? What is your name? What is your detective serial number?" I am amazed how many people in this country are in a sense subtly restrained from that, as if they had better talk. (p. 1513)

Glancing at the thick sheaf of detective reports, Ribicoff told Nader, "You and your family can be proud. They have put you through the mill and they haven't found a damn thing wrong with you" (p. 1513).

Nader stated that he did not represent clients involved in Corvair design suits or work for their attorneys. Nader in fact had said this to GM executives when he visited the Technical Center in January; apparently, involvement would have prohibited his seeing certain Corvair technical exhibits at the center. According to Nader, Bridenstine had indicated that he believed what Nader said. That GM's actions proved they did not take him at his word only demonstrated to Nader that

> General Motors' executives continue to be blinded by their own corporate mirror-image that it's "the buck" that moves the man. They simply cannot understand that the prevention of cruelty to humans can be a sufficient motivation for one endeavoring to obtain the manufacture of safer cars. (p. 1469)

Nader added that contrary to Roche's earlier statement, he was "singularly unimpressed" at GM's presentation, which included an "outrageously erroneous assertion" and "evasive responses" (p. 1469).

As for the similarity of his writings and plaintiff's language in design cases, Nader said these resulted from "a common design defect" in the cars. Indeed, some of Nader's material came directly from GM's patents and trade journals! (p. 1507).

THE CASE IN RETROSPECT

Despite Nader's tormenting by the investigation and hearings, Ribicoff said he could not help "but feel that what this hearing has achieved will have a salutary effect on business ethics and also the protection of the individual" (p. 1513).   Kennedy felt that Roche had raised his stature by appearing (p. 1564). Perhaps the most important results of the hearings were the auto safety laws. Kennedy said that were it not for

Nader and Ribicoff, Congress would not even have considered an auto safety law (p. 1515).

According to the *Atlantic,* the March 22 hearings

> did as much as anything to bring on federal safety standards. One Senator said, "Everybody was so outraged that a great corporation was out to clobber a guy because he wrote critically of them. At that point everybody said what the hell with them." Another Capitol Hill man said, "When they started looking in Ralph's bedroom, we all figured they must really be nervous. We began to believe that Nader must be right." [16]

Although the Justice Department decided that "criminal prosecution is not warranted in this matter" (p. 1591), in November 1966 Nader filed his $26 million invasion-of-privacy suit in the Manhattan State Supreme Court of New York, this suit resulting in the out-of-court settlement award of $425,000. Nader said the suit was brought to "remedy a wrong inflicted upon one individual and the public interest, in the freedom to speak out against consumer hazards."

As for Nader personally and his credibility as a consumer advocate, the hearings made him front-page material, the underdog miraculously defeating the giant of the automotive industry. According to *Newsweek,* "After his confrontation with GM, Nader's public image was more like that of a knight in shining armor." One auto man grumbled, "If GM hadn't beatified him, where would he be today?" [17]

SELECTED REFERENCES

INGRAM, TIMOTHY, "On Muckrakers and Whistleblowers," *Business and Society Review,* Autumn 1972, pp. 21–30.

MILLER, ROGER LeROY, "The Nader Files: An Economic Critique," paper presented at the Conference on Government Policy and the Consumer, Center for Research in Government Policy and Business, October 27–28, 1972.

PETERS and BRANCH, *Blowing the Whistle: Dissent in the Public Interest* (New York: Praeger, 1972).

SCHWARTZ, LOUIS, "Institutional Size and Individual Liberty: Authoritarian Aspects of Bigness," *Northwestern University Law Review* (March–April 1960) pp. 4–20.

WALTERS, K., "Your Employees' Right To Blow the Whistle," *Harvard Business Review,* (July–August 1975) pp. 26–35.

U.S. Congress, Senate, *Federal Role in Traffic Safety, Hearings Before the Subcommittee on Executive Reorganization of the Committee on Government Operations,* 89th Cong., 2nd sess., March 22, 1966.

[16] Drew, "The Politics of Auto Safety," p. 99.
[17] *Newsweek,* January 22, 1968, pp. 65–66.

Corporations and
the Consumer

STEVENS VERSUS PARKE, DAVIS & COMPANY, AND A. J. BELAND, M.D.

AN EVALUATION OF PRESCRIPTION DRUG PROMOTION AND DISTRIBUTION PRACTICES— ETHICAL AND SOCIETAL IMPLICATIONS

The record of chloramphenicol production, promotion and prescribing is one compounded in part from complacency, laziness, stupidity, carelessness, deceit, and greed. It likewise poses questions that must be answered by physicians. Why did all the efforts of the AMA, the National Research Council, the FDA, and even the courts fail for almost two decades, and why did the promotional strategy of the drug company succeed?

—Dr. Harry Dowling, one of the
leading experts in the United
States in the field of infectious
diseases 1

Reprinted from S. Prakash Sethi, *Images and Products: Marketing, Institutional Advertising, and Public Interest* (Santa Barbara, Calif.: Wiley/Hamilton, 1976). Copyright © 1976 by John Wiley & Sons, Inc., New York. Used by permission.
   The author is grateful to Mr. Robert L. Charbonneau of the law firm of Harney, Ford, Charbonneau & Bambic, Los Angeles, California, attorneys for the plaintiffs, for generously providing material which assisted in the preparation of this case study. The attorneys for defendant Dr. A. J. Beland—Ball, Hunt, Hart, Brown, and Baerwitz of Long Beach, California—also furnished relevant material and their assistance is appreciated. Parke, Davis & Company supplied some supporting material useful to the study.
1 Dr. Dowling is professor emeritus of medicine at the University of Illinois and former chairman of the AMA Council on Drugs.

On March 14, 1973, the California Supreme Court upheld a jury verdict of $400,000 against Parke, Davis & Company and Dr. A. J. Beland. This was one of the largest such awards in similar cases in the United States. The award for damages was made because of the wrongful death of Mrs. Phyllis Stevens. Her death was the result of using Chloromycetin,[2] a brand name antibiotic manufactured by Parke, Davis & Company and prescribed for Mrs. Stevens by Dr. A. J. Beland, her physician. The Supreme Court held that Parke, Davis & Company was guilty of so over-promoting the drug as to induce physicians to prescribe it more widely than should be warranted in terms of sound medical practice (and also to minimize, if not ignore, the dangerous side effects arising from the usage of such drugs).[3]

ISSUES FOR DISCUSSION AND ANALYSIS

This case raises some important issues relating to the practice of medicine in the United States, the nature of the pharmaceutical industry, and the role of various regulatory bodies in providing adequate safeguards. A careful analysis of the circumstances surrounding the case, the facts as

[2] Chloromycetin is the trade name for chloramphenicol. It is a wide-spectrum antibiotic, i.e., an antibiotic that kills or stops the growth of a great number of different disease-causing organisms.

[3] The narrative in this case study is primarily derived from the following legal briefs and court decisions. Rather than cite them repeatedly, each source is identified by a letter and followed by a page number. The sources are as follows:

(A)   *Stevens et al.* v. *Parke, Davis & Co. et al.,* Ca. 2d App. Dist. 2 Civil 38475. Opening Brief of Appellants (Stevens), June 1971.

(B)   *Stevens et al.* v. *Parke, Davis & Co. et al.,* Ca. 2d App. Dist. 2 Civil 38475. Respondent's Reply Brief (Parke-Davis), September 1971.

(C)   *Stevens et al.* v. *Parke, Davis & Co. et al.,* Ca. 2d App. Dist. 2 Civil 38475. Opening Brief of Appellants (Parke-Davis), September 1971.

(D)   *Stevens et al.* v. *Parke, Davis & Co. et al.,* Ca. 2d App. Dist. 2 Civil 38475. Reply Brief of Respondent (Beland), December 1971.

(E)   *Stevens et al.* v. *Parke, Davis & Co. et al.,* Ca. 2d App. Dist. 2 Civil 38475. Closing Brief of Appellants (Stevens), January 1972.

(F)   *Stevens et al.* v. *Parke, Davis & Co. et al.,* Ca. 2d App. Dist. 2 Civil 38475. Brief of Respondents (Stevens), January 1972.

(G)   *Stevens et al.* v. *Parke, Davis & Co. et al.,* Ca. 2d App. Dist. 2 Civil 38475. Reply Brief of Appellants (Parke-Davis), March 1972.

(H)   *Stevens et al.* v. *Parke, Davis & Co. et al.,* Ca. 2d App. Dist. 2 Civil 38475. Court of Appeal Decision, March 1972.

(I)   *Stevens et al.* v. *Parke, Davis & Co. et al.,* Ca. 2d App. Dist. 2 Civil 38475. Petition for Rehearing (Stevens), April 1972.

(J)   *Stevens et al.* v. *Parke, Davis & Co. et al.,* Ca. 2d App. Dist. 2 Civil 38475. Answer to Petition for Rehearing (Beland), April 1972.

(K)   *Stevens et al.* v. *Parke, Davis & Co. et al.,* 9 Cal. 3d 51 (1973). Petition for Hearing in Supreme Court (Beland), May 1972.

(L)   *Stevens et al.* v. *Parke, Davis & Co. et al.,* 9 Cal. 3d (1973). Answer to Petition for Hearing in Supreme Court (Beland), May 1972.

(M)   *Stevens et al.* v. *Parke, Davis & Co. et al.,* 9 Cal. 3d 51 (1973). Supreme Court Decision, March 1973.

determined by the courts, and the decisions of the court can help us in understanding the nature and magnitude of the conflicts that arise between the individual and the corporation, between a corporation's desire to increase its profits and society's expectations for a high level of ethical standards of performance, especially where an individual's health and safety are at stake. The case may also be used to study the effectiveness of various control mechanisms, e.g., the marketplace, self-regulation, and regulatory agencies, in safeguarding the public interest.

The questions related to Parke, Davis's liability go beyond the legal considerations in the California Supreme Court decision. While it is not intended here to question the Court's decision, we must analyze what behavior should be expected of a company beyond the strict governmental regulation, existing market constraints, and in terms of controlling the behavior of persons over which it may have only partial control or no control at all. For example:

1. Was Parke, Davis negligent in preparing or using the material that described the drug in 1964? Did the company, by its actions, "water down" the warning label?

2. Did Parke, Davis promote or contribute to the overprescription and overuse of chloromycetin for unindicated purposes?

3. To what extent can a company actually control the activities of its detailmen in their communications with physicians? Remember, the personal and career goals of a salesman are only partially in congruence with those of the company.

4. How can a company be made accountable for the activities of independent intermediaries such as the physician, the hospital, and the pharmacist? These intermediaries are professional individuals and organizations and have legally and socially recognized independence in their operational spheres. Such accountability may require total control on the part of the manufacturer over all the elements of the distribution channel leading to the final consumer. Even if such a control were possible, is it socially desirable? What are its implications?

5. How should a company develop its marketing strategy, in a heavily regulated environment, to protect itself from situations in which it may be held responsible for the activities of others?

In addition, there are some technical questions that have bearing on management decision making and long-range planning. For example:

1. It is not clear whether the California Supreme Court made its decision solely on procedural grounds, substantive facts and applications of laws thereto, or both.

It would be interesting to speculate what the court would have done had the trial court judge specified the grounds on which he was rejecting the jury's decision. The importance of this case as a precedent for future cases and also as a determining variable for management policy depends heavily on this interpretation.

2. Stevens' attorneys cited three specific causes for action against Parke, Davis: negligence, breach of warranty, and strict liability. An analysis of the evidence and the court's decision seems to indicate that negligence and breach of warranty, as legally defined, would not be the probable causes and the decision against Parke, Davis rested primarily on the application of strict liability. However, strict liability as a legal concept is of more recent origin and is constantly evolving. Since legal cases take a long time before their final disposition, it is quite likely that a case may be decided based on the concept of strict liability as it existed at the time of the incident but which might not be prevalent by the time the court made a decision. An analysis of legal definitions and their implications for negligence, breach of warranty, and strict liability would be helpful in understanding the implications of this case for management policy.

We should also realize that a corporation does not act in a vacuum; its practices are largely determined and constrained by the nature of marketing practices employed by the industry as a whole and also the economic and sociopolitical environment in the country. Thus an understanding of the industry is important for an evaluation of the activities of a particular company.

THE CIRCUMSTANCES OF THE CASE

The facts of the case are simple and straightforward and were not contested in the courts by the defendants. What *is* in dispute are the causes that led to the occurrence of the facts. Most important is the question of the responsibility of the various parties—the patient, the doctor, and the manufacturer—in causing these facts to take place and how the consequences or costs of such acts should be borne or apportioned by the various parties. Of equal importance are two related questions: One, could this tragic event have been avoided if one or more parties had exercised prudent and reasonable care in performing their relative roles; and two, what might be done to minimize, if not completely avoid, similar occurrences in the future? In other words, to what extent is this an isolated incident caused by the failure on the part of one or more parties to behave prudently, and to what extent could the incident be attributed to the structure and the process of interaction between the patient, the doctor, and the drug manufacturer, and the environment in which this triad of interactions takes place?

On Christmas Day, 1965, Phyllis Stevens died of pneumonia as a result of aplastic anemia—the failure of the bone marrow to produce enough white blood cells to ward off infection—caused by the administration of Chloromycetin.[4] At the time of her death she was thirty-eight years old.

Phyllis Stevens was born in 1927. When she was twenty she developed

[4] Aplastic anemia is the depression or destruction of the bone marrow caused by a drug or chemical or radiation damage.

a chronic lung condition called bronchiectasis. However, this did not prevent her from entering into any normal activities, and in 1948 she married and subsequently had three children. Testimony at the trial by the plaintiffs and the deceased's doctor established that Mrs. Stevens had been leading a normal and active life as a housewife and mother. She was proficient in cooking and camping and enjoyed partaking in them. She had hoped to enjoy even more recreational activities with her family after her surgery. The family spent two weeks each year camping in national parks. In addition, they spent weekends and holidays at Big Bear Lake, where they owned a cabin. Mrs. Stevens also found time to return to college, where she completed the courses required for a teaching credential and in fact taught for five days prior to entering the hospital. In sum, despite her lung condition Phyllis Stevens enjoyed a full, rich life.

On May 25, 1964, she visited Dr. Arthur J. Beland to see if he could recommend some treatment for her bronchiectasis that would make it easier for her to teach. Dr. Beland described her as "being a well-developed, well-nourished, intelligent lady who does not appear acutely or chronically ill" (E–3). He did recognize a lung abnormality which, upon X ray examination, was diagnosed as bilateral bronchiectasis, the same condition Mrs. Stevens had had for 18 years. Dr. Beland recommended surgery, which he subsequently performed on September 1, 1964. (Surgery had also been recommended 18 years previously.) Due to complications resulting from the operation, he prescribed Chloromycetin shortly thereafter. The drug was given to her six times between September and November 20, 1964. She was also operated on two more times— October 23, 1964 and February 18, 1965—for further removal of portions of the afflicted lung. Her condition failed to improve and in June 1965 Dr. Nathaniel Kurnick, a hematologist, was brought in on the case. Dr. Kurnick's tests showed that Mrs. Stevens was suffering from bone marrow failure, that is, aplastic anemia. Her bone marrow was unable to produce enough red cells, white cells and platelets, the three components of blood. Her body lacked the ability to produce white cells in sufficient numbers to ward off infection. Mrs. Stevens consequently died on December 25, 1965.

THE CASE AGAINST BELAND
AND PARKE, DAVIS & COMPANY

The case for the wrongful death of Mrs. Phyllis Stevens was filed by and on behalf of her three children, Janet Stevens, Suzanne Stevens, and Kennon Stevens, all minors, and her husband, John Stevens, in Los Angeles Superior Court.

Based on the plaintiffs' briefs and the testimony of various witnesses during the trial, the plaintiffs' case can be summarized as follows:

1. Dr. A. J. Beland (hereinafter referred to as Dr. Beland) was accused

of malpractice and was called negligent in prescribing and administering the drug Chloromycetin, which has known dangerous side effects. A less dangerous antibiotic could have been used just as effectively.

2. Parke, Davis & Company (hereinafter referred to as Parke, Davis) was charged with negligence in failing to sufficiently warn the medical profession of the dangers of the drug and in so overpromoting it as to negate the effect of the written warnings that were available to the prescribing physician. Such negligence in this case was the proximate cause of the death of Phyllis Stevens. The plaintiffs cited three specific causes of action against Parke, Davis: negligence, breach of warranty, and strict liability (C–3).

During the trial Dr. Beland testified to the fact that he was indeed aware of the dangerous side effects of repeated and/or prolonged use of Chloromycetin; the drug's being the most dangerous antibiotic available; Parke, Davis's warnings with respect to its use; the information contained in the 1964 PDR (Physician's Desk Reference) [5] concerning its dangers; the risks attending its use and the recommendation for adequate blood studies; and the drug's association with aplastic anemia. He also testified that in prescribing drugs he did not rely on drug company detailmen or magazine advertising and had no recollection of talking to Parke, Davis detailmen or their leaving literature for him to read (C–7, 8).

The plaintiffs contended that, Beland's testimony notwithstanding, he could not help but be influenced by the promotional bombardment directed by Parke, Davis at the medical profession and aimed at negating the effect of "warnings" concerning the use of this drug. Thus, the plaintiffs maintained that Dr. Beland's testimony should be ignored as it related to Parke, Davis and that the company should be held liable as charged.

HISTORY OF CHLORAMPHENICOL

To understand the allegations made against Parke, Davis, it is necessary to briefly narrate the history of the development of chloramphenicol.[6]

[5] *The Physician's Desk Reference* is a reference book used by doctors to obtain information on various drugs. It is published yearly. The information contained therein is supplied by the drug manufacturers on a voluntary basis.

[6] The history of chloramphenicol and the studies relating it to aplastic anemia, including the numbers and types of articles published, is well documented in U.S. Congress, Senate, Subcommittee on Monopoly of the Select Committee on Small Business, *Competitive Problems in the Drug Industry: Present Status of Competition in the Pharmaceutical Industry*, Part 6, 90th Cong., 1st and 2nd sess., November 1967 and February 1968. Part 5, 90th Cong., 1st and 2nd sess., December 1967 and January 1968, and Part 11, 91st Cong., 1st sess., February and March 1969, are also cited in this study. All citations from this source are hereinafter referred to in the text as *Hearings, Competitive Problems in the Drug Industry*, followed by part and page number. For a more favorable discussion on the use of Chloromycetin and arguments against further restrictions on its usage, see Marvin Henry Edwards, "Chloromycetin: Special Report," *Private Practice*, 3, 3 (March 1971), 42–56.

Chloramphenicol was discovered in 1946 and put on the market under the trade name of Chloromycetin three years later after it was tested by Parke, Davis as to its efficacy. It was found to be an extremely effective wide-spectrum antibiotic. However, by 1952 there were so many reports about its possible association with the development of blood disorders (also known as blood dyscrasias), including aplastic anemia, that the Food and Drug Administration, in conjunction with the National Research Council, began an investigation. Until the investigation was completed, the FDA stopped further certification of the sale of the drug. This research resulted in a "recommendation." (C–5, 6) to Parke, Davis to include the following warning on each label of the drug: "Warning—Blood dyscrasias may be associated with intermittent or prolonged use. It is essential that adequate blood studies be made" (M–4).

However, the drug continued to receive scrutiny and widespread comment as a result of its association with aplastic anemia. Literally hundreds of articles concerning the possible development of aplastic anemia after treatment with Chloromycetin appeared in medical journals.

In 1961 the Kefauver hearings in the Senate on the drug industry [7] resulted in the FDA's requirement that Parke, Davis strengthen the warning on the label. The warning label commencing in 1961 read as follows:

> Warning—Serious and even fatal blood dyscrasias (aplastic anemia, hypoplastic anemia, thrombocytopenia, granulocytopenia) are known to occur after the administration of chloramphenicol. Blood dyscrasias have occurred after short term and with prolonged therapy with this drug. Bearing in mind the possibility that such reactions may occur, chloramphenicol should be used only for serious infections caused by organisms that are susceptible to its antibacterial effects. Chloramphenicol should not be used when other less potentially dangerous agents will be effective, or in the treatment of trivial infections such as colds, influenza, viral infections of the throat, or as a prophylactic agent.

> Precautions: It is essential that adequate blood studies be made during treatment with the drug. While blood studies may detect early peripheral blood changes, such as leukopenia or granulocytopenia, before they become irreversible, such studies cannot be relied upon to detect bone marrow depression prior to development of aplastic anemia. (C–6, 7)

The plaintiffs pointed out that Parke, Davis did not take adequate steps to bring this warning to the attention of the medical profession. In fact, it took a Senate investigatory hearing to even get Parke, Davis to

---

[7] Senator Kefauver headed the following two investigations into the drug industry: U.S. Congress, Senate, Subcommittee on Antitrust and Monopoly of the Committee of the Judiciary, *Drug Industry Antitrust Act Hearings*, 7 parts, 87th Cong., 1st sess., 1961; and U.S. Congress, Senate, Subcommittee on Antitrust and Monopoly of the Committee of the Judiciary, *Administered Prices in the Drug Industry*, 29 parts, 85th, 86th, and 87th Cong., 1957–61.

include a truthful warning about the drug. Between the time of the FDA's 1952 recommendation and its 1961 order, Parke, Davis avoided the issue. In the 1952 PDR there was no warning about the link between Chloromycetin and blood disorders. In 1953 a warning was included but it did not state that the blood disorders could be fatal. The same was true of the 1955 entry, which read:

> Chloromycetin is a potent therapeutic agent; and because certain blood dyscrasias have been associated with its administration, it should not be used indiscriminately nor for minor infections. Furthermore, as with certain other drugs, adequate blood studies should be made when the patient requires prolonged or intermittent therapy. (F–10)

Even after the 1961 order, Parke, Davis was not disseminating the information. The 1962 entry read:

> Chloromycetin. Chloramphenicol. Parke, Davis & Co. Product Information Section. Detailed information on Chloromycetin, including dosage, administration, contraindications and precautions, may be obtained by consulting the package circular or by contacting your local Parke, Davis representative or the Office of Medical Correspondence, Parke, Davis & Co., Detroit 32, Michigan. (F–10, 11)

When called upon to testify, Mr. Bradshaw, chief attorney for Parke, Davis, said that no warning information was included because the company concluded that it would have been an "unwarranted expense" to have it printed in the book. The same reason was given for its exclusion in the 1963 book as well. The warning was finally included in the 1964 edition but only because of criticism aimed at Parke, Davis by physicians who wanted the warning included.

ADVERTISING AND PROMOTION

Soon after the FDA directive in 1952, Parke, Davis took steps to minimize the effect of the warning labels on potential sales. The testimony at the trial brought out the following evidence:

In 1952 the president of Parke, Davis issued a press release to all salesmen which stated that "Chloromycetin has been officially cleared by the Federal Drug Administration and the National Research Council with *no restrictions* on the number or the range of diseases for which Chloromycetin may be administered" (F–5).

In another letter dated November 20, 1952, the medical director of Parke, Davis wrote to all the company's salesmen attesting to the fact that

Chloromycetin is "well tolerated" and in the hands of the physician is an extremely valuable therapeutic agent. Some physicians are of the opinion that Chloromycetin has been taken off the market or its use restricted. Some physicians have formed the impression that this antibiotic has been associated with the development of blood depression in large numbers of patients, and will be amazed when we point out the facts. Tell the Chloromycetin story to every physician in your territory in the shortest possible time. If the situation is understood, physicians will readily use this valuable therapeutic agent when indicated. (F–6)

Additional plans are under study and in preparation in behalf of Chloromycetin products, which will support your detailing efforts in a substantial way, such as a major Chloromycetin hospital display program, a Chloromycetin issue of Therapeutic Notes, literature, Chloromycetin products brochures, special promotion pieces, samples, and standard packages, new Chloromycetin product forms, general advertising, direct mail advertising, laity promotion of an institutional character, plans for pharmaceutical meetings, and plans for medical meetings. (F–8)

In another document, "Suggested Details for the Benefit of Salesmen in Promoting This Drug," salesmen were told that

Intensive investigation by the Food and Drug Administration carried on with the assistance of a special committee of eminent specialists appointed by the National Research Council resulted in unqualified sanction of the continued use of Chloromycetin for all conditions in which it had previously been used. (F–7)

Salesmen's visits to doctors urging them to prescribe the drug were frequent and took place constantly from 1956 on. Although literature left with the doctors apparently did contain warnings about possible side effects, the salesmen themselves never voiced any warnings. Giveaway calendars, rulers, and other materials were used in the promotion campaign as well as full-page ads in medical journals. None of these contained any mention at all of the possibility of harmful side effects. Doctors were thus bombarded with personal visits and promotional material. Medical journal ads also added to a distorted view of the drug.

The trial testimony showed that not a single piece of promotional material or instructions received by the field salesmen from the home office contained any mention of a warning as to the drug's side effects, nor were the salesmen ever asked or reminded to mention to the physicians, on their sales calls, the dangerous side effects of Chloromycetin.

The only other warning issued by Parke, Davis, in addition to the one contained on the label, was a mass-produced "Dear Doctor" letter cautioning the physicians about the danger associated with the use of Chloromycetin. When asked why the full-page advertisements for Chloromycetin in medical journals did not contain any warning language, the attorney for the defendants replied that those ads were in the nature of reminders and therefore did not contain any warning of the side effects of the drug.

Parke, Davis was clearly concerned about the effect of its promotional material on the case. In 1968, Mr. Donald Swanson, a regional sales manager for Parke-Davis whose territory was the Los Angeles/Long Beach area, received a letter from Walter Griffith, the director of promotion, stating that all materials concerning the promotion of Chloromycetin should be destroyed. This was done. Parke, Davis's attorney also testified that all the promotional material relating to Chloromycetin during the 1960s was destroyed by Parke, Davis and thus was not available. The only evidence produced at the trial by Parke, Davis to support its contention of additional warnings were a "Dear Doctor" letter dated 1962 and a products information brochure.

THE RESPONSE BY DR. BELAND
AND PARKE, DAVIS & COMPANY

Dr. Beland admitted that he was fully aware of the dangerous side effects associated with the use of Chloromycetin but nevertheless maintained that he was not negligent in his prescription and administration of the drug to Mrs. Stevens. He filed a motion for nonsuit.

Parke, Davis made the following points in its defense:

1. As a matter of law, the company was not guilty of negligence either in the distribution of the product or in the failure to adequately warn of its dangers. Also, there was a complete lack of evidence that any act on the part of Parke, Davis caused injury to Mrs. Stevens. Exclusion of any warnings from the advertisements and other promotional material was perfectly legal. The FDA directive stipulated that a warning must be included only in advertising material that stated specific recommendations as to proper use and dosage.

2. Hundreds of articles relating the link between aplastic anemia and Chloromycetin appeared in medical journals. Parke, Davis wrote letters to doctors about the link. The medical profession further learned about it "through teaching, symposiums, lectures and the general methods by which the medical profession self-instructs itself" (F–6), and the warning label, used from 1961 on, was extremely explicit.

3. Dr. Beland was fully aware of the dangers of the drug and admitted that "in prescribing drugs he did not rely on drug company detailmen or magazine advertising, and has no recollection of talking to Parke, Davis detailmen" (F–8).

4. All of the ten doctors who testified at the trial, both for the plaintiffs and for the defendants, agreed on the following points: Mrs. Stevens's death was caused by aplastic anemia resulting from the administration of Chloromycetin; the association between aplastic anemia and Chloromycetin was well known to the medical profession in and before 1964;

and the 1964 warning label painted an adequate picture of the inherent dangers. Dr. Phillip Sturgeon, one of the plaintiff's witnesses, stated (with no disagreement expressed by either side) that by 1964 sufficient information had been disseminated so that doctors should have known that Chloromycetin could cause fatal aplastic anemia and that it should not have been used unless it was the only drug effective in a certain situation (Chloromycetin is extremely effective in treating Rocky Mountain Spotted Fever, typhus, and typhoid). There were other drugs available by that time that would have been as effective in treating various infections.

THE SUPERIOR COURT ORDER

After a three-week trial, the jury returned a verdict in favor of the plaintiffs and awarded them $400,000 in damages. However, Superior Court Judge Shea ordered the amount reduced to $64,673.42 ($60,000 in general damages and $4,673.42 in special damages), stating that the verdict "is not sustained by the evidence, and that it is based upon prejudice and passion on the part of the jury" (A–2). He therefore ordered a new trial to be granted on the issue of damages unless the plaintiffs would accept the reduced amount. He also denied the motion for a new trial on the issue of liability and the motion for judgment notwithstanding the verdict (A–1, 2).

The plaintiffs did not agree to accept reduced damages and instead chose to appeal the case. Defendants Beland and Parke, Davis also chose to appeal for reasons that will be shown in succeeding pages.

ARGUMENTS MADE BY THE PLAINTIFFS IN THEIR APPEAL

1. Judge Shea's order for a new trial was invalid because it did not contain the specific written reasons required for such an order by the Code of Civil Procedure, Section 657 (as amended in 1965 and 1967).[8]

2. Plaintiffs contended that Judge Shea was "guilty of a gross abuse of discretion in attempting to grant a new trial on the issue of damages or in the alternative reducing a verdict of $400,000 to $60,000 in general damages." Such an attempt to reduce the verdict by 85 percent, said plaintiffs, is "virtually unprecedented" (A–11). In one of the first cases ever argued before the California Supreme Court, the situation presented was quite similar to that of *Stevens* v. *Parke, Davis,* in which the trial judge ordered the jury award vastly reduced. In its decision, the Supreme Court stated that a judge

---

[8] Section 657 was dealt with at length and interpreted by the Supreme Court in *Mercer* v. *Perez,* 68 Cal. 2d 104, and *Scala* v. *Jerry Witt and Sons,* 3 Cal. 3d 359. (See A–5–11 for a detailed discussion.) In both cases the court reversed orders granting new trials because of the violation of section 657.

ought never to set aside a verdict for such a cause, unless, beyond doubt, the verdict be unjust and oppressive, obtained through some undue advantage, mistake or in violation of law, as upon questions so peculiarly pertaining to the powers and investigation of the jury, it ought to be presumed that the verdict of the jury is correct. (A–12) [9]

3. The right of trial by jury in civil cases as well as in criminal cases is secured by the Bill of Rights. The Seventh Amendment of the United States Constitution states: "The right of trial by jury shall be preserved, and no fact tried by a jury, shall be otherwise re-examined in any court of the United States, than according to the rules of the common law." Article I, section 7 of the California Constitution provides that the "Right of trial by jury shall be secured to all and remain inviolate." Based on these provisions, plaintiffs declared that any attempt on the part of the trial judge to disturb the jury's findings would be in violation of these rights.

4. The trial judge made the following statement at the time of the proceedings on the hearing regarding the motion for a new trial:

> Actually, had I been making a finding on this thing in my own judgment, it would have been in the neighborhood of $25,000. . . . All I can say is, gentlemen, I have not been able to find any case that would sustain a verdict anywhere near approaching this, and that is why I have taken the tactic that I have. (A–14, 15).

The trial judge's instructions to the jury stated that, according to a mortality table, the life expectancy of a female person aged forty years is 37.5 additional years. Thus the verdict for general damages in the amount of $400,000 averaged $100,000 per plaintiff. Over the life expectancy of the deceased, the award amounted to approximately $2,600 per year per plaintiff (A–17). The plaintiffs argued that there was no legal, factual, or reasonable basis for holding that each of the plaintiffs would not be entitled to $200 per month for the losses sustained due to the death of Mrs. Stevens:

> [She] died in the prime of her life and during the prime of her husband's life and during the adolescent and maturing years of her children. Each of the plaintiffs suffered a profound loss and the translation thereof into monetary damages totaling $400,000 makes much more sense than the unfounded conclusion of the trial court that damages should have been in some far lesser sum (whether the same be $60,000 or $25,000). (A–18)

[9] *Payne* v. *Pacific Mail Steamship Co.,* 1 Cal. 33.

ARGUMENTS MADE BY DR. BELAND
AND PARKE, DAVIS IN THEIR APPEAL

Defendant Dr. Beland appealed from the judgment against him but filed no brief in support of his appeal. Also, he contested plaintiffs' appeal from the order granting a new trial on the issue of damages.

Defendant Parke, Davis appealed on the following grounds:

1. The jury's verdict for damages was indeed excessive, and plaintiff's appeal for a new trial on the issue of damages should be denied.
2. The court committed reversible error when ruling on evidence and when instructing the jury as well as allowing misconduct by plaintiffs' counsel.
3. Parke, Davis was not negligent, and therefore the company should have been granted a directed verdict or judgment, notwithstanding the verdict on all issues, i.e., the trial court judge should have directed the jury to bring in a verdict of not guilty (A–1, 2).
4. In case the appellate court were to disagree with the company on this subject, a new trial on all issues should be granted.

In support of its appeal, Parke, Davis made the following arguments:

1. Parke, Davis was not negligent in preparing or using the warning label that accompanied the drug in 1964. The warning labels clearly spelled out that aplastic anemia had been associated with the use of chloramphenicol and that chloramphenicol should not be used when other less potentially dangerous agents would be effective. The essence of the plaintiff's case against Dr. Beland was that, considering the nature of the decedent's illness, he should have used other drugs. This again was precisely the point covered in the warning label.

2. Dr. Beland was aware of the warning label. Dr. Beland's testimony left no doubt in anyone's mind as to whether he was aware of the dangers inherent in the drug. He was 100 percent aware of it and had been in 1964 when he prescribed it. Plaintiffs' counsel contended time and again, in arguments, that it was Parke, Davis's duty to disseminate the information on the warning label. Parke, Davis contended that it had met its duty by placing the warning label in the package inserts and by the distribution of "Dear Doctor" letters. It also argued that the issue of the method of dissemination of the warning label was meant to mislead the jury so that plaintiffs' counsel could assert that Parke, Davis should have done something else they did not do. The law was clear. If the doctor was aware of the information, it made no difference how he acquired it (C–17).

3. The warning label to Dr. Beland was not watered down. Parke, Davis asserted that plaintiffs' counsel was allowed to introduce into

testimony events of alleged overpromotion and watering down by Parke, Davis by assuring the court that he would connect this evidence with Dr. Beland's prescription of Chloromycetin in 1964 in order to come within the statement in *Love* v. *Wolf* [(1964) 226 C.A. 2d 378]· "If the over-promotion can reasonably be said to have induced the doctor to disregard the warnings," then, under certain circumstances, the drug company would be liable along with the prescribing doctor. Note, however, that in *Love* v. *Wolf*, Dr. Wolf testified that he had been influenced by Parke, Davis's promotion of Chloromycetin. In 1958, the year he prescribed it for Mrs. Love (who subsequently contracted aplastic anemia), the warning label was not specific enough to have led him to choose another drug. Dr. Beland, on the other hand, specifically testified to no causal link between the drug promotion and his prescription of it. Dr. Beland's testimony in this connection was uncontradicted and should have supported defendant Parke, Davis's motion for a directed verdict.

Assuming that plaintiffs were correct in finding that Parke, Davis was guilty of a "breach of duty" in overpromoting the drug, that breach must be the proximate cause of the injury.[10] Although Dr. Beland stated he was not influenced by alleged overpromotion, plaintiffs' counsel argued that maybe that wasn't true. In denying defendant's nonsuit, Judge Shea stated:

> It is a question of the measure of conjecture and speculation, and this lays in the use of the word, inferences to be deduced from the testimony. The rule is that we do not allow speculation and conjecture, but what else is an inference predicated on? Is there evidence here from which an inference may be drawn that this was what happened? (C–26, 27)

Parke, Davis believed that the trial court misunderstood the permissible inferences that may be drawn from evidence. While permissive, logical inferences may be drawn, speculative possibilities did not really constitute a true inference and, in any event, the inference must fail when it was confronted with clear, explicit testimony (C–27).

Parke, Davis contended that the evidence on record clearly demonstrated that Dr. Beland prescribed the drug Chloromycetin with full knowledge of the side effects suffered by plaintiffs' decedent. In this situation, the intervening acts of Dr. Beland superseded any possible negligence on the part of Parke, Davis and insulated Parke, Davis from liability. California courts have consistently held that a warning given

---

[10] In *Spencer* v. *Beatty Safway Scaffold Co.* [(1956) 141 Cal. App. 2d 875], the court said: "The plaintiff in a tort action must establish the presence of every fact essential to his cause, especially that the negligence complained of was the proximate cause of the injury and not a mere speculation." See also *McKellar* v. *Pendergast* [(1945) 68 Cal. App. 2d 485]; *Reese* v. *Smith* [(1937) 9 Cal. 2d 324]; *Puckhaber* v. *Southern Pac. Co.* [(1901) 132 Cal. 363, 366]. See also (C–24).

to an intermediate third party or his discovery of the danger relieves the original supplier from liability.[11]

4. Parke, Davis also contended that plaintiffs' counsel prevented defendant from receiving a fair trial by making inflammatory statements and playing on the emotions of the jury, and was therefore guilty of gross misconduct.

COURT OF APPEALS DECISION

The appeal decision was filed on March 21, 1972. Justice Roth reversed the judgment against Parke, Davis with directions to the trial court to enter judgment in favor of Parke, Davis. However, the court did not dismiss the lawsuit against Dr. Beland but granted an order to him for a new trial.

Judge Roth said that the trial judge's decision to lower damages "was an appropriate exercise of its discretion" and that it was "based in part on the vague showing in respect of decedent's earning power and primarily on passion and prejudice equating with the desire of the jury to punish and resulting in a verdict far in excess of what would have been reasonable and just" (H–4). Judge Roth also said that Section 657 had not been violated.

SUPREME COURT DECISION

The attorneys for the Stevens family appealed to the California Supreme Court, the highest state court. They appealed from an order granting the defendants a new trial on the issue of damages. Defendant Parke, Davis appealed from the judgment entered on the verdict in favor of the plaintiffs and against Parke, Davis, and from the order denying its motion for judgment notwithstanding the verdict.[12]

Supreme Court Justice Raymond L. Sullivan's decision, filed on March 14, 1973, affirmed the verdict of the jury which granted the plaintiffs $400,000 in damages. In rendering its decision in favor of plaintiffs, Judge Sullivan concluded that all the arguments made by Parke, Davis were without merit and therefore its appeals were denied.

---

[11] The brief quotes decisions to substantiate this: *Youtz* v. *Thompson Tire Co.* [(1941) 46 Cal. App. 2d 672]; *Boeing Airplane Co.* v. *Brown* [(1961) 291 F.2d 310, 318–19]; *Stultz* v. *Benson Lumber Co.* [(1936) 6 Cal. 2d 688, 693]; *McLaughlin* v. *Mine Safety Appliances Co.* [(N.Y. 1962) 181 N.E. 2d 430]; etc.

[12] Dr. Beland also took an appeal from the judgment but later abandoned it.

THE SUPREME COURT'S RATIONALE FOR ITS DECISION

It is not necessary to review the briefs submitted to the Supreme Court by the various parties as they cover essentially the same ground and use similar logic applied in their briefs to the court of appeal. Instead I will summarize the reasons and logic employed by the court in rendering its decision.

The court agreed with the plaintiffs' contention that the order for a new trial should be reversed "because it fails to contain an adequate specification of reasons in compliance with Code of Civil Procedure section 657" (M–9).[13]

The court stated that while it had not laid down any hard and fast rule as to the content of such a specification, it had emphasized on several occasions [14] that, if the ground relied upon was insufficiency of evidence, the trial judge's specification of reasons "must briefly identify the portion of the record which convinces the judge 'that the court or jury clearly should have reached a different verdict or decision' " (M–10).

The objective of specificity in section 657 was to encourage careful deliberation by the trial court before ruling on the new trial motion and to make a sufficiently precise record to permit meaningful appellate review (*Mercer* v. *Perez*, 68 Cal. 2d 104 at pp. 112–116). Furthermore, a specification that merely recited the court's view of evidence as to whether "the defendant was not negligent or the plaintiff was negligent" was of little if any assistance to the appellate or to the reviewing court (M–12).

The court also held that the same rules that apply to a specification of reasons in respect to the ground of insufficiency of the evidence should apply to a specification of reasons in respect to the ground of excessive or inadequate damages. Indeed, to state that the damages awarded by the jury were excessive is simply one way of saying that the evidence does not justify the amount of the award.[15] The same statutory test applied in determining whether a new trial should be granted either on the ground of excessive or inadequate damages, or on the ground of insufficiency of the evidence.[16]

13 Section 657 provides in relevant part as follows: "When a new trial is granted, on all or part of the issues, the court shall specify the ground or grounds upon which it is granted *and the court's reason or reasons* [original italics] for granting the new trial upon each ground stated" (M–9, 10).
14 *Mercer* v. *Perez* [(1968) 68 Cal. 2d 104]; *Miller* v. *Los Angeles County Flood Control District* [(1973) 8 Cal. 3d 689]; *Scale* v. *Jerry Witt & Sons* [(1970) 3 Cal. 3d 359].
15 *Doolin* v. *Omnibus Cable Co.* [(1899) 125 Cal. 141, 144]; 5 Witkin, Cal. Procedure (2d ed. 1971), p. 3618.
16 Section 657 states in relevant part: "A new trial shall not be granted upon the ground of insufficiency of the evidence to justify the verdict or other decision, nor upon the ground of excessive or inadequate damages, unless after weighing the evidence the court is convinced from the entire record, including reasonable inferences therefrom, that the court or jury clearly should have reached a different verdict or decision" (M–12, 13).

The court stated that the trial judge's order for a new trial made no pretense of specifying reasons upon which the judge based his decision to grant the defendants' motions. The statement that the verdict was excessive, that it was not sustained by the evidence, was a statement of ultimate fact that did not go beyond a statement of the ground for the court's decision. It did not indicate the respects in which the evidence dictated a less sizable verdict, and failed even to hint at any portion of the record that would tend to support the judge's ruling. The mere statement that the amount of the verdict was "based upon prejudice and passion on the part of the jury" was not a "reason" that provided an insight into the record (M–14).

The new trial order in this case was based solely upon the ground of excessive damages. Since no reasons were specified, the conditions under section 657 were not met. The order granting a new trial could not be sustained on this ground. Therefore, the judgment would be automatically reinstated as to both defendants (M–16).

Noting that Dr. Beland abandoned his appeal from the judgment, Justice Sullivan stated that the judgment would thus be automatically final.

THE SUPREME COURT'S OPINION
OF DEFENDANT PARKE, DAVIS'S APPEAL

The court rejected Parke, Davis's contention that (1) the record showed that as a matter of law Parke, Davis was not negligent; and (2) that the court committed reversible error in respect to rulings on the evidence, rulings as to the alleged misconduct of plaintiffs' counsel, and instructions to the jury (M–17).

In rejecting Parke, Davis's contention of not being legally negligent, the court provides us with an excellent statement as to the circumstances under, and the extent to which, a producer is liable for the harmful effects of its products.

One who supplies a product directly or through a third person "for another to use is subject to liability to those whom the supplier should expect to use the [product] with the consent of the other . . . for physical harm caused by the use of the [product] in the manner for which and by a person for whose use it is supplied, if the supplier . . . knows or has reason to know that the [product] is or is likely to be dangerous for the use for which it is supplied, and . . . has no reason to believe that those for whose use the [product] is supplied will realize its dangerous condition, and . . . fails to exercise reasonable care to inform them of its dangerous condition or of facts which make it likely to be dangerous." (M–19, 20) [17]

It is established that in the case of medical prescriptions, where adequate warning of potential dangers of a drug has been given to doctors, there is no duty by the drug manufacturer to ensure that the warning reaches the doctor's patient for whom the drug is prescribed. The courts have nevertheless held that mere compliance with regulations or directives as to warnings, such as those issued by the United States Food and Drug Administration in this case, may not be sufficient to immunize the manufacturer or supplier of the drug from liability. The warnings required by such agencies may be only minimal in nature, and when the manufacturer or supplier has reason to know of greater dangers not included in the warning, its duty to warn may not be fulfilled. What is more to the point, these warnings can be considered to be eroded or even nullified by an "over-promotion of the drug through a vigorous sales program which may have the effect of persuading the prescribing doctor to disregard the warnings given." [18]

It is ironic that the two earlier court decisions most cited by all the parties (*Love* v. *Wolf* and *Incollingo* v. *Ewing*) and the ones from which this case also drew heavily involved Chloromycetin and Parke, Davis, and in both cases the verdict went against Parke, Davis. A careful reading of these decisions leads one to wonder why Parke, Davis did not change its marketing practices for promoting and distributing Chloromycetin or, failing that, why the company did not try to settle the case out of court instead of fighting it all the way to the state supreme court. The answer may perhaps lie in two sets of interrelated factors. One, the industry practices for the promotion and distribution of drugs are so well entrenched that it is extremely difficult, if not impossible, for one company to go against industry trends either for all or one of its products. Two, the profit margins and potential for promoting and selling ethical drugs in the present manner are so high that companies are willing to risk lawsuits and often absorb the costs of adverse judgments rather than tamper with a tried and proven success formula. However, these suppositions need further substantiation through a rigorous analysis of the drug industry before their causative extent can be established.

In the first case, *Love* v. *Wolf* [(1964), 226 Cal. App. 2d 378], the plaintiff sued her physician, Dr. Wolf, and Parke, Davis & Company for damages for personal injuries after she had developed aplastic anemia following the administration of Chloromycetin. The court rejected as without merit Parke, Davis's contention that the trial court should be

[17] Rest. 2d Torts, § 388; see also *Love* v. *Wolf* [(1964) 226 Cal. App. 2d 378, 395]; *Tingley* v. *E. F. Houghton & Co.* [(1947) 30 Cal. 2d 97, 102]; *Gall* v. *Union Ice Company* [(1951) 108 Cal. App. 2d 303, 209–310]; *Yarrow* v. *Sterling Drug Co.* [(D.C. S.Dak. 1967) 263 F. Supp. 159, 162], affd. in *Sterling Drug Inc.* v. *Yarrow* [(8th Cir. 1969) 408 F. 2d 978, 993]; *Sterling Drug Inc.* v. *Cornish* [(8th Cir. 1967) 370 F. 2d 82, 84–85].
[18] *Love* v. *Wolf* (266 Cal. App. 2d, 226, 395–96); *Yarrow* v. *Sterling Drug Co.* (263 F. Supp. at pp. 162–63); *Incollingo* v. *Ewing* [(Pa. 1971) 282 A.2d 206, 220].

directed to enter a judgment for Parke, Davis, because, so it was argued, the record showed as a matter of law that such defendant was liable neither for breach of warranty nor for negligence. After taking note of the numerous warnings distributed by Parke, Davis, the court nevertheless stated: "[W]e must accept the evidence leading to justifiable inferences that Parke, Davis, believing otherwise, had watered down its regulations-required warnings and had caused its detailmen to promote a wider use of the drug by physicians than proper medical practice justified" (M–21, 22).[19]

In *Incollingo* v. *Ewing* [(Pa. 1971) 282 A.2d 206], the Supreme Court of Pennsylvania refused to reverse a judgment against Parke, Davis for damages arising from plaintiff's death as a result of the administration of Chloromycetin. Parke, Davis's evidence of warning was similar to that introduced in the present case. The court held:

> We think that whether or not the warnings on the cartons, labels and literature of Parke, Davis in use in the relevant years were adequate, and whether or not the printed words of warning were in effect cancelled out and rendered meaningless in the light of the sales effort made by the detailmen, were questions properly for the jury. . . . [I]f detailmen are an effective means of selling a product and explaining its nature, a jury could find that they also afforded an effective medium of conveying a warning. (M–22, 23)

In reviewing the evidence within the framework of the principles alluded to in these two cases, the judges stated that they were satisfied that the jury could draw a reasonable inference that Parke, Davis negligently failed to provide an adequate warning as to the dangers of Chloromycetin by so "watering down" its warnings and so overpromoting the drug that members of the medical profession, including Dr. Beland, were caused to prescribe it when it was not justified.

The Supreme Court also rejected Parke, Davis's contention that, even if it did overpromote the drug, it was exonerated from any liability because the testimony in the case clearly established Dr. Beland's negligence thus making him, as a matter of law, an intervening cause in Mrs. Stevens's death. (See *Magee* v. *Wyeth Laboratories,* 214 Cal. App. 2d at pp. 251–352.)

The court based its dismissal of Parke, Davis's argument on two grounds. One, it was the province of the jury to resolve the conflicts in the evidence and to pass upon the weight to be given the evidence. Citing various legal authorities, the court stated that it was within the province of the trier of fact to accept one part of the testimony of a witness and reject another part even though the latter contradicts the part accepted (M–26). The court concluded that there was adequate circumstantial

---

[19] On retrial, Parke, Davis was again found liable and judgment against it was affirmed on appeal. *Love* v. *Wolf* [(1967) 249 Cal. App. 2d 822].

evidence on the record to support a reasonable inference by the jury that Dr. Beland was induced to prescribe the drug for Mrs. Stevens because of Parke, Davis's overpromotion. Like many others of the profession, he had been exposed to the promotional tactics employed by Parke, Davis. It was reasonable to assume that the company's heavy advertising and promotion efforts for the drug consciously or subconsciously influenced him.

The court's second argument had to do with the definition of the "legal" responsibility of a producer. The court stated that even if the jury were to accept Dr. Beland's testimony that he was cognizant of the dangers of the drug, *nevertheless his negligence was not, as a matter of law, an intervening cause which exonerated Parke, Davis* (M–28). According to the court:

> It is well settled that "an actor may be liable if his negligence is a substantial factor in causing an injury, and he is not relieved of liability because of the intervening act of a third person if such act was *reasonably foreseeable* at the time of his negligent conduct. [Citations.] Moreover, 'If the likelihood that a third person may act in a particular manner is the hazard or one of the hazards which makes the actor negligent, such an act whether innocent, negligent, intentionally tortious or criminal does not prevent the actor from being liable for harm caused thereby.'" [*Vesely* v. *Sager* (1971) 5 Cal. 3d 153, 163–164, quoting Rest. 2d Torts, § 449; italics added.] Thus, if it was reasonably foreseeable that physicians, despite awareness of the dangers of Chloromycetin, would be consciously or subconsciously induced to prescribe the drug when it was not warranted, Parke, Davis cannot be relieved of liability because of the intervening act of Dr. Beland in prescribing the drug while cognizant of its dangers. If there is room for reasonable men to differ as to whether the intervening act was reasonably foreseeable, then the question is properly left to the jury. [*McEvoy* v. *American Pool Corp.* (1948) 32 Cal. 2d 295; Rest. 2d Torts, § 453, com. *a.*]

> We are satisfied from a review of the evidence set forth in detail, *supra,* that the jury could reasonably find that Dr. Beland's negligent prescription of Chloromycetin for Mrs. Stevens was a foreseeable consequence of the extensive advertising and promotional campaign planned and carried out by the manufacturer. The record reveals in abundant detail that Parke, Davis made every effort, employing both direct and subliminal advertising, to allay the fears of the medical profession which were raised by knowledge of the drug's dangers. It cannot be said, therefore, that Dr. Beland's prescription of the drug despite his awareness of its dangers was anything other that the foreseeable consequence—indeed, the desired result—of Parke, Davis' overpromotion; this intervening act was "one of the hazards which makes [Parke, Davis] negligent." [*Vesely* v. *Sager, supra,* 3 Cal. 3d at p. 163.]

Having rejected Parke, Davis's substantive arguments against the jury's verdict, the court also dismissed as without merit the company's contentions that (1) the trial court erred in denying its motion for a judgment notwithstanding the verdict, and (2) there were flagrant examples of misconduct of plaintiffs' counsel to compel a new trial.

The court's decision was thus stated: "The order granting a new trial is reversed. The order denying defendants' motion for judgment notwithstanding the verdict is affirmed. The judgment is affirmed" (M-37).

EPILOGUE

In a communication to the author dated January 27, 1975, concerning the Stevens case, a spokesman from Parke, Davis stated: [20]

> Parke, Davis does not agree that the promotion or marketing of any of its products, including Chloromycetin, has ever been improper. The promotion of prescription drugs is so regulated, as to what can be written, that it precludes any thought of over-promoting.

> The Food and Drug Administration first issued regulations in December 1960, later revised in October 1968, covering promotion literature. These regulations required that in detailing a product to a physician, the brochure given to the physician contain the full disclosure of the product, or a package insert be left with the doctor.

> There have been changes, approved by the Food and Drug Administration, in the labeling of chloramphenicol since 1965, when the Stevens litigation had its origin. However, these changes were not the result of the lawsuit. All labeling, promotion and advertising is reviewed with the FDA prior to its release.

> Parke, Davis' promotion and distribution of ethical drugs through physician detailing and pharmacy contact has remained much the same. . . . Parke, Davis does not feel that its prescription drugs have been over-promoted, nor has it made any changes in its marketing of these products as a result of the Stevens lawsuit.

SELECTED REFERENCES

BALL, ROBERT, "The Secret Life of Hoffman-LaRoche," *Fortune,* 84 (August 1971), 130.

BARTENSTEIN, FRED, JR., "Images of the Drug Industry: The Industry View," in *The Economics of Drug Innovation,* ed. Joseph D. Cooper (Washington, D.C.: American University, Center for the Study of Private Enterprise, 1970).

BOYD, ELDON M., "The Equivalence of Drug Brands," *Rx Bulletin,* 2 (July–August 1971), 101.

[20] Letter from M. Thorn Kuhl, public affairs division, Parke, Davis & Company, Detroit, Michigan, dated January 27, 1975.

BUCHAN, J. W., "America's Health: Fallacies, Beliefs, Practices," *FDA Consumer,* 6 (October 1972), 4.

CBS Reports, "Prescription: Take With Caution," CBS Television Network, January 10, 1975.

COOPER, MICHAEL H., *Prices and Profits in the Pharmaceutical Industry* (New York: Pergamon, 1966).

DOWLING, HARRY F., *Medicines for Man* (New York: Knopf, 1970).

"Drug Substitution: How to Turn Order into Chaos," *Journal of the American Medical Association,* 217 (August 9, 1971), 817.

EDWARDS, MARVIN H., "Chloromycetin: Special Report," *Private Practice,* 3 (March 1971), 3.

FIRESTONE, JOHN M., *Trends in Prescription Drug Prices* (Washington, D.C.: American Enterprise Institute for Public Policy Research, 1970).

FLESH, GEORGE, "Pharmaceutical Advertising," *New Physician,* 20 (March 1971), 137.

FUNK, EDWIN, "Yesterday, Today and Tomorrow in Drug Advertising," *Pharmaceutical Marketing and Media,* 2 (March 1967), 13.

GARAI, PIERRE R., "Advertising and Promotion of Drugs," in *Drugs in Our Society,* ed. Paul Talalay (Baltimore: John Hopkins Press, 1964).

HARRIS, RICHARD, *The Real Voice* (New York: Macmillan, 1964).

————, *A Sacred Trust* (Baltimore: Penguin, 1969).

HOGE, JAMES F., "Legislative History of Home Remedies," *Annals of the New York Academy of Sciences,* 120 (1965), 833.

Incollingo v. *Ewing,* (Pa. 1971) 282 A. 2d 206; 444 Pa. 263.

"In Whose Hands?" *Economic Priorities Report,* 4 (August–November 1973), 4–5.

JICK, HERSHEL, OLLI S. MIETTENIN, SAMUEL SHAPIRO, GEORGE P. LEWIS, VICTOR SISKIND, and DENNIS SLONÈ. "Comprehensive Drug Surveillance," *Journal of the American Medical Association,* 213 (August 31, 1970), 1455.

KIEFER, DAVID M., "Risk and Reward in Ethical Drugs," *Chemical and Engineering News,* 46 (January 29, 1968), 22.

Love v. *Wolf,* (1964) 226 Cal. App. 2d 378; 38 Cal. Rptr. 64.

Magee v. *Wyeth Laboratories,* 214 Cal. App. 2d.

MARONDE, ROBERT F., STANLEY SEIBERT, JACK KATZOFF, and MILTON SILVERMAN, "Prescription Data Processing: Its Role in the Control of Drug Abuse," *California Medicine,* 117 (September 1972), 22.

MAY, CHARLES D., "Selling Drugs by 'Educating' Physicians," *Journal of Medical Education,* 36 (January 1961), 15.

McEvoy v. *American Pool Corp.,* (1948) 32 Cal. 2d 295.

Mercer v. *Perez,* (1968) 68 Cal. 2d 104.

MINTZ, MORTON, "Drug Ad Exports Pose a Problem," *Washington Post,* May 21, 1968.

————, "The Pill: Press and Public at the Experts' Mercy," *Columbia Journalism Review,* 7 (winter 1968–69), 4.

MODELL, WALTER, "Editorial: Requiem for the FDA," *Clinical Pharmacology and Therapeutics,* 11 (January–February 1970), 1.

MYERS, MAVEN J., "Distribution Aspects in the Potential Misuse of O-T-C Preparations," *American Journal of Pharmacy,* 142 (January–February 1970), 29.

NORWOOD, G. JOSEPH, and MICKEY C. SMITH, "Market Mortality of New Products in the Pharmaceutical Industry," *Journal of the American Pharmaceutical Industry*, N.S. 11 (1971), 592.

Opinion Research Corporation, *Physicians' Attitudes Toward Drug Compendia, A National Survey Sponsored by Pharmaceutical Manufacturers Association,* Princeton, N.J., 1968.

OPPENHEIMER, ROBERT, "Ethics Is Alive and Well in Medical Ad-Land," *Pharmaceutical Marketing and Media,* 3 (April 1968), 9.

PEARSON, MICHAEL, *The Million-Dollar Bugs* (New York: Putnam, 1969).

Pharmaceutical Manufacturers Association, *The Medications Physicians Prescribe: Who Shall Determine the Source?* (Washington, D.C., 1972).

SESSER, STANFORD, "Peddling Dangerous Drugs Abroad: Special Dispensation," *New Republic,* 164 (March 6, 1971), 17.

SILVERMAN, MILTON, *Magic in a Bottle,* 2nd ed. (New York: Macmillan, 1948).

————, and PHILIP R. LEE, *Pills, Profits, and Politics* (Berkeley, Calif.: University of California Press, 1974).

Sterling Drug Inc. v. *Yarrow,* (8th Cir. 1969) 408 F.2d 978.

STOLLEY, PAUL D., and JAMES L. GODDARD, "Prescription Drug Insurance for the Elderly Under Medicare," *American Journal of Public Health,* 61 (March 1971), 574.

TEELING-SMITH, GEORGE, "The British Drug Scene," *The Economics of Drug Innovation,* ed. Joseph D. Cooper (Washington, D.C.: American University, Center for the Study of Private Enterprise, 1970).

U.S. Congress, Senate, Subcommittee on Antitrust and Monopoly of the Committee on the Judiciary, *Physician Ownership in Pharmacies and Drug Companies,* 1965.

U.S. Congress, Senate, Subcommittee on Monopoly of the Select Committee on Small Business, *Competitive Problems in the Drug Industry: Present Status of Competition in the Pharmaceutical Industry,* Parts 5, 6, and 11, 91st Cong., 1st and 2nd sess., 92nd Cong., 1st sess., 1967, 1968, 1969.

U.S. Congress, Senate, Subcommittee on Monopoly of the Select Committee on Small Business, *Advertising of Proprietary Medicines: Effect of Promotion and Advertising of Over-the-Counter Drugs on Competition, Small Business, and the Health and Welfare of the Public,* Part 3, 92nd Cong., 2nd sess., December 1972.

U.S. Congress, Senate, Subcommittee on Health of the Committee on Labor and Public Welfare, *Examination of the Pharmaceutical Industry, 1973–74,* Parts 1–6, 93rd Cong., 1st and 2nd sess., December 1973, February, March, and May 1974.

Vesely v. *Sager,* (1971) 5 Cal. 3d 153.

VOGT, DONALD D., and NORMAN F. BILLUPS, "The Merger Movement in the American Pharmaceutical Complex," *Journal of the American Pharmaceutical Association,* N.S. 11 (November 1971), 588.

WAITE, ARTHUR S., "The Future of Pharmaceutical Drug Promotion," *Medical Marketing and Media,* 6 (June 1971), 9.

WASSERMAN, BENNETT, "The Ubiquitous Detailman," *Hofstra Law Review,* 1973.

Yarrow v. *Sterling Drug Co.,* (D.C. S.Dak. 1967) 263 F.Supp. 159.

Youtz v. *Thompson Tire Co.,* (1941), 46 Cal. App. 2d 672.

ZALAZNICK, SHELDON, "Bitter Pills for the Drugmakers," *Fortune,* 77 (July 1968), 82.

Corporations and Their Authorized Dealers and Franchises

MOBIL OIL COMPANY

AND ITS FRANCHISED DEALERS

BIG CORPORATION, SMALL ENTREPRENEUR, AND CONSUMER INTEREST AND CONVENIENCE

> Big oil isn't out to get the independent gasoline dealers out of a sense of malice or anything like that. It's just good business. . . . they don't renew leases. They say they're eliminating uneconomic stations. But why should the uneconomic stations *always* be independents?
>
> —MARTIN LOBEL, lawyer and a former executive assistant to Senator William Proxmire (D, Wis.) [1]

In February 1974 Mr. Lawrence Ancker, the owner of North Avenue Service Center, a Mobil gas outlet, joined twenty other Mobil dealers in a class action suit to prevent the company from canceling their leases. Mr. Ancker had been notified by Mobil in October 1973 that the lease would not be renewed.

Reprinted from S. Prakash Sethi, *Images and Products: Marketing, Institutional Advertising, and Public Interest* (Santa Barbara, Calif.: Wiley/Hamilton, 1976). Copyright © 1976 by John Wiley & Sons, Inc., New York. Used by permission.
1 "Gasoline Stations Threaten to Close in Protest to U.S., Squeeze on Independents," *The New York Times,* February 16, 1974, p. 1.

THE INDEPENDENT DEALER'S POSITION

Mr. Ancker's case against the company can be summarized as follows:
In April 1972 Mr. Ancker entered into an agreement with Mobil Oil to
lease Mobil-owned land, a building on that land, and the use of Mobil
trademarks and advertising in order to operate a gas station and affiliated
service facilities in Norwalk, Connecticut. The lease was to run one year
and was subject to renewal every year.

Ancker contends that with an investment of money, time, and effort,
he built his station into a high-volume dealership (over 500,000 gallons a
year). He regards himself as the Lord & Taylor's of Norwalk's gas stations.[2] His lease was renewed for a second year. However, in October 1973
he received a letter from Mobil simply saying that his lease was being
canceled and that it was inadvisable to renew it. "That's all. No cause. No
nothing." [3]

Mobil offered him a job with the company to run the same station as
contract manager. Ancker maintained that Mobil was following a similar
policy in Connecticut and New Jersey and had canceled the leases of a
majority of their lessee dealers who were operating gas stations with high
sales volumes.

> Under this plan, Mobil will *own* the gasoline that the station will
> sell, *fix* the price at which it will be sold and reap the profit there-
> from. The contract manager selected will be an *employee* of Mobil.
> He will be paid a weekly salary, and as additional income will keep
> the profit he makes on the sale of tires, batteries, accessories and
> repairs.[4]

Ancker contended that Mobil's move was directed at controlling the
movement and disposal of gas and its pricing at every point from the oil
well to the gas pump and would result in "a monopolistic bonanza" for
the oil companies. The independent retailer would be the loser but the
public would be the real victim, "as it would be at the mercy of the major
oil companies, which would control prices." [5] Ancker further maintained
that although he would be making essentially the same amount of money
under the new arrangement, he could not go along with it because he
wanted to retain his "independent status and continue to serve the community on that basis." [6]

2 "Service Stations Battle Mobil Oil in Connecticut," *The New York Times,* March 19,
1974, p. 47. See also "Dealer Claims Mobil Oil Forces Him to Clear Out," *The Hour*
(a Norwalk, Connecticut, daily newspaper), February 28, 1974, p. 1.
3 *The New York Times,* March 19, 1974, p. 47.
4 Letter dated February 20, 1974, from Lawrence Ancker to Fred Ferretti, staff reporter
of *The New York Times.*
5 *The Hour,* February 28, 1974, p. 1.
6 *Ibid.*

MOBIL OIL COMPANY'S POSITION

Mobil contended that the company's action was in response to the Franchise Act amendments enacted in 1973. (As of February 1974, Mobil had canceled 14 of its 200 franchises in Connecticut and had sent notices of cancellation to another 90 dealers.) This act prohibits an oil supplier from failure to renew a service station lease except for "good cause." The act does not define the phrase "good cause." In a communication to the author, Mr. J. William Dalgetty, a Mobil Oil regional attorney, stated:

> The 1973 Connecticut Franchise Act had the effect of giving a dealer, who had invested approximately $10,000 in inventory and equipment, the same long term property rights in a service station as an oil company supplier that had invested $300,000.
>
> . . . the supplier/landlords did not know under what conditions they would be able to discontinue doing business with a service station dealer once they entered into a lease arrangement.
>
> . . . this legislation is basically anti-consumer because it denies an oil company landlord the flexibility to discontinue doing business with those dealers that operate a dirty service station, and engage in price gouging and other practices not in the best interests of the consuming public.[7]

The company further stated that this law removed nearly all control that the company then had over such an investment "even to the extent of preventing us from choosing not to continue doing business with a dealer after a lease or a supply contract has expired." [8] The company was left with "no alternative but to work out a new relationship with dealers in Connecticut." [9] The dealers so chosen were invariably high-volume, high-value stations.

The company's response implied that it was simply taking defensive measures, confined to Connecticut, to protect its long-term interests as well as those of the consuming public. However, a perusal of news reports and a flurry of private and government civil and criminal lawsuits indicated, at least on the surface, that Mobil's activities were not confined to Connecticut, nor was it alone in its efforts to increase the number of company-owned stations. It seemed that most of the major oil companies were taking advantage of the fuel shortage and endeavoring to squeeze out the independent operators by denying them adequate fuel supplies and by other practices aimed at making these dealers' operations unprofitable (Appendix).

[7] Letter to the author dated October 21, 1974.
[8] *The New York Times,* March 19, 1974, p. 51.
[9] *Ibid.*

THE STATE OF CONNECTICUT STEPS IN

The Connecticut State Assembly responded to the complaints of many dealers by introducing a new bill—5096—which would amend the 1973 Franchise Act and make a material alteration of a franchise an unfair trade practice. The bill also provided for compulsory arbitration in case of contract disputes between the dealer and the company. The bill had the support of an overwhelming majority of the state's independent gasoline station operators (those opposing it felt it did not afford them enough protection), the state's Department of Consumer Protection, and Connecticut Governor Thomas J. Meskill.

The hearings were held before the General Law Committee of the Connecticut State Assembly.[10] The only organized group objecting to the bill was the petroleum industry, which instead supported bill 328 (discussed later in this section). It is interesting to briefly review the arguments both for and against the bill because they throw a great deal of light on the practices of the oil industry as seen by the industry and the independent dealers. Equally important, it tells us something about the rhetoric employed by various parties.

Arguments against Bill 5096

The representative from Mobil Oil made the following arguments:

1. Bill 5096 suffers from the same defects as the 1973 amendment to the Franchise Act: there is no definition of "good cause." What would constitute good cause? An oil company's wish to sell a service station when a lease has expired? The company's desire to convert the property to another use? If poor appearance constitutes good cause, who determines the standards of poor appearance?

2. The purpose of this bill is to give franchisees more security when dealing with their franchisors. However, the bill will actually have the opposite effect. By not being able to make any materially different changes in the terms or conditions of the agreement, the franchisor might simply have to change its way of doing business. The term "materially different change" is too vague and only adds to the uncertainties already present in the 1973 Franchise Act.

3. The bill would make an unfair trade practice out of the termination, nonrenewal, or modification of a franchise. The Unfair and Deceptive Trade Practices Act passed last year is a consumer protection act. Franchisees, including service station dealers and vari-

[10] Transcripts of hearings before the General Law Committee on bills 5096 and 328 dated March 19, 1974, pp. 256–84; April 1, 1974, pp. 114–20; April 23, 1974, pp. 1280–1336; May 3, 1974, pp. 2462–63.

ous restaurant and hotel/motel operators, are not consumers but businessmen and as such they should be regulated by laws affecting trade and commerce.

4. Compulsory arbitration is not a good solution. The courts are better equipped and qualified to resolve such disputes as might arise and thus should be used.

The above arguments were supplemented by those given by a spokesman for Shell Oil. The gist of his arguments is as follows:

1. The provisions of bill 5096 were discriminatory, confiscatory, and vindictive and therefore undesirable and unnecessary.
2. A group of dealers misled the committee. Good dealers don't need the protection of this bill—it is only the "unprofessional, inept, inefficient" dealer who needs it in order to remain in business.
3. The rights of the dealers and the suppliers must be balanced so that the interests of the gasoline consumers can be protected.

Arguments for Bill 5096

The Department of Consumer Protection presented these arguments in support of the bill.

1. The State of Connecticut had the power to enact legislation involving a contract which in turn involved a trademark.
2. The so-called ambiguity about the definition of "good cause" was a red herring on the part of the oil companies to direct attention from the main issue of protecting the rightful and legitimate interests of gas station operators.
3. "Good cause" is a positive declaratory statement of conduct and accepted as such in a great number of other states, e.g., Iowa, Nebraska, Florida, and New Jersey. There are many similar phrases in existing state and federal statutes, e.g., undue influence, unfaithfulness, unfair use, unreasonable rate, unfair competition, unjust discrimination, and the like, which have been left undefined. They have been constantly interpreted by reasonable men operating in good faith throughout our history and at all levels of our judicial system.
4. It is not a question of semantics but of motives, to wit, why a company would or would not renew a franchise.
5. Mobil was not concerned with the provisions of the Franchise Act or bill 5096. Its concern lay with the acquisition of high-volume, high-value stations, part of the company's long-range plans. For example, on February 5, 1974, a Mobil representative testified before the district court in Hartford that the company made an analysis of all the 175 Mobil stations in Connecticut and discovered

that some 40 percent of them were grossing over 500,000 gallons a year. He further testified that Mobil's policy was that any station doing business of over 500,000 gallons a year would be taken over by Mobil and run by a Mobil employee. Mobil would renew the license of anyone doing less business.

6. There is nothing in the bill that will interfere with the free enterprise system. The oil companies want to choose for themselves how "free" it should be.

A host of retail gas station operators and representatives of retail gas station dealers testified in support of the bill. It appeared that Mobil was not particularly concerned about the welfare of the gas-buying public. There were recorded instances of the company congratulating a station operator for doing an excellent job in running his station and building volume sales. The congratulations were shortly followed by a terse letter indicating that the operator's lease would be canceled or that the terms of the lease would be radically changed. Other operators testified that their leases were canceled because of "poor performance." They contended that the company used this as an excuse. The real bone of contention was that the dealers had refused to carry Mobil's other items for sale—products they thought were overpriced and uncompetitive. It should be noted that forcing dealers to carry these items is against the law. The company representative denied pursuing such practices.

Bill 328

Notwithstanding all the testimony supporting bill 5096, it was not reported out for action by the assembly. Instead, the committee reported out bill 328, amended per the suggestions of the Mobil representative. It was signed by the governor and became effective as Public Act No. 74–292 on May 10, 1974. The main provisions of this act are as follows:

An Act Concerning the Relationship Between a Franchisor and a Franchisee

Summary: The bill defines "good cause" for cancellation, termination or failure to renew a franchise, requires six months notice of failure to renew because of change of use of the property used in the franchise, removes a requirement that notice of termination, cancellation or non-renewal be filed with the Department of Consumer Protection, and requires franchise renewals to be for a term of three years.

Content and Operation: *Good Cause.* Good cause includes, but is not limited to, failure to comply substantially with any material and reasonable obligation of the franchise agreement. Good cause also includes conversion of the property involved in the franchise to a different use by the franchisor, sale or lease of the property, and failure of the property owner (other than the parties themselves) to renew the lease. If the property is sold or leased to a subsidiary or affiliate of the franchisor, however, it would not be able to be used in the same business as the franchise agreement. *Notice of Intent Not to Renew.* Written notice of intent not to renew because of a different use of the property is required to be given to the franchisor six months prior to the expiration of the franchise agreement. Notice of cancellation or nonrenewal no longer has to be filed with the Department of Consumer Protection. *Term of Franchise.* Franchise renewals are required to be for a term of three years.

MOBIL'S REACTION TO PUBLIC ACT NO. 74–292

With the passage of the new bill, Mobil began offering for lease those stations that it had earlier converted to salary operations from franchise operations. Larry Ancker, who had operated his station for six months without any contract, also received a new lease and is now operating his station at the same location.

But Mobil's views about such laws remain unchanged. J. William Dalgetty, the company attorney who took an active part in the Connecticut assembly hearings and also offered amendments that were incorporated into the law, stated in a communication to the author:

> . . . we are still philosophically opposed to any law that restricts a landlord's right not to renew a lease agreement after it has expired. . . . We believe that this type of legislation unconstitutionally transfers long term property rights from a land owner, who has invested substantial sums of money to acquire the property, to a lessee dealer who has put up little or no capital that he can't otherwise get back out of his business.[11]

11 Letter dated October 21, 1974.

APPENDIX

RELATIONSHIP BETWEEN MAJOR OIL COMPANIES AND THEIR FRANCHISED DEALERS

It appears that the problems of Mobil dealers in Connecticut were not isolated cases spawned by the Connecticut Franchise Act. During the energy crisis, there were nationwide complaints that major oil companies were trying to use the gasoline scarcity as a means of eliminating competition at the retail distribution level.

The retail distribution of gasoline is essentially carried out by three types of operators. First, there are company-owned and operated stations selling branded gasoline and other products known as TAB (tires, accessories, and batteries) supplied by the company. The second type of station is operated by independent dealers who have franchises to sell the branded gas at a certain location. These are the franchised dealers. Quite often the property and equipment are owned by the company, which then leases them to an independent operator who works on a commission. He is free to raise or lower prices even in competition with company-owned stations selling the same brand, in response to market conditions. The third type is an independent dealer who sells private brand (nonmajor) gasoline and competes primarily on the basis of price. These operators buy gasoline from independent refiners or wholesalers who, in turn, may have bought their supplies from major oil companies trying to unload surplus inventories.

An issue arising out of the energy crisis of the winter of 1974 concerns marketing practices of the major oil companies. While consumers were noticeably upset by the rapidly rising price of gasoline and long lines at the pumps, dealers were voicing their displeasure over aspects of their relationships with the big oil companies. There were allegations that the major companies were engaged in an ambitious campaign to drive the independent dealers out of business.

There were widespread complaints of gas station closings. However, evidence indicates that most of the closings were concentrated among small independent stations selling private brands or off-brand gasoline, and among franchised dealers.

During the peak years of 1969–70, there were 222,000 gasoline stations. As the fuel crisis of 1973–74 worsened, the number dropped to 216,000. The drop is even larger than the 6,000 indicates, however, because as many small stations closed they were replaced by fewer but larger stations. In Los Angeles County alone, the world's largest single gasoline market, there were 7,076 service stations before the crisis. Of these, 6,028 sold major brand names and 1,048 were independents. After the crisis had peaked, 704 big brand stations and 270 independents had closed. While independents and franchised dealers were dwindling in number, company-owned outlets were becoming more numerous. Before 1973, Shell owned only 174 of the 9,500 stations selling Shell gasoline. But then in

1973 it opened 163 more—an almost 100 percent increase in just one year.[1]

Complaints reverberated throughout the ranks of the independent dealers. They accused the oil companies of using the oil crisis to squeeze the independents out while setting up their own company-owned and operated stations. Other complaints included that of independents having to stock their stations with company-owned TAB upon threat of loss of lease. Mobil Oil and Union Oil have been charged in suits on this point.

The independents selling nonmajor gasoline exhibited higher failure rates than did the other independents. By 1973 these independents constituted approximately one-sixth of the stations in the United States, but accounted for roughly one-fourth of all the gasoline sold. Nearly 12 percent were forced to close during the oil crisis, as compared with only 9 percent of the major brand name stations.[2]

To these dealers, the gasoline shortage that occurred in the winter of 1974 was contrived by the major oil companies as a way of forcing the nonbrand independents out of business. With a shortage, of course, the major companies would not be able to provide excess gasoline to the independents. Thus the stations would be forced out of business. Presently the independents' share of the retail market has shrunk from its high of 25 percent to half that, and it will get even smaller, some sources say.[3]

The reaction of the oil companies to these complaints was to insist, first of all, that the oil shortage was indeed real and that they allocated fuel as equitably as possible. As to not renewing leases, they said that they were changing their marketing practices and the station closings were part of a tightening-up process. "We were overbuilt," says one executive; "What we're doing is eliminating uneconomic stations." [4]

In September 1974 *The New York Times* published the remarks of Z. D. Bonner, president of Gulf Oil Company, U.S. In his remarks Mr. Bonner said that the major oil companies shared the frustration felt by the American public brought about by the previous winter's gasoline shortage. He indicated that although charges of a created shortage had been shown to be without basis, there had been a persistent trend to lay all the blame on the major oil companies. Mr. Bonner stated that punitive measures instituted by federal authorities had occurred and would continue to occur. If regulatory agencies would refrain from exerting any influence on the operations of American business, in particular the oil companies, the free enterprise system would work as advertised. Mr. Bonner seemed to imply that the gasoline shortage was not contrived by the oil companies, but instead resulted as a consequence of the activities of federal regulatory agencies. He called for business to enter into a practice of stewardship for the free enterprise system, so as to educate the public concerning the functioning of the market economy and the need to deregulate industry. Nowhere in his remarks was there any attention

---

[1] Fred Ferretti, "Gasoline Stations Threaten to Close in Protest to U.S.—Squeeze on Independents," *The New York Times*, February 16, 1974, p. 1.

[2] *Ibid.*

[3] *Ibid.*

[4] *Ibid.*

paid to the claims by the various dealers that the major companies were attempting to create an anticompetitive industry. Instead, the tone of Mr. Bonner's remarks seemed to be that if left alone, American business, i.e., the oil industry, would operate efficiently and in the best interests of the consumer.[5]

Some legal action has been taken by various groups to counter these assertions. The situation of the independent dealer spawned a hearing in Salt Lake City in March 1973 before the Consumer Subcommittee of the Senate Commerce Committee. The hearings contained testimony by several local and independent dealers, one of them a lessee of two Texaco stations. At one time this individual had been a district sales representative for Texaco. He testified that during the time he worked for Texaco there was a 30 to 40 percent annual dealer turnover rate. After two years, only five of his original dealer accounts were still maintained. He indicated that the reason for the turnover could be explained by the company's marketing practices: "It is a common occurrence for a major oil company dealer to find himself competing with some gasoline marketing by his own company at prices from 4 to 10 cents below the price at which he is asked to sell." [6] The various other individuals who testified at the hearings presented similar stories. It was suggested that although the issue of dealer/company relationships had appeared to surface in Utah, there was reason to expect that a nationwide trend was developing.[7]

In March 1974 a grand jury was impaneled at the request of the New York State attorney general's office to investigate alleged criminal activities in New York State by the petroleum industry. One of the resulting indictments charged Mobil Oil with "restraint of trade and competition" between May 1972 and April 24, 1974, in four New York City counties. The specific charges stated:

> . . . certain agents and employees of Mobil attempted, by means of threats, to coerce certain Mobil dealers to purchase automobile tires, batteries and accessories solely from Mobil. [This was done] even though the prices charged by Mobil for such articles were higher than the prices for which such articles could be purchased elsewhere, and even though said dealers had no legal obligation to purchase [them from Mobil].[8]

In September 1974 seven oil companies—Mobil, Exxon, Shell, Gulf, Sunoco, Amoco, and Texaco—were indicted and charged with "criminally

[5] Z. D. Bonner, "How Industry Can Regain Public's Trust—Point of View," *The New York Times,* September 1, 1974, Sec. 3, p. 10.
[6] Statement of Gary Anderson before the Consumer Subcommittee of the Senate Commerce Committee, March 17, 1973.
[7] Statement of Charles Binsted, president of the National Congress of Petroleum Retailers, before the Consumer Subcommittee of the Senate Commerce Committee, March 17, 1973.
[8] "Mobil Oil Is Arraigned, Pleads Innocent to Forcing Dealers to Buy Its Products," *The Wall Street Journal,* July 2, 1974, p. 4.

acting together to restrain competition in the sale of gasoline" in New York City.[9] Another indictment accused Exxon, Mobil, and Gulf of entering into an agreement in order to thwart open bidding for the gasoline sold to government agencies throughout New York State.[10]

In October the same grand jury suggested but did not formally charge that more than a year before the 1973–74 Arab oil embargo, the major United States oil companies conspired to create a fuel shortage so that prices could be driven up and independent dealers would be forced out of business. Because the oil companies created the shortage in 1972, the United States was much more vulnerable to the Arab oil embargo later on.[11]

In other actions against the oil industry, a state suit was filed in California against Union Oil for trying to force the operators of a service station to stop selling other firms' products.[12] A $200 million suit was filed against Mobil Oil by a former California service station operator who charged that his lease had been illegally terminated because he sought to buy his TAB supplies from a source other than Mobil.[13] A provisional consent order was arrived at between the Federal Trade Commission and Phillips Petroleum in order to free 1,400 of Phillips' 26,000 retail outlets from practices that the FTC deemed anticompetitive. These included allowing the outlets to purchase TAB supplies from non-Phillips sources, easing restrictions on purchasing gasoline from other suppliers, and renewing leases for at least five years in most cases and giving dealers the right to arbitrate disputes about lease cancellations. James T. Halverson, director of FTC's Bureau of Competition, hopes that the consent order will serve as a model for other oil companies in their dealings with their retail outlets.[14]

SELECTED REFERENCES

ALLVINE, FRED C., and JAMES M. PATTERSON, *Competition Ltd.: The Marketing of Gasoline* (Bloomington: Indiana University Press, 1975).

———, and ———, *Highway Robbery: An Analysis of the Gasoline Crisis* (Bloomington: Indiana University Press, 1975).

American Motor Inns, Inc. v. *Holiday Inns, Inc.*, 365 F. Supp. 1073 (D.N.J. 1973).

9 Oil Companies Are Indicted Here in Gasoline Sales," Fred Ferretti, *The New York Times,* September 1974, p. 1.

10 "Seven Major Oil Concerns Plead Innocent to Antitrust Charges in New York City," *The Wall Street Journal,* September 6, 1974, p. 8.

11 "Jury Hints Big Oil Plot by U.S. Firms," *San Francisco Chronicle,* October 8, 1974, p. 8.

12 "Antitrust Suit Against Oil Firm," *San Francisco Chronicle,* December 25, 1974, p. 14.

13 William Moore, "Ousted Gas Dealer Is Suing Mobil Oil," *San Francisco Chronicle,* January 8, 1975, p. 2.

14 "Phillips Petroleum to Free 1,400 Dealers from Curbs FTC Calls Anticompetitive," *The Wall Street Journal,* September 18, 1974, p. 5.

COMANOR, WILLIAM S., "Vertical Territorial Restrictions and Customer Restrictions: *White Motor* and Its Aftermath," *Harvard Law Review,* 81 (1968), 1419.

GTE Sylvania, Inc. v. *Continental R.V., Inc., et al.,* No. 71–1705 (9th Cir., May 9, 1974).

GRETHER, E. T., *Marketing and Public Policy* (Englewood Cliffs, N.J.: Prentice-Hall, 1966).

HUNT, SHELBY, "Socio-Economic Consequences of Franchise System of Distribution," in *Contractual Marketing Systems,* ed. Donald L. Thompson (Lexington, Mass.: Heath, 1971).

KITSON, PETER W., "Trademark Franchising and Antitrust Sanctions: The Need for a Limited Rule of Reason," *Boston University Law Review,* 52 (1973), 463.

LaFortune v. *Ebie,* 26 Cal. App. 3d 72, 102 Cal. Rptr. 588 (1972).

McGUIRE, E. PATRICK, Franchised Distribution (New York: The Conference Board, 1971).

MOYER, REED, "Competitive Impact of the Emerging Energy Company," *California Management Review,* 16 (summer 1974), 4.

POSNER, RICHARD A., "Exclusionary Practices and the Antitrust Laws," *University of Chicago Law Review,* 41 (1967), 506.

PRESTON, LEE E., "Restrictive Distribution Arrangements: Economic Analysis and Public Policy Standards," *Law and Contemporary Problems,* 30 (summer 1965), 506.

Sealy Mattress Company of Southern California v. *Sealy, Inc.,* 346 F. Supp. 353 (N.C. Ill. 1972).

THOMPSON, DONALD N., *Franchise Operations and Antitrust* (Lexington, Mass.: Heath, 1971).

TIMBERG, SIGMUND, "Territorial Restrictions on Franchisees: Post-Schwinn Developments," *Antitrust Law Bulletin,* 19 (1974), 205.

U.S. Congress, Senate, Judiciary Subcommittee on Antitrust and Monopoly, *Hearings on Exclusive Territorial Allocation Legislation,* 92nd Cong., 1972.

United States v. *Topco Associates, Inc.,* 319 F. Supp. 1031 (1970).

United States v. *Topco Associates, Inc.,* 405 U.S. 596 (1972).

Corporations, Ethnic Minorities, and Discrimination

EASTMAN KODAK COMPANY (A), ROCHESTER, NEW YORK

CONFLICT WITH A MINORITY GROUP—FIGHT

> It is beneficial for businessmen to indulge in introspection and in the words of Robert Burns, "see ourselves as others see us." It seems ironically fitting that the line should be from Burns' poem "To a Louse," because that is precisely how some people do see businessmen . . .
>
> —GEORGE R. VILA,
> Chairman and President, Uniroyal Inc.

Eastman Kodak is the largest producer of photographic equipment and supplies in the world. In *Fortune's* list of five hundred corporations in 1972 Kodak ranks twenty-third, with yearly sales in excess of $3.47 billion. It has over 114,000 employees in all its plants and offices.

Kodak, headquartered in Rochester, New York, is that city's largest employer, its more than 44,000 employees being about 13 percent of the entire work force in the area. Kodak's influence on the Rochester community is such that merchants schedule sales to coincide with Kodak bonus checks.[1]

In 1918 founder George Eastman started the Rochester Community

This case material has been adapted from S. Prakash Sethi, *Business Corporations and the Black Man* (San Francisco: Chandler Publishing Company, 1970). Copyright © 1970 by Chandler Publishing Company. Used by permission.

[1] Jules Loh, Associated Press for Sunday A.M. papers, April 23, 1967.

Service (later the Community Chest).[2] He also founded the Eastman School of Music and made large grants to medicine and to the community theater.[3] The company enjoys a close relationship with Rochester University and other local organizations,[4] donates employee time to work in civic causes, and is considered both a good place to work and a good corporate citizen: "Evidence of the company's philanthropy is visible everywhere." In the decade of the sixties Kodak pumped nearly $22 million into the city's hospitals, schools, and Community Chest. The company sponsors a fellowship program for black teachers, and in 1964 alone it gave $1.5 million for aid to education.

Because it is nonunionized, Kodak is unusual. More than half the companies in Rochester, (including General Motors, General Dynamics, and Xerox) are unionized. One Kodak executive says, ". . . the only explanation is that . . . the laws being what they are . . . people don't feel the need to be represented." The company says that "Kodak continually reviews its employment policies to assure that they do not present any barriers to the employment of anyone because of race, creed, color, sex, or age. Pre-employment testing is limited to a few jobs which require specific skills or aptitudes." [5]

The company has long had a skilled trades apprentice program which, according to one Kodak brochure, consists of up to four years of "combined classroom and on-the-job training leading to a skilled craftsman career as an electrician, instrument mechanic, machinist, pipe fitter, sheet metal worker, or tool or instrument maker. A high school diploma or equivalent and demonstrated mechanical ability are required." [6]

Kodak was one of the first one hundred companies to join President Kennedy's Committee of Equal Employment Opportunity "Plans for Progress Program," in June 1962.[7] Its brochure "How Kodak People Are Selected" says, "For any particular job, the person is chosen who appears best fitted to do that job. . . . Such things as race, creed, color or national origin neither help nor hinder in getting a job at Kodak."

Kodak has been making efforts to ensure that blacks are aware of opportunities at Kodak. In recruiting nonprofessionals, the company uses a number of community agencies, such as the Human Relations Commission, the New York State Employment Service, the Urban League, Rochester's five settlement houses, high school counselors (with emphasis on inner-city schools), and adult education program administrators. In 1966 Kodak, which contributes to the Negro College Fund, expanded the range of its recruitment of professionals to include thirteen predominantly black colleges. During that year the company was involved with career centers in a program to help place college-trained Negroes.

2 "There's a FIGHT in Kodak's Future," *Factory,* June 1967, p. 69.
3 "Meeting of Minds," *Forbes,* October 1, 1965, pp. 37–38.
4 *Ibid.;* also see *Yearbook of American Churches* (New York: National Council of Churches of Christ in the U.S.A., 1965).
5 "Equal Employment Opportunity. Eastman Kodak Company's Positive Program" (Rochester, New York: Public Relations Department, Eastman Kodak Company, 1967).
6 *Ibid.*
7 *Ibid.*

A former Eastman Kodak board chairman stated in a letter of April 25, 1966:

> You will recognize that our efforts to provide equal employment opportunities are increasingly more positive and far-reaching than in past years. Previously our policy had been simply to try to employ the person best fitted to do the work available without regard for his or her background. We have moved actively beyond that position. We now seek to help the individual who lacks the necessary qualifications *to become qualified*. In other words, we are contributing to the training of the individual so that he or she can qualify for employment.

However, Kodak's sense of social responsibility, though contributing to the betterment of community life, resembles that of the benevolent Puritan father who, while making sure of his children's welfare, does not hesitate to discipline them should they fail to measure up to his standards and values. By keeping its employees happy with generous bonuses, good working conditions, and other benefits, the company has remained free of unions and has carefully guarded the established prerogatives of management.

The benevolent father image is very strong in Rochester and has been fostered so assiduously and for such a long time that to some extent both the community and the company have become its captives. As William C. Martin puts it: "It is inaccurate to think of Rochester as a company town but he who underestimates the devotion Rochesterians feel toward Eastman Kodak does so at his own peril. . . ." [8]

ROCHESTER

According to the 1970 United States census, Rochester is the forty-ninth largest city in the country. *The World Almanac* says that New York's third largest city is a "world leader in the manufacture of precision goods and a major eastern U.S. cultural center. Located on Lake Ontario, it leads the world in the manufacture of photographic film and cameras, optical goods, dental equipment, and thermometers." [9] Rochester's largest employers are Eastman Kodak (41,757), Xerox Corporation (13,000) and Bausch and Lomb (5,300).

In a public relations ad in *The New York Times* Rochester said of itself that it was "a community [metropolitan area] of more than 700,000 people with the highest percentage of skilled, technical and professional employees of any major U.S. metropolitan area; more engineers than any one of 23 states; the highest median family income of any city in the state,

---

[8] William C. Martin, "Shepherds vs. Flocks, Ministers vs. Negro Militancy," *Atlantic*, December 1967, pp. 53–59.
[9] *The World Almanac, 1970* (Cleveland, Ohio: Newspaper Enterprise Association, Inc., 1970).

sixth highest in the nation . . . 67 percent of the residents owning their own houses. For the Negro, it would seem that things never looked better. Employment of whites in the county had increased by 11 percent since 1960 but employment of nonwhites had gone up 43 percent—more than four times the national average." [10] The city housed some of the most enlightened corporations in the nation, with enviable records in labor relations and social welfare policies.

Rochester, in 1966, was suffering from all the malaise of a city in the doldrums. The vigor of its industry, high income, and employment for the majority of its work force were matched by the recurrent and persistent problems of its poor, whose lives were not being improved by the city's antipoverty and civil rights programs. Significantly, public housing units numbered 450, with only 1,400 more in the planning stage. One school board member stated that school segregation was "more severe than ever." [11] A few organizations, such as the NAACP and the Urban League, spoke for the poor and underemployed, but according to a *New Republic* article "the other civil rights organizations don't amount to much. An NAACP rally last year [1966] drew eight people." [12]

Reporting for *The New York Times* on June 20, 1966, John Kifner quoted the Reverend Herbert D. White, a young clergyman who headed the Rochester Area Council of Churches Board of Urban Ministry, on the state of the city:

> This is a city with five settlement houses, whose Community Chest Drive always goes over the top, and which prides itself on having every available service. And it's a city which has gone on line— against a lot of opposition—to have an open enrollment plan in the school and a police review board. But one thing that is crucial here is the high degree of affluence in this community. If you are poor in this town, you really know you are poor.[13]

Affluence was everywhere—for the whites. For blacks it was a mirage, unreal, unattainable. In April 1965 there were no blacks on the city council, none on the board of education or the planning commission. In the fire department 2 of 604 were blacks and on the police force 25 of 515.[14]

BIRTH AND GROWTH OF FIGHT

Rochester's race riots (July 23–26, 1964) had made it evident that something must be done to avoid a recurrence. Most citizens of Rochester

[10] Barbara Carter, "The Fight Against Kodak," *The Reporter*, January 21, 1967, pp. 28–31.
[11] *Ibid.*
[12] James Ridgeway, "Attack on Kodak," *New Republic*, January 21, 1967, pp. 11–13.
[13] John Kifner, "Negro Federation Points to Advances in Its First Year in Rochester," *The New York Times*, June 20, 1966, p. 26.
[14] James Ridgeway, "Saul Alinsky in Smugtown," *New Republic*, June 26, 1965, pp. 15–17.

were embarrassed and shocked that this could happen in "their" city. They believed that Rochester had adequate welfare programs, far superior to those of most other cities. Most leaders were against any radically different or innovative measures, believing that the 1964 riots could not happen again.

The majority of the local clergy felt differently. They felt it necessary to inspire in blacks a feeling that they had some control over their own destiny, and they believed this could best be achieved through a viable local organization. The Rochester Ministers' Conference (RMC), an association of black church leaders, sought assistance from Dr. Martin Luther King's Southern Christian Leadership Conference. As the standard "King" approach did not spark much fervor among the black community, the SCL team suggested that Saul Alinsky might be able to help.

The RMC obtained help from the interdenominational Board for Urban Ministry, which was affiliated with the Rochester Area Council of Churches. The board believed that the crux of the black problems was the "lack of a potent organization to raise his hopes and needs." [15] They felt that Alinsky could channel black hatred toward whites into constructive action through an organization similar to those he had started in other cities. The Board for Urban Ministry, with help from the Council of Churches, raised $100,000 for a two-year contract ($90,000 for expenses and $10,000 for salaries). The necessary funds flowed in from local and national church bodies and from many white liberals.

Alinsky's fame was based on his Woodlawn Organization, which began in the Chicago slums in 1960. Alinsky later expanded his activities to Detroit and Kansas City. Alinsky's *modus operandi* was to seek out "natural leaders" and aid them in forming a "people's organization" whose goal was "self-determination." Alinsky's methods might polarize a community; nevertheless they were defended as being the only hope for ethnic minority poor. Alinsky believed that "people do not get opportunity or freedom or equality or dignity as a gift. . . . They only get these things in the act of taking them through their own efforts. . . . The haves never do anything unless forced."

In April 1965 FIGHT (Freedom-Integration-God-Honor-Today) was formed, allying 134 black organizations. The press warned that Alinsky's methods would result in future riots. Alinsky made an analogy between Rochester and a Southern plantation in his reply.

On June 11, 1965, the first FIGHT convention was held. The 1,000 delegates adopted a constitution, set policy goals, and elected a minister, Franklin Delano Roosevelt Florence, as temporary chairman.

Shortly after Alinsky arrived, local businessmen raised $40,000 to open an office of the moderate Urban League. In the past, funds for such an office had been unavailable. The manager of the Community Chest, threatening to withhold previously committed funds from a settlement house that had tried to join FIGHT, stated: "Chest funds could not be

[15] Loh, Associated Press.

used to support FIGHT . . . in fulfillment of promises made to contributors." Florence accused the Community Chest of discrimination.

The *New Republic* quoted Florence as saying: "The establishment feels it can plan for us and not with us. . . . The only thing the white paternalists want to know about Negroes is whether they will riot again this year. And that all depends," he added, "on how soon the whites learn black men are human beings. They are not their simple children." [16]

In the beginning, Florence's leadership and indeed FIGHT's very survival were in jeopardy. Opposition came not only from the "white establishment" but from the "black community" as well, largely from middle-class blacks who felt that FIGHT's leadership was too militant. During its first eighteen months, FIGHT concentrated on federal antipoverty programs and urban renewal. It succeeded in getting the city to increase the number of planned low-cost housing units and also gained control of the urban renewal Citizens Committee. FIGHT obtained a $65,746 federal antipoverty grant for an adult education program and three seats on Rochester's antipoverty board. FIGHT's picketing of landlords was successful in getting slum apartment buildings fixed up.

FIGHT organized a recruitment and training program with Xerox, starting with sixteen trainees and expanding to thirty the number of jobs for hard-core unemployed workers in 1967.

FIGHT claimed to represent three-quarters of Rochester's black community through its component Negro organizations—churches, settlement houses, and Black Panther clubs. Many disputed this claim. FIGHT accepted few whites, but a "Friends of FIGHT" was formed to give whites a chance to lend support. Before December 20, 1966, FIGHT's active membership was small, but it eventually increased to about three hundred. According to an Associated Press feature story, directors of a settlement house that belonged to FIGHT said that the organization represented less than one percent of the black community. Florence denied this but offered no hard membership statistics.

In its June 1966 convention, FIGHT resolved that "Eastman Kodak be singled out for special investigation this year." According to Alinsky, "Rochester . . . is under the thumb of Eastman Kodak, which also controls the banks, local university, hospitals, etc. The effect of its rule is to shut Negroes away from the rest of the community."

THE CONFRONTATION

Florence's first meeting with Kodak Board Chairman Albert Chapman, President William Vaughn, and Executive Vice-President Louis Eilers, which took place on September 2, 1966, was deceptively harmonious. Florence talked about the problems of the ghetto blacks. He demanded that Kodak implement a new training program to recruit and train blacks

---

[16] Ridgeway, "Saul Alinsky in Smugtown."

who could not meet regular recruitment standards. Vaughn stated that Kodak had such a program and suggested that they talk further on the proposal.

In preparation for the second meeting on September 14, 1966, Alinsky put FIGHT's proposal in writing. At the meeting, Florence read from a written statement that was distributed to everyone present. He admitted that Kodak's special preemployment training programs were a start but that the number of persons had to be increased to between five hundred and six hundred over an eighteen-month period so that they could qualify for entry level positions across the board. Florence further stated that FIGHT, as the only true representative of the unemployed in the Rochester area, should be solely responsible for recruiting and counseling the trainees. Vaughn's reply, also in writing, neither accepted nor rejected FIGHT's demands. Vaughn described the existing programs for the unqualified and spoke of plans to expand them:

> The company hopes to benefit from suggestions which FIGHT may offer, as it has in the past been helped by the advice of a number of organizations on these matters. FIGHT and other interested organizations are invited to refer possible applicants for all these programs.

Vaughn noted that the FIGHT proposal and Kodak plans had much in common and that the company would be interested in meeting again to discuss ways in which "FIGHT might cooperate in the implementation of Kodak's plans."

Kodak seemed in no way to want to end the talks. It was obvious that Kodak had stiffened its resistance to the FIGHT proposal by repeatedly stating "its intention to retain control of all hiring. At the same time, it urged FIGHT to refer people to existing programs designed for the under-skilled." [17] FIGHT rejected Vaughn's proposal to work within the existing Kodak framework for assisting hard-core unemployed. Vaughn refused to bind the company to hiring a specific number of people, pointing out that "jobs aren't something you turn out on a machine." [18] Among the reasons given by Kodak for not accepting FIGHT's demands were:

1. Kodak could not enter an exclusive arrangement with any organization to recruit candidates for employment and still be fair to the more than sixty thousand people who apply each year.
2. Kodak could not agree to a program that would commit it to hire and train a specific and substantial number of people in a period that would extend so far into the future.[19]

[17] Martin, "Shepherds vs. Flocks, Ministers vs. Negro Militancy."
[18] "The Fight That Swirls Around Eastman Kodak," *Business Week*, April 29, 1967, pp. 38–41.
[19] "And Kodak Will Ask, 'How High?' " *Fortune*, June 1, 1967, p. 78.

Florence and Vaughn agreed to meet the following day, but further talk was doomed. The unreconcilable difference was whether FIGHT could *demand* anything by right and whether Kodak could concede FIGHT's demands without abrogating its own rights and obligations. At future meetings, Kodak's leading representative was a second-echelon executive, Kenneth Howard of the Industrial Relations Department.

At one of the meetings, while Howard was explaining Kodak's training program, Florence repeatedly interrupted, asking, "Are we talking about FIGHT's proposal?" [20] Howard unequivocally expressed Kodak's view that the subject was the ways in which FIGHT might cooperate in Kodak's expanded recruitment and training plans. Florence made it clear that he was "not interested in Kodak's plans." He insisted that the discussion be limited to the FIGHT proposal. Howard restated Vaughn's reasons; nothing was accomplished.

The fourth meeting was held September 19. Howard called upon Florence at FIGHT's headquarters. Florence declared that he would deal with no one lower in rank than President Vaughn. Howard then presented a letter from Vaughn to Florence restating Kodak's position and informing him that if FIGHT were willing to cooperate, further discussion could be held; otherwise Kodak would proceed without FIGHT.

Between September 22 and October 22 two letters were exchanged. In one letter Florence stated:

> Use of terms like "exclusively," "monopolistic," "arbitrary demands," etc., in reference to the FIGHT proposal does an injustice to the careful thought and consideration that has gone into our suggestions. We have not even had opportunity to discuss the details of our approach with Eastman Kodak.[21]

Vaughn replied:

> Meanwhile, you and other members of FIGHT might be interested in knowing that while these discussions and subsequent correspondence have been going on the Kodak company has continued to employ a substantial number of people in this community, including many Negroes.[22]

Negotiations broke down completely.

On October 22 Kodak announced that it had made arrangements with the Board of Fundamental Education (BFE), a professional adult education concern, for help in expanding Kodak's training programs. One hundred people would be enrolled. FIGHT was enraged and declared the "deal" to be a fraud perpetrated on the poor. Florence then led a

---

[20] *Business Week*, April 29, 1967.
[21] Letter to William L. Vaughn, president of Eastman Kodak, from Minister Franklin D. R. Florence, president of FIGHT, October 7, 1966.
[22] Letter to Mr. Florence from William L. Vaughn, October 21, 1966.

forty-five-man group to Kodak's office to seek "clarifications" of the program. On his arrival, he found that all the trainees had already been selected.[23] "It's a fraud—It's a trick," Florence immediately declared. And he went on the radio to say: "We can't understand, for our lives, how a company with their creative ability can . . . take pictures of the hidden side of the moon . . . but can't create Instamatic jobs." Saul Alinsky, who was with Florence on the program, said: "I can tell you this. Eastman Kodak has plenty to be concerned about, because this kind of an issue . . . if it ever develops . . . and it may well develop . . . will become a nationwide issue across the board to every Negro ghetto in America." [24]

FIGHT retaliated with an intensive campaign in the news media abusing Kodak and threatening dire consequences for the peace of the city and other ghettos all over America.[25] Alinsky bitterly accused Kodak of playing "an out-and-out public relations con game with FIGHT" and considered the hiring of BFE (rather than the acceptance of FIGHT's programs) a "backdoor deal." [26]

To the management of Kodak, it was inconceivable that their organization, with its enviable record of good corporate citizenship and assistance to minority groups, should be accused by a militant group backed by local churches and other community organizations of not helping the cause of the Negro. Kodak's incredulity was reinforced by growing evidence that the company was not holding its own in the contest. In the public forum, FIGHT repeatedly outmaneuvered and outclassed Kodak.

The human element played its role, too. Florence—described in an AP story [27] as stocky, bullnecked, with a dry voice and unpolished manners— used communications media with dramatic effect on every possible occasion. He held press conferences after every meeting with company officials, sometimes in the lobby of Kodak's headquarters building. Vaughn, on the other hand, a quiet and somewhat aloof man who found Florence's manner "intimidating—a lot of finger-pointing and all that," [28] maintained a cool, dignified posture. Some Kodak employees attempted to help break the impasse between Kodak and FIGHT. In early December, for example, John Mulder, a Kodak assistant vice-president, met for lunch with his friend the Reverend Marvin Chandler, a member of FIGHT, and considered ways in which discussions might be resumed. Mulder had been active in civil rights causes, and his wife was a member of the Friends of FIGHT.[29] He felt that men directly responsible for hiring and training might be the most appropriate company representatives in future discussions with FIGHT.[30] He submitted this idea to Vaughn, who agreed, and on December 16, 1966, he appointed Mulder to head a new Kodak team.

[23] Carter, "The Fight Against Kodak."
[24] *Ibid.*
[25] *Ibid.*
[26] *Rochester Times-Union*, October 24, 1966.
[27] Loh, Associated Press.
[28] *Business Week,* April 29, 1967.
[29] Loh, Associated Press.
[30] Ridgeway, "Attack on Kodak."

KODAK'S ABORTIVE AGREEMENT AND ITS REPERCUSSIONS

On December 19 and 20, Mulder and other Kodak representatives met secretly with FIGHT spokesmen. Mulder had expected to meet with Chandler to pursue further their earlier luncheon discussion. Instead, although Chandler was present, Florence took charge.

At 2 P.M., December 20, the two parties signed the following agreement:

A special committee appointed by Eastman Kodak president, William Vaughn, has been meeting Monday and Tuesday with officers of the FIGHT organization.

Kodak representatives stated that they have not employed traditional standards of hiring for the last two years. FIGHT hailed this as a step in the right direction as well as the Kodak officers' statement that they will deal with the problem of hard-core unemployed.

Job openings, specifications, and hourly rates were discussed and agreed upon by the joint group.

January 15th was agreed upon as the date for a beginning of the referral of 600 employees, the bulk of which would be hard-core unemployed (unattached, uninvolved with traditional institutions).

Under the agreement, the FIGHT organization and Kodak agreed to an objective of the recruitment and referral (to include screening and selection) of 600 unemployed people over a 24-month period, barring unforeseen economic changes affecting the Rochester community. FIGHT, at its own expense, would provide counseling for the employees selected by Kodak.

Kodak agrees to the following: join with FIGHT in a firm agreement to

A. Continue semi-monthly meetings between Kodak and FIGHT to increase the effectiveness of the program.

B. Kodak will familiarize FIGHT counselors with the foremen and work skills required, and in turn FIGHT will familiarize Kodak foremen with the life and environment of poor people.

C. Kodak and FIGHT will share information on the referrals.

D. Kodak and FIGHT will issue a 60-day community progress report.

> JOHN MULDER
> Asst. Vice President,
> Eastman Kodak
> Asst. General Manager,
> Kodak Park Works
> FRANKLIN D. R. FLORENCE
> President of FIGHT

Florence was extremely pleased and repeatedly asked Mulder if he was authorized to sign for Kodak. Upon Mulder's confirmation, FIGHT made a radio announcement of the agreement.

The nature of the content and timing of the agreement were most unusual and were indicative of Kodak's inexperienced negotiating personnel and their general handling of the situation. As Barbara Carter pointed out in "The Fight against Kodak":

> It was a strange agreement at best. One of the six paragraphs mentioned the "referral of six hundred unemployed people," another the referral of "six hundred employees," a distinction of some importance. For a non-union company, the briefest paragraph was by far the oddest. It said simply, "Job openings, specifications, and hourly rates were discussed and agreed upon by the joint group." Moreover, semimonthly meetings on the program's "effectiveness" were also agreed on.

On December 21, 1966, Kodak's executive committee met and voted unanimously to repudiate the agreement. The following day the board of directors met and concurred with the executive committee's decision. In a statement issued by the company the executive committee stated that "for all its ambiguities [the December 20 document] violated antidiscrimination laws." [31] The committee stated that Mulder had not had the authority to bind the company. The company apologized profusely for the mixup but flatly repudiated the whole arrangement.[32] There was no record of any written instructions from Vaughn to Mulder about the extent of the latter's authority in conducting the negotiations. Mulder, after the incident, did not talk to the press or anyone else and his side of the story remained a mystery.

William S. Vaughn, newly elected chairman of the board, said that Kodak had

> two fundamental and critical objections to the FIGHT proposal: (1) We could not enter into an arrangement exclusively with any organization to recruit candidates for employment and still be fair to the more than 60,000 people who apply each year. . . . (2) We could not agree to a program which would commit Kodak to hire and train a specific and substantial number of people in a period which would extend so far into the future. Obviously, our employment needs depend on the kinds of jobs available at a particular time, and on the demand for our products.[33]

According to an Associated Press release describing the events directly following December 20, 1966, "another aspect of the agreement plainly horrified at least one high Kodak executive, who detected the faint odor of a 'labor contract.'" [34]

[31] Loh, Associated Press.
[32] "Fight at Kodak,"*Newsweek,* May 8, 1967, pp. 81, 83.
[33] *Fortune,* June 1, 1967.
[34] Loh, Associated Press.

The community reaction ranged from incredulity to anger. The involvement of a large corporation and the controversial Alinsky resulted in national attention to what Kodak believed was a local issue.

Kodak took double-page advertisements in both morning and afternoon papers and said that it "sincerely regrets any misunderstanding." The ads repeated the company's earlier position that it could not have "an exclusive recruitment" arrangement with any group nor could it commit itself to any specific number of jobs "owing to the uncertainties of economic conditions." Furthermore, the ads gave the company's oft-stated position on social responsibility—Kodak was "deeply concerned to do all that we reasonably can to meet a pressing social need in this community, namely, to try and develop employment opportunities" and "many positive steps" had already been taken by the management.[35]

Although neither FIGHT nor Kodak made it public at this time, it seems that immediately following the repudiation of the agreement by Kodak, and after Kenneth Howard was back in control as Kodak's chief negotiator, FIGHT desperately tried to patch things up and salvage the agreement on almost *any terms acceptable to Kodak but was rebuffed by company officials.* Earl C. Gottschalk, Jr., writing in *The Wall Street Journal* on June 30, 1967, gave the following account of Kodak's attitude:

> On December 23, a delegation headed by Mr. Chandler met with the executive committee. According to Mr. Chandler's account of the meeting—which Kodak agrees is accurate—FIGHT asked Louis D. Eilers, president of Kodak, to sign the agreement. He declined, saying the company simply could not give a second party any voice in determining its labor relations and employment practices. Then, says Mr. Chandler, "We asked them to put into the agreement anything they wanted to, or to change it in any way they desired. Again, Mr. Eilers said no."
>
> "At that point," says Mr. Chandler, "Mr. Florence even suggested that the entire document could be dispensed with if he and either Mr. Eilers or Mr. Vaughn could go on television and make a joint statement saying simply that FIGHT and Kodak would work together to get more jobs for ghetto Negroes. This idea met with no enthusiasm either." [36]

The issue of whether Kodak should accept FIGHT demands merged, in some people's minds, with the personality of Ken Howard. Howard said that he didn't know how widespread this feeling was. "I am aware of some of it, but most of the people who are mad at me do not talk to me about it. It has been the same here since I got this assignment. People who do not agree with you do not talk with you about it because essentially you are following the management policy and position in this area."

35 "Sheen Appoints a Vicar for Poor," *The New York Times,* January 4, 1967, p. 4.
36 Earl C. Gottschalk, Jr., "Kodak's Ordeal," *The Wall Street Journal,* June 30, 1967, pp. 1, 14.

It would be erroneous to assume that Howard had something to do with the repudiation or that he was a better negotiator than Mulder. It would be more accurate to say that Howard's views of the situation and what Kodak ought to do were more congruent with those of the top management than Mulder's. Howard may have been wrong for the situation but he was right for the management. Being a second-echelon official, he was simply presenting the management's views as well as he could. The fact that he happened to agree with the position only made him more suitable for the job.

Kodak did not visualize the effect of its repudiation on the nation. For a company of its size and resources it is hard to see how it could have been so wide of the mark in taking the pulse of the social system. While the company was handling the problem as a local issue, the controversy received national attention largely because of the efforts of FIGHT and its supporters, the National Council of Churches, the Catholic Church, and the very fact that it involved a large United States corporation. To an outsider it seemed like a fight between David and Goliath. According to Edward L. Bernays, a well-known public relations counsel and author:

> [It] fell like a bombshell into the pro-civil rights milieu of contemporary America. A company dependent on good will went against all the current social mores and folkways. It was a colossal public relations blunder that will go down in history.[37]

Alinsky caustically suggested, "Maybe their executives ought to enroll in the Head Start Program and learn to read." He charged Kodak with "playing into the hands of those who say you can't trust the white man. I don't know how much [strife] Kodak will be responsible for this summer."

Both Kodak and FIGHT held news conferences in which angry words were exchanged. In his news conference on January 6, 1967, Kodak's new president, Dr. Louis D. Eilers, charged that FIGHT's "talk about employment" was "being used as a screen" for "making a power drive in this community."[38] As reported by *The New York Times,* Dr. Eilers stated that "since the Alinsky forces were brought to Rochester, FIGHT has run a continuing war against numerous institutions that help build Rochester—the school system, the Community Chest, the city government, and even organizations especially set up to help solve minority group problems." Dr. Eilers's statement characterized FIGHT's demands as "arbitrary and unreasonable," and he asked if the group's "goal was really to get jobs for those who need them. . . . To the best of our knowledge, FIGHT has not sent anyone to us to apply for work." Concerning Mr. Mulder, Dr. Eilers said, "We all expressed the greatest of displeasure at the signing," but added that he "didn't envision any change in Mr. Mulder's job."

---

37 *Ibid.,* p. 14.
38 John Kifner, "Critics Assailed by Head of Kodak: He Accuses Negro Group of Power Drive Upstate," *The New York Times,* January 7, 1967, p. 25.

In a news conference held later in his storefront office, Minister Florence (he insisted on being addressed as "Minister," rather than "Reverend") said that Dr. Eilers's statement was that "of an hysterical and insecure man." He said that his group was trying to get Negroes into the "[melting] pot at Kodak." As to Eilers's statement that no one had applied for jobs through FIGHT, Florence flourished what he said were duplicates of the applications of forty-five people.

Eilers and Florence met twice, but at the third meeting Eilers was not present and Kodak's representatives were members of the Industrial Relations Department. Florence left in a huff saying, "We thought we were going to meet with Dr. Eilers, and they sent in a group of janitors." [39]

In January Saul Alinsky began a campaign to round up national support for FIGHT. On January 3 representatives of the National Council of Churches Commission on Religion and Race, the Board of National Missions of the United Presbyterian Church, and the Board for Homeland Ministries of the Church of Christ visited Rochester and expressed their support of FIGHT in the Kodak dispute.[40] On January 10 the Citizens Crusade Against Poverty, a private group working with funds of the United Auto Workers Union, convened a closed meeting at which it was decided to support FIGHT. At the meeting were delegates from the National Association for the Advancement of Colored People, the National Council of Churches, the Protestant Episcopal Diocese of New York, and the United Presbyterian Church.[41]

Hoping to make peace, the Area Council of Churches took a full-page ad urging FIGHT to endorse Kodak's training programs and Kodak to endorse FIGHT's proposal. A few days later the president of the council, a Kodak employee, and two directors, one also a Kodak employee, resigned from the council in protest against the ad, which they felt favored FIGHT. FIGHT became more "hardnosed":

"We're not interested in white hope," Florence told a FIGHT meeting. "FIGHT asks Kodak where is the black hope for the underprivileged and unemployed in Rochester."

"Tell it, Brother," yelled the crowd. "Sock it to 'em."

"They talk about America being a melting pot," said Florence, "but the question right now is not whether black can melt, but whether they can even get into the pot. That's what FIGHT has been trying to do—get some of them into the pot at Kodak." [42]

As a result of its abrogation of the December 20 agreement, Kodak's corporate image was extremely tarnished. As a letter to the editor illustrates: "It is inconceivable that a man of Mr. Mulder's position could so

---

39 "Kodak Job Plan Rejected," *The New York Times,* January 11, 1967, p. 19.
40 *The New York Times,* January 4, 1967, p. 4.
41 *The New York Times,* January 11, 1967, p. 19.
42 Ridgeway, "Attack on Kodak."

misunderstand what he was or was not authorized to do." [43] Despite Kodak's insistence that it had not intended Mulder to initiate a new policy, *Business Week* quoted Vaughn as saying that Chandler and Mulder's decision to resume talks between FIGHT and Kodak "gave us some hope that there was a new deal here." [44]

On January 19 television reporters followed Black Power leader Stokely Carmichael into town. That night the leader of the Student Nonviolent Coordinating Committee told a FIGHT rally (approximate attendance, two hundred) of plans for a national boycott of Eastman Kodak products vowing to "bring them to their knees." [45] Carmichael said, "We have been looking for a fight against a big company, and you've got everything we want. . . . When we're through, Florence will say 'Jump,' and Kodak will ask 'How high?' " [46] Carmichael's national boycott turned out to be picketing in four cities and involved only several dozen citizens of Detroit, Chicago, San Francisco, and Atlanta.[47]

During the first week of February Kodak announced openings for 137 to 158 unskilled persons in training programs leading to regular jobs. Kodak requested referrals from eleven agencies including settlement houses, the State Employment Service, the Urban League, and FIGHT.[48]

Four days later, Florence brought 87 people to the Kodak employment office. Kodak interviewers were ready with application forms. Describing the meeting, a Kodak official said the FIGHT people engaged

> in an hour-long demonstration, constantly interrupting our attempt to describe these programs to the group; they demanded that we provide jobs on the spot for those present. Our industrial relations people offered to accept applications and interview that day any members of the group who were seeking employment. Several stepped forward to volunteer only to be warned by Minister Florence, President of FIGHT, that they should not accept the offer.

The Associated Press reported that "after an hour and a half in a closed conference room, Minister Florence said his group had been offered neither jobs nor interviews, and if Kodak claimed the opposite, which Kodak did, it was 'an out and out lie.' " (The Associated Press learned that a Kodak spokesman had in fact told Minister Florence that applicants must first be interviewed and offered the chance. Minister Florence had replied, "We didn't come here to talk about interviews, we came for work.") [49] Florence also said that agencies who cooperated with Kodak in referring people for jobs were joining in a "conspiracy" (FIGHT had such

[43] Paul A. Mallon, "But and Rebut," Letters to the Editors of *America*, May 6, 1967, p. 37.
[44] *Business Week*, April 29, 1967.
[45] Loh, Associated Press.
[46] Carter, "The Fight Against Kodak."
[47] *Ibid.*
[48] *Ibid.*, also see Loh, Associated Press.
[49] Loh, Associated Press.

an arrangement with Xerox at the time)[50] and that Kodak's training programs were "a sham and a disgrace."[51] Referrals were made and the program moved along.

Kodak decided to break off the meetings. Florence warned Kodak that it might be to blame for a "long, hot summer" in 1967.

Eilers regarded such threats as irresponsible and stated:

> To tell the truth, I don't know what they want. Certaintly not jobs—they could have had those, and still can. Every one of the ten referring agencies in Rochester has placed people in jobs at Kodak and none has asked for an exclusive deal. This year we'll have about 300 more in our training program. It's too bad FIGHT doesn't want to participate.

"We don't want any of Kodak's paternalism," said Florence. "The training program we've proposed is something we can do ourselves. We know ourselves better than anybody from Kodak does, and better than any Black Man who goes home to the suburbs every night and pretends he's white. We have to help ourselves by ourselves. That's what self-determination is."[52]

The New York Times described FIGHT's next move:

> In March, FIGHT bought ten shares of Kodak stock, at a cost of $1,442.65, to gain a voice at the stockholders' meeting. The organization sent out 700 letters to clergymen and civil rights groups urging them to contact fellow stockholders to protest the company's action at the annual meeting.[53]

In response to FIGHT's call, various church organizations announced that they would withhold from the management their proxies for more than 34,000 shares. In addition, twenty-one private investors accounting for 5,060 shares announced that they would withhold proxies from the management. John Kifner, writing in *The New York Times*, pointed out that "those proxy withholdings (about 40,000 shares in all) are largely symbolic since the company's latest annual report lists 80,772,718 shares of stock."[54]

A group of influential ministers developed a compromise program that they believed would bring an end to the Kodak-FIGHT controversy. Representatives from many local industries joined the ministers and agreed to hire and train 1,500 hard-core unemployed over an eighteen-

[50] Carter, "The Fight Against Kodak."

[51] "Equal Employment Opportunity, Eastman Kodak Company's Positive Program" (Rochester, N.Y.: Public Relations Department, Eastman Kodak Company, 1967).

[52] Loh, Associated Press.

[53] John Kifner, "21 Churches Withhold Proxies to Fight Kodak Rights Policies," *The New York Times,* April 7, 1967.

[54] John Kifner, "21 Kodak Investors Withhold Proxies," *The New York Times,* April 17, 1967, p. 25.

month period. Kodak also agreed to join Rochester Jobs, Inc., as this program was known.

FIGHT complained that this was another example of the white establishment's doing something for the poor without giving them an adequate voice in the process, but finally joined the program. Florence was elected a vice-president and named to key committees. Clearly, FIGHT had gained an impressive victory and was undeniably, if indirectly, responsible for a precedent-setting partnership between private industry and the poor. Though no hiring quotas were announced, Kodak's share was approximately 600. The poor—not 600, but 1,500—had the promise of jobs; FIGHT had its victory; and Kodak was apparently doing all FIGHT had ever asked of it. Florence announced that the new program would not affect FIGHT's dispute with Kodak and that the protest at the stockholders' meeting at Flemington would occur as scheduled. *FIGHT wanted some kind of direct concession from Kodak.*[55]

As far as Florence was concerned, the issue was no longer jobs but dignity. He maintained that Kodak had arrogantly broken a moral agreement. He said that FIGHT was only trying to solve local problems in partnership with business, instead of by resorting to the federal government. He recalled that in a previous crisis situation, during World War II, industry had turned farmers into tradesmen overnight because the national good demanded it. A similar crisis situation, he said, exists today.[56]

On April 25 Kodak's annual stockholders' meeting was held in Flemington, New Jersey. Buses and carloads of white and black demonstrators from Rochester and other cities and from Cornell, Princeton, Yale, and Dartmouth arrived in Flemington during the morning, and were met by a force of state troopers, local police, and Kodak guards. There were no incidents.

Also in attendance were the ten FIGHT members who had each purchased one share of stock plus the stockholders who had withheld their proxies in support of FIGHT. William S. Vaughn, chairman of the board, opened the meeting at one o'clock.

Florence was on his feet immediately. "Point of order," Florence shouted. "I'll be heard as long as I'm on the floor." To cries of "Throw him out," Florence shouted, "We will give you until two o'clock to honor that agreement," and then walked out of the building. Outside, Florence told his followers, "This is war."

Precisely at 2 P.M. Florence returned to the meeting, crying "point of order" until he had Vaughn's attention.[57] Florence pointed a finger at the chairman and asked, "Are you going to recognize the December 20 agreement?" Vaughn's reply was firm: "No sir, no we are not." [58] With this Florence and some of his followers walked out. FIGHT's attempts to

55 Martin, "Shepherds vs. Flocks, Ministers vs. Negro Militancy."
56 Raymond A. Schroth, "Self-Doubt and Black Pride," *America*, April 1, 1967, p. 502.
57 *Business Week*, April 29, 1967.
58 "Fight at Kodak," *Newsweek*, May 8, 1967.

disrupt the meeting were not successful. The meeting was not halted nor was the management challenged.

Vaughn's defense of Kodak's record as well as its reasons for repudiation drew cheers from most stockholders present.[59] Nor did the withholding of proxies present any serious difficulties for management. Of Kodak's 80.8 million shares, 84 percent were voted for management. All Kodak officers were reelected. A month later the company took away from John Mulder his assistant vice-president title, although he retained his job as assistant general manager of Kodak's Park Plant.

. Outside the meeting Florence's and Alinsky's statements received national coverage from television, radio, and the press. Kodak's corporate image suffered considerably.

Following the annual meeting Kodak tried to upgrade its public image by hiring Uptown Associates, a Manhattan-based black public relations and advertising concern specializing in "ethnic marketing." According to a story in *The New York Times:*

> A Kodak official in Rochester said the company contract with Uptown Associates was not related to its current conflict with FIGHT.
>
> Reuben J. Patton, head of Uptown Associates said "the company did not seek me out" because of the FIGHT controversy. He stated that he had first offered his services to Kodak in June 1964 when they were turned down by the company advertising director, who wrote to Patton saying:
>
> As you know we are very much interested in the Negro market. . . . At the moment we do not require extra services. . . . and if the occasion arises where we feel you can be of additional service to us, please be assured that you will hear directly from us.
>
> Florence said he was "glad to hear that Kodak can sign contracts with Negro firms specializing in face-saving. This is proof that Kodak was never in good faith with the poor, but only wanted to hire 'instamatic' Negroes." [60]

Kodak eventually realized the ineffectiveness of its public relations strategy and consequently tried to amend it by hiring outside agencies such as Carl Byoir and Associates for help in dealing with ethnic groups. Kodak also approached other professional experts in urban and ghetto problems to help it specifically in dealing with FIGHT. Consequently, in May 1967, Kodak invited Daniel P. Moynihan, former assistant secretary of labor and then the chairman of the President's Council on Urban

[59] *Ibid.*
[60] John Kifner, "Negro Ad Agency Hired by Kodak," *The New York Times,* April 28, 1967, p. 46.

Affairs, for consultation. Mr. Moynihan talked with both Kodak officials and FIGHT members to seek out ways of possible compromise. A week of secret meetings followed between the two parties, which resulted in an agreement.

On June 23 President Filers sent a telegram to Minister Florence in which Kodak recognized

> that FIGHT, as a broad-based community organization, speaks on behalf of the basic needs and aspirations of the Negro poor in the Rochester area . . . that both FIGHT and Kodak support RJI which promised to be an effective way of providing job opportunities for the hard-core unemployed . . . that FIGHT and Kodak establish a relationship under which Kodak would send employment interviewers into selected places in inner-city neighborhoods in cooperation with FIGHT . . . that it may be helpful to the people referred by FIGHT and employed by Kodak to have special guidance and advice from your organization [and that there be a] continuing dialogue between FIGHT and Kodak [to] cover various areas bearing on the economic needs and aspirations of the Negro community.[61]

At FIGHT's third annual convention, held that same evening, Kodak's telegram was endorsed.

In the fall of 1967 talks were renewed on Kodak's promotion of inner-city small business. FIGHT suggested that Kodak build a plant in a ghetto area and allow FIGHT to operate it. Kodak refused to do this but suggested something in the scope of small business. FIGHT was interested, so Kodak prepared a forty-page booklet entitled "A Plan for Establishing Independently Owned and Operated Business in Inner-City Areas." [62] The plan stated that Kodak would take the initiative in organizing a Community Development Corporation (CDC) and would assist in its financing along with other organizations that would be encouraged to join it. The objective of the CDC would be to support small businesses, and the plan suggested three types: wood products, vacuum-formed plastic items, and equipment service. In addition, Kodak suggested forming a microfilming service, which the company considered particularly desirable since it was labor-intensive, equipment could be rented, and required training took only a few weeks. The jobs involved would not be menial. Kodak foresaw a good-sized market in microfilming government documents.

FIGHT showed interest in the microfilming service, was disappointed that under 150 jobs were involved, and suggested an operation that would employ 500 people. Kodak estimated that it would need between $2 mil-

---

[61] From copy of telegram dated June 23, 1967, sent by Dr. Louis K. Eilers, president of Eastman Kodak, to the Reverend Franklin D. R. Florence, president of FIGHT.
[62] "A Plan for Establishing Independently Owned and Operated Business in Inner-City Areas" (Rochester, N.Y.: Eastman Kodak Company, November 1967).

lion and $3 million in sales to employ 500 people and emphasized that it considered such an operation unrealistic as there was no possibility of finding such a large market.

On November 4 *The New York Times,* giving FIGHT as its source, stated that Kodak would build a finishing plant for photographic facilities employing 100 to 150 people and that the factory would be "black-operated." A November 18 article quoted the new FIGHT president, DeLeon McEwen, as saying, "Kodak will join FIGHT in developing a microfilming factory that will hire and train 400 to 500 unskilled Negroes."

The two stories put Kodak in an awkward position: to continue talks with FIGHT would be by "deeds reinforcing their exaggerated claims"; to break off talks would contradict Kodak's desire to help FIGHT. Kodak asked FIGHT to announce the misunderstanding, but it refused—even after Kodak said it would not be able to continue talks if this were not done. FIGHT, in preserving this "barrier" to talks, kept the issue alive.

On December 5 Kodak announced the "details of a plan to combat poverty in Rochester." The plans called for starting small businesses in the city's predominantly black slums, with each business employing nine to fifteen workers. Although these businesses would be started with Kodak's help, they "would eventually be independently owned and operated by employees." [63]

On April 1, 1968, Kodak announced that its program to train jobless persons from Rochester's inner city would continue in 1968. Monroe V. Dill, Kodak director of industrial relations, said that the company expected to hire 200 persons for the program during the coming year, the same number as the preceding year. He also said that since the inception of the on-the-job program in 1964, 500 men and women, many lacking industrial skills or adequate education, had been trained in special classes. FIGHT's president, DeLeon McEwen, responding to Kodak's announcement, said that the results of the education program were "known only to Kodak" and "they have not been enlarged to the black hard-core unemployed." [64]

This program was not connected with Rochester Jobs, Inc. (RJI). Earlier, in January, Rochester Business Opportunity Corporation (RBOC) had been formed "to promote and encourage independent business in and for the inner-city." Kodak joined with sixty of the city's largest companies to provide collateral to guarantee bank loans to finance business among the inner-city residents. RBOC's twenty-eight-member board also included several blacks and a Puerto Rican.

On April 17 Kodak announced a gift of $150,000 to the Community Chest's Martin Luther King Memorial Fund. RBOC's largest venture has been a $600,000 joint venture by FIGHT, the U.S. Department of Labor, and Xerox to start a FIGHT-managed metal stamping and electrical transformer manufacturing factory expected to employ one hundred people.

---

[63] "Handicraft Plan Offered by Kodak," *The New York Times,* December 16, 1967, p. 37.
[64] "Kodak to Continue Training Program," *The New York Times,* April 2, 1968.

SELECTED REFERENCES

ACKERMAN, ROBERT W., "How Companies Respond to Social Demands," *Harvard Business Review*, July–August 1973, pp. 88–98.

ALLEN, LOUIS L., "Making Capitalism Work in the Ghettos," *Harvard Business Review*, May–June 1969, pp. 83–92.

ALLUME, FRED C., "Black Business Development," *Journal of Marketing*, 34 (April 1970), 1–7.

"A Plan for Establishing Independently Owned and Operated Business in Inner-City Areas" (Rochester, N.Y.: Eastman Kodak Company, November, 1967).

BAHR, HOWARD M., and JACK P. GIBBS, "Racial Differentiation in American Metropolitan Areas," *Social Forces*, 45 (June 1967), 521–32.

BEARDWOOD, ROGER, "The Southern Roots of the Urban Crisis," *Fortune*, August 1968, p. 84.

BERMAN, JEFFREY A., "The Birth of a Black Business," *Harvard Business Review*, September–October 1970, 4–6ff.

BIRCH, DAVID L., *The Businessman and the City* (Boston: Harvard Graduate School of Business Administration, 1967).

BRIMMER, ANDREW F., "The Negro in the National Economy," in *The American Negro Reference Book*, ed. John P. Davis, Chap. 5 (Englewood Cliffs, N.J.: Prentice-Hall, 1966).

BROWER, MICHAEL, and DOYLE LITTEL, "White Help for Black Business," *Harvard Business Review*, May–June 1970, pp. 4–6ff.

BROWN, CLAUDE, *Manchild in the Promised Land* (New York: Macmillan, 1967).

BUNKE, HARVEY, "Negro Must Be Full Partner in Market," *Business and Society Review*, 5, 2 (spring 1965), 3–9.

CAMPBELL, ANGUS, *White Attitudes Toward Black People* (Ann Arbor, Mich.: Institute for Social Research, 1971).

CLOWARD, RICHARD A., and FRANCES FOX PIVEN, "Corporate Imperialism for the Poor," *Nation*, October 16, 1967, pp. 365–67.

COHEN, OSCAR, "The Responsibility of American Business," in *The Negro Challenge to the Business Community*, ed. Eli Ginzberg (New York: McGraw-Hill, 1964).

COHN, JULES, "Is Business Meeting the Challenge of Urban Affairs?" *Harvard Business Review*, March–April 1970, pp. 68–82.

CROSS, THEODORE L., *Black Capitalism* (New York: Atheneum, 1969).

DAVIS, JOHN P., ed., *The American Negro Reference Book* (Englewood Cliffs, N.J.: Prentice-Hall, 1966).

DOMM, DONALD R., and JAMES E. STAFFORD, "Assimilating Blacks into the Organization," *California Management Review*, 15, 1 (fall 1972), 46–51.

DOWNS, ANTHONY, "Alternative Futures for the American Ghetto," *Daedalus*, 94, 4 (fall 1965), 771–814.

"Equal Employment Opportunity. Eastman Kodak Company's Positive Program" (Rochester, New York: Public Relations Department, Eastman Kodak Company, 1967).

FINLEY, GRACE J., *Mayors Evaluate Business Action on Urban Problems* (New York: The Conference Board, 1968).

FLOWER, BARBARA J., *Business Amid Urban Crisis: Private-Sector Approaches to City Problems,* Public Affairs Study No. 3 (New York: The Conference Board, 1968).

FOGELSON, ROBERT M., "From Resentment to Confrontation: The Police, the Negroes, and the Outbreak of the Nineteen-Sixties Riots," *Political Science Quarterly,* 83 (June 1968), 217–47.

———, "White on Black: A Critique of the McCone Commission Report on the Los Angeles Riots," *Political Science Quarterly,* 83 (September 1968).

FOLEY, EUGENE P., "The Negro Businessman: In Search of a Tradition," *Daedalus,* Winter 1966, pp. 107–44.

FRANKLIN, RAYMOND S., "The Political Economy of Black Power," *Social Problems,* 16, 3 (Winter 1969), 286–301.

GASSLER, LEE S., "How Companies Are Helping the Undereducated Worker," *Personnel,* July–August 1967, pp. 47–55.

GINZBERG, ELI, ed., *The Negro Challenge to the Business Community* (New York: McGraw-Hill, 1964).

GOODE, KENNETH G., "Query: Can the Afro-American Be an Effective Executive," *California Management Review,* 13, 1 (fall 1970), 22–26.

HANRAHAN, GEORGE D., "Why Social Programs Fail," *Economic and Business Bulletin,* spring–summer 1972, pp. 51–59.

HODGSON, JAMES, and MARSHALL H. BRENNER, "Successful Experience: Training Hard-Core Unemployed," *Harvard Business Review,* September–October 1968, pp. 148–56.

"Is Black Capitalism the Answer?" *Business Week,* August 3, 1968, p. 60.

"Is Business Meeting the Challenge of Urban Affairs?" *Harvard Business Review,* March–April 1970, p. 68.

JANGER, ALLEN R., and RUTH G. SHAEFFER, *Managing Programs for the Disadvantaged* (New York: The Conference Board, 1970).

KAIN, JOHN H., and JOSEPH J. PERSKY, "Alternative to Guilded Ghetto," *Public Interest,* winter 1969, pp. 74–87.

KUHN, JAMES, and IVAR BERG, *Values in a Business Society* (New York: Harcourt, Brace, Jovanovich, 1968).

LYFORD, JOSEPH P., "Business and the Negro Community," in *The Negro Challenge to the Business Community,* ed. Eli Ginzberg (New York: McGraw-Hill, 1964), pp. 96–100.

MACK, RAYMOND W., "Riot, Revolt or Responsible Revolution or Reference Groups and Racism," *Sociological Quarterly,* 10, 2 (spring 1969), 147–56.

"Making Capitalism Work in the Ghetto," *Harvard Business Review,* May–June 1969, p. 83.

McELRATH, DENNIS C., "Urban Differentiation: Problems and Prospects," *Law and Contemporary Problems,* 30 (winter 1965), 103–10.

McFARLANE, ALEXANDER N., "Leaping the Ghetto Gap," *Vital Speeches,* December 15, 1968, pp. 157–60.

McKERSIE, ROBERT B., "Vitalize Black Enterprise," *Harvard Business Review,* September–October 1968, pp. 88–99.

MOYNIHAN, D. P., "Toward a National Urban Policy," *Public Interest,* fall 1969, pp. 3–20.

NADLER, LEONARD, "Helping the Hard-Core Adjust to the World of Work," *Harvard Business Review*, March–April 1970, pp. 117–26.

National Industrial Conference Board, *Company Experiences with Negro Employment*, No. 201 (1966), pp. 1–55.

PALMERI, RICHARD A., "Business and the Black Revolt," *California Management Review*, 11, 4 (summer 1969), 31–36.

PARENTI, MICHAEL, "Ethnic Politics and the Persistence of Ethnic Identification," *American Political Science Review*, 61 (September 1967), 717–26.

PASCAL, ANTHONY H., "Black Gold and Black Capitalism," *Public Interest*, spring 1970, pp. 111–19.

PERLOFF, HARVEY S., ed., *The Quality of the Urban Environment* (Baltimore: Johns Hopkins Press, 1969).

PETTIGREW, THOMAS, *A Profile of the Negro American* (Princeton, N.J.: Van Nostrand, 1964).

———, "White-Negro Confrontations," in *The Negro Challenge to the Business Community*, ed. Eli Ginzberg (New York: McGraw-Hill, 1964), pp. 39–55.

PURCELL, THEODORE V., "Break Down Your Employment Barriers," *Harvard Business Review*, July–August 1968, pp. 65–76.

———, "The Case of the Borderline Black," *Harvard Business Review*, November–December 1971, pp. 128–33, 142–50.

———, and GERALD F. CAVANAGH, *Blacks in the Industrial World* (New York: Free Press, 1972).

———, and ROSALIND WEBSTER, "Window on the Hard-Core World," *Harvard Business Review*, July–August 1969, pp. 118–29.

REDDING, SAUNDERS, "The Methods," in *The Negro in America*, ed. John Hope Franklin and Isidore Starr (New York: Vintage, 1967), pp. 113–16.

ROSE, ARNOLD M., "The Negro Protest," *Annals of the American Academy of Political and Social Sciences*, 357 (January 1965), 1–126.

SETHI, S. PRAKASH, *Business Corporations and the Black Man*. (San Francisco: Chandler, 1970).

———, and DOW VOTAW, "Do We Need a New Corporate Response to a Changing Social Environment?" Parts I and II, *California Management Review*, fall 1969.

SPRATLEN, THADDEUS H., "A Black Perspective on 'Black Business Development,'" *Journal of Marketing*, 34 (October 1970), 72–73.

STERNLIEB, GEORGE, "Is Business Abandoning the Big City?" *Harvard Business Review*, January–February 1961, pp. 6–12, 152–64.

STURDIVANT, FREDERICK, D., "The Limits of Black Capitalism," *Harvard Business Review*, January–February 1969, pp. 122–28.

SUNDQUIST, JAMES L., "Jobs, Training, and Welfare for the Underclass," in *Agenda for the Nation*, ed. Gordon Kermit (Washington, D.C.: Brookings, 1968), pp. 49–76.

TOBIN, JAMES, "On Improving the Economic Status of the Negro," *Daedalus*, fall 1965, pp. 878–98.

U.S. Departments of Labor and Commerce, *The Social and Economic Status of Negroes in the United States, 1969*, BLS Report No. 375, Current Population Reports, Series P–23, No. 29.

WEISS, NANCY J., "The Negro and the New Freedom: Fighting Wilsonian Segregation," *Political Science Quarterly*, 84 (March 1969), 61–79.

Corporations and the News Media

ABC + ITT $\overset{?}{=}$ FREE PRESS [1]

CORPORATE PRESSURE
FOR FAVORABLE REPORTING
AND MANIPULATING OF NEWS

News is nothing more than any other thirty minutes of TV programming, and when it starts getting bad ratings it's going to go off the air.

—Anonymous observation

Journalists were never intended to be the cheerleaders of a society, conductors of applause, the sycophants. Tragically, that is their assigned role in authoritarian societies, but not here—not yet.

—CHET HUNTLEY

INTRODUCTION AND BACKGROUND

What exactly is the public interest in the news media? This question is open to many interpretations, but the new media themselves use the criterion that news be covered "fairly," with no one business, government, or interest group controlling media coverage.[2] Competition among enterprises engaged in the communications business ensures the use of technological improvements and up-to-date services and helps to minimize the

---

[1] Title adapted from Eileen Shanahan, "Comment: Merger Issue. A.B.C. + I.T.T. = ?" *The New York Times,* July 30, 1967, Sec. 4, p. 5.
[2] S. Prakash Sethi, *Business Corporations and the Black Man* (San Francisco: Chandler, 1970), Chap. 6.

influence of any one group. Likewise, the public interest is served by corporations with sufficient financial resources to assume risks in introducing new processes and techniques and in expanding into pioneer communications fields.

The following case concerns the thwarted merger between two communications companies, ABC and ITT. In the events surrounding the proposed merger the issues involved in defining the public interest in news broadcasting were thoroughly scrutinized, with implications not only for the immediate question of the conformity of the merger to government regulations, but also for the long-term issues of control, autonomy, and quality performance of broadcasting enterprises.

BACKGROUND OF ABC AND ITT

International Telephone and Telegraph (ITT) is one of the largest conglomerate corporations in the world. Since its formation about fifty years ago, it has primarily operated as a holding company for foreign telephone equipment and operating companies.[3] At the time of the proposed merger, ITT had interests in at least sixty-six countries and was engaged in domestic and foreign manufacturing, the operation of telecommunications utilities, and financial and other service activities. A leading international record carrier, ITT also claimed to be the world's largest manufacturer of telecommunications equipment.[4] Of its domestic manufacturing activities, about 40 percent was done under government contract related to space programs and defense. Sixty percent of its net income came from abroad and, according to the company, it had "extensive investment and responsibility in the economies and societies of the countries in which it operates." [5]

In 1959 ITT hired Harold Geneen as president. To balance the corporation's domestic and international operations, Geneen activated a vigorous policy of growth, primarily through the acquisition of domestic industries, including Alexander Hamilton Life Insurance, American Universal Life Insurance, Avis Rent-A-Car, and Aetna Finance Company. The goal of doubling sales and earnings in the first five-year period was achieved, and ITT's acquisitions have continued unabated. Much of the

3 "Dissenting Opinion of Commissioner Nicholas Johnson," Part IV of *ABC-ITT Merger Proceedings,* Federal Communications Commission, Washington, D.C., rev., December 21, 1966, p. 15.
4 "Dissenting Statement of Commissioner Robert T. Bartley," *ABC-ITT Merger Proceedings,* Part II, pp. 2–3.
5 *Ibid.,* Part IV, pp. 8, 11, 21. For example, directors of foreign ITT subsidiaries include three legislators, a former premier, and foreign ministry employees. Eventually seven of fifteen board members of the Chilean subsidiary will be government appointed (pp. 19–20).
The Indian government owns 75 percent of one ITT company, and the company cannot sell any of the stock to an Indian or to a citizen of a country not approved by the Indian government.

success of ITT's growth policy has been attributed to Geneen and the taut system of control that he exerted over ITT's previously autonomous operating managers.

The American Broadcasting Companies, Inc., is a child of the government's concern for the maintenance of freedom of the press. In response to the Federal Communications Commission's (FCC) chain broadcasting rules of 1941, the Blue Network Company, one of two networks owned by the Radio Corporation of America (RCA), was offered for sale and was purchased by Edward J. Noble, who created the American Broadcasting Company. ABC has since substantially increased its operations and by 1966 owned 399 theaters in thirty-four states, five television stations (most ABC affiliates are independently owned as per government regulation), and six AM and FM stations in the top ten broadcasting markets. ABC was capable of reaching 93 percent of 50 million American homes with television sets and 97 percent of those with radios.

In addition, ABC subsidiaries produced records on six different labels, published three farm newspapers, and distributed filmed television programs to stations, networks, and advertisers. ABC was active in foreign markets through a wholly owned subsidiary which acted as program purchasing and sales representative for foreign stations in twenty-five nations.[6]

HISTORY OF THE MERGER

On December 3, 1965, ITT publicly announced that representatives of the two companies had met several times and agreed that ABC would be merged into ITT as a wholly owned subsidiary with control passing from ABC stockholders to a new group composed of both ABC and ITT stockholders.[7]

The two companies entered into the agreement on February 14, 1966, and on March 31, 1966, ABC filed the necessary applications with the FCC for its approval of transfers of licenses for ABC broadcasting stations to the new ITT subsidiary corporation. Proxy statements describing the details of the merger were sent to the shareholders of both companies, who voted overwhelmingly to approve the merger.

In July 1966 the FCC requested information from the presidents of ABC and ITT regarding the proposed future operations of the new broadcasting company. Replies were soon received by the commission, which then accepted the bulk of the data as authentic and accurate statements of fact. The FCC ordered that a hearing before the full seven-member commission be held on September 19, 1966; any party interested in the case could appear and be heard at that time.

As in all merger cases, the FCC considered the possibility of potential antitrust effects, and in keeping with policy, maintained a continuing liaison with the Antitrust Division of the Department of Justice with

[6] *Ibid.*, Part II, Attachment A; Part IV, pp. 12–15.
[7] *Ibid.*, Part IV, p. 85.

regard to the case. The division itself had been independently collecting data on the case since the two companies' first announcement but continually put off the commission when it requested Justice's views. Thus the department made no statement regarding the matter prior to the FCC's hearing on September 19, 1966, did not appear at the hearing, and commented only that it had the matter under study.[8]

It was not until November 3, after the commission had notified Antitrust Division Chief Donald Turner that an FCC decision was imminent, that Turner replied that there was a "sufficient possibility of significant anticompetitive effects"[9] which could result from the merger. He suggested that the commission hold off its decision until the department had arrived "at a final decision on the anticompetitive aspects of the merger."[10] The commission then asked the division to make a more definite statement and notified it that it was preparing to issue its decision on December 21, 1966. The commission noted, however, that whereas a Justice Department report would be significant, it would not be binding.[11]

Finally, on December 20, 1966, Turner submitted to the commission the Antitrust Division's decision that the department did not have the grounds to seek to block the merger in court, but it saw a number of possible anticompetitive consequences in the proposed merger that the FCC should explore.

The commission, having been prepared for weeks to act on the proposed merger, approved it the next day, noting that the questions Justice raised had already been carefully considered. The commission also criticized the Justice Department for waiting as long as it had before expressing its views. The commission's vote was four to three, with Commissioners Bartley, Cox, and Johnson dissenting.

Promptly following the commissioner's decision, the Justice Department, in a Petition for Reconsideration, asked the FCC to review its decision and to hold a full and evidentiary hearing (which had not been done earlier) and to permit the Antitrust Division to participate as a party.[12] The department hinted that if the FCC did not reopen the case, it might bring suit under Section 7 of the Clayton Act to nullify the merger on anticompetitive grounds.[13]

On February 1, 1967, the FCC ordered ABC and ITT to delay the

---

8 *Ibid.*, "Memorandum Opinion and Order," Part I, pp. 1, 2, 5.

9 *Ibid.*, Part IV, p. 80.

10 *Order on Petition for Reconsideration,* Federal Communications Commission, February 1, 1967, Part I, p. 2.

11 *ABC-ITT Merger Proceedings,* Part I, pp. 1, 5; Part IV, pp. 80–84. This was the first time that the Justice Department had sought to intervene in a case involving FCC's handling of broadcast properties. Traditionally, the courts had recognized that in the regulation of broadcast media considerations other than competition should also prevail in the general public interest. For example, in the case of *FCC* v. *RCA Communications, Inc.,* the court agreed with FCC that "encouragement of competition as such has not been considered the single or controlling reliance for safeguarding the public interest." 346 US 86 (1953).

12 *Order on Petition for Reconsideration,* February 1, 1967, p. 4.

13 *ABC-ITT Merger Proceedings,* Part I.

merger until a reconsideration hearing had been conducted.[14] The companies called the department's intervention an "unprecedented attack" on the commission's competence and urged the FCC to reject the department's allegations.[15] The FCC said that the delaying action was taken because of the unique status of the Justice Department and the particular nature of the case but pointed out that this procedure set no precedent whatsoever. The commission further indicated that Justice would have to supply it with documentary evidence to support its charges.[16]

The commission held a thirteen-day hearing during April 1967, in which the Justice Department was a party. The commission again approved the merger on June 22 and the vote was again four to three with the same dissenters.[17]

Subsequent to this second approval, the Justice Department appealed the case to the United States Court of Appeals in Washington, and the unlikely happened: The U.S. (Justice), as it were, was opposing the U.S. (FCC) in a court case.[18] Prior to a court decision, however, ITT withdrew from the ABC merger agreement on New Year's Day, 1968.[19] The merger agreement had given either party the right to cancel after New Year's Eve. ITT exercised this option because it felt that terminating the merger would best serve the interest of its stockholders as the stock price of ABC had risen tremendously during the long delays plaguing the merger. The potential cost to ITT of the merger had risen from $380 million to $660 million.[20]

SOME KEY ISSUES

It would be impossible to present all the issues involved in the proposed merger, but some of the most important are discussed below.

During the first hearing, the majority of the commission was of the opinion that since ITT and ABC were not competitors in any market, the merger would not increase the concentration of control in the broadcasting industry, hence it would not have anticompetitive effects. Indeed, the merger would benefit the public interest for three reasons. First, the increased financial resources available to ABC through ITT would result in better programming. ABC's financial need was great. Although NBC

14 "Dissenting Opinion of Commissioners Robert T. Bartley, Kenneth A. Cox, and Nicholas Johnson," *The ABC-ITT Merger Case Reconsideration,* Federal Communications Commission, June 22, 1967, p. 135.
15 Eileen Shanahan, "Merger Defended by ITT and ABC," *The New York Times,* February 24, 1967, p. 1.
16 *Order on Petition for Reconsideration,* February 1, 1967, pp. 3–4.
17 *ABC-ITT Merger Case Reconsideration,* Sec. 2, pp. 137–38.
18 "ITT-ABC Merger Is Held Up by Federal Court," *The New York Times,* July 22, 1967, p. 53.
19 Jack Gould, "ITT Calls Off ABC Merger Bid," *The New York Times,* January 2, 1968, p. 1.
20 "A Broken Engagement for ITT and ABC," *Business Week,* January 6, 1968, p. 24.

and CBS were very profitable operations, ABC had been in the red for the past four years. Second, ABC stated that more cash would better its competitive position with respect to the other networks, and ITT promised to help in this area. Third, ITT had decided to attempt to make technological advances in UHF broadcasting, an area that would help the network to become more competitive with CBS and NBC.

Some observers felt that one reason for ABC's enthusiasm for the merger was the fear that a prominent industrialist, Norton Simon, was attempting to take control of the company. Simon had begun buying ABC stock in March 1964, and by July 1964 he was the largest single stockholder, with 9 percent of the company's outstanding stock. It was rumored that he wanted a seat on the network's board of directors. Speculation abounded that ABC wanted to merge (which would dilute Simon's ownership percentage) to prevent his control of the company.[21]

Both the Justice Department and the dissenting commissioners raised another issue. The original hearing had consisted of only two days of oral hearings before the commission *en banc,* and not before an examiner who customarily heard the arguments. The FCC felt this to be a more direct and public way to study the issues. However, the antagonists said that the commission had "failed to conduct the type of full hearing required by the Federal Communications Act of 1934"[22] and had not given sufficient warning for those opposed to the merger to prepare their arguments. Indeed, no opposing arguments were made.[23]

The antagonists felt that the merger would eliminate ITT as a potential independent entrant into broadcasting. They said that ITT was one of the relatively few firms with the resources, technical capability, interest, and incentive likely to make a significant contribution to diversification in broadcasting and to activities directly competitive with broadcasting. The merger would reduce the likelihood of this occurring. It was said that ITT had been considering entering the broadcasting industry prior to the merger agreement. Without the merger, the argument ran, ITT would have entered TV broadcasting on a significant scale.[24]

The same argument was said to apply to ITT's CATV and Pay-TV efforts. If the merger were approved, ITT would probably drop its efforts in this area, as CATV would conflict with ABC's broadcasting aspirations.[25] That is, the company would have an interest in the status quo technology and would be less interested in research and development

21 *ABC-ITT Merger Proceedings,* Part I, pp. 8–13; Part IV, pp. 15–17.

22 *Ibid.,* Part I, p. 4. According to dissenting Commissioner Johnson, the commission was not originally planning to hold hearings at all as the outcome had "been a foregone conclusion." Only Commissioner Bartley's insistent request for "a full evidentiary hearing" led to the compromise "oral hearing" (Part IV, p. 2).

23 Department of Justice, *Proposed Conclusions and Brief,* May 29, 1967, p. 82. See also *ABC-ITT Merger Proceedings,* Part IV, Sec. 2, pp. 68–70.

24 Department of Justice, *Proposed Conclusions and Brief,* May 29, 1967, p. 87. See also *ABC-ITT Merger Case Reconsideration,* pp. 43–47.

25 CATV, or Cable TV, transmits programs by telephone wires rather than by air and usually increases the number of stations available to a particular area. James Ridgeway, "The Voice of ITT," *New Republic,* July 8, 1967, pp. 17–19.

aimed at promoting Pay-TV and CATV. Merger opponents rejected this on the grounds of ABC's financial needs. They said that open-market financing was available and that despite ABC's nearness to the debt limit, that limit could probably be extended. Furthermore, ABC's deficient performance was due not to insufficient funds but to operational difficulties.[26] Finally, the opposition accused ABC and ITT officials of making misleading and erroneous statements and of lacking general candor while testifying.[27]

The commission majority replied that ITT's decision to merge with ABC came *after* its decision not to enter the broadcasting industry and *after* it had begun moving out of CATV. In addition, the majority held that there were "hundreds" of other companies capable of doing valuable research and development in broadcasting technology and that the merger would induce ITT to do research that might benefit ABC.[28]

The three commissioners who wrote the minority opinion disputed ITT's statement that it had decided not to enter the broadcasting industry, citing an offer the company had made to an independent television station. Also, if the merger were allowed, ITT would pursue research in general broadcasting which could help ABC, but it probably would not do research on Pay-TV and CATV, media competitive with ABC's general broadcasting. On the other hand, if the merger were prohibited, ITT would be one of the most likely contributors to Pay-TV and CATV technology.[29] Also, ABC should not look to ITT for help with its cash flow problem, as ITT documents had projected a net cash flow *from* ABC to the parent company.[30]

THE ABC-ITT MERGER AND THE INDEPENDENCE
OF THE NEWS MEDIA

The primary issue of this case, and indeed one of the primary issues of the merger agreement, was the degree of autonomy that ABC would maintain as a wholly owned subsidiary of ITT. ABC President Goldenson, in an interdepartmental letter sent before the agreement, stated:

> While I cannot at this time discuss the details of these continuing negotiations, I thought you would like personally to know that a prerequisite of any proposed merger, as far as I am concerned, will be the continued autonomous management and operation of Ameri-

[26] *ABC-ITT Merger Case Reconsideration*, Sec. 2. See also Department of Justice, *Proposed Conclusions and Brief*, April 29, 1967.
[27] *ABC-ITT Merger Case Reconsideration*, Sec. 2.
[28] "Opinion and Order on Petition for Reconsideration," *ABC-ITT Merger Case Reconsideration*, Sec. 1, pp. 14, 38.
[29] *ABC-ITT Merger Case Reconsideration*, Sec. 2, pp. 13–14, 43–45.
[30] *ABC-ITT Merger Proceedings*, Part IV, p. 10.

can Broadcasting Companies, Inc., and its divisions and subsidiaries.[31]

ABC later won assurances from ITT that it would remain autonomous under its present management and Goldenson's leadership. Doubts were expressed, however, that ITT President Geneen would stand idly by as a titular head of "that third network" after a record of wanting the top position in everything he did.[32] Shortly after the agreement was made, Wall Street observers anticipated "that the strong personalities of Mr. Geneen and Mr. Goldenson will clash and that the ITT image will intrude heavily into ABC, particularly in programming." [33]

In any case, the merger agreement provided that ABC would retain its own independent board of directors and management, with some cross representation on the two boards, for at least three years. During those three years, however, matters of major ABC importance were to be submitted to the ITT board before becoming effective.[34]

THE FCC MAJORITY OPINION

The majority opinion in the FCC's first ruling of December 1966 pointed out that the key issue of the proposed merger was whether the extensive business interests of ITT might influence ABC's broadcasting activities, and particularly whether there would be any commercial influence on the journalistic function—the reporting of news and news commentary—or on the selection, scheduling, or treatment of public affairs programming. The majority recognized the large stake our society has in preserving the freedom of broadcast stations and networks from the intrusion of extraneous private economic interests upon programming decisions. Thorough, fearless, and unbiased collection, dissemination, and analysis of news is, they said, crucial to a free society. There is widespread and growing reliance by the public upon broadcast sources of news and news commentary and upon public affairs programming and other kinds of informative programming. They were, therefore, attentive to the positive assurances that both ABC and ITT gave the FCC and the public on this score.

The majority opinion affirmed that the commission's own criteria for freedom of the press would not be violated by the merger because of ABC and ITT's repeated assurances that ABC would operate as a substantially

[31] Gene Smith, "Defines Merger Proposal," *The New York Times,* December 3, 1965, p. 55.
[32] Gene Smith, "New Role Looms for IT&T Chief," *The New York Times,* December 12, 1965, Sec. 3, p. 1.
[33] Gene Smith, "Personality: The Empire Builder at I.T.T.," *The New York Times,* February 20, 1966, Sec. 3, p. 3.
[34] "Dissenting Statement of Commissioner Robert T. Bartley," *ABC-ITT Merger Proceedings,* Part II, p. 8.

autonomous subsidiary and that ABC's operations as a broadcasting licensee would not be affected by the commercial, communications, or other similar interests of ITT. Both ITT and ABC officials were examined at length on this matter, and the assurances and representations set forth were considered sufficient guarantee that the autonomy of ABC's news department was not in jeopardy.[35]

As to the hazard of alien influence on the broadcasting operations of an American subsidiary of ITT, the majority opinion stated:

> We know from our experience in the regulation of communications that many of our large broadcasting licenses and the two other television networks also have substantial foreign interests, including subsidiary corporations in many countries. We have seen no evidence at any time that any of these foreign interests have influenced any of the programming presented in this country. There is no reason to assume or suspect that any such influence will occur in the case of ITT.

> Nothing of which we are aware in the history of ITT's operations abroad or in the United States suggests that it has ever been or would in the future be neglectful of its loyalties or responsibilities as an American company, or that aliens associated in the ownership and management of overseas ITT companies would by some sinister and unexplained means exert influence upon the interests of the United States broadcast public.[36]

THE DISSENTERS

The key difference between the majority and minority opinions was in regard to the *possibility* of dangers resulting from the merger as opposed to the *probability* of such. The minority was concerned with the *"potential* conflict of interest between the business interests which comprise ITT and ABC's broadcasting responsibility to the public, especially in news and public affairs," whereas the majority was concerned with the *likelihood* of such. This is why dissenting Commissioner Johnson felt that it was ITT and ABC's burden to show that the merger was in the public interest, and not as the majority felt, that any merger is in the public interest unless proof to the contrary is brought forth.

Johnson said:

> ITT as owner of ABC constantly will be faced with the conflict between its profit maximizing goals—indeed obligations to shareholders—which characterize all business corporations, and the duty to serve the public with free and unprejudiced news and public

---

[35] *Ibid.*, Part I, p. 10.
[36] *ABC-ITT Merger Case Reconsideration*, Sec. 1, pp. 16–17.

affairs programming. The issue is both whether anything damaging to ITT's interest is *ever* broadcast, as well as *how* it is presented.

The number of such potential conflicts is "endless." How, for example, was ABC to report foreign affairs when 60 percent of ITT's earnings was from foreign subsidiaries and investments? More specifically, how should ABC report on the possible nationalization of ITT property in foreign countries? (It had occurred in eight countries.) In the past, ITT had encouraged such laws as the Hickenlooper amendment calling for reduction of United States aid in countries not paying for nationalized property. How should ABC News view such laws in the future? How should the network report widespread dissent movements in Brazil if the government outlawed reports favorable to the dissenters? "Would anyone in ABC News be inclined or feel free to propose the show in the first place?" said Johnson. "Would they be able to withstand suggestions from within or without ITT that ABC news' resources might better be used on other assignments?" How should ABC report government defense and space policy when space-related contracts accounted for 40 percent of ITT's domestic income? Or, how should the network view truth-in-lending legislation while parent ITT operated several finance companies?

The mere promise of ITT officials that they would not interfere with ABC news and public affairs programming was not sufficient, Commissioners Johnson and Bartley asserted. Both Goldenson and Geneen might be out of a job tomorrow, but the corporation would continue. "These assurances are given by men—and we are turning these broadcast properties over to corporations," which would continue to influence the public after present officials were gone.

Even assurances by present management would not guarantee the independence of ABC during their periods in office:

> Subtle pressures on ABC officials to serve ITT interests cannot be eliminated by the most scrupulous adherence to formal independence for ABC and its editorial staff. ABC personnel will, on their own initiative, consider ITT's interests in making programming decisions. Institutional loyalties develop. These are often reinforced by the acquisition of stock in the employing company—now ITT stock, not ABC. And most important, it will be impossible to erase from the minds of those who make the broadcasting decisions at ABC that their jobs and advancement are dependent on ITT.[37]

With awareness of ITT's foreign interests, even the most conscientious news official would be less objective than he would be if ABC remained unaffiliated, and he would not forget that his future in the company could be affected by his handling of ITT-sensitive issues. Thus, the threat was less that items would be filmed, killed, or slanted, as that ideas or new

[37] All these quotations will be found in *ABC-ITT Merger Proceedings,* Part IV, pp. 6, 18, 20–29. See also Part II, p. 4.

coverage would never even be proposed. It was also possible that materials would be considered that were in essence simply public relations pieces for ITT or its interests. These were real threats, but the more probable abuse was that reporters might overcompensate by stressing or suppressing developments embarrassing to ITT. Whichever way the programming leaned, the public would suspect that ITT interests governed ultimate selections. "The risks which this suggests are of a kind that should be taken only with the greatest caution and only with a showing of extraordinarily compelling countervailing benefits." [38]

Johnson added that ITT was like most companies that spend "vast sums to influence its image and its economic relations—through advertising, public relations, and Washington representation."

Are we to accept, on the parties' own self-serving assurances, that although ITT may continue to exert pressure as an advertiser on the programming of CBS and NBC, it will exert none as an owner on the programming of ABC?

I am afraid I must concede that the assurances we have been provided—that ITT will be totally oblivious to the image created for it by its own mass media subsidiary, ABC—simply strain my credibility beyond the breaking point.

It seems elementary to me that the only real way to find adequate safeguards for the public's interest in programming integrity is to give attention to the structure of the industry, not to assurances, albeit sincere, of interested parties who may be gone tomorrow.

[Thus] the best we can do is to try to provide as much insulation as possible for the industry's programming from extraneous economic considerations. The worst we can do is to encourage mergers like this, which expose businessmen to the daily temptation to subvert the high purpose and indispensable role of the broadcast media in a free society. [39]

Bartley, who agreed with Johnson that industry *structure* was paramount, in his dissent referred to other cases in which nonbroadcast corporate interests have intruded into broadcast operations. For example, RCA-NBC exerted pressure on Westinghouse to "swap stations in Cleveland and Philadelphia so RCA could have an outlet in Philadelphia where its laboratories were located." [40] Bartley concluded that "as bankers think like bankers, I believe we can expect that corporate conglomerates will think like corporate conglomerates rather than like objective professional broadcasters."

The majority did not feel structure to be that critical, as it did not

---

38 "Dissenting Opinion of Commissioners Robert T. Bartley, Kenneth A. Cox, and Nicholas Johnson," *ABC-ITT Merger Case Reconsideration,* p. 85.
39 *ABC-ITT Merger Proceedings,* Part IV, pp. 28, 30.
40 *Business Week,* January 6, 1968, p. 14.

treat the matter as closed. It demands "eternal vigilance" by all broadcast licensees and will receive our continuing scrutiny for indication that our reliance upon the assurances and safeguards set out on this record was not warranted.[41]

To the majority's promised scrutiny, Bartley retorted:

What tools do they have to make the vigilance meaningful? . . . Such policing would be a near impossibility. When such eternal vigilance demands our continuing scrutiny of the particular situation, I believe the better course is to protect the public interest by not allowing it in the first place.

The majority pointed out, however, that since the beginning of broadcast licensing, the commission had licensed enterprises involved in a vast number of activities. Proposals excluding particular business interests (such as those in foreign countries) could not now be adopted unless they were applied to other cases, which would require the FCC to restructure the broadcasting industry, in turn requiring the FCC to refuse to renew licenses held by other networks and by numerous large conglomerate corporations. The majority said that such actions would not be in the public interest. But Bartley was suggesting this restructuring of the industry when he said, "This merger presents the Commission with the very basic and fundamental question of whether licenses should be granted to corporations involved in business other than broadcasting."

ITT PRESSURE ON NEWS MEDIA

In April 1967 the FCC held hearings on the Justice Department's request for a reconsideration of the merger. During these hearings, ABC President Goldenson testified that the president of ABC News would still have unquestioned authority over news programming and his decisions "wouldn't have to be cleared with anybody." [42] ITT President and Chairman Geneen testified before the commission that his company had "absolutely no intention of interfering in any way with the content of news programs" on ABC. The "composition and status" of ABC's board of directors would be unique among ITT subsidiaries, and present "operating personnel and general policies" would be continued. Geneen said, "We have considerable confidence in ABC's management or we wouldn't have entered into the merger."

This confidence in ABC's management, it turned out, was not unconditional. Geneen's original position was that, as a member of ABC's new

[41] All the quotations will be found in the following sequence in *ABC-ITT Merger Proceedings:* Part II, p. 4; Part I, p. 10; Part II, p. 13; Part I, p. 18; Part II, p. 14.
[42] Fred L. Zimmerman, "Managing the News?" *The Wall Street Journal,* April 17, 1967, p. 18.

board and executive committee, he would refrain from voting on matters likely to involve conflict of interest. However, *The Wall Street Journal* reported that Geneen, under pressure by an FCC attorney, admitted "it would be his duty to vote on all matters before ABC's board or executive committee." ITT would have the final say in the network's programming and selection of ABC directors. Geneen also said other "matters of major importance" would need his company's approval.[43]

Only a few days after Geneen testified that his company would not unduly influence ABC's news programming, an article in *The Wall Street Journal* quoted three reporters who said ITT officials had requested them to alter news stories in various ways. The article gained wide publicity for the issue of freedom of the press in the proposed merger.

THE *JOURNAL* ARTICLE

The Wall Street Journal article of April 17 quoted one reporter as saying, "It's incredible that guys like this want the right to run ABC's news operation." This criticism was in response to an ITT representative's complaint to the reporter's editor about his articles.[44]

A public relations official of ITT said, "We've been dissatisfied with some of the coverage. . . . Some of it has been incomplete and unfair." Indeed, by late February various company officials had complained about the coverage of *The New York Times,* the Associated Press, United Press International, *The Wall Street Journal,* and the *Washington Post.* According to *The Wall Street Journal:*

> The complaints were made through calls and letters to reporters and editors, and at meetings, with editors here [Washington, D.C.] and in New York. Occasionally factual inaccuracies were alleged, but more often the complaints were that reporters weren't writing balanced accounts or were obtaining information from unreliable sources.

Eileen Shanahan, who had been covering the proposed ITT-ABC merger for *The New York Times,* said that in January two ITT officials came to see her to complain about an article and to suggest "in imperious tones" that *The New York Times* carry the full text of a long FCC order issued that day. Later on, a third ITT representative telephoned her, criticizing an article and saying that the subject matter "wasn't worth a story." Miss Shanahan said, "He questioned my integrity and that of the *Times.*" The official in question, in denying Miss Shanahan's allegations, said he only "objected to one or two sentences."

Morton Mintz of the *Washington Post* found ITT's Public Relations

[43] "ITT Says Its Control of ABC Won't Alter Network's News Policy," *The Wall Street Journal,* April 17, 1967, p. 3.
[44] Zimmerman, "Managing the News?" p. 18.

Department's actions "rather unusual" when they first called him in November 1966 to suggest that he cover a certain congressman's speech, which was expected to be favorable to the merger. Mintz replied that he was busy and did not intend to cover the speech. At that point the ITT representative asked to speak to the editor and executive vice president of the *Post* who, however, never mentioned this to Mintz.

A UPI reporter said he was subject to "an obvious economic threat" from ABC, a big customer of the press service's radio and television news reports, after various stories he wrote concerning the merger appeared. Jed Stout, another reporter from UPI, said that John Horner, Washington, D.C., director of news media relations for ITT, telephoned him and cited a *Wall Street Journal* article dated February 6, which stated that the Justice Department would bring ITT to court if the FCC did not rule against the proposed merger. Stout said, "As I interpreted it he was asking me to write a story 'knocking down' the Journal piece. I declined to do so." [45]

The night that the FCC announced another delay of the ITT-ABC merger to hold further hearings regarding the Justice Department's evidence, a Washington-based AP reporter, Stephen M. Aug, was dictating the story over the phone. As he was in the middle of his sixth paragraph he was told that ABC had seen the story over the AP wires and had called from New York requesting he change his first paragraph.[46] Network officials wanted the paragraph changed from the FCC "ordered" a delay in the merger to the FCC "suggested" a delay. Aug. refused to change the wording.[47]

REACTION TO THE WALL STREET JOURNAL ARTICLE

Two days later, on April 19, the Justice Department requested the FCC to subpoena three of the reporters quoted in the article, Messrs. Aug and Stout, and Miss Shanahan, to "explore matters raised by a *Wall Street Journal* article Monday, reporting on efforts to affect press coverage of these proceedings and the independent news judgment" of these reporters and their organizations.[48] According to the department such "alleged pressure" might be improper [49] and might be related to the company's promise not to interfere with ABC news coverage.[50] The FCC chief examiner complied with the department's wishes.[51] Also, an FCC

45 *Ibid.;* see also "ITT Inquiry Calls Three Reporters," *The New York Times,* April 20, 1967, p. 28.
46 Zimmerman, "Managing the News?" p. 18; see also Fred P. Graham, "3 Reporters Allege Pressures by ITT about Their News Coverage of Its Merger Plan with ABC," *The New York Times,* April 21, 1967, p. 45.
47 Graham, "3 Reporters Allege Pressures by ITT."
48 "Reporters Are Subpoenaed for Hearing on ABC-ITT," *The Wall Street Journal,* April 20, 1967.
49 *The New York Times,* April 20, 1967, p. 28.
50 Graham, "3 Reporters Allege Pressures by ITT," p. 45.
51 *The New York Times,* April 20, 1967, p. 28.

Broadcast Bureau attorney said the bureau intended to call on John Horner, the ITT official mentioned in the article, to testify before the commission concerning his reported activities.[52]

The reporters were reluctant to give information to other reporters until after their testimony. Miss Shanahan did say, however, that the *Journal* article was "correct, as far as it went—there was more."

Horner issued a statement saying:

> . . . we have made no effort to manage the news. We at ITT believe wholeheartedly in the right of free speech and we have the greatest respect for members of the press and other news media. Historically, the company has been able to communicate its views to the press without any difficulty.
>
> As a publicly held company, we regard it as our duty to supply the fullest information possible on news stories and when occasional errors occur, to assist correspondents in correcting the record. In so doing over many years, we have enjoyed excellent cooperation from the media.

The day the subpoenas were issued, James Hagerty, an ABC vice-president who had been President Eisenhower's press secretary, said it would be "impossible" for ITT to influence ABC news coverage—and "if it did I would resign." [53]

THE REPORTERS TESTIFY

The three reporters testified at hearings held on April 20. Stout of UPI added greater detail to the allegations made in *The Wall Street Journal* article of April 17.[54] He said Horner had talked to him in February about the *Journal* article of February 6 and had asked him about the *Journal's* sources of the rumor that the Justice Department would probably challenge the merger in court if the FCC approved it. The article was not free to name the officials who had given the information. Stout, who regularly covered the Justice Department, said at the hearings that Horner "asked me to make inquiries in the Department of Justice as to whether or not this decision [to go to court] had [actually] been made." Stout refused Horner [55] and told the FCC he had never before received such a request.[56]

ITT had already complained to *The Wall Street Journal* about the February 6 article. The *Journal* said of the complaint that

52 *The Wall Street Journal*, April 20, 1967.
53 *The New York Times*, April 20, 1967, p. 28.
54 Graham, "3 Reporters Allege Pressures by ITT," p. 45.
55 "Reporters Tell FCC That ITT, ABC Tried to Influence Press Coverage of Merger," *The Wall Street Journal*, April 21, 1967, p. 10.
56 Graham, "3 Reporters Allege Pressures by ITT," p. 45.

Mr. Horner said then that it was a "speculative story" and that it didn't seem right for the Journal to print "speculative" stories.

He said the Journal shouldn't write stories having an adverse effect on the stock market. He noted that ABC stock had dropped $4.50 a share the day after the article was printed. The same day, however, ITT common stock rose $1.625 a share.

ITT succeeded in getting the Justice Department to send the company a telegram stating that a decision hadn't been made on whether to take the case to court. ITT itself promptly issued the telegram to the press. But a Justice Department official told the Journal privately that the telegram to ITT shouldn't be construed as a denial of the Journal's report.

Stout said that Horner telephoned him again concerning the *Journal* article, calling its author a "hipshooter" and saying "there had been a great deal of inaccurate reporting on the merger." Also, Stout's own reporting came under fire. On February 3, two of his superiors discussed his "choice of words" in a story concerning the merger proposal. They explained to him that "there have been complaints received from officials of ABC about the accuracy of the story." The reporter's superiors told him the phrase in question was not accurate.[57]

Miss Shanahan testified that ITT representatives had contacted her five or six times. During one brief encounter, an official, whose identity the reporter did not remember, talked to her of a recent development in the merger case favorable to ITT saying, "I expect to see that in the paper, high up in your story." [58]

On February 1, at about 8 P.M., Edward Gerrity, senior ITT vice-president for public relations, and another ITT official delivered a company statement to Miss Shanahan's office.[59] According to the reporter, Gerrity indirectly requested to see the story Shanahan was then writing, which she thought he should have known was "an improper thing to ask a reporter." He asked if her paper was going to run the text of a recent FCC statement criticizing the Justice Department for being late with its evidence in the case. Shanahan thought that document insufficiently important, but Gerrity asked in an "accusatory and certainly nasty" tone, "you mean you did not even recommend the use of text?" Shanahan said, "He badgered me again to play up favorable developments in the case." Gerrity also inquired if she had been following the stock market prices of ITT and ABC. Shanahan told him she had not [60] and later told the commission that "he asked if I didn't feel I have a responsibility to shareholders who might lose money from what I wrote. . . . I told him no.[61] . . . My responsibility was to find out the truth and print it." [62]

[57] *The Wall Street Journal,* April 21, 1967, p. 10.
[58] *ABC-ITT Merger Case Reconsideration,* Sec. 2, p. 29.
[59] *Ibid.;* see also *The Wall Street Journal,* April 21, 1967, p. 10.
[60] *ABC-ITT Merger Case Reconsideration,* pp. 29–30. See also Graham, "3 Reporters Allege Pressures by ITT," p. 45.
[61] *The Wall Street Journal,* April 21, 1967, p. 10.
[62] *ABC-ITT Merger Case Reconsideration,* Sec. 2, p. 30.

Gerrity then asked if she was aware "that Commissioner Nicholas Johnson was working with some people in Congress on legislation that would forbid any newspaper from owning any broadcast property." [63] (*The New York Times* owns an AM-FM radio station in New York.) When she told him she was unaware of such a bill he replied, "I think this is some information you should pass on to your publisher before you write any more about Commissioner Johnson's opinions." [64]

During the hearings the *Times* reporter identified one of the congressmen alleged to be working with Johnson as Senator Gaylord Nelson of Wisconsin.[65] In response to this testimony, the FCC later issued a statement saying:

> Commissioner Johnson will have no statement to make on this charge, at this time, while the merger case is under consideration by the Commission. Neither Mr. Johnson nor any other official Commission spokesman has ever talked with any person at any time about legislation prohibiting newspaper ownership and no change in that policy is now under consideration.[66]

Johnson later personally denied "collaboration" with Nelson, and Nelson denied ever having met Johnson.[67] According to the July 8, 1967, issue of the *New Republic*, *Variety* discovered that ITT public relations officials had given the same story about Senator Nelson to reporters for the *Milwaukee Journal*, which owns a radio and TV station. The newspaper, however, discovered that the ITT information was incorrect.[68]

According to the reporter's testimony, later in February the Justice Department filed its report with the FCC and Miss Shanahan wrote an article on the department's evidence.[69] John Horner then told her that her coverage of the merger "has been unfair right from the beginning." [70] According to Horner the most objectionable part of her recent story was her statement that the department would take the merger to the courts if the FCC did not reopen its hearings. Horner said the department "had issued a statement saying that it would not go to court." The *Times* reporter asked him to read her that statement, which she testified only said that "the Department had not decided what it would do if the Commission refused to reopen the hearing." When she said that he had "improperly characterized" the statement, Horner again told her her reporting was unfair, a remark that angered her. According to her colleagues, she yelled at Horner [71] that he had insulted not only her but also her editors, and she hung up the phone.[72] Miss Shanahan then called the Justice Depart-

63 *Ibid.*
64 *The Wall Street Journal,* April 21, 1967, p. 10.
65 *ABC-ITT Merger Case Reconsideration,* Sec. 2.
66 *The Wall Street Journal,* April 21, 1967, p. 10.
67 *ABC-ITT Merger Case Reconsideration,* Sec. 2.
68 James Ridgeway, "The Voice of ITT," *New Republic,* July 8, 1967, pp. 17–19.
69 *Ibid.,* p. 31.
70 *The Wall Street Journal,* April 21, 1967, p. 10.
71 *ABC-ITT Merger Case Reconsideration,* Sec. 2.
72 *The Wall Street Journal,* April 21, 1967, p. 10.

ment and inquired about the statement Horner had read to her over the phone. As it turned out, such a "statment" had never been released—the information was a private communication to the company from the department.

Continuing her testimony, Miss Shanahan said that during one of the commission's earlier hearings she had missed a brief portion of the testimony. Upon her return Horner informed her of what she had missed. He supposedly told her, in an "insistent and nasty" tone, that "I expect to see headlines just as big on this one as on what happened the other day," [73] presumably referring to an article that Horner considered unfavorable. [74] Miss Shanahan said a similar incident had only happened once in her five years with the *Times*. [75] Her editor, she said, also told her that this was uncharacteristic of the paper's previous contacts with the company. [76]

PRELUDE TO DECISION

During the April 20 hearings, ITT counsel attempted to question the reporters about their sources within the Justice Department, [77] on the grounds that the company was "entitled to show that the Department of Justice has had conversations with the press [also]. This bears directly on ITT's efforts to get two-sided coverage." However, the hearing examiner sustained a Justice Department objection of immateriality. [78] The ITT lawyer himself then objected on the grounds that ITT and ABC were being denied their right of free speech in getting their side of the merger to the public while secret government sources were allowed to present their own side.

In general, ITT spokesmen would not comment about the testimony after the hearings were over, but James Hagerty of ABC said he accepted Aug's statement that someone from the network had asked him to change a story before it was finished but that the company was unable to determine who made the call. [79]

On April 21 the president of ABC News, Elmer Lower, testified before the commission. In reference to Hagerty's reported statement that he would resign if ITT attempted to influence the network's news policies, Lower said, "I think I would hear about it before Mr. Hagerty did and I would be out the door ahead of him." According to Lower, no one of his superiors in the ABC hierarchy had ever exercised any control over the network's news programming, and he did not expect any change in this policy in the future. [80]

73 *ABC-ITT Merger Case Reconsideration*, Sec. 2.
74 Graham, "3 Reporters Allege Pressures by ITT," p. 45.
75 *ABC-ITT Merger Case Reconsideration*, Sec. 2.
76 Graham, "3 Reporters Allege Pressures by ITT," p. 45.
77 *Ibid.*
78 *The Wall Street Journal*, April 21, 1967, p. 10.
79 Graham, "3 Reporters Allege Pressures by ITT," p. 45.
80 "A.B.C. Station Aid on Merger Urged," *The New York Times*, April 22, 1967, p. 36.

Arguments for both sides in the merger case continued until June 2, when ITT concluded its oral arguments with assurances that "the independence of ABC programming from any other ITT commercial or similar interest shall be inviolate."

According to the attorneys for the two companies, the "built in guarantees of independence for ABC news"—sections of the merger agreement and internal policy documents signed by ITT President Harold Geneen—answered "the major issue the Justice Department relies on" in attempting to prevent the merger. Accordingly, any changes in this policy would be communicated to the commission.[81]

The Justice Department maintained, however, that the commission would not "find it possible to monitor . . . on a day to day basis," ITT's pledge of a hands-off policy.

In answer to questions from the commission, ITT attorneys said that the company's actions regarding attempts to influence the news coverage of the merger hearings "were more than the normal kind of public relations [in] one or two instances" and did not represent company policy.

Commissioner Johnson asked if the FCC could believe that ITT "will follow higher principles with ABC," with whom it had economic influence, than with reporters such as those covering the FCC hearings, over whom it had no control. ITT counsel replied that the company now had "a greater sensitivity and a greater awareness" of the need for a free press.[82]

FCC'S "RECONSIDERED" OPINION

On June 22 the FCC announced its decision to allow the merger.[83] The commission agreed with ABC News President Elmer Lower that the greater financial resources available to ABC if the merger took place "would increase, rather than decrease, the independence of the new gathering organization." Without ITT's finances, the commission stated, the network would not be able to undertake the "cultural programming innovation, news and public affairs expansion" necessary to compete with the other two TV networks, CBS and NBC.

The commission added that "news and public affairs programs are not profitable and that the ability of a television network to produce and present such programs depends in large part on its financial prosperity and resources." The majority opinion cited Fred Friendly, former head of CBS News, as saying that NBC, with the financial strength of RCA behind it, was in a more advantageous position regarding the type of non-profit public service programming it could present and initiate.

---

81 "ITT Gives Pledge on News Policy," *The New York Times*, June 3, 1967, p. 63.
82 *Ibid.*
83 All quotations in this section will be found in Federal Communications Commission, "Opinion and Order on Petition for Reconsideration," *ABC-ITT Merger Case Reconsideration*, Sec. 1, pp. 30, 31, 34.

Thus, since ABC was not as highly profitable as NBC and CBS, "it is obvious that ABC is at a tremendous disadvantage."

Finally, that the heightening of competition between the networks will serve the public interest needs no exposition. Therefore, based on our knowledge of the industry and the present network situation, we find on the supplemental record that there will be a significant benefit to the public interest in this respect.

In regard to ITT's and ABC's alleged pressuring of news reporters, the commission cited only one instance of improper conduct. In general,

> there is no evidence that either ITT or ABC did any more than ask reporters covering the proceeding to be factually accurate in their reporting. It is clear that there was some difference of viewpoint as to what the significant facts were, and this difference persists among the parties, counsel, reporters, and others concerned with the case. There is no impropriety in approaching the press to inform or to attempt to correct supposed inaccuracies. All of the reporters testified that this is a common, even daily, occurrence for reporters. The Commission's own "fairness doctrine" is premised on the right to do just this with respect to broadcast reports of news and commentary concerning controversial matters.

Only Gerrity's relating of false information to Miss Shanahan was cited as "improper" and only an "isolated incident."

The majority dismissed Justice's fears of ITT pressure on numerous grounds, including (1) "the Commission's experience with similarly situated enterprises in the industry," (2) "the past performance of both applicants as long time licensees of the Commission," and (3) the fact that "the area of broadcast reporting of news and public affairs is a field in which the Commission has experience and special competence and in which the Department has no special qualifications."

DISSENTING OPINION

Commissioners Bartley, Cox, and Johnson dissented from the FCC majority opinion in the reconsideration.[84] The actions of the two companies with regard to alleged pressuring of news reporters and other incidents

> show the disdain in which ITT holds the Commission, and other persons and institutions in our society, seen as bothersome obstacles

---

[84] All quotations in this section will be found in Federal Communications Commission, "Dissenting Opinion of Commissioners Robert T. Bartley, Kenneth A. Cox, and Nicholas Johnson," *ABC-ITT Merger Case Reconsideration*, Sec. 2, pp. 27–29, 31, 33, 34–37, 40.

in the way of their merger or other ITT design. Such conduct is relevant to the credibility of ITT's self-serving statements generally, and especially its assurance to this Commission of its regard for the integrity and independence of ABC programming decisions and of its sense of responsibility in making commitments to this Commission as a broadcast licensee.

The minority opinion characterized ITT's "treatment and attitude towards the working press reporting these proceedings [as] shocking."

During reporters' testimony before the FCC, it was brought out that ITT public relations men had at various times called reporters at their homes: "Such repeated remonstrances and requests, and the willingness to contact the reporters at home, indicate a zealousness which we believe, at least, an unusual evidencing of extraordinary sensitivity to press treatment."

The incident involving Gerrity and Shanahan

evidences (1) overbearing behavior generally, (2) an insensitivity to the independence of the press, (3) a contempt for the proper functioning of government, (4) either a willingness to engage in deliberate misrepresentations of fact, or incredible naïveté in accepting and spreading unsubstantiated rumor, and (5) an attitude completely accepting the propriety, indeed the inevitability, of news reports reflecting the extraneous economic interests of a reporter's friends or employers.

The conduct of John Horner, ITT's head of PR in Washington, and other officials in pressuring Miss Shanahan regarding the Justice Department "statement"

demonstrates an abrasive self-righteousness in dealing with the press, a shocking insensitivity to its independence and integrity, a willingness to spread false stories in furtherance of self-interest, contempt for government officials as well as the press, and an assumption that even as prestigious a news medium as The New York Times would, as a matter of course, want to present the news so as to best serve its own economic interests (as well as the economic interest of other large business corporations). Despite this, ITT offered no rebuttal of any of the testimony of Miss Shanahan.

The minority opinion went on to say that it was not clear if the ITT public relations department had acted on its own or "was ordered, encouraged, or merely condoned by the top management of ITT. The least that can be said is that the officials involved presumably thought they were acting in accord with the wishes or policies of top management, or in the interests of the corporation." Indeed, ITT merely characterized the public relations Department's behavior as "overzealous," and no apologies or reprimands were made public. Even if public relations was acting outside of company policy (and ITT did not make this clear), "ITT would then be left with the fact that it cannot guarantee ABC's autonomy. If it cannot control its own senior vice president's conduct it has little hope of controlling lesser officials and employees."

The minority opinion also cited previous instances in which ITT allegedly had behaved illegally or improperly. In one, the company acquired an international carrier and transferred control of it from one subsidiary to another, before the required FCC approval, *then* sought the commission's permission to perform an act already accomplished. Another instance was cited in which ITT, even though it had not yet been merged with ABC, used the economic pressure of its advertising accounts to influence other corporations to benefit the network. The behavior of ITT lawyers during the supplementary hearings was also characterized as "high-handed," and reference was made to a company lawyer who telephoned a Justice Department witness

> and, in a two-hour conversation, tried to get him to change three sentences in the testimony which he was proposing to give. On cross examination, when asked if he felt he had been pressured, his first reaction was: "It depends, I am fairly tough, but two hours on a telephone, you know. I don't know. You can interpret that in your own way."

The opinion cited the chief hearing examiner's characterization of ITT lawyers' behavior as "improper" when they were delivering notes to witnesses who had not yet testified and who were excluded from the hearing room by order of the examiner himself. ABC lawyers were also accused of proffering witnesses with "positively misleading information" and making no attempt to set the record straight.

In regard to ITT's behavior with respect to the news media and FCC witnesses, the three commissioners said:

> ITT officials performed these acts and displayed these attitudes in a period which should have been filled with incentive for the most exemplary behavior because of the company's assurances about ABC's freedom from news management and pressure. Certainly it is likely that never again will there be such a depth and immediacy of public scrutiny of ITT's posture in this regard. Yet, with full knowledge of this public attention, ITT not only failed to match its assurances about the future with its deeds of the present, but actually conducted itself in a deliberate manner that gives these assurances a distinctly hollow ring. If ITT behaved this way with the spotlight on it, how much credibility can be given to assurances that ITT would not be led to similar conduct when the pressures, subtle and overt, can be transmitted with a minimum of visibility and accountability? It is not unreasonable, therefore, to believe that ITT would evidence similar disdain for ABC as a press medium, whether arising from

such misguided managerial élan or conflicting business goals inherent in its conglomerate and international operations.

In our view, this recurrent conduct on the part of ABC and ITT officials and attorneys has gone far beyond the bounds of natural prejudice and advocacy. The examples are far more numerous than we have recited. . . . We cite this deeply disturbing pattern of behavior because we believe it makes it impossible to approach the self-serving testimony of applicants' officials with anything but skepticism. And it is that testimony which constitutes a major part of the majority's "justification" for this merger.

SHADES OF RALPH NADER

On July 8 *The New York Times* and the *New Republic* reported Eileen Shanahan as saying that John V. Horner had been making inquiries about her "professional and personal life."

She said that three different persons, two of them her former employers, had told her of the inquiries and that in one of the cases she had been told that Mr. Horner had made a telephone call whose sole purpose was to inquire about her.[85]

After hearing from the second person approached, Miss Shanahan contacted ITT's counsel for the FCC hearing and "demanded that the investigation be stopped." The attorney called her the next day and said that he did not think there had ever been a "systematic investigation" and that no further inquiries would be made anyway. According to Horner, there was, and there had been, no investigation. He admitted that Miss Shanahan's name might have come up in "normal chitchat" with people, but no inquiries were made that were not "entirely normal, clean and above board." Horner said he "couldn't say" if he had contacted her former employers, as "I don't know who her former employers were." [86]

On September 7 the *New Republic* said that ITT had been investigating, through third parties, the personal life of James Ridgeway, whose articles in that magazine had been critical of the proposed merger.[87] One of the third parties was James Mackey, a researcher for *Army Times* of Washington, D.C. According to the *New Republic,* Mackey called the magazine's office and asked

what sort of articles did [Ridgeway] write, how often did they appear, how long had he worked there. . . . What was his height and

85 "Reporter on Times Says ITT Made Inquiries about Her," *The New York Times,* July 8, 1967, p. 22.
86 *Ibid.*
87 Eileen Shanahan, "Justice Department Disputes Faith Shown by FCC in Its Approval of ITT-ABC Merger Proposal," *The New York Times,* September 8, 1967, p. 30.

weight, what restaurants did he frequent, did he drink, was he married, . . . was his wife a reporter. Did she help out with his work, was he friendly with the other employees (Does he say good morning), did the editor care much for him and so on.

Later on, Mackey said that one of ITT's advertising agencies had asked him to "find out anything, everything I could about a guy named James Ridgeway." Mackey had never done this before, but his newspaper depended heavily on its advertisers and wanted to please their ad agencies.

Ridgeway questioned Mackey, who replied, "This is all above board as far as I know. Gee, don't think your name is Ralph Nader or anything like that." An ITT representative told Ridgeway, "We're not conducting any investigation of you, and we have no reason to . . . I don't know anything about the *Army Times.* It seems to me that if you have an argument with somebody, it's them not us." [88]

In a letter in the September 30, 1967, issue of the *New Republic, Army Times* Vice-President William F. Donally said that Mackey "undertook the investigation . . . entirely on his own and without authorization from *Army Times* or anyone connected with *Army Times*" and was dismissed for his "incredible behavior." Donally said it was his opinion that neither ITT "nor anyone else" authorized the investigation. Mackey, according to the vice-president, refused to discuss the matter with his former employer, though the *Times* continued to try to get an explanation from him. According to Donally, the newspaper was "totally unaware" of Mackey's investigation and had "never done any investigation of any individual for anyone: not for advertisers, not for editors, not for anybody." [89]

JUSTICE RETURNS

Also on September 8, the Justice Department brought the FCC decision to the court of appeals on the grounds that the commission could not ensure that ITT would maintain a hands-off policy regarding ABC News if the merger were to take effect. According to the department, any attempt to "enforce" ITT's promise not to influence ABC public affairs and news programs for its own interest was an "impossibility" and "would come dangerously close to the kind of program censorship which is barred by the First Amendment and the Communications Act." [90]

The company also came under fire. "It is plainly absurd to think that the FCC will receive advance written notice [as ITT promised] before ITT tries to kill an ABC documentary or before ABC officials, on their own, shelve subjects which would be embarrassing or detrimental to

[88] "ITT's Press Relations," *New Republic,* September 16, 1967, p. 6–7.
[89] "The Ridgeway Caper," *New Republic,* September 30, 1967, p. 36.
[90] All quotations in this section will be found in Shanahan, "Justice Department Disputes Faith Shown by FCC."

ITT." The Justice Department also challenged the commission's contention that ITT did not differ from RCA as a television network parent
company, although RCA had extensive business with foreign countries.
Unlike RCA and CBS:

> ITT is, in origin, a foreign operating company and its predominant
> source of profit overseas is in the sale of telecommunications equip-
> ment.

> Since the postal, telephone and telegraph functions in other coun-
> tries are almost invariably performed by governmental entities,
> ITT's position in these markets is largely dependent upon its success
> in dealing with the officials of governmental or quasigovernmental
> bodies.

> [Thus] ITT could have strong motivation to use a news medium
> affirmatively to promote certain of its investments, by showing offi-
> cials or programs of a foreign government in a favorable light.

Dangers exist in that "internal corporate pressures" and "subtle influences" may result "in avoidance of subject matter, blunting of criticism,
the treatment of controversy in a noncontroversial manner, because of the
economic interest of the company."

The Justice Department attacked the FCC majority opinion's statement that there was only one "isolated" instance of improper conduct in
regard to ITT's pressuring reporters covering the hearings. Indeed, certain activities of ITT officials were "outrageous conduct" and were central
to "the very matter" of the Justice Department's worry over "ITT's assuming responsibility for ABC's news and public affairs activities."

The FCC filed its brief with the court of appeals during the first part
of October and said the Justice Department erred in its contention that
the commission could not enforce ITT's promise that it would not interfere with the network's news and public affairs programming.[91]

The merger was canceled by ITT on January 1, 1968, before the court
of appeals had made its decision.

SELECTED REFERENCES

CRANDALL, ROBERT W., "FCC Regulation, Monopsony, and Network Television
    Program Costs," *The Bell Journal of Economics and Management Science,*
    autumn 1972, pp. 483–508.
GRAHAM, GENE S., "History in the (Deliberate) Making: A Challenge to Modern
    Journalism," *Nieman Reports,* September 1966, pp. 3–7.
"Is the Press Biased?" *Newsweek,* September 16, 1968, pp. 66–67.
KELLY, FRANK K., "Second Edition/Who Owns the Air," *Center Magazine,*
    March–April 1970, pp. 27–33.

[91] "ITT Scores Suit to Block Merger," *The New York Times,* October 3, 1967, p. 28.

SETHI, S. PRAKASH, Business Corporations and the Black Man (San Francisco: Chandler, 1970).

U.S. Congress, Senate, Committee on Judiciary, Subcommittee on Antitrust and Monopoly, *Economic Concentration*, Part 8A, Appendix to Staff Report of the Federal Trade Commission's *Economic Report on Corporate Mergers*, Part 8, 91st Cong., 1st sess., 1969.

EASTMAN KODAK COMPANY (B), ROCHESTER, NEW YORK

CONFLICT WITH A MINORITY GROUP—FIGHT: THE ROLE OF THE NEWS MEDIA

The media report and write from the standpoint of a white man's world. The ills of the ghetto, the difficulties of life there, the Negro's burning sense of grievance are seldom conveyed. Slights and indignities are part of the Negro's daily life, and many of them come from what he now calls the "white press"— a press that repeatedly, if unconsciously, reflects the biases, the paternalism, the indifference of white America. This may be understandable, but it is not excusable in an institution that has the mission to inform and educate the whole of our society.

—Report of the National Advisory
Commission on Civil Disorders (1968)

From the very beginning the news media played an important part in the Kodak–FIGHT controversy. Both protagonists were aware of the role mass media could play in informing and influencing public opinion. The news media were therefore an important variable for Kodak and FIGHT, and the strategies of the two parties were carefully designed to *manipulate* and *use* the media to their best advantage.

This case material has been adapted from S. Prakash Sethi, *Business Corporations and the Black Man* (San Francisco: Chandler Publishing Company, 1970). Copyright © 1970 by Chandler Publishing Company. Used by permission.

Would the Kodak–FIGHT altercation have received national attention had not radio and television, wire services, national newspapers, and magazines covered Stokely Carmichael's visit to Rochester, Minister Florence's press conferences, and the demonstrations at Kodak's annual stockholders' meeting? The news media apparently played an important role in bringing the issue before the public. Furthermore, it is becoming apparent that the media's role in molding public opinion is increasingly critical in similar situations and that all parties to a conflict must consider the media before deciding on a course of action.

The news media are of interest in this case because to some extent they helped to create the news they reported. FIGHT's attempts to make its disagreements with Kodak a nationwide controversy were aided by the media. Several times throughout late 1966 and the first half of 1967, Florence was able to win support among various segments of the American public because he kept the issue at a controversial level. This strategy, to a large degree, accounts for the often bizarre manner in which FIGHT's spokesmen and supporters acted before television cameras to attract public attention. By focusing solely on its sensational aspects, the news media chose to elevate the controversy to a national level and at the same time distorted and exaggerated its impact.

The conflict between Kodak and FIGHT was covered nationwide by the major news services and by national magazines and journals of all types and political persuasions. Although events were reported throughout the controversy, national coverage was heaviest immediately after Kodak repudiated its agreement with FIGHT and at the time of the stockholders' meeting in Flemington, New Jersey.

THE LOCAL NEWS MEDIA [1]

The only English-language daily newspapers in Rochester—the *Democrat & Chronicle* and the *Times-Union*—were both part of the Rochester-headquartered Gannett newspaper chain and were both published by Paul Miller, president of the chain.[2] Before the FIGHT–Kodak controversy erupted, the Gannet chain had a reputation for progressive thinking

[1] The accounts of coverage by local television and radio stations reported in this section were indirectly obtained through newspaper reports and magazine articles.
[2] Gannett Co., Inc., is a chain of newspapers and radio and television stations located in small- and medium-size cities primarily in the northeastern states. In 1967 it had 30 newspapers (29 owned and one affiliated) with circulation ranging from 6,500 to 218,600. In addition, Gannett owned AM radio and VHF television outlets in Rochester and Birmingham, New York; AM-FM radio outlets in Danville, Illinois, and Cocoa, Florida; and a VHF television outlet in Rockford, Illinois. Of the two Rochester newspapers, the *Democrat & Chronicle* was published mornings and Sundays (circulation 142,794 and 218,586, respectively), and the *Times-Union* was an evening paper (circulation 143,855). See *Ayer Directory of Newspapers and Periodicals, 1967* (Philadelphia: N. W. Ayer and Son, 1968); *Broadcasting Year Book, 1968* (Washington, D.C.: Broadcasting Publications, 1968), p. A–112; *Editor and Publisher Year Book, 1968* (New York: Editor & Publisher Co., 1968), p. 312.

and constructive work in the area of civil rights. In 1962 the *Times-Union* published an updated version of a 1960 series under the title "Winds of Revolt," which showed "how badly the Negroes were housed in a city famous for its homes, its trees and lilacs, its culture, its generosity, and its depression proof economy." [3]

In 1963 Paul Miller assigned Gannett's executive director, Vincent Jones, to investigate the different ways Northern cities were coping with racial unrest and urban crisis. More than forty editors and reporters contributed to the investigation, and more than one hundred articles were prepared and distributed within a year, starting in July 1963 under the general title of "The Road to Integration." This series won journalism's highest award, the Pulitzer Prize, the first ever awarded to a group or chain.[4] The same series won a Brotherhood Award from the National Conference of Christians and Jews.

However, when the Board of Urban Ministry invited Saul Alinsky to Rochester, Gannett raised a strong protest. The reaction probably reflected the views of publisher Paul Miller who, since 1966, had led a one-man crusade against FIGHT, church organizations supporting FIGHT, Saul Alinsky, and all other persons sympathetic to FIGHT.

The *Times-Union* and its radio and television affiliate WHEC dispatched a three-man team to Chicago to study the operations of Alinsky's Industrial Areas Foundation in the Woodlawn section of Chicago. The outcome was a three-part series in the paper and two one-hour television documentaries during prime time. According to Vincent Jones, "both sides praised these presentations as objective and informative."[5]

However, neither this series of articles nor the opinions expressed by local clergy changed any minds at Gannett. As Jones put it:

> We have tried to keep our feet on the ground and to pursue a moderate, practical policy. . . . The invitation [to Saul Alinsky] was issued by the Council of Churches without first consulting the community. Because of the way it was handled, and a belief that Alinsky's controversial methods would do more harm than good, the *Times-Union* questioned the whole project. It was a moderate editorial stand, but left no doubt of the newspaper's belief that the move was risky at best.[6]

Miller's wrath was directed as much, if not more, against the Rochester Area Council of Churches (RACC) as it was against FIGHT and Saul Alinsky. According to an article in the *New Republic:*

> At the church breakfast in late 1966, Miller was once more belaboring the ministers for "sneaking" the organization past responsible

---

[3] Vincent S. Jones, "How Rochester Reacted," *Nieman Reports,* June 1965, pp. 16–17.
[4] *Ibid.*
[5] *Ibid.*
[6] *Ibid.*

citizens, and bringing into their midst this "ill-mannered tiger" [Alinsky] to preach "his hate."

"Rochester, New York, is not Rochester, Alabama," said Miller, who sounds like an undertaker. "We have primarily a refugee problem, not a racial problem." How inappropriate it was, he went on, for church people to cultivate in Negroes the idea that in Rochester as in the South, they must take something away from somebody to make progress. Miller recommended to the ministers an article in the December *Reader's Digest* entitled "Are We a Nation of Hoods?" It provided a valuable perspective on the teachings of Jesus.

"If the organization you finance be continued," he said, "why not see that it gets a name somewhat less offensive to the total community. How about W-O-R-K instead of F-I-G-H-T, how about L-O-V-E, how about T-R-Y, how about D-E-E-D-S?" [7]

Again in January, Miller made an editorial attack in the *Times-Union* on those of the clergy who had supported FIGHT. The editorial, entitled "The Gulf Between Pulpit and Pew—One Layman's View," drew a large number of letters to the editors of both papers, and most of the letters were critical of FIGHT and its supporters. However, it was not so much the letters as how they were headlined that reflected the bias of the editorial staff and management.

The two papers gave extensive coverage to Kodak and generally accorded front-page space to its press releases. Again the titles were invariably pro-Kodak or anti-FIGHT. The newspapers' coverage on FIGHT's activities and its position was small compared to that on Kodak or to that accorded FIGHT by the national news media. This bias was carried further into 1967 when an editorial in the *Democrat & Chronicle* of June 16, 1967, entitled "Council's Defense," derided the attempt of the Rochester Area Council of Churches to defend their support of FIGHT.[8]

Gannett newspapers were not the only media that did not like Alinsky and FIGHT. As noted in part C of the Kodak study (page 473), radio WHAM canceled a free hour it had been giving to the RACC. In an editorial attack on the council, reported in the *New Republic*, WHAM said:

Thinking members of Rochester area churches have admitted many times over that the solution to the plight of any minority cannot be solved overnight—that demands are one thing, but that people do not become economically equal just because the various members of the Christian faith would have it that way. More realistically,

[7] James Ridgeway, "Attack on Kodak," *New Republic,* January 21, 1967, pp. 11–13.
[8] "Alinsky Defends Black Power" and "Kodak Reviews Record on Job Talks with FIGHT," *Rochester Times-Union,* October 24, 1966, and September 21, 1966; "FIGHT Vows New Push for Kodak Jobs," "Kodak Questions FIGHT Job Demands," and "Council's Defense," *Rochester Democrat & Chronicle,* October 26, 1966, September 8, 1966, and June 16, 1967.

members of the human race must prove their capacity to compete and to want to be part of the community.[9]

FIGHT's only local outlet was WBBF, which Kodak people called "the Voice of FIGHT." This station presented FIGHT's publicity releases as news copy and made no attempt to give Kodak's viewpoint to listeners.

Coverage by the wire services and the nationally prominent newspapers was quite extensive, and most leading metropolitan dailies reported the conflict at its various high points, many relying on the wire services for their information. The biggest coverage by the press, radio, and television was accorded the stockholders' meeting. The proceedings of the meeting, the demonstrations outside the auditorium where the meeting was held, and the pronouncements of the spokesmen for Kodak and FIGHT were reported by all the national television networks, radio stations, and newspapers across the country. The only other occasion when network television cameras visited the scene was to record Stokely Carmichael's visit to Rochester in January 1967.[10] The role of television seems to have been crucial to Minister Florence's strategy. To some extent he was able to use television networks to escalate the issue to national prominence, and he believed that only in this way could he pressure Kodak into conceding FIGHT's demands.

NATIONAL NEWS MEDIA

To get a better idea of the emphasis given to the Kodak–FIGHT controversy, it is necessary that we make a detailed analysis of the nature and extent of coverage accorded the incidents by various news media.

The New York Times, perhaps the most influential newspaper in the country, was constantly on the scene. Starting with the first FIGHT convention in June 1966, the paper continuously reported the story as it developed. Immediately after Kodak's repudiation of the agreement of December 20, the *Times* published a long article, followed by four more related articles in January 1967 (three in the first week alone), two in February, nine in April, and three in May. The coverage thereafter declined in quantity but was adequate for reporting all the relevant news.

A close reading of the *Times* coverage reveals certain interesting points. First, the reporting was carefully balanced and "objective." John Kifner, who did most of the reporting, as well as Edward Fiske and M. J. Rossaut, presented opposing views in every story. The captions for different articles were either neutral or balanced to give equal billing. Nevertheless, the complete lack of the interpretive articles or in-depth analyses generally associated with this paper is striking. Not a single editorial was written on the controversy, which had vast social implications and had received so

9 James Ridgeway, "Saul Alinsky in Smugtown," *New Republic,* June 26, 1965, pp. 15–17.
10 The account of coverage by network radio and television described here was gathered only indirectly through a study of the press reports.

much national attention. Moreover, the reporting appeared to be somewhat indifferent, in that it was confined to merely quoting the spokesmen for Kodak and FIGHT. (As will be shown in the following section, *The Wall Street Journal* did the best investigative job of reporting, although it printed fewer stories than the *Times.*)

The *Washington Post* presented the other extreme. Nicholas Van Hoffman made no secret of where his sympathies lay. In a long article on January 9, 1967, entitled "Picture's Fuzzy as Kodak Fights FIGHT," he blamed Kodak for a large part of the conflict. In colorful language he suggested that the Kodak management was "out of focus" and hinted darkly that if the situation did not improve soon, "Negroes may again be out on the streets shooting, and not with Brownie Instamatics!" [11]

Among the national news magazines and general periodicals that covered the story at various times were *Time, Newsweek,* and *U.S. News and World Report.* Of the three, *Newsweek's* coverage was more extensive, with sufficient interpretive material to enable readers to see the conflict in its proper perspective. However, there was no expressed opinion by any of the magazines.

In contrast, the national magazines with liberal leanings were full of interpretive articles by well-known writers. The *New Republic* carried two articles by James Ridgeway, "Attack on Kodak" and "Saul Alinsky in Smugtown." The *Reporter* had two articles, one by Barbara Carter entitled "The FIGHT Against Kodak" and the other by Jules Witcover entitled "Rochester Braces for Another July." The *Atlantic* had an article by William C. Martin entitled "Shepherds vs. Flocks, Ministers vs. Negro Militancy." Although most of these articles listed the contributions made by Kodak to Rochester's civic causes, they minimized their real value in the light of changing social conditions. These authors also faithfully reported Kodak's position but berated its rationale and were generally pro-FIGHT in their writings.

The conservative magazine *National Review,* in an article entitled "The FIGHT–Kodak Fight" by Dorothy Livadas, took a strong pro-Kodak position and largely blamed "the starry-eyed churchmen," Saul Alinsky and Florence, for aggravating racial tension in Rochester. The article implied that most Rochester blacks wanted "no part of FIGHT" and suggested that Saul Alinsky was a man who "capitalized on the plight of the downtrodden and made a hero of himself while exploiting their misery." [12]

In a personal interview, a Kodak public relations executive expressed the conviction that the company's position in the controversy was not being fairly reported in the national press:

> It always makes good copy for David to be throwing a stone at Goliath. If Minister Florence were anywhere in the vicinity, the reporters would go after him to say something and he would take full advantage of this opportunity. . . .

11 "Picture's Fuzzy as Kodak Fights FIGHT," *Washington Post,* January 9, 1967.
12 "The FIGHT–Kodak Fight," *National Review,* June 27, 1967, p. 683.

The problem was primarily local in nature until the stockholders' meeting when, despite the 116 newspaper people present, the national press reported the thing so poorly that most people who read the account that appeared in a local paper hadn't the slightest idea what it was all about except that Kodak was having some trouble with Negroes.

According to an article by Raymond A. Schroth in the magazine *America*, "Kodak officials are still smarting from stories by James Ridgeway in the *New Republic* (January 21, 1967) and by Nicholas Van Hoffman in the *Washington Post* (January 9, 1967), in which Kodak claims to be misquoted." [13] In an interview with Schroth, Kodak spokesmen again repeated this charge.

THE BUSINESS NEWS MEDIA

The Kodak–FIGHT controversy was of special interest to the business community, as businessmen all over the country were asking themselves, "Will this happen to my corporation?" Alinsky himself saw Kodak as just the beginning of a pattern of attacks by racial minorities against outmoded corporate behavior.

The business news media covered the controversy extensively as news, provided their readers with in-depth analyses and interpretive articles, and also wrote policy editorials. The opinions of most business magazines ran from sympathy for Kodak to extreme hostility toward FIGHT in terms of both its objectives and its tactics.

The news coverage by *The Wall Street Journal* was perhaps the best of any newspaper in the country. For example, it was the *only* newspaper to report that after the Kodak repudiation, Mr. Florence offered to amend the agreement in any manner acceptable to Kodak or even to scrap it if Kodak officials would jointly announce with him on television their willingness to cooperate with FIGHT "to get more jobs for Negroes."[14] This was indeed an important concession by FIGHT, asking to do only what the company had said all along that it was willing to do. Yet Kodak officials turned down FIGHT's offer.

Why did FIGHT not choose to publicize Kodak's refusal? Florence was desperate after Kodak's repudiation and was probably willing to go to great lengths to salvage at least something from the situation. He might also have realized FIGHT's lack of staying power in a long contest. However, after his turndown Florence kept this incident quiet for fear it would appear to his followers as a "sellout" and would show lack of courage and militancy on his part. Kodak was not interested in publicizing the event because it would make the company look stubborn and unreasonable and

13 "Self-Doubt and Black Pride," *America*, April 1, 1967, p. 502.
14 Earl C. Gottschalk, Jr., "Kodak's Ordeal: How a Firm That Meant Well Won a Bad Name for Its Race Relations," *The Wall Street Journal*, June 30, 1967, pp. 1ff.

would refute all the pro-cooperation propaganda it had been making in public.

The kind of coverage given the Kodak–FIGHT controversy by the business news media is exemplified in some of the story titles and excerpts from these stories:

> *The Wall Street Journal:* "Eastman Kodak Accuses Rochester Rights Groups of Pushing for Power," "Kodak Refuses to Restore Negro Job Pact; Rights Group Vows 'War' Against Concern," "Eastman Kodak and Negro Group Reach Compact to Work in Harmony," "Kodak's Ordeal: How a Firm That Meant Well Won a Bad Name for Its Race Relations," "Kodak Announces Plan to Help Slum Dwellers Start Own Business." [15]
>
> *Business Week:* "The Fight That Swirls Around Eastman Kodak," "Kodak and FIGHT Agree to Agree," "What the Kodak Fracas Means." [16]
>
> *Fortune:* "And Kodak Will Ask, 'How High?' " (a reference to Stokely Carmichael's inflammatory statement in his Rochester press conference on January 19, 1967).[17]
>
> *Factory:* "There's a FIGHT in Kodak's Future." [18]
>
> *Barron's National Business and Financial Weekly:* "Who's Out of Focus? A Note on the Harassment of Eastman Kodak" (an attack on FIGHT and the church organizations supporting FIGHT).[19]

Reviewing Kodak's handling of the situation, *Business Week* [20] commented that after the second meeting, "Kodak was admittedly sidestepping FIGHT's demands. . . . [No] major company could remain union-free in New York State, as has Kodak, without considerable skill at evasive tactics." On Kodak's repudiation of the agreement, *Business Week* said: "While the agreement clearly ran counter to what Kodak had insisted all along, disavowing it weakened the company's position." Quoting an executive, the same periodical stated: "At least one executive thinks Kodak's lack of labor negotiating experience explains some of its clumsiness. 'Union negotiating teaches you when your name is on something, you have got an agreement.' "

Fortune, on the other hand, confined itself to quoting Kodak spokesmen and wrote:

> Two days later, Kodak declared that the agreement was "unauthorized" and unacceptable. Chairman William S. Vaughn subse-

[15] *The Wall Street Journal*, January 9, 1967; April 26, 1967, p. 7; June 26, 1967, p. 9; June 20, 1967, pp. 1ff.; November 20, 1967, p. 15.
[16] *Business Week*, April 29, 1967, pp. 38–41; July 1, 1967, p. 22; May 6, 1967, p. 192.
[17] *Fortune*, June 1, 1968, p. 78.
[18] *Factory*, June 1967, p. 69.
[19] *Barron's*, May 1, 1967, p. 1.
[20] *Business Week*, April 29, 1967, pp. 38–41.

quently issued a statement saying that Mulder . . . had acted "through an overzealous desire to resolve the controversy." [21]

Barron's presented the extreme end of the continuum on anti-FIGHT opinion. In an article on May 1, 1967, it stated: "Legally and morally, however, the company could not make the commitment demanded by FIGHT." *Barron's* thought Kodak had a lot to learn about labor relations: "If anything, it has taken not too hard a line, as its radical critics aver, but too soft. The presence on the pay roll of an executive who failed to grasp the elementary principles cited above suggests as much." [22]

Although some of the business magazines recognized the need for change in corporate behavior and suggested more positive action in the area of assistance to minorities, most of them were editorially critical of FIGHT and its supporters.

In an editorial entitled "What the Kodak Fracas Means," *Business Week* called the Kodak–FIGHT conflict the forerunner of similar conflicts. The editorial further stated:

> The demand that Kodak simply put to work whatever Negroes FIGHT produces is preposterous. . . . It is not the business of any corporate management to run a public welfare establishment. Efficient production of goods and services is the name of the business game. Personnel policies that are violently inconsistent with profitability violate one of the private corporation's cardinal rules. Management must retain its rights to hire, fire, promote, and assign work in ways that serve business objectives. [23]

The editorial urged business to understand and appreciate the objectives of civil rights groups in Rochester—the main objective being blacks —but said that "hiring unskilled Negroes cuts into profits, at least in the short run," and argued that "business must be paid for undertaking what is in the end a public responsibility." It exhorted civil rights groups to abandon their militancy and warned them that like the Wobblies and the Knights of Labor, "they will get nowhere unless they avoid inflicting serious injury on the effective operation of private business in this country. . . . Black Power won't work any better than did labor power, when directed at radical objectives."

In another article *Business Week* commented:

> Alinsky—and FIGHT—are intent on using Kodak to press their conviction that corporations must assume more responsibility for the poor in their communities than business customarily takes on. Says Alinsky: "American industry had better recognize—and some do— that they have a special obligation. . . . [The] Kodak situation

21 *Fortune,* June 1, 1968, p. 78.
22 *Barron's,* May 1, 1967, p. 1.
23 *Business Week,* May 6, 1967, p. 192.

dramatically reveals that today's ghettobound, militant urban Negro may generate even more problems for business than the civil rights struggle in the South created."

No business would find it easy to keep pace with Alinsky's fast-moving, bare-knuckles style of civil rights campaign. . . .[24]

Kodak's dealings with FIGHT, in fact, starkly dramatize the clash of modern radical black tactics with well-meaning but traditionalist business attitudes.

An editorial in *Fortune* described FIGHT's action at the stockholders' meeting as a harassment and described the Kodak–FIGHT situation so that businessmen would understand "what the battle is really about." The editorial agreed that

> many U.S. industrial corporations are failing to move fast enough to help Negro applicants qualify for employment. No company can be expected to "create instamatic jobs," as Minister Florence has said Kodak should. But in one way or another, industry should try to help unskilled and uneducated Negroes who want jobs to qualify for jobs. What makes FIGHT's "war" against Kodak appalling is that Kodak has recognized its obligations here. It is hard to imagine a worse way for Negro organizations to try to beat down employers.[25]

The clergy's desire to support better job opportunities was good, but *Fortune* questioned their use of stock-voting proxies to achieve these objectives. However, in the Kodak case, a proxy for FIGHT was not a vote for blacks but a vote for giving FIGHT power. "And that cause imposes no moral claim upon churchmen or businessmen or anybody else."

Barron's rebuked Kodak for its softheadedness in dealing with FIGHT and questioned the logic of the concept of social responsibility for corporations:

> The time has also come to do a little soul-searching with respect to corporate responsibility. Companies want to be good citizens, and, by providing jobs, paying taxes and the like, they generally succeed. However, management is the steward of other people's property. It can never afford to forget where its primary obligations lie.
>
> [The] company policy as outlined in a 1966 Management Letter . . . speaks of going beyond selection of the best qualified person, to seeking "to help the individual who lacks the necessary qualifications to become qualified."
>
> More suited to a sociology text than a corporate manual, the Letter adds: "Industry must look less critically at the individual's school

[24] *Business Week,* April 29, 1967, pp. 38–41.
[25] *Fortune,* June 1, 1968, p. 78.

record and work experience and more at his potential." Throughout the protracted dispute with FIGHT, Kodak's executives have chosen to ignore repeated provocations, insults and lies, an excessive forbearance which has merely incited their tormentors. In the corporate realm, as in any other, appeasement is a losing game. For Kodak and the rest of U.S. industry, it's time to stop turning the other cheek.

The clergy is in bad company. In taking issue with the employment policies of Eastman Kodak, moreover, the churchmen stand on very shaky ground.[26]

THE RELIGIOUS PRESS

The religious press not only actively participated in informing its audience about the Kodak–FIGHT conflict but also contributed to molding the opinion of the nationwide clergy. Generally speaking, it supported the stand taken by national church organizations in assisting FIGHT and also supported FIGHT's demands against Kodak.

In an editorial entitled "Economic Leverage of the Churches," *America,* the national Catholic weekly, supported the stand taken by Protestant groups in withholding their proxies from the management of Eastman Kodak and further asserted:

Anyone who believes that it is morally reprehensible to buy the products of a firm that discriminates against colored workers must hold that passive, uncritical ownership of the firm's securities is also wrong.

It must be admitted, however, that in many cases it simply has not occurred to managers of church funds or purchasing agents to use their economic power for moral goals. Like other investors, they have single-mindedly sought security and a satisfactory rate of return. Similarly, purchasing agents have felt that they discharged their duties when they obtained goods and services at a favorable price.

All this leads one to wonder why a theology of consumption and investment for modern market societies has not been more intensively cultivated. The humbling fact is that before the civil rights movement challenged God-fearing people to practice what they preach, most of us in transacting business performed as economic men. Or, which is nearly as bad, we absentmindedly followed the rule attributed to the late Henry Ford: "Whatever is good business is also good morals." [27]

---

26 *Barron's,* May 1, 1967, p. 1.
27 "Economic Leverage of the Churches," *America,* May 13, 1967, p. 714.

The *Episcopalian* echoed similar views,[28] as did the *United Church Herald,* which commented on the involvement of the churches in the Kodak–FIGHT conflict:

> Nor will the role of the churches in these developments go unnoticed. The Christian community often has been called the conscience of America but seldom has its voice been heard so clearly. Such a role is bound to be controversial—especially when the church challenges the intentions of its own members. But in a nation where the structures of power are increasing rapidly in size and influence, the corporate body of Christ must speak its convictions and may occasionally need to flex its muscles.[29]

The Belgian *Chronicles and Documents* commented in an editorial on the economic wealth of the church and its possible uses:

> But, have the Church administrators always been aware of the duties imposed by the possession of this wealth? In countries where the economy rests greatly on private initiative, shouldn't it be necessary that the Church herself show some initiative, and set an example wherever the possession of certain resources gives her the right to be present? The Kodak case shows very clearly the positive role that the ecclesiastic structures could play in a business concern.[30]

The religious press, however, did not unanimously support church involvement in racial problems, issues of job discrimination in general, and FIGHT in particular. The *Christian Century* for one did not agree with either FIGHT or its church supporters and editorialized:

> But one wing of the clergy—greatly and properly concerned and determined to do something, even if it is the wrong time—gulp and swallow what in the opinion of many of us is a highly dubious nostrum. Moreover, this minority is enraged by those of us who, having studied the Alinsky method closely and for a long time, resolutely refuse to gulp and swallow. What amazes and puzzles us is not Alinsky—he declares himself most forthrightly—but the hypnotic effect he has on some members of the clergy.[31]

In another editorial entitled "Episcopal Editor Denounces Saul Alinsky," the *Christian Century* concurred with the opinion of another Alinsky critic, Carroll E. Simcox, editor of the *Living Church,* by saying:

> And Simcox, with whom we are not always in agreement, said a great deal more to which we found ourselves tapping our feet, in-

[28] "Church vs. Kodak: The Big Picture," *Episcopalian,* June 1967, pp. 43–44.
[29] "Rare Days in Any Month," *United Church Herald,* August 1967, p. 23.
[30] "The Church and Capitalism," *Chronicles and Documents,* Brussels: Auxiliaire de la Presse, S.A. Bureau voor Persknipsels, N.V., 1967.
[31] "Alinsky Denounces Reconciliation," *Christian Century,* July 5, 1967, p. 861.

cluding his statement: "I don't want one nickel of my church offering ever to find its way to anything that this man Alinsky administers or even comes near, and if I learn in advance that it has an Alinsky-related destination I won't offer it." [32]

The editorial policy of *Christianity Today* also did not support FIGHT. In "Church Leaders Put the Squeeze on Kodak," the paper cautioned:

> Members of denominations backing FIGHT must consider whether their churches should be so deeply involved in big business, and whether their stock voting power should be used to harass responsible private enterprise. . . .
>
> Every Christian must be committed to equal-employment opportunities for men of all races. But race is not the only issue in the Rochester controversy. The basic issue in all agitation aroused by the Saul Alinsky forces centers on changing the economic structure of our nation. Church members should repudiate and withhold financial support from leaders who back such rabble-rousing causes. All Christians should become involved in the Church's foremost enterprise sharing with men poor in spirit the unsearchable riches of Christ.[33]

In another editorial, "A Fight Church Officials May Regret," [34] *Christianity Today* said:

> Denominational officials are rendering a great disservice to the cause of Christ and the betterment of the Negro's status in American life by supporting the Saul Alinsky FIGHT organization in its calculated controversy with the Eastman Kodak company. . . . In its zeal to aid the Negro, the Church must exercise care that it does not promote organizations that sow disruption and seek political power while professing to help the less fortunate.

The *Presbyterian Journal* was perhaps the most vocal and vociferous in its attack against those clergy who sympathized with FIGHT or supported their churches' involvement in seeking economic justice for the poor. In a strange indictment of FIGHT supporters, it said:

> *Notice that the people on whose behalf the Church was called to picket were not necessarily Christians.* No. The Church merely considered that its mission was to decide between two contending factions in a business dispute, and join the picket lines across the nation against one faction. [Emphasis added] [35]

[32] "Episcopal Editor Denounces Saul Alinsky," *Christian Century,* November 15, 1967, p. 1452.
[33] "Church Leaders Put the Squeeze on Kodak," *Christianity Today,* April 28, 1967, p. 1.
[34] "A Fight Church Officials May Regret," *Christianity Today,* May 12, 1967.
[35] "Re: Church Strikes and Boycotts," editorial, *Presbyterian Journal,* March 8, 1967.

Dr. L. Nelson Bell, in an article in the *Presbyterian Journal,* stated his views on the blacks. They sounded like an echo of the apologetics of the segregationists of a (hopefully) bygone era. Among other things, he stated:

> Perhaps Eastman Kodak Co. has been too slow in making use of all available labor. On the other hand, some may be demanding "rights" for which they are not equipped. We do believe the Church in its eagerness to promote civil rights may have omitted an even greater duty—the promotion of a sense of responsibility which can only be attained by hard work.[36]

THE BLACK PRESS

The Kodak–FIGHT conflict was covered for the black press by the Negro Press International. Its reporting—quite sparse compared with other special-purpose media—was confined to the statements made by the spokesmen for FIGHT and Kodak on different occasions during the dispute. The only black paper of national repute, the *Chicago Daily Defender* (national edition), carried a total of eight stories on the dispute, only three of which related the background in any detail. The paper also carried an editorial entitled "Economic Justice." [37] However, this editorial was devoid of any statement of position or philosophy by the editors or publisher of the newspaper and was just a brief summary of events.

Crisis, the official organ of the NAACP, published only one article on the problems of Rochester, Arthur L. Whitaker's "Anatomy of a Riot," [38] and carried two short news items ("NAACP Hits Rioters" and "Rochester NAACP Aids in Bringing Peace to Riot-Torn City") in the news section under the heading "Along the NAACP Battlefront." [39] The news items appeared in the August–September 1964 issue. Mr. Whitaker's article appeared in the January 1965 issue and preceded the Kodak–FIGHT conflict by at least six months.

SELECTED REFERENCES

ADLER, NORMAN, "The Sounds of Executive Silence," July–August, pp. 100–5.

ARMSTRONG, R. W., "Why Management Won't Talk," *Public Relations Journal,* November 1970, pp. 6–8.

[36] L. Nelson Bell, "Church Activities Have Gone Wild," *Presbyterian Journal,* March 8, 1967.

[37] "Economic Justice," editorial, *Chicago Daily Defender,* nat. ed., May 20–26, 1967, p. 10.

[38] "Anatomy of a Riot," *Crisis,* January 1965, pp. 20–25.

[39] "Along the NAACP Battlefront," *Crisis,* August–September 1964, p. 470.

GRAHAM, GENE S., "History in the (Deliberate) Making: A Challenge to Modern Journalism," *Nieman Reports,* September 1966, pp. 3–7.

HOBBING, ENNO, "Business Must Explain Itself," *Business and Society Review,* 1972, pp. 85–86.

"Is the Press Biased?" *Newsweek,* September 16, 1968, pp. 66–67.

LEONARD, RICHARD, "Role of the Press in the Urban Crisis," *Quill,* May 1968, pp. 8–11.

WAYS, MAX, "Business Needs To Do a Better Job of Explaining Itself," *Fortune,* September 1972, p. 85.

Corporations and the Church

EASTMAN KODAK COMPANY (C), ROCHESTER, NEW YORK

CONFLICT WITH A MINORITY GROUP—FIGHT: THE ROLE OF THE CHURCH

> The church is not an impersonal edifice, although all too often it seems that way. The church is what we have made it. The dilemma is that while its mission should be the righting of wrongs and the active pursuit of the great Judeo-Christian values, we have instead made it for the most part a force for the status quo.
>
> —JOHN D. ROCKEFELLER, JR.

The activities of the church [1] played a very important role in the Kodak–FIGHT controversy. It was an agency of the church that was instrumental in bringing Saul Alinsky to Rochester and thus creating FIGHT. Moreover, it was the local clergy who provided FIGHT with its initial momentum and sustained it in the early stages. Even after FIGHT was a going concern, the church was one of its strongest supporters at both local and national levels. Protestant and Catholic church organizations consistently supported FIGHT, although their membership was predominantly white. These groups were under constant pressure, especially at the

[1] *Church* is defined here as all organized Christian religious organizations in the United States.

local level, to disengage themselves from this controversy. Obviously, it was not the most usual activity for the church to engage in. Although members of the clergy had been involved in civil rights actions in the South and had participated in sit-in demonstrations and peace marches, their action in Rochester was unprecedented in many ways. It involved a deliberate attempt at organizing local minorities through techniques that were unorthodox and unacceptable even to some of the most liberal groups in the United States. These techniques carried with them the potential for violence. In a city like Rochester, which had been the scene of race riots, this action seemed particulary foolhardy. It was sure to incur the displeasure of a majority of the town's citizens who were, after all, church members and had the right to ensure that the churches satisfy their spiritual needs rather than become rabble-rousers.

Why then did the church become involved in the controversy? To understand this, we must realize that in Rochester the various elements of the church, ranging from the Rochester Area Council of Churches to the individual ministers and priests, had somewhat different, at least short-run, objectives and more often than not were subject to different pressures or allegiances.

The Board for Urban Ministry was the organization originally responsible for inviting Saul Alinsky and his Industrial Areas Organization to Rochester with a view to encouraging organization among the local minorities and giving them a new voice in representing their views to the city and its establishment. The board realized that this action might not be acceptable to the city's other powerful and equally well-meaning groups because of Alinsky's reputation as a radical. To understand the board's action, it is necessary to consider the circumstances and the source of the board's authority.

The Board for Urban Ministry was a semiautonomous offshoot of the Rochester Area Council of Churches (RACC). Although RACC endorsed the board's action, it was the board and not the council that was actually responsible for bringing Alinsky to Rochester. The distinction between the two, often overlooked, is strategically important. As William C. Martin, writing in the *Atlantic,* put it:

> The Council is composed of more than 200 member congregations and is ultimately answerable to them. The Board for Urban Ministry is composed of representatives from eight denominations and is thus not directly answerable to individual churches. According to the policy of the two organizations, the Board could have invited Alinsky without the Council's approval, but the Council was not obligated to poll its member churches as to their desires in the matter.

> The Board for Urban Ministry issued the invitation to Alinsky and led in providing his fee. Over half the fee came from church agencies such as the Presbyterian Board of National Missions. Much of FIGHT's most articulate support at Flemington came from similar denominational offices. These agencies and their staffs are ultimately

responsible to a constituency, but even if that constituency opposes a policy decision strongly enough to try to countermand it, it is likely to move too late or hit the wrong target.[2]

THE ATTITUDE OF THE NATIONAL CHURCH ORGANIZATIONS

Only during the past twenty years or so have American churches become conspicuous in causes against race prejudice and economic inequality. Thus the National Council of Churches went on record in 1954 as working against those forms of economic injustice that are expressed through racial discrimination.[3] It is also on record in support of equal employment opportunity for all,[4] the use of nonviolent demonstrations to secure social justice,[5] the elimination of segregation in education,[6] and the prevention of discrimination in housing.[7]

The use of economic pressure in racial issues was specifically proposed and approved in a background paper prepared for the National Council of Churches:

We believe it is of primary importance that Christian people everywhere recognize that what may be called bread-and-butter injustice can be equally as devasting to human life and well-being as civil injustice, if not more so, largely because bread-and-butter pursuits are so necessary to the maintenance of life. Because these forms of injustice are so closely related to habit, local mores, and man-to-man relationships, they can only partially be opposed or regulated by law or civil authority.[8]

The General Board, therefore, resolved on June 8, 1963:

[2] William C. Martin, "Shepherds vs. Flocks, Ministers vs. Negro Militancy," *Atlantic,* December 1967, pp. 55–59.
[3] National Council of Churches of Christ in the United States of America (NCCCUSA), "Christian Principles and Assumptions for Economic Life." Resolution adopted by General Board, September 15, 1954.
[4] NCCCUSA, "Christian Influence Toward the Development and Use of All Labor Resources Without Regard to Race, Color and Religion or National Origin." Resolution adopted by General Assembly, December 9, 1960.
[5] NCCCUSA, "The Church and Segregation." Resolution adopted by General Board, June 11, 1952. Also see "Resolution on the Sit-In Demonstrations." Adopted by General Board, June 2, 1960.
[6] NCCCUSA, "Statement on the Decision of the U.S. Supreme Court on Segregation in the Public Schools." Adopted by General Board, May 19, 1954.
[7] NCCCUSA, "The Churches' Concern for Housing." Resolution adopted by General Board, November 18, 1953.
[8] NCCCUSA, "Background Paper of Information Relating to Resolution on the Use of Economic Pressures in Racial Tensions." Prepared by Department of Church and Economic Life in consultation with Department of Cultural Relations of Division of Christian Life and Work, June 9, 1963, p. 5.

When other efforts to secure these rights do not avail, to support and participate in economic pressures where used in a responsible and disciplined manner to eliminate economic injustice and to end discrimination against any of God's people based on race, creed, or national origin.[9]

The National Council of Churches has gone even further by recognizing that the churches' own purchases must be based on other than strictly economic criteria. The basic philosophy of the council was very well articulated in the policy statement adopted by the General Board on September 12, 1968:

The institutional church enters into the economic life of society in a variety of ways. . . . The economic activities and financial transactions of the church total many billions of dollars annually. As a result, the church is inevitably involved in the exercise of substantial economic power. . . . We reaffirm that all economic institutions and practices are human structures conceived and designed by men; that they affect the conditions and quality of life of persons, many of whom cannot exercise any control over their functioning. . . . The market system which characterizes the American economy is one such institution. When the church approaches the marketplace in its role of purchaser of goods and services, it inevitably becomes a participant in an intricate network of economic forces involving ethical issues, policies and decisions. . . .

Most purchasing decisions by the church involve a selection among competing vendors. Such factors as quality, performance, convenience and price—conventional determinants of most purchasing decisions—although relevant to the economic activity of the church, are not sufficient criteria for its selection among vendors. The nature of the church requires that as an economic institution it also consider the social impact of its purchasing decisions in terms of justice and equality. . . .

In cases where injustice is found to exist, the church should make vigorous efforts through moral persuasion to secure correction of the abuses. . . . Where such measures prove to be inappropriate in securing justice, or where past experience demonstrates that these means alone are ineffective, the church is not only justified, but in faithfulness to its nature, is required to give its patronage to sources of goods and services which it finds to have policies and practices that better serve social justice. . . .

When such action is taken, the church is free and indeed may be impelled, as a form of witness, not only to inform the vendors

9 NCCCUSA, "The Use of Economic Pressure in Racial Tensions." Resolution adopted by General Board, June 8, 1963.

involved but also to announce publicly the nature of its action and the reasons for it.[10]

The problem of the church's concern for economic issues and its involvement in conflicts where it is not a direct party has another dimension which is equally explosive: the choice of strategies. The National Council of Churches has supported the use of nonviolent methods in securing economic justice for minorities.[11]

However, what should the church do if nonviolent and peaceful means do not succeed? When is a violation of man-made laws justified if there is a superior law of conscience? Economic pressures can be used not only by the church but also by other groups that the church is opposing. If these measures by the church can be justified because of the righteousness of the cause, how can they be condemned when used by other groups if the latter are equally honest in their belief of the justness of their cause and are not motivated by bigotry, selfishness, or prejudice? The mere existence of power, be it legal or implied, is not enough justification for its use. However, if ends are to be used as criteria for legitimizing means, the church as a party to the conflict has no more right to proclaim that its values are the "justifiable" ends than have the other parties to the conflict.

The National Council of Churches, recognizing some of these issues, justified its approach thus:

> Use of economic pressures also involves the possibility of violence. Though violence may sometimes result from an action, this possibility does not necessarily call for opposition to such action, particularly on the part of those who seek to use non-violent economic means to eliminate or decrease discrimination.[12]

The council also recognized that there might be occasions when a company might lose its regular clientele if it were to cater to the special needs of a particular group. It thus argued that such a company was only an innocent bystander, not the offending party, and should therefore not be subjected to economic pressures by the church. These measures might involve yet another party—those people who give tacit support to discriminatory practices of some businesses by not actively opposing those companies and their activities and by continuing to patronize them. Notwithstanding, the council maintained:

> These factors make more difficult, but no less necessary, the understanding of and resistance to the use of economic pressures as a means to enforce racial discriminations or oppression. They serve to highlight the importance of looking with broad historical perspective at the full sweep of economic injustice which the victims of

10 NCCCUSA, "The Church as Purchaser of Goods and Services." Policy statement adopted by General Board, September 12, 1968.
11 "The Use of Economic Pressure in Racial Tensions," NCCCUSA, June 8, 1963.
12 "Background Paper of Information," NCCCUSA, June 9, 1963.

economic injustice now seek to remove, or at least alleviate through the use of economic pressures being made against them.

It is, therefore, no wonder that the board was more in tune than the council with the trends of national church organizations and more willing to use less conventional approaches to solving the problems of Rochester's minorities. The board was assured of the support of the National Council of Churches in view of the latter's public statements and official resolutions favoring the use of economic pressures and other direct action to promote the cause of the minorities. Moreover, financial independence and only indirect representation of the local churches insulated the board from local pressures and in a sense made it insensitive to the feelings and desires of the local clergy and citizens.[13]

In inviting Alinsky, the board knew that it was creating "an atmosphere of controversy," [14] but the ferocity and, to some extent, the direction of opposition were unexpected. RACC and its member congregations came under immediate attack from media and laymen alike. The local newspapers accused the council of bringing in "outsiders" and troublemakers and of supporting militants who were intent on creating unrest among the people of Rochester. As reported in the *New Republic*, the city's most powerful radio station, WHAM, an ABC affiliate, in an editorial warned that

> if the clergy persisted in bringing Alinsky into town then the ministers must start paying $275 for the hour-long Sunday morning church service the station had been broadcasting free. WHAM said Alinsky was a "troublemaker." . . . The Council held its ground against WHAM and the Sunday morning radio program was cancelled.[15]

Commenting on the intensity of local hostility to the council's action, the same observer stated:

> In the face of this intensive barrage, many laymen found themselves in a quandary over the role their pastors and denominational leaders were playing. For weeks, representatives of the Board for Urban Ministry and the Council of Churches spent their evenings interpreting the realities of life in the ghettos and the dynamics of the Alinsky approach to groups of troubled laymen.[16]

It was easy and perhaps spiritually comfortable for most of the educated, suburban, affluent laymen to support their clergy's involvement in

---

13 *Ibid.*
14 "The Fight That Swirls Around Eastman Kodak," *Business Week,* April 29, 1967, pp. 38–41.
15 James Ridgeway, "Saul Alinsky in Smugtown," *New Republic,* June 26, 1965, pp. 15–17.
16 *Ibid.*

social action, as long as it did not go beyond the discussion stage and as long as any action was confined to peaceful methods of protest. However, these parishioners could not reconcile themselves to the idea of their clergy being involved in an open struggle for power between different groups in the community. The lack of precedent, the absence of a clear-cut philosophy, and the feeling of uncertainty about possible achievements further added to the laymen's confusion and frustration, as reflected in the nature and intensity of their response. There was a widespread cancellation of pledges—sometimes running into thousands of dollars. William C. Martin reported: "Resentment of church involvement ran so high in some congregations that church leaders would not pass out brochures presenting FIGHT's request for third-year funding until after the annual pledge drive." [17]

There was a serious question as to how long clergymen could function under strain and still maintain their sanity. One minister, tormented by threats and telephone calls, took his own life; the calls were then made to his wife.[18] Others were victims of anonymous letters circulated among the congregations and of telephoned threats against their families. A minister who had been attacked for supporting FIGHT found that the lug bolts had been taken off the wheels of his car.[19] In a large number of cases, parishioners simply stopped talking or being friendly to their clergymen. William Martin, writing in the *Atlantic,* commented:

> The loss of members and money affects a minister because they are tangible signs of his professional "success," however much he may wish they were not. But the confusion, bitterness, and hostility that he sees in his people cause him the greatest pain. In [one] case, members made a point of telling the minister's children that the church could never make progress until their father left. In some churches dissident laymen organized attempts to get rid of the offending minister. In others, leaders withheld salary increments or warned the pastor not to spend too much of his time in activities related to FIGHT.[20]

The resentment of the local citizenry against the Rochester Area Council of Churches was even more vocal and violent. According to William Martin:

> Letters and telephone calls—some reasonable, others obscene and threatening—poured into the council office. Numerous churches and individuals decided to "teach the council a lesson" by lowering or canceling contributions for the coming fiscal year. One church, recognizing that FIGHT was only one part of the council's activity, raised its contribution $500, but accompanied its pledge with a letter

17 Martin, "Shepherds vs. Flocks," pp. 55–59.
18 Jules Loh, Associated Press Feature Story for Sunday A.M. papers, April 23, 1967.
19 James Ridgeway, "Attack on Kodak," *New Republic,* January 21, 1967, pp. 11–13.
20 Martin, "Shepherds vs. Flocks," pp. 55–59.

strongly critical of the council's stance. Others were not so charitable. At the final tally, the council's annual fund drive for the coming year :nissed its goal by $20,000. Ironically, the attempt to punish the council has had no effect whatever on FIGHT, which has in fact been guaranteed third-year funding by the various denominational bodies and church agencies, nor on the Board of Urban Ministry, which is also funded denominationally and has never been more secure financially.[21]

CHURCH ACTIVITIES AFTER
THE AGREEMENT OF DECEMBER 20

When the executive committee of Kodak's board of directors repudiated the agreement signed by John Mulder, RACC found itself in a worse dilemma than ever before. The community was already hostile to RACC's earlier actions, and any support of FIGHT would further intensify the conflict. FIGHT's actions immediately following the repudiation did not help. On January 19, 1967, against the advice of many of his supporters, Minister Florence invited Stokely Carmichael to Rochester. In his speech Carmichael made inflammatory statements against Kodak, Rochester, and every other organization that did not agree with FIGHT.

The council was really concerned about the danger of the situation getting out of hand; yet it could do nothing but support FIGHT's cause, since it felt that Kodak had indeed broken a promise which the other party had accepted in good faith. The council's hand was further forced when Kodak took full-page ads in the local newspapers to publicize its reasons for rejecting the agreement. The council wanted to avoid a further deterioration of the situation, but it could not desert FIGHT's cause without losing all the work done so far and perhaps permanently discouraging the minorities from putting any faith in the white man's promises. The council took double-page ads in the papers urging Kodak to honor the agreement and at the same time asking FIGHT to support Kodak's training programs. However, with supporters of both factions having raised community passions to a high pitch, the council's appeal to patience and reason was lost to the hysteria, while its support for FIGHT was overblown. The reactions were predictable though unfortunate.

DENOMINATIONAL DIVISION OF OPINION ON FIGHT

The controversy caused division among individual denominations in the Council of Churches. Stokely Carmichael's visit prompted six of Rochester's eighty Presbyterian churches (FIGHT's largest church supporters) to consider withdrawing their support of FIGHT, while their parent body's Health and Welfare Association condemned Kodak.[22] The Episcopalians were reportedly the second largest church supporters of FIGHT. In response to criticism of FIGHT by the Gannett newspapers, the bishop of the Episcopal diocese of Rochester appointed a committee to "assess FIGHT and to determine," by April 1967, "whether the diocese which has already contributed $19,000 should continue its support."[23] The third largest church group, the Baptists, decided to continue their contributions, but a third of the delegates voted against the proposal.[24]

The Reverend Elmer G. Schaertal, pastor of the Lutheran Church of the Redeemer, openly dissented with the council's stand in a letter to the *Rochester Democrat & Chronicle*. Schaertal equated the disrespect for authority that was sweeping the country with that of FIGHT for Kodak:

> . . . the disrespect sweeping our country of youth, of college students, of ministers, and leaders like Adam Powell and James Hoffa for the law and courts and of FIGHT for Kodak which is the most community minded company that I know. . . . The demands of FIGHT call for a special privilege because of color. . . . This seems crazy to me and would do great harm to both company and all the workers who would resent the man coming in by paternalistic power rather than qualifications for the job. If one asks why Florence and FIGHT are so insistent in this, one can only answer that it is for power and would be used in that way rather than for benefit of workers, or company or Rochester. . . . As to the Council of Churches and the denominations supporting FIGHT, I do not believe the majority of either their ministers or their people are in sympathy with the stand their leaders have taken or the support they have given.[25]

Several other ministers used their pulpits to advocate reason and even some rethinking on the part of the church. However, none took as harsh a stand as Mr. Schaertal. One minister said that many church people were "facing the future with some misgivings" and that "we must find our way back to the true image of the church and lessen the gap between clergy and laity." Another minister commented that "part of the reason why we have this controversy and the strong difference of opinion within the church is that we are in new times and the church is facing new and greater issues for which we have no sharp guidelines from the past." Another minister asked that Kodak and FIGHT "call it a draw," saying that the struggle was "like that between the elephant and the whale, which are different animals living in different environments and moving in

[22] Barbara Carter, "The Fight Against Kodak," *Reporter*, January 21, 1967, pp. 28–31.
[23] Raymond A. Schroth, "Self-Doubt and Black Pride," *America*, April 1, 1967, p. 502.
[24] "And Kodak Will Ask, 'How High?' " *Fortune*, June 1, 1967, p. 78.
[25] Elmer G. Schaertal, "A Pastor Speaks Up for Kodak," *Rochester Democrat & Chronicle*, January 15, 1967.

different worlds."[26] Some ministers, even had they wanted to, could not support FIGHT because of individual circumstances, such as age, health, or special situations in their churches.[27]

There followed a spate of letters to the newspapers by irate citizens opposing the church's stand on the controversy. Many strongly supported Mr. Schaertal's views. Few, if any, sympathized with the position taken by the Rochester Area Council of Churches. Here is a representative sample of the comments made by some of the readers:

I commend Pastor Elmer Schaertal for expressing his opinion so clearly in his letter to the D. & C.

In the long run more could be accomplished if everyone were allowed to devote full time and attention to his own problems. Eastman Kodak to the business of manufacturing and selling its products, FIGHT to sending its people to the proper place—the school—for education, the Rochester Area Council to preaching the Gospel.

The local crusading knights of the cloth, johnny-come-latelys in the civil rights bandwagon, cloaked in their spiritual aura of infallibility, are quite ready to order others to place their houses in order according to their views, integratively speaking, but have woeful shortcomings in their own houses of worship.

Every day we read that more and more people believe that religion is becoming less meaningful. Therefore, why don't preachers either return to the pulpit and extol an almighty and just God, or leave the church to campaign for Minister Franklin Florence, Saul Alinsky and other radical dissidents under their own names. Let those disenchanted clergy look about them. Hardly an area in or about Rochester has not benefited from the Eastman Kodak Company. There isn't a major company in the United States with a more liberal and higher standard of employment ethics.[28]

The expression of resentment and dissent also took other forms. The president of the Council of Churches (a Kodak employee) and two directors of its board (one of whom was a Kodak employee) resigned from the council in protest.

Fundamentalist and Evangelical churches kept out of the Kodak–FIGHT controversy, perhaps because of theological conviction. These groups believed the primary function of the church was to prepare individuals for life after death and saw no relationship between socioeconomic and religious issues. The deed of one church specifically prohibited the

---

26 "Pastors Refer to FIGHT Case," *Rochester Times-Union,* January 23, 1967.
27 Martin, "Shepherds vs. Flocks," pp. 55–59.
28 "The Ordeal of the Black Businessman," *Newsweek,* March 4, 1968, p. 34.

discussion of social or political issues anywhere on church property. According to William Martin:

> Some are simply not aware of what is going on in their city. One insisted that Negroes "are basically a happy, satisfied people who like to work as servants and live in a haphazard way." He doubted many in his church would object if Negroes tried to become members, "but, of course, if too many came, then we'd start a colored work." Another admitted he was not too well informed about FIGHT, but he hoped Hoagy Carmichael would not get to be its president. Most, however, are as concerned as their more liberal colleagues but cannot reconcile conflict tactics with their understanding of the gospel. "We feel," one evangelical minister said, "that you will never get rid of slums until you get rid of the slum in men. You have to start with the individual man, and you don't start by teaching him to hate." [29]

THE POSITION OF THE CATHOLIC CHURCH

For the most part, the Catholics (not represented in the Protestant Council of Churches, of course) steered clear of the Kodak–FIGHT dispute. However, on January 3, 1967, when the turmoil in Rochester was at its peak because of Kodak's December 20 repudiation, Bishop Fulton J. Sheen asked the Reverend P. David Finks—a FIGHT sympathizer—to advise him on the problems of the poor by appointing him an episcopal vicar of urban ministry. Finks was a member of FIGHT's advisory council and was on the executive board of Friends of FIGHT at the time of his appointment. Bishop Sheen admitted that the appointment was "a very unusual step" but said, "I do not follow traditional methods, except in the faith." He also raised the possibility of strong cooperation with other faiths "even to the sharing of houses of worship . . . in poor neighborhoods." According to *The New York Times:*

> Spokesmen for the Roman Catholic diocese declined to say whether the priest's appointment was connected with the current controversy between the Negro group and the Eastman Kodak Company. They commented that the letter naming Father Finks to the post speaks for itself.[30]

Speaking before the city's Chamber of Commerce on January 23, 1976, Bishop Sheen said:

> As the Church had to learn that the world was the stage on which the gospel was preached, so the world has to learn that the inner city

29 Martin, "Shepherds vs. Flocks," pp. 55–59.
30 "Sheen Appoints a Vicar for Poor," *The New York Times,* January 4, 1967, p. 4.

is the area where the secular city will find God. Could not all the industries of the secular city begin to give a proportion of their blessing to the inner city—not just "tokens" but something more substantial? The whole world looks at Rochester, . . . but it does not see the city's beauty: it sees the blemish on its face.[31]

Father Finks expressed his views on FIGHT and his philosophy on religion and church in an address to the Pittsford-Perinton Council on Human Relations:

Those seeking social justice for the have nots of this world should support a viable community organization of minority groups dedicated to bring about the necessary social change. The most viable group here is FIGHT. . . . Christianity is not a mere belief or ritual, but is basically living like Christ did. We will be judged on whether we respond to the urgent call for social justice. . . . Tensions are necessary and can be used creatively in making the democratic process work. . . . Members of the clergy have been chaplains of the establishment too long.[32]

THE PART PLAYED BY NATIONAL CHURCH ORGANIZATIONS

Florence was quite successful in his appeal to various organizations to withhold their proxies from the management and also to boycott Kodak's products and demonstrate against its plants in all parts of the country. At the Kodak stockholders' meeting in April 1967, seven of the eight dissenting groups, which represented 40,000 of the 80.7 million outstanding shares, were religious organizations. Although the stock represented by these groups was but a small fraction of the total, it would be misleading to measure the impact only in terms of the number of shares. Unlike FIGHT, these organizations were well-established institutions representing a large number of churches. They had access to the public forum which, though not equal to that of business institutions, was quite important. Kodak—or for that matter any other business corporation— could not afford to treat the voice of this group as representing merely one-half of one percent of their stock.[33]

Bishop Dewitt, who represented the Episcopal Church at the annual stockholders' meeting, read a statement prepared by the church's execu-

[31] Schroth, "Self-Doubt and Black Pride," p. 502.
[32] Chuck Boller, "Priest Backs FIGHT," *Rochester Democrat & Chronicle*, February 2, 1967.
[33] For example, the Episcopal Church had 3,340,759 members in 7,547 churches and the United Church of Christ had 2,067,233 members in 6,957 churches. John Kifner, "2 Churches Withhold Proxies to Fight Kodak Rights Policies," *The New York Times*, April 7, 1967, p. 1.

tive council for the press. This statement perhaps sums up the feelings of many other churchmen who were also present at that meeting:

> Possession of power conveys the obligation to use that power reasonably. Corporations—and indeed investing churches—must measure the responsible use of their resources by social as well as financial yardsticks. . . . We stand with Negro communities in their real grievances and their urgent need for organizational power to participate in an open society. And we stand with the management of corporate enterprises which seek to manage their affairs for the well-being of the total community.[34]

FIGHT's request for national demonstrations against Kodak's plants was not enthusiastically received by some of the church organizations. In an editorial entitled "Re: Church Strikes and Boycotts," the *Presbyterian Journal* rejected that church's activities in the area of community organization:

> For those who see the church as an organization existing for the purpose of helping achieve certain needed social, economic and political objectives (in much the same way Kiwanis Clubs work for the betterment of boys generally) these developments are a logical outgrowth of their concern. But for those who still hold to the Scriptural mission of the church, to win men to salvation in the Lord Jesus Christ, these developments must be viewed as radical departures from the assignment given the church by her Lord.[35]

The same editorial reported that the Nashville Presbytery, when asked to support Project Equality, which involved sponsoring official boycotts of businesses that did not practice fair employment, turned it down by a vote of two to one.

FIGHT's popularity waned somewhat among the clergy when Florence escalated his demands to Kodak and threatened to start a nationwide demonstration that summer. The Rochester Area Council of Churches, in its first official criticism of FIGHT, passed a resolution criticizing the organization's intemperance and urging a cancellation of a candlelight demonstration.[36] Church pressure, as well as lack of interest in Florence's planned demonstrations, may well have speeded the "reconciliation" between FIGHT and Kodak on June 23, 1967.

Kodak officials were also not happy with the stand taken by RACC in the Kodak–FIGHT controversy. During an interview with the author, some Kodak spokesmen expressed the opinion that RACC's involvement in originally hiring Alinsky kept it from objectively assessing the company's side of the dispute. This bias spread to other churches locally and to the communication RACC had with the National Council of

---

[34] "Church vs. Kodak: The Big Picture," *Episcopalian*, June 1967, pp. 43–44.
[35] "Re: Church Strikes and Boycotts," editorial, *Presbyterian Journal*, March 8, 1967.
[36] Martin, "Shepherds vs. Flocks," pp. 55–59.

Churches. As evidence of this bias, the Kodak men stated that in only a handful of instances across the country did clergymen attempt to look into the Kodak side of the story. Even when Kodak officials tried to present the facts as they saw them, their efforts were rebuffed by the clergy.[37] Kodak spokesmen gave the impression that RACC was not only primarily responsible for creating FIGHT and for the resulting tension in the community, but also largely instrumental in engaging the National Council of Churches in the conflict and in generating adverse national publicity and reaction against Kodak.

THE RAMIFICATIONS OF CHURCH INVOLVEMENT

Where has the involvement between Kodak and FIGHT left the church? The Rochester Area Council of Churches certainly has not won any kudos for its efforts from any group in the community. In fact, as the Reverend Paul R. Hoover pointed out, "the loudest condemnation of the RACC's actions has come from inner-city citizens of all races." [38] The dissatisfaction of the community's affluent is reflected in the financial problems of RACC. Referring to the slump in the council's financial support, the *Rochester Democrat & Chronicle* said that it indicated disillusionment with sponsorship of FIGHT and disappointment in an approach to helping blacks based on acrimony and upheaval rather than on goodwill and orderly processes. The newspaper further said that it would be more in keeping with reality "if the Council just admitted a misjudgment and went on from there." [39]

According to one observer, one of the key factors in the Rochester situation was the presence of a closely knit group of activists in the Board for Urban Ministry who were instrumental in inviting Alinsky and also in attracting like-minded ministers from the local clergy. This group did not share the apprehensions of the local people nor did it identify with their

[37] Kenneth Howard of the Industrial Relations Department, Eastman Kodak Company, said in an interview with the author that a "member of the Presbyterian clergy in Missouri was urged to send us a telegram by a clergyman in New Orleans. The clergyman in Missouri called Kodak to hear our side of the story. I had a long talk with him and sent him some information. He never sent the telegram to Kodak.

"The amusing sideline to this is that I am also a graduate of a divinity school. In the middle of this network of communications, we discovered that a former very close friend of mine in the divinity school was sending out his literature to clergymen all over the country. So I called him and said that I had heard he was interested in the Rochester situation and asked him whether he had ever visited Rochester and he said 'yes, oh yes.' So I told him that since I was also involved in this issue from the other side, it might be worthwhile if we got together sometime and talked about it. I pointed out to him that I believed there were certain inaccuracies and half-truths that were being circulated about Kodak and that I was sure he wouldn't want to be a party to them. But he never called me, he never came to see me, he wouldn't send me a copy of what he sent out around the country. This was typical of the whole problem. He wasn't in the least bit interested in knowing the facts."

[38] Paul R. Hoover, "Social Pressures and Church Policy," *Christianity Today*, July 21, 1967, pp. 12–14.

[39] "Council's Defense," *Rochester Democrat & Chronicle*, June 16, 1967.

objectives. Those in the group believed themselves to be working for a great cause and had a different and more radical outlook as to what ailed society and how it could be cured. Equally important in their indifference to the local pressures was the fact that their personal advancement and goal achievement depended on satisfying a peer group that was national in character and was not likely to be influenced by the opinions of the Rochester power elite.

Reviewing the situation in Rochester, the Reverend Paul R. Hoover wrote in *Christianity Today:*

> The frightening events in Rochester have left behind two tragic consequences: (1) a growing lack of confidence in churches and church leaders, not excluding inner-city ministers whose motivation and actions over the years were hardly open to question; and (2) a growing fear of what the future may hold in view of the reckless threats of members of the FIGHT organization at the Kodak annual meeting in Flemington, New Jersey. . . . Part of the soul-searching on the part of ministers, particularly those working within the city, centers on how long they can physically and mentally stand the pressures that stem from the difference in attitudes and professional experiences between the suburban congregation and the mission-oriented inner-city congregation.[40]

SELECTED REFERENCES

"The Church and Capitalism," *Chronicles and Documents* (Brussels: Auxiliaire de la Presse, S.A. Bureau voor Persknipsels, N.V., 1967).

Cox, Harvey G., "The 'New Breed' in American Churches: Sources of Social Activism in American Religion," *Daedalus,* winter 1967, pp. 135–50.

Fichter, Joseph H., "American Religion and the Negro," *Daedalus,* fall 1965, pp. 1085–106.

McDonald, D., "The Church and Society," *Center Magazine,* July 1968, pp. 28–35.

Mowry, Charles E., *The Church and the New Generation* (Nashville: Abingdon Press, 1969).

Niebuhr, R. H., *Christian Realism and Political Problems* (New York: Scribner's, 1953), pp. 149–96.

O'Dea, Thomas F., "The Crisis of the Contemporary Religious Consciousness," *Daedalus,* winter 1967, pp. 116–34.

Rahner, Karl, ed., "Christians in the Modern World," in *Mission and Grace,* Part I (London: Sheed & Ward, Stag Books, 1963).

Sethi, S. Prakash, "The Corporation and the Church: Institutional Conflict and Social Responsibility," *California Management Review,* 15, 1 (fall 1972), 63–74.

Sleeper, C. Freeman, *Black Power and Christian Responsibility* (Nashville: Abingdon Press, 1969).

[40] Hoover, "Social Pressures and Church Policy," pp. 12–14.